POLITICAL ECONOMY
An Introductory Text

Edmund S. Phelps

MᴄVɪᴄᴋᴀʀ Pʀᴏꜰᴇssᴏʀ ᴏꜰ Pᴏʟɪᴛɪᴄᴀʟ Eᴄᴏɴᴏᴍʏ
Cᴏʟᴜᴍʙɪᴀ Uɴɪᴠᴇʀsɪᴛʏ

POLITICAL ECONOMY
An Introductory Text

W·W·NORTON & COMPANY · New York · London

ILLUSTRATION ACKNOWLEDGMENTS

Page 1 and cover: Albert Lorenz.
Page 83: West façade of Chartres Cathedral. Rendering by de Lassus. Courtesy Bibliotheque Nationale, Paris.
Page 155: Chateau de Verneuil-sur-Oise. Designed and rendered by Jacques Androuet Du Cerceau, the Elder. Courtesy Cooper-Hewitt Museum, The Smithsonian Institution National Museum of Design. Gift of the Council of the Museum.
Page 233: The Customs House, Dublin. Designed by James Gandon. Courtesy Warder Collection.
Page 349: Crystal Palace, London. Designed by Joseph Paxton. Courtesy Warder Collection.
Page 377: Dulles Airport. Designed by Eero Saarinen. Rendered by J. Barr.
Page 469: "Indeterminate Façade." Designed by and rendering courtesy of SITE/Alison Sky, Michelle Stone, and James Wines.

Copyright © 1985 by W. W. Norton & Company, Inc.

Published simultaneously in Canada by Penguin Books Canada Ltd, 2801 John Street, Markham, Ontario L3R 1B4
Printed in the United States of America

The text of this book is composed in Sabon, with display type set in Fritz Quadrata. Composition by Vail-Ballou Press. Manufacturing by The Maple-Vail Book Group. Book design by Nancy Dale Muldoon. Line art by Danmark & Michaels.

FIRST EDITION

Library of Congress Cataloging in Publication Data

Phelps, Edmund S.
    Political economy.

    1. Economics.   I. Title.
HB171.5.P488   1985   330   85-5151
ISBN 0-393-95312-2

W. W. Norton & Company, Inc.
500 Fifth Avenue, New York, N. Y. 10110
W. W. Norton & Company Ltd.
37 Great Russell Street, London WC1B 3NU

1 2 3 4 5 6 7 8 9 0

Contents

Part 4 CLASSICAL MARKET THEORY AND ECONOMIC POLICY 233

Part 7   THE ELEMENT OF DISEQUILIBRIUM IN MODERN MARKET THEORY   469

Preface

This book is an introduction to economics for the university student and general reader. The focus, in common with other such texts, is on political economy. Economics arose in response to questions of political interest about the national economy; and though economics has since found other applications as well, its vitality and development continue to stem from this central concern. The causes and effects of the way society organizes and regulates its economy—and the resulting debates over instability, inequality, joblessness, inflation, organizational incentives, and the rest—are the main stuff of economics from here to China.

ORGANIZATION AND AIMS

The material in this text has been organized to begin at the beginning, even if that means saving the best for later. First comes the object of study: the behavior of rational and self-interested individuals more or less on an equilibrium path, and particularly the society's method of coordinating and rewarding the contributions of those participating in the social economy. The economic roots of society and the theory of collective action through government are early chapters in this story. So are the theories of failure to cooperate, the explanations of wasteful public actions, and the various notions of fairness that may sometimes limit or contain these difficulties. We are brought by this material to the borders of economics with sociology, political science, and moral philosophy, and thus not left to feel that economics is unattached to these other fields.

These basic matters, treated early in the text, lay the ground for the main subject in political economy—the *choice* of economic systems and public laws and policies that society has available for coordinating and rewarding its members' participation in the economy. This text emphasizes the great theme running through Western economics: the question of the desirable role for free markets in goods and in productive services and the desirable role for the government. The argument is between the classical case for "the market" and the post-classical critiques that advocate extensive governmental intervention to replace the market or repair its defects. This theme leads inevitably to the two clashes occurring in economics today—the contest between the *neoclassical* model of the marketplace and the *modernist* models of imperfectly informed markets developed in the past two decades, and the dispute between the *New Classical* and the *New Keynesian* schools over the stability, or resilience, of the market economy and the utility of "activist" countercyclical government policies.

In Part 1, the book takes up the scope and characteristic methods of economics, particularly the concepts of rational choice and equilibrium. Part 2 examines the sources of cooperation and the obstacles to cooperation that may arise even in bilateral, two-person situations. Multilateral cooperation, particularly the rise of law and markets, and some of the difficulties of such cooperation arising from "politics," occupy Part 3. The classical case for reliance on markets within certain limits, and the classical role for the state outside those limits, are the subject of Part 4. The next part considers the critique of the market by Marx and subsequently by the New Left. Part 6 then presents the modernist market models of recent years, with their unclassical stress on the incomplete or unequal information possessed by buyers and sellers. Finally, Part 7 introduces the criticism that Keynes leveled against the market, especially a market economy unaided by activist governmental intervention, and the controversy that it has sparked among the monetarist, New Classical, and New Keynesian schools of thought.

Chapters 4, 8, 13, 16, 18, and 19 are followed by appendices on the open economy—the national economy that is open to foreign trade and to foreign lending or borrowing. These can be saved for the end and read in sequence. Or they can be read as they appear so that readers do not have to wait to see applications to foreign relations of the economic principles that arise and to see whether the propositions encountered about closed economies carry over to an open one or need to be modified.

With one question answered—What is this book about?—two further questions crowd in: Why read political economy? And why this text rather than some of the others (of which there are quite a few)? A response seems necesssary, even though the proof of the pudding is in the eating.

The best reason for reading introductory economics, and for most readers the only reason, is that it will help them to understand better a large part of their world—the everyday world in which they must make their career and lead a civic life. Besides helping to sort out issues of fact, the study of economics is nearly indispensable for sorting out the ethical issues raised by political questions. In fact, the English economist John Maynard Keynes felt, as have others, that economics was developed for just that purpose: ". . .[E]conomics, more properly called political economy, is on the side of ethics. Marshall always used to insist that it was through ethics that he arrived at political economy . . . and nearly all English economists . . . reach economics that way. There are practically no issues of policy . . . which do not involve ethical considerations."* Since this economics text aims to discuss political economy in an especially focused and up-to-date way, it is reasonable to expect that it will help readers with their decisions as voter, investor, and career maker at least as much as any other would.

To do this job as well as it can this new text has started from a rethinking of what is essential in an introduction to economics. The existing introductory texts all contain excessive accumulations of unnecessary material. The compulsion to cover every topic, at least superficially, no matter how ephemeral the topic, turns the book into an encyclopedia and the course into a trial. Readers have trouble seeing the forest for the trees. An objective of this text has been to scrape away much of the unnecessary material: The number of chapters has been cut by nearly half, and almost every chapter makes a primary point, sometimes also a secondary point, but never a catalogue of points. These main points constitute the two dozen or so great ideas in economics.

Teachers of the introductory course report a disturbing stress on the formal, purely technical, side of economics and a consequent submersion of substance. "I supressed nature's design for me, untested; subordinated all meaning to form, unhesitating." So runs a confession in an oratorio by Arnold Schoenberg. Perhaps today's textbook writers need not make so terrible an admission! But texts do subordinate meaning to form when they devote a chapter to analyses, geometric and algebraic, of the *size* of the effect of government spending on national output but not so much as a sentence to the foundations for the view that there is any effect at all after all things are considered. And writers do supress part of their nature when they avoid the hot potato of taxation. The primacy given to formal analytics leaves the impression that quantitative problems—curve shifting and numerical or algebraic calculations—are the very heart of economics rather than an occasionally employed arm of economics. An objective of this text has been to banish some of the formal constructs not required in an introduction to the subject—though a great many technical terms are too convenient to do without, as in any field.

Nevertheless, the uses of political economy and the hoped-for advantages

* J. M. Keynes, Letter to William Temple.

of a concise development of economic principles are not the sole reasons for this text. Another purpose is to communicate, at an introductory level, the fundamental changes ocurring in economic theory in recent decades and thus to convey a sense of the creativity in economics that has made it exciting for economists. Economics is always a cumulative collection of portraits of the way economic institutions, such as competitive markets, appear to work. The wave of modern portraits of the market-based economy—beginning with the distinctive visions of Keynes and Schumpeter a few decades ago and then sweeping over all of economics in the past twenty years—constitutes a revolution in the perspective of economics that is not unlike the modernist revolutions that struck some other fields this century, from physics to music and art.

In the past couple of decades, economics has added a whole new vocabulary: incomplete information, transaction costs, customer markets, "asymmetric" information, incentive compatibility, reputation, incentive- (or efficiency-) wages and job rationing, statistical discrimination, implicit contracts, macroeconomic-equilibrium and the accelerationist hypothesis, the island parable, rational expectations, the policy ineffectiveness proposition, disinflation, and credibility. These modernist concepts and others are introduced (not always by name) in this book.

The desire to present these basic advances in economics, most of which are contributions of my generation (and some of which I had a hand in), alongside older themes and earlier findings, provided much of the constructive energy needed to carry out so large-scale a project. The hope, and an assumption behind liberal-arts education, is that there are readers who will take pleasure in finding out what economics is like.

ACKNOWLEDGMENTS

In the course of this project a great many others besides the author have played a necessary role. I hope that the following acknowledgments provide a reasonably full accounting of my debts to them.

The broad plan of the book (with the theme of classical versus modern) was conceived in the late 1960s, and the publishing agreement with W. W. Norton & Company was reached in 1970. In the following years of delay after delay, my advocate at the publishing house, Donald S. Lamm, remained loyal, patient, and seemingly confident, for which I am most grateful. His thoughtful editorial work on the manuscript that eventually materialized is also appreciated.

Real progress began in 1979 when, sink or swim, I jumped into an experimental introductory course at Columbia without the life preserver of a textbook to teach from. Each lecture required preparing the material that would make up another chapter. The students in that class deserve my thanks for serving as live subjects of that experiment. With the lecture notes as a base, the writing proceeded relatively smoothly from early 1980 until completion some four years later.

The organization and aims of the book owe much to conversations with a great many people, more than can be listed here. But a few stand out in my memory. There is George Stigler, who gave me the key to the arrangement of the early chapters when he told me he would start with two-person situations and graduate to many-person ones if he were rewriting his own text. There is Amartya Sen, who persuaded me that a text in political economy would be starting off on the wrong foot if (carrying Stigler's idea to the extreme) it started with the economics of one-person situations. There are also my colleagues at Columbia, all of whom, I think, have contributed something to this text in innumerable conversations about economics and teaching over the years. (The influence of their writings is all over the book—expanded choice instead of utility, election strategies, paradoxes with three agents, rent seeking, supervision, adverse selection, export crowding out, and so forth—but that is another story.)

At an early stage in their development the various chapters received a close reading from a number of scholars, and I am grateful for their scrutiny and criticism. Edward Gramlich and Amartya Sen reviewed approximately the first half of the original manuscript. Steven Salop and Andrew Weiss read the part on modern equilibrium models and some earlier chapters. Nearly all of the manuscript was read by Arnold Collery, Roman Frydman, Alvin Marty, and Mancur Olson. Some of the appendices on foreign trade were read by Robert Feenstra. I also want to thank Janet Byrne for her careful copy editing and Nancy Palmquist for her reliable handling of communications about the manuscript over so many years.

Although much of the book was written at my home base, Columbia, the hospitality of several universities abroad provided opportunities to work on the manuscript with little or no interruption. For their invitations I am grateful to Jan Cramer at the University of Amsterdam, Mario Simonsen at the Vargas Foundation in Rio, Heinz König and Jürgen Schröder at the University of Mannheim, and Marcello deCecco at the European University Institute in Florence.

Such a demanding project is hard on family members as well as the author. Over the years my wife, Viviana, and my step-daughter, Monica, coped with the strains on my time and mood, as did my mother and father. As this preface was being finished my father died, knowing that the book was at last done. His dedication and integrity set a standard in my life and in my work on this book.

Part 1

Introduction

CHAPTER 1

The Rules of the Game

A society is held together by the mutual advantages its members find from exchange with one another, from collaborating in production and trading the products. A society's economy is the meeting ground for such exchange. By participating in this economy, pooling their efforts in exchange for claims to the resulting goods, the members of society can expect to do better than by living apart. If exchanges could not occur, the society would not function and would dissolve into ones that could.

For exchange to develop people need to be guided by laws and incentives in choosing what part to take in the economy. There have to be "rules of the game" so that people have an idea how to play their cards. Recognized rights and prohibitions, expected rewards and penalties, trusted conventions and norms are necessary to encourage and to coordinate efforts—to achieve an economywide division of labor. The deliveryman counts on the employer to pay him the wage agreed upon, on the state to settle for the enacted taxes, on his neighbors not to steal what remains; in return, the employer expects him to deliver the goods.

> Every society needs its economy and, to operate the economy, a structure of opportunities relating prospective reward to role performed: a set of activities, or exchanges, that a participant is permitted to have (rights to enter into certain contracts, own certain properties), and for each permitted activity the likely reward (pay, security, job satisfaction).

A society's economy, then, operates by presenting the participants with a structure of opportunities which determines, given people's goals and capacities, who does what. In affecting the tasks that people choose to do it thus determines the efficiency with which the society produces and delivers to people the goods they want. And in setting the rewards obtainable for the various tasks it thus determines, given people's skills and other resources, the distribution of benefits to the participants in the economy.

But by what mechanisms or system of mechanisms are the prevailing opportunities for reward determined? How do they work? How efficiently do they perform compared to others? Why not other (or modified) mechanisms?

> Political economy is the study of the conflicting reward structures that society can (and hence must) choose among: How do the mechanisms in an existing or potential system—legal rights, certain markets, taxes and subsidies, decrees and duties, etc.— operate in shaping people's opportunities? And how well or badly do they tend to perform?

Inequality, unemployment, inflation, pollution. . . . In all cases the political economist seeks to explain what is necessitated by economic factors, what is the result of political factors, and what might be changed.

THE ECONOMICS OF SCARCITY

Goods, to be goods, must satisfy wants of one or more persons—wants for security, comfort, discovery, expression, achievement, and so on. Goods are the vehicles that carry satisfactions of human wants. A plot of land is not a good, then; it is a resource capable of producing goods. Money, stocks, and bonds represent financial assets that are expected to be exchangeable for goods.

Goods, by their nature, must also be available from current resources. A good is either produced currently from existing resources, or it is itself an existing resource, such as sunlight or foodstocks stored from previous production. Here is the Canadian economist Robert Mundell waxing poetic on this trinity of terms in the economic lexicon:

Hunger is a want . . . and food [in stock] a resource. Hunger creates the desire for food. Thus the availability of food for reducing hunger, combined with the ability to eat it, implies that food is a good. Available food, drink, and shelter are goods that can eliminate hunger, thirst and cold; a symphony concert is a good that can satisfy a listener's love of music and a toy train is a good that can satisfy a child's taste for play. The concept of a good in economics is a very broad one. A loaf of bread is a good; and so is a car, a house, a painting, a Beatles record, a bed, and a dog. So might be air, a date with a girl, a swim in the sea, a conversation with a genius. . . .*

Not all goods gratify our self-interest in the narrow sense of that term. Giving a gift is a good if it satisfies the giver's desire to express affection. Volunteering unpaid labor is a good if it satisfies the volunteer's desire to express a sense of belonging.

Nor are all goods outputs rather than inputs. It has long been recognized that in some jobs the work is itself rewarding. Sociologists speak of job satisfactions, and economists of nonpecuniary rewards—rewards other than those provided by the pay. The best jobs have a wide assortment of characteristics, *some* of which are actually goods for the job holder.

Many jobs are still pure tedium or drudgery, of course. Yet it would be difficult to underestimate the importance of nonpecuniary rewards, since jobs differ so much in this respect and the differences can be worth a lot. To create something, anything, or to share with others in the production of something—such goods are of great value to virtually all of us. The importance of work is noted by the Swedish economist Gunnar Myrdal:

[It] is a stock phrase of . . . textbooks in economics [that] consumption is the sole end of production. . . . In other words: Man works in order to live. This is a possible philosophy of life. But . . . there are many people who live in order to work. . . . Most people who are reasonably well off derive more satisfaction in their capacity as producers than as consumers. Indeed, many would define the social ideal as a state in which as many people as can live in this way.†

When the late-nineteenth-century English economist Alfred Marshall argues how central the economy is to people's lives he remarks that

. . . the business by which a person earns his livelihood generally fills his thoughts during by far the greater part of those hours in which his

---

* Robert A. Mundell, *Man and Economics* (New York: McGraw-Hill, 1968), p. 5.

† Gunnar Myrdal, *The Political Element in the Development of Economic Theory*, (Cambridge, Mass.: Harvard University Press, 1954, tr. by Paul Streeten from the 1932 German ed.), p. 136.

mind is at its best; during them his character is being formed by . . . his work . . . and by his relations to his associates in work. . . .*

These observations of Marshall's are reason enough to study political economy.

Thus goods are the stuff of which rewards are made. The rewards from participation in the society's economy, paid or unpaid, pecuniary and non-pecuniary, all take the form of goods or the means to acquire goods.

An economy is where wants interact with resources to yield the production of goods for the participants. Since goods require resources to produce, the production possibilities of an economy depend upon its endowment of resources. These resources may be classified into three categories corresponding roughly to the famous trio of labor, land, and capital:

- Labor. There are the human resources—the physical and mental capacities of the participants in the economy. A few goods require no human involvement in their production (sunsets, running water from a natural well, exhibitions of memorabilia in unmanned museums), but they are exceptions.

- Land. There are the natural resources—consisting of land, atmosphere, water and other minerals, fish and wildlife. It has been observed that rich natural resources are not necessary for a rich standard of living—witness Israel and Japan (which are not well endowed in those respects); yet water, for example, can limit the growth of cities and farms.

- Capital. There are the artificially produced resources built up in the past for subsequent use—collectively called capital. The accumulated capital of an economy includes both material resources, such as plant and equipment, and intellectual resources, such as arithmetic and navigation. In a society's economy the capital also includes its moral and political resources; without its elemental customs and institutions to draw on a society would not be able to create and maintain any set of rules for participation in the economy—there would be chaos and strife or retreat into self-sufficient enclaves.

When economists speak of the allocation of the resources of an economy they mean how each unit of these resources is used—which good it is engaged in producing—and how the resulting output of goods is distributed to the participants.

While an economy without wants would be a contradiction, there could exist, at least in our imaginations, an economy in which wants for all the

---

* Alfred Marshall, *Elements of Economics* (London: Macmillan and Company, 1892), p. 2.

available goods were *limited*. In such an economy it *could* be that the existing resources for producing these goods were so plentiful that each person's
wants for all the producible goods were satisfied in full—an economy of
plenty: Everyone would work only to the point where working longer would
not be enjoyable, so all available job satisfactions would be completely realized. And thanks to these efforts, the technology, and the plentifulness of
natural and capital resources, everyone's desires for the outputs produced
would also be completely satisfied. Everyone would be satiated with goods—
the goods the economy was capable of producing.

An economy of plenty might not be as contented as might be supposed at
first. Plenty of *what*? Vast resources are not sufficient to make anyone happy—
the sated noblemen in Mozart's comic operas and the stuffed bourgeoisie in
Buñuel's satirical films brilliantly dramatize that. There might be no possibility of creativity at work, and no songs to sing after work. Still, it would
be an extraordinary economy: Though each of its existing resources is *limited* in quantity, wants have not pressed up against the limits of its existing
resources. Though the quantity of land is limited, not infinite, the *limit is
not binding*. Hence no existing resource is *scarce*—scarce in the economist's
sense that having more of it, even just a little more, would make a difference.

> In a land where there was enough for all, enough of whatever
> goods the economy was able to produce, the resources and goods
> would not be scarce. None would have any scarcity value, since
> having more of them would not matter to anyone. Thus an econ-
> omy without scarcity would have no opposing interests, no bones
> of contention.

This hypothetical economy of plenty has been a recurrent dream for centuries. The vision of a society with "enough for all" may have beckoned
many settlers to the New Land in the frontier days of the nineteenth century.
Such an economy is nevertheless only a mirage, if human experience to date
is any guide to human prospects. Not even monks and mystics have enough—
not as long as they could meditate longer or better with the help of more
capital or land or the assistance of others. To have run out of uses for additional rewards is to suffer from a failure of the imagination. For most people
there are not enough hours in the day, and never enough income.

- ◆ Heinrich Schliemann, the Hamburg merchant turned archeologist, hurriedly
  amassed a great fortune to spend searching for the ruins of ancient Troy.
- ◆ Eleanor Belmont, the New York actress and heiress, worked tirelessly into
  her nineties raising resources to rescue the Metropolitan Opera.
- ◆ Paul McCartney, the British songwriter and recording artist, uses his vast
  income to keep his independence from "the big guys."

FIGURE 1–1: Scarcity and Nonscarcity Illustrated

PANEL A

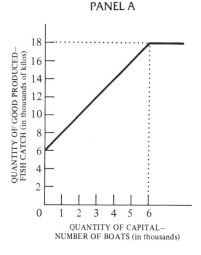

QUANTITY OF GOOD PRODUCED—
FISH CATCH (in thousands of kilos)

QUANTITY OF CAPITAL—
NUMBER OF BOATS (in thousands)

number of boats exceeds (or equals) the number of fishermen—here 6 thousand—fishing boats become a *nonscarce* resource: Having more would make no difference.

Panel B depicts a slightly less obvious case: Society might not want to consume more fish just because there are more boats. Here it is supposed, at the other extreme, that only 6 thousand are going to be produced, because no more of that good (fish) is wanted. In this case, an increase in the number of boats, up to 2 thousand boats, results in a reduction in the *number of fishermen.* Released from fishing, these ex-fishermen then produce *other* goods—bread, circuses, or take early retirement for leisure-time pursuits. Thus boats are a scarce resource up to that point; having more makes a difference. But with 2 thousand or more, boats would become nonscarce.

The diagams illustrate scarcity and nonscarcity of a resource by showing how the available quantity of the resource, the number of fishing boats, might alter the economy's capacity to produce. The diagrams measure the effects of a change on the number of boats *alone,* with all *other* resources—the number of fishermen, the coastal waters, and so on—being unaffected. ("Other things equal," as economists say.)

First, the most obvious of cases. Panel A depicts the effect of the number of boats when the total effect is on the capacity output of *fish* (the production of the other goods, and leisure, are not altered). Here, with each additional boat one more fisherman can take to the fishing waters in a boat instead of being restricted to netting fish on the shoreline and thus catch 3 kilos of fish per day instead of 1, for a gain of 2 kilos per day. As long as having more boats around means catching more fish, by liberating more fishermen from the shore, boats are still *scarce.* But once the

PANEL B

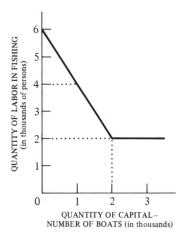

QUANTITY OF LABOR IN FISHING
(in thousands of persons)

QUANTITY OF CAPITAL—
NUMBER OF BOATS (in thousands)

♦ J. Paul Getty, the Texas oil billionaire, declared he never felt rich because he always had use for every penny.

The prodigious appetites for rewards and talents for using them of these heroic spenders are merely spectacular examples of the truth that, in our world, resources are scarce—that having more (no matter how much already) makes a difference. A general increase of the rewards offered in an economy enhances the ability of people to pursue their preferred careers; it improves the opportunities they can provide their children, family, and friends; and it permits them to lead a richer social and cultural life.

> In the economies that people have actually experienced, there are *always unfilled wants for more*—more of the goods produced by the existing resources.

Economics studies the *economy of scarcity*—where unfilled wants for the economy's goods press the economy to the limits of some of its resources, leaving wants still unfilled. Recognizing that the wants for an economy's goods seem never to be filled, economics supposes that these wants are unlimited. The encounter of limitless wants with limited resources inevitably results in scarcity. Of course, every resource in any earth-bound economy is limited: there is only so much topsoil, so much iodine in the sea, so many sands in the desert, and so on. That much is geology. But if there are unlimited wants, hence always unfilled wants for more of some of the economy's goods, then *at least some* of the economy's existing resources must be scarce: If the supply of all resources were somehow increased—so that there was more land, more capital, and even more time in the day—it is certain that *some* of these extra resources would find uses in filling some of the unfilled wants—*which* resources depending on which wants are most unfilled.

> Political economy focuses on economies in the grip of scarcity, where *some* resource limits are *limiting* the economy's capacity to satisfy the wants for the goods it produces, leaving *unfilled wants* for these goods. If these *scarce* resources were more abundant, more wants would be satisfied; if less abundant, there would be less satisfaction of wants. Figure 1–1 expresses this concept of scarcity in geometric terms, as does Figure 1–2.

> There is no telling in general—for all economies and all time— *which* resources will be scarce and which not scarce. There is a theoretical possibility of a time when there is no more scarcity

FIGURE 1–2: Scarcity and Nonscarcity, a More Realistic View

PANEL A

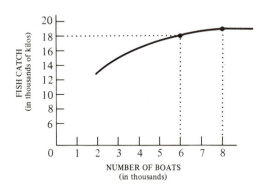

sent out when some of the others were found needing repairs and hence not available for the day's work. Yet at some point having more boats would make no more difference; in Panel A that level is reached once there are 8 thousand boats. Beyond (or at) that point fishing boats become *nonscarce.*

Panel B illustrates the same ideas in the case where it is desired to have a fixed catch of fish— say, 6 thousand kilos on the average. As before, 2 thousand boats would require 2 thousand fishermen. But here, having a few boats less would not require *so many more* fishermen to reach the target output as in Figure 1–1's Panel B, where men without boats can catch only 1 thousand each; they could help out with the remaining boats. And here, having spare boats would reduce time lost through "down" boats and thus actually reduce the labor needed.

These diagrams illustrate scarcity and nonscarcity more realistically. Panel A records that 6 thousand boats and 6 thousand fishermen produce 18 thousand kilos of fish—exactly as in the previous example depicted by Figure 1–1, Panel A. But there are two differences. First, if a few of the 6 thousand boats are *lost,* say 1 thousand, capacity output does not fall by as much as before. Why? The 1 thousand fishermen thus stranded *could* cast their nets from the shore, catching a total of 1 thousand instead of 3 thousand—which was the case in Figure 1–1, Panel A. But here, in Figure 1–2's Panel A, those stranded fisherman can produce *more* than 1 thousand by teaming up with the others to help with repairs or other work. *Second,* if a few boats are *added* to the 6 thousand, capacity output is increased. If there are, say, 7 thousand boats for only 6 thousand fishermen, the extra boats contribute spare capacity. The spare boats could be

PANEL B

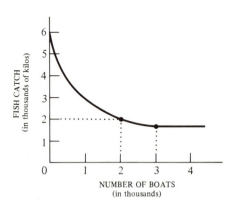

of labor: Abundant robots would do everything, with robot mates getting us through the days.

The list of resources that turn out to be scarce will vary from economy to economy. It will depend on the nature of people's wants—on tastes. The salt mines will not be a scarce resource, and salt will have no scarcity value, in an economy where everyone is on a sodium-free diet. It will depend also on the technology: The supplies of the various minerals in ocean water are (for the most part) totally unused, hence these resources are not scarce, because extracting them for the production of goods, such as drinking water, would require prodigal amounts of *other* resources that *are* scarce and already used to better advantage in other ways. It will also depend on the quantity of each resource available—on endowments. Prairie land and mountainous acreage are only partially used, and hence not scarce, in economies where their supplies are plentiful in relation to wants for the goods they are used to produce.

How could there be an economy in which there is no scarcity of *labor?* Certainly the human resources of a society stop being scarce when there are no longer enough of all the other *complementary resources* that each worker needs to be outfitted with in order to produce. It may be that in the past such nonscarcity occurred when primitive agricultural societies were struck by drought or floods. Now the development of a "high technology" in microcomputers and robotics has raised fears in the minds of some, as did earlier waves of mechanization, that human labor everywhere in advanced economies will again cease to be scarce—this time made obsolete by an *abundance* of supermachines that serve as *substitutable resources* for labor. Impossible? Theoretically, no! By itself, economic theory does not rule out the existence of an economy where robots can do anything that humans can and have proliferated to the point where they, and human labor as well, are no longer scarce. (In this exotic economy humans would engage in production, alongside their humanoid robotic colleagues, only for the job satisfactions in it; but without pay, since no employer, not even a government employer, would have reason to pay for work that robots can do without cost, because they are not scarce.) In fact, such an economy is a most unlikely prospect! Robots may some day grind out good tunes and even embryos, but never make good musicians and mothers. Reflecting on the question of man and machines, a great economist (who turns up in chapter 19) said, in a small joke, that there will always be a servant problem. Nevertheless, now there are robots to clean house and walk the dog. Thus robotics are *reducing* the scarcity value of some unskilled labor, which is no joke for unskilled workers (unless the savings are steered their way).

The essence of an economy, then, is the activity of purposeful "actors" striving to meet their wants in the face of limited resources. (Regions do not have economies, only individuals and societies have economies.) There is an economy wherever there is management of available resources to satisfy wants—where "economy" in the homey sense of using resources to best advantage is being practiced. The very word *economy* comes from the Greek word *oikonomos,* which means one who stewards, or husbands, resources toward some end. To "economize" means to use each scarce resource with regard to the other ends that the resource could serve instead.

Scarcity and Choice for an Individual

If the essence of an economy is economizing, then there can be one-person economies as well as social economies. And there are, of course. The most famous example of a one-man economy is found in fiction—the figure of Robinson Crusoe created by the eighteenth-century novelist and economist Daniel Defoe. In fact, not long ago there was the sad figure of the Japanese soldier Hiro Onodo, who, having become separated from his comrades and fearing enemy capture, lived alone on the resources of a Philippine jungle for most of his adult life. These are closed economies—they have no trade with the world outside—and a bizarre case. However, one-person economies that "export" or "import" something are not uncommon. The home is such an economy: A person when at home has to decide how best to allocate his limited time and other resources between recreation (watching a television show or reading the newspaper) and doing domestic chores, and between doing one chore and another. The single-operator farm is a one-person economy: The farmer has to choose how to allocate his working time and his land between raising wheat, say, and raising sheep to produce wool.

Scarcity arises in these one-person economies as in social economies. The individual's own labor—his or her time—is scarce, and so may be other resources as well. Hence the individual has choices to make about how to use those scarce resources: More labor devoted to raising sheep leaves less working time for raising wheat; more acreage for wheat means less for sheep. More time spent watching football on television leaves less time for vacuuming rugs or washing socks. Thus a decision to produce more of a good is a decision to produce less of some other good.

A consequence of scarcity, in any one-person economy as well as any social economy, is that production possibilities are limited—so that producing more of one thing decreases the amount that can be produced of something else, given the amounts of the various resources available.

The relationship between the possible output of one good and the possible output of some other good is captured by the *production possibility curve*. Figure 1–3, Panel A, depicts such a curve for the solitary farmer choosing between wheat and wool, given the labor-time he makes available. There is a similar production possibility curve for a *social* economy, given total employment (or the total number of "manhours" employed) in such production. Panel B depicts another curve that describes the choice between wheat and hours worked, given the time spent producing wool.

Since producing more of a good requires producing less of another, given the resources available, the true cost of an extra unit of a good is the amount of the other good that is given up; this is called the *opportunity cost* of a good—the cost of producing one unit more of a good measured by the size of the alternative opportunity that is sacrificed as a result. The opportunity cost of a resource (or a resource input) has a similar meaning—it is the cost of using one more unit of a certain resource in producing something, such as an additional acre devoted to wool production, as measured by the consequent loss of output of the other good that the resource unit would otherwise be producing, such as wheat. Our farmer, when he considers giving an extra acre or extra day to wool, will consider these opportunity costs. They are basic to deciding whether extra wool is best produced through extra labor or extra land, and whether the extra wool produced the best way would be worth that extra cost.

These concepts—scarcity, the set of production possibilities, opportunity cost—lead naturally to another basic economic concept. A person is producing *inefficiently* if there is a different way of using the available resources that would produce more output of some good without causing reduced output of any other good. The farmer, for example, is allocating his resources inefficiently if by using less labor with more land in producing wool and less land with more labor in producing wheat he can produce more of one (or both) without less of the other. And production is *efficient* if there is *no* other way of using the available resources that would produce more of something without reducing the output of something else—without an opportunity cost. In Figure 1–3 efficiency in production means being *on*—not inside—the production possibility curve. One of the big questions in political economy is whether a *society* might be inefficient—and exactly what that means.

FIGURE 1–3: The Production Possibilities of a Lone Farmer

PANEL A

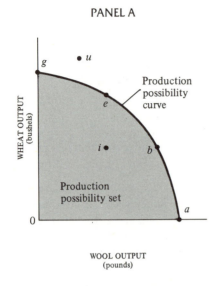

WOOL OUTPUT
(pounds)

points on or inside the production possibility curve is usually called the production possibility set; it is represented by the shaded area. Output combinations corresponding to points outside the set, like *u*, are unattainable—impossible to produce if no more labor is made available.

Obviously the farmer is misusing, or misallocating, his resources if he succeeds only in producing a combination inside the curve. Point *i* is inefficient.

Panel B: GIVEN THE TIME DEVOTED TO PRODUCING WOOL, MORE WHEAT OUTPUT IMPLIES MORE WORK, LESS LEISURE TIME

The curve in Panel B takes another view of production possibilities of the farmer. This curve shows for each possible amount of total *work* (hence leisure) the largest output of wheat that is possible—given the amount of time devoted to producing the other good, wool. As before, point *e* illustrates efficient production, and point *i* inefficient production.

Panel A: GIVEN THE LABOR TIME DEVOTED TO PRODUCTION, MORE WHEAT IMPLIES LESS WOOL

The production possibility in Panel A shows for each possible amount of *wool* output the largest possible output of wheat—and vice versa—given the total amount of his time that the farmer devotes to such production.

Thus the farmer could choose to produce the combination of outputs represented by the point *e* which is *on* the production possibility curve. Or he could choose any other point on the curve. For example, starting from point *e* the farmer could shift some more of his labor and land over to producing wool—at a cost in terms of wheat output—in order to produce the combination indicated to point *b*. The table (below) gives numerical illustrations.

Alternatively, he could produce the output combination represented by a point that is *inside* the curve, such as the point *i*. The whole set of

PANEL B

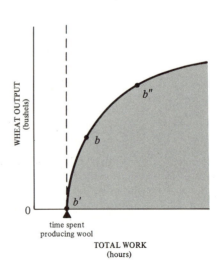

TOTAL WORK
(hours)

Do people typically attain efficiency in the province of their one-person economies? If they do it is not with a how-to-do-it manual. Yet if an individual holding sway over a micro-economy does manage to allocate his time and other resources efficiently, such an allocation will obey certain principles; and these efficiency principles might actually help a person to achieve efficiency.

- If Crusoe, contemplating a more berry-rich diet, considers switching a nearby field from apples to berries, he should calculate the opportunity cost (in apples lost) of reallocating that land, hence the "rent" he should charge himself for that land. Then he should calculate the cost of reallocating instead some of his *labor* from apple picking to berry gathering— the time needed to gather the desired increase in berries from distant fields and the opportunity cost of withdrawing that labor from apple picking, hence the "wage" to charge himself for that labor. By such calculations Crusoe might manage to produce each good at the lowest possible cost— thus achieving efficiency in production.

- If Crusoe, contemplating the consumption of more leisure time—a slower-paced life-style—considers lying in bed an extra hour each morning, he should calculate what the opportunity cost of that hour would be measured in terms of reduced fish in the morning catch, hence the "wage" he should charge himself, in units of fish, for that hour of his time. Then he should calculate the cost if instead he reduced the time spent producing each of the other goods, hence the "wage" to charge himself, in units of apples, if he takes the hour out of apple growing. By such calculations Crusoe might be able, after some trial-and-error, to achieve what could

Table 1–1: PRODUCTION POSSIBILITIES OF THE ILLUSTRATIVE FARMER

Bushels of Wheat		Pounds of Wool	Total Hours Worked	Point in Panel A
0	if	70,000	2,000	a
10,000	if	60,000	2,000	b
20,000	if	40,000	2,000	e
30,000	if	0	2,000	g

Bushels of Wheat	Total Hours Worked	Pound of Wool	Points in Panel B
0	1,500	60,000	b'
10,000	2,000	60,000	b
15,000	2,500	60,000	b''

be called efficiency in the level and direction of his production activities. If Crusoe misperceives these opportunity costs of his time he will be led to choose inefficiently his use of time, and thus to make himself worse off than need be.

But anyone who has spent a Saturday dashing from washer to stove to barber (with newspaper) to dryer to stove knows that programming one's activities efficiently is a complicated business.

THE FUNCTIONING OF A SOCIAL ECONOMY

When we pause to reflect on how intricate and interwoven the social economy is, at least in most countries today, we have to marvel that these elaborate structures managed to develop and continue to survive. (It is even more amazing if, as some political economists contend, societies are capable of organizing their resources perfectly efficiently, at least within a wide sector of the economy; but more of that later.)

What makes these present-day social economies incredibly complex, especially in recent times, is the extent to which labor and other resources become specialized and thus highly interdependent. To realize even a fraction of the mutual gains that a social economy offers its participants—to come anywhere near to achieving an efficient use of its resources—labor and land and capital must be employed in different jobs and industries; and then the goods produced must be somehow divided and exchanged. Some of the advantages are obvious enough:

◆ By specializing, each individual and region can use to best advantage special skills and resources. So miners are short and lamp lighters tall; northern regions grow grains and the south green vegetables; and farmers do not waste their time alternating between north and south to be self-sufficient.

◆ Specializing permits a person to become more proficient, through prior training and on-the-job experience. So a doctor and dentist together know more than would two doctor-dentists.

Another advantage of specialization was the one that struck Adam Smith, founder of classical political economy, two centuries ago. In a famous passage from *The Wealth of Nations,* Smith recounts his visit to a new pin factory in the early years of the Industrial Revolution*:

---

* Adam Smith, *An Inquiry into the Nature and Causes of the Wealth of Nations* (London: Strahan and Caddell, 1776). References here will be to the Modern Library ed., Random House.

... [I]n the way in which this business is now carried on, . . . making a pin . . . is divided into about eighteen distinct operations, which, in some manufactories, are all performed by distinct hands. . . . I have seen a small manufactory of this kind where ten men only were employed. . . . But though indifferently accommodated with the necessary machinery, they could . . . make among them . . . upwards of forty-eight thousand pins in a day. . . . [I]f they had all wrought separately and independently . . . they could certainly not each of them have made twenty, perhaps not one pin in a day. . . .*

In explaining precisely how this great feat of productivity resulted from such a "division of labor," Smith notes that "time is not lost in passing from one species of work to another" (point 1 above) and that each workman acquires increased "dexterity" (point 2 above). But he emphasizes a third factor, "the great number of machines which facilitate and abridge labor. . . ." Smith had witnessed, he knew, a breakthrough in the design of machinery—in the use of capital:

◆ By dividing the work into several repetitive and simultaneous operations, the machine designed for each operation could be used continuously— without interruption for the length of the day, or shift; if an artisan made the whole pin (or shoe or whatever) in solitary isolation, then each such specialized machine would be idle most of the time or machines would be shipped back and forth from artisan to artisan.

The mention of capital brings up another dimension in which people specialize—the time dimension. Some people work at producing goods for consumption immediately or in minutes, such as film projectionists and waiters. But the vast majority of people are producing goods for consumption at future times, often the distant future: Each day there is trucking, production of trucks, production of tires and rolled steel sheet, coal mining and rubber growing, production of mining machinery, and so on. Thus goods are produced by an indirect, or roundabout, process: An input today, such as a tree planting, may take years to show up in a finished consumer good, such as the morning's newspapers.

◆ In a society that has a lot of accumulated capital with which to produce its consumer goods, people specialize at different stages of a lengthy production process: some replace buildings, some repair machines, some produce to replace unfinished goods-in-process. So there is a division of labor *over time*, as today's people attempt to coordinate with tomorrow's and succeeding days' people, in order to produce future consumer goods.

*Smith, *The Wealth of Nations*, Book I, chap. 1, p. 5. It is interesting that Smith, prophet of the benefits of specialization, also foresaw the dark side: "The man whose life is spent in performing a few simple operations, of which the effects . . . are always the same, has no occasion to exert his understanding or to exercise his invention" (p. 734).

The achievement of such specialization, however, raises an obvious problem for every society to solve one way or another: People performing the various specialized tasks in a bakery, say, require some bread (literally and figuratively) for their efforts. The people specializing in wheat growing, and in trucking, want to consume bread, not wheat or trucked wheat—not the unfinished, or intermediate, good they happen to specialize in producing. Further, people generally want to consume a variety of things—everyone wants bread *and* circuses. The wheat grower and the circus worker want to use their pay to obtain bread, and the baker to buy admissions to the circus. Thus specialization requires a method of *exchange*. People must be able to receive in exchange for their labor inputs (and any nonlabor inputs) some good or goods they desire to consume.

♦ In certain cases, such exchanges are conducted by barter. A farm worker may be paid "in kind." Bus rides and theater tickets are frequently swapped for chickens in rural Bolivia, and The Barter Theater in North Carolina got its name that way. In the "underground economy," a dentist and a carpenter may swap their services in order to dodge taxes.

♦ For the most part, exchanges in the social economy are made with the aid of money—paper money, or "bank money," (the balances in people's bank accounts) that people accept as payment for their inputs and that is accepted in turn as payment for finished goods. Thus the swap of inputs (and unfinished goods) for finished goods is turned into a two-step process: inputs-for-money, then money-for-goods.

Either way, the worker producing wheat is paid with some sort of *property* that can be used to acquire bread or other finished goods and that the worker alone has the right to use. Figure 1–4 depicts the circular flow of such wealth.

Four Trade-offs: Choices Facing Every Social Economy

Although a *method* of exchange—some system of property—is necessary for specialization and exchange, it does not by itself determine the "division of labor" among the various specialized tasks nor the distribution of the various goods obtained in exchange. To achieve the benefits of specialization and exchange, the social economy must somehow answer the basic questions about *how* resources and the resulting goods are to be *allocated*: How—with what batch of resources—is each good going to be produced? How—for what basket of finished goods—is each person's pay to be spent? How much of each finished good—consumer good and capital good—is going to be produced? How much pay is each resource going to be rewarded with? The answers to these questions will decide how fully the society realizes the potential benefits of specialization and how the realized benefits are distributed.

FIGURE 1—4: The Wheel of Wealth

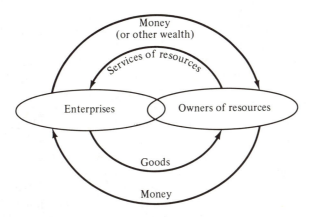

Once a system of legal ownership and property rights has been instituted exchange can commence.

Producing enterprises, private and public, obtain productive services from resources. Then the enterprises supply finished goods to resource owners. This is shown by the *counterclockwise* circular flow.

Resource owners, private and governmental, receive payments in the form of money (or IOUs or other claims) for the use of their resources.

Then they exchange this money (or another sort of wealth) for finished goods produced by the enterprises. This is represented by the *clockwise* circular flow.

Because all enterprise revenue becomes income paid to somebody and all income payments must come from enterprise revenues, the total income in the social economy must equal the total enterprise revenue—which is the money value of the total output of finished goods produced by the enterprises in the social economy.

It is clear that these allocation questions facing every social economy have to be answered by some social mechanism for people's cooperation and interaction. Take the question of the way each good is to be produced. In a social economy, the resources available to each producing unit, or operation—to a coal mine, an air shuttle service, a radio station, etc.—are *not given*, unlike the situation of Crusoe. Some mechanism must determine the *amounts* of labor, land, and capital resources going to each individual producing unit. How well this mechanism does its job will determine the extent to which the social economy achieves efficiency in production. It is not enough that every producing unit be using efficiently the resources it happens to have; it is necessary as well that resources be allocated efficiently *among* the various producing units. (It won't do for one sheep rancher to have a lot of labor and little capital while another otherwise identical rancher has little labor and lots of capital.) For *efficiency in production*, each resource should go to the producer who can make the most productive use of it.

Similarly, there must be a mechanism to determine (since people want more than one good) the way each person's income is divided among the different goods produced. In the social economy, the goods available to a person with a certain income are *not given,* unlike Crusoe, who could eat only the fish he produced and who could not return merchandise for a store credit. (The *total* consumption of fish is given by total output, but one *individual's* consumption is not given by his or her own output.) If some people's income is half that of another group's, shall they get half as much fish and half as much of everything else too? Or shall they be allowed, in effect, to *trade in* some opera tickets for more fish and movies? Whatever the answer society gives, the question must be answered. Some mechanism must determine the amounts of each of the finished goods that each person's income is exchanged for or spent on. The mechanism chosen will determine how nearly the social economy attains *efficiency in trade:* For such efficiency, each unit of each good should go to the consumer willing to pay the most for it, given the total amounts of each good supplied and given people's incomes; then there would be no unexploited opportunities for mutually beneficial trade. To realize that efficiency, clearly, it is not enough that each consumer avoid waste through spilled milk and forgotten opera tickets; consumers must allocate goods efficiently among themselves through some cooperative mechanism.

The determination of how much is produced of each good likewise requires a mechanism to coordinate the participants' different specialized efforts. Chaos would result if the participants all left their choice of a specialty to chance. They have to be guided by some mechanism in choosing whether to join the circus or stay on the farm. Even if the social economy were producing just one good, bread, say, decisions to keep wheat fields in cultivation or not, to maintain or to close down rail lines, to replace or to scrap bakery ovens, etc. have to be coordinated (at least to a degree!). The efficiency of the economy is greatly dependent on the performance of whichever coordinating mechanism society adopts: Does it turn the wheat land into a dust bowl and leave bakery workers and ovens idle? Does it create a boom in farm equipment making and other agricultural investments that will be regretted later? Does it produce too much bread and not enough circus? Evidently the success of the economy in meeting people's wants for various goods (including leisure) also depends on the degree to which the economy attains this third kind of efficiency—*efficiency in the level and direction of economic activity.*

The Big Trade-off

Lastly, the social economy needs a mechanism for determining the reward to each resource owner for the input contributed—hence the amount of pay that is spendable on finished goods (including any government subsidy and net of all taxes). This is a problem for society that is famous for the conflicts and controversy it has aroused. In human societies, at least, the participants in the social economy have opposing interests when it comes to the rewards. If society were to add successively to the reward for one kind of resource in a certain use—say, unskilled farm labor engaged in wheat growing—there must come a point after which each further increase in bread for that resource necessitates cutbacks in bread for truckers, bakers, and the rest. At some point more for them spells less for us. That would not be so in a world that somehow escaped scarcity, where wants for the producible goods were sharply limited. Nor would it be so in a society in which people did not seek to be rewarded with goods for their own private use—where they were content to work for shared national objectives (and took food only to keep going). But individualism and scarcity are normal features.

It may be this individualism—the desire of the individual for autonomy within the group—that most distinguishes human societies from nonhuman societies, at least those at the primitive end of the biological spectrum. In their studies of the flock of birds, the school of fish, etc., zoologists and ethologists and sociobiologists adopt a view that has points in common with economists' view of human society. These primitive societies are seen as collections of purposeful and cooperating agents that find themselves up against the problem of scarcity. Further, these societies manage to make remarkably effective use of their scarce resources by developing a division of labor (achieved by mechanisms that are still under study). In their researches on the insect colony, however, sociobiologists arrived at a novel hypothesis: These social creatures devote the resources of their society to the sole objective of propagating the society's genes, risking their lives when that may help to save the colony from invaders.

In this view, what is totally alien about these fanatical social creatures is that none has an apparent desire for any *individualistic*, or *private*, good—a good having the ordinary property that, like a raincoat or a raisin, it can be used by one individual or another but not both. Instead, they have an overriding desire for a *collective*, or *public*, good—a good that any member of society can join in sharing, like a fireworks display or radio broadcast, without thereby causing less of the good to be available to the others sharing in the good—namely, the growth of their genes. Since there are no individualist desires for private consumer goods—or any such wants are overriden by desire for the collective good—there is no tug-of-war over the distribution of consumable goods among the members. (Food is distributed among the participants as oil is distributed over the moving parts of a machine—as a means to a higher end.) And since members' wants converge on the same collective good, there are not even opposing interests over which collective good to produce. Lacking politics, these organizations resemble cult societies.

Yet individual interests are surely not opposed on every matter at each step, even in the most individualistic human society. The economy of a society is not a big-stakes bingo game in which one player's winnings constitute the other players' loss. The social economy presumably offers the prospect of *mutual gain* to some or all the participants—a gain compared to dropping out of the social economy or emigrating to another one. So, provided that the participation in the economy is voluntary, the potential gainers must have some *common interests* as well as opposing interests. They have common interests in obtaining one another's participation and cooperation—up to the point where the benefit to each person no longer exceeds or covers the cost—for the sake of their mutual gain.

- There are undoubtedly common interests in taking a variety of collective actions that make economic cooperation more reliable and efficient. Certain public-health measures, prohibitions against theft and fraud, enforcement of certain kinds of contracts, and so on almost surely produce a gain for all or most and a loss to no one (not even thieves, after toting up all benefits and costs).

- There are also common interests when it comes to rewards—to the spendable pay offered for services contributed. Beyond some point, lowering the pay to some kind of resource might so reduce the incentive of the owners of that resource to contribute to production that everyone's reward is lowered as a consequence—a case of killing the goose that laid golden eggs. There is a common interest in avoiding the booby traps of mutual harm.

The difficulty faced by human societies is that at some boundary the members run out of common interests to exploit and run into zones of opposing interests. Figure 1–5 depicts graphically the two sides of the coin.

Thus every social economy faces four sorts of trade-offs—choices to be made about production, trade, employment, and distribution. Clearly one choice will influence the other choices to be made. The way rewards are distributed will influence the supply of labor and production, for example. Yet all four sorts of decisions are made, no matter what the system for making them.

FIGURE 1—5: The Trade-off between One Resource's Reward and Another Resource's Reward

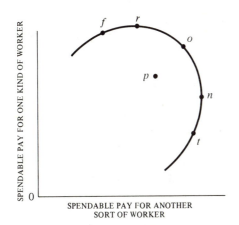

The curve depicts the maximum reward that can be offered to one resource on a certain use, *given* the size of the reward to be offered to some other resource on some other use—and taking as constant the rewards to all the other resources.

Each point, such as *p*, represents a pair of rewards—a structure of rewards—one reward to the one resource, one reward to the other resource. But at point *p*, and at any other point inside the curve, the economy is inefficient. If the economy eradicates all inefficiencies (other than the ineradicable ones), the pair of rewards will correspond to a point *on* the curve. We can deduce that point *p* is inefficient because there exist alternative points, such as point *o*, which offer higher rewards to both of the resources. Point *o* is efficient in the sense that, as a practical matter, society cannot do better for both individuals.

In the choice between point *r*, say, and point *o*, the two resources can be seen to have *opposing* interests. They have *common* interests on escaping from point *f* northeastward to *r*.

THE CHOICE OF MECHANISMS: ALTERNATIVE ECONOMIC SYSTEMS

How to cope with the mind-boggling complexity of all this?

In medieval Europe there were the mechanisms of the feudal system. The manorial economy of the villages was subject to extensive regulation by the feudal lord and the manorial court. In the towns there was the self-regulation of the guilds: craftsmen and merchants were permitted by the lord to form an association called a guild to protect themselves from theft, extortion, and unwanted competition. There might be a fair *contest* for each position but not unregulated freedom for anyone to enter an industry in *competition* with existing producers. The guiding principle, or ethos, of medieval life was that each person had duties and rights corresponding to that person's station in the society: to give the service that was conventional in that position and in return to receive protection in this employment from suppliers, competitors, and so on.

With the rise of the nation-state and the growth of commerce, dating from the Renaissance, the power of the local regulators declined, as did the influence of medieval morality. National rulers began to regulate on a national scale. They granted monopoly rights to certain companies, outlawed or restricted some industries for the benefit of other industries, protected certain guilds from potential competitors, sought to legislate wage rates, and protected certain domestic industries from foreign competition—the stiff tariff duties on imported grain decreed in Britain's "corn laws" being the classic example. The advocates of such legislation were called *mercantilists,* their ideas and policies *mercantilism.* (This approach to organizing the economy was reincarnated in Mussolini's Italy under the names corporativism, state capitalism, and fascism.)

A fundamentally new kind of economic system was outlined in Smith's *Wealth of Nations.* Smith argued for a system in which production and exchange would be determined through the mechanism of *free and competitive markets*—markets free of mercantilist interferences that protected some industries and restricted others and, above all, markets in which all buyers and sellers were free to enter and to compete without licenses or charters or other sponsorship of the state.

To argue his case Smith had to offer a theory of how such a system would work. (Many of the succeeding disputants in the debate Smith started did not really argue, they just banged on the table.)

Smith takes it as an axiom of commercial life that enterprises are always striving for bigger profits and resource owners are constantly looking for better terms. In commerce at least, rationality and self-interest reign. Second, Smith supposes that resource owners (workers, land owners, etc.) become informed of any differences that just arose in the rates of remuneration in the various enterprises or industries, and know what new rate of pay to expect now.

Hence if labor or land or capital brought momentarily higher rewards in one employment than another the owners of this productive factor will transfer it from the less remunerative to the more remunerative employments to the point where the prospective rate of pay is again *equal* in every use. Thus, there is an equilibrium in which each employer knows he has to pay labor (and likewise land, etc.) the same going rate, neither more nor less than the best price it can command in other uses.*

In Smith's theory, the equilibrium rates of pay to the factors of production (wage rates, land rents, etc.) determine the equilibrium price of each commodity. And the market "demand" for

---

* The notion of equilibrium found in economics is defined in chap. 3, and the concept of rationality (or rational choice) is developed in chap. 2.

each good determines, given the price, how much of it, in equilibrium, will be produced.*

Thus Smith founded the idea of a social equilibrium despite considerable freedom of action by society's members:

[With] all [mercantilist] preferences . . . or restraint . . . being . . . taken away, the obvious and simple system of natural liberty establishes itself. . . . Every man, as long as he does not violate the laws of justice, is left perfectly free to pursue his own interest [in] his own way, and to bring both his industry and capital into competition with those of any other man or order of men.†

Smith furthermore claimed that this competitive market mechanism is a *desirable* one for organizing the economy.

. . . the annual revenue [or national income] of every society is always precisely equal to the exchangeable value of the whole annual produce of its industry, or rather is the same thing as that exchangeable value. As every individual eneeavors, therefore, as much as he can both to employ his capital . . . and to direct [his] industry that its produce may be of the greatest value, [he] necessarily labors to render the annual revenue of the society as great as he can. He . . . neither intends to promote the public interest, nor knows how much he is promoting it. . . . [H]e intends only his own gain, and he is in this, as in many other cases, led by an invisible hand to promote an end which was no part of his intention.‡

Smith's contention, in other words, is that the profit motive of enterprises and the quest of resource owners for the best available terms, if operating in free and competitive markets, would serve to eliminate inefficiencies: Profit-minded producers would seek to produce at the smallest possible cost and thus economize on each resource according to its costliness, or price; and income-minded resource owners would make sure that no producer is offered a bargain price below the going rate, thus below opportunity cost; so only the producers with the most productive uses for a resource will be able to afford to employ it. And consumers, choosing according to their tastes and appetite for income and work, would determine the output of each good. The government will only create inefficiencies where there would have been none if, in mercantilist fashion, it intervenes in the resource allocation of the market with assorted restrictions and privileges.

. . . every system which endeavors, either, by extraordinary encouragements, to draw towards a particular species of industry a greater share of the capital of society than what would naturally go to it; or, by extraordinary restraints, to force from a par-

---

* In explanation, Smith writes: "If at any time [the quantity brought to market] exceeds the effectual demand, some of the [employed factors] must be paid below their natural rate . . . [which] will prompt . . . laborers [or owners of capital] . . . to withdraw a part of their labor or capital from this employment. If the quantity . . . should at any time fall short . . ." (*The Wealth of Nations*, Book 1, chap. 7, p. 57).

†Ibid., Book 4, chap. 9, p. 651.

‡Ibid., chap. 2, p. 423.

ticular species of industry some share of the capital which would otherwise be employed in it; is in reality subversive of the great purpose which it means to promote. . . . It diminishes, instead of increasing, the real value of the annual produce of its land and labor.*

Thus was born the classical doctrine of laissez faire—of noninterference with competitive markets.

Within a century there was much disenchantment with this classical vision of an efficient economy resting so much on individual freedom and rationality. The view grew that Smith's theory of the competitive market system was seriously in error or incomplete and had to be rejected. Out of the criticisms new systems developed, in thought and in experience. In the early twentieth century there began to be invented—on paper—a system called liberal socialism, in which most producing enterprises would be state-owned and private property owning would be confined to paper money, government bonds, and consumer durables. The proponents of this socialism claim it is superior to competitive capitalism in that it makes possible reduced economic instability, reduced unemployment, the least possible income inequality, and efficiency in the kinds of goods (from education to the environment) it would produce.

In the twentieth century, as everyone knows, the system widely called communism (which is one kind of socialist state) has developed as Marxist regimes have arisen over much of the globe. This communist system is certainly not the one imagined to be the ultimate destination of societies by Karl Marx in *Das Kapital.*† Yet this system (as well as Marx's visionary system) does owe much of its rationale—the justification it offers on its behalf—to Marx's radical break from the suppositions of Smith. Marx departed on the question of the sources of human fulfillment, seeing class divisions and "alienation" where Smith saw only freedom and personal growth. This Marxist system also differs from Smith's in preferring to centralize most production decisions—in the ministry of planning of the national government.

WHAT POLITICAL ECONOMY IS ABOUT

Political economy is the study of society's operation of its economy. The object under the lens is the structure of rewards available to the participants in the social economy.

The "political" in political economy is a recognition of the fact that the

---

* Smith, *The Wealth of Nations*, Book 4, chap. 9, pp. 650–51.
† *Das Kapital*, Volume 1, Hamburg, 1867. English tr., *Capital* (Chicago: Charles H. Kerr Publishing Co., 1906).

performance of the economy, as observed in the size of the rewards, is only in small part dependent on inalterable nature factors—that is, natural resources. The performance depends largely upon the institutional mechanisms that society chooses to use, as a matter of policy, to motivate and to coordinate the participation of resources in the social economy—the property rights to hold and spend certain forms of wealth, the rights of individuals to market (that is, sell) certain services to the highest bidder, laws defining the roles of public enterprises and private enterprises, the methods of taxation and public-enterprise charges and conscription (drafting) used to raise resources for public programs, and so on. (Some of these mechanisms actually describe, or define, people's opportunities in certain respects, so some of the links between institutions and reward are direct ones.) *Political economy is ultimately the study of the effects of various mechanisms, and systems of mechanisms, used (or usable) by societies to operate their social economy.*

Thus the political economist is concerned with understanding the various mechanisms in a society that shape the structure of rewards—the causes of the wealth of nations, in Smith's simplified formulation. Do we owe our rewards to our economic system, or would some other mechanism (here and there) perform equally well for us? Is it true as has been contended that our system is *efficient*? Many observers imply that it is when they say that there is no such thing as a "free lunch." Or are there better mechanisms for coordinating and motivating resources that would offer greater rewards for *everyone*?—and if so what has stymied society from introducing such mechanisms? Could poorly paid workers have their rewards increased, at the expense of the better rewarded, through a different method of taxation (perhaps simply a change in tax rates)? Or does "economics," not "politics," rule out greater rewards to the least rewarded? Of course, political economy is not the same as political science, or the study of politics. Yet, inevitably, the explanation of the reward structure by reference to the *effects* of society's chosen economic institutions and policies sheds some light on the *causes* of those institutions and policies. The function served by an institution may provide at least some explanation of it.

The objective of explanation is one side of political economy. But just as it would be strange to have physics without engineering or biology without medicine, political economy has a second, more practical side. The side called *positive* political economy studies the determination of the rewards *as they are*. The side called *normative* political economy studies the structure of rewards (and accompanying institutions) *as they would be* if the society introduced different economic institutions or government policies, in the hope of reducing inefficiency, or if society implemented this or that moral standard for choosing among alternative feasible reward structures, in the desire for some brand of justice. Normative political economy *criticizes* the prevailing reward structure and the underlying economic mechanisms—

inspecting them for any way in which they fall short by society's existing, professed standards; and analyzing how the rewards would change if society adopted new policies or moved to one or another proposed principle of economic justice that departs from existing standards. The driving idea behind normative political economy is the belief that societies can change their economic institutions—not without premeditation and discussion, of course, but certainly in response to persuasive objections to the prevailing mechanisms and compelling arguments for different ones.

The two modes of analysis—positive and normative, explanatory and critical—have counterparts in psychological development. Some educational theorists find that our capacity for moral reasoning develops like our powers of mathematical reasoning—in stages. By adolescence we realize that some kind of law and order is needed for supporting any brand of justice; and that if society were to judge the deservingness of each violator before deciding whether to enforce the laws, obedience to the law could not be counted on and everyone might suffer as a result. Next is a higher stage of moral development that is reached when we grasp that the individual rights protected by the law are ultimately based on an implicit agreement, or compromise, by society's members over the rights that all the members shall be accorded; that the law tends to change once a different set of laws is seen as better reflecting the conception of justice by which people judge themselves, other persons, and the society itself. At this mature stage we recognize that society's institutions are manmade and and can always be unmade, or replaced by something else, if and when people's notions of justice have evolved with accumulated thought and experience.

The two modes of political economy also correspond to the two sides of a person's social life: one's purely individual or private satisfactions derived from career and family and friends, and one's interests in the social or public sphere, in political and esthetic involvements yielding a different sort of satisfaction. Just as one who never cared a whit about the terms offered by society except insofar as they affect his or her own benefit would not be regarded by most judges as a whole person, or a fully realized human being, so a concern with only the "what is?" of economics and never the "what if?" and "why not?" would fail to represent the whole of political economy, and the most human part.

Having said all that, we can safely say what political economy is really about. It is a long-running debate over the mechanism of competitive markets—markets for the factors of production (labor, land, etc.) in which employers have to bid for resources and resource owners compete for employment, and goods markets in which consumers have to buy their goods but can shop around for offers and enterprises compete for consumers with quality and price. It is the debate over *economic liberalism* started by Adam Smith. Although two centuries old, the debate has intensified in this century as Marxist regimes abolished or curtailed competition and generally narrowed the role of markets in favor of central planning. Now the view is widespread that no goods or resources that are critically important should be left to the market—from housing to nuclear energy, from milk to human kidneys.

> Smith argued that enterprises and resources (including human ones) can be forced to compete in the marketplace, and this would be good because competitive markets, if left free of government interference, are efficient. The critics of this liberalism declare that real-life markets are grotesquely *in*efficient, in part because they are (unavoidably) not very competitive either. The economic liberals reply, "Inefficient compared to what other mechanism? Markets, made as competitive as is practicable, are relatively efficient, there being no way in practice to improve on them." The critics retort, "Perhaps relatively efficient if we care only for the rich, but not so for the poorest." And so on.

The political economist is largely engaged in clarifying and weighing the pros and cons of markets, regulated or unregulated, as devices for the operation of the economy.

RESEARCH METHODS: THE USE OF THEORETICAL MODELS

Both enterprises in political economy, the positive and the normative, are unscientific in one respect. The trouble is the obstacles to testing ideas. A researcher can attempt to appraise hypotheses about the effects of the existing tax policy by testing the implications, or predictions, of these hypotheses against the evidence, or data; but obviously this is not remotely as conclusive as a before-and-after experiment. Sometimes a group of normative political economists can persuade a country to adopt some *new* economic policy or mechanism. An example is the supply-siders' tax cut program in the early 1980s in the United States. Yet this is not the "controlled experiment" of the laboratory sciences. (It is not surprising, then, that there is controversy among political economists over many unsettled points; but not more, perhaps, than among paleontologists disputing Darwin's views on evolution and astrophysicists over the origin of the universe.)

In another respect, both enterprises in political economy are quite scientific. Both involve the constructing of *theoretical models*. Any such economic model consists of a description of the economic mechanisms through which the individual (and the government) interact and certain premises about individual motives and attitudes. Such a model, if simple enough to be analyzable, can then be shown to have various implications, or "predictions," about the outcome or possible outcomes of the mechanisms modeled. (An output of numerical predictions requires an input of numerical assumptions.) The model-builder's creativity—and presuppositions and possible biases!—come into play when, forced to simplify reality to manageable dimensions, the modeler chooses which things to eliminate and thus which unreal abstractions to leave in. Two of these abstractions, rational choice and equilibrium, are the subjects of the next two chapters.

SUMMARY

1. Political economy is the study of the determination of the structure of opportunities, and resulting pattern of rewards, for those participating in the social economy. There are both economic and political factors to sort out.

2. All resources are limited. Hence the possibilities for production of goods, being limited by resources, are also limited. But human wants for some goods appear to be limitless for practical purposes. Hence there is bound to be scarcity of some goods—leaving unsatisfied wants—and of some (or all) of the resources that would be useful in producing more of them.

3. Since wants press up against the limits of one or more resources, every society faces trade-offs in how to use these scarce resources and how to allocate the scarce goods they produce among the participants. Four trade-offs were distinguished.

4. How these choices, or trade-offs, are made will determine the economy's efficiency—in production, in trade, and in the level and direction of economic activity—and the distribution of rewards.

5. An economic system is a system of mechanisms for making these trade-offs. Several systems, from state capitalism to communism, were noted.

6. Political economy in general, and this text in particular, is primarily about the successes and failures of the competitive market mechanism first envisioned by Adam Smith.

CONCEPTS INTRODUCED

goods
resources
scarcity
production possibilities
opportunities
collective, or public, good

an economy
choice
opportunity cost
allocation of resources
efficiency
  of the individual
  of the social economy

a social economy
exchange
  collaboration
  trade
property rights
distribution of rewards
market mechanisms

STUDY QUESTIONS

1. What are the unusually scarce resources possessed by the richest country? the most prosperous city? the most successful income earners? How might these scarcities change if tastes changed in some way? If the world became richer or poorer?

2. An eccentric named Magoo from Los Angeles announces establishment of a foundation to provide "free lunches" for life to the ten professors designated the best lecturers in the principles of political economy course around the world. Are these lunches *free goods* in the economist's sense of being nonscarce? Are they the product of resources that are nonscarce?

3. Why can it be said that there is a free lunch or two (or more) available in an economy that is inefficient?

4. Discuss how Smith's advantages of specialization are illustrated by Henry Ford's conveyor-belt system of automobile assembly and the Japanese method of rushing materials to the assembly-line worker "just in time."

5. According to the Lucius Littauer Professor of Political Economy at Harvard University, "A wood cutter wouldn't cut wood if bystanders were free to carry it away as fast as he could cut it" (T. C. Schelling, *Micromotives and Macrobehavior*, New York: W. W. Norton & Co., 1978, p. 33). What point was the professor apparently making about specialization and exchange in the social economy?

6. In the movie quotation that opens this chapter, the famous "brother scene" in *On the Waterfront* ("You was my brother . . ."), Marlon Brando:

   a. exults over the happy fact that between brothers there cannot be conflicting, or opposing, interests.

   b. acknowledges that his brother (Rod Steiger) faced a conflict between his own interest and his brother's (Brando's) and concedes that his brother (Steiger) had balanced the two opposing interests in a just way.

c. expresses gratitude to his older brother for having taught him that work, participation, personal development, and other rewards of a career could not be of importance to him.

d. reproaches his brother for having been unwilling to inconvenience himself out of brotherly love

CHAPTER 2

Rational Choice and Individual Gain

JACK (to waitress):
Hold the mayonnaise, hold the lettuce . . . now all you have to do is
hold the chicken, bring me the toast, [and] bring me a check for the
chicken-salad sandwich . . .

Jack Nicholson (to Lorna Thayer) in *Five Easy Pieces* (1970)

THE previous chapter depicts society as a cooperative enterprise for the mutual gain of the participants. It tells of participants offered opportunities from which they make choices of tasks and goods. It suggests that a society's economic system could be inefficient, could be offering opportunities to everyone that are worse than need be, so that everyone could be made better off. It suggests also that individuals' opportunities may not be equal, or equivalent.

But can these terms of political economy—opportunities, gains, worse-off and better-off, inefficiency, inequality—be given precise meaning? And how can political economy amount to anything if the economist cannot predict what exactly the consumer and worker will choose, cannot measure people's sense of well-being at all accurately, does not know how to compare people's happiness, and cannot even be sure that people are happier now than centuries ago! The political economists have a lot of explaining to do before they can confidently trot out their wares.

The time has come, then, to examine the distinctive way that political economy treats matters of individual choice and welfare. There is first the concept of rational choice, of trying to make the best of one's opportunities.

The notion of an individual's demands for consumer goods and supplies of effort—a person's demand curves and supply curves—emerges from this discussion. Next there is the concept of the gain to a rational person from an enlargement of his or her opportunities, from obtaining better terms (better wages, better prices, etc.), for example. The further idea that people gain from such "expanded choice" can be seen to be a powerful analytical tool: We could use it to calculate (on paper, anyway) whether some reform of the tax laws or some reduction of tariff protection would cause everyone to gain by providing everyone with expanded choice—thus testing the efficiency of the existing system; or to calculate whether some particular group, such as the poorest-paid workers, would obtain expanded choice and hence gain. And to make these calculations we do not have to know people's underlying goals, or preferences. Then there is the concept of the surplus that a person obtains from a transaction—the total gain. With all this as background we are in a position to discuss how the political economist might analyze inequality in terms of unequal opportunities.

RATIONAL CHOICE: THE MODEL OF "ECONOMIC MAN"

When we think of physical matter interacting, particles like molecules joining up or getting in the way of one another, it certainly does not occur to us that this molecule scored a big gain or that one suffered a small setback. No doubt the reason we do not think that way about inanimate matter is that we suppose molecules are not trying to "get anywhere," that their behavior is not purposeful—whether or not they're tough-skinned and would have no feelings on experiencing defeat. By contrast, when in our inquisitive childhood we experimented with a garden ant by placing a ruler, or straightedge, in front of the ant at one distance and angle after another, we all must have noticed the ant's ceaselessly calculating behavior. The ant retreats only as much as it is forced and advances as much as permitted. Most important, when the ruler is rotated to make the ant's way faster, the ant never perversely chooses to reverse its direction along the ruler's edge. It never chooses belatedly to go in the other direction when it could have done so before at a better angle and it didn't choose to do so then—only a very neurotic ant would be so mindless! It is the presence of such purposefulness in behavior that makes possible the measurement, at least the approximate measurement, of the gain or loss to the individual from a new opportunity, a lower price, a withdrawn barrier.

Granting that there is something we would want to call purposeful, or rational, behavior (by ants or humans or any sentient creature), which are its essential features? One trait that is basic to rationality is taking advantage of any opportunity that would be an advance toward one's goals whenever doing so would not cost anything; when it would not require foregoing any other opportunities. If the meaning of rationality includes paying attention and thinking, then it certainly implies not passing up opportunities that have a zero "opportunity cost."

The folk axiom that "you can't take it with you" and the business maxim to "buy cheap" (and its corollary, "sell dear") are reminders to behave rationally in just this respect. It would not be rational, in the above sense of that term, to put aside some income into a miserly hoard that is never to be spent or given away. Similarly, it would not be rational to shop at one supermarket if the identical bundle of goods can be bought at another supermarket, just as convenient and pleasant, at smaller cost; nor to accept a job when there is known to be another one just like it, with the same job satisfaction, that offers more pay. In all these examples of irrational choice making there is at least one *other* (not chosen) opportunity that *dominates* the *chosen* opportunity—that is, it offers *more* goods *without* less leisure or less job satisfaction (which is another good)—without an opportunity cost.

Figure 2–1 expresses in diagrammatic terms this property of rationality—the idea of not neglecting a dominating opportunity. It means always choosing from among the opportunities on the upper boundary of the set of opportunities—the so-called *frontier* of the *opportunity set*.

This trait of operating at the frontier of one's opportunity set is a necessary characteristic (a sort of test) of rationality in choice making no matter what opportunity set faces the individual, no matter how many times it might move. If the opportunity set confronting our hypothetical rational individual shifts out, as depicted in Figure 2–1, Panels B_1, B_2, and B_3, then the point that would have been chosen from the former opportunity set will be rejected in favor of some point on the frontier of the new opportunity set. The rational choice maker will choose to *realize the gain*—the advance toward his or her goals—which such an expansion of the opportunity set makes available by rejecting the position that would have been chosen had the set not shifted in order to take advantage of the new opportunities. Just which position on the new frontier will be chosen by the individual is another story (and not always crucial for the particular question being asked). The individual will choose from the points on the frontier according to his preferences. (In what may be called the normal case, the individual will respond by choosing more goods and less work (i.e., more leisure time not working)—if, as depicted in Figure 2–1, Panel B_1, there is an exactly parallel upward shift of the frontier.)

FIGURE 2–1: A Property of Rational Choice: Not Choosing An Opportunity over Another Opportunity that "Dominates" the Former—Illustrated by the Work-Income Choice

PANEL A

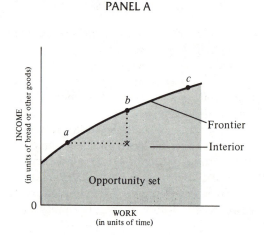

Each diagram shows an individual's perceived opportunities for work, measured in hours over a year, say, and the corresponding income, measured in units of some good—say, bread. For simplicity, it is supposed that the individual can work a 2 thousand-hour year, or 2001, or 2001.333 ...—as much as the individual likes up to the total time available. And jobs are all alike with respect to "job satisfaction."

Each job available or collection of jobs, with its total number of hours and the corresponding total amount of pay—hence *each opportunity*—can be represented by some corresponding *point* in the diagram. The collection of such opportunities—the collection of such points—is the *opportunity set.* The upper boundary of the opportunity set—the locus of uppermost points—is called by economists the *frontier* of the opportunity set.

Rationality, in these diagrammatic terms, implies that the individual would not choose to operate in the interior of the choice set, such as at the point marked with an x in Panel A. To choose such a point would mean accepting unnecessarily low wages or paying unnecessarily high prices for bread and other purchases. The point *b* is unambiguously better—it dominates the point marked x—since it offers more goods for the same work and same job satisfaction. Rationality requires one to operate on the *frontier* of the opportunity set, choosing a work-income pair such as at point *c.*

Hence, if the opportunity set expands in such a way that the frontier *shifts up,* as illustrated by Panels B_1, B_2, and B_3 below, then rational choice requires rejecting the work-income pair that would have been chosen had there been no shift—a point like *c* on the old frontier—in favor of a point on the *new* frontier, such as *c'.*

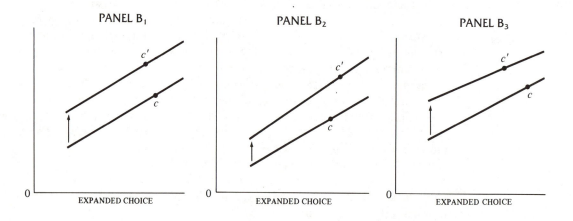

That rationality implies always choosing to have more (not less) of a good—as long as it is a good and if it does not cost anything—may seem reasonable enough. Yet it is apt to provoke complaints. "You mean it would be rational for me to rob and steal if I knew I wouldn't be caught?" The concept of rational choice does sound a bit "cut-throat" on the first exposure. But rationality here means opting for more of a good in situations where doing so would not require foregoing any consumption of other goods—where "other things are equal," as economists are fond of saying. If a person's self-respect is a good (for him or her), and if robbing or stealing would cost the person some self-respect, then rational choice making does *not* mean seizing every or any opportunity for a risk-free holdup or burglary. Thus rationality in choice making does not imply *greed*. The point can be expressed graphically as in the diagram below. Without scruples a person's opportunity set might be the entire shaded area, thanks to lucrative targets of opportunity. But a self-imposed constraint against stealing would rule out these highest-paying opportunities, which correspond to the darker shaded area, and leave the individual's earnings and consumption of bread constrained by the wages and prices available from "legitimate" jobs and exchange—without embezzling and shoplifting. In fact, economists usually suppose that each person's consumption expenditure is "constrained" by his or her income from legitimate activities—although black-market or criminal activities must sometimes be taken into account.

On the other hand—a phrase economists are often forced to use—the notion that there are opportunities and preferences among them *and that's that* may sometimes be oversimple when it comes to a person's transactions with others. If I would accept a stranger's offer of a game of tennis, even though I know that ten dollars will fall out of my pocket on the way to the court, does rationality compel me to accept an offer of a game with him for a price of ten

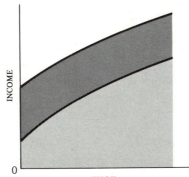

INCOME

0

WORK

dollars (which I might think unfair!)? If you would accept a stranger's offer to carry you the last yards after a tiring trip when you know that ten dollars will fall out of your pocket as a result, must you (being rational) be willing to *pay* the stranger the same ten dollars to carry you (which you might think exploitive)? Perhaps there are some things we feel we *ought not* to do no matter that everyone would prefer the consequences of doing them.

Not choosing an opportunity that is dominated by any other one is a very modest standard of rational behavior. It is the least we could mean by rationality. It seems natural that political economy adopt as part of its *method of analysis* the postulate that people are rational in that sense—even though there may be quite a few persons in any society who are not, and everyone miscalculates from time to time. Yet this minimal notion of rationality is too little to ask. There is an additional standard by which to judge the rationality of a person's choice making—that the choices the person would make from different opportunity sets not "contradict" each other; that while tastes may evolve with age and experience, there is at any particular time a certain logical consistency in a person's choice-making behavior under hypothetical experiments.

The other characteristic that we may associate with rationality in individual choice making may be expressed in terms of a formal axiom: If a rational individual would choose *a* over *b* when faced with *one* opportunity set that made both those opportunities available, then such an individual faced with a *different* opportunity set would not then choose *b* if it *also* made *a* available as well. The psychological sense of this axiom is that people like what they like: An individual does not recast his or her preferences in response to any alteration in opportunities. The *choices made* may very well respond—it would be a special case when the choice made did not respond—but not the *preferences*. It should be noted that an individual might choose *a* over *b* "at random" because he or she is really indifferent or not sure which of them is preferable, in which case choosing *b* over *a* the next time would not actually be contradictory. But such a case seems to be sufficiently rare that it is not worth modifying the second rationality condition to allow for that possibility.

This second property of rationality is expressed in Figure 2–2. An opportunity that would have been rejected in one situation is not selected in another situation if the opportunity that would have been chosen is still present.

FIGURE 2–2: A Property of Rational Choice: Not Switching from One Opportunity to Another Merely Because a Third (Unchosen!) Opportunity Arises

PANEL A: Expanded choice
due to rotation
plus upward shift

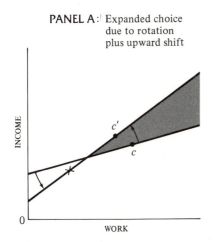

PANEL B: Expanded choice
due to rotation

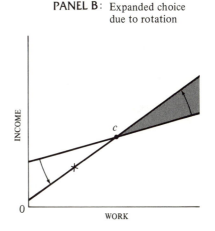

In each diagram there is good news and bad news for our hypothetical worker. The good news is that the wage (in terms of goods) offered in all the job opportunities has risen by a certain percentage amount; hence the frontier has *steepened.* The bad news is that the worker's nonwage income (in terms of goods) has fallen; so the point where the frontier intersects the vertical axis (the vertical intercept) has *moved down.* But in Panel A and Panel B new opportunities are gained and the opportunites lost would not have been chosen. This also is expanded choice.

In Panels A and B, then, the opportunity that would have been chosen from the "old" frontier, point *c,* is available in the "new" opportunity set as well. In these cases it would be irrational for the individual to choose a point like the one marked x over *c* if offered the "old" frontier—which reveals that x is not as good as the still available *c.*

Panel C presents a quite different situation. There a point like *c'* is rational to choose, since it was previously rejected in favor of a point like *c* that is no longer available.

PANEL C: Not expanded
choice

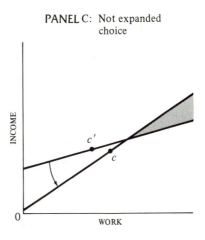

FIGURE 2–3: Rational Choice—Illustrated by a Consumer's Choice

PANEL A

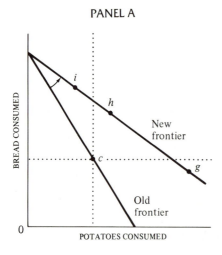

PANEL B

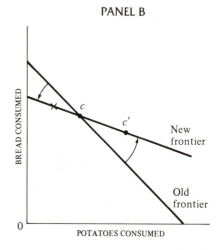

The properties of rational choice making apply to any choice. Figure 2–3, Panels A and B, depict the opportunities of a consumer with a given budget to spend on bread and potatoes. The *frontier* is downward sloping—that is, negatively sloped—since buying more potatoes leaves less of the budget for bread. It is a straight line if the consumer's budget is too small to give him any power over the prices—a case of "small potatoes."

In Figure 2–3, Panel A, a fall in the price of potatoes is depicted. This swings out the frontier. So the bread-potato basket that would have been chosen, labeled *c*, is rejected in favor of *g* or *h*—or even a point like *i*—on the *new* frontier. Can you explain why *i* does *not* violate either condition for rationality? In Figure 2–3, Panel B, potatoes have again become cheaper but bread more expensive; the budget in terms of bread is down. But point *c* can still be chosen. Here, more potatoes can rationally be consumed—but not less! Can you see why not?

So much for the meaning of rational individual choice. How bad an assumption, or postulate, is it? Certainly not as bad as it first looks. As we have just seen, the second property of rational choice making boils down to the assumption that an individual's preferences (the rankings of rival assortments of goods) are independent of the *terms* at which the available goods can be exchanged for one another—the preferences are *given* in that sense. ("If I prefer *c* to x in one experiment you won't find me choosing x over *c* in some different experiment in which 'third' opportunities are different.") This may suggest that rationality requires preferences to be "given" in the sense of being inborn and immutable—and we can all agree that our preferences are not all innate, that they are largely acquired. But rationality does *not* require that preferences be innate and immutable. Preferences can be *given at each moment* (in the sense of not being influenced by the terms at which goods can be exchanged) even if they are entirely acquired, the result of previous education and the example of others—and even if tomorrow's preferences will be different because of what is learned today.

On the other hand, few economists would be prepared to argue that the rationality assumption is highly realistic. Not everyone is rational and presumably no one is rational in all situations at all times. Research psychologists are producing evidence from laboratory subjects that suggests people do sometimes, in some situations, behave contradictorily. If they lose their ten-dollar tickets at the theater they choose not to buy a replacement (they go home); but if they lose the money for the theater ticket at the theater they reach down into their pockets for more money to buy the ticket. They do not see, it seems, that they could as well think of the lost ticket as lost cash. The two losses, while superficially different, produce the *same* downward shift of the opportunity cost. Hence it would not be rational to choose an option x over another option *c* in one case while revealing that in the other case the option *c* would be chosen over x.

What is to be done? The political economists adopt the model of "rational man," or "economic man," because it is a powerful tool for achieving their objectives—it performs even though it may be quite inaccurate—and because there is so far no alternative to it. The hope is that using the "economic man" assumption, though inaccurate, does not lead to crucial errors on the big questions.*

INDIVIDUAL SUPPLIES AND DEMANDS

The concept of the opportunity set and the notion of a preferred opportunity in the set lead naturally to another concept: the relation between the wage rate available to the individual and the quantity of work-time, or labor, that the individual supplies—for short, the individual's labor-supply curve.

---

*The term *economic man* is so prevalent in political economy, and in the social sciences generally, often in its Latin translation, *Homo economicus,* that its appearance somewhere in this volume is almost obligatory. The "man" in economic man denotes a member, male or female, of the human species, *Homo sapiens,* and not in particular the male member, *vir.* Nowhere do advocates of the economic man concept of human behavior suggest that the female of the species is less calculating than the male. The concept had always traveled safely under its Latin name until a generation ago. But *Homo economicus* had to be retired from service with the abandonment of the Latin requirement in the secondary schools.

FIGURE 2–4: The Individual's Labor-Supply Curve

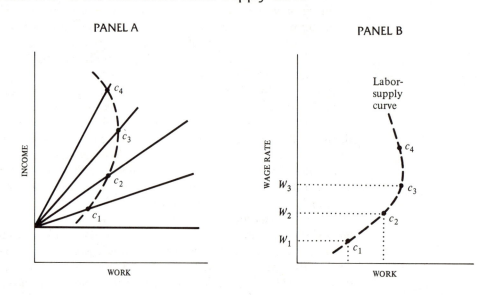

As the wage is increased, more income is earned and the quantity of labor supplied is increased or decreased.

Suppose the social economy offered our hypothetical individual a zero wage rate. The individual would then have some corresponding opportunity set—with a perfectly flat frontier, since more work would bring no more income. If the individual is offered a positive wage rate the frontier of the opportunity set swings up—it slopes upward, since more work would bring more income. Each hypothetical increase of the wage rate produces another upward swing of the frontier. And each new (and steeper) frontier leads the individual to choose some corresponding amount of labor to supply. So there emerges in this way the relationship between the level of the wage rate and the quantity of labor supplied—the labor-supply curve. Figure 2–4 illustrates the emergence of the individual's labor supply curve.

The properties of rational choice also apply to choosing how much of a good to sell, or supply—and how much to demand. Consider a farming family deciding how much of their farm-grown crop to market in exchange for factory-made cloth and therefore how much of the crop to retain for their own con-

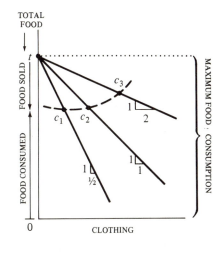

sumption. The family faces "constant" terms of trade, or price; i.e., each additional unit of food sold exchanges for a constant number of additional units of cloth (2, or ½, or whatever) no matter how many units of food are brought to the market. Then the opportunity-set frontier between food consumption and cloth consumption is a straight line as shown in the figure, left. If $0t$ is the crop of food, then, in the absence of any taxes or license fees, the frontier originates at point $t;$ the family could consume their entire crop (and so have nothing left for clothing or taxes). Any improvement in these terms of trade—from 1 to 2, or from ½ to 1—is represented by a swing of the frontier to the right—i.e., by a counterclockwise pivot around the point t. Successive improvements of the price lead to a sequence of points chosen by the family—first c_1, then c_2, and so on. Because such improvements enable the family to consume more cloth *and more food too* it is questionable whether any particular improvement will induce the family to supply more food to the market. The move from c_2 to the *higher* c_3 increases the food consumed and *decreases* the amount *marketed*.

If an improvement in their terms of trade happens to be accompanied by a drought or a property tax or a bridge toll or a marketing license fee or any other setback that shifts inward the frontier to such an extent that the net result is a *rotation* of the frontier around the former choice point, like c_2, then the possibility of consuming more cloth *and* more food is *removed;* there is only the relative cheapening of cloth in terms of food. If they are going to take advantage of that cheapening, by stepping up their consumption of cloth, they must supply more food. Certainly it would be irrational of the family to supply less food, as Figure 2–3, Panel B, with its analogous rotation, illustrated.

THE NOTION OF INDIVIDUAL GAINS

We could hardly expect a person to choose rationally if the person did not have well-ordered goals, tastes—hence, preferences among the opportunities—on the basis of which to make choices. The properties of rational choice, captured in Figures 2–1 and 2–2, seem rational to us precisely because they are hallmarks of choice-making behavior by anyone who is trying to advance toward certain goals or to retreat from them as little as possible. These so-called axioms of rational choice earn the name rational because they are characteristics of the choice-making behavior of any person aiming to "make the best" of the available choice set according to his or her preferences.

The notion of a rational person as one engaged in gainful, or purposeful, behavior, subject to existing opportunities, leads naturally to a further notion: The rational individual *gains* whenever presented with an opportunity set that, according to the individual's preferences, is *preferable* to the opportunity set previously available. And since a rational person chooses the most preferred position within the available choices, the opportunity set is preferable if (and only if) the position that is chosen from it is *preferred* to the position that was chosen (or would have been chosen) from the other opportunity set. Thus, for example, to say that someone gains from belonging to his or her society instead of living in isolation or in another society means that he or she prefers the position chosen from the choice set made available by society to the position that would be chosen anywhere else. So far, so good. The above notion of an individual's gain is straightforward, commonsensical. Yet it brings us to some important questions.

How do we *tell*, the question arises, when an individual's gain from participating in society goes up or down? Imaginably, we could sit down with the person and ask him whether he prefers his new opportunity set to his old one—although it might be necessary to persuade the person that no harm will come from being truthful, because we are not tax collectors. Or, if we think we know the person's preferences we could ask ourselves whether we would prefer with that person's preferences the new opportunity set over the old choice set. In a wide range of cases, however, we do not need to know the person's preferences beyond knowing the position the person chose from the old opportunity set in order to establish that there is a gain for the individual in having the new choice set. These are cases involving *expanded choice*.

◆ If the new opportunity set is a case of expanded choice with *room to spare*, as in Figures 2–1, Panels B_1, B_2, and B_3, and 2–2, Panel A, where there is an upward *shift* on top of any rotation, then the individual gains from having the new opportunity set—because the new opportunity set offers the position that would have been chosen from the old opportunity set and *still better points* out on the frontier, so the new set is preferable.

♦ If the new choice set is a case of expanded choice with *no* room to spare, as in Figures 2–2, Panel B, and 2–3, Panel B, which show unadulterated rotation, then we can say that the rational individual must either gain (because the rotation has opened up one or more preferred positions to which he can move) or at any rate not lose.

While it is true that there is a gain or at any rate no loss *if* the new opportunity set results in expanded choice, it is *not* true that there is a gain or at least no loss *only if* expanded choice results.

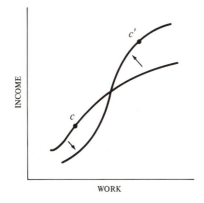

Thus expanded choice is a sufficient condition but not a necessary condition for a non-negative gain. To grasp that, we merely need to imagine the appearance of a new opportunity set that is a slight case of *contracted choice*—the position that would have been chosen from the old set *is* snatched away—yet this contraction is so slight in comparison to the degree of rotation that the individual nevertheless finds the new opportunity set preferable: The newly chosen point, labeled *c'* in the diagram above, is preferred to the point, labeled *c*, that would have been chosen had the old opportunity set remained available. It follows that contracted choice is a necessary but not a sufficient condition for a loss. With this point in mind and the diagram as illustration, it becomes obvious that the radically new opportunity set obtained by *joining* society may contract choice for the individual—maybe he will miss the good tomatoes—while at the same time the act of *leaving* society to return to the old opportunity set may *also* contract choice. Migration either way would entail abandoning the previously chosen position. Nevertheless, one of the opportunity sets may be preferable—the new one, for example—so there may very well be a gain to the individual from belonging to society *despite* some contraction of choice.

The previous examples of expanded choice all involve an improvement in the terms at which "work," conceived as the duration or intensity of a person's effort, can be exchanged for "income," as measured by the amount of some good or package of goods that can be obtained in return. There is no need to specify by what mechanism those terms of exchange have improved. The improvement might have originated in some new social policy aimed at better rewards for certain individual activities or simply more goods for certain people. Or the improved terms of exchange may have occurred because the productivity of the individual in performing some task went up and society was unwilling or unable to skim off all of the increase in income that potentially went to the individual as a result. A person's productivity might rise because his or her labors were assisted by more or better capital equipment, by more or better co-workers, or because the technology available to the individual has somehow improved. Or the improved terms of exchange may have resulted from a favorable change in the terms of trade between one product and another: There is a rise in the terms at which the good that the individual finds it best to work at producing exchanges for goods that the individual likes to obtain for consumption.

Expanded choice through trade: food costs only 2 cloths per square meal instead of the old 4 cloths per meal. A classic illustration of the gain to a lone producer from joining society is based precisely on the expanded choice that results for the individual upon discovering that the terms at which goods are being exchanged for one another in society—these are called relative prices or exchange ratios—are not generally identical to the terms at which the individual had to "trade" one good for another when operating as a solitary producer-consumer. The mountain man who can grow some crops and raise some sheep but has less time for the one the more time he spends on the other is going to find that in the valley either wool clothing is surprisingly cheap in terms of

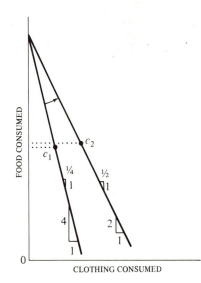

food, or food is surprisingly cheap in terms of wool clothing. The former case means that obtaining an extra coat costs fewer square meals than the mountain man would have had to sacrifice in order to produce an extra coat; the latter case means that an extra meal costs fewer square meters of wool cloth than mountain man would have needed to sacrifice to obtain that meal—if, in the interests of straight thinking, the individual holds constant the total amount of work allocated to the two activities. The figure illustrates the case where food is found to be comparatively cheap in society: So mountain man swaps some bolts of cloth for some bargain-price food and may step up cloth output besides.

Expanded choice is a useful indicator of individual gain where the social question to be studied does not require quantifying (i.e., measuring quantitatively) the gain to an individual (or gains to a group of individuals) from some proposed or actual social change beyond establishing that there is a gain or at least no loss. And there are in fact several sorts of problems in political economy in which attention focuses on whether there *is* a gain, not how large is the gain.

- One such kind of problem arises whenever it is desired to ascertain that a social action will be in the common interest, so that some individuals gain from it and no one loses. When some economic guru comes off a high to tell us that his reform of the tax system or overhaul of commercial regulations would yield a gain for all, we hope he has based his claim on an argument that the resulting alteration in the structure of opportunities offered people would mean expanded choice *for all*—at least for some, and contracted choice for none—or that those persons not winning expanded choice will gain nevertheless.
- Another kind of problem in which only the existence of a gain or loss matters, not the magnitude, arises when the members of society or some element of them do not want certain *underdogs* in society—persons whose opportunities have been diminished by natural handicaps or social disadvantages—to suffer a loss on top of the meager position from which they start.
- There may be the political question of whether a social change would produce a gain for some *majority* of society's members.

Quantifying the Gain by "Willingness to Pay"

There are other problems, however, in which it is necessary somehow to quantify the gain or succession of gains (and losses) going to an individual.

When a social program (administered by the government, say) contains more than one element it may be necessary to weigh gains and losses in the balance in order to ascertain whether there is a resultant gain or loss.

◆ A program of no-charge crop dusting to control the boll weevil might be of common *benefit* to cotton growers; but at what *cost?* A question that arises then is whether there is a way of taxing the growers that pays the cost of the program without causing a welfare cost, or burden, that outweighs the benefit received—so that the rest of society is not stuck with part of the tab and no grower ends up with a loss instead of a gain from the program. It is necessary to quantify the benefit of the program and the burden (or welfare cost) of the tax for each grower in order to determine whether an individual gains or loses.

◆ Similarly, an overhaul of the tax system that would leave some tax rates lower but other tax rates higher prompts the question: Do the welfare gains from the tax rate cuts add up to more for each individual than the welfare losses from the tax rate hikes? And if not, what are the circumstances or preferences of the individuals who come out losing?

To gauge the magnitude of an individual's gain from one or more new opportunities we ask *how much* (of some good) *the individual would be willing to pay for access to the new opportunity set.* Hence, to measure the gain to a person from belonging to the society of his or her choice we may ask how large a membership fee (payable in some good or other) the person would be willing to pay before exclaiming, "A higher charge than that and I will be driven to live and work elsewhere." Similarly, the gain to a consumer from a drop in the price of jeans may be measured as the amount of some good that the consumer would be willing to pay for the license to buy jeans at the lower price instead of the higher one (without need for the license).*

---

*The size of the gain to an individual from *slightly* better terms of exchange obeys a convenient and often useful formula:

◆ The gain to a consumer from a small reduction of the price of a consumption good is approximately proportional to the volume of the good that is to be purchased—and the approximation approaches perfect accuracy as the price reduction considered is made successively smaller and smaller. That means that the gain from a two-cent cut in the price of laundering shirts would be approximately offset by the loss from a one-cent rise in the price of bus trips for an individual taking two bus rides for every clean shirt.
◆ The gain from a small rise in the reward per unit to a person's hours worked or income saved is approximately proportional to the volume of labor or volume of saving that the individual is going to supply. Hence the gain from a 2 percent rise in the return to saving (from 1 percent per month to 1.02 per month, say) would be approximately offset by the loss from a 1 percent fall of after-tax wage rates for any individual saving half his wage income.

Thus the size of the gain from a *small* improvement in an individual's terms is (approximately) proportional to the size of the exchange.

Measuring the gain to an individual from expanded choice by his "willingness to pay" may be illustrated as follows. Take our worker-consumer supplying labor in exchange for bread. Suppose, for simplicity, that the wage rate (per hour or month) is the same on all the jobs available to the individual—so the wage rate is a constant, being independent of the amount of work supplied. An increase of the individual's wage rate, from w_1 to w_2, would obviously enlarge his opportunity set—a clear case of expanded choice.

What is the most that the individual would be willing to pay in order to have the improvement? The answer, it might seem, is simply the *increase in income* that would result *without any change in the amount of labor supplied*. This income increase is the increase in "bread" that would be obtained if the individual happened not to increase or decrease the labor he supplies in response to the higher wage rate. And since either response is possible, this answer might seem a smart guess.

This is the right answer if the individual cannot supply more labor. But it is not quite right otherwise. This increase in income is, generally speaking, an underestimate of the individual's willingness to pay. Why? If we could collect a *fixed payment* of exactly this amount from the individual, no matter whether he works more or less, the individual would still be *left with some expanded choice* relative to the original opportunity set with its old wage rate. Proof: The individual could still consume and work as he did originally, handing over the whole resulting increase in wage income to pay the fixed charge. Or he could take advantage of the new opportunities to earn extra income for less extra work than before that are provided by the higher wage rate—and he would also be willing to pay something for this enlargement of his opportunity set.

The increase in income without working more does measure the gain from a higher wage rate if the individual cannot supply more work. But, otherwise, the true gain can be seen to be larger. The improved terms on which the person can "trade" his leisure for income creates an incentive to substitute extra income for some leisure, and the new incentive is worth something. See Figure 2–5.

Quantifying the gain from a reduction in the price of a consumer good proceeds in the same way. Consider a farming family completely specialized in the production of food that swaps some of their crop for store-bought clothes. A reduction in the price of clothing in terms of food due, say, to cost-saving innovations in clothing manufacture, swings out the farming family's

FIGURE 2–5: Measuring the Individual's "Willingness to Pay" for Expanded Choice— The Case of an Increased Wage Rate

PANEL A

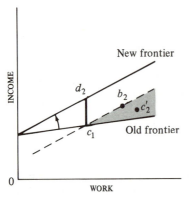

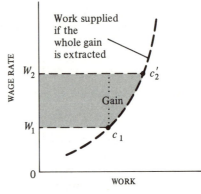

If a demonic experimenter, *intending* to take away the entire gain from the increased wage rate, collected a fixed payment of only d_2c_1, the individual could still gain from the remaining expanded choice by opting for a new opportunity, like b_2, not originally available, which is better than the originally chosen c_1. So the gain exceeds d_2c_1.

Exactly the whole gain could be extracted by levying a somewhat larger fixed payment, which would drive the disappointed individual to choose a point, c_2', which is barely as good as the originally chosen c_1.

PANEL B

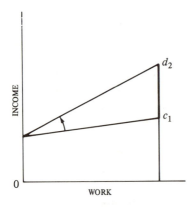

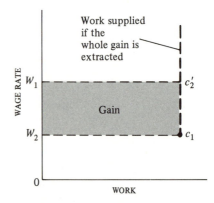

Only in the extreme case where the amount of labor cannot be increased would collecting the income increase d_2c_1 extract—and hence be a measure of—the whole gain.

When the whole gain is extracted in this case, the individual would respond by choosing the same work and bread consumption.

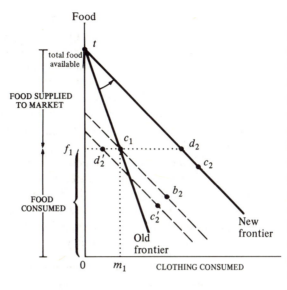

opportunity frontier between clothing consumed and food consumed as shown in the diagram to the left. It is clear that the size of the rightward shift as measured by the line segment d_2c_1 is exactly proportional to the amount of food marketed, f_1t, and to the volume of clothing, $0m_1$. But that measure, d_2c_1, is only an *approximation* to the gain in the sense of "willingness to pay." If the payment extracted from the individual to "compensate" for the lower price were only d_2c_1 the individual could move rightward along the post-payment frontier, passing through the old c_1 to a point that would ordinarily be better, like b_2—thus to take advantage of the small remnant of expanded choice that would be left after the payment had removed most of the expansion. The reduced price of clothing creates an *incentive to substitute* food for clothes. Hence the measure of the gain from the reduced price is ordinarily a greater distance, like d_2d_2'. A fixed payment of that size permits the individual to choose a point, labeled c_2', that is no better or worse than the original point c_1.

WATER VERSUS DIAMONDS: THE "SURPLUS" OBTAINED FROM CONSUMING

The origin of the notion of an individual's gain from lower prices for things bought and higher prices for goods or services sold is a story in itself. The analysis of such gains was stimulated by a puzzle that bothered Adam Smith. Common sense, he thought, indicates that the price of a good will depend upon its usefulness—what Smith called its value in use. But consider how much is spent on diamonds and how little, if anything, is spent on water.

Yet the benefit we derive from the quantity of water we drink surely dwarfs the benefit that even the most bejeweled ladies derive from the diamonds they wear. As Smith wrote: ". . . the things which have the greatest value in use have frequently little or no value in exchange. Nothing is more useful than water but it will purchase scarce anything; scarce anything can be had in exchange for it."* Smith was right in insisting on the distinction between value in use and value in exchange; for if the value in use of the goods we buy did not exceed the value in exchange—what we pay for them—nothing could be gained from trade, from buying and selling! And Smith may have worried that it would appear to people that political economy has its "values" upside down—that it celebrates expensive goods and has no place for the goods that are free, some of which are the most important things in life.

It took a century for Smith's puzzle to be solved, and decades more to reduce the solution to its simplest essentials. Now the resolution of the water-diamond paradox is obvious enough.

♦ If water was initially supplied, whether by public or private enterprises, at a high price, consumers would have been driven to spend a lot for it. If the price is then reduced or eliminated, the individual consumer—even before considering altering his drinking habits—would clearly gain: The *benefit* from the unchanged water consumption would be the *same* as before, but the *cost* would be *down* (by the amount of the consumption *times* the price cut); so there would be a gain to the consumer equal at least to these savings from the price cut. In Smith's terms, value in use is the same while value in exchange falls.

♦ In addition, because incentives are altered, there is a *further* gain—which is clearest to see if we imagine that the government sends out a fixed tax bill to the water user equal to the above savings from the price cut. Because water is cheaper than before, the consumer will have an incentive to substitute some water for some milk; more water will be consumed. In view of these new opportunities to consume extra water more cheaply than before, the individual could afford to pay a *further* tax—and be no worse off than originally. Thus—a further gain.

Conclusion: The total benefit from our consumption of water is enormous in part *because* the price is so low; we can afford to wallow in it. The beneficial properties of a good determine the quantity demanded *given* the price—not directly the price. If the price of *diamonds* collapsed, due to technical breakthrough in production or a curious government subsidy, the same things would happen: Consumers' expenditures on diamonds might fall— *would* fall certainly if the price fell to zero or sufficiently close to zero. But

* Adam Smith, *The Wealth of Nations*, Book I, chap. 4, p. 28.

the consumer's benefit would not fall—it would increase, and by more than any increase in expenditure since the consumer will only gain from the extra purchases in response to the incentives of the lower price.

Thinking about Smith's paradox led inevitably to the application of rational-choice analysis to the question: Can we *measure* the level of benefit, and hence the excess of benefit over cost? What exactly is the *total gain* that results from being able to buy a good at the prevailing price instead of being faced with a price so high that the good cannot be afforded, cannot be bought at all? We may interpret the question to mean this: What is the welfare loss, or negative gain, that would result from a price increase (or series of price increases) so large as to make the individual give up the good? Such a *loss* could be measured by the fixed payment the individual would have to *receive* in order to make him willing to accept the higher price—to *compensate* him for the higher price, so that he would not be left worse off as a result. *This loss* that would be suffered if the price of the good put it out of reach is a notion of the individual's *surplus* from being able to buy the good at the actual, affordable price.

> The notion of the consumer's surplus from purchase of a good is a humbling reminder that, thanks largely to the low prices (in terms of labor time) the social economy can offer to the participants, we do *not* get what we pay for—we get *more* than we pay for: What you consume of a good is worth to you what you pay for it *plus* the *surplus*. If a price increase made the good no longer affordable, you would lose that surplus. For the farmer consuming food and diamonds, this surplus is equal to the amount of extra food he would have to be paid to compensate him for being "priced out" of the gems.

Thus we can say to Smith: The great decline in the price of water has increased the surplus of total benefit over total cost, by producing the obvious cost savings and by creating new incentives—that is, by expanded choice. The surplus from anyone's consumption of diamonds, meanwhile, remains small because the price remains high.

COMPARING INDIVIDUAL WELFARE BY COMPARING OPPORTUNITIES

The economic concept of an individual's gain has been introduced. We can conceive how to measure an individual's gain from taking advantage of the opportunities of a social economy (compared to others or possibly a solitary existence). We can even conceive how to measure an individual's total gain from being able to buy, with his earnings, a good at the affordable price that prevails—the so-called surplus. This surplus, somehow measured, might be considered the right measure of the individual's welfare. (We can imagine economists engaged in comparing one person's surplus of, say, 17 with another person's surplus of 17 or 12 or 20—in units of labor time, perhaps.) But it would not be practicable to obtain estimates of these surpluses.

Psychological comparisons seem no less fraught with difficulties. When we think about two people we know well, it is certainly possible that we will disagree over which of them has the greater contentment, sense of reward, feelings of gratification, and so on. And if we agreed we might still confess to being uncertain. No wonder that economists are uncomfortable with attempts to compare individuals' happiness, well-being, or "utility"—to use the word for well-being that came into use in the nineteenth century (and which is still used a little). If we do not know the two people at all well, of course, the difficulties are much greater.

In fact, economists have begun to suspect that there may be rather little connection between happiness and cumulative economic progress. Was the middle-income Canadian less happy a century ago? We cannot be sure, although we do commonly think that acute poverty—neglect and deprivation—is rarer now in the "welfare state." Are the handicapped less happy than the able-bodied or simply less advantaged? We are uncertain.

What then? The political economist can reformulate the problem of comparisons by looking not at people's happiness but at their opportunities. The focus is on their capabilities and the rewards offered for what they are capable of doing—hence their options, as represented in the concept of the opportunity set. Then, in comparing people's opportunities, the question is whether one person's opportunity set can be seen to be preferable to another person's—whether it can be shown to offer a gain—and, possibly, by how much. In the same way that we look at the inequality in a person's opportunities "before" and "after" a change in the individual's opportunity set, we can look at the inequality *between* persons.

◆ We may say that the people in one situation are better off than the people in another situation if the former have opportunities that dominate those of the latter, and not vice versa (the latter do not have opportunities dominating some opportunities of the former).

◆ And in cases where it makes sense to suppose that the people in two different situations have the same preferences—the same tastes and standards—we may say that people in a certain situation are better off than those in another if their opportunity set shows expanded choice compared to the others' opportunity sets.

That way we do not get into the murky subjectivism of happiness and utility. Nor do we lurch to the other extreme of pretending that the opportunities to make one's way in life don't matter and that inequality is a figment of the imagination.

SUMMARY

1. Political economists traditionally suppose, or postulate, in their method of analysis (as distinct from their day-to-day personal dealings) that the individuals who participate in the economy satisfy the conditions of rational choice (or choice making).

2. One condition for rational choice making is that the individual does not accept an opportunity when he perceives that there are one or more other opportunities—alternative options—that dominate the former one—that is, that are superior in some or all respects and less preferable in no respects.

3. A necessary condition for rationality, thus, is that the individual should operate on the frontier of the individual's opportunity set.

4. Another condition for rational choice making is that the individual does not accept any opportunity that would have been rejected in favor of another opportunity if, when faced with a different opportunity set containing the same two opportunities, the individual would have *accepted* the latter opportunity—thus "revealing a preference" for that latter (second-mentioned) opportunity.

5. A further necessary condition for rationality, thus, is that if the frontier rotates in some way, the individual will not choose a new point on the new frontier that "contradicts" this choice from the old frontier.

6. The two conditions for rationality mean that an individual will "take advantage" of expanded choice, not respond perversely, dysfunctionally.

7. An individual can be viewed as gaining from expanded choice. The gain can be viewed as gaining from expanded choice. The gain can be measured by how much the individual would be willing to pay for it (in units of one good or another)—willingness to pay.

8. The total gain from access to a good at its prevailing price—the surplus of benefit over cost—is called the individual's surplus. Smith's water-diamond paradox is cleared up by formulating this gain, or surplus.

9. But when discussing economic inequality we are generally content to compare people's opportunities.

CONCEPTS INTRODUCED

opportunity set*
frontier of the opportunity set
upward (or outward) frontier shift
dominating opportunity
frontier rotation
expanded choice
individual's labor-supply curve and
    consumer-good demand curves
individual's gain from expanded choice

willingness to pay
the measure of gain
expanded choice from trade
water-diamond paradox
benefit and cost
surplus of benefit over cost
comparing persons' opportunity sets
happiness, or "utility," vs. capabilities and
    rewards

STUDY QUESTIONS

1. If the government raises taxes in order to provide "free" food and clothing for the populace, rational worker-consumers will:

    a. work less hard because the incentive is reduced

    b. work harder in order to contribute more tax revenue for food and clothing

    c. work as before, since nothing is free

    d. it's a toss-up

2. If the government raises taxes in order to buy bread to hurl it at an advancing enemy, rational worker-consumers will:

    a. work less hard because the rate of pay (after tax) is reduced

    b. work harder so as not to have to tighten their belts so much

    c. work as before and try to keep their minds off the war

    d. can't tell

3. Observing the effects of the potato famines in mid-nineteenth-century Ireland, Sir Robert Giffen noted a paradox: The Irish peasants actually consumed more, not fewer, potatoes as their price rose. Were they irrational? What do you guess happened to their consumption of bread?

4. "Since successful and prosperous people are mostly workaholics who are not visibly 'happier' than the rest of society, there is no substance to notions of 'inequality' and 'the less advantaged'; nor to notions of efficiency and progress since we are no happier than before the Industrial Revolution." Discuss.

* Sometimes called the choice set.

5. A person who had often lunched at Mama's and always tipped exactly 15 percent stops going there upon finding that Mama now adds a 15 percent service charge in lieu of a tip. Is this irrational or is it a case of contracted choice?

6. A young Italian economist, told she has only another year to live, is choosing between a fellowship in political economy in London and one in Milan. She decides she prefers the more convenient and luxurious situation in Milan to the more interesting and challenging appointment in London—until news arrives of an offer from New York. Imagine—political economy in New York! Pondering the new information and bolstered by this vote of confidence, she reevaluates her prospects in each place. Reluctantly discarding New York as too far, she decides upon London. What property, or axiom, of "rationality" does this decision violate? Is it truly irrational of the signorina to behave this way? What does the question suggest is an implicit assumption in the theory of rational choice about a person's information on the elements in her opportunity set and about her capacities to derive satisfaction from each of these elements?

7. Consider a farmer who was a self-sufficient producer of his own bread until he discovered a society in which to specialize. By producing only wheat and exchanging it for bread in the market he finds his "rate of pay," per hour, rises from w_1 to w_2, as in Panel A of Figure 2–5. Explain why (in the case of Panel A) the farmer's *gain* is *greater* than the wage-rate change times the *initial* amount of hours worked, though *less* than the wage-rate change times the *subsequent* number of hours worked and *less* than the increase in the farmer's consumption of bread.

Now suppose that the market price of bread somehow goes up to the point where the farmer's rate of pay (in bread per hour) is back to the original w_1 so that, as a result, he drops out of the market and returns to producing his own bread (or he may as well do that). Consider then the lump sum bread payment that the farmer would have to receive to be exactly compensated for this rise in price. Explain why this compensating payment is exactly the aforementioned gain that he has now lost.

Suppose finally that, due to a climatic change or some other cause, the farmer's rate of pay in the production of bread actually falls from w_2 not to w_1 but rather to a level, w_0, just low enough that he stops producing and consuming bread (though continuing with his usual brook trout and berries for nutrients). Explain why the bread payment the farmer would need to compensate him for this rise in price to the prohibitive level is (or was!) the farmer's consumer's surplus from being able to consume bread at an affordable price (namely, at the price $1/w_2$ hours worked per unit of bread). Identify graphically, using Panel A of Figure 2–5, the size of this compensating bread payment, or surplus. Prove that it is *greater* than zero, though *less* than the farmer's former consumption of bread.

CHAPTER 3

Economic Equilibrium
and the Theory of Supply and Demand

OCTAVE:
On this earth there is one thing which is terrible, and that is that everyone has his own good reasons.

Jean Renoir in *The Rules of the Game* (1939)

Economists call attention to a feature of economic life that, to a degree, is normal in every society. It is a feature that people are rarely conscious of in the day's transactions—much as some ways people talk and look go unnoticed until recognized in paintings and poems. Yet it is of fundamental importance to the analysis of any economic system: Each workday millions of Parisians find their morning croissant and the croissants find them. London theater lovers without "tickets" go elsewhere or stay home, so ticketholders may keep their seats unchallenged for the whole performance. In New York and almost everywhere sellers of goods commonly accept "money" in payment, often the mere promise of "money," and this "money"—this paper or promise of paper, which is utterly unproductive and unsatisfying itself—is then accepted in turn as payment for others' services or others' goods. In mines and mills and most plants everywhere, the output is unfinished goods—gas, metal, chemicals, etc.—that no consumer has contracted to buy. *There is a remarkable degree of order in any social economy, especially when it has been operating under its accustomed mechanisms and has not been disturbed by any extraordinary shock.*

There is orderliness too in the normal operations of armies and corps de ballet, of course, but no one exclaims over it. We may admire the strategy or the choreography, but we take accomplishments of coordination for granted where there is a command structure with a single director at the top. What is impressive about the orderliness found in most economies is that so much of it is achieved without any need—possibly without any use!—for comprehensive directives from a central ruling authority attempting to ensure the coordination of people's production and consumption of each good. A degree of order is achieved with considerable individual autonomy.

Much of our education and experience in childhood suggests to us that individual autonomy is permissible only if everyone exercises that autonomy in a collective spirit: for the sake of the family or the good of the team. We are taught to obey authority and to learn to share. (So we are prepared from childhood to accept that socialism might work, but only if the autonomous production managers are "team players" acting "for the good of society.") Capitalist enterprises, however, exercise their autonomy in the quest for their own profit. They decide what to produce and what jobs to offer, with scarcely a thought to whether it might be "good" for the country, and usually without really knowing. And yet food and drink reliably reach the stores and homes. That such profit seeking is no bar to order is driven home by Smith: "It is not from the benevolence of the butcher, the brewer, or the baker, that we expect our dinner, but from their regard for their own interest. We address ourselves not to their humanity but to their self-love, and never talk to them of our own necessities but of our advantages."* Smith thought the economy would flourish if its members were given wide autonomy to pursue their own interests. Order would be achieved, for people would soon learn to coordinate their activities by themselves.

Smith's bold claims for enterprise capitalism have led to most of the central questions of political economy: Whether it is possible that a capitalist enterprise system—under current operating rules anyway—might remain in *dis*order, in chaos or muddle. Whether the same might be true of a socialist enterprise system, so-called market socialism. Whether, under prevailing laws, etc., there even exists a potential state of order that could ever be reached. And whether, if order prevails, the order produced by the "best" of capitalist rules is good enough.

There is a prior question with which we must deal, however. What is the meaning of "order" here? How could we tell, if we could gather all the information we wanted, that order prevails? Economic order is apparently not law and order. It is not a political balance between haves and have-nots, between sun belt and snow belt. It is not just industrial peace at every factory between workers and owner. But what is it? Having a clear concept of

* Adam Smith, *The Wealth of Nations*, Book 1, chap. 1, p. 14.

order—a clear notion of *equilibrium,* as economists call it—is important because (as indicated above) it is basic to every expert discussion and every reasoned argument in political economy. It is a key notion in the way political economists organize their analyses of how the economy would function, and how well it would function, under this or that set of rules. The concept of equilibrium (and disequilibrium) is as basic to political-economic theory as the postulate of rational choice.

> The notion of a societywide economic equilibrium together with the concept of rational choice are the postulates that give political economy its methodological distinctiveness. Psychology has rational choice but not social order. Sociology has equilibrium but no emphasis on the voluntary and rational.

THE CONCEPT OF EQUILIBRIUM

The technical concept of *economic equilibrium* gives a precise meaning to the intuitive notion of total economic order. Equilibrium simply means correct expectations. An *economy* is said to be in equilibrium if, and only if, the outcomes of the participants' attempts to carry out their individual plans are going to be consistent with the participants' expectations. Of course, the individual plans on which the outcomes depend are based on certain expectations; so the concept of equilibrium contains the idea of a loop. The economy is in equilibrium if and only if expectations are such as to generate individual plans or strategies that produce outcomes that "validate," or "confirm," those expectations:

$$\text{expectations} \rightarrow \text{strategies} \rightarrow \text{outcomes}$$

Thus equilibrium is characterized by the presence of expectations that, by helping to produce the "right" individual plans, contribute to their own realization. An equilibrium, then, is *a case of self-fulfilling expectations* in this sense: The particular expectations that prevail there are such—given the participants' preferences, and their technological and institutional possibilities—as to make them self-fulfilling. To say that an equilibrium exists does not mean that any and all expectations are self-fulfilling—that "believing makes it—anything!—so."

> Of course we should not presume that any real-life economy is *exactly* in equilibrium, which would be a case of total order. But the concept serves to clarify the meaning of order.

Goods and things, then, are not capable of economic equilibrium—only people's expectations are. There is a human, mental element to economic equilibrium, since it means a consistency between *people's beliefs* and what happens. The "order" in an orderly market for croissants, according to this concept of equilibrium, is the realization of the expectations on which suppliers and consumers of croissants based their current (croissant-related) decisions:

- In equilibrium, suppliers find that they are selling the volume they expected to sell and find that their competitors have set the prices they were expected to; so the expectations on which the suppliers based their production decisions are realized. And consumers find croissants at the prices they expected to encounter and find the work and income waiting for them that they expected to obtain to pay for croissants (and their other planned purchases); so the expectations on which croissant buyers based their buying plans, when they left home on an empty stomach, are realized too.
- In disequilibrium, by contrast, the expectations of some (or all) of the participants in the market are wrong. Perhaps consumers will be surprised to discover a reduction of price, and each supplier will be disappointed to learn that the other suppliers have cut their prices as much as he reduced his price. Some of the transactors may have differing expectations, so someone is going to be wrong; or all the transactors may form mistaken expectations, even making the same mistake.

In most markets, though not all, data showing a marked increase in unsold goods, or unhired labor, for example, serve as useful indicators of the presence of disequilibrium in that market. An abnormally large stock of unsold croissants at the end of the morning indicates that suppliers have overforecast the quantity of croissants their customers are willing to buy at the current price; a general sellout, or stock-out, of croissants by mid-morning indicates an underforecast of the croissants demanded. However, there can be a disequilibrium even when there is no surplus and no shortage (beyond what might be normal in the market being studied). In some *other* markets—for many widely traded metals and staples—there can occur last-minute price adjustments that serve to avoid surpluses and shortages—and thus "clear the market"; but those unanticipated price adjustments mean disequilibrium for the suppliers or consumers who didn't expect them. There is a more general point worth making: We cannot necessarily detect the presence of a disequilibrium just from looking at current data on production, consumption, and prices.

It might be that production and consumption are at perfectly normal levels, but only because producers all underpredicted the rise in the average price—they would have set still higher prices, and sold less, "had they known." Or, it might be that all the data show sharp changes; but if these changes were expected beforehand, it is no disequilibrium.

When the economy is in disequilibrium, so the expectations of some or all the participants are incorrect in some respect, the people who have mistaken expectations may sooner or later come to suspect that there is something wrong with their expectations. They *may* become aware that they have been unrealistic—optimistic (or pessimistic), not just unlucky (or lucky). They will then attempt to correct their expectations, to find the error or errors in their assumptions, estimates, and theories about their world. Some estimate might be recalculated, some forecast remade, in the light of recent experience: Poultry producers might reduce their forecasts of the normal price, families might resign themselves to higher prices (in terms of their labor time) and reduced rewards for working (in terms of goods). Or there might be some fundamental rethinking of beliefs about how some part of the economy behaves: people might stop believing that government officials will move to reduce the inflation. In any case, such revisions of people's expectations may—and usually will—lead them to alter their behavior accordingly—to choose a different plan or different strategy. In such a disequilibrium scenario, then,

$$\text{expectations} \rightarrow \text{strategies} \rightarrow \text{outcomes} \rightarrow \frac{\text{revised}}{\text{expectations}} \rightarrow \frac{\text{revised}}{\text{strategies}}.$$

By contrast, an economy in equilibrium does not motivate people to review their beliefs—to rethink and react.

THE INDIVIDUAL IN DISEQUILIBRIUM AND EQUILIBRIUM

The simplest examples of disequilibrium, and of equilibrium, are those involving the expectations and consequent behavior of just one person. The other persons in society are not going to react to that behavior, or their reactions are going to be small enough that we can afford to neglect them. So there are no reactions by others, in games with two or more "players," to complicate the story.

Perhaps the most familiar illustrations of disequilibrium are about children. The child who has won a triple ice cream from her indulgent parents and who won't be able to finish it is in disequilibrium, suffering from a disequilibrium (or disequilibrating) expectation—her eyes are too big for

FIGURE 3–1: Expected vs. Actual Opportunities

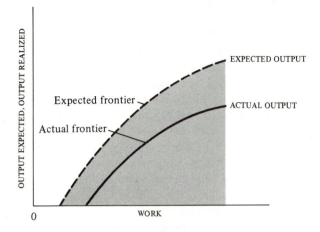

In planning how many hours to devote to some activity, a person will form some expectation of the amount of time required to produce any given amount of output—say, the number of cords of wood chopped, square meters of wall painted, or chapters written. The expected work-output relation may differ, however, from the true rela-tion. In the case illustrated, the individual under-estimates the work required to produce every level of output that might be planned. In the resulting disequilibrium the individual will either have to work more than he planned, or produce less than he planned, or both.

her stomach. Such experiences teach children, who are not born knowing the costs and benefits of everything (and who are therefore uncertain of their true preferences) to develop equilibrium expectations about their options. People, adults as much as children, sometimes have disequilibrium expec-tations about the "technology"—the costs of producing. The companies that have designed new aircraft are famous for their "cost overruns" and so are individuals: The scholar starting to write a textbook does not know he will be in chapter 3 when he expects to be in chapter 10. The family buying a home does not know they will find themselves "house-poor," unable to afford anything but the mortgage payment because they underestimated the expenses. The students starting to smoke do not know how difficult it will be to stop—the cost of quitting.

Quite a lot of fiction grows out of the fascination with the irony, often poignancy, of disequilibrium. X is unaware that his (her) love for Y is not reciprocated, that U is "using" X's naïve misimpression for her (his) own ulterior motives, etc. In the movies there is Laurel and Hardy's *Blockheads* in which Stan has spent twenty years in the trenches thinking that the war is still on. In real life there was the celebrated flight from Brooklyn to Ireland in 1938 by the test pilot for Republic Aircraft, Douglas Corrigan—dubbed "Wrong Way" Corrigan when, after the flight, he explained that his intended destination was California. (Not that all disequilibrium situations turn out undesirably.) Many disequilibrium phenomena resemble what analysts in the operations-research area call the two-armed bandit problem. Some slot machines offer two arms for the player to choose between with each coin. The player who has been lucky with the left arm may decide that it will not pay (on average) to experiment with the right arm—and hence continue that strategy indefinitely—even though, in fact, the right arm might be more favorable to the player. In sticking to option y^1, the gambler never gets to compare other options, y^2, y^3, and so on. (The ad agency's problem is to persuade such satisfied consumers to switch brands.)

Equilibrium and Chance

When there is no element of chance standing between a person's actions and the final outcome, no random events that could alter the outcome in an unanticipated way, then a person who is in equilibrium finds that everything is working out exactly as expected—as if he or she is blessed with "perfect foresight." When there is an element of randomness in the outcome of the individual's actions, however, we should say that the person is in equilibrium if and only if that person has *correct expectations about the chances*—correct beliefs about the probability that the outcome will be this one, the probability it will be that one, and so on for each possible outcome.

Clearly we would not want to say of some professional fisherman that he is in disequilibrium—that he is in the wrong business—just because he came home with an empty boat today. (But it is another matter if he is fishing in the Dead Sea.) A Canadian prospector was reported a few years ago to have reached eight-eighty and to be still looking for his first gold strike; but we would not want to say that he has been in disequilibrium all his life unless we thought we knew more about the chances of finding gold in the Yukon than he does. Neither is it necessarily a case of disequilibrium when a businessman, encountering unusually heavy traffic to the airport, on one occasion misses his plane. But it *is* a disequilibrium, in fact, if he has been regularly underestimating the traffic; then the unexpected frequency with which he finds he is late for planes may cause him to revise his traffic expectations—and to leave home earlier.

ECONOMIC EQUILIBRIUM IN A SOCIETY

The economy of a society is in equilibrium if and only if all the persons participating in the economy are in equilibrium. A fundamental property of the economy in any society, of course, is that the outcome resulting from a participant's actions depends upon the other participants' actions as well as the person's own—unlike the situation for Crusoe. Every participant is guided by his or her own interests, which are not generally parallel to those of the other participants, and no one's interests govern the actions of all (except in a voluntary and autocratic cult-society, like a bee colony). So each person, in figuring the outcome of any strategy of his own, must reckon the actions (and perhaps the reactions) of other persons, or certain effects of those actions; each person will be influenced by his expectations about the other participants' behavior.

The extra dimension in a society's equilibrium as compared to an individual's, therefore, is that each participant has correct expectations about how the actions of the others are going to impinge on him. In equilibrium a person's expectations somehow take adequate account of the other persons: their expectations and their behavior and its effects. Such correct expectations play the role (for good or ill) of arranging (or coordinating) people's interactions in a surprise-free—in that sense "orderly"—way. But what coordinates the expectations? Some social institutions—laws, conventions, markets—must grow up for "expectations" to apply to.

Classical economics focused on social interactions in which the actions of one person have little effect on anyone else: what one corn grower among many does has negligible effect on one corn-flakes consumer because there are so many such producers and consumers. Nevertheless, some social interactions of crucial importance involve only a few persons (as poets and dramatists have long noted). Quite a lot of actions a person might take have only one victim or beneficiary—no third party is significantly affected. The employee bargains and dissembles against just one employer (his or her own); a mugger usually mugs one person at a time, and a "muggee" seldom has two muggers to play against each other; the bidder for a contract may know it has a single competitor for the job.

Interactions between two "players" (or at most a few players) are especially intriguing because they exhibit a kind of conjectural interdependence: "My move is going to be influenced by the move I expect her to make, and I believe that her move is likewise going to be influenced by the move she expects me to make. So what I expect her to do is influenced by what I expect she expects I am going to do." An example is the pitcher trying to figure out in which way the batter supposes he has outguessed the pitcher—but it is not economics, because there is no room for collaboration: one's gain is the other's loss. When an interpersonal interaction involves such a conjectural element it is called a "game of strategy," or simply a *game*.

GAMES PEOPLE PLAY: COINCIDING AND OPPOSING INTERESTS

Many problems of coordination can be viewed as two-person games. When two ships are found by their pilots to be heading straight toward one another, they want to coordinate their moves to avoid collision. To simplify a little, let us suppose that each pilot has to choose between two moves—to turn to the left or to the right, to port or starboard as old salts like to say. If they both turn to their right collision will be avoided, and the same is true if they both turn to their left; collision results, we shall assume, if either pilot turns in a direction opposite from the other.

The situation and the outcomes from each possible pair of moves by the pilots are illustrated with the use of the "pay-off matrix" in Figure 3–2. The characteristic of this game, and of coordination games generally, is that each player wants to do what the other player expects him to do—for it is mutually disastrous for either player to choose the move that the other player was

FIGURE 3–2: The Boaters' Dilemma

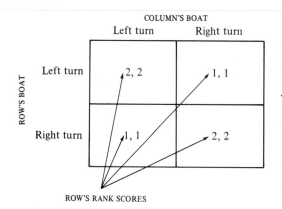

ROW'S RANK SCORES

One of the pilots—call him Row—"plays" the rows. The other pilot, called Column, is pictured as playing the columns.

The matrix records the players' respective evaluation of each possible outcome: first Row's evaluation, then Column's. Row ranks at the bottom the outcome in which both turn left, so Row gives it a rank score of 1. Row gives the same rank score to the other collision outcome in which they both turn right, since it is tied for bottom. Row gives a rank score of 2 to the other two outcomes, which are tied for next-to-bottom rating in Row's evaluation. In this purest of all coordination games, Column's rankings of the possible outcomes are identical to Row's.

An equilibrium exists in the case where Row expects Column to turn right and Column expects Row to turn right: Then Row will turn right, as Column expected, and Column wil turn right, as Row expected. If those are the players' expectations they will be shown to be correct. Another equilibrium exists when instead each player expects the other to turn left. Although these two equilibria exist, at most one of them will actually take place in one play. (Clearly disequilibrium exists in the two cases where the expected turns are different directions: The players' resulting strategies will prove those expectations to be incorrect.)

FIGURE 3—3: Coordination Game between Farmer and Rancher

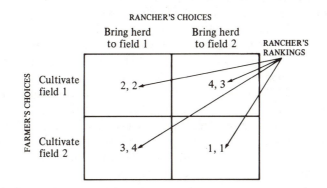

In this coordination game, Farmer ranks as worst (at the bottom) the outcome in which Rancher brings his cattle to field 2 after Farmer has chosen to cultivate that field rather than the other; so Farmer gives this outcome a rank score of 1. For Farmer the next worse outcome is a collision with the cattle at the superior field 1, so he gives that outcome a rank score of 2. He ranks highest the outcome in which he cultivates field 1 while Rancher grazes his cattle in field 2. But Rancher, who also covets field 1, ranks highest the outcome in which his cattle graze there while Farmer uses field 2. (To keep the example as simple as possible, it is assumed that Rancher, like Farmer, ranks collision on field 1 ahead of collision on field 2; but this assumption is inconsequential.)

There exists an equilibrium in which Farmer expects Rancher to bring his herd to field 1 and Rancher expects Farmer to locate at field 2; then Farmer calculates that the better outcome, of the two that remain available, is the one where he farms field 2, which is what Rancher expects him to do, and Rancher figures that his best move is to take his herd to field 1, just as Farmer expects him to do. There is clearly another equilibrium, in which Farmer expects Rancher to take field 2 and Rancher expects Farmer to farm field 1. (Of course, when Farmer and Rancher each expect the other to go to the same field, whether it is 1 or 2, there is a disequilibrium in which both players' expectations are disappointed.)

It is a distinctive characteristic of these coordination-game equilibria that not only does each player not want to deviate from his calculated course of action, given his expectation of the other's action, but he also does not want the other player to deviate from his expectation of what the other player will do. And that other player does not wish to deviate from that expectation either.

counting on him not to choose. But which of the two moves is expected? If we look at the matter in a nonhistorical or purely technical way there is no answer: There are two equilibria, one if both pilots expect the other to turn left, and the other if both expect a turn to the right. Fortunately, ships' pilots have solved this coordination problem over the centuries by the adoption of a convention. Both ships should turn to the right. And since each pilot will expect the other to adhere to that convention, he is motivated to turn to the right himself. Successful conventions are thus self-reinforcing.

Most coordination games are marked by an additional feature. While each player wants to "coordinate" his strategy with that of the other player(s), the player is not generally indifferent as to which equilibrium outcome to "coordinate on." Even in a team effort two or more members may want to play the leading role; they agree only that it is worst to lose. Competing subway builders agree they do not want two subways, but if just one, whose? If two back-to-back skyscrapers would be worse than none, and none worse than one, then which one is it to be? One solution to such a coordination game may be illustrated by the time-worn story of the farmer and the rancher: there are two bodies of land available, one of them better than the other both for growing crops and for grazing cattle. The farmer would rather not plant where the rancher is going to invade with his livestock, whichever field that is; and the rancher would rather not take his herd to the field where the farmer has planted, with its barbed-wire fences and risk of bullets, whichever field that is. Obviously there are two possible equilibria, one of them preferred by the farmer and the other preferred by the rancher. Here society has stepped in to ensure that some equilibrium occurs (partly because of the interests of third parties). Figure 3–3 illustrates this game.

Property Rights as Devices for Coordination

Could this latter sort of coordination game, with its conflict over the choice of equilibrium, be resolved by a convention? Sometimes a convention does solve a coordination problem despite such conflicts: when a man and a woman arrive at a revolving door at the same instant, the purely arbitrary convention called "ladies first" works pretty well in avoiding collisions. The earliest societies, and those few primitive societies still surviving today, are often termed traditional societies because they employed conventions to resolve conflicts much more extensively than contemporary societies do: When the father died tradition often dictated that the family business go entirely to the eldest son (the convention of primogeniture). Two persons aspiring to the same office or the same advantage, such as the better plot of land, might find that some code of chivalry would award the prize to the older or the weaker—perhaps on the theory that with luck the loser would have another opportunity (and such sharing was a desirable principle).

In the simplest societies such conventions might have worked: A person would not want to break a convention if it would cost him the esteem of the community or if it would jeopardize his prospect of being treated chivalrously himself in the future. But there seems little possibility that such conventions might work to resolve differences between Rancher and Farmer in a frontier society, or between drilling rigs on the high seas, or contesting squatters in an urban jungle. Out there conventions won't police themselves, and so they will not work.

A system of property rights, enforced by society, can solve this coordination game. If the fields are "owned," so that the rights to graze and cultivate in a field are likewise owned, the user of that field will have to buy or lease those rights to avoid the penalty for violating another's property rights. The prior requirement of obtaining these rights ensures that rancher and farmer will not both plan to use the same field. It does not matter here whether Farmer and Rancher own the land they use or instead lease the land from an absentee owner. And it does not matter here whether the land is under private ownership or public (state) ownership—or some of both.

Thus the institution of property rights can often serve to coordinate the expectations of individuals so as to prevent their having costly collisions. But this institution characteristically requires social enforcement. Otherwise, the rancher, wondering why the farmer should get the better land (just because he can better afford it), would be tempted to unseat the farmer—figuring that he has an equal chance of winning in a showdown. Third parties who want to see ranchers and farmers produce and send their foodstuffs to market therefore have an interest in stopping such collisions; and third parties make their own property rights more secure by showing readiness to intervene in the defense of others' property rights: hence there is willingness to enforce property rights. So the reliable delivery of croissants to every Parisian, while an impressive achievement no doubt, is not a miracle in which governmental power plays altogether no part. The government is needed to establish and enforce one or another system of property rights if the economy is to deliver any good.

THE "MARKET GAME": EQUILIBRIUM AND DISEQUILIBRIUM OF ENTERPRISES

Without property rights and their social enforcement, then, living a hand-to-mouth existence might be the only prudent strategy. A person would find it risky to produce goods in excess of what he needed to survive, since any surplus goods might be pirated or demanded as extortion. (You might lose half your goods every time you ran into anyone as well armed as yourself.) *With* property rights and the prospect of their effective enforcement, however, people will be motivated to adopt a more venturesome, more enterprising strategy. If working harder or longer will earn a person property rights that can be exchanged for additional goods, it is rational to seize the expanded opportunity. If specializing in the production and sale of goods that a person is comparatively talented at producing will earn a person property rights that can be exchanged for the other goods wanted, it is rational to abandon self-sufficiency in favor of a strategy of specialization. Cobblers will have an incentive to stick to their lasts and mitten makers to stick to their knitting.

The institution of property rights of some sort leaves open in many respects the kind of economic system that a society may have. There may be purely private ownership or purely public ownership, as already noted; or there may be a mixed system of public and private ownership. A second dimension is the mechanism for allocation. Under a commercial market mechanism, the owners of resources supply them largely in order to earn income with which to buy final goods—as between two identical jobs, at any rate, the supplier takes the better-paying one; and the suppliers of final goods produce for sale "in the market," aiming for the highest possible profit (for the governmental or private owners). Under a command mechanism, such as the army or pure communism, the workers donate their services and final goods are "allocated," as though they were experimental drugs, "on merit." Then one's TV set will not likely be stolen, because it is the property of the state. A third dimension of any economic system is the direction of resources: Resources will not organize themselves into producing and delivering units—a circus needs an impresario, a croissant business an entrepreneur. At one extreme there is a perfectly centralized governmental authority doing all the employing and producing (other than what friends and family can produce by themselves). At the other extreme we find many enterprises each taking initiatives independent of the others: the enterprises in such a "decentralized" system may be under private ownership or owned by the government.

To give further illustrations of economic equilibrium in a society, examples involving interactions among many (even all) participants, we want now to focus on just one economic system: one in which everyone is the (private) owner of his own labor—no prison labor for use by the state, no slave labor for use by a slave owner; in which everyone works, among other reasons, for income to spend buying final goods for consumption; and in which production and marketing decisions are undertaken by a number of independent enterprises each seeking maximum profit. Of course this is like the standard brand of capitalism—enterprise capitalism, it might be called, as distinct from state capitalism in which a single monopoly firm (or a very few monopoly firms) can operate under license from the state without fear of a new entrant trying to obtain a share of the market.

But the system just specified is also like what is called market socialism—a system in which socialist enterprises, although ultimately returning any profit to their government owner, compete with one another just like private enterprises: meeting customers' demands at a competitive price in order not to lose a share of the market, and paying employees competitive wage rates so as not to suffer a draining away of employees (called "attrition") to other enterprises.

It is clear that in such an enterprise market system, the existence of property rights merely lays the ground for the possibility of an economic equilibrium. To be in equilibrium it is not enough that the theatrical producer have a lease to the theater and exclusive contracts with the actors and playright; these property arrangements ensure correct expectations in only a few respects—the theater will not be double-booked, the same play or the same stars will not appear in another production (and thus divide the potential audience). To be in equilibrium the producer must also have correct expectations about the "market" for his production: That involves the ticket price(s) that producers of rival productions will be charging—and thus the price(s) he can charge while remaining competitive—and the number of admissions he can sell at such competitive prices. The producer must also have correct expectations about the "market" for the inputs needed to produce—the competitive scale of wage rates needed to retain cast and staff of the planned caliber. (One can imagine that producers would contract with ticket buyers in advance of any production. But then it is the ticket buyers who run the risk of finding themselves in a big disequilibrium.)

What has all this to do with the phenomenon of order in a largely unplanned economy? What is its bearing on the celebrated smoothness with which croissants and their consumers seem to meet, the serenity with which suppliers of real goods and hard work accept in payment a thing (called money) of no intrinsic worth or satisfaction? Just this: The great entrepreneurs of the croissant industry supply their product in the amounts they do because they have certain expectations about the "market" for croissants—the average price, total number of purchases. Sellers of services (and final goods) accept money in payment because they have certain expectations about the terms at which they can in turn exchange this money for croissants and other goods they want to buy. The economic system is in an equilibrium— there is a kind of order—when such expectations of enterprises and households are generally correct. The order we see in the croissant market arises because the enterprises and consumers who participate in that market have somehow acquired a set of correct expectations regarding that market. While there is no economic czar to coordinate suppliers in the croissant market, it is conceivable that they nonetheless achieve an equilibrium by learning to coordinate themselves.

EQUILIBRIUM PRICE: THE CLASSICAL CASE OF SUPPLY AND DEMAND

One hundred years or so after Smith's *Wealth of Nations* classical economics entered a new stage of development. Starting on the Continent and spreading through Britain finally to America, a new wave of analysis arose—often called neoclassical economics—on the determination of the prices and amounts produced of the various goods in an economy operating under free markets. One of the late-classical masters, at the end of the nineteenth century, was the English economist Alfred Marshall. It was Marshall who, more than anyone before him, developed the classical analysis of how price and output are determined in a single industry, viewed in isolation from other industries producing other goods. The object of Marshall's theoretical study was an important, though evidently special, case—an industry in which all the suppliers are *pure competitors:* Each producer is so small that what it does will have a negligible effect on the other producers. (The small-scale producer of Soave wine in Italy knows that his output is too small a drop in the bucket to be able to affect the price that this year's harvest will sell for at the auction.) Moreover, the *pure* competitor knows that he need not lower his own price to sell more—he can sell all he wants at the common market price—because his product is indistinguishable from the others' product and there are no "frictions" making it costly to find more buyers quickly, so there is no reason why he must accept (even briefly) a lower price than any of the other sellers (no matter how much more he wants to sell).

In a market characterized by pure competition those participants on the buying side of the market find themselves in a similar situation. Each buyer is conscious of being too small to affect the price. So no one fears that by buying more the price will be driven up, and no one hopes that buying less will push the price down. And each buyer knows that to obtain the good it is not necessary to pay a higher price than anyone else, nor is it possible to get away with a lower price. Under pure competition, the transactors are faceless, the transactions impersonal—no one is a pleasure to deal with or a pain, either.

> In a purely competitive market, then, there operates what is called the *law of one price*. If some seller were to enjoy an advantageous price, one or more of the competing sellers would rush in to spoil it; and if a buyer were to find a bargain, one or more of the competing buyers would ruin it. Second, each buyer and seller takes the market *price as given,* since each is too small to be able (with his minuscule purchases or sales) to affect it appreciably.

The equilibrium price of a good produced and sold in a purely competitive market is determined by two forces—*supply* and *demand*. The same is true of the equilibrium output of the good, the output level associated with that same equilibrium. Demand summarizes all the forces acting on the behavior of buyers, and supply summarizes all the influences upon the behavior of the suppliers. Of course, *every competitive market outcome is going to be marked by some price and output:* suppliers bring so much to the market, and this output is sold for some price. All the output is marketed at the price it will bring. But an equilibrium outcome is special. The enterprises supplying a good to a purely competitive market are in equilibrium if, but only if, they have correct expectations about the market price that is going to result. Hence *in equilibrium the actual price is going to be equal to the expected price*—the price expected by suppliers when they made their production decisions. The equilibrium price is the correctly expected price—an instance of fulfilled expectations.

The determination of the equilibrium price and equilibrium output is best illustrated diagrammatically.

The demand curve. Consider first the role of demand. According to rational choice theory, it was seen in the previous chapter, a person with a particular opportunity set makes a unique choice—there is nothing indeterminate about it. Thus a person faced with observable prices for this and that good, and having a certain amount of wealth and certain expectations of future income and future prices, will choose definite amounts of each good to buy. Plunk a Martian down in a market economy and that extraterrestrial being may in desperation flip a coin to decide which goods and how much to try; but earth-persons, having been around, have no such difficulty deciding. This functional relationship between what each person would like to buy of a good and the price of that good (and the prices of all the other goods) is the basis of the market demand: *The total amount of a good that all market participants in the aggregate wish to buy is called the* QUANTITY DEMANDED *of that good in the market. This quantity depends on the price of the good, just as each person's desired purchase depends on the price. The functional relationship between the quantity demanded and the price of the good is called the* DEMAND CURVE, *or* DEMAND SCHEDULE.

A hypothetical demand schedule is tabulated in Figure 3–4. It shows the amount demanded of a good, tomatoes in the illustration, at each of several different prices per bushel. Each pair of price and corresponding quantity demanded is plotted as a point in the diagram. Each of these points must lie on the demand curve—the demand curve must contain these points (and more). The smooth curve shown is the hypothetical demand curve: It registers the quantity demanded at any price, including the several prices singled out in the table.

FIGURE 3–4: A Demand Curve for Tomatoes

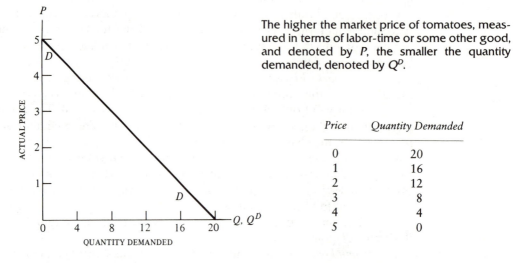

The higher the market price of tomatoes, measured in terms of labor-time or some other good, and denoted by P, the smaller the quantity demanded, denoted by Q^D.

Price	Quantity Demanded
0	20
1	16
2	12
3	8
4	4
5	0

The hypothetical example of a demand schedule displays a property found to be true of the demand schedule for virtually every good: The lower the price, the greater is the quantity demanded. This inverse relationship between price and quantity demanded is reflected by the negative slope of the demand curve: as we move along the demand curve, each small increase in the quantity demanded is associated with a *decrease* (a negative change) in price. Or as informal economists are fond of saying: the demand curve is "downward sloping" as we travel along it from left to right. The apparent reasons for this downward or negative slope are: Ordinarily each person will wish to buy less of a good—at any rate, not more of the good—when its price goes up. And even if the good is a raincoat, which it is not possible to buy less of (short of not buying it), more people will be willing to go without one or postpone getting one the higher its price.

Coupling the hypothesis of a downward-sloping demand curve to the pure competitiveness of the market we are discussing leads to a significant implication: All the transactions in the market at any moment—all the current purchases and sales—will be made at the price that makes the quantity demanded just equal to whatever quantity of the good has been brought to market for sale. For if the price were so low that the quantity demanded exceeded the amount available for sale, some buyers would be unable to buy as much as they wished. But that cannot happen under pure competition—the frustrated buyers would not stand still watching, they would attempt to bid away some of the quantity that others were at the point of getting, and in so doing they would bid up the price. And if the price were so high that the quantity demanded were less than the quantity available to be sold, some buyers would see that one or more sellers were going to be left with a quantity unsold; and that cannot happen under pure competition either— since buyers would welcome the opportunity to make their purchases at lower prices, the sellers having unsold quantities would divert purchases from their competitors by offering lower prices. *Under pure competition, the price is at just the level that equates the quantity demanded to whatever quantity has been produced and brought to the market. That price is said to "clear the market," preventing both shortage and surplus. With a downward-sloping demand curve, this market-clearing price is lower the larger is the quantity of the good brought to market.*

FIGURE 3–5: Under Pure Competition, Price "Clears the Market"

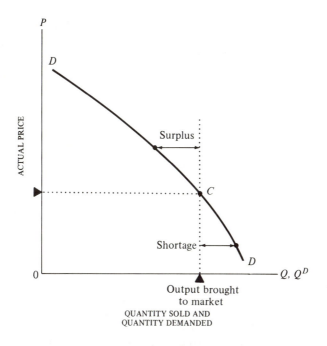

Suppose that the quantity of the good brought to the market happens to be the amount indicated in the diagram. All of this quantity is to be sold in the current period, no matter what the price. So the amount for sale may be represented by a vertical line, which shows the same amount available at every price.

To find the price that will be established in this purely competitive market one needs only to locate the price at which the quantity demanded just equals the quantity available in the market. This equality occurs at the point c on the demand curve. The height, or ordinate, of this point is the competitive price. At a lower price there would be a shortage, at a higher price a surplus. Competition prevents such nonclearing prices.

♦ Caution: This *actual* price is not necessarily the equilibrium price, as we shall soon see.

The supply curve. Granted, the quantity of a good supplied determines its price in a purely competitive market. But what determines the quantity of the good supplied? Answer: the price that suppliers expect and the supply curve that depicts their resulting production response.

Each enterprise has the problem of deciding which goods to produce, if any, and how much of each. Such decisions will determine whether a plot of land is used for potato growing or cattle raising and whether a city loft is leased for ballet classes or karate lessons. The classical hypothesis is that capitalist enterprises decide such questions on the basis of expected profitability: * If the expected price at which the enterprise will be able to sell the good once produced is low, then the profitability consideration warns the enterprise away from committing itself to producing that good; at a higher expected price, the enterprise will be willing to produce more—up to the point consonant with achieving the maximum expected profit. The supply response of each enterprise to the expected price (and expected price of the other goods) determines the amount marketed: *The total amount of a good that all market participants in the aggregate wish to supply is called the* QUANTITY SUPPLIED *of that good in the market. The amount supplied depends on the expected price of the good. The functional relationship between the amount supplied and the expected price of the good is called the* SUPPLY CURVE, *or* SUPPLY SCHEDULE.

An example of a hypothetical supply schedule is given in the table accompanying Figure 3–6. It shows the amount supplied of the good, the same tomatoes under discussion, at each of several different expected prices. Each pair of expected price and corresponding quantity supplied is plotted as a point on the supply curve.

The supply schedule shown has a property that is typical, though not necessarily universal, among supply schedules (if economists' impressions over the centuries are a good judge): The higher the expected price, the larger is the quantity supplied. This "direct" relationship between expected price and quantity supplied is reflected by the positive slope of the supply curve: Each small increase in the quantity supplied is associated with an *increase* in (a *positive* change of) the expected price. In other words, the supply curve is "upward sloping" as we "read" it from left to right. The reason for this upward, or positive, slope is that the supplying enterprises will be willing to produce more of the good only with an increase in the

---

* A not so different hypothesis might be entertained regarding socialist enterprises. The museum director may ask himself what kind of exhibition will sell the most admissions, and the restaurant manager what kind of cuisine promises to fetch the fanciest prices.

FIGURE 3–6: A Supply Curve for Tomatoes

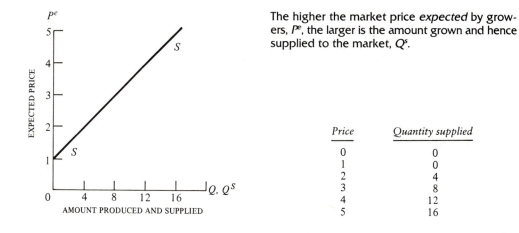

The higher the market price *expected* by growers, P^e, the larger is the amount grown and hence supplied to the market, Q^s.

Price	Quantity supplied
0	0
1	0
2	4
3	8
4	12
5	16

price they expect to receive for it; and that is so because the producers know that the cost of producing more (one more unit, say) is higher the larger the amount already being produced—each unit costs the enterprise more than the previous one.

It will be recalled that the *equilibrium* price means a correctly expected price. When the enterprises supplying the market have all hit upon the right price to expect, that is the equilibrium price; when they are guessing wrong, they (or their price expectations) are not in equilibrium. To calculate the equilibrium price it is necessary to ask: What price expectation if shared by all the supplying enterprises would cause them to supply an amount of the good just large enough to make the actual market price *equal* to this expected price? Clearly, if expectations of price are high, the enterprises will be encouraged to bring a large quantity of the good to the market, so the actual price will be low—a disappointing disequilibrium for suppliers. And if expectations of price are low, the quantity supplied by the nervous enterprises will be accordingly small, so the actual price will be high—an exhilarating disequilibrium for the downcast suppliers. *The apparatus of supply and demand may be used to calculate the equilibrium price. It is located at the intersection of the supply curve and demand curve. If all the suppliers expect that price, the resulting amount supplied when sold in the market will cause that same price actually to occur. That expectation, and only that one, will thus prove self-fulfilling.*

FIGURE 3–7: The Equilibrium Price Level Is Determinable from the Supply and Demand Curves Jointly

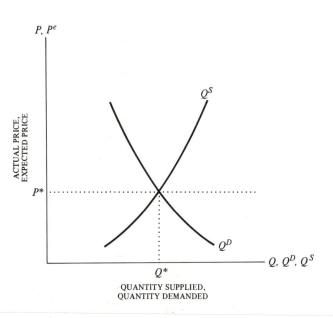

QUANTITY SUPPLIED,
QUANTITY DEMANDED

The equilibrium price, P^*, has the property that if $P^e = P^*$ then $P = P^*$ likewise, so that $P = P^e$—correct expectations. It can be seen that P^* must be at the level where Q^D and Q^S are equal. For suppose P^* were higher, say. Then Q^D corresponding to this price level would be less than the corresponding Q^S, so P would have to be *lower* in order to increase Q_D—so P would be less than P^e, a case of incorrect expectations. At P^*, $Q^D = Q^S$. Only if $P^e = P^*$ will the actual price *(P)* equal the expected price P^e and hence quantity supplied *(Q^s)* equal quantity demanded *(Q^D)*.

A very simple diagram suffices to capture the two essential themes in the equilibrium analysis of a purely competitive market: The actual price depends on—is some function of—the price expectations of the suppliers. And the equilibrium price, if there exists one, is the price expectation that, if held by all the suppliers, will be "self-fulfilling." For purposes of the accompanying diagram, suppose that all suppliers expect the same price, correctly or not. The supply-demand analysis showed that the greater this *expected* price the smaller will be the resulting *actual price*. Consequently the curve that depicts the actual price resulting from each expected price is downward sloping, as shown. The equilibrium occurs in the diagram where the curve intersects the 45° line—for it is along that line that actual price equals expected

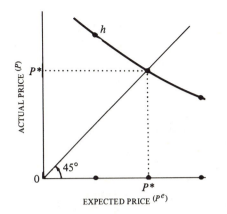

price. If the expected price is less than this equilibrium price, actual price will be greater than expected price; this outcome is like point h lying above the 45° line. If the expected price is greater than the equilibrium price, actual price will be smaller than expected price; that is a point below the 45° line. In algebraic terms, the actual price is a decreasing function of the expected price. Hence $P = f(P^e)$, with a negative "derivative," or slope, $f'(P^e)$. Then the equilibrium price, denoted by P^*, is implicitly determined by solving the equation $P^* = f(P^*)$ for the unknown P^*.

EPILOGUE TO PART 1: SOME CENTRAL ISSUES IN POLITICAL ECONOMY

People are forever saying that the economy (ours or some other) would benefit from functioning under some different "system"—more socialization of certain enterprises or desocialization of certain enterprises, more central planning or less of it—or under the same system with changes in the operating rules—more steeply progressive taxation or less progressive taxation, more protection of industry from competition or less regulation of industry, and so on. To analyze how a given set of rules and institutions "works," or would work if established, it is natural to want to postulate that the economy will settle into equilibrium. Confident of our hypothesis of equilibrium, we can turn our eyes from all the myriad disequilibrium outcomes that might have won equal attention; we can focus instead on the equilibrium outcome (or the equilibrium outcomes, if more than one exist).

It would be false to think that equilibrium is inherently desirable. When Moscovites who fancy certain specialty goods queue up for their weekly rations the system is operating in equilibrium: the ones who queue up find the waiting generally no worse than they expected and are content to go on with their strategy of queueing up; and the ones who refuse to join the lines, seeing or hearing that they are saving the time they expected to save by not queueing, are content to maintain their strategy. But few would say that this equilibrium is superior to every disequilibrium that might have occurred instead. (If a person overestimated the queueing time and stayed home, he would save other people's time besides his own—the people who would have been in line behind him—so maybe all would gain from queueing up less often "by mistake.") Quite a few observers of modern social life, in fact, have been appalled at what they believe to be the equilibrium of the system they are living under: How terrible that *this* is our equilibrium!*

The classical economists, however—Smith and the rest—evidently felt that the equilibrium of a capitalist enterprise economy was a good thing. A large part of twentieth-century political economy has been devoted to interpreting and evaluating their enthusiasm: In what sense good? And good compared to what? When capitalism is in disequilibrium it still "works" for those who happen to profit from others' mistakes; so one wonders—is there some fair test, some acceptable standard, by which capitalist enterprise equilibrium "beats" every disequilibrium? Does the capitalist enterprise equilibrium, given the right book of operating rules, likewise "beat" any noncapitalist or nonenterprise equilibrium? Adam Smith apparently thought so:

> The individual . . . neither intends to promote the public interest, nor knows how much he is promoting it. . . . He intends only his own security . . . his own gain . . . and he is led by an invisible hand to promote an end which was no part of his intention. . . . Pursuing his own interest he frequently promotes that of society more effectually than when he really intends to promote it.†

Yet plenty of critics of capitalism have thought otherwise. Karl Marx, for example, decried enterprise capitalism as anarchic because its development is dictated by "capital" rather than "reason." And the first half of the twentieth century saw demands for reducing the degree to which society's economic development is dependent on the not centrally coordinated investment decisions of capitalistic enterprises—for greater socialization of national investment. A real achievement of modern political economy has been to "make sense" of Smith, to make what may be the best possible, the most sophisticated defense of his claims for a competitive capitalist economy; and, in so doing, it has at the same time identified some of the limitations of Smith's vision.

But the grand debate with Smith is still not over. Some of that debate is over the question of whether a highly capitalist economy normally experi-

---

* When director Jean Renoir's character (played by Renoir) in *Rules of the Game* remarks, despairingly, that in this world "everyone has his own good reasons" he means (presumably) that people are acting quite realistically—with correct expectations about human behavior and the "system"—as well as self-interestedly and rationally. Although it might be in our mutual interest to do so, we lack the trust and the conscience to expect and to act differently.

† Smith, *The Wealth of Nations*, Book IV, chap. 2, p. 423.

ences its equilibrium outcome. A visitor from some more tranquil place, seeing the ups and downs of unemployment and inflation, could be pardoned for supposing that the Western economies these days have been in the violent throes of disequilibrium. But that is *not* the obvious question it may appear to be, as part 7 will help show.

SUMMARY

1. An individual, in his use of resources to obtain goods (his economic actions), is said to be in *economic equilibrium* if he is acting on the basis of correct expectations; if not, he is in *economic disequilibrium*.

2. An *economy* is said to be in economic equilibrium if all the participants are in economic equilibrium. Presumably it is not typical of economies that they are *exactly* in equilibrium; presumably some of the people are in disequilibrium some of the time. But when building a theoretical model of a social economy the economist finds it tremendously convenient to suppose—at least as a starting point—that the economy is in economic equilibrium.

3. The idea of economic equilibrium is first illustrated by reference to some two-person situations—games of strategy. The boaters' game is a game of pure coordination, of perfectly parallel interests by the two players. The farmer-rancher game is a coordination game displaying opposing (as well as parallel, or coinciding) interests. Some mechanism of *property rights* will be *necessary* if disequilibrium collisions are never to occur. (In these simple games of coordination, property rights are enough to do that—they are sufficient. But in the big game, there is a competition for property and hence the possibility of disequilibrium in that game.)

4. The idea of economic equilibrium, and disequilibrium, is then illustrated by reference to the traditional "market game"—a single market with many sellers, all small and frictionlessly competing with one another for the purchases of many small sellers. In this auction-type market, the price tends to "clear the market"—to find the market-clearing level. But this price may or may not be the equilibrium price. The enterprises are in equilibrium if, and only if, they forecast correctly the market-clearing price. The higher is their forecast of the next market-clearing price, the more they produce for sale next period and thus—given the demand curve— the lower will be the actual price. The forecast that would cause the actual price exactly to *equal* that expected price is the equilibrium price; it is the expectation of *that* price level that will be self-fulfilling.

CONCEPTS INTRODUCED

economic equilibrium	pay-off matrix	market-clearing price
economic disequilibrium	market demand curve	expected price
game	market supply curve	equilibrium price and quantity

STUDY QUESTIONS

1. "We can prove that people are *not* in economic equilibrium because every day in a big city there are hundreds of still-vacant apartments that were not rented and scores of people who miss their trains." Where is the mistake?

2. "The theory that price and quantity, in equilibrium, are determined by supply and demand says on the one hand that an increase in the quantity demanded may increase the price, and then it says that an increase in the price will decrease the quantity demanded; so it is self-contradictory gibberish." Discuss.

3. "The amount of a product supplied to a market depends, as everyone knows, on the price(s) that producers expected to be able to obtain for the output supplied. Since supply-and-demand theory does not predict or explain what these price expectations are it does not explain the amount of the product produced and the price obtained. So the theory is as empty as a vacuum jar." Evaluate these statements.

4. The late Joan Robinson, professor of economics at Cambridge University, has been cited as an opponent of the view that the social economy is typically and approximately in equilibrium. She is quoted as having declared: "Once we admit that an economy exists in time, that history goes one way, from an irrevocable past into the unknown future, the conception of equilibrium based on the mechanical analogy of a pendulum swinging to and fro in space becomes untenable." (*New York Times*, December 14, 1983, p. D2)

   a. Is an economic equilibrium *defined* to be a constant state of affairs or, more generally, a course of events that is tending (with or without oscillations) to a steady state?

   b. What does economic equilibrium have to do with pendulums? Can a pendulum have expectations? Can it be in disequilibrium?

5. Robert Lucas, distinguished service professor of economics at the University of Chicago, has championed the view that economics should assume the realization of equilibrium, offering on behalf of that view a novel defense: "Why is it that arctic animals have white fur? [Zoology teaches] it is handy if you are trying to escape predators to be able to blend into the snow. But that doesn't explain anything about how it came about. A lot of our theorizing [in economics] is about *outcomes* and it is very weak on process . . ." (R. A. Klamer, *Conversations with Economists*, Totowa, N.J.: Rowan and Allanheld, 1983, p. 47). Is that true of zoology? If true, is it satisfactory? Discuss.

Part 2

Simple Exchange: The "Gothic" Economics of Two-Person Transactions

CHAPTER 4

The Gains from Cooperation

CHARLIE (to Rosie):
All right. It'll be you at the tiller and me at the engine, just like
it was at the start.

Humphrey Bogart (to Katharine Hepburn) in *The African Queen* (1951)

WHAT is the economic glue that holds the members of society together? A seventeenth-century school called Harmonism thought it had the answer. In the Harmonist theory, there are born composers, born surgeons, and so on; it is these heaven-sent differences among persons that make belonging in a society advantageous. But this theory was seriously inadequate. It failed to explain the interactions of peoples whose natural talents and acquired skills are not observed to be different. Nor could it cope with the possibility that the composer would *also* make the better surgeon, the actress *also* the better writer.

Today we recognize that the transition from a population of nomadic food gatherers, and later self-sufficient farmers, to a society is largely a response to the opportunity to achieve various economies—savings of resources—through collaboration and through specialization and trade. Economies in production are frequently obtainable if people combine their efforts. Sometimes a qualitatively different product is thus made feasible: Together people can build a bridge or produce a play that they cannot do working alone. And having combined forces, people can achieve other economies by agreeing to specialize and trade: That saves the lost time and confusion that would be caused if people had to alternate between city and farm, office and factory, computer and typewriter. Adam Smith saw these advantages of collaboration and specialization and noted another one. The worker who specializes in a single task is apt to become more proficient at it. But these centuries-old explanations of collaboration and specialization still leave us short, in both breadth and depth, of an adequate theory of the gains from cooperation.

The economic roots of human societies are the subject of this chapter. The gains from collaboration in production are examined with the help of two concepts, the production function and marginal productivity. Then some gains from other social interactions that Smith missed will be taken up: the gain that noncollaborating producers can obtain by efficiently dividing their use of capital and natural resources; the gains that arise from people's differences (the differences in their natural abilities or acquired skills); the gains that arise from the opportunity for trade in the different goods produced. These last two gains from social cooperation are examined with the aid of another concept, the notion of comparative advantage.

The sources of cooperation between societies is the subject of the appendix to this chapter. It uses the concept of comparative advantage to study how countries can find mutual gains from foreign trade or foreign investment.

> The focus here and in the next two chapters is on simple exchange—the interactions between any pair of persons. There will be opportunities later (in Part 3) to bring in the distinctive gains and losses that can arise from interactions among three or more persons.
>
> In the following analysis of simple exchange, we need not imagine Crusoe and Friday stranded on an island. The method of analysis here merely supposes, for purposes of simplicity, that the bilateral transactions under study are independent of any relationship with third persons and they have no third-party effects that would bring third persons into the transaction.

COOPERATION IN PRODUCTION: AGGLOMERATION OF IDENTICAL RESOURCES

Production is commonly a group activity. One reason is that often a combination of diverse talents is essential to the product. A product as sophisticated as *Star Wars* could not have been home-made by any one person. Composers of opera (from *Orfeo* to *Evita!*) have generally required a librettist or even a team of them. Chemists, biologists, and geneticists might combine for a research project in microbiology.

Collaboration is also the rule in the most routine, cut-and-dried activities. The air frame, engines, and instrumentation of a Boeing 747 could be assembled by one worker; it would take months to do it, of course. The plane is not assembled that way, for an obvious reason. The total workhours required per aircraft assembled are much reduced if there is another worker (or more) to hold the ladder or work the crane for the first. In his day, Adam Smith found it astonishing that even in the production of a pin the latest methods utilized many workers specializing in different tasks. If Smith were alive today and toured the new Sony cathode-ray tube factory in Osaka or even the much older Rosa Luxemburg light-bulb factory in Warsaw, he would no doubt be impressed again at the remarkable extensiveness and intricacy of what he called "the division of labor."

It may seem plausible that now, in the last decades of the twentieth century, automation is rapidly turning the factory back to an establishment with few workers and turning the retail service sector back into small specialty shops. In this view, automated and computerized machinery has begun to perform the specialized functions formerly performed by labor. Some social observers see a return of "domestic industry," previously driven out by the factory system at the onset of the Industrial Revolution, as the home becomes a computer-equipped "electronic cottage." Whatever the future may hold, however, history records that the past trend has been quite the reverse. Today factories of two thousand strong are a commonplace; even in the nineteenth century they were still a rarity. In Spain as late as 1850, there were more employers (including the self-employed) than there were employees.* The twentieth century marks the waning, not the rebirth, of the artisan's shop and the ma-and-pa retail establishment.

THE STAGE OF INCREASING RETURNS

There is a potential gain from collaboration between two persons in the production of a good whenever the resulting output level obtained through collaboration exceeds the total of the outputs that each would produce working alone. Then, and only then, there is enough output from the col-

---

* Hugh Thomas, *A History of the World* (London and New York: Harper and Row, 1979), p. 527.

laboration—compared to the sum of what the two persons can produce independently—that either person can be rewarded with more output than he can produce alone while the other person is rewarded with no less than (or even with a little more than) he can produce alone. If you can produce 5 hats and I can produce 2, and together we can produce 8, then clearly there is room for a mutually gainful arrangement between us—one in which neither of us loses, and one or both of us gains.

How is it that the extra product resulting when a second person joins the first—3 in the above example—might be greater than what the second produces without the first—2 in the example? Was the second person technologically inferior to the first? Not necessarily. There can be gains from collaboration, or combination, even if people are *identical*. Then if you can produce 5 so can I, but I might be able to add more than 5 by joining you.

In political economy there is a hypothesis bearing the shorthand label "the stage of increasing returns." This hypothesis is *one* explanation of why production is a collaborative effort.

Consider the addition of one worker to the existing inputs—the assemblage of land, capital (plant and equipment), and any workers already present—that are engaged in the production of a good somewhere. The increase of output that results, given the other inputs, is called the *return* from adding that worker's labor—or, more simply, the return from the added worker. One can also speak of the return from adding acreage, floor space, lathes, staplers, fuel—though it is the return from adding *labor* (of a specified kind) in which we are interested here.

◆ The *return* from adding an extra unit of labor to a given collection of cooperating inputs is the *extra* output resulting from the extra worker.

If a succession of workers (of a given kind) are added, one after the other, there results a *series* of returns—increasing or decreasing or fluctuating as the case may be. The hypothesis of *increasing returns* to labor states that introducing the second worker to a given production process would increase output *more* than the introduction of the first worker increased it. And if "increasing returns" continues, the return from adding a third worker would exceed the return from adding the second. (There can be increasing returns from the successive addition of further units of *any* kind of output, in fact.)

◆ The hypothesis that there is a stage of increasing returns to labor says that, up to a point, as successive workers are added to the other inputs of land, capital, energy, and so on (including possibly other kinds of labor), the return from each added worker is *greater* than the return from the previous addition of a worker. So the second worker adds more to output than the first does. And if increasing returns *continue*, a third worker adds more than the second—and so on until "increasing returns run out." See Figure 4–1.

FIGURE 4–1: The Stage of Increasing Returns

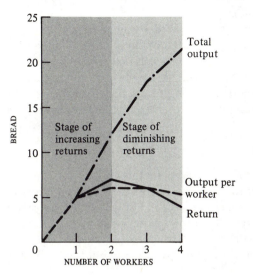

	Number of Workers (Amount of Labor)	Return from Added Worker (Marginal Product of Labor)	Output Produced (Total Product)	Output per Worker (Average Product of Labor)
A stage of	0	–	0	0
increasing	1	5	5	5
returns	2	7	12	6
	3	6	18	6
	4	4	22	5.5

In the numerical example the returns from adding labor are at first increasing—from 5 to 7 with the addition of a second worker. But the stage of increasing returns ends there. Thereafter there are diminishing returns: The third worker brings a return less than the second did, and the fourth less than the third.*

With the precise meaning in economics of the term "return" to an input having been given, it should be noted that the term has a variety of other meanings in everyday use. For that reason economists frequently use another term, one not found in everyday speech, for the same concept—the *marginal*

---

* The table and diagram also illustrate a relationship between *average product* and *marginal product* that always holds as a matter of math: Average product is *rising* (with increased output) if marginal product is *greater* than average product; is *constant* if marginal product is *equal;* and is *falling* if marginal product is *smaller*. (Verify by explaining the table.) The explanation is that an additional dose of the input—here, labor—pulls up (down) the average product if its contribution—i.e., the marginal product—is above (below) the previous average, just as a batter pulls up his season's batting average by having a better-than-average day.

product of the input. Thus, another name for the return from adding the labor of another worker (of a certain kind) is the *marginal product of labor* (of the given kind).

It is clear, then, that if there are increasing returns, at least up to the second worker, then production of this good will not be with just one worker: Since a worker producing alone can produce only what the first worker can produce, namely 5 in Table 4–1, while by joining the second worker he would add *more* to total output, namely 7 in the example, it would be a waste or their resources for the two workers not to team up.

> The existence of a stage of increasing returns to labor implies that total output will be increased if workers collaborate.

Do returns have to *go on* increasing to warrant a team of three workers? No. If adding a third worker does not add a still larger increase in output than adding the second did—even if it was somewhat smaller than the extra output produced by the second worker—it might nevertheless be larger than what the first worker could produce, and hence larger than what the third person could produce alone. So there would be room for a deal with the third worker.

Is there some explanation of the phenomenon of a stage of increasing returns? *Why* should we expect that up to a point each addition to input should add *more* to output than the previous addition to input? One can think of increasing returns as the result of some hurdle that the inputs have to surmount before they can be successful in producing any output at all. Imagine a cowboy attempting singlehandedly to bring a herd of irritable steers to market. Until there are enough cowboys to encircle the herd the task is hopeless. The lone cowpoke would be lucky to have a single steer in tow by the time he got to Kansas City. Obviously the return to a second cowboy is greater than that meager return to the first cowboy. And returns might continue to increase: Perhaps the return from having a third cowboy might exceed the return from adding the second, since it is awfully hard to encircle a herd with just two cowboys. (It is necessary to *fool* the cattle into thinking they are surrounded.) But eventually, as with all good things, increasing returns come to an end: With the third, or tenth, or hundredth cowboy, the return stops increasing and starts to decrease. If that did not happen, all the world's cowboys would be working together in one gigantic round-up.

INCREASING RETURNS TO SCALE

For collaboration in production to be profitable it is not essential that there should be increasing returns (at least up to a point). If increasing returns were the only basis for collaboration, many enterprises would still be one-person affairs. In some resource situations, returns are never increasing, not even "up to a point." There may be decreasing returns from the start.

Imagine two identical farmers with identical capital resources situated on identical farms, back to back. Suppose that these farms are small, with meager resources. Then it might very well happen that if one farmer joined the other *and* left his own land and capital behind, the return from the input of the second farmer would be less than the return from the input of the first. Instead of increasing returns there would be diminishing returns. Although the second farmer worked as hard, the small farm would not offer a second worker the same opportunities it presented to the first. In that case, there would be no gain from collaboration *if*, as we were supposing, a farmer had to abandon his farm and capital in order to work with another. (If the return to the input of the second farmer is less than the return to the first then, since both farmers were producing the same before collaboration, the return from adding a second farmer to one of the farms would be less than what that farmer could produce alone.)

But there is no reason why a worker considering joining another worker could not bring with him the land and capital he would use if working alone. The workers can cooperate in production by combining the land and capital they were using in addition to pooling their efforts. So consider again the identical farmers on identical farms. Joining forces leads to a production activity on twice the scale of what either farmer had before—an activity with twice the number of farmers, twice the land, and twice the amounts of the various capital resources. If such an equal-percentage increase of all the inputs leads to an exactly proportional increase of the output, there are said to be *constant returns to scale*. And if such an equiproportionate increase of all the inputs yields a more than proportional increase of output, there are said to be *increasing returns to scale*. It should now be clear that if the pooling of resources by the two farmers yields only constant returns to scale, their farms may as well be operated separately, since the output of the combined farm is just equal to the sum of the farms' outputs when operated separately. But if the pooling of their resources results in increasing returns to scale, then there is a gain from collaboration involving all the inputs: The output of the combined farm is then more than twice the output each farmer would produce if he worked alone—so the increase of output from the second farmer's contribution (including his land and equipment) exceeds what he would have produced alone. Hence, either or both farmers could gain from the cooperation.

A rather similar conclusion follows if we apply these concepts instead to a single producer, or entrepreneur, deciding how much land, labor, and capital to hire for the production of some farm product or other good. If there are constant returns to scale, operating with a larger tract of land (through consolidation of adjacent tracts, say) would *not* reduce cost per unit—but under increasing returns to scale it would, since all the cooperating factors (labor and capital) would not have to be increased in the same proportion. See Figure 4–2.

FIGURE 4–2: The Concept of Returns to Scale

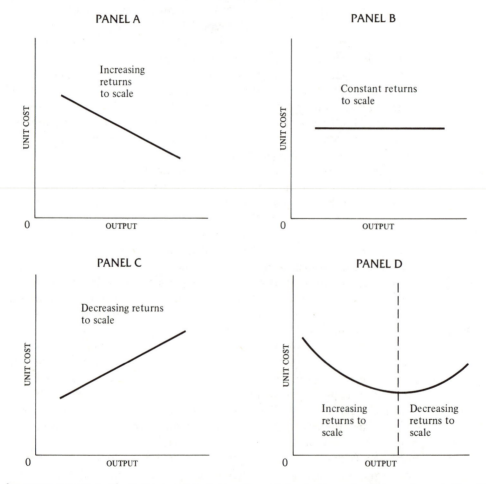

A way to conceive of returns to scale is to ask what happens to total costs per unit of output, if capital and land as well as labor are allowed to increase, when output is increased. When there are increasing returns to scale, as in Panel A, *unit cost* is *decreasing* because total cost is not increasing in proportion to output. Panels B and C depict the other cases.

Sources of Increasing Returns to Scale

Casual observations of production processes in various industries suggest that increasing returns to scale are quite common—at least up to a point at which the sources of the increasing returns to scale have run out. One source of increasing returns to scale—one of the economies of scale, so-called—arises when some existing plant or piece of equipment can serve to produce a larger volume of output with little or no modification. Doubling the capacity of a factory may not require a larger generator for electricity, and doubling the output that a ranch can supply to the market may not require widening the road to the city. Such mass-production economies are called "internal" if the benefits accrue to the production enterprise that increases its scale of operations and not to neighboring enterprises.

Another source of increasing returns to scale arises if a change in the inputs (and hence output) of some producer would permit a gain in the productivity of some neighboring producer—a gain, that is, in *his* (the neighbor's) output without any increase in the inputs over which he has control, or takes initiative. Then the producers have a motive for coordinating some or all of their input decisions. By consolidating their inputs in some respects, two identical producers can take advantage of the effects of one on the other to produce more than twice what each was producing alone. The presence of a "neighborhood effect," or "externality," either in the form of an external economy in production (in the beneficial case) or an external diseconomy in production (in the harmful case), generates a gain from consolidation—an "external economy of scale."

> It should be clear from the factory example above that increasing returns to scale does not characteristically manifest itself when there is an equiproportionate increase—say, a doubling—of literally every input, from boilers to night watchmen. The more than proportional increase of output that results under increasing returns to scale is really due to the possibility of redesigning some of the jobs or some of the capital equipment to take advantage of the increased scale of operations. A more descriptive *name* for the phenomenon called increasing returns to scale, therefore, is "decreasing cost." As output rises by successive proportional amounts—growing in the manner of a geometric series, 1, 2, 4, 8, . . . —the *total* cost of producing, using the best designs, rises at a *slower* proportionate rate—for example, the series 10, 18, 28, . . . —at least at first. In other words, as output increases by successive amounts, the successive levels of cost per unit are *decreasing*.

The many examples of increasing returns to scale all have in common the feature that when the scale of operations is increased a cost saving results because some input can be "shared" among the increased units of output being produced.

- ◆ To build a giant aircraft having twice the passenger-carrying capacity of the previously largest aircraft it is not necessary to double the number of engines and the number of wings. The additional passengers being accommodated can "share" the four engines and single wing of the "previous" contingent of passengers (although some increase of horsepower and wing span may still be desirable).

The sharing of an input is obvious when some externality accounts for the increasing returns to scale.

- ◆ Two producers operating alone may each find that a dock or a road would not raise his own output by enough to repay the cost of the investment; the private benefit to a producer falls short of the cost. But if the use of the dock or road were shared (as it would be if the producers merged), the combined output of the two producers might rise by more (and never by less) than if the builder kept exclusive use for himself; the social benefit, then, would exceed the private benefit.

COOPERATION IN PRODUCTION WITH DIFFERING HUMAN RESOURCES

Even if, we saw, a society consisted of identical people identically endowed—the same talents and skills, and the same access to land and capital and techniques of production—people would not want to work on isolated homesteads. People would make shoes and can fruit in factories, mine and fish in crews, form assembly lines to construct cars. There would be an agglomeration of people to form a town—even a sparsely settled society might have a giant city—in order to obtain the economies from having one airport, one water system, one telephone exchange instead of several. But there is no important reason other than simplicity of the analysis to assume, as we have been doing, that people are identical in their abilities and situations (as if they were cloned from the same person and were all handed equal resources to work with).

An important reason why people produce in groups, we shall see, is that they are different: They are *not* identically endowed with each and every natural attribute and acquired skill that might be useful in production. They can take advantage of their differences in order to produce together more effectively than separately. By dividing up the production process into separate tasks and assigning these tasks in a way that recognizes the differences among workers, more can be produced by a given group of nonidentical workers than could be produced (in the aggregate) if each worker tilled alone, making the best of his strengths and weaknesses. To find collaboration advantageous it is not necessary that there be increasing returns to labor or increasing returns to scale. A difference in people's endowments will nevertheless make collaboration beneficial.

COORDINATING NONLABOR RESOURCES

There is one way in which two persons might differ that does *not* point the way to collaboration between them—but it does make beneficial another mode of cooperation between them. It could be that, when it comes to the production activity (or activities) they are engaged in, one person is simply "more of a worker"—a bigger producer—than the other one. If the production process involves just one task, like fruit picking, it is possible that one worker can always perform that task faster than the other worker—so he or she is always twice the worker or 50 percent more worker. Can such workers usefully cooperate? Yes, certainly. If the land and capital they have at their disposal are scarce resources, the two workers will have a *mutual interest* in having every such resource allocated between them so as to make their aggregate output as large as possible—and dividing (as they choose) any resulting gain in the "total pie." Hence, they will want the "big producer" to have an appropriately larger allotment of the complementary resources with which to work.

Under constant returns to scale, a worker who is twice the other should be alloted twice the land and twice the capital allocated to the other; how they divide the gain in total output is another matter. To see this, consider identical triplets who, finding it efficient to work apart, divide the family farm into equal thirds. If a pair of these workers is replaced by a new worker who is identical in capabilities to the other two, it remains true that the total output (which is to be shared somehow between the two workers) will be largest if the third triplet works with one-third and the fast worker farms the other two-thirds.

There is a rule for allocating a given amount of a scarce resource—land, oil, clay—between two workers (or between two crews of workers) in such a way as to make the aggregate output—the sum of their individual outputs—as large as possible. Suppose there is a rectangular strip of homogeneous land to be allocated between our fast worker and his slower neighbor. We know that the faster worker will be allotted at least half, so consider, as a beginning, the provisional allocation in which the land is split down the middle, half to the faster and half to the slower worker. Then compare the effects of moving the border by successive equal amounts in such a way that, each time, the faster worker's land is increased by a square yard and thus the slower worker's land is decreased by the same amount. At what point will the aggregate output reach a maximum? Economists call the change in output resulting from an one-unit change in an input the *marginal product* of that input as noted earlier. In terms of that concept we may say that the point at which aggregate output reaches its maximum has the following character:

> The increase in the output of the faster worker from having an extra unit of land *just balances* the decrease in the output of the slower worker from having one less unit of land. *That is,* the marginal product of land used by the faster worker is *equal* to the marginal product of land used by the slower worker. The latter marginal product is the opportunity cost of land allocated to the faster worker and hence the marginal product of land for the fast worker just covers the opportunity cost of an extra unit of land for his use.
>
> *or*
>
> The marginal product of land used by the faster worker exceeds the marginal product of land used by the slower worker, but the faster worker already has received all of the land. But this is not a possibility under constant returns to scale. As long as land is not indivisible, like a blast furnace or a shovel, even the slow-moving worker will be assigned a little space to lumber around in.

It follows that, under constant returns to scale, the worker with the greater "labor power" is assigned a proportionally larger plot of land to work with. That will be larger by just enough to equalize the marginal products of land in the two uses.

COMPARATIVE ADVANTAGE

We have been discussing some implications of a simple difference between workers: There is a single task or else just a single skill or single talent involved in the work, and one of the workers is better at it than the other. Such a one-dimensional difference in ability does not by itself offer any motive for collaboration in production, for working shoulder to shoulder. There is only a motive to coordinate the use of complementary resources like land and capital. These two implications remain when there are two tasks—or, for that matter, two hundred tasks—if the fast worker is "equally faster" than the slow worker at each of these tasks. But when the slow worker is "comparatively fast" at some task, there arises a motive for the two workers' collaboration—despite constant returns to scale from the start and no stage of increasing returns.

"Absolute advantage." One way in which differences between persons can make their cooperation mutually beneficial is rather extreme. It arises, for example, if the production of some good requires a talent or skill that is present in one worker and missing in another. Then the latter person will need the former if he is to engage usefully in the production of that good. Such an example evokes the image of master and slave or sorcerer and apprentice. Independent production is impossible. A situation of less one-sided dependency is one where the worker without the one skill has another skill that the *other* worker does not have. Then neither person can produce the good without the collaboration of the other. In less extreme cases, one person is merely *more* productive in one task while the other person is merely *more* productive in another task. In all these cases each person has an absolute advantage (or at least no absolute disadvantage) in one task and *not* in the other task. Such collaborations are uncommon. They often arise where a range of unusual talents or skills is required. In opera and song, the collaborations of Lennon & McCartney, Lerner & Lowe, Gilbert & Sullivan, Verdi & Boito are clearly of this sort.

The Theory of Comparative Advantage

It is just common sense that if some production process involves two tasks, and one person is better at one task while the other is better at the second, those persons can produce more working together than they can working alone. Political economy was well into the nineteenth century without having progressed beyond that common sense. In the seventeenth century, the Harmonists held that a benevolent deity had endowed the earth with hardy men to farm the land, fearless men to sail the ships, stalwart women to bear children—every person is better than the rest at some task or other. This was a theory of exchange, of collaboration and trade, based on absolute advantage. The limitations of this theory, however, finally became too apparent for it to survive. Plainly there were (and continue to be) people who lacked any absolute advantage and who had an absolute disadvantage in everything; the old absolute advantage theory could not explain how such people might find a role in society's production. And there have always been conspicuous people who are protean talents, polymaths, jacks-of-all-trades; the absolute advantage theory could not explain why such persons tended to specialize, nor could it predict in which direction the specialization would take place.

It finally came to be realized that it is not really "absolute advantage" that creates an opportunity for a gain in efficiency through collaboration. It is not necessary that a worker be "faster" in some task in order that his collaboration with another worker result in a larger total output between them. By contributing to the task at which he is *comparatively fast* (hence the other worker comparatively slow) he can release some time previously spent by the other worker on that task and thus increase the time that worker has available for the task at which that *other worker* is *comparatively fast*. By contributing to the task at which he has the comparative advantage he can (although he is slower at that task than the other worker is) permit the other worker to devote more effort to the task at which that other worker has the comparative advantage. As a result, more is accomplished at both tasks, because each worker is employed at the task for which he is comparatively well suited. With faster performance of both tasks, a larger rate of output is possible. This idea is illustrated in Table 4−1.

There is a further point worth making to complete the analysis. We have seen that the worker who is comparatively fast at one task can contribute to efficiency by allocating more of his effort to that task and less effort to another task (or other tasks). But *how much* more effort at that task? Should that worker *completely* specialize in the task at which he has the comparative advantage? And likewise the slower worker? The question here is the optimum degree of specialization by the two workers. This much is clear from the start: If the slower worker continues to have the same comparative advantage he started with even after he was completely specialized in that task, he can contribute most to the combined output of the two workers by specializing completely where he has his comparative advantage. (In terms

Table 4−1: AN ILLUSTRATION OF COMPARATIVE ADVANTAGE

Gains from collaboration arise from comparative, not absolute, advantage. Consider Bernstein and Sondheim, producing lyrics and tunes (or melody).

Bernstein has an absolute advantage in both tunes and lyrics. The comparative advantage in tunes belongs to him because the ratio 9/3 is greater than the ratio 4/2. The comparative advantage in lyrics belongs to Sondheim because the ratio 2/4 is greater than 3/9. Now if Sondheim would give up two weeks of tune writing to produce lyrics instead, and Bernstein were to give up one week of lyric writing to compose tunes instead, the results would be as shown below.

An Extra Week of Time Will Produce	Bernstein	Sondheim
Lyrics	3	2
Tunes	9	4

	Bernstein	Sondheim	Aggregate
Lyrics	−3	+4	+1
Tunes	+9	−8	+1

of the example, Mr. Sondheim will write only lyrics—as long as Mr. Bernstein is interested in producing show tunes.) But unless he has an *absolute* advantage in this task, he will thus help the other (faster) worker to specialize only *incompletely;* he can spare the faster worker some, but not all, of the task at which the fast worker is at a comparative disadvantage. (Mr. Sondheim would have to be able to produce 9 lyrics a week to free Mr. Bernstein completely of that task.) The more general answer to the question of optimum specialization must allow for the possibility that a worker's comparative-cost advantage in moving out of one task into another declines with each increase in his specialization. Then we may characterize the optimum degree of specialization by our two workers—the point where their combined output is at its maximum—thus:

- *either:* the opportunity cost that is incurred if the slow worker performs another unit of the task at which he "had" the comparative advantage has *risen* to the point, and the opportunity cost of an extra unit of that same task performed by the fast worker has *fallen* to the point, that these two opportunity costs are *equal.* That is, the slow worker's marginal product at his comparative-advantage task considered as a *ratio* to his marginal product in performing the other task—in Mr. Sondheim's case, the ratio was originally 2/4—has fallen to the point, and the other worker's marginal-product ratio in these same two tasks has risen to the point, that these two marginal-product ratios are *equal.* From this degree of specialization, no further degree of specialization (possible or not) would be desirable. At this pattern of specialization, the two workers have specialized to such an extent that their comparative advantages have "run out"— there is no more advantage to be exploited.

- *or:* the opportunity cost of the slow worker's performing another unit of his comparative-advantage task is *still* below the opportunity cost of the fast worker's performing that same task—so the slow worker's comparative-cost advantage has not yet "run out"—but the slow worker has no *more* time to give to that task: he is already completely specialized, spending no time on the task at which he is at a comparative disadvantage.

LEARNING BY DOING

If a person has a comparative advantage in some activity there is an efficiency gain from his specializing in it—up to a point, anyway. That is the classic comparative-advantage theory of the "division of labor." For centuries, however, social observers have noticed that a line of causality runs in the other direction as well: If a person specializes in some productive task, for any reason or no reason at all, that person develops a comparative advantage—or a stronger one—as the result of the work experience acquired. Thus there is room for a second theory of the division of labor: People decide to specialize in order to acquire a comparative advantage in the future. By concentrating on one job a person has a better chance, at any rate, of becoming comparatively efficient at it than if he tries to be a jack-of-all-trades.

By the Middle Ages there was in Europe an elaborate network of specialized trades—butcher, baker, candlestick maker, and so on. And though an apprenticeship was often required, so that a novice would not practice on the public without instruction and supervision by an expert, most of the skill and knowledge acquired by the craftsman, tradesman, artisan, and artist of those times developed through on-the-job experience more than prework schooling and innate aptitudinal advantages. By the seventeenth century, however, manufacturing began to evolve from the "domestic system," the system of so-called cottage industry in which production took place in family homes, to the "factory system" in which the production process was divided into distinct tasks and each worker became specialized in one of them. A few years before his 1776 classic was published, Smith visited one of the new factories in Northumberland and marveled at the extent to which the "division of labor" had gone in that humble pin factory:

... in the way in which this business is now carried on, not only the whole work is a peculiar trade, but it is divided into a number of branches, of which the greater part are likewise peculiar trades. One man draws out the wire, another straights it, a third cuts it, a fourth points it, a fifth grinds it at the top for receiving the head; to make the head requires three distinct operations; to put it on is a peculiar business, to whiten the pins is another; it is even a trade by itself to put them into the paper; and the important business of making a pin is, in this manner, divided into about eighteen distinct operations, which, in some manufactories, are all performed by distinct hands, though in others the same man will sometimes perform two or three of them. I have seen a small manufactory of this kind where ten men only were employed, and where some of them consequently performed two or three distinct operations. But ... those ten persons ... could make among them upwards of forty-eight thousand pins in a day. ... But if they had all wrought separately and independently, and without any of them having been educated to this peculiar business, they could certainly not each of them have made twenty, perhaps not one pin in a day. ....*

---

* Smith, *The Wealth of Nations*, Book I, chap. 1, p. 5.

Smith gives a triad of reasons for division of labor. In our terms, they are learning by doing, increasing returns, and increasing returns to scale:

> This great increase of the quantity of work which, in consequence of the division of labor, the same number of people are capable of performing, is owing to three different circumstances; first, to the increase of dexterity in every particular workman; secondly, to the saving of the time which is commonly lost in passing from one species of work to another; and lastly, to the invention of a great number of machines which facilitate and abridge labour, and enable one man to do the work of many.*

Smith evidently felt this first factor to be the most important:

> The difference of natural talents in different men is, in reality, much less than we are aware of; and the very different genius which appears to distinguish men of different professions, when grown up to maturity, is not upon many occasions so much the cause as the effect of the division of labor. The difference between the most dissimilar characters, between a philosopher and a common street porter, for example, seems to arise not so much from nature as from habit, custom and education.†

While Smith and succeeding classical economists all celebrated the benefits from the division of labor, later social critics, from the nineteenth century onward, came to bewail its drawbacks. In primitive societies there was some natural basis for most specialization. Bony men did the hunting, fleshy women the pearl diving, old people raised the children, and so on. And a person used a wide range of talents and skills to produce the whole good, not just one of many operations going into the manufacture of a finished good. One's special attributes determined what one produced, and what one produced had an understood and respected place in the natural order of things.

In technologically advanced societies, by contrast, the work that many people do gives no indication of their aptitudes and education. A worker might be engaged in a single repetitious operation that makes no use of the bundle of attributes that distinguishes him from other workers. He has no room to produce the good his way, exercise his intelligence, test his endurance—he is effectively a robot, as much a part of the machinery as the lathe, typewriter, or computer he works with. The most graphic depiction is Charlie Chaplin's *Modern Times,* in which the central character, a Ford assembly-line worker, spends his whole life accomplishing nothing more than turning bolt 999. And numerous writers have satirized the mindlessness of

* Smith, *The Wealth of Nations,* Book I, chap. 1, p. 7.
† Ibid., chap. 2, p. 15.

office work. It was the political economist Karl Marx, however, who (even before he had got much into political economy) most forcefully protested how modern industrial life might virtually "alienate" a person from his own personality. Marx therefore looked forward to a future society in which industry would be forced

... to replace the detail-worker of today, crippled by the life-long repetition of one and the same trivial operation, and thus reduced to the mere fragment of a man, by the fully developed individual, fit for a variety of labours, ready to face any change in production, and to whom the different social functions he performs are but so many modes of giving free scope to his own natural and acquired powers.*

Now the workplace is, for most participants in the economy, a vastly less unpleasant environment than it was in Marx's time. The interesting questions are whether the workplace could be made more stimulating for the people working *without* a sacrifice of the output of the products (other than job satisfactions) that are being produced; and if *not,* whether the workers would be *willing to pay* that much or more in reduced income and hence consumption for the enhancements of work.

COOPERATION IN CONSUMPTION

Up to now the main sources of gain from cooperation in production have been expounded "as if" there is just one good in the society that people want to consume, hence just one commodity or service to be produced. But people want a variety of goods—meat and drink, bread and circus. The Europeans seemed to value their discovery of America and Asia more for the added supplies of tobacco and spices than anything else. It will be realistic, therefore, to bring in this further dimension of economic cooperation in a society—cooperation in regard to the consumption of two or more goods.

The gains from cooperation in consumption stem from the inefficiency that would result if each of two (or more) persons were to limit himself to consuming only those goods he chose to earn through his efforts in production. To consume only the goods you are talented at producing would be to miss an opportunity for expanding your consumption choices: Any two people who are *different* in some relevant respect, regarding their tastes or their abilities, can gain from trading goods with each other.

The most important application of this principle involves again the concept of comparative advantage. Here we consider a case in which a person

* Karl Marx, *Capital*, volume 1, Berlin, 1867. English trans. Chicago: Charles H. Kerr Publishing Co., 1906.

has a comparative advantage over another person in the production of some final good—cheese, say—and the latter person has a comparative advantage in producing some other final good, say wine. What does this mean? We take it to mean that if the producer who is comparatively good at producing wine reduced his output of cheese by one kilo, the increase in the liters of wine he could produce would be greater than the corresponding increase that the producer who is comparatively good at dairying could achieve if he likewise reduced cheese output by a kilo—and this no matter how much (or how little) wine the first producer makes and no matter how much (or how little) cheese the second producer turns out. That is what it means to say the one producer has a comparative advantage over the other in producing wine (or cheese). In such a case there can be a mutual gain for the two persons from a bit of trade: Since the producer comparatively good at dairying pays a stiff price in terms of cheese for every extra bottle of wine he decides to produce and consume while, at the same time, the producer skilled in viniculture faces a higher opportunity cost in units of wine for each kilo of cheese he elects to make, the viniculturist can afford to offer his wine to the

FIGURE 4–3: The Mutual Gain from Trading by Two Parties—The Simplest Case Where Outputs Are Fixed

PANEL A   PANEL B

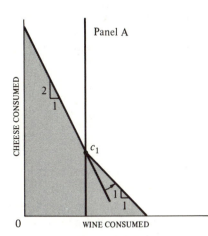

Panel A's Mr. Juan chose c_1 before discovering a trading partner, trading off 2 kilos of cheese to get each liter of wine. If offered terms of only 1 kilo of cheese for 1 extra liter of wine, Juan would swap some of his cheese crop to obtain more wine. It is a textbook case of *expanded choice.*

Panel B's Miss Tu chose c_1 before discovering the trading opportunities, sacrificing 2 liters of wine for each kilo of cheese. But Tu will gladly sacrifice more wine to get more cheese once offered terms of exchange like 1 liter of wine for 1 kilo of cheese. Hence there can simultaneously be expanded choice for Tu too—since Tu can trade for the price of Juan.

dairyman at a lower cheese price than what the dairyman was paying to himself and in so doing be obtaining cheese from the dairyman at a lesser unit cost (in terms of wine) than he was bearing before! *Both* parties by trading their unchanged outputs of the two goods can obtain better terms than what they can each do singly by only "trading with himself." Figure 4–3 drives home the point, making use of the notion of expanded choice.

The gain opened up by the possibility of trade does not stop there, however. There is no reason why each producer should stick to the pretrade output mix of wine and cheese. The producer comparatively good at wine making can reduce his cheese output by a kilo and the *other* producer raise his output by a kilo, so as to preserve the aggregate output of that good. Then the additional output of wine that the viniculturist will find possible to make will exceed the reduction of wine output that will be suffered by the farmer comparatively good at dairying. So aggregate output of wine will be increased. The viniculturist can ship enough wine to the dairyman to restore the latter's consumption of wine—while the dairyman ships to him the kilo of cheese to restore the viniculturist's consumption of cheese—and still have some wine left over. However the two producers share between them the extra number of bottles, there is clearly the possibility of a mutual gain. Likewise, the producers could instead maintain the aggregate production of wine and increase their aggregate production, and mutual consumption, of cheese. Or they can do something in between—dividing the opportunity for specialization by producing more aggregate cheese and more aggregate wine. This is just another application of the lesson that specialization can produce mutual benefits when there is comparative advantage. But where that advantage occurs in *different* goods, *trade* is needed to realize those gains.

SUMMARY

1. The chapter takes up the roots of cooperation—the sources of mutual gain—that cause people to work and live together.

2. Some of the roots of cooperation do not depend upon people being different—having identical resources and tastes. Even if people were identical they would not all work in solitary fashion on separate homesteads and word processors. People would agglomerate in groups—in factories, mines, offices, and so on. The advantages of such collaboration are increasing returns (up to a point) and increasing returns to scale.

3. People would also have reason to cooperate in the way nonhuman resources—land, capital, energy—are allocated. It makes sense for the

engineer not to drive the tractor to work and the farmer not to use the convertible as a tractor.

4. Then there are all the opportunities for mutually advantageous cooperation that arise from people's differences in resources and tastes. There are tasks that only a short person can perform and others that only tall ones can do. These are cases of absolute advantage. Then there are the cases of comparative advantage. It may be that, as the song says, "I can do anything you can do better," but you and I could both be better off by cooperating, you specializing in one thing and I in another. Then there will be more for both.

5. Furthermore, by specializing it is possible that a person will become more proficient—learning by doing.

6. Finally, there is the gain that people can obtain from trading. Even if each producer went on producing exactly the same outputs of these products as always, when both producers discover that they have been "trading off" at different terms of exchange, there are some common terms of exchange that will give both of the producers expanded choice and thus make both producers better off through trade at those new terms.

CONCEPTS INTRODUCED

return, or marginal product	decreasing, constant, and	absolute advantage
stage of increasing returns	increasing costs	comparative advantage
stage of diminishing returns	production function	learning by doing
increasing, constant, and		
decreasing returns to scale		

STUDY QUESTIONS

1. "There may be a political theory of why a society was able or unable to be formed, or a cultural theory of why cooperation could or could not occur (say, the members spoke the same language). But there cannot be a noneconomic theory of why people are motivated to (try to) form a society—a noneconomic impetus to social interaction." True or false?

2. The allocation of resources between two individuals is efficient in the practical sense if

   a. the two persons have not so far thought of a better way to cooperate

   b. there exists no other arrangement compatible with the incentives as well as the resources of each self-interested party—hence no other enforceable bargain, or contract—that would achieve a mutual gain over the present arrangement (if any) between them

And the allocation is efficient in the *ideal* sense—there is ideal efficiency in the resource allocation—if

a. the two parties have not hit upon any cooperative arrangement that is better for both of them than their present arrangement

b. there exists no other arrangement compatible with their incentives and resources that would achieve a (further) mutual gain

c. there exists no other arrangement consistent with their resources that, if achieved, would yield a (further) mutual gain.

3. An agglomeration of people into collaborative teams may be necessary for efficiency, ideal and practical, because of

a. a stage of increasing returns to labor

b. a stage of increasing returns to scale

c. the heterogeneity of workers with respect to talent and skill

d. people who like people

e. all of the above

f. none of the above

4. Suppose that the application of extra labor in Florida in the production of orange juice has a marginal product of 20 and in the production of fish has a marginal product of 40 while in Massachusetts the corresponding numbers are 10 and 30. In which state does labor have a comparative advantage in the production of fish? In which state an absolute advantage in producing fish? If labor is immobile between the two states, from which state would comparative-advantage theory predict that fish would be "exported"? If labor is perfectly mobile between the two states, from which state will labor migrate? What will tend to be the effect of such migration on the states' absolute advantage, or absolute disadvantage, in fish?

APPENDIX:
THE POTENTIAL FOR MUTUAL GAIN FROM FOREIGN TRADE AND INVESTMENT—THE OPEN ECONOMY

There are opportunities for mutual gain from cooperation across national boundaries as well as from cooperation inside national borders. In fact, the advance over the past two centuries in the understanding by economists of the potential gains from international cooperation, much of it stimulated by the issues of the day in foreign economic relations, has contributed greatly to the economic theory of social cooperation within a country.

A distinctive feature of international cooperation is that labor is not highly mobile across national borders—much less mobile than within national borders, at any rate. The costs of migrating to another country are greater, generally speaking, than the costs of moving to another region of the same country. Furthermore, many countries place barriers to immigration, and some to emigration. In the traditional analysis of international trade, which we adopt here, it is supposed that labor is unwilling or unable to move internationally. (Now that the great waves of migration that began in the nineteenth century have stopped, the international immobility of labor is not so unrealistic on assumption.)

The thought that the trade of one country with another—both countries being previously closed to trade—could simultaneously generate gains in both countries was not always understood. The realization that there would be mutual gains available from such trade dawned with the discovery of the concept of comparative advantage (defined above, p. 98). The discoverer was the early nineteenth-century English economist David Ricardo.

Consider England and Portugal, Ricardo said. Both produced cloth and wine by means of their respective endowments of fully-employed land and labor. Possibly England is able with a batch of land and labor to produce more cloth *and* to produce more wine than can Portugal, in which case England is said to have an *absolute* advantage in producing both goods; or possibly Portugal happens to enjoy such an absolute advantage. Such absolute advantage, if it exists, tells us nothing about the opportunities that may exist for gainful trade between the two countries. What matters for trade is *comparative* advantage. Undoubtedly Portugal is *comparatively* the more productive at producing the other of the two goods. If Portugal is comparatively productive at growing wine, that country is said to have a *comparative advantage* in producing wine—and England then has a comparative advantage in producing cloth.

Ricardo then demonstrated that, as a result of such comparative advantage, Portuguese wine producers and English cloth producers can reach terms at which to exchange wine for cloth that are *mutually beneficial*. Such trade can yield gains in both countries. Why? With Portugal comparatively productive at producing wine, wine must be comparatively cheap in Portugal* and cloth comparatively cheap in England—that is, the comparatively low cost of making *wine* in Portugal will be reflected in a *lower* cloth price of wine in Portugal and a lower wine price of cloth in England—provided the two governments do not intervene with controls or sales taxes or other instruments in such a way as to interfere with this effect on prices. But if wine is comparatively cheap in Portugal—1 jug selling for ½ bolt of cloth, say—and cloth comparatively cheap in England—1 bolt exchanging for ½ jug, say—then *both* the Portuguese wine sellers and the English cloth sellers can obtain better terms for themselves by agreeing to exchange with one another at any exchange ratio *between* Portugal's pretrade wine price (½ bolts) and England's pretrade wine price (2 bolts)—say, 1 bolt for 1 jug. Moreover, with the discovery of better terms abroad, the domestic price of wine in Portugal will be pulled up to equality with the foreign price (since a wine seller there would be unwilling to sell for less at home than abroad, if transport costs are negligible); thus Portuguese wine producers, and by the same argument English cloth makers as well, can obtain better terms on *all* sales, not just export sales.

So, provided the two governments are content to permit such trade, wine will be exported from Portugal to England and cloth exported from England to Portugal. What came to be known as the *law of comparative advantage* states just that: A country in its trade with another country will export the good at which it has a comparative advantage in producing and import the good in the production of which it has a comparative disadvantage. (As we have just seen it is a corollary of this law that there are individual gains as a result.)

If the implications of Ricardo's discovery of comparative advantage stopped there his achievement would be less celebrated than it is. The implications went beyond the simple though valuable truth that trade lowers the price of cloth to the Portuguese (which is a gain for Portuguese wine growers) and lowers the price of wine in England (which is a gain for English cloth makers). Ricardo's theoretical model of a two-good two-country world clearly implied that *national consumption* of both goods in *both countries* could be increased by means of comparative-advantage-based trade. Figure 4A–1, which is an adaptation of Figure 4–3 in the text of this chapter, tells the story.

But Ricardo left unexplored a thorny issue. Would all the Portuguese who were engaged in the production of cloth (at least until the onset of trade) gain from the opening up of foreign trade? Would all the English in the wine-growing business be better off? Not necessarily. Take the case in which land (scarce land at any rate) is not used in making cloth—only labor is used to make cloth. If the Portuguese government does not intervene with taxes, subsidies, tariffs, quotas, and whatnot—if the government permits free trade—then the workers who make Portuguese cloth will be made worse off as a result of the trade with England: each Portuguese worker in the cloth industry would continue to make the same "wage" as before *when measured in terms of cloth;* since workers can still make one bolt of cloth per day they will still earn that much as their daily wage expressed in cloth. But the influx of English cloth, by lowering the price of cloth in terms of wine, will necessarily increase the price of wine in terms of cloth. Hence Portuguese cloth makers will find their wages *reduced* in terms of wine— and thus reduced overall; and the same goes for Portuguese workers who happen to be engaged in wine growing, since their wages, expressed in terms of cloth (or wine), are going to be no higher than those in cloth making.

---

*That is, the *ratio* of the price (in terms of some money) of wine to the price of cloth is lower in Portugal than the same ratio in England.

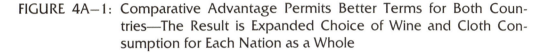

FIGURE 4A–1: Comparative Advantage Permits Better Terms for Both Countries—The Result is Expanded Choice of Wine and Cloth Consumption for Each Nation as a Whole

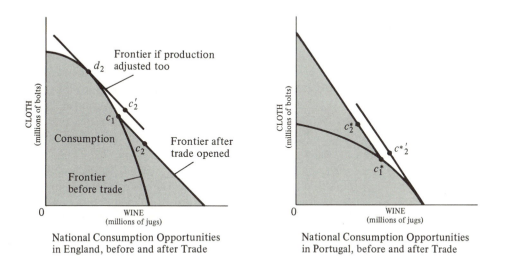

National Consumption Opportunities
in England, before and after Trade

National Consumption Opportunities
in Portugal, before and after Trade

In England, without foreign trade, production and consumption correspond to some point designated c_1. At that output combination, the cost in terms of cloth of an extra unit of wine is high—say 2 bolts of cloth for a jug of wine. In Portugal the no-trade outcome is designated c_1^*. Without trade, the cost in cloth of an extra unit of wine is lower—say ½ bolts for a jug of wine. This is reflected in the greater slope of the before-trade frontier in England at c_1 than in Portugal at c_1^*. (The former slope is −2, the latter is ½.) But by trading at some intermediate price—say, 1 bolt for 1 jug—England can obtain extra wine more cheaply and thus move out along the *new* consumption frontier to a point like c_2; Portugal can obtain extra cloth more cheaply and thus choose c_2^*. By moving resources out of wine into cloth in order to produce the combination at d_2, England could then export some of the *extra* cloth produced and thus end up consuming more wine *and* more cloth—at a point like c_2'.

It is precisely the adverse effects of imports upon wages that prompts opposition in many third world countries (and first world countries too) to opening their economies to cheap manufactures from abroad. The land owners will gain, it is argued, at the expense of the urban (and ultimately the rural) worker.

Similarly, the English gentry who own the land that is needed to grow English wine will find that the decreased price of wine in terms of cloth, thanks to Portuguese imports, means an increased price of cloth in terms of wine. So the same land rent in terms of wine translates into reduced income in terms of cloth.*

Present-day economic theorists point out, however, that Ricardo's model does lend support to a carefully qualified pro-trade position: That foreign trade *can* and *will* yield a gain for *everyone*—provided that the government takes the necessary steps. The government of Portugal could arrange for everyone in Portugal to gain from some trade with England if so desired. And the same is true of England. In each case, the government has to use taxes and subsidies (or some equivalent fiscal instruments) to make sure that labor or land—whichever is adversely affected by the influx of imports—will suffer no loss *after* account is taken of subsidies and taxes. It "makes sense" that such a government program is feasible, since the total national consumption of both goods is up as a result of trade; the only problem is to make sure that everyone's consumption is up.

> *How*, exactly, can the government prevent a loss to anyone from the opening up of foreign trade? A detailed proof would require more space than appropriate here, but the gist of the argument can be outlined: Let the Portuguese government tax the purchase (in Portugal) of cloth, foreign and domestic, by just enough to drive the wine price of cloth back to its pretrade level. Let the tax revenue collected be used to subsidize the employment of labor in the domestic production of cloth by just enough to bring the cloth-makers' wage including the subsidy back to its pretrade level in terms of wine. Then land owners in wine growing will gain from the fall of the wage rate in terms of wine; but that gain can be taxed away to provide a similar subsidy to workers employed in wine growing. But this tax will still leave land owners with the net gain arising from the opportunity presented by the lower wage rate to hire more workers away from the cloth industry for a net increase in their land rents. The land owners can thus gain, the workers can be protected, and the "government" can break even on the deal; or the land owners can be more heavily taxed so that the workers will have some or all of the gains.†

---

*Moreover, even English land rents in terms of *wine* would fall as a result of this trade as some labor left the land to make cloth for export.

†A socialist or communist state that operated all the producing enterprises yet did not own the land nor control the workers could accomplish the same "gains for all" more directly: It could maintain the pretrade price of cloth and offer temporary inducements to workers to move to wine growing. Out of the cost savings from obtaining some cloth by *trading* some wine for *imported* cloth the government could increase both its wage and rental payments to workers and land owners: more wine and cloth for all.

We have been discussing the gains to a country from opening up its economy to foreign trade in consumer goods. There are also gains available from opening up the economy to foreign capital flows. A century after Ricardo's time, Britain, having already discovered Portugal, discovered Argentina. Evidently the rate of return on capital was higher than the level to which it had fallen in Britain. British savers were able to gain by investing in Argentina—in railways and livestock industries—instead of Britain, and Argentine workers gained by finding their productivity—and hence their wages—higher as a result. Both countries were able to consume more wool and mutton! (But if British workers and Argentine savers are not to lose out, the two governments must take steps to redistribute the gains.)

CHAPTER 5

Obstacles to Efficient Cooperation

FOREMAN:
Boys, boys! You'll get your money as soon as I have it.

Barton MacLane (to Humphrey Bogart and Walter Houston) in
Treasure of the Sierra Madre (1948)

EVERY society rests, as we recognized at the start, on the mutual gains it permits its members over what they would have if they settled in another society or lived alone as nomads and hermits. The previous chapter showed that where there are two or more persons faced with scarcity and able to interact, there is usually room for such mutual gains. Various mutual gains are likely to be available under ideal cooperative arrangements at any rate, whether or not they are achievable through workable and acceptable understandings and bargains.

What we might call the *pure* theory of cooperation postulates that the ideal cooperative arrangements needed to achieve every available mutual gain can and do prevail. Wherever the resources and tastes of any two persons leave open the possibility of a mutual gain, that potential gain will be realized by the required cooperation between them. Thus, in every bilateral exchange, actual or potential, the two parties to the transaction achieve an allocation of resources that is efficient in the full, or *ideal,* sense of the term. Such a pure theory explains the impetus to the formation of human societies by showing, as does the previous chapter, that there would *not* be ideal efficiency in resource allocation if people opted for self-sufficiency: Some ideal planner could lay out one or more ideal arrangements for cooperation that would make *all* the participants better off.

But what if the ideal arrangements are not workable, so that people will not be willing to follow them or to rely on other parties to follow them? To be *practicable,* a cooperative arrangement between two or more persons has to be not only consistent with their resources and tastes, it has to be *compatible* with the individuals' respective *incentives* and *disincentives* to uphold their end of the agreement.

Where the ideal cooperative arrangements are not practicable, because of the temptations or fears of the parties to a potential exchange, there arises the question of whether there are any practicable arrangements that would permit a mutual gain. It could be that some *dis*incentives operate to discourage cooperation altogether.

Another problem may stand in the way of cooperation. What is there to ensure that the persons searching for gainful cooperation will succeed in *agreeing* to a mutually practicable and gainful arrangement, assuming such arrangements exist?

With this chapter we examine some of the difficulties in contracting and problems of bargaining that may prevent cooperation of an ideally efficient kind or even block cooperation altogether. This material may look like a handbook of pathological cases. However, it also describes most potential social exchanges to some degree.

MORAL AND PSYCHOLOGICAL BARRIERS TO COOPERATION

Exchange between persons, especially continuing exchange, is not primarily a matter of reciprocal gift giving except in so-called traditional societies of the cultural anthropologist. (Gifts are commonly a feature of courtship, of course, and are often part of commercial efforts to sell an unfamiliar product to potential buyers.) Nor is cooperation between persons typically a case of perfectly parallel self-interests—of sink-or-swim together. Typically, because of competing self-interests, cooperation requires reliable agreement over contributions and rewards. And it requires that each party be confident somehow that the other party will keep his end of the bargain.

Ensuring that the other party is adhering to the agreement presents no difficulties in some cases. I will do the dishes and eat only half the food if you will cook the dinner. You will cook and eat half the food if I supply clean dishes and pans. If you don't cook, I will and then eat it all, so you will cook as agreed. If I don't do the dishes, you won't; nor will you cook, so I will wash as agreed. Here each party can cancel the agreement, in time to avoid any irrecoverable costs, as soon as the other party is observed not to be fulfilling the agreement; the partner's behavior is fully observable. But in many cases, ensuring that the partner is complying with the agreement would be too costly or too unreliable to be worth the benefit. Such agreements, when foreseen to be unworkable, will be avoided.

Parables of Greed and Moral Hazard

One of the first to recognize that ensuring compliance with an agreement is often a problem, so mutually gainful collaborations sometimes fail to go through, was the famous Scottish philosopher-economist David Hume, in his treatise in political economy.* Hume imagines two sheep raisers both bordering a swamplike meadow. They recognize the engineering possibility of a joint undertaking to drain that watery fen, a collaboration that, if scrupulously carried out, will cause them both to gain—that is, to benefit more than it will cost (in bales of raw wool). Will they venture into this undertaking, and will it succeed? Hume makes it clear that each man will be *motivated to look for pretexts not to fulfill his part of the job*—to plead sick, say, and invite the partner to finish the work. It is a weakness of human nature, Hume supposes, that each person will want to be a free rider—to get something for nothing—although preferably not to be known as such.

Actually, Hume remarks that good friends would indeed go ahead with such an agreement and without risk that the partner-friend would shirk his or her obligations; but perhaps he concedes that only in order not to distract attention from his argument about how difficult it would be to avoid free riders when many collaborations would have to be among nonfriends. We are left with the implication that where the potential collaboration would be only a casual encounter, rather than an undertaking between neighbors for life, the free rider problem might scare them from collaborating.

Hume did not stop to be explicit about the many possible "pretexts" that a person might offer for having contributed less than was agreed upon. I was sick, and now it is the busy time, so you must do my part if you want the work finished. Or—there were technical difficulties, and while I put in as many hours as you, I am sure, the work at my end progressed unexpectedly slowly on that account.† The modern economic theorist encounters similar "incentive problems" in many—perhaps most—examples of collaboration.

*David Hume, *A Treatise on Human Nature*, London, 1739. Hume, already renowned for his early work on the philosophy of knowledge, considered that this book would lay the foundations for the "moral" (or, as we might say today, humanistic) sciences, including "politics," by which Hume meant the study of the political-economic relations that may exist between "men as united in society and dependent on each other."

†It might be thought that the incentive problem can be solved by our arranging that you pay me a bonus if I do my share, and I will pay you a bonus to do yours. But maybe you can't afford to pay me unless and until I pay you—since you can't *count* on me to pay if you can't expect me to count on you and hence to do my share.

- Two farmers know that there is an advantage from merging, helping each other with planting and harvests, provided that each does not appreciably slacken his effort. But each farmer then has an incentive to do less than he has agreed, while claiming that he has put in the amount of effort agreed upon and is therefore entitled to the share of the outputs agreed upon. And the solution, to watch each other carefully and have a physician certify complaints of ailments, may be more costly than the problem. Monitoring—watching each other closely, calling in expert observers in disputed cases—might help, but it is costly: when will the one farmer do his work if he must always be standing over the other? Foreseeing these incentive problems, the farmers may wisely decide to drop their projected collaboration—and remain family enterprises. (Maybe your mother will doze off, but she will not rob you blind.)
- Two ship owners, fearing loss, would like to have a mutual insurance plan under which each would cover half the losses of the other if the latter's ship went down. But each owner then has less incentive than he had when he bore by himself the costs of his decisions to avoid dangerous cargo, perilous routes, etc.

There is a common thread running through Hume's example and the added ones: Although there would be a mutual gain from some agreed collaboration, each person (acting alone) would gain still more from applying less effort than was agreed; since his partner would not learn in time (if ever) the extent of that effort, the partner's effort would not be tied to his own effort—so there would be no risk of retaliation, nor hope of reciprocity, from the partner.

Where the collaboration is all-or-nothing, the nature of the problem—the simultaneous presence of a mutual opportunity and the snag—is summarized by two inequalities:

benefit from the   cost of   benefit from his
output added by   <   contributing   <   own agreed input
his own agreed input   the agreed input   *and* the other's input

If either person anticipates this problem—the moral hazard, as it came to be called centuries ago in the insurance business—he will shy from entering into that partnership. The failure to cooperate occurs because one or both of the potential collaborators foresees that he is defenseless against the other, or that (at least) the cost of defending himself against the other would cost him too much, eating up the gain from the cooperative enterprise.

The best-known examples of the difficulties of cooperation, however, describe an external diseconomy. The notion of an external diseconomy, also called an *external cost,* has been made familiar by popular discussions of conservation and pollution problems. My acting to drill oil faster from a deposit I share with my neighboring producer, to sink another artesian well to tap the common water table beneath us, to take more fish from the sea we share, to spill more fertilizer into the stream we both border on—all these acts would be an external diseconomy for my neighbor. Each would have an external cost on top of the internal one that I bear. The external cost of an individual's act is the excess of the sum total of the costs caused to each person affected over and above the cost caused to the individual who is acting—the discrepancy between the *social cost* and the *private cost* of the act. When something you do has an external cost, some person or persons would be willing to pay you something not to do it, if they knew you intended to do it.

In contrast: If you work harder on the land you are already using in order to grow another bushel of some crop or obtain another kilo of some ore, the total cost is borne by you; neither a neighboring producer nor anyone you exchange goods with is affected. If you obtain that extra bushel or extra kilo by simply arranging to sell 1 bushel or kilo less than before, again the cost is borne by you: Whatever the price I was getting for each kilo sold—measured in socks or shrimp or books, or the money to buy those things—I will have to pay that price, being able to buy that much less in the way of socks or shrimp or books; the person who trades with me is "down" by 1 kilo, but he is "ahead" by the price it would have cost—and since the *last* kilo he used to buy can be presumed to have been just barely worth the price he was paying, the deprivation of that last kilo will not be appreciable enough to have a place in our calculation of the total cost. Hence he would not be willing to pay you something (on top of the price) for that missing bushel or kilo, because he was already paying (in the form of the price) what that last bushel was worth. In these cases, there is no external cost or diseconomy—it is all internal cost.

The presence of an external diseconomy in the relationship between two or more persons inicates the desirability of their cooperation. A utopian solution would call for the perpetrator of the external diseconomy to receive some compensation, some subvention, for not doing it; or to pay a penalty for doing it. But the costliness of ensuring compliance in interaction with raw self-interest may cast the feasibility of cooperation into doubt:

- Two fishermen share waters where they have been overfishing. Each one sees that with every additional fish caught the expected number of fish *he* can catch in the future is *not* reduced by one fish or more—because the other fisherman will suffer the same reduced stock of fish and will be as likely as he to pay the consequences in the future. Although they might contemplate a tax agreement, in which each fisherman agrees to pay to the other a fraction of his catch, each one would be tempted to evade the agreement by underreporting the size of his catch. It is possible, therefore, that such a bargain will not be reached and that, if reached, it will not be closely complied with.

- Two city dwellers sharing the same park recognize that they would be better off if they would refrain from incinerating their trash, littering the park, unleashing their dogs, etc. But each knows that obtaining conclusive evidence of cheating would usually be impossible: Each one could always answer, if presented with evidence of dog litter, that "it must have been a stray dog that left that, or maybe it was your dog that left that—since *I* always pick up after *my* dog." Neither party can effectively bribe the other to cooperate by threatening to punish a violation when a violation—and for that matter a punishment—cannot reliably be determined.

Although there would be a mutual gain from some form of cooperation, scrupulously carried out, each person would gain more from evading the terms of the agreement than from complying with them—given the behavior of the other party (or parties) to the agreement. Since A realizes that B would not learn of A's evasion, A would not have to anticipate that B (if not evasive himself) would suspend his compliance in response to A's evasion. Therefore, A need not expect to suffer any penalty for his own evasion. If either person anticipates that he cannot enforce the other person's observance of their agreement, there is no purpose served by his entering into such an agreement—after all, he can decide unilaterally not to pollute, without consultation with neighbors; for if the other fellow finds it convenient to pollute (or, contrastingly, morally satisfying not to pollute) that person can go on doing so with impunity.

In cases where the cooperation is all-or-nothing, like "pollute or don't pollute," the opportunity for mutual gain and the "hitch" or pitfall may be captured by these two inequalities:

benefit to the person from restricting *his* *own* pollution or extraction to the agreed amount	<	cost to the person of observing the agreed restriction	<	benefit to the person from his own restriction of pollution *and* the other person's agreed restriction

The theme of all these tales is familiar enough. It is an element of anyone's tragic sense of life: We have met the enemy and they are us; the best for each is the enemy of the good for all, our self-seeking is sometimes the undoing of us all. Some years ago, in the early development of game theory, it was noticed that parables of greed like the ones we have been discussing are illustrations of a certain type of two-person game. It is a game in which the players, with a mixture of opposing and parallel interests, cannot cooperate in certain respects: they cannot watch and warn each other because monitoring and communication is impossible or too costly. Each player, therefore, is in the dilemma of not being able to *bargain* and *contract*. This Dilemma Game, as we shall call it, has the characteristic pay-off matrix shown in Figure 5–1.

A comparison of the players' respective preference rankings shows that each of them would prefer the outcome in which both observe the terms of the agreement to the outcome in which both breach the agreement for individual gain. But *given* the decision by the player called Row, whether that be a decision to observe the agreement or to break it, the player called Column prefers to break the agreement; the corresponding statement is true of Row's preference given Column's decision. It makes sense in this game that each player takes the other's decision as given, uninfluenced by his own decision, since the other player cannot detect his decision and he cannot convincingly communicate it—and even if he could, he could not tell the response.

This game was dubbed the Prisoner's Dilemma by its originator, the American mathematician A. W. Tucker. The name comes from the example widely used to illustrate the game: The district attorney takes two suspects into custody and keeps them separated. He is sure they have perpetrated a certain crime, but he lacks sufficient evidence for a conviction. He talks to each of them separately and tells them that they can confess or not; that if neither confesses he will book them on a minor charge and both will receive a minor punishment. If both confess to the crime they have committed, he will prosecute but recommend less than the maximum sentence. If either one confesses and the other one does not, the confessor will receive lenient treatment for turning state's evidence, while the latter well get "the book" thrown at him.

Unfortunately the label "dilemma" has caused a generation of students to misunderstand the game and its lessons. If a dilemma is a hard choice between unattractive alternatives, then neither prisoner, once arrested, has a dilemma. Neither prisoner, in particular, has to ponder what his partner in crime is going to do.

FIGURE 5–1: The Dilemma of Parties to an Unenforceable Contract—Often Known as the Prisoner's Dilemma

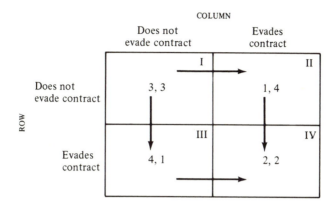

The first number in a cell indicates the rank score of the corresponding outcome for Row, the player playing the rows. The worst outcome is scored 1, the next a 2, and so on. The second number in a cell records the rank score of the associated outcome for Column, the player deciding between the columns.

For Row, cell III with its score of 4 ranks higher than cell I, which scores 3, and cell IV ranks higher than cell II. Hence a play of the game by rational decision makers would not result in either cell I or cell II. The reason is that the player, in this case Row, can gain from evading certain terms of the contract no matter which decision has been made by Column.

For Column, cell II ranks higher than cell I and cell IV ranks above cell III. Hence a play of the game would not result in the outcome of either cell I or cell III. This reflects the gain to Column

from evading certain terms of the contract given whichever decision has been reached by Row. (Because evading is preferred in all cases, that decision is a dominant strategy for Column—and likewise for Row.)

If these self-seeking players were to play this game and make the rational decisions, therefore, the result could only be the outcome represented by cell IV. (Neither player could intelligently expect cell I, and if Column expected cell II or if Row expected cell III—perhaps under the misimpression that his partner was a different sort of fellow from himself—he would be disappointed. Cell IV is the equilibrium in the sense of correct expectations.)

The paradox is that this outcome is worse for both than the one in cell I. It may also be worse for both than the outcome from avoiding the game. Caveat contractor!

For each partner has a "dominant strategy"—to confess is the better decision if the partner has independently decided to confess and better also if the partner has decided not to confess. So neither prisoner—both hardened criminals, schooled by hard knocks in the theory of rational choice—will have any difficulty at all reaching the right decision. The pay-off matrix tells us from the beginning that for each partner the length of the jail sentence weighs more heavily (at least in the case at hand) than brotherhood, pride, honor among thieves, etc. If either partner had a difficult choice to make, it may have been in deciding upon the rank ordering of the four cells in the pay-off matrix. The game called Prisoner's Dilemma shows how the outcome will be determined if the two prisoners each resolve that "dilemma" in the way described by the pay-off matrix.

FEAR OF RENEGING: PARABLES OF DISTRUST

It is often objected that the model of interpersonal behavior portrayed by the Prisoner's Dilemma takes too bleak a view of human nature. People, even "jailbirds," do not commonly "rat" on each other—consider the saying "Honor among thieves." People do not necessarily just litter because they find a self-advantage in littering. Witness Toronto and Buenos Aires: In those places people do not litter because "One does not litter" is a norm of social behavior that they expect the others to obey, and they do not wish to feel like social deviants or antisocial deviants. In Switzerland, it used to be said, you could leave your wallet on a park bench and be certain of finding it there hours later.

An explanation that has been given for such pro-social behavior is that a person's self-image is among a person's self-interests. One who is "not that sort of person" finds that the cost in lost pride from breaking some understanding or convention may outweight the benefits (net of any other costs). There may be a desire for "integrity": If I would not want to be found out having done that, I would not want to do it when I could not be caught either. The idea was formulated in Plato's book on morals, *The Republic*: Thrasymachus says that a man would rape and steal if he could make himself invisible to avoid detection and Socrates replies that a just man would not do that in order to avoid self-hatred.

It is often thought that the logic of economic theory would have the theorist assume that people are honest only when they have incentive to be. This is quite an inaccurate impression, however. To apply the concepts and techniques of economic theory it is not necessary to suppose that people's individual choices are constrained only by their need to limit themselves to what they can beg, borrow, or steal. As noted in chapter 2, they can be viewed as constrained also by self-imposed restraints not to lie, cheat, steal, murder, etc.; then people make their choices subject to more than one constraint.

It would be more accurate to charge economics with optimism and naïveté. Economics does not have a model of a world ruled by protection societies, professional extortion rings, and paid terrorists. In fact, the economist is inclined to infer from the parables of moral hazard and greed that such a world—an underworld without any honor and trust—would not last long.

It is then natural to suppose that a party to an agreement or tacit understanding will not, if he is self-respecting, feel comfortable about evading that understanding in some way that is "not done." On the other hand, no self-respecting person would enjoy having done the right thing if he found that the other party had been cynically evading the understanding; he would feel exploited, used, taken. These two considerations—wanting to do the right thing but not wanting to be duped—are introduced in the Assurance Game.

The characteristic pay-off matrix of this Assurance Game is shown in Figure 5–2. It shows that each player would prefer not to evade *if he knew*

FIGURE 5–2: The Assurance Game

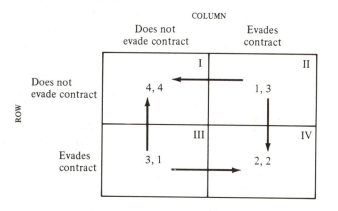

For Row, cell I with its top score of 4 ranks above cell III, while cell IV ranks higher than II. Hence the rational decision for Row is to choose to evade if he expects the other player to evade but to choose not to evade if he expects the other player not to evade.

Similarly, for Column, cell I ranks above cell II, while cell IV ranks higher than cell III. Hence Column will accordingly choose not to evade if he expects the other player not to evade. (Because evading is not preferred in the case where the other player does not evade, that decision is

not a dominant strategy for Column—or Row.)

If the two persons playing this game act in the assurance of the mutually desired outcome—each one confident that the other will not cheat—the result will be the successful outcome described by cell I. But if they lack all trust in one another, each one expecting the other to do the wrong thing, the result will be the unfortunate cell IV. That latter, tragic outcome stems from a failure to communicate—since each would have volunteered his full cooperation had he believed the other intended to cooperate fully.

that the other player had decided not to evade. Yet each player would prefer to evade if he knew that the other player had decided to evade. The effect of this feature of the pay-off matrix is to bring in the expectations of each player about the play of the other one. If each player feels assured that the other is not going to evade the contract, then each will choose not to evade. It is another example of a self-fulfilling prophecy. But there is in this game another possible equilibrium: If each player feels certain that the other is going to evade the contract, then each will be driven—as a defensive move to avoid being "taken"—to evade himself.

We have seen that the mere technical *possibility*—resources and engineering ability, plus some suitable division of the pie—of a mutual gain does not guarantee that the interpersonal cooperation needed to secure that mutual gain will actually be forthcoming. The first sort of parable, above, turns on the premise that the persons presented with the technical possibility are susceptible to the moral hazards—they are vulnerable to temptations or they are simply unscrupulous opportunists. The second sort of parable, above, centers around the premise that one or both of the persons acts defensibly out of fear and suspicion, and in so doing impairs the cooperative effort. Clearly it is right to be clear about the difference between these two parables. It is no wonder, though, that they tend to blur into one another. In the film *The Treasure of the Sierra Madre* we see Humphrey Bogart portray the slide of Fred C. Dobbs from a loner incapable of any warmth or affection into a raving paranoid whose mad assumption that everyone wants 100 percent of the gold ultimately leads to a total loss. But Dobbs had been gulled out of his pay in his previous venture at cooperative enterprise, and it was probably not the first time he had been cheated. (In Dobbs's stratum of society, peopled with adventurers whose sole aim was to obtain the riches they could get out of it, larceny was endemic. Freud remarked that a difficult aspect of paranoia is that the paranoid is right about one time in ten.) The prospecting venture is an Assurance Game, but Dobbs is then unable to trust and to believe the trust of his partner.

BARGAINING: THE POSSIBILITY OF AN IMPASSE

Put aside now the disheartening possiblity that no contracts can be found to extract mutual gain from a technological opportunity—whether because no such contract is compatible with people's incentives or because people have not been clever enough to hit upon such contracts. At the other extreme there is the possibility that *more* than one contract offering mutual gain can be found. The availability of more than one contractual arrangement can turn out to be all too many. When there exists a range of ways to apportion the tasks and rewards, hence the costs and benefits, of a joint undertaking, the problem of somehow arriving at *one* contractual agreement among the more than one available may stand in the way of reaching *any* agreement at all.

To have a definite example we consider the case of increasing returns: two miners, or hunters, or sit-com writers find that by combining their efforts they can produce a larger output per year than the sum of their individual outputs when working separately. To make it simple, we assume that each must toil just as hard, from sunrise to sundown, say, either way, so there is no saving of time or energy. Then the *range* of possibilities by which the mutual gains may be divided by the collaborators can be summarized neatly by a diagram—see Figure 5–3.

- The graph identifies the points representing contractual arrangements that are *efficient*. An efficient contract, it may be recalled, is one that cannot be improved upon for one party without worsening the terms of the arrangement for another party. In our simple example—fixed labor inputs, hence no incentive problems—a contract will therefore be efficient if its rewards exhaust output.
- Some of these efficient contracts can be blocked by the bargaining parties: The reason is that each party would refuse contracts offering lesser rewards than he could earn operating alone. The collection of unblocked contracts constitutes the *core*.

The question to be considered is whether hard bargaining by our two potential collaborators will necessarily lead them to an agreement to proceed with the joint undertakings—or whether instead there is the possibility that they will become locked in stalemate.

Our problem is called, not surprisingly, a bargaining game. Bargaining games belong to the class of games in which the players can and do communicate freely—huffing, blustering, and bluffing as they like—which is unlike the class of game (often called "noncooperative") sampled earlier in this chapter. Two types of bargaining games are the variable-threat game and the fixed-threat game. In the former type of game, the players can calibrate and adjust their strategies, threatening to contribute less effort, less care, etc., if they do not get a larger reward. In the latter type of game, the players have only the choice of whether to contribute a fixed labor input or not—although each player can threaten the other that he will go to work with less probability if he does not receive a larger reward. Our example above, with its supposedly fixed labor inputs, is evidently of this latter, fixed-threat type.

FIGURE 5–3: The Range of Possible Bargaining Outcomes

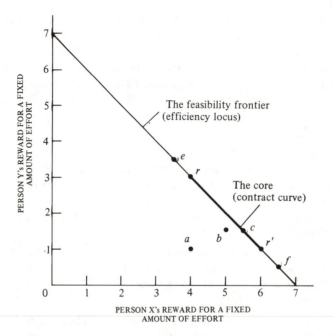

Working separately, the two persons can produce 1 and 4, respectively, by their own efforts—hence an aggregate output of 5. Working together they can produce a total output of 7—an increase of 2.

If they succeed in working together, any pair of rewards—meaning the reward to Person X and the reward to Person Y—summing to 7 would therefore be technically feasible (excluding negative rewards). Every such pair of rewards corresponds to a point on the straight line having slope −1 that is labeled the feasibility frontier. Of course, any pair of rewards that add to less than 7 would also be feasible, since claims to some of the output could be disputed and the output thus wasted. Hence all the points interior to the straight line feasibility frontier would be perfectly feasible also if X and Y work together.

If instead they continue to work separately, Person X might reward himself with 4 units, the amount he would produce, provided he could avoid Y or resist Y's appeals and threats; similarly, Person Y might be rewarded with 1. That pair of rewards corresponds to point a.

All the efficient reward pairs lie on the feasibility frontier. Point a is inefficient—hence it is inefficient of them not to work together—and so is point b. Points e and f, for example, are efficient.

But Person Y could block the reward arrangement corresponding to f because f would give him less than he would have at a, obtainable by working alone. Likewise Person X could block e because it is worse for him than a. Person Y would not be similarly motivated to dismiss c or even r or X to reject r'. All the points from r' to r are in the core—not blocked from consideration.

Some bargaining theorists have argued that this bargaining game has a definite solution—*one in the core,* hence an efficient outcome. According to that proposed solution, a player who tried to get more by yelling louder or who demanded more "because I'm me" would not succed. But a player will win a larger proportionate rise of his reward than the other one if more willing to risk the collapse of the cooperative undertaking; a player's relative share of the total output from cooperating will exceed his relative share of the aggregate output from not cooperating if and only if he is more willing to bear risks. So if X and Y have the same aversion to risk taking, they will split the cooperative output (of 7) in the same old 4-to-1 ratio in which they were rewarded before they discovered the mutual opportunity and agreed to cooperate.

It is an ingenious theory. It abstracts from many considerations—the players' liking of or distaste for conflict, their differing skills in communication, the possibility of pretending to have more daring than actually possessed, and so on; yet any theory, if it is to shine a penetrating light on the problem in need of illumination, must abstract from much of the detail and clutter of everyday real life. The evidence, however, suggests that this proposed solution leaves out too much.

If this solution were a satisfactory theory, then outbreaks of industrial and marital strife would be nonexistent or rare enough to neglect; they would be unimportant aberrations, anomalies. Certainly, negotiations would never end in a deadlock, an impasse—for according to the theory, the contestants will ultimately find the solution to their problem. The fact that, in actuality, cooperative relationships end in unresolved disputes—wasteful industrial strikes or lock-outs, destructive wars, and expensive divorce contests—indicates that bargaining can utterly break down.

When bargainers finally abandon their attempts to reach agreement the cause of the failure to settle may be that each party has underestimated the other's alternative opportunity or his target share of the cooperative gain. Why don't they keep trying and learn to revise their estimates? Perhaps they would learn if they bargained long enough. However, even so, one (or both) of the parties may eventually come to expect that the cost of going ahead without the other party—making certain investments, incurring sunk costs— would be less than the cost of waiting until such time as an agreement is reached. By insisting in your final offer on some positive share of the cooperative gain you do not foreclose the possibility of winning it, which is a better policy over a lifetime of deals.

An examination of bargaining theory, however brief, would be incomplete without noting the views of the very inventor of the contract curve, the neoclassical mathematical economist Francis Ysidro Edgeworth. Edgeworth also presumed that the two parties would bargain their way to a point in the core—would land, that is, somewhere on his contract curve. Moreover, Edgeworth too had a theory of which point on the contract curve would be chosen: the determining principle he called the greatest sum-total of happiness. But the application of that Utilitarian principle, which was first conceived by Jeremy Bentham earlier in the century, is to be constrained by the condition that any bargain outside the contract curve would be rejected by one or the other of the two contracting parties. Referring to his book *Mathematical Psychics,* Edgeworth wrote: "The present author has suggested, as the principle apt to be adopted by two (or . . . a few) self-interested parties contracting in the absence of competition, the greatest-happiness principle, slightly modified: that arrangement to be made which conduces to the greatest sum-total welfare of both parties, subject to the condition that neither party should lose by the contract." * Unfortunately, Edgeworth is not convincing as to why his self-interested parties, who may not care for one another's friendship, would be inclined to adopt that principle—assuming they could interpret it.

When bargainers reach a deadlock, the sticking point may be a matter of principles—the principle to apply in setting their respective rewards from the collaboration. If Person X's demand and Persons Y's demand add to more than 100 percent of what together they would produce in collaboration, the explanation may lie in their having inconsistent notions of what would be a "just" apportioning of the rewards. In Figure 5–3 Person X might insist on the outcome at point *c,* believing it to be the natural solution to their bargaining problem, while Person Y might reject those terms (and worse ones) *not* because he imagines his opponent has the greatest aversion to risk taking but because he is unwilling to accept terms that he regards as unfair. Of course Y does not deny that *c,* while offering him the short end of the deal, is better than *a* with respect to the material rewards involved: point *c* may permit him to write more poetry, support a daughter's mathematics studies, pay for the husband's overdue dental work; yet Y may very well feel compelled to reject X's terms because they would cost too much in self-respect. The previous analysis of the problem of distrust suggested that it is not at all impossible, and maybe not uncommon, that a person would

*F. Y. Edgeworth, *Mathematical Psychics.* London, 1881 (London School of Economics reprint series, 1932, p. 56).

refrain from seizing a gain for himself if he thought it would be unjust to the other party; the motive, it was suggested, was a desire to preserve an image of himself as a fair and respectable person. It is equally possible that a person would not tolerate having a gain unfairly seized from him. Many people want to treat others fairly and to be treated fairly in return.

In the classical view, as formulated by Smith, it is beneficial for all to let each member of society seek out the exchanges that are in his self-interest. More than a century later, neoclassical economists isolated and identified the germs of truth in the classical doctrine: they argued that unrestricted exchange between persons will typically serve efficiency but not generally society's notion of fairness—so redistribution is needed; and, second, that unrestricted exchange is *not* appropriate where there are external diseconomies—for then some sort of governmental intervention is needed to modify what and how much is produced and exchanged.

Still, with all its many qualifications, neoclassical economics left the impression that if people will use their government to intervene in free market exchanges with wisdom at those few places in the economy needing corrective intervention, ideal economic efficiency will result. Perhaps what people want may be bad for them or they may be in disarray over the right social goals to pursue. But the government will have done what little needs to be done to eliminate inefficiencies. Then, truly, it can be said that there is no such thing as a "free lunch."

Private exchange and the needs for governmental intervention are viewed in a different light by modern economic theorists. There are so many "hazards" in everyday exchange that it is a wonder that any transactions take place! Those who want to play fair or not play at all, and decide to take a chance on their partner's fairness, risk being the victims of a confidence game. In the modern theory of transactions and contracts, incentives are as important as resources. When the two parties to a transaction, actual or potential, are unable to create incentives for one another to act nondestructively, the prospect of shirking, chiseling, welching, and so on is apt to arise; then the two parties are apt to be deterred from a transaction or else driven to take costly measures to lessen the damage from one another's behavior. Market life is rife with "market failure" of this modern type.

In this modern view, private transactors can greatly benefit from governmental measures for their protection. Certain kinds of public regulation, from truth-in-advertising to food-and-drug laws, can operate to reduce economic inefficiency, making possible a gain for everyone. The government can be considered to be on a treasure hunt through woods stocked with "free lunches."* Nor is protection from the other party the only rationale

---

*Third parties and the theory of government are the subject of Part 3. The modern economic theory of private market transactions is developed in Part 6.

for such government regulation. *Third* parties have a self-interest in the efficiency which other parties are cooperating in production.

SUMMARY

1. The previous chapter considered some theories of cooperation, explaining why certain cooperative activities, if arranged, would make possible a mutual gain—and hence are necessary for economic efficiency. This chapter considers some theories of the failure of certain cooperative activities to occur, despite the possibility of a mutual gain that they hold out if they could be arranged. In this chapter, as in the previous one, the focus is on two-party transactions.

2. Hume's image of the two sheep raisers, each wary of the other's temptation to shirk his obligations, is one of the earliest analyses (or models) of a contract that, although mutually beneficial, cannot be relied upon by either party because it is not self-enforcing—neither one can monitor and threaten the other in order to force compliance with the agreement; and there is no third party (or court of law) to enforce the contract. So unless the sheep raisers are friends who can count on one another to want to maintain the other's admiration, they will not engage in the mutually beneficial project.

3. More familiar examples of this dilemma—the inability to contract, or bargain, with the other party in an enforceable way—involve an external diseconomy, like my smoke getting into your eyes and yours into mine. I would agree not to pollute if the agreement forced you not to pollute—but not if it is unenforceable.

4. In these games the players are in a noncooperative environment: Each player wants most his share of the benefits from the mutually gainful project. But the players are in a "dilemma" (perhaps not the best word, but the traditional one)—faced with the impracticability of a contract, or bargain, that the parties can mutually enforce. If, without enforceability, each does what is "best for him," the cooperation does not occur.

5. Quite different is the sort of situation, or game, in which each player would *prefer* to do the cooperative thing, even if the other party could not enforce that, *if* he knew that the other party was going to cooperate (also without being forced to). Here the stumbling block to cooperation is not the temptation to shirk or generally to act selfishly. The obstacle to cooperation is the lack of confidence, or assurance, that the other party is going to cooperate because he or she is confident of the first party's cooperation.

6. The phenomenon of feuds between neighboring lords, labor disputes, strife between partners—in short, open conflict—emerges from interactions in a cooperative setting where there *are* bargaining, threats, and the rest. Here a mutual test of one another's resolve to hold out for the terms of the bargain demanded can lead, for a time at least, to a deadlock, conceivably a stalemate.

7. It is clear that *third* parties, through the institution of governmental agency, have a self-interest in enforcing contracts made by pairs of individuals since, in general, the rest of us can earn a consumer's surplus from the cheap availability of their goods—but not if they cannot get together; and further, a self-interest in "knocking heads together," in mediating disputes between deadlocked negotiators.

CONCEPTS INTRODUCED

free rider	Assurance Game	core
external diseconomy, economy	mutually enforceable contract	aversion to risk taking
Dilemma Game (Prisoner's Dilemma)	bargaining game (cooperative game)	deadlock, or impasse

STUDY QUESTIONS

1. What sort of bargaining problem may prevent two persons, each one seeing room for mutual gains, from arriving at a cooperative arrangement?

2. What sort of cooperative difficulties may prevent the cooperative arrangement between two parties to a transaction, though the arrangement is efficient in the practical sense, from being ideally efficient?

3. A recent book by the game theorist Robert Axelrod, *The Evolution of Cooperative Behavior* (New York: Basic Books, 1984), reported experiments in which the "players" are engaged in a *version* of the Prisoner's Dilemma game in which the "play" is repeated over and over again. It was found that the strategy of "tit for tat"—of punishing (just once) the partner every time he made the selfish move by doing the same to him in retaliation—worked very well against an assortment of strategies used by opposing players. Discuss. Do these results suggest that there is no "problem" of cooperative behavior in the original, nonrepeated Prisoner's Dilemma game?

CHAPTER 6

Ideas of Fairness

GENTLEMAN:
Madam, I think you are very beautiful.
CLIO DULAINE:
Yes, isn't it lucky!

Claude Rains and Ingrid Bergman in *Saratoga Trunk* (1945)

WHEN a wealthy young signora and her butler become stranded on
a desert island in Lina Wertmüller's film *Swept Away*, the core of bargaining
outcomes they can choose among opens wide, and once rescued it snaps
shut again: the butler's choice is reduced to accepting her employment or
taking a similar one, hers to employing him again or someone like him.
However, it is an exaggeration, for art's sake, to suggest that a person in
normal life has nothing to bargain over, no influence over the terms. Right
here, as well as on desert islands, cooperative relationships between persons
often leave considerable leeway for bargaining. The valued employee senses
the possibility of a further raise in pay without causing the concern to top-
ple, or the company knows it could pay less without causing the employee
to quit, or both. The husband could do more of the chores without divorc-
ing, or the wife could do more, or both.

It is thus not unusual that the parties to a contract—at least one and
commonly both of them—are recipients of what is called *monopoly rent*:
The size of this rent to a party measures the amount by which the reward
from the contract exceeds the next-best possibility for the same kind of

work—the excess of income over opportunity cost. A resource's income contains monopoly rent if the income exceeds the minimum level needed to attract it from any alternative use—the rent being the excess.*

Where there are rents to be captured, and thus some room for bargaining, it is not unusual for the parties to the contract to appeal to notions of a "fair bargain," of justice, in attempting to win a more favorable bargain. Similarly, whole countries are being heard nowadays protesting what they regard as the unjust terms of their relations with trading partners. The poorer, typically southern, nations have sought a North-South dialogue on a "new order" for the division between rich and poor countries of the gains from international trade. Of course, talk of fairness is often empty mumbo-jumbo— mere posturing to wear the opposing party down. But if *we* want to be able to talk meaningfully and intelligibly about fairness, about justice, and to be able to tell when others are not talking so, we need to learn something of the distinct conceptions of fairness that have arisen in political economy and that continue to be invoked in present-day discussions.

It is perfectly true that the policy adopted in a many-member society toward the distribution of rewards could not resemble in every respect the policy toward the apportionment of rewards in two-person situations. The two-person society has no possible "competition" from a third person, and no government to intervene and modify or redistribute rewards between contracting parties. Yet the elemental cooperation between *two* persons is the natural starting point for any discussion of economic fairness, or justice, *in general*. The principles of distributional justice that have been proposed for use by a society in the design of public programs and economic institutions have typically derived from parables of justice between two persons.

THE STANDARD OF EQUALITY

It is pretty well agreed that no rule—no law, convention, formula for setting rewards—could qualify as a moral principle that was not impartial, that did not apply equally to similar people in a similar situation. The English philosopher of law and morals R. M. Hare called this quality of moral principles universality, and illustrated nonuniversality with a story: A man in a compartment of the train to London remarks to the other occupant, who is about to light a cigarette, that he ought not to smoke in that compartment— and then he (the first man) lights a cigarette himself. Only a social psycho-

---

* A resource's income is said to contain *economic rent* if the income exceeds the minimum level needed to elicit the current supply of the resource in *any* similar use—the economic rent being the excess. The rents received on unimproved or improved land and existing structures are extreme examples of economic rent, since the owner will supply the whole of the resource in return for any rental income rather than leaving the property unleased. Clearly, an economic rent contains some monopoly rent when the alternative uses are nil or less well rewarded.

path would use the word "ought" like that. Anyone using the word "ought" in the normal way would be intending to convey something like: "Stranger, it is a principle not to smoke in that compartment, and like any moral principle it applies to everyone, including you and even me." It is clear from the story that Hare wants us to think of the two men as morally equal, so that universal or impartial application of the no-smoking rule restricts the smoking of both men equally. If the first man would suffer life-threatening convulsions in the event he did not take a puff or two, and that extenuating circumstance were known to the other occupant, then it would be a different story! Then it wouldn't be crazy (though it would be a bit much) for the first man to remind the second man of the rule (with its exception in life-or-death cases).

Economic egalitarianism, the proposed principle of equal reward for equal effort, has its roots in the impartiality of moral principles. If laws should provide equal protection for all, why not equal rewards? If justice is blind, why not also the paymaster who fills the pay envelopes? Certainly egalitarianism makes a valid point. It would be morally outrageous of someone to say that he deserved more than the others just because he is the person named Fred C. Dobbs (or some other name). There has to be some justification for inequality of rewards, some reason for accepting the inequality that remains—if, in fact, the remaining inequality could be reduced. Consider two partners who are identical twins, with identical talents and energy and identical preferences and situations; both would be willing to exchange assignments in their joint enterprise. If one of the partners were to demand an income of 60 thousand (dollars or pounds or whatever) in a situation where the total income produced was 100 thousand, the response of the partner would be predictable: "You have no right to more than half, since I am just as able to contribute as you, and (being just as hungry and just as industrious) also just as willing to work as you are. Maybe you are more reckless or arrogant—your demand for more than half makes me wonder about you. However, we are equals in every morally relevant respect, so we ought to be rewarded equally for our equal effort."

Few people would refuse to join the economic egalitarians on that point. But what of partners who are not equals? Two twentieth-century egalitarians, the historian R. H. Tawney and the playwright George Bernard Shaw, seemed to favor equality *no matter* whether persons cooperating in society were equals in ability or circumstance. They envisioned a society in which the contributors were rewarded equally because they understood that they were all *morally equal*—that their differences have no just relevance for their individual shares of the total pie produced by the society to which they belong. Such a social design might very well be considered the ideal, although no society would know how to achieve exact equality even when every member was devoted to that goal. (Who could prove that some group, electricians or oboists, was not better off than the average, unless they were observed turning in their pliers and reeds?) The age-old question, however, is whether such an egalitarian design of society would be compatible with the *incentives* of the society's self-interested members and therefore attainable, workable. Aristotle, who was perhaps the first great mind to think about that, thought not. "Justice," Aristotle wrote, "consists of treating equals equally"—but he added, "and treating unequals unequally." Evidently Aristotle believed that the rule of equal rewards would not work out desirably if the partners, the members of a society, were markedly unequal in abilities or circumstances.

Aristotle sought to produce a "political economy" of the traditional society—societies built on status or position rather than government-enforced contract as in the modern society. In such a traditional society, there is barter of a sort; but it is not the outcome of higgling by two traders out to obtain the best bargain. In the world described by Aristotle, exchange arose from the needs of an "extended family" who once shared certain resources, using them in common. But as the size of the extended family grew and they were compelled to settle apart, they found themselves short of some of the goods they formerly used in common, so they acquired the needed goods from each other. One might share his water, another might share his fields. Such a transaction was a nonsynchronized gift exchange, as distinct from an ordinary commerical exchange where no antecedent trading relationship between the parties to the exchange exists.

Yet, while Aristotle held an idealistic vision of the human community, he was realistic about the unavoidability of inequalities. The economic anthropologist Karl Polanyi summarizes Aristotle as follows:

The rate of exchange must be such as to *maintain the community* . . . not the interests of the individuals, but those of the community were the governing principle. The skills of persons of different status had to be exchanged at a rate proportionate to the status of each: the builder's performance exchanged against many times the cobbler's performance; unless this was so, reciprocity was infringed and *the community would not hold.**

In this interpretation, Aristotle held the view that a builder would not operate in a society on equal terms when, because of the

---

* Karl Polanyi, "Aristotle Discovers the Economy," in *Primitive, Archaic and Modern Economies: Essays of Karl Polanyi*, ed. George Dalton (New York: Doubleday, 1968; reprinted from chapter 5 of Karl Polanyi, Conrad Arensberg, and Karl Pearson, eds., *Trade and Market in the Early Empires* (Glencoe, Illinois: The Free Press, 1957). The passage Polanyi cites is from Aristotle's *Nichomachian Ethics*.

scarcity of his skills, he could do better elsewhere—on his own or, more likely, in another society. The cobbler has to recognize that the builder must receive the larger reward in their transactions because of the builder's greater opportunity cost.

A difficulty in attempting to treat unequals equally—it is the problem Aristotle apparently had in mind—is that the more-than-equal, faced with the prospect of equal rewards, may find a greater reward elsewhere: The greater reward might be obtainable in another society of similar more-than-equals, or another society where more-than-equals are rewarded with greater-than-equal rewards, or—necessarily in the case of the two-person world—by working independently.

This difficulty with equality is illustrated in the accompanying Figure 6–1 (which happens to be similar to the previous Figure 5–3). Equality of rewards corresponds to point *e*. Person X, whose reward is measured along the horizontal axis, would have a reward of 4, corresponding to point *a,* upon deciding not to join the cooperative enterprise with Y; that is, X's opportunity cost, or foregone reward from joining forces, is equal to 4. It so happens that the egalitarian point *e* lies left of point *a*. That is, the reward to X if Y were to cooperate under the principle of equality would be smaller than X's opportunity cost. In this case, then, equality is not in the core; so X has a motive to "block" such an arrangement. (The total gain to be divided is only 2, so if Y were to move up from 1, which is his reward if there is no cooperation with X, all the way to 3.5, the point of equality, then X would have to miss all the gain—receive no part of the total gain of 2—and relinquish .5 of the 4 he could earn without Y's help.) This hard case for egalitarians is a real possibility, no less possible than the "easy" case in which *a* lies below and left of *e*. It is the case, typically, when the high-technologist works with the unskilled.

What said the egalitarians in response to this hard case? After all they were not fools—they were in fact brilliant!—so they must to some extent have anticipated this difficulty with equality even as they were proposing this principle. Evidently the egalitarians had in mind a new breed of human beings who would take satisfaction from participating in a good society, and this satisfaction would more than compensate those who would suffer a reduction of their rewards. And of course there are instances of that sort of behavior even among the present standard breed. When a man of modest means, say, marries a successful soprano, he does expect to enjoy the same standard of living as she—to

FIGURE 6—1: A Case in Which Equality Is Outside the Core

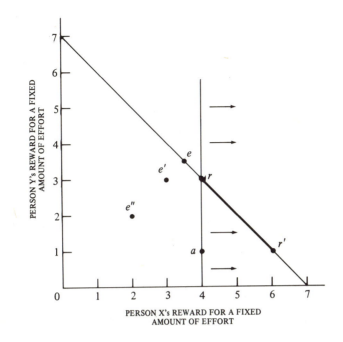

Working separately, the person whose reward is measured along the horizontal, or X, axis can obtain a reward of 4, and the other person, whose reward is measured along the Y axis, can obtain a reward of 1.

Working together, the two persons can have any pair of rewards corresponding to any point on the feasibility frontier. Every efficient pair of rewards lies on this feasibility frontier; hence the reward pairs located inside the frontier are inefficient. And the converse is true: every reward pair on the frontier is efficient; hence the efficiency locus is the entire frontier.

The egalitarian reward pairs are represented by points on the 45° line from the origin. The point e″ on that 45° line corresponds to a reward of 2 to each person. That point is feasible since it does not lie beyond the feasibility frontier. But

e″ is inefficient since there is at least one other point, such as e′, that is also feasible (through collaboration) and is more rewarding for both persons. The pair of rewards that is both egalitarian and efficient is the one that corresponds to e. That is the point of intersection of the efficiency locus with the 45° equality locus. The rewards at e are 3.5 to each.

While equality is feasible from a technological and organizational standpoint, all the feasible egalitarian points lie outside the core. Since Person X, whose reward is measured along the horizontal, can obtain a reward of 4 operating independently of Person Y, whose reward is on the vertical, X could block any of those egalitarian arrangements to his own advantage. Person X would rather not collaborate than accept equal rewards.

drive a comparable car and wear comparable clothes and dine at similar places, to have similar access to friends and ideas; in the event of divorce, he will expect to share equally in the property accumulated during their marriage. It is very awkward, apparently, to treat unequally someone you love. But most economists have found it impossible, up to the present time at any rate, to imagine modern-day societies operating on the principle of love. Adam Smith had a poignant remark to make here. Any individual living in society, Smith wrote, ". . . at all times stands in need of the cooperation and assistance of great multitudes while his whole life is scarce sufficient to gain the friendship of a few persons. [Rather than depending on the kindness of strangers, anyone] will be more likely to prevail if he can interest their self-love in his favor, and show them that it is for their own advantage to do what he requires of them."* However, even if people were generally willing to sacrifice to raise the standard of living of others, to accept the rightness of giving away every unequalizing piece of good fortune, there is a subtler problem awaiting the egalitarians—the problem of incentives.

Another difficulty with equality is that the practicable sharing arrangements that would be necessary to achieve equality tend, in nearly all cooperative enterprises, to impair people's incentives to contributive efficiently to such an extent that they would be *counterproductive*: both partners in the enterprise, including the one *intended to be the beneficiary of equality*, would benefit by settling for some less egalitarian reward structure.

Of course, in cooperative situations where the partners can effectively plan together their separate and joint activities, agree on the "wage" to assign to each task and any lump-sum side payments, and be able to count on the plan's being carried out, the partners might expect to achieve equality—and even to achieve it with ideal efficiency. But this sounds like a marriage more than the less intimate sorts of cooperative enterprise, and a dream marriage at that. In most areas of real life, there is too much uncertainty to permit the "central planning" of each person's contributions; there are more unanticipated disturbances than could be dreamt of in any contingency plan. Further, deciding on the worth (and hence the appropriate wage) of each task might be tedious, and the burdensomeness of each task a source of

* Adam Smith, *The Wealth of Nations*, Book I, chap. 2, p. 14.

contention for the partners. And it may be too time-consuming, and hence too costly, for the partners to monitor each other's activities to verify that the assigned tasks are being done. (Recall the example in chapter 5 of the two farmers contemplating a merger in which they would be unable to observe each other's efforts.)

In most cooperative situations, therefore, the partners have to choose among reward structures of less intricate design—ones involving wage rates, or tax rates, in a manageable fashion. But a simple structure cannot typically be designed to achieve equality except wastefully—if achieve it at all.

Equal Pay

Consider two collaborators in production of unequal productivity. To implement their desire for equality they might think of the principle "equal pay for equal work." But work to be declared equal (or not equal) must be compared somehow. How to measure work? Work in the sense of effort expended or tedium felt is apt to be unobservable and impossible to estimate reliably; only in a variety of special cases would it be clear that one person's work was greater than the other's. To put the above principle into practice the partners might consider the more operational rule of "equal pay for equal time on the job." (Under that rule, the partners would receive the same "wage rate" for the first hour or day worked, the same "wage rate" for the second, and so on; thus incomes could be unequal, but not the opportunities for reward.) If the partners have the same tastes—the same preferences between income and leisure—they would choose to be working equal time and hence receive equal pay (in the sense of equal income).

The defect of the equal pay for equal time rule is that it would pay a partner the same wage rate no matter which task the partner performs. The reward structure offers no incentive—no incentive to take up a more productive task in preference to a less productive task, no matter how much more productive. Hence the partners will naturally gravitate to doing the tasks that are most attractive—the most painless, least stressful, most fun, least demanding—with no regard to the productivity of the task. Certainly, then, the equal pay rule is not efficient in the ideal sense: An omniscient being could issue directives that would cause both partners to be better off—to enjoy expanded choice—provided the partners obeyed them. It is a reward structure that is inefficient in the practical sense as well: There exist reward structures giving each partner a share in the gain of output resulting from performing a more productive task, and giving the partners some incentives to take on the most productive tasks (in relation to their unattractiveness), that would be better for both partners. The partners would be motivated to perform some less attractive tasks but they would be more than compensated with increased pay.

What holds here for two persons holds with greater force for societies of many persons:

- Productivity would suffer from equal pay, since pay prospects would not tend to lead people into their best assignments.
- Performance would suffer from equal pay, since higher pay would not provide incentives to work with the right energy and care.

Equal Sharing

An income-sharing rule has the advantage, compared with the equal pay rule, of leaving people with some incentive to take into account the productivity—hence the potential for income—of the tasks from which people must choose. In the case of collaborators in the production of a single good, such a rule states how the output is to be shared, or how a person's contribution to that output is to be shared, among the partners; in the case of two goods being produced, like wine and cheese, the price at which the two goods are exchanged must be used to figure the wine specialist's income in terms of cheese (or the cheese producer's cheese output in terms of wine). Obviously, among the many "settings" to which such arrangements might be tuned, many settings are hugely inegalitarian. The madman scientist and his half-wit servant may divide the income from their fiendish plot in the ratio of 99 to 1; similarly, the clever viniculturist and the cheese maker who knows nothing but cows. To implement their ideal of equality, two producers might opt for equal sharing of their collaborative output, or of their respective incomes (if working separately).

The defect of the equal-sharing rule has already been anticipated in the dilemma of the two farmers who could, so far as technological consideration are concerned, gain from a merger if they collaborated efficiently but who, if they merged, would have little or no incentive to work efficiently (see chapter 5). A point of that discussion was that the loss of incentives resulting from a sharing rule might very well make infeasible any collaboration. The point to be made *here* is a different one, having to do in particular with the equal-sharing rule: There is the striking possibility that the "disincentive effects" of having to share half the yield of one's efforts with the partner may leave *both* producers worse off than they would be under some other arrangement—some other "setting" of the percentages to be shared, or some basically different kind of rule for distributing income—that tolerates more inequality.

- Any income-sharing rule is a form of taxation. The percentage fraction of the first unit of income earned by a producer that must be handed over to others (to his collaborators or trading partners) is the tax rate on his first unit of income; the tax rate on the second unit of income, on the third, and so on are all defined analogously.

- In these fiscal terms, the equal-sharing rule may be described as a flat tax rate—the percentage rate being the same for every unit of income earned from first to last, with both partners facing the same tax rate. Obviously, that tax rate is 50 percent under equal sharing: Each producer must throw the whole of any additional units of income earned into the general treasury; but since each producer is to receive half the treasury's revenue, each will get back half of his own payment as a tax refund (while in addition receive half the other's payment as a "transfer"); so the true tax rate, after allowance for the refund, is one-half.

It should be clear that there must be some scheme of sharing on a less equal basis, meaning a lower tax-rate—say, a lower tax rate on additions to income that were out of reach under egalitarian rule—which would bolster incentives to produce strongly enough to be *mutually* beneficial.

To achieve a mutual improvement over the results of the equal-sharing rule, any of several alterations in the reward structure might be tried. Economic theory does not promise, *a priori,* that every one of these inegalitarian alterations, even if tried a little bit at a time to avoid overdosage, would improve both partners' rewards. Yet there is one such alteration predicted by theory to succeed for sure, provided the big earner has some hours left in the day to work harder. Once the little earner sees that the big earner is working less than he could, the former will be wise to offer a mutually beneficial deal: "I know that you, like me, prefer equality to inequality, but evidently you are only human. You would give more effort if you had the incentive. So I am offering you on any additional income beyond the amount you have chosen to earn under equal sharing a reduced tax rate." By this device the big earner can be coaxed to earn some additional income, income that would not otherwise have been produced at all. Hence, as long as that reduced tax rate is still positive (greater than zero), some additional tax payment will be made as a result. The little earner thus wins a larger reward via the increased transfer from the big earner, and the big earner seizes the gainful opportunity to produce a larger reward for himself.

The basic idea of this scheme is illustrated in the accompanying diagram. Under equal sharing, Person X chooses to earn 4 thousand and Person Y, 2 thousand. They nevertheless receive the same disposable income of 3 thousand after taxes and transfers. X, for example, receives 1 thousand from Y as a transfer and receives 2 thousand after tax from his own earnings. The lower of the two solid straight lines is X's budget line (opportunity locus). It shows that if X were to earn an extra 1 thousand his reward (in disposable income) would rise only 5 hundred—to 3 thousand 5 hundred; earning an extra 2 thousand would raise his reward by only 1 thousand—to 4 thousand. But a reduction of the tax rate on *extra* earnings, say to 25 percent, would induce X to earn additional income. If X responded by earning 2 thousand more, which is the response illustrated, X would be rewarded with an extra 1 thousand 5 hundred; certainly X gains by virtue of his expanded choice. And since X would then pay an extra 5 hundred in tax, Y's transfer would rise by 5 hundred; hence Y gains too.

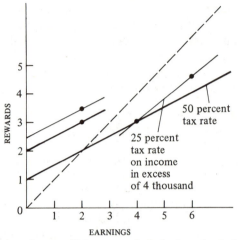

The proposition that gearing the reward structure for equality of rewards must spell smaller rewards for everyone concerned is even more striking, and obvious, when we come to societies with larger numbers. And the magnitude of the effect is greater: An enterprise of two persons, like a marriage, might suffer only small mutual losses in reward from the yen of equality. ("Darling, I won't do the play unless they give you equal billing.") In large enterprises, however, the damage is devastating.

- Applying the equal-sharing rule to an enterprise of four persons, say, would subject each member to a flat tax rate of 75 percent on the "wage" from any extra effort; a member would be permitted to keep only one-quarter of the marginal product of any extra effort.

- Instituting the equal-sharing rule in an enterprise of a hundred—not a large society by today's standards—would imply a tax rate of 99 percent; each member would receive only one-hundredth of the additional output contributed by any additional effort and would lose only one-hundredth of the lost output caused by a lessening of effort.

- As we consider larger and larger societies, the difference that any member's own efforts can make to that member's income completely vanishes!

In any populous society that operates on the principle of equal sharing, the effect on a person's own income of the contribution the person makes to the enterprise would be negligible; and the self-seeking member would *choose* to neglect the effect of his contribution on the aggregate of the others' income—the person may favor egalitarianism but presumably not heroism. So no member would have an appreciable incentive to work beyond what was motivated by the desire for amusement, comradeship, challenge, personal development. Everyone would try to be a free rider, refusing to contribute to the performance of the less attractive tasks no matter how productive, yet wanting to share the production of the others. But there would be nothing to share.

Figure 6–2 illustrates the conclusion that a movement toward either equal pay or equal sharing would, by decreasing incentives, after a point lower everyone's rewards.

FIGURE 6–2: Beyond Some Point Further Reduction of Inequality Would Entail Inefficiency

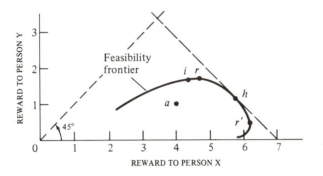

By cooperating, the two persons can have any pair of rewards represented by a point on or inside the curve labeled the feasibility frontier. For example, the partners can have the rewards 5.5 and 1.5, respectively, as indicated by point *h*. We may interpret that reward pair as the outcome when the partners do not share their incomes with one another. There are no taxes or transfers involved in that distribution of rewards.

To achieve a less unequal distribution of rewards, arrangements involving tax rates that weaken incentives have to be used. As a consequence, the redistribution of rewards is accompanied by some frictional loss in the total of the two rewards: The increase in the reward to Person Y is smaller (if positive at all) than the decrease in the reward to Person X. Eventually the point *r* is reached at which a further reduction in the reward to X cannot accomplish an

increase in the reward to Y. Beyond that point *r*, further adjustments of the reward structure in the interests of lessening inequality further, while causing a further reduction in the reward to Person X, have the effect also of reducing the reward to Person Y as well.

Every efficient pair of rewards must lie on the hump-backed feasibility frontier, just as in the example of Figure 6–1. But the converse is not true. Not every reward pair on the frontier is efficient. Only the points on the northeast sector of the frontier are efficient; that is, the efficiency locus is only the indicated segment of the feasibility frontier from *r'* up to *r*. The point *r* is efficient; the point *i*, for example, is clearly not efficient. (The point *r* is efficient in the practical sense only, since among points on the feasibility frontier only *h* is ideally efficient.)

Because equality is recognized to be counterproductive, and quite destructive in large groups, every country of which we have any knowledge makes it a rule to permit a person to keep more when more is earned—not all of any additional income, but at least a fraction. Not to do so would appear to be an act of spite, for it would be hard to understand what else but sheer spitefulness could motivate a national policy that by withdrawing an incentive to earn operates to pull everyone down. For decades, Great Britain was closest to an exception, with its tax rate of approximately 100 percent at the upper levels of wage and salary income (called earned income in Britain), but the rate at the top has recently come down. Certainly the Soviet Union is no exception, where the successful manager of a large state enterprise and the popular soloist in the performing arts can expect to live like royalty in comparison to the rest of the population.

No one claims that outsized rewards are "deserved," as if they were the product of heroic efforts—the runners-up, after all, have often worked as hard or harder, and the greatest violinist avoids practice as ingeniously as does any child. But outsized rewards have a necessary role to play wherever there is the potential for outsized income: the government can collect nothing in taxes from high incomes for the benefit of the other members of society if by confiscatory taxation of income above a certain level it leaves no one with any incentive to earn a high income. The assumption, to the contrary, that pride in one's work and position or one's income *before* tax would prove to be a sufficient incentive may be valid in some cases: For artists and authors, income may be a lesser motive than fame and recognition, yet with success many of them take refuge in tax havens, despite their ties with family and friends back home, in order to protect their incomes after tax.

Karl Marx was something of an egalitarian, perhaps the most egalitarian of the important nineteenth-century economists. While admiring the Promethean achievements of capitalism over the century that had just taken place when he was writing, he condemned capitalism for its glaring income inequality and forecast its eventual replacement by a sort of bourgeois socialism and ultimately what he called pure communism. Yet Marx, for all the defects in his futurology, was insightful on equality. In his comments published years later on a utopian blueprint of the day called the Gotha Plan, of 1875, he implicitly conceded that the world was not ready for equality; that until the spirit of pure communism finally reigned in people's hearts there would have to be inequalities to provide incentives—even if, as in a socialist system, all or most of a country's capital is owned by the state rather than, as in capitalism, by persons. In his own words, describing his own plan, he wrote:

... the individual producer receives back from society—after the deductions have been made—exactly what he gives to it. ... He receives a certificate from society that he has furnished such and such an amount of labour (after deducting his labour for the common funds), and with this certificate he draws from the social stock of means of consumption as much as costs the same amount of labour. ...

Here obviously the same principle prevails as that which regulates the exchange of commodities [i.e., one gives more to get more] ...

This *equal* right is an unequal right for unequal labour.*

Most political economists of the twentieth century have thought that Marx's understanding of the role of inequality continues to be applicable with no prospect in sight of the pure communism he prophesied. This much might be agreed between orthodox Marxists and political economists of more modernist persuasions: If there should ever come a time when technological and artistic progress reaches an end, so that the production of a country becomes routine, because the best way of doing it has been thoroughly learned, *then* unusual talent would not enjoy much scarcity value in most cases; those performers whose looks or voices have something oddly attractive about them would earn high incomes, but the possibilities for inequalities would be very much narrowed. Although pecuniary rewards—incomes— would have to differ across jobs to provide incentives to get production tasks done, people would be effectively equal to a much greater degree. Then the issue of equality will be moot. But will artistic and technological change ever subside? And if so, when?

THE NEO-EGALITARIANS' NOTION OF "FAIRNESS"

We ought not to conclude our consideration of equality without recording the recent revival of egalitarianism in a new form. The motto of the neo-egalitarians is divide and trade: if I have one apple orchard and you have three orange orchards, you can assure yourself a trading outcome that is better for you (at least in my eyes) than for me—at worst, by refusing to trade any of your mountain of oranges for my humble apples. And if these endowments of ours were the product of sheer chance (rather than, say, a different willingness to make sacrifices when we were younger), that result is bound to seem unfair to me. So "fairness," according to the neo-egalitarians, dictates that we divide our endowments equally between us, *then* trade, in the event that we have different tastes. If it turns out that you have still come out ahead after trade, because I really do not care for apples much at all, at least it cannot be said that we started from an unfair distribution of

* Karl Marx, "A Critique of the Gotha Plan," *Neue Zeit*, Stuttgart, 1891. English tr. Robert C. Tucker, ed., *The Marx-Engels Reader* (New York: W. W. Norton & Co., 1972), p. 387.

endowments—we do not envy one another our endowments, no one begrudges the other's endowment.

How does this notion of "fairness" apply to societies like ours in which, among other things, a person's initial endowment upon entering the world of work consists largely of time and energy, talent and skill? Knowledge is not divisible and tradable in the way apples and oranges are, nor is the human drive and energy to make use of one's knowledge. The theoreticians of "fairness" have responded to the problem with a vision of a society in which every member is a sort of corporation and every member of society is made an equal shareholder in each such corporation.

♦ Certainly there is something attractive about such an arrangement when the group is small, at any rate. Imagine three filmmakers—Francis, George, and Steven—all equally good bets. By exchanging percentage-point shares in the income of each other's projects on a one-for-one basis, they can spread the risk that one (or even two) of their current projects will be a flop; and that risk-sharing arrangement may encourage them to take bigger risks in the interests of having a great success. Possibly they would enjoy becoming equal (one-third) partners in one another's projects.

Perhaps such a solution is workable in some sectors of some economies. But imagine a million farmers all equal partners in each of a million farms: no farmer would have an incentive to farm any better than he could get away with in his year-end corporate report to the board of directors. And there would be no gain if a farmer saw a better use for his talents. We are brought back to the incentive difficulties that were the trouble with "equal sharing." The idylls of equality between couples and within small groups, which have left on all of us an imprint of what is ideal in human life, do not apply readily to the workaday societies of real life. They are not even a reliable guide to cooperation between two partners who are not friends.

JUSTICE ACCORDING TO RAWLS

Granted that equality of rewards works out badly—it may be unworkable—what then? The failure of egalitarianism has left moral philosophers groping for some notion of justice in the distribution of rewards to take its place. Surprisingly, one of the most arresting notions of justice is of fairly recent origin (as these things are measured). It is the "difference principle" developed by the American philosopher John Rawls. Economists often call it the maximin principle. Baldly stated, the principle calls for selecting the reward structure that favors the underdog, the person or persons at the bottom rung of the ladder, as much as is feasible—taking into account the foregone opportunities (the opportunity costs) of the cooperating parties and their responsiveness to incentives.

Every human society in Rawls's view is a cooperative enterprise for mutual gain—for the gain of some or all members, at any rate, and a loss for none. More precisely, making use of the technical terms, a society permits its members to escape from the inefficiency of what they could achieve by going their separate ways—to escape from point *a* in Figures 6–1 and 6–2 on to the efficiency locus. The source of the trouble is that more than one cooperative reward structure is efficient, so there is the need to choose the structure. The members of society, if they have any moral sense, will understand the desirability of having some principle, or set of principles, by which to choose from among the potential reward structures. Those principles of justice would provide a way of assigning rights and duties to society's members and of determining the distribution of "burdens and benefits" of social cooperation. These principles would comprise society's economic constitution; such a constitution would constrain the government's management of taxation, public services and subsidies, and so on, in the same way that a society's political constitution constrains governmental legislation and administration affecting political rights.

What principles would people designing a society agree to adopt? Right from the start, in his liberal conception of a society as a voluntary association for mutual gain—or, at any rate, for gains to some or all persons joining and losses to no one—Rawls implies that people would rule out any distribution of tasks and rewards that, if it were tolerated, would leave one or more members worse off than they would be working independently of that society. Of course, a person who preferred the prospect of living apart to the position offered by a society might nevertheless be coerced to participate; but such a society would be a slave state rather than a voluntary association. Rawls takes it that the very first principle adopted by people forming a society would protect each individual's freedom from coercion, especially by the government:

Each person is to have an equal right to the most extensive basic liberty compatible with a similar liberty for others.*

Since everyone would be free to emigrate—to vote with his or her feet—no person would stay to participate if the terms, the prospective burdens and benefits, spelled a loss over what could be obtained by working apart. The losers would opt out, and the cooperative arrangement making them lose would be unworkable. "The scheme of social cooperation," Rawls writes, "must be stable: it must be more or less regularly complied with and its basic rules willingly acted upon. . . ."†

> If those arrangements that would involve anyone's participation at injurious terms are to be disqualified, then all the eligible out-

---

* John Rawls, *A Theory of Justice* (Cambridge, Mass.: Harvard University Press, 1971), p. 60.
† Ibid., p. 6.

comes must lie north or east or northeast of *a*, the outcome from not participating, in Figures 6–1 and 6–2. (Egalitarian reward structures would therefore be ineligible if, as these figures depict, any feasible equal-rewards outcome is worse for Person X than not participating.) If arrangements that would be inefficient are also to be disqualified, it follows that all the eligible outcomes lie on the efficiency locus and in the core—hence on $r'r$ in Figure 6–1 and Figure 6–2.

The second principle that designers of society's reward structure would agree to adopt, according to Rawls, blends regard for equality with respect for efficiency. Granted that unbridled egalitarianism would be mutually destructive, possibly even infeasible; still, each step away from equality needs justification. What position toward inequality will the designers of the reward structure come to agree upon, after their impartial and thoughtful deliberations? The designers will agree, Rawls argues, that each strengthening of incentives, and consequent widening of inequality, is justified if and only if it makes everyone better off:

... social and economic inequalities are to be arranged so that they are both (a) reasonably expected to be to everyone's advantage, and (b) attached to positions and offices open to all.*

The principle is simply illustrated in the two-person case (see Figure 6–3). As society contemplates successive reward structures offering the members ever greater incentives, the succession of reward outcomes travels upward, northeast, along the feasibility frontier; in this phase, everyone benefits from the strengthening of incentives, despite the evident widening of inequality. The widening of inequality continues to be justified until finally one of the members ceases to benefit. At that point efficiency prevails, in the practical sense of the term: It is not possible from that position to make either person better off without making the other person worse off. In this two-person case, it is clear, the less well off member is as well off as possible at this point; it is the "maximin" outcome because at this point the minimum of the two rewards (that is, the smaller of the two) is at a maximum.

On Rawls's difference principle, it would be unjust for a person or group *already at least as well off as another* to demand a greater reward for cooperation *if at the other's expense.* Thus X would accept *r*, and only *r*, as just in Figures 6–1, 6–2, and 6–3.

JUSTICE AS RAWLSIAN "FAIRNESS"

The difference principle is one conception of distributive justice. It is Rawls's intuition of the principle that men and women would agree to choose for

* Rawls, *A Theory of Justice*, p. 60.

FIGURE 6–3: Rawls's View of Fair Inequality

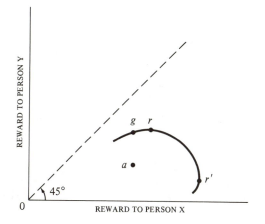

event the persons did not reach an agreement, is inefficient. It is not as good for Person Y as *g*, for example, the point due north of *a* on the feasibility frontier. So a move to the point *g* represents both less inefficiency and less inequality.

In the case illustrated, though, point *g* is itself still inefficient. The reward structure that generates the outcome at *g* is counterproductive for Person Y: Reward structures offering more incentives to Person X would cause both X and Y to receive higher rewards—although the reward to Y would increase less than that to X.

Once point r is reached, any further alteration of the reward structure in the direction of offering greater incentives to X would raise the reward to X only at the expense of lowering the reward to Y. Hence the point r is efficient.

The points down the "right face," or northeast sector, of the feasibility frontier, called the efficiency locus, are also efficient. But these outcomes represent a widening of inequality in comparison with *r* that is unjustified, since the one person gains at the expense of the other.

Widening inequality is consistent with people's sense of justice only up to the point r, since the less advantaged member would lose ground beyond that point.

The point *a*, representing the outcome in the

their society if, in their deliberations, each of them were to consider the matter with fairness to the others, with the appropriate impartiality. That leads to the question of what is involved in thinking fairly. What sort of mental exercise, of thought-experiment, must a person do? The Biblical injunction, do unto others as you would have others do unto you, contains a basic insight—that deciding what is fair requires imagining ourselves in other people's shoes.

Of course, this venerable golden rule would be quite silly if interpreted to imply: "The rich man ought to give all his wealth to the poor man because, were their positions reversed, he would certainly prefer the other's gift of all his wealth to any smaller gift—he's no dummy." On that interpretation, the poor man ought to reject the gift, because if he were the rich one he would certainly prefer the other one to reject such a gift. So the conflict would remain—only each man would be taking the side of the other. This interpretation of the golden rule would make the rich man and the poor man exchange places and leave them there— no closer to a solution.

Sensibly interpreted, the Biblical injunction expresses the point that moral rights are general, unlike the special privileges claimed by despots and zealots. I must acknowledge your right to this share from our partnership under the circumstances if I would demand as my right that same share were our situations reversed. The same point is made by the Talmudic injunction, do not do unto others what you would not have them do unto you. I have no right to that share from our partnership if I would not accept as right your demand for that same share were our situations reversed. But, with regard to the Biblical advice, what would be my right in the present circumstances? And, with regard to the Talmudic prohibition, what would it be not right of you to do were our positions reversed (and hence not right for me in the actual situation)? Certainly it is *necessary* to put ourselves in the other person's shoes in order to think fairly about interpersonal conflicts. But obviously is *not sufficient.*

To grasp the notion of thinking fairly, Rawls, along with other economist-philosophers of recent decades, direct us to imagine ourselves being in the shoes of all of the other members of society as well as our own *and* not knowing *which* of those shoes we are destined to wear, or even the personality of the wearer. We are to choose our principles of fairness in ignorance of our own individual vested interests. (We are to know only that more reward will be preferred to less, whoever we are, because a larger reward to a job makes it easier to pursue an interesting career and satisfying personal life.) The just distributive principle, for Rawls, is the one that "free and rational persons concerned to further their own interests" would choose in that hypothetical situation of shared ignorance of one's advantages and predilections, that "initial situation of equality."

It has now been shown that the maximin principle can be deduced from a set of postulates, or axioms, expressed in mathematical terms. If we find those axioms acceptable, we are compelled by mathematical logic to accept the implied maximin principle. But such formal logical analysis has not brought economists closer on the question.

People deliberating over the principles of justice in a setting of impartiality might also be attracted by the example of the children deciding how to cut an irregularly shaped cake "fairly." They see that by having the one who was unlucky enough to draw the second piece—the less advantaged child, in this case—be the one who cuts the cake, the disadvantage of the unlucky one is minimized. This parable works just as well if the size of the total cake will depend upon the willingness of the cake cutter to cut the cake in unequal shares.

Moral philosophers and other theorists of social choice are still considering Rawls's striking thesis that people in such an impartial setting would be led to choose Rawls's principle.

UTILITARIANISM: ANOTHER VIEW OF ECONOMIC JUSTICE

There existed before Rawls a quite different view of distributive justice. It is the view of the early nineteenth-century philosopher Jeremy Bentham and followers who came to be called utilitarians. For utilitarians, that reward structure is best that yields the greatest sum total of human happiness. Corresponding to each reward structure is some distribution of rewards and tasks among the members of society; the resulting happiness of each member—the "utility" that the person derives from the reward net of the "disutility" of the task performed to earn it—can be recorded like a person's weight or temperature. The utilitarians then argue that these happiness readings, these individual utilities, can be made commensurate with one another, in the same way that Fahrenheit thermometer readings can be compared (even when the numbers have been rubbed off) as long as they have one and the same scale (the same length corresponding to a degree). So if a new reward structure is tried, we could determine whether the sum of the utilities is increased—because we could compare the increases of utility (of the gainers) to the decreases of utility (of the losers). Associated with each reward structure, then, is a sum of the corresponding utilities. One reward structure is better than another in the utilitarian calculus if the former produces a larger sum of utilities; and two structures are equally good if they produce the same sum. The reward structure (or structures) associated with the largest attainable sum of utilities, the maximum total utility, must be just, since no other structure is better. Justice in the utilitarian view requires society to *maximize* the sum of utilities.

It is therefore clear how the utilitarians would diverge from the Rawlsians in a case like that in Figure 6–3, with its recognition of the importance of incentives. While Rawls's principles justify a widening of inequality only up to point *r* in that case, the utilitarian principle would justify some further widening of inequality. As society experiments with successively larger doses of incentives, Rawls would have society stop once the "utility" of the less well off person has peaked and would decline if incentives were strengthened further. But at that point the "utility" of the better-off person would

FIGURE 6–4: The Utilitarian View of Fair Inequality

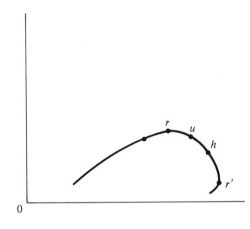

People would accept a widening of inequality beyond *r* up to the point—like *u*—where the increase of utility to Person X from still further widening would no longer be able to counterbalance the decrease of utility to the unfortunate Person Y.

still rise with a further dose of incentives. So *total* utility must still be climbing as incentives are increased at the point where Rawls would stop. Therefore further doses of incentives must, up to a point, increase the sum of utilities. The point labeled *u* in Figure 6–4 illustrates the conclusion that utilitarianism would go farther in the toleration of inequality than would Rawls.

It is this willingness of utilitarianism to sacrifice, to "trade away," one person's gain for the sake of another person's gain that Rawls objects to—no matter that the latter gain is greater than the gain sacrificed, and that (of course) there was nothing personal about it. Rawls's view is based on "rights," the utilitarians' on the "public convenience." A person, if he is to be tried, has the right to a fair trial, no matter how expensive, as Rawls would see it; and the utilitarians would say that fairness must be weighed in the balance along with cost. The competition between these two contending views continues.

SUMMARY

1. In two-person situations, even in the context of a large society, there is generally a range within which the mutually beneficial bargain may fall; and it is presumably the case that deadlocks and conflicts, as well as chiseling and reneging on agreements, would occur far more frequently than they do in the world if it were not that, in the more successful societies at any rate, some degree of consensus exists over the principles of

justice. When an individual tries to extract the best possible terms for himself, he may make a case in terms of the justice of his claims, precisely because he assumes the other party will be moved by considerations of justice. So there are ample reasons why prevailing ideas about economic justice inevitably come up in a study of the way social economies behave. In addition, of course, society has recourse to ideas about justice in determining, by one or another political process, how and to what extent it will intervene in the distribution of rewards among the participants.

2. Economic equality as the conception of justice—the economic egalitarianism of the socialists G. B. Shaw and R. H. Tawney, for example—originates in the moral premise that an ethical standard to be acceptable must be universalizable, that is, applicable to all persons alike—such as the belief that a law or decree can be just only if it is just to apply it to everyone. ("If it is just for *me* to get less than half, despite my equal effort, it must be just for *you* to get less than half—and how would *you* like to receive less than half? Right, so it can't be just.") Thus it is argued that persons are *deserving* of equal rewards, at least for equal efforts (relative to capacities).

3. But if people are allowed to choose what jobs they work at and how hard they work (which may very well be necessary for anything approaching economic efficiency), then collaboration by individuals on the basis of equality of reward (or at least equality of pay) may fail to be workable—it may fail to be compatible with individuals' respective incentives—even when the individuals are equal in their abilities at the cooperative undertaking. One of the individuals may back out if equality of reward is required because he can do better than that elsewhere. Or, one or both of the partners might suffer a lack of motive to work hard since the costs of not working hard would be shared equally (as was seen in the case of Hume's two neighboring sheepmen). Hence cooperation on the basis of equality may be incompatible with individual incentives.

4. Suppose that two or more individuals do find it advantageous to cooperate, notwithstanding a reward structure geared to equality. If the partners are unequal in ability, drive, etc., it may be that such an equal pay or equal-sharing arrangement is *worse for everyone* in that it produces a smaller reward for everybody that some reward structure that leaves individuals with greater incentives to earn more. Insistence on a structure of equal rewards will pull down everyone's rewards by weakening incentives to work harder (for the sake of the extra benefit produced) if, as can usually be assumed, all or most of the partners are working to earn pay for themselves rather than for the rest of the group.

5. A recent notion of economic fairness, known as "fairness," rests on the idea of "divide (equally) and trade." This standard of justice also raises

questions of whether its implementation would be compatible with individual incentives. What would ensure that a farm manager, owning an equal share of all the farms, would use well the resources allocated to him on the farm he manages and that he would contrive to obtain the right resources?

6. The notion of economic justice developed by Rawls says this: If the individuals engaged in a cooperative enterprise *start* from a hypothetical, and regrettably inefficient, position of equality or something close to it, then the creation of larger and larger individual incentives to work hard, etc., although inequality-causing, are perfectly just as long as everyone gains—indeed, as no one objects that a further move in this direction would cause him some reduction of his reward (from its previous level)—in that sense, a loss. Practically speaking, this criterion of economic justice amounts to saying that widening inequality is justice as long as it leads to the largest possible reward to the least well rewarded—to the working poor. Thus the criterion is usually called the maximin criterion because the minimum of the rewards is maximized—that is, made as large as possible.

7. The standard of economic justice called utilitarianism differs significantly: It says that it is quite alright to widen incentives further than Rawls's stopping point *as long as the gains to the gainers outweigh* (on some comparison) *the losses to the losers.* Rawls, in contrast, argues it is *not* right to "trade off" (that is, to trade away) one person's reward for the sake of a larger reward for another person, no matter how large the gain compared to the first person's loss. (See study question on this issue.)

CONCEPTS INTRODUCED

economic justice, or fairness	divide-and-trade "fairness"	maximin criterion
conceptions, or notions, of justice	Rawlsianism	utilitarianism
economic egalitarianism		

STUDY QUESTIONS

1. Economic analysis, using the premises of self-interested individuals operating in an equilibrium state, argues that equality of opportunity:

   a. is not feasible because, in general, some people are born or raised with advantages over others;

   b. *is* feasible, but only through genetic engineering or surgery;

    c. could be achieved, if it is feasible at all, only by "leveling" methods that would pull everyone else down to the level of the lowest;

    d. could be achieved, if feasible, only by methods that at some point would perversely pull everyone down from where they just were;

    e. could be achieved, if feasible, only by methods that would pull everyone down from their original levels.

    Identify the correct statement and explain why the other options are incorrect.

2. George Bernard Shaw has one of his characters in *Man and Superman* say, "Some donkeys have the damndest luck." To what extent, judging from your own general knowledge and experience, are personal fortunes a matter of chance and to what extent a matter of advantages from early life?

3. To what extent are the advantages and disadvantages of persons in your society a function of differences in people's *drive*—their diligence in acquiring skills and their industriousness in applying them—and to what extent is the inequality of advantage a matter of luck—luck in genetic inheritance, parental upbringing, and social class?

4. "In utopian-egalitarian communities, productivity and performance are not observed, so there is inevitable inefficiency. In capitalism, people's hours worked and the ease with which they earn are not measured, so inequality is unavoidable." Discuss.

5. Contrast the Good Samaritan with the Good Rawlsian.

6. Use Figure 6–1 and the Rawlsian principle of choosing among points that do not damage either party, hence from the locus of points $r'r$, to discuss Rawlsian justice in trade and investment between the North and the South.

7. "Since economists are not agreed on an exact conception of justice, there is no legislation that, provided it does not hurt anyone, they can agree is unjust." Discuss.

Part 3

The Political Economy of Multilateral Exchange: The "Baroque" Economy

CHAPTER 7

Gains from Multilateral Exchange: Law, Organization, and Markets

BANDIT CHIEF:
Badges? Badges? Badges?! We don't need no stinkin' badges!

> Alfonso Bedoya (to Bogart and Walter Huston) in *The Treasure of the Sierra Madre* (1948)

No one would speak of a "government" in a two-person society, and for good reason. Two-person enterprises may have a leader or a tyrant, but not a government in the normal sense. Their behavior may be subject to agreements, but not laws. It may be a clause in their contract that neither will wear overshoes to bed, but there is no law against it. By its nature, a law is external to any pair of persons in a society, whether determined dictatorially or democratically. Hence the concept of a government is tied up with societies of three persons or more—with societies of many or at any rate several members. Government is intrinsically multilateral.

The same multilateral character may be found in two other institutions—the managerial organization and the market.* It would be an unusual organization in which one partner was accountable to "the manager" while the other partner went unmanaged. The managerial structure, clearly, develops in an organization of several or more persons. Similarly, it would be strange

---

* The term *organization* encompasses all enterprises and agencies, private or public, profit-seeking or not.

of Farmer Jones, hauling some of his produce to Farmer Brown for a possible exchange, to say that he was bringing goods "to the market." Markets grow out of the gains from three-person (or more-person) exchange, and the clustering of sellers (and of buyers) in competition with one another.

With this chapter we begin to consider the society of several persons, or many. The focus of attention in the present chapter will be on the rudimentary beginnings of the three aforementioned institutions—the government, the organization, and the market. We start with the government, with how the government grew out of the widespread demand for a protection agency into a public institution for collective protection, for the protection of all, paid for by involuntary assessments on society's members. Once a government is in existence to protect life and limb, it can be made available to protect against theft and embezzlement, against fraud and other breach of contract. The stage is thus set for the extensive development of organizations and markets.

COST SHARING IN THE ENFORCEMENT OF RIGHTS: THE RISE OF LAW

Even when there are only two persons in a society, some of one's resources might have to be spent in protecting certain rights against violations by the other. The other guy may find one's existence inconvenient, or want to poach one's holdings of wild game, or pay for his surgery with spoiled wine. There are means by which one might hope to deter such violations—the threat of a penalty after the fact, such as a reprisal or merely withdrawing one's cooperation for a while as a punishment, or the threat of some counterforce before the fact, like molten lead over the castle walls. But such deterrents, whether or not effective, are not generally without their costs: my punishing you may hurt me too, my reprisals have opportunity costs for me, and castle walls are expensive.

When there are *three or more* persons in a society, they may come to realize that such individual rights will be better protected—defended with less inefficiency, with smaller total resource costs—if each person, through a mutual defense pact, can count on allies to share the cost of deterring any violation of his rights. For then, if a person is known to belong to a mutual defense pact, it will be understood that the cost to that person of deterring an attack has been reduced, since the cost of the deterrence is spread over all the pact members. So anyone contemplating an attack can expect that the pact members will be willing to spend more to repel such attacks than would the victim if he had no allies. The horse thief will expect a longer chase by a bigger posse if he knows the costs will be shared by all the ranchers, not just his victim.

By this reasoning we reach a theory of mutual protection associations, of private protection clubs—not yet a theory of government protection. The road is open, nevertheless, to that latter destination. One line of argument visualizes a struggle until victory among warring protection associations. Suppose that, at first, there is more than one protective club in operation. If none offered protection from its own members, any member would be willing to pay for membership in an additional club that did not contain all the members of the club (or clubs) already joined; seeing that, a protective club would see a mutual advantage in offering protection against its own members as well—in return for higher assessed contributions to the club. So it will be sufficient for any person to belong to one club—at any rate when there are large numbers of people around, not just three! Hence, assuming the service offered is much the same, a person need only look for an association offering protection at the lowest cost. That would be the *largest* association, since *it* could spread the cost of defending against any violation over the largest number of members and therefore could afford to mount the most intimidating defense of the members' rights. Leaving freak cases aside—like two equal-sized associations poised in delicate balance pending the first disturbance—we are led to the conclusion that the competition between protective associations would be ruinous, causing only one association to survive. (Of course, geographical barriers like a river may permit two associations to coexist in their separate adjacent spheres. But they make two societies, not one society with two protective clubs.)

The proposition that a single sovereign government will arise to meet people's demands for protection against violations of what they deem to be their rights is espoused in the provocative book on political philosophy by the American philosopher Robert Nozick. Nozick writes:

A theory . . . [of] how a state would arise from [a theory of a] state of nature will serve our explanatory purposes *even if no actual state ever arose that way.* . . . A fundamental potential explanation, an explanation that would explain the whole realm under consideration [had the specified explanatory process been at work rather than some other], carries important explanatory illumination even if it is *not* the correct explanation. . . . We learn much by seeing how the state could have arisen, even if it didn't arise that way. If it didn't arise that way, we also learn much by determining why it didn't; by trying to explain why the particular bit of the real world that diverges from the state-of-nature model [of the rise of the state] is as it is.*

---

* Robert Nozick, *Anarchy, State and Utopia* (New York: Basic Books, 1974), pp. 7–9.

This view has brought criticism from some political scientists. They contend that the rise of governments did not in fact occur in the way that this "philosophy" of government appears to suggest it did. It is true, apparently, that much of the world's history is a story of existing governments with their armies expanding their sovereignty until the globe was covered; this is not a story of free competition, actual or potential, between indigenous and endogenously arising protection agencies—and to this extent the simple philosophical theory is inaccurate as a causal account of history. Many societies found their protection through foreign governments imposed from outside. But how did the *first* government arise? Or the *second* government survive, if two managed to coexist? A theory of government-in-general does not have the same purpose and subject matter as the theory of national borders.

Of course, no association could long establish itself as the sovereign protector of people's rights in a society if the character of the protection it offered were seen by all to be inferior to that available in some other society or that expected to be obtainable from some other sort of protection association; otherwise, the members of the society would exit, or they would revolt against the established association and thus reopen the competition. To be viable, therefore, the association must be perceived as administering its protection dependably and with care that regular procedures are followed. This observation suggests two virtues that a protective association must have to succeed.

- It must offer "equal protection," including equal protection of accused persons. For if the association were to offer its protection unequally to the citizens, either capriciously or with bias, all or most people would worry that they would not be among the lucky beneficiaries of the unequal protection. It is comparatively easy for people to check that protection is being offered equally, comparatively hard to verify that it is being offered unequally in the promised way.

- It must offer protection of one's rights from violations by anyone. Hence no person could be above the law, exempt from the rights of others. Of course, those holding administrative office in the protective association are in special situations and may be accorded certain prerogatives of office. But if the association head were the king, people would still have rights against the king.

Beyond these points, it may be suggested, people would demand that the structure of assessments to pay for the association also meet their sense of fairness.

We thus arrive at a "theory" of the rise of government. It arose, organically rather than by design, out of the possibility of supplying on a sharing basis—and therefore at a cost that people could afford—the protection of certain rights. The resulting mutual protection associations were engaged in governing—in making and enforcing laws. Foremost among the rights for which protection was desired, we may suppose, was the right to personal safety—safety from being killed, raped, tortured, assaulted. A close second must have been the right to keep one's own produce and any goods for which it had been exchanged—hence rights against theft, trespass. Inevitably, however, the protection associations must have been drawn into a further definition of people's property rights—from the right not to be held up by highwaymen to the right to levy a toll for access to one's road or stream. Pretty soon the protection association needed legislators to set the rules and judges to decide the cases.

KINDS OF PROPERTY RIGHTS

Out of the conflict between the rights claimed by one person and those of another there will emerge a more elaborate specification of what people have the right to do. Here we may distinguish between private rights and communal property rights. Both kinds of rights set boundaries on the permissible use of resources.

Private property rights are reserved for the owner of the property. Such rights might include the right to drill for oil on the property but not to operate a glue factory, the right to drive a car or operate a bus but not recklessly, to own and read a book but perhaps not to sell it to a minor. In every case the rights to a property are limited, qualified by ifs and buts:

> In common speech, we frequently speak of someone owning this land, that house, or these bonds. This conventional style is undoubtedly economical from the viewpoint of quick communications, but it masks the variety and complexity of the ownership relationship. What is owned are *rights* to *use* resources, including one's own body and mind, and these rights are always circumscribed, often by prohibition of certain actions. To "own land" usually means to have the right to till (or not to till) the soil, to mine the soil, to *offer* those rights for sale, etc., but not the right to throw soil at a passerby, to use it to change the course of a stream, or to force someone to buy it. What are owned are socially recognized rights of action.*

Note that an essentially private property right—the right of the bus owner, say, to sell rides on the bus and not to have it "borrowed" for a joy ride without permission—can belong to a branch of government, such as a city-owned transit authority, as well as to a person or company of persons.

---

*Armen A. Alchian and Harold Demsetz, "The Property Rights Paradigm," *Journal of Economic History*, 33 (March 1973):17.

To the statement by Alchian and Demsetz it might be added that often the lengths and limits of the rights to a property are not, and could not have been, spelled out in advance of the outbreak of a dispute over the question. The reason is that future circumstances affecting the property in all their novelty and variety could not have been fully foreseen or comprehensively taken into account beforehand. Hence the owner's plans or even his development of a property may be influenced less by a literal reading of the rights conferred by the title of ownership than by what he or his attorney expects he can "get away with." And that is often a matter of conjecture, for if the dispute goes to the lawyers for a settlement they may find wide latitude under the law and have little more to go on than their creativity and instinct for compromise—often expensive for one of the disputants; at the same time, judicial decisions and legislative acts are constantly reinterpreting property rights and redrawing the line between one property's rightful uses and another's. Both the looseness of legal rights and their state of flux were emphasized by the economist-sociologist Gunnar Myrdal:

Popular ideas tend to be formalistic and to mistake the form for the reality. . . . (Lawyers . . . know that no one is more legalistic than the non-lawyer. . . . [A]lthough one might expect that [a nonformalistic doctrine of lawyers called bona fide] would appeal to the common man's dislike of formalism and to his sense of equity . . . this is due to a mistaken notion about the common man. He, more than the expert, is prone to think in legalistic forms and stereotyped conventions.)

Nothing has confounded discussions and muddled political attitudes so much as the traditional method of thinking in terms of "systems". To take an example: Our economic "system" is often described as based on private property. This generalization, which may have some historical justification if numerous qualifications are added, is quite misleading as it stands, for the relevant social factors can be altered *by degrees* without changing the system as such. . . .

In reality there is no such thing as a "system". It is at best an analytical tool for analysing social phenomena. From a system no conclusions can be derived about what is or about what ought to be. Thus one cannot deduce the right of inheritance from the right of private property. Such concepts as "right of private property", "freedom of contract", "inheritance", etc., so common in abstract economic analysis, are, in this abstract sense, quite unknown to lawyers and sociologists. Thus there has never been a free market in the sense in which the term is used in economics. Long before there was any market to speak of, exchange transactions had been subjected to rules by those in power. These regulations . . . have always influenced the content and the results of the transactions. The "system" of private property is modified by every session of Parliament and often by judicial acts. . . . The political choice is never one between a number of abstract, logically coherent social orders, as economic theory tends to present it, such as free competition, communism, etc.*

Nowadays, of course, no professional economic theorist—and certainly not the present author!—would present the political choice of a society in the simplistic, discontinuous terms that Myrdal complained of decades ago.

A communal property right is a right to a use of a resource that is shared with other persons—so they are said to have "rights in common" to that use of the resource. Defined more fully, a communal property right may legally be exercised by any qualified person, without charge for the act of use, on a first-come, first-served basis—up to the limit, if such exists, of what is available. Such communal rights include certain uses of the river and lake, the city streets and sidewalks, the village green and the old path up to sheep meadow—space permitting; also, the right to watch the sunset, to listen to the sound of the band marching by, to tune in a satellite television transmission (but perhaps not to record it).

Is there a communal right to a certain use—namely, prompt ingestion—of Hans's corner-store chocolate ice cream on a hot day, as long as the supply lasts? Certainly not if Hans has a private property right to his holdings of the ice cream, and he has not decided to give it away. Yet if Hans must *sell* to anyone, and on a first-come, first-served basis—perhaps that is a condition for his town license to operate a store—then we may say that there is a communal right *to buy* the ice cream, provided the town does not charge one a fee for exercising that right to buy. Similarly, there is a communal right to buy a ride on "common carriers" licensed by the town, but no such right to lease Andrew's cherished 1926 Silver Streak for a Sunday outing with the kids—Andrew may lease only to close family.

With the increases in population and congestion, there has been a tendency in the world for community property rights to be repealed, replaced by private property rights. There were *communal* rights to graze sheep on the English commons until the Enclosure Acts sanctioned private holdings; but

*Gunnar Myrdal, *The Political Element in the Development of Economic Theory*, Stockholm, 1929. English tr. by Paul Streeten (Cambridge, Mass.: Harvard University Press, 1954), p. 197 and footnote (placed in parentheses above).

with individual shepherds having little or no incentive to conserve on grass, the result was overgrazing. Ultimately most of the common grazing land was converted to private property.

Paying for Law Enforcement by Compulsory Contribution

If, every time his horse was stolen, the hapless cowboy had to pay the protection agency he had joined the whole cost of the posse, the trial, and property attachments necessary to get his horse back (or enough goods to buy a new one), he would have no more incentive to catch the horse thief than he would if he did not belong to the association. It would defeat the purpose of the association to charge a price equal to the entire cost of organizing the posse—where, in figuring that cost, account would be taken of the output lost by the cattlemen who had to leave their ranches and herds to join the posse. If the cowboy had to pay the whole cost of pursuing the thief, he could simply hire his own posse at no greater price to himself—and cancel his membership in the association; then, horse thiefs would flourish, knowing that the victim would be unlikely to try to apprehend them.

If no user of the protection is himself to pay for any of the extra cost—or perhaps for not more than a small fraction of the extra cost—incurred when an enforcement action is taken on his behalf, how are the costs of operating a protection association to be paid for, to be "financed"? The cattlemen's associations of the Old West, in nineteenth-century America, were largely do-it-yourself organizations: Each cattleman was assessed a contribution in the form of doing his own share of the work of protecting the herds against rustlers. Similarly, the members of the voluntary firemen's associations in colonial America had to put in their time at the firehouse if they were to be bailed out when their own houses were ablaze.

Alternatively, the members of a protection association can be assessed a monetary contribution to pay professionals to perform the services of the association. This modern-day method has the advantages of the division of labor. In this case, there is an additional reason for not charging a member for each act of enforcing the member's rights: Possibly the enforcers—police, judges, and so on—might have been idle otherwise, or possibly they can work on a case without affecting their capacity to respond to a new alarm requiring enforcement; so the opportunity cost of enforcing the member's rights may be quite small. What needs to be paid for mostly is the "overhead" cost of just "being there."

◆ There is some analogy here to the way a country club operates. It could charge as much for each play as would have to be paid for a use of commercial tennis courts or golf courses. But each member of the club, generally speaking, is willing to subsidize the use of the club facilities for two reasons: it will make the members more willing to play, so each member will more easily find a willing partner; and it is inefficient to discourage using the courts and the course by charging for play at times when there is excess capacity—better to charge a membership fee with which to cover the overhead cost of maintaining the facilities.

Whether the services of the protection agency were paid for solely by membership dues or by some mix of dues and user charges for services rendered, an agency in the business of protecting large numbers of people—more than a handful of cattle raisers or townhouse owners—would face a difficult problem: How would a mugger, burglar, poacher, or kidnapper know whether the prospective victim under surveillance was under the protection of the agency? Unless members in good standing could be issued counterfeit-proof certificates proclaiming "I Give to the Agency" for them to wear on their sleeves and stick on their windows, so that among nonmembers these paraphernalia would be conspicuous by their absence, nonmembers would enjoy much the same protection—the same deterrence, anyway—as members would. Nonmembers would receive a "free ride." True, it is not necessarily wrong to offer free rides, nor to accept them when offered. However, the feasibility of riding free might create a financial problem for the agency: Who would pay dues if paying up would bring little, if any, extra protection? This has become known as the *free-rider* problem.

Thus the protection agency, with its monopoly of force, would have to use its force to make the payment of assessed contributions *compulsory*. If one wants to live and work in the jurisdiction of the agency, inevitably receiving the benefits of some or all its services, one will be assessed a tax—with penalties for tax evasion and for refusal to pay. The cattlemen were able to discourage free riding by the threat of withdrawing their protection, leaving the ostracized free rider a sitting duck. Apparently the colonials were able to exert social pressure on people to pay their dues; but that system did not survive as populations grew in size and mobility. As towns grew, governments, in order to protect the rights of townspeople, were driven to coerce the payment of taxes—on penalty of expulsion or jail.

COST SHARING IN MANAGEMENT: THE RISE OF ORGANIZATION

When there are three or more persons available for cooperation in the production of something, they can form a production unit that we would recognize as a company or bureau—an organization with a management or administration to coordinate and oversee the contributions of the persons working in it. A group of hunters on an expedition; a band of soldiers guarding the settlement—these are primitive examples. At the other extreme we have the complex examples of the modern age—the conglomerate corporation with its hierarchy of personnel, from the chief executive officer and division presidents to the office messengers and elevator operators; the government agency with its equally elaborate bureaucracy of civil servants. A company, private or governmental, is engaged in selling its product—as in everyday usage of the word—while a bureau, philanthropic or governmental, is engaged in giving its product away.

♦ In what follows, our focus will be not on the general question of why three or more persons may collaborate in their production—one general answer to that is economies of scale. The focus will be on the organizational economies of scale, or managerial economies of scale, that arise when three or more can join together, and on the question of why they may adopt an organizational structure having specialized management personnel.

Organization? What is an organization, anyway? In any system of thought there must be a few terms that go undefined. The notion of an organization, as that term is used here, has been illuminated by the English economic theorist John Hicks:

It is quite clear that the manager does not make all the decisions himself. There is delegation of decision-making. Only some decisions are made centrally; the rest are left to be made by the lower orders in the hierarchy. The need for delegation is commonly explained in terms of limited capacity for oversight. The manager cannot be everywhere at once; and he cannot know everything at once. That by itself is a sufficient reason for delegation. But it is probable that there is a further reason. The power to take decisions, even over a limited field, is a thing on which the normal person sets considerable value; he has to be called on to be something more than a mere automaton if he is to give of his best. He needs, at the least, a little freedom to do his job his own way. It is only by the most iron discipline that he can be deprivated of that freedom. Why should one take the trouble to exercise such pressure, unless it is needed? It is simpler to delegate.

If the delegation of decision-making is not to lead to chaos, it must proceed by rule. There must be rules which circumscribe the fields in which individuals are free to take decisions; rules which will commonly take the form of prescribing the place of the individual in the organization. They may be written rules; but for the most part they are understandings, implications of the job the individual is set, which will serve in the place of written rules . . . if they are understood well enough. A production unit . . . may be defined in terms of the things it produces . . . ; but we get nearer to its essence if we regard it as an *organization*, now revealed as a structure of rules and understandings, the rules and understandings by which the various grades in its hierarchy are fitted together.*

True, it is at least imaginable that even a two-person collaboration would name a "manager" and a "managed." But few people would be content always to be managed, never a manager. "You mean you will direct me, supervise me, monitor me—while you shirk your duties and rob the till without my seeing?" Such a division of tasks would be in name only, because the managed partner to avoid being cheated would have to spend time overseeing the manager—who else would? In the two-person partnership, therefore, management is very much a two-way street. Each partner must spend time overseeing the contribution of the other. So there cannot be anything closely resembling a "management" or "administration" in the ordinary sense. It is pertinent also to recall a point made earlier, in chapter 5, about the problem of trust in cooperative projects: If each partner—or even just one of the partners—must spend a great deal of time monitoring and verifying the work of the other, the prospect of a mutual gain from their collaboration may vanish. Two people are rarely *enough* people to be able to afford a management, particularly its supervisory or overseeing function. (A recent national security advisor to the United States President, Zbigniew Brzezinski, commented that he had spent almost all his time making sure the policy would be carried out, and little of his time making the policy.)

Once there are three or more potential collaborators, it may pay to set up a system of supervision to guard against shirking and pilfering—against malfeasance and embezzlement. "I won't have to watch you half the time, and you me half the time, because we'll have a third person to watch us both." If the person brought in to supervise, to carry out the overseeing function of management, can effectively monitor the performance of both the original collaborators for the same time that he can monitor either one, we have a case of increasing returns to scale. More generally, if 2 (or 3 or N) workers can be supervised at *less* than 2 (or 3 or N) times the cost of monitoring 1 worker, there is an economy of scale from having the larger number of workers sharing the same monitor or monitors.

♦ The gains from collective supervision to protect against shirking and pilfering are analogous to the gains from collective policing (that is, guard and patrol) to protect against robbery, extortion, and assault. In both cases, people see that by huddling together under the watchful eye of the same "guard"—whether it be the supervisor or security guard at the fac-

*John Hicks, *A Theory of Economic History* (Oxford: Oxford University Press, 1969), pp. 10–11.

tory or the cop on the beat—they can achieve a given level of protection from each other at less cost than if they operated in pairs (or, more generally, in smaller groups).

There is more to a system of overseeing performance than the workers' supervisors—those who peer over the shoulders of the workers to check their work, or pace the catwalk watching for a worker asleep at the switch. The supervisors on the front line themselves need supervising. (If their success in maintaining adherence to the rules is not monitored, there is nothing to prevent them from taking bribes not to report infractions of the rules by the workers under their supervision.) Evidently the ancient Romans thought about the problem: *Cui custodiet custodien?*—Who oversees the overseers? The supervisors who monitor the workers at their workbench, or in the chorus line, will report to their own "higher order" supervisors, of course. In a large enough organization, there is more than one of these super-supervisors, and they must report to the next higher order; and so on, all the way to the top. Thus the system of supervision may be described as a pyramid of personnel. At the top of the pyramid is the chief executive officer in the management structure. He cannot supervise the performance of everyone with the best results. By delegating the supervision of the workers to an echelon of vice-chiefs, who may in turn delegate, and focusing his own overseeing on their performance, the manager will obtain benefits from closer supervision that—in many cases, anyway—can more than repay the cost of the extra layers of personnel.

The image of the managerial pyramid fails to answer the question of who will oversee the manager, the chief officer. If the manager's performance is to be satisfactory, the manager must have an incentive to perform well and need to give an account of that performance. If the company is an enterprise for the gain of its owners, be they private individuals or some governmental unit, it is the owners who must hold the chief executive accountable for his managerial performance. If the agency is a governmental organization operated for the benefit of some or all the citizens, it is the responsible governmental unit that must hold the manager accountable.

There are two kinds of *incentive pay* by which the manager may be motivated to perform up to a certain standard. First, the manager's reward can be graduated according to his performance: a better than average performance is rewarded with bonuses and honors, and a still better performance is rewarded still more. However, no purpose would ever be served by punishing the manager with a reward so small that he is not motivated to take the unusual care demanded of a manager. Managers are "overpaid"—willingly and deliberately paid a premium by the owners of the enterprise or the legislators overseeing the government agency—so that they have a lot to lose if and when they lose their positions. Chief managers are overpaid most of all for the reason that the damage their laxity would cause would be the most costly. This is the second way by which the manager is given an incentive. The manager can be replaced in the event of a demonstrably poor performance, or inability to demonstrate good performance. (Becoming the chief operating office has its dangers for the employee.)

The theory of organization has become a vast subject, and a challenging one. The above discussion is no more than an introduction to a central part of that theory. Yet this brief discussion is enough to raise a puzzle. If the economy of scale offered by the possibility of working under the same management impels three persons to form one producing company instead of two—leaving aside cases like the lone trapper, where no management would be useful—then does not the same economy of scale (alongside any others) dictate that three hundred million persons would also find mutual advantage in operating under just one management structure? The economist shifts uneasily in his chair, casting about for a worthwhile reply.

First of all, the economist may reply, there may very well *be* a tendency for the producing companies to merge into one general company—in the very long run. For the past two centuries, a company has had to grow pretty fast just to keep the same relative share of the world's output. Once the growth of world output, due to rising population and productivity, finally approaches an end, we may very well find that the more aggressive companies drive out the others from the field, and merge with one another, until, possibly, there is just one giant conglomerate in place of the many existing companies. In a sense, such a state of affairs has already been reached in the socialist countries of Eastern Europe and Asia. There the managers of the various state enterprises report to the apparatus of the central planners—in a way that is not altogether different from the ways that the presidents of the subsidiary companies belonging to a conglomerate report to the central executive body of the parent organization. In both the socialist and the capitalist cases, the managers of the subsidiary enterprises are permitted a certain amount of autonomy under the rules and understandings of the organization.

On the other hand, the economist may add, there may be diseconomies of scale that, beyond some size of the organization, begin to outweigh the economies of scale—including, in particular, the managerial economies under discussion. It may often happen that as an organization grows to a large enough size it loses the speed, versatility, and creativity needed to compete effectively with those organizations, at least the better managed of them, that have remained smaller—slimmer, more agile and alert. Of course, we must be on guard against implicitly assuming that "whatever happens is for the best." Should the large companies be left to die, or to shrink, just because they cannot compete successfully *if unaided by the state?* Maybe the large organizations are worth assisting, like eagles and whales. (When the government of France socializes—or "nationalizes"—its banking industry, it thus ensures that new, upstart banking enterprises that are privately financed will be unable to enter the French banking business. When the United States government took over the mail delivery business, it also declared that competition by private letter-carrying companies is illegal. In these cases, evidently, some advantage for some people was seen in putting a stop to competition. It is possible, however, that the advantage seen is only a mirage, and the costs to other people entirely real.)

INFORMATION SHARING IN EXCHANGE: THE RISE OF THE MARKET

A society is imaginable—the totally collectivist society that ants and bees establish, for example—in which not a single part of a person's life is left to the person's own discretion. Government managers would direct what a person produced and what a person consumed. The French have the word *dirigisme* for that thoroughly "directed" kind of society; the nearest English word seems to be totalitarianism. Whatever we call it, it is safe to say that the members of any society would find intolerable a style of government that left them no private sphere. So let us consider a society in which the laws and regulations that people live under leave them with some personal space, some preserve, within which they have the freedom to make their own decisions. There is some protected domain in which individuals are accorded certain rights—the right to certain uses of their own bodies, the right to certain uses of their own lawful produce or earnings, the right to certain uses of goods obtained in lawful sales, etc.; and consequently certain actions are up to each person's discretion—the selection of a mate, job, town, soft drink, . . .

In this world of individual choice, which is our world, a person is not compelled to buy (or use) an airplane ticket to Miami; a person has to be sold on the idea. No one is conscripted into piloting airline flights or building aircraft; a person has to be bought, so to speak—attracted, induced, persuaded. A good of this discretionary sort, in order to be sold, is commonly "marketed"—made available to the set of potential buyers or an appreciable subset. Similarly, the discretionary job opening is commonly brought to the labor market. ("I got my job through the classified ads in the *New York Times*.")

Barter Trade

In a society where individuals have a domain of free choice, in which they are free to buy and sell certain goods from one another, it is possible, even likely, that each person will be related "by trade" to everyone else. The *simplest* network of trading relations is this: A "exports" enough to B to pay for A's "imports" from B, and similarly for every pairing of persons, A and C, B and C, and so on. There is a balance of trade between each pair of traders. This sort of trading pattern is often called *barter*. When the White Sox trade two pitchers for three outfielders in a straight player swap it is a barter deal—and when there is an "undisclosed amount of cash" in the bargain, it isn't. Here are two illustrations of barter trade:

In both cases some of the individuals have more than one trading partner—just one of the individuals in the left-hand case, all of the individuals in the right-hand case.

THE SOURCES OF MULTILATERAL TRADE

Evidently a barter trade pattern is composed only of bilateral exchanges—exchanges between two parties with no third party involved. While a network of trade that is purely bilateral might be attractive for its simplicity, it would be a rarity for trade to remain bilateral. If exchange relationships happened to begin bilaterally, in their early development, it is likely that unexploited opportunities for gains through multilateral trading would soon be noticed and seized upon. One route by which trade would become three-way is through the emergence of a "trader" who sells not from what he produces (if anything) but from what another produces.

Arbitrage

Consider two buyers of, say, apples—one could as easily think of two groups of apple buyers—who are paying *different consumer prices*. Any third person observing this discrepancy between the two prices will see the opportunity for a trading profit through the process called *arbitrage*. A profit can be made by buying apples from the low-price buyer at some intermediate price and selling them at some higher, yet still intermediate, price to the high-price buyer. (Clearly both apple buyers enjoy "expanded choice" as a result of the trader's alertness in bringing them into indirect contact with each other; possibly one of the suppliers of apples, or the common supplier if there is only one, loses, since the formerly high-price buyer will now buy fewer apples at the high price—though buy more apples altogether.)

Consider the analogous situation of two suppliers, or two groups of suppliers, who are paying *different marginal costs of production*: The extra cost that, say, grower B must pay to produce the last kilo grown, *b*, exceeds the extra cost, *a*, that the other grower, A, must pay to produce the last kilo he has been growing. (Perhaps B, while not stretching to produce any more than A, is saddled with inferior land or location or talent. Or perhaps B, although no less able, etc., has to strain to meet the large and lucrative orders he has stumbled onto, and so he must use expensive doses of fertilizer, water, etc. to stretch his already mammoth crop.) Any third person discovering this situation would likely see the profitable opportunity for an arbitrage operation: He could buy some apples from the low-cost grower, A, at a price that is intermediate between the two marginal cost levels *b* and *a,* and sell them to high-cost grower B at some higher, yet still intermediate, price—and thus make a profit for all three parties to the transaction. Or the third person, called the arbitrageur, can try to buy the A operation, manager

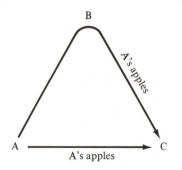

and all (lock, stock, and barrel), and sell it to the owner of the B operation—in effect acting as a broker in a merger of the two operations. (Either way, clearly, both apple suppliers will enjoy added profit as a result of the arbitrage: the same aggregate production and sales can take place, but at an extra profit because of the more efficient allocation of production as between the two suppliers. Possibly one of the buyers of the apples, or the common buyer, loses, since the low-cost supplier will now charge a higher price.)

Brokerage

The implication is that 2, 3, or N consumers or suppliers of the same good can benefit from being connected to one another. Imaginably, such a connection might be like the links in a chain: B links A to C, C links B to D and so on; here B "arbitrages" between A and C, C "arbitrages" between B and D, and so on. At the same time, B may be a producer himself and sell some of his produce—not a specialist in arbitrage. Or, at the other extreme, all the linkages might be effected by a single individual who specializes in "trading," in "buying low and selling high." The specialist trader, or *broker,* serves as a third-person intermediary between the final buyers and the original sellers. Through the intermediation of a broker or group of brokers there is, in effect, a public dissemination of information: For example, the people who would have consumed at a low price in the absence of the intermediary learn (or are made to feel) the presence of consumers who would have been faced with a high price; and the consumers who would have faced a high price learn of the presence of consumers (possibly consumer-producers) who would have been faced with a low price. The latter group, rather than continuing to consume the good themselves at the low price, are led to sell their old car, rent their summer homes, pawn jewelry, and sell Grandma's primitive paintings *at a higher price* via a broker; and the former group, rather than buy at the high price, if buy at all, buy these goods via the broker *at a lower price.* (Of course, brokers will not stay in the business if their fee and the volume of business do not yield enough revenue to cover their opportunity costs. So selling prices normally exceed buying prices.)

The Coalescence of a Market

The second stage in the development of the trading network is locational. Where does one find a trader? Most likely where other traders are, of course: at the trading post, in the town market. The concentration of traders in the same known place results in a substantial saving of costs for final buyers and original sellers alike. Before the establishment of the trading site, a seller had to incur significant costs in searching for a buyer offering satisfactory terms, be it a final buyer or a trader; with the rise of the trading post, each seller shares free of charge the information that the good supplied can be sold there—and at the average price—since that is where most of the buyers and other sellers will go to transact. Similarly, before the appearance of the public market, a buyer had to incur search costs to find a seller, whether a trader or an original seller, offering satisfactory terms; with the establishment of the market, the buyers share free of charge the knowledge that the good they demand can be purchased there, if anywhere—and at the most common price. Knowledge of the whereabouts of the trading place, and of its prices, constitutes a collective, or public, good: You can draw on that knowledge without anyone else's having to stop drawing on it or another's having to produce more of it. Once that collective good is produced, its use, by anyone or everyone, requires no resource cost.

Thus the introduction of a market possesses the feature raised by every collective, or public, good: Every user would benefit but everyone would prefer the others to pay for it. How does the developer of a market expect to be repaid, and possibly to gain? The answer in many cases is that the developer of a trading post earns a return through the additional rent that traders will pay for the land on which the trading post is developed. A race may occur among developers to try to capture these enhanced land values, each developer hoping to make his land the site of the shopping center of the area. Alternatively, the race might be between hamlets and villages, represented by their local governments, in the interest of enhancing their tax collections.

Why this agglomeration of traders in one place? There must be some sort of mechanism, an "invisible hand" process, that causes the "market"—an abstract idea, a metaphysical idea—to take shape in the form of a square, stalls, shops, milling crowds, etc. The process of competition among sellers, and among buyers, provides the needed explanation. When a seller of a good discovers another seller of that good with a high marginal cost, with an ability to sell additional units only at great cost, the former seller can reasonably expect to profit by going into competition with the latter. Such a high marginal-cost seller is a better candidate to compete against than one whose marginal cost is small and who can therefore better fight off competition. By this sort of process, concentrations of sellers tend to emerge. Rather than spreading themselves evenly like band members on a parade ground, sellers will cluster in twos and threes. The successful seller of burgers with standing room only can expect another burger seller nearby. Similarly, the buyer with the good fortune to be obtaining a low price can expect other buyers to move alongside in the hope of competing for such low-price supplies. Once an area has become known as the site where there is competition between two or more sellers of a good, be they traders or the original sellers, still other sellers may be drawn to the site—because that is where buyers will be. Rather than attempt to draw buyers to a site where there are few or no buyers initially, the seller choosing a location will be drawn to a site where it is easy to raid the other sellers for their patrons; that saves start-up costs. As the number of sellers at a particular site increases, buyers find increasing reason to concentrate their comparative shopping among the buyers conveniently in that same vicinity. (It may very well be that *if* the seller can find a buyer or two in the hinterlands, away from the main market, the seller can play the role of the "monopolist," raising prices above what would be paid in a highly competitive market—by the device of restricting output, thus keeping the good scarce to the buyer; but charging such an "above market" price would not be tenable indefinitely, as customers would drift away to the main market—neglecting, as we have been doing, the transportation costs of commuting between home or office and this or that seller.)

There is another reason why a new seller would prefer a big lake to a little pond—certain other things being equal, or, as the ancient Romans said, *ceteris paribus.* Although the average price in two spatially distinct markets might tend always to equality, following a disturbance in either market, a gap between the two prices, once created, does not vanish instantly. The new seller entering either market must figure that his additional supply will drive down the price in the market he chooses to enter; only gradually will that price tend to rise partially, and the other price fall somewhat, as the water levels in the lake and the pond come back into equality through the seepage between them. That being the case, the seller will fear that the price reduction he causes would be larger if he enters a "thin" market, with few sellers and buyers, than a market with more numerous sellers and buyers. Worse, the seller might also fear that by elbowing into the thin market he will provoke a collusive effort by the sellers already occupying that market to retaliate, with the purpose of driving him out—which would not be the case if he slipped into a less thin market, where he would barely be noticed.

- ◆ Having recognized the tendency for traders to congregate, we should not assume that the result is a single market site in the world or in every population center. (When people say "there is a market for that" we know better than to ask where it is.) The market for weekly magazines, say, may be confined to only one place or instead consist of a few sellers close to one another in every town or perhaps one seller on every corner of a city. Clearly there are counter-tendencies toward the dispersion of a market.

A role for government in the operation of markets. Governments make use of markets much as any nongovernmental enterprise uses them. The government may coax workers into this or that employment, through the inducement of wages and other attractions, much as any other enterprise does. The government may also supply certain products to the market, such as electricity, for a price, like private enterprises. Moreover, when the government does not own and operate the entreprise, it can still intervene to alter its production and prices by the device of a tax or subsidy. (What difference does it make if the Royal Ballet Company of Covent Garden is a government enterprise running a deficit covered by taxes or, instead, a private enterprise receiving a subsidy that permits it to sustain a loss? In either case the management has to serve two masters, the public and the government.) As a participant in the market, the government is unique in having the latitude to sustain losses indefinitely—hence to give goods away, not merely to sell them—in view of its monopoly over the power to tax.

The converse is also true: Markets make use of the government. In fact, markets could not get beyond the stage of swapping between people who know each other were it not for the intermediation of some kind of government. When Smith wrote that "It is not from the benevolence of the butcher . . . that we owe our supper . . . ," he was not telling the whole truth. The healthy self-interest of butchers may be a necessary condition for putting meat on the table—although totalitarian countries have found other methods than Smith's of appealing to their self-interests—but it is certainly not sufficient. How do I know, in deciding whether to sell some of my fish to buy beef, that the the butcher does not "short-weigh" (so much that if I knew beforehand I would not make the trade)? Or that the meat sold is not really horse meat? Or is diseased? Of course, each person would be free to take unilateral defensive measures at a cost: People could bring their own scales to market, buy books on food chemistry and animal pathology, etc. In other cases, however, consumers would be defenseless: How does the consumer ascertain that the aircraft flying to Miami is as safe as the consumer has been led (or asked) to believe? The typical consumer cannot afford the training to make the tests himself—and the airline could hardly offer an inspection with each passenger ticket sold. Planes will not take off until the consumer is assured that they will not come apart in midflight.

The consumer needs the assurance of some disinterested third party, or some third party who will perform disinterestedly for the sake of gain, that the product is what it is claimed to be. Certainly the seller of the goods cannot generally be relied on—the seller is the other party, and may be terminally ill, with plane tickets to Timbuktu. Another person, or group of persons, might in some cases be able to serve the needed function. (Private testing companies have been able to cover "opportunity costs" by selling their test results to consumers. But they cannot cover the cost of testing jumbo jets and butchers in the millions.) However, it is the sellers themselves who have the major stake in such assurance, since the consumer can always buy something else.

In the Middle Ages, a producers' association could take collective action (in their own self-interest) for the protection of their quality standards—the medieval guild. By promising to blow the whistle on any member who let down standards, and to withdraw their warranty as punishment, the guild was acting as a miniature government for mutual protection.

The medieval guild survives, here and there. We send our kid sister or son to the neighborhood movie house assured that it will not prove emotionally shattering, since we know the motion-picture association has inspected each new film for its potentially destructive influence and graded it accordingly. We hire a band for the big dance assured that the musicians' union will not admit players into membership who are atrocious. Here the self-interests of the producers, whom the government has permitted to act collectively, is relied upon. Nonetheless, in matters of aircraft, butchers' scales and meat inspection, surgeons' certification, and a host of other products, the enforcement of standards— and to some extent the setting of standards—has been put under the administration of the government rather than a private industry association.

Three Goods: The Case of "Triangular" Trade

No discussion of the gains arising from the multilateralization of exchange would be complete without including the most famous schoolbook example of multilateral exchange—triangular trade in three goods. In the "pure" case, B exports only to A, C exports only to B, and A exports only to C. Hence A imports only from B, B only from C, and C only from A.

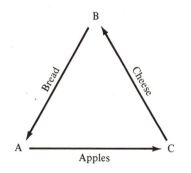

Historians noted such a trade flow in the seventeenth century involving Europe, America, and the Caribbean. Its basic characteristic is that the bilateral "balance of trade" is broken: There is a trade surplus with one trading partner—B runs a surplus with A, since B doesn't spend its revenue from the sale of its bread to A on A's apples—and a trade deficit with the other partner—B runs a deficit with C, since C doesn't buy B's bread with the revenue from its sale of cheese to B. (Piracy and shipwrecks aside, the one surplus must just offset the other deficit, thus leaving an overall balance of trade—over the "lifetime" of the transactors, at any rate.)

How may such a triangular pattern come about? Earlier, we considered the possibility of multilateral exchange even when there are only two goods: some of A's produce may be shipped by an arbitrageur from B to the final buyer, C. Some of the reasons for the rise of such intermediaries were discussed. But here there are three goods involved, and, accordingly, a new reason why trade may break out of the bilateral mold.

The triangular pattern may arise because, owing to differing preferences and/or costs, there are no bilateral trading arrangements that would make both parties to any bilateral arrangement (with its balance of trade) better off. As shown by the table below, B and A, neither of whom has any cheese, *both* rank "having more bread" above "having more apples." So there is no way that B and A can reach a bilateral deal. An analogous problem stands in the way of a bilateral arrangement between B and C, and between A and C. Only by sitting down together to forge a three-way trading agreement can any party obtain an improvement over what is obtainable with no trade whatsoever.

Preference Orderings			Preference Rankings			
B	A	C		B	A	C
more cheese	more bread	more apples	buy cheese	1st	3rd	2nd
more bread	more apples	more cheese	buy bread	2nd	1st	3rd
more apples	more cheese	more bread	buy apples	3rd	2nd	1st

How can this multilateral trading pattern be achieved? How can the apple seller's bread purchases be paid for when the bread seller does not accept apples in payment? The pattern can be achieved by the use of credits—IOUs. A, the apple seller, can pay B by turning over the credit he accepted—C's IOU— in payment of his apple sale to C. B, the bread seller, will accept that IOU of C's as payment, because B can use it to pay for his purchase of cheese from C. C, the cheese seller, will accept his own IOU as payment for his cheese sale. (That payment must be just sufficient, since everyone's exports are worth just enough to pay for what is imported, there being overall balance of trade. The IOU might read, "Pay to bearer 30 kilos of cheese" when B has agreed to buy that much from C.)

♦ What if B were afraid that C might repudiate his IOU? Then B might balk at accepting that IOU from A in payment for the sale of his bread, and the multilateral pattern could not get started. What may be needed is some governmental arrangement that threatens C (and anyone else) with penalties—in effect, a ganging up by A and B—in the event of C's willful default of his debt.

The other method by which the multilateral pattern may be achieved is through the use of money. If there exists some asset, like currency or deposit balances at a bank, that is readily accepted as a means of payment, that "money" can be used to pay the bread seller, who will accept it knowing he can use it to pay the cheese seller, who will accept it knowing he can use it to pay the apple seller . . . and so on in an indefinite circuit.

♦ At one time, gold coin and bullion circulated as money. Governments assisted by enforcing debts contracted in terms of gold and by accepting tax payments in gold. Later, governments replaced gold money with paper money (and gold replaced wood and tin in people's teeth).

A RIDDLE OF ECONOMIC HISTORY

Which came first: the government or the market? A large governmental bureaucracy is observed as early as the Bronze Age, a notable example being the government of the pharaohs in ancient Egypt. On the other hand, evidence of markets can be traced as far back as the Stone Age. It is difficult to imagine the growth of any extensive and regular amount of trade without the protection of law, however.

What must have happened is that the development of the market and of the government were tied together. Markets, having passed a certain number of stages, could not advance very far into the next stage in response to the next innovation without some further development of the goverment. Once that further development of the government took place, markets were able to complete that stage. Similarly, innovations in the management of the government might lead to further development of the market.

Fortunately, we can understand how the chicken serves the egg, and how the egg serves the chicken, without knowledge of their beginnings. Analogously, we need not think of the government as the response to the market, nor the other way around, in order to have insights into how the government serves the market and the market serves the government.

SUMMARY

1. The government, organizations, and the market—key institutions for political economy—are multilateral in the sense of involving several or more persons in interrelated ways. This chapter is the first to take up the distinctive features of economies with opportunities for multilateral exchange.

2. In a multiperson society there are desires for certain mutual protections from intrusions and encroachments by one another, which can be seen to create opportunities for the formation of "protective associations." The competition among such associations is likely to leave only one standing, although the winner may then have to contest the territory with foreign governments that would like to extend their sovereignty. The reigning protective agency can then be seen as meeting various demands for laws, adjudication, and other collective goods—thus becoming, in every way, a government. A large range of its activities will be financed by dues, called taxes—rather than a user fee being charged whenever someone makes use of the government. One reason for that (taken up in this chapter) is the same reason that club members do not pay enough on each visit to the pool or museum, and cattlemen do not pay enough for each posse to retrieve their stolen cattle, to cover the costs (and thus prevent an operating deficit); if they did, there would be no gain from being a member of the association—they could buy the service when needed.

3. One theory of the large organization, such as a large producing enterprise, rests on the similar phenomenon of cost sharing. In an operation with only two or a few persons, the costs of supervising—monitoring and directing—may be prohibitive. But a larger organization permits these costs to be spread over a greater number of workers, and hence a bigger volume of potential output. Every organization, then, can be viewed as a protective association in which the members, or partners, seek to protect themselves from pilfering, shirking, etc. In short, there are increasing returns to scale because of *management* economies. (These are not the only large-scale economies, of course.)

4. Lastly, the chapter introduced the theory of a "market"—an inherently multilateral mechanism in which arbitrageurs and brokers play the role of linking buyers to one another, and similarly linking sellers, thus bringing all transactions into the market. An historic example of a market serving to integrate transactions is the case of triangular trade, beginning in colonial times.

5. It is noted that just as governments have prospered with the development of markets, so markets have needed the development of a helpful government to flourish. In many cses it is in the collective interest of the producers that the government intervene to protect the consumer.

CONCEPTS INTRODUCED

communal property rights	cost sharing	bilateral versus multilateral trade
private property rights	incentive pay	arbitrage
free-rider problem	barter	brokerage

STUDY QUESTIONS

1. What is the common feature—the common denominator—of the government, the market, and the organization?

2. What is the "free rider" problem in the financing of collective projects requiring scarce resources? Is the spirit of the free rider dominant in all of us or only enough of us to be a problem? Is the problem that free riding makes voluntarism uneconomic, even infeasible? Or that the risk of free riding demands monitoring one's neighbors' contributions and struggling with one's own temptation to "free ride"? Discuss.

3. Is a tax on consumer purchases coercive, or compulsory? A "tax" on the holding of government currency via inflation? Is an income tax more compulsory?

4. If governments have to extract their financing coercively, can it be that any collective project thus financed by a government would lead to expanded choice for every one of the taxpayers?

5. If an economy had just one scarce factor of production—say, labor—and had just one produced good—say, bread—and this bread was not storable, how many markets would there be in this economy? (A labor market and a goods market? Or what?) Assume to begin with that there is nothing serving as "medium of exchange"—or, more, that labor is bartered for bread and bread for labor. What if there is money?

6. "After the liberation of Europe [in 1945], the revival of intra-European trade was almost solely on the basis of bilateral payments agreements. . . . 'The central bank [of a country] supplied its own currency at a fixed rate of exchange against that of the partner up to a certain limit, called swing, which was intended to afford room for minor fluctuations in commercial deliveries.' . . . [Under] the machinery of the European Payments Union [in 1950], the Union took over all bilateral surpluses and deficits of each member. If during July 1950 Belgium ran a surplus with Britain, this would be treated as a surplus with the Union for Belgium and a deficit with the Union for Britain" (Brian Tew, *International Monetary Cooperation*, London: Hutchinson, 1967). Why was the EPU a great advance?

CHAPTER 8

Problems of Public Choice

> NORA CHARLES:
> Say, are all these things really true?
> NICK CHARLES:
> I dunno.
> NORA CHARLES:
> Then why are you saying them?
> NICK CHARLES:
> Because it's the only thing that makes sense!
>
> Myrna Loy and Wiliam Powell in *The Thin Man* (1934)

THE previous chapter dealt with a central problem in the theory of government: how a coalition within a population—a coalition of some or all the members—might find mutual gain from coercing themselves into participating in a collective action. How could anyone gain from a law coercing him or her to do more or pay more than he or she would pay voluntarily? The discussion showed the "logic" of acting collectively, even if that entails coercion, in various sorts of circumstances:

- When my fraudulent business associates cheated me there was little I could afford to do alone (besides changing associates), since prosecution was so costly. But the deterrent effect of a district attorney's office has saved me more than enough to repay my share of the cost.
- While it does not pay me to have the local clams tested at the nearby lab, I and everyone else would be glad to share the cost via taxes of government inspection of food and drugs.

The motive to act collectively is not confined to laws providing protection from others—to laws against theft, fraud, and negligence. The logic of being willing to act collectively applies wherever a law could bind people to act together.

- Left alone, I would never pick up after my dog Shag. Yet I would favor a government ordinance backed with penalties requiring me to pick up after my dog, provided this same ordinance would have the effect of making enough other dog walkers pick up after their dogs.
- The owner of the old Interborough Rapid says that, since he automated, all his costs are overhead: if he charged each rider only what the ride cost him he wouldn't collect a penny of revenue. As a user who would ride more often if the fare could be cut, I would favor the city's buying old Rapid and eliminating the fare, provided the other riders in the city share adequately with me the extra taxes necessary to compensate the owner of Rapid and his creditors for the expropriation.
- Up to a point I would be willing to pay the additional price of having a safer car—safer than what "the market" indicates people are willing to pay for—provided the other car buyers have to buy cars with the same safety features; for if all the cars on the road are safer, my insurance rates will go down more than if I alone switch to a safer car.

Thus the "logic of collective action" resolves a central paradox in the theory of government: Why may some persons in a society *welcome* being coerced into doing a thing that their individual unilateral actions did not reveal they wanted to do? Because their own coercion may be a price they are willing to pay to obtain the coercion of the others. "I'm out for myself as, I guess, the rest are. Still, I favor society's requiring me to operate under rules of the game that are just (as I see it), since the application of those rules to me (and everyone else) is necessary to getting them applied to the other people in society."

Some social theorists—the Austrian economist Friedrich Hayek dubbed them design theorists—have sought to explain the existence and functioning of the government (in any society) as the product of the "coalition" of *all* the members of society, as an institution for the gain of all. Without any government, they say, there would be economic inefficiency: Deprived of a governmental institution, we would have to go without collective actions that make all persons better off—or actions that *could* make all persons better off, at any rate. Thus government is necessary for efficiency. Perhaps the most venerable statement of this theory is the celebrated tract *Leviathan* by the seventeenth-century political philosopher Thomas Hobbes. Seeking to justify the rise of the sovereign nation-state with all its coerciveness, he posed as the alternative his famous image of a "state of nature" where people are without the devices of government:

> ... during the time men live without a common Power to keep them in awe, they are in that condition which is called Warre; and such a warre, as is of every man, against every man. ... In such condition, there is no place for Industry; because the fruit thereof is uncertain; and consequently no Culture of the Earth, no Navigation, ... no Instruments of moving, ... no Arts, no Letters, no Society; and which is worst of all, continuall feare, and danger of violent death; And the life of man, solitary, poore, nasty, brutish, and short.*

The theory that governments serve to eradicte inefficiency is better than no theory at all, but it is seriously incomplete. Even if everyone does gain from the government's total program, possibly a quite different program would have been a gain for everyone too. Further, many individual actions of the government are certainly not a gain for everyone: The Swiss social thinker Jean Charles Sismondi claimed that the laws against theft made thieves worse off. The only realistic view, then, is that collective actions serve coalitions—sometimes, though perhaps rarely, the coalition of all society.

What the theory of collective action tells us is that, in the typical society, there is room for a deal—or, since collective actions may be taken in many areas, a package of deals. But which deal or deals? There has to be some sort of bargaining, some exercise of power or principle, to determine which deals are made and at what terms. For one thing, citizens will not generally have the same preferences with regard to proposed packages of collective actions—all favoring roads over ports, orphanages over jails, etc. For another, the highest objective of any special interest group is to obtain the preferred collective action at other people's expense—the rich wanting the poor to support their airports, the poor wanting the rich to support urban renewal. The theory of collective action discussed above falls short of being a full theory of what happens in another way: Before the bargaining can begin, there has to be some mechanism by which citizens can express their interest in this or that collective action. The political institutions that represent members of society who wish to express their interest in collective actions inevitably play a role in the outcome.

---

*Thomas Hobbes, *Leviathan*, London, 1651. Ed. C. B. MacPherson (Harmondsworth: Penguin Books, Inc. 1968), pp. 185–88.

There is, thus, another chapter to the theory of government: a study of *collective choice making* by members of society having conflicting individual interests and operating within existing political institutions.

POLITICS AS USUAL: OBSTACLES TO EFFICIENT SOCIAL CHOICE

We know something about any *individual's* choice behavior, if rational. What can be said about *social* choice behavior? Here we take up the theory of social choice in its descriptive—though not uncritical—life-as-it-has-been-to-date chapter. How, it asks, are collective actions arrived at?—or not arrived at? (Clearly, collective actions *not* taken are also the subject of the theory of social choice.) And what can be said by way of an appraisal, or critique, of the results of that process?

◆ With regard to the first question, the process of social choice, it is clear that the government's decision to subsidize mail delivery or to subsidize the employment of low-paid workers is not like consumers' outlay for postage or producers' outlay of wages to low-paid workers; the latter are simply the aggregate of individual actions, while government actions are seldom reached by adding up the individual expressions of desire by the members of the society.

◆ With regard to the second question, the "goodness" of the results, it is also clear that to postulate—to suppose for the sake of argument—that society (via the government) acts rationally and invariably chooses an efficient outcome might be an untenable assumption: whether it is possible for the group to behave rationally or efficiently (or both) when the individuals comprising the political process are rational self-interested persons is an assumption needing to be confirmed or refuted.

To raise the question of the rationality, efficiency, and justice of the results of the political process might raise some eyebrows—and hackles. "What do you mean by such a question? Those in governmental authority came by their powers legitimately, didn't they? The king was legitimate heir to the throne, the legislature duly elected, the administration lawfully appointed. The methods of governmental decision making were freely chosen, weren't they? If the *process* is good, its *results* must be good." It is true, of course, that a society would be foolish to throw out a political process merely because some (or even all) or its results were less than ideal according to one or another moral judgment, since no political process can be expected to be perfect. The trouble with the statement quoted is that it mistakes procedural justice for justice overall—and procedural justice is not enough. If the only moral requirement a process had to satisfy were procedural justice, *all* political processes that passed the test of legitimacy, due process, tradition, constitutionality, and so forth would be deemed just; there would be no moral basis for rejecting any of them, no matter how wasteful or repugnant some of them might be. To ask whether the results of the political process under consideration are substantively just can be regarded as the first step in an inquiry into whether that procedurally just process might be less satisfactory, less good, than some other procedurally just process that could be adopted instead.

Absolute Rule

The simplest form of government is autocracy in the strict sense: one-man rule without any concessions or compromise. Absolute dictatorship may be likened to absolute zero in molecular physics—it can only be approximated. Yet it is instructive to consider, briefly, this "ideal type," or extreme.

If interested only in his *own* comforts and possessions—his own private goods, that is, and not the private goods of his subjects—the absolute dictator will choose those collective actions that provide him with the largest possible tax revenue to spend after expenses. With that maximum budget to allocate, the dictator can enjoy the maximum number of homes, or yachts, or vacations (from the tedium of dictating). Thus in deciding on government expenditures and subsidies the dictator's only criterion would be their effect on tax revenue net of the expense. And in setting tax rates, the dictator would be careful not to overtax, stifling with too little incentive the geese that lay the golden eggs. If also interested in certain collective goods, such as the way of life of the society, the dictator may spend some of his budget on subsidies to foster the "public interest"; possibly some tax concessions will be a convenient way to encourage the desired use of resources.

Authoritarianism need not spell totalitarianism. A despotic regime secure in its power might see that it stood to benefit from enterprises competing and innovating in the sale of goods and the hiring of talent, and from households competing for better jobs and cheaper goods; that way, very possibly, the economy will have a larger "taxable capacity," perhaps a vastly greater capacity, to fill up the treasury's coffers. (But although authoritarian regimes need not be totalitarian, in fact they tend to be. The extent to which enterprises in authoritarian countries require government permission to open or close a business is perhaps underestimated.)

Since being an autocrat can be so lucrative, the absolute ruler is a sitting duck for a coup. The hallmark of the autocratic regime, thus, is its suppression of criticism, rivals, and challenges to any part of its authority. An authoritarian government needs "security" personnel to enforce the suppression. A high level of security is often prohibitively expensive, though, especially when an external or exogenous shock causes a crisis; so the authoritarian regime can expect to be the object of peasant revolts, guerrilla attacks, military insurgencies, foreign liberation, and the rest. Pure autocracy, then, is an unstable substance.

POWER POLITICS: RULING OVER PRESSURE GROUPS

Niccolò Machiavelli, the Italian Renaissance figure, is the person we generally regard as the first sophisticated political theorist. Machiavelli saw clearly that the ruler cannot expect to be an absolute dictator but must win and maintain support in order to rule at all. Machiavelli's *The Prince* is not a manual on how to maximize tax revenue; it is a survey of the successful stratagems for staying in power. Underlying Machiavelli's analysis of political success was his modern recognition, in contrast to the vision of the ancient and medieval philosophers, of conflict between factions as a natural condition of society.

The ruler who has rivals, and who therefore must compete to stay in power, will have to "buy" sufficient political support. In the pursuit of political support, the ruler can expect to find that making concessions that are in the general interest will buy much less support (if they buy any) than concessions costing the same amount of revenue that appeal to special interests.

POLITICIAN: I will enact a general lowering of taxes and a general raising of the fight against disease and squalor, of which you and indeed all the other factions of society have complained, if in return you spurn my rivals, send your sons to the militia, and stop shooting at my tax inspectors.

PRESSURE GROUP: Ruler, if you have any intention of doing those fine things you'll do them with or without the small help that the support you seek from us would provide you. So we will play the free rider. To win our support you must do for us something that we can see you would not have done anyway, except for our support. A special favor.

Thus the various factions, each one wanting to increase its economic rent— its surplus of benefit over cost, or required compensation—will be willing to "sell" its political support only in exchange for *special interest* legislation.

What are the results of this interaction of support-seeking politicians and rent-seeking special interests? The government favors bestowed upon special interests in return for their political support are not likely at the same time to make a contribution to economic justice as anyone conceives it. The rent-seeking pressure groups that will benefit the most are those that happen to be in the best strategic positioin. A more striking point concerns economic efficiency. There will be a *loss of efficiency if* the special favors to special interests are not straightforward, fixed payments for "services rendered." And there are, in fact, two obstacles to "lump sum" payments to interest groups:

- The government may have no way of identifying the persons who are music lovers, airplane travelers, dressmakers, and so on in order to buy their support except by undertaking actions causing these groups to *select themselves* by stepping forward to take advantage of the government's generosity—subsidies to televised concerts, subsidies to airport operations, tariffs protecting against importation of foreign-made dresses, etc. Thus the government in dispensing favors will often use this method of *self-selection*.

- The government does not want to be seen as offering a public dole to any particular subgroup within the nation, nor does the group wish to be seen as receiving such a dole, because it would incite other groups to demand the same dole—so the dole would end up having to be spread thin over the populace, too thin to achieve its purpose of buying the original group's support. The government prefers productive-seeming programs that have the *latent function* of providing favors. A merchant marine to benefit domestic ship builders and military bases to boost local interests are classic examples.

As a result of these considerations, the buying of support from one or more pressure groups tends to use up resources or divert resources in the process. The government buys the interest group's output or subsidizes its sale to other groups who would not otherwise buy it.

In recent years another source of inefficiency arising from pressure-group politics has been noted. Pressure groups and individual enterprises not only invite the government to aid them in wasteful ways. In actively seeking higher rents for themselves they directly waste resources of their own in the process.

- An industry need not wait for the ruling group in power to notice the latest opportunity for a political deal. The industry can organize a lobby to attempt to persuade legislators and bureaucrats of the mutual advantages of certain special interest legislation in the form of government investments, subsidization, and import protection for the benefit of the industry. Likewise, an enterprise can lobby the government for the award of a government contract. Although large amounts of resources may be spent in these activities, no output is produced that way—only some information that could generally be made available to the government with less expense.

- Often the government benefits that an organization can obtain depend upon its scale in some respect. Thus a private or city-owned hospital may increase the number of its beds in order to win a larger share of aid from the central government. As all hospitals adopt this ploy, there may very well result an excess of beds in all hospitals.

Thus the vying for government benefits by rent-seeking private interests tends to result in a wasteful duplication of efforts and investments.

It is quite possible, as a consequence, that every faction in society will receive government favors—morsels from the public pork barrel—providing some amount of benefit (measured by what people would pay to keep those favors) in return for its support of the government (which may very well cost it nothing); yet at the same time, every faction's benefit from the pork barrel could be *less* than the cost to it of its tax contribution to the barrel. Because the factions all find it politically risky or infeasible simply to receive their favors in the form of tax refunds, each is induced to accept instead its share of the pork barrel despite the low benefit per unit cost. *Each faction, acting unilaterally, would be irrational to turn down the "pork barrel projects" offered to it* in return for its support, since there is no way of "trading in" the pork barrel items for a lump-sum payment (of the same cost) with which to buy bread and circus. *But if all factions were to refuse* offers from the pork barrel, the ruler would find it feasible out of his savings to institute a general reduction of tax rates—even lump-sum payments to everybody—that would generate benefits worth every bit of what they cost the ruler (in lost tax revenues); *then all the factions would receive a larger benefit,* at no extra cost to the ruler, *than the pork barrel projects offered.*

> The opportunity for a mutual gain from *everyone's* somehow agreeing to refuse the porkbarrel (and demand general tax relief instead), and the "hitch" standing in the way, is captured thus:
>
> | benefit obtained by a faction from *its own* refusal of the pork barrel (via the *general* tax relief that would result) | < | cost, or benefit fore-gone, to the faction from *its own* refusal | < | benefit to the faction from its refusal *and* the other factions' similar refusal at the same time (via the resulting general tax relief) |
> |---|---|---|---|---|

The conclusion, then, is that the political equilibrium that results from the separate striving of benefit-seeking pressure groups for special favors from the power-seeking government suffers from inefficiency—it fails to possess efficiency in the ideal sense. For if only the factions would all forgo those favors, and the ruler would pay back the savings in the form of tax rate reductions or general subsidies that were worth at least what they cost the ruler, all would be better off and the ruler no worse off.

> This conclusion, the paradox that everyone's quest for self-advantage works to the disadvantage of all—this time through the mechanism of the pork barrel—is illustrated by the now-familiar Dilemma Game in Figure 8–1.

Human knowledge, though, is fallible. The above conclusion derives from a model, however informal a model, of political life—and no model can be guaranteed to have "thought of everything." A whole career could be spent

FIGURE 8—1: The Dilemma of Two Factions Tempted by the Ruler's Pork Barrel

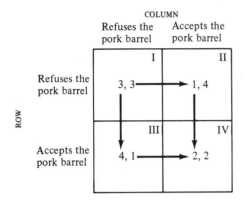

The first number in a cell indicates the rank score of the corresponding outcome for Row, the player playing the rows. The worst outcome is scored 1, the next worst 2, and so on. The second number in a cell records the rank score of the associated outcome for Column, the player deciding between the columns.

For the faction labeled Row, cell III with its score of 4 ranks higher than cell I, which scores 3, and cell IV ranks higher than cell II. Hence a play of the game by rational decision makers would not result in either cell I or cell II. The reason is that the player called Row can gain from evading any social compact aimed at achieving cell IV no matter which decision has been made by Column.

For the faction named Column, cell II ranks higher than cell I and cell IV ranks above cell III. Hence a play of the game would not result in the outcome of either cell I or cell III. This reflects the gain to Column from evading certain terms of the contract given whichever decision has been reached by Row. (Because evading is preferred in all cases, that decision is a dominant strategy for Column—and likewise for Row.)

If these self-seeking players were to make the rational decisions, therefore, the result could only be the outcome represented by cell IV. (Neither player could intelligently expect cell I, and if Column expected cell II or if Row expected cell III—perhaps under the misimpression that his partner was a different sort of fellow from himself—he would be disappointed. Hence cell IV is the equilibrium in the sense of correct expectations.)

The paradox is that this outcome is worse for both than the one in cell I. It may also be worse for both than the outcome from avoiding the game.

fielding, and perhaps sometimes bobbling, the many what if's that could be fired:

Q: What if the factions convened to draw up a social compact that would make the pork barrel unconstitutional?

A: They might be unable to reach such an agreement, for if the members of society have no widely shared conception of justice they may find themselves unable to agree on how to divide the gains from the constitutional bar.

Q: What if, nevertheless, the factions did agree to declare pork barrel projects unconstitutional? Maybe their differences over justice were not huge, or some of them were apparently willing to swallow injustice as they saw it.

A: There is still the free-rider problem, especially if some factions feel unjustly treated by the deal that was made when all pork barrel projects were banned. As with disarmament agreements, there would have to be policing of the agreement. Enforcing the agreement might be prohibitively costly.

Q: But what if the costliness of monitoring, etc. happens in fact to be low?

A: Then we would still run up against the difficulty that a law making the pork barrel illegal would be too vague to be enforceable. The manifest intention of subsidies to merchant vessels is to have a shipping capacity in the event of war. But perhaps that rationale masks the true purpose—the latent intention to provide the shipping interests with special favors in return for their political support of the government in power.

Some of the worst abuses in the campaign for political support may be preventable with the glare of publicity brought by an opposition political party—or by a free press, the security of which is dependent upon the existence of such opposition. But the opposition party, being unable to win power yet, is not in a position to enforce purity by the party in power.

If to abolish the inefficiency caused by the pork barrel the government is required to allocate its public projects "fairly," through a competitive process to select the beneficiary, the inefficiency springs up again from a new source. Under the good-ol' pork barrel system, a town, say, would be designated the site of some desirable government operation—a sports complex or a research laboratory or whatever—without incurring any costs for the favor, other than loyally supporting the government in the future if it wants to keep the operation there. But if the award of the government facility is to be determined by an open competition among towns on the basis of their apparent suitability and perhaps their persuasiveness, one or more towns will be led to spend resources (or promise to do so) in order to enhance their suitability for the award and to persuade the government of their suitability. To obtain a benefit for which each of the towns would have paid 100 pesetas, every one of the towns may have incurred lobbying costs of 20, and the winning town may have had to promise to pay another 40 if awarded the government facility. In the aggregate, the costs incurred by the competing towns may entirely eat up the benefit. The fair and open competition for the various government awards by "rent-seeking" pressure groups may prove to be a source of inefficiency: Were the towns able to cooperate, to act together, they could have reduced their costs without diminishing the benefit.

DEMOCRATIC METHODS: MAJORITY RULE

A democracy, of course, decides a great deal of the actions of the government by vote—a representative democracy by vote of the citizens' representatives. What kinds of actions may be decided by vote are circumscribed in the articles of the constitution, or some equivalent tradition. The selection of the representatives is itself determined by a popular election. Usually legislation is required to pass by a simple majority; the same is true of votes of confidence ratifying the party in office under the parliamentary system. Often elections to office may be won by a plurality; in a two-party system, however, a plurality is a majority.

Election for office when there are just two candidates and just one issue is a predictable and straightforward story. One of the candidates wins, and the gist of the winning strategy is clear enough. The voters can be ranked according to how far to the "left" or "right" each one stands on the issue. If one of the candidates were to adopt an extreme position—appealing to the right, say—the other candidate could take a less extreme position and thereby capture the middle voters and all those at the other extreme, hence a majority. Anticipating this, the former candidate will optimally attempt to stake out the center, as best the candidate can estimate it. Like two gasoline stations that locate next to one another on a stretch of highway, the two candidates are led to squeeze together at the political center.

THE SWING VOTING OF THE MIDDLE VOTER

This "model" of political election does not explain why there are just two parties, and just one issue. But it does offer insight into why in a two-party system the parties are not perceived as being radically different, and why when one party loses administrative office and a majority in the legislature there is seldom a radical shift in administration policy and legislation. In particular, it offers some insight into how democratic societies determine the redistribution of income from high-income to low-income receivers. If a candidate proposed so high a tax rate that, despite the governmental subsidies and public projects that would result, many of which would benefit everyone, the *middle voters* would lose on balance, then that candidate would be vulnerable to a winning strategy by the opposing candidate—namely, cut tax rates.

The swing-voter model applies in an interesting case: people care only about taxation, *and* a single tax rate is to be chosen—a flat proportional tax of 1, or 2, or 3, . . . percent on all income of certain kinds. By implication, the way the tax revenue collected will be spent has already been determined somehow—on public education, say, or subsidies to raise the rewards available to low-paid workers. Then voters whose incomes (net of any subsidy) were tiny would figure that the benefit to them from a higher tax rate would outweigh the tax cost to them—as long as a higher tax rate resulted in increased tax revenue collected. At the other extreme, voters whose incomes were gigantic would figure that the benefit to them, if any, from a higher tax rate would always be less than the tax cost to them.

This standard result in the theory of elections contains an important truth: Voters whose views are extreme on an issue of great interest to all voters will have little influence compared to the voters who are in the "middle of the road." The party of the "left" on the issue need not bend its platform to please left-wing extremists, because they have nowhere else to go—their only threat is to abstain, while the voters in the middle threaten to swing the election to the party of the right if the former party is too far to the left for their taste. But the further result—that the voter or voters precisely in the middle of the voting population will determine the platform of the winning party—is a result deriving from very special assumptions: *if* there is a single issue on which voters are divided, and *if* there are just two candidates, *then* the median voter calls the tune. The great issue of economic justice in the structure of rewards does not reduce to a single matter.

Special Interest Voting by "Single Issue" Voters

It is clear, to take a fundamental example, that the matter of "economic justice"—the choice of the structure of rewards in society, and all that— does not boil down to a single issue. Where there are two or more types of income, there is not just *one* tax to be determined; there are as many taxes to be determined as there are types of income that are taxable. Suppose that the two election issues are the size of the proportional tax rate to be applied to wage-type income *and,* in addition, the size of the proportional tax rate to be applied to interest-type income—and that, up to a point, an increase of either tax rate makes possible an increase of some governmental service, like anti-poverty programs, that are generally welcomed. It is clear, in that situation, that the middle voter does not necessarily exist: The voter who stands in the middle on the question of the wage-income tax rate may be somewhat extreme on the question of the interest-income tax rate, and vice versa.

Similarly, where there are two or more ways to spend tax revenue, there is not just one total-spending decision to be made—there are as many decisions as there are types of spending. Again, it is quite possible that there is no voter who stands in the middle on every issue. Voters, like the doughnut, do not require a center.

Just for fun, consider the example of a collection of voters who cluster into three groups: liberals, leftists, and rightists. The leftists want high taxes and big government spending on health, education, and other "welfare" programs. The liberals want high taxes too but favor a smaller government that turns back the tax revenue to low-income individuals (and maybe community governments) in the form of subsidies and transfer payments and subsidies to low-wage employment. The rightists, finally, want low taxes as well as low government expenditures. These contrasting preferences are depicted in the diagram to the left. Farthest out from the origin are the leftists. Directly below them are the liberals, since they want the same tax revenue collected but want lower welfare-type spending than the leftists do. Directly west of the liberals are the rightists; like the leftists, they want tax revenue spent on "welfare," such as social security for the old and disabled, not "redistribution"—but they want much less of such spending (and therefore lower taxes) than the leftists do.

In this situation, assume one of the candidates were to announce a position on how much tax revenue to raise and how much welfare-spending to do (with the balance going for redistribution) that was *equidistant* from the three polar opinions—the position indicated by *a* in the diagram. Would the other candidate then find it best to adopt the same central position—to stand likewise at *a*, smack in the center of the triangle? Of course not! The latter candidate could do better by moving northeast to steal away the votes of both the leftists and the liberals—if the latter groups together make up a majority. Similarly, by moving southwest that candidate could do better if rightists and liberals together outnumber the leftists; and if leftists and rightists outnumber the liberals, the latter candidate could do better by taking a position northwest of the former candidate. We see, therefore, that it would be a mistake for either candidate to stake out a position in the center. To do so would leave the opponent with a winning strategy—perhaps two or even three winning strategies.

What is the position that the first-mentioned candidate should adopt so as to avoid certain defeat?

Rather than pretend when thinking about election contests that there is only one issue dividing the voters, it would be just as useful to imagine that political reality is at the other extreme: Every voter has one particular interst—an interest that is special, or unique, to himself or herself—and one interest that is general, common to all. For example, every voter might prefer the candidate that promises the lower tax rate—provided the two candidates score equally on the matter of special interest to him or her. There is a general interest, then, in having a lower cost of government, other things being equal. At the same time, if the two candidates do not differ or differ sufficiently little) on the tax rate, the dairyman will vote for whichever candidate promises the larger subsidy to the consumption of milk, the working parent will vote for whichever candidate promises the larger subsidy for use of day-care centers, the biochemist will vote for the candidate promising the larger subsidy to biochemical research, and so on. Note that not all producers are dairy farmers, or working parents, or biochemists; so any such subsidy will benefit the recipient more than the recipient's share in the resulting tax cost. What will happen in this electoral setting?

Will both candidates, in that setting, hope to ride to victory on a platform of no subsidies and (accordingly) a zero rate of tax? Not likely! It is likely that each candidate will attempt to "buy" a majority of the voters with promises of support for their respective special interests. Each voter will be wiling to "sell" his or her vote in return for the subsidy (or whatever the special interest requires); for the individual voter will understand that the effect of the special subsidy on the general tax rate will be too small to eliminate the gain. To be sure, the candidate who appeals to half or more of the special interests of the voters may be readily identified as a big spender, since tax revenue will have to be raised to pay for the promised subsidies. But as long as the candidate's capture of each additional voter necessary to compile a majority does not increase the tax rate so much as to leave the voters previously captured ready to revolt in favor of no taxes and no subsidies, the candidate will be driven to pursue his quest of buying up a majority of the votes. Thus the election may go to the candidate who is first to "purchase," at the expense of the voters' tax bill, a majority of special interest voters.

Thus the competition of candidates for a majority of special interest voters invites the same factionalism, the same rule of the pork barrel, discussed earlier. It is quite possible that each voter who sold his vote would be willing to buy it back *if doing so would compel the others who sold their votes to do the same.* The tax costs saved would exceed the benefit lost—for every voter.

We have been examining the process of election to office by majority vote. We have found that in one respect the outcome of the process—namely, the feature of vote buying—leaves something to be desired. Of course, such an analysis would be of little significance if the voters, having spent their votes, always found to their surprise that the goods were not delivered—that the promises made were worthless as guides to the actions the government would take. In fact, however, the voters often know pretty well what they are voting for.

- In a legislative system of the American type, the voter understands that victory of one presidential candidate over another will make more likely certain legislative initiatives and vetoes by the president as well as certain moves and policies that are within the discretion of the executive branch of government.
- In a parliamentary system such as the British and the Canadian, voters have an idea of the agenda of legislation that will be enacted by each of the contending parties in the event it wins a majority of the seats in the parliament.

On the other hand, much legislation in a democracy is decided not by a monolithic majority party (nor by a monolithic presidency) that is of one mind on every issue but, rather, by majority voting among many legislators of varied opinions or representing diverse regional interests. In addition, some legislation is decided by majority voting on popular referendums submitted directly to the citizens themselves. Understanding the process of legislation by majority vote—the process by which proposals, rather than candidates, are voted up or down—is therefore part of any understanding of how democracies work.

LEGISLATING BY MAJORITY RULE

When there is the possibility—with perfect social management, at any rate—of a mutual gain for three or more groups, it may nevertheless be that decision making by majority rule will stand in the way of realizing any such mutual gain. It was noted earlier, in chapter 5, that even in the simplest of bargaining situations, the bilateral case, a possibility for mutual gain may fail to materialize because of conflicting judgments or pride on the part of the bargainers. That an impasse may occur when there are three or more persons, or groups, engaged in making a decision is also true. Committees, legislatures, groups are famous for being *unable to make up their collective minds*—because they haven't any. Still, manifestations of the difficulty, when they come along, do not lose their capacity to surprise and annoy.

Imagine that members of the Dutch legislature contemplate the creation of a national opera house. Where to put it? A bill to locate the new house in Amsterdam would be defeated by a majority coalition of partisans from Rotterdam or The Hague who want the house in their home city. Similarly, a bill to build the house in The Hague would be voted down by Amsterdamers and Rotterdamers, while a bill to locate it in Rotterdam would be blocked by Amsterdam and The Hague. Thus it can happen, as the example shows, that no national opera house is constructed—even if, as is possible, every member of the legislature would rather have an opera house in *any* of the three cities than not have it at all.

The above example is fiction, inspired by the impression that Holland has no national opera house. But whether fictional or factual, advanced students of political decision theory will argue that the example is too simple to capture the requisite reality. The example tells us simply that in the preference ranking of the A group (such as the Amsterdam contingent) the outcome *a* (such as the opera house in Amsterdam) ranks first, and the other two outcomes, *b* and *c,* are tied for second. The B group ranks outcome *b* first, and ranks *a* and *c* second. The C group ranks *c* first, *a* and *b* second. This information is tabulated below in the standard format. The only other information is that the three groups are more or less equal in number.

	A	*B*	*C*
a	1st	2nd	2nd
b	2nd	1st	2nd
c	2nd	2nd	1st

The example omits the information that (presumably) the various groups also like other things besides opera. If that is so, might not the Rotterdamers, say, bribe one of the other groups to vote with them on a bill to locate the opera house in Rotterdam? Amsterdam, say, could "trade" its votes on the opera in exchange for Rotterdam's yes-votes on something—improved port facilities, say—that was likewise blocked by a majority vote. In fact, such vote trading, or "log rolling," does often happen; an opportunity for a trade of votes may arise that serves to break the impasse (to break the logjam). But it is *not* a sure thing that there will exist opportunities for vote trading. Scholars in game theory point to the elementary case of three persons (or cities) trying to divide a billion dollars among them. No solution to that classic game exists!

When each one of several options, all desirable, is unable to command a majority of the vote, the result is not always an impasse. The result may be the adoption of some compromise proposal that is generally preferred to an impasse but which is possibly inferior to each of the original options—inferior in everyone's preference ranking. Imagine the Brazilian legislature deciding anew on the seat of government back in the 1950s. The prime options might have been São Paulo, the rising business center, or Rio, which was the capital, or Salvador in the northeast, which was the first capital city. If any pair of these coastal cities could have blocked selection of the third as the nation's capital, the best solution—better than no solution, which would have been untenable—might have been to compromise by inventing and selecting a new option: a site in the interior, to be named Brasilia. (Imaginably, the founders of the European Economic Community, the so-called Common Market, faced a similar problem in deciding on the location of the new organization: not Milan or Rome, obviously, because of French and German opposition; and not any French or German city either for reasons of Italo-German or Franco-Italian resistance. Therefore Brussels.)

Quite another defect afflicts majority decision making when the members of the group are not indifferent to the options they do not prefer. Imagine that the citizens of Zurich, say, can build a youth center or an opera house or save the expense. The good burghers fall neatly into three groups—each of which is a minority, so any two of them is large enough to constitute a majority of the citizenry. One of these groups, the A group, prefers the youth center to the opera house and the opera house to saving the money. Another group, the B group, prefers the opera house to saving the money and prefers saving the money to building a youth center. There is, lastly, the C group, which prefers avoiding the tax expense to having the youth center and prefers the youth center to the opera house. We could think of the A group as hippies, the B group as well-off bourgeoisie, and the C group as skinflints who would like to see the kids off the streets; but just who they are, and what their motives are, do not figure in the point that the example makes.

It goes without saying here that a person who prefers x to y and prefers y to z also prefers x to z. That property of preferences is called transitivity. Obviously, comparisons commonly have that property: If Rio is hotter than Los Angeles and Los Angeles is hotter than Toronto, then Rio is hotter than Toronto—heat relations are transitive. On the other hand, if Navratilova can beat Shriver and Shriver can beat Evert, it may or may not be that Navratilova can beat Evert—there is no guarantee of transitivity there. The very same thing is true of majority decision making by a group, as will be shown.

Now a remarkable implication can be developed: Note first that if there were to be a referendum on whether to build an opera house, and if no one had any prospect of any future referendums on anything else that might be built instead (in the event the opera house was voted down), the A group would add their votes to the B group in favor of building the opera house.

That follows from the information that both the A and B groups prefer the opera house to saving the tax expense; to them the opera house is worth the tax expense—their share of the expense, at any rate. So, if such a referendum were to take place, the opera house would carry by a majority vote— over the opposition of the expense-conscious C group.

But note also that if instead there were to be a referendum on whether to build a youth center *or* an opera house, and no one had any prospect of being able in the future to vote against both, the C group would add their voices to the B group in favor of building the youth center. That follows from the information that both of these groups would rather have a youth center than an opera house. So, in such a referendum, the youth center would carry by a majority vote—over the opposition of the elegant B group.

Does it follow from this information that the "will of the people"—or, at any rate, the "will of the majority"—is to build the youth center? It is tempting to conclude that, for if the community would choose by majority rule the opera house over saving the money and choose the youth center over the opera house, wouldn't the community choose by a majority the youth center over saving the money? *If* so, and if it is all right to decide these matters by majority rule, we could then say that either project, the opera house or the youth center, is "preferable" to saving the expense, and of the two projects the youth center is the "preferred" one! But the argument will not work. It trips over its key assumption before it has gotten to first base. The assumption that if a community would choose b over c by a majority and choose a over b then it would choose a over c is indefensible. It is not necessarily true that the community would choose a over c. The Zurich example is proof of that: If there were to be a referendum on whether to build the youth center or save the money, the youth center would *not* win a majority of the votes. The B group, who least wanted a youth center, would cast their votes with the C group, who most wanted to save the tax expense, in favor of saving the money.

Some students of voting problems, and problems of social choice in general, like to see the logical structure of the problem—to see the problem divorced from the "local color" of the particular example. Never mind poignant pictures of Zurich burghers trooping to the operas of Richard Strauss! To write down the logical structure of the example, do the following. Let the three options confronting the community be denoted a, b, and c. Let a be the option ranked highest by the voters belonging to the faction A, b be the option favored by those belonging to B, and c be the top-ranked option for those in group C. Letting 1st denote the highest-rank option, 2nd the second rank, and 3rd the third, we may then summarize the entire preferences of each of the groups by the tabulation directly below. In addition, the example contains the information that either pair of groups—but neither group alone—is enough to constitute a majority. In our example, *a* is the youth activities center, the favorite of the youth activist A's, *b* is the opera house dreamed of by the bourgeois B's, and C is saving the tax expense of both.

	A	B	C
a	1st	3rd	2nd
b	2nd	1st	3rd
c	3rd	2nd	1st

Another way to tabulate the information about preferences is to record the rank order of the options for each group, A, B, and C, in a separate column for each of these groups. Such a tabulation is shown below. The column under the heading A indicates that voters in that group prefer *a* to *b* and *b* to *c*. The old skinflints prefer *c* to *a* and *a* to *b,* as shown by the column under C. It is especially easy to see, on inspecting this matrix of rank orderings, that proposal *b* would beat *c* and that *a* would beat *b* and that—the paradox—*c* would beat *a*.

A	B	C
a	c	b
b	a	c
c	b	a

Of course, this sort of tabular formation, with its abstract notation, has the advantage that one can see why one sort of example (such as the Zurich example) gives rise to the paradox that no proposal can survive a run-off against some other proposal, while another sort of proposal does not. Also, the use of such matrices facilitates the analysis of larger problems with many proposals and groups of voters.

This famous result is devastating to the idea that a society might rely on majority rule, could appeal to the "will of the majority," in deciding public questions. The paradox just analyzed shows that it is not really a coherent idea. How do we know, in any particular problem to be decided, that there *is* a will of the majority? In the Zurich example, no will of the majority exists: "the" majority depends on *the either-or choice* (the referendum) *being made.* There is a *cycle* from one majority to a second to a third as the either-or choice moves from pair to pair of alternatives. (When *b* is preferred to *c* by one majority, and *a* is preferred to *b* by a distinct majority, the *former* majority need not prefer *a* to *b* and the *latter* majority prefer *b* to *c*. No wonder, then, that there may fail to be a majority that prefers *a* to *c*, that some coalition drawn from the two aforementioned majorities may actually prefer *c* to *a*.) Consequently, when a community is deciding on some public question—such as whether to do *a* or *b* or neither—there is no guarantee *that there exists a will of the majority* that could be used to decide the question.

People's reactions to this paradox—called Condorcet's paradox of voting—commonly fall into a familiar pattern. "Yes, I see the possibility of what you call 'cycling', but isn't it a rarity in real life to find a case in which a majority prefers *b* to *c*, another majority prefers *a* to *b*, and a third majority prefers *c* to *a*? In most cases, the C group, for example, might prefer *b* to *a*, not *a* to *b* as in the Zurich example." The first thing that scholars of social choice say in answer to that reaction is that no society can be altogether content to operate by majority rule once it understands that some of the time no majority exists and a series of votes would produce "crazy" cycling—especially if society does not know beforehand whether the problem coming up is one of those times. Furthermore, it may be answered, the instances where cycling would result from a series of votes are not rare at all. Whenever we have a first prize, a second prize, and a third prize to be allotted to three individuals, any allotment *c* can be defeated in majority voting by an allotment *b* that awards to the second prize winner under *c* the first prize and awards to the third prize winner under *c* the second prize; but so likewise can the allotment *b* be defeated by the allotment *a* under which the new first-prize winner under *b* is demoted to third prize and the other two individuals move up; but, then, by the same reasoning, it can be seen that the allotment *a* could be defeated in majority voting by the original allotment *c*. Who can doubt that there are myriad public-expenditure decisions to be made in any society that have this paradoxical cycling feature? And tax decisions too.

The other common reaction is: "In the real world, we seldom see a series of votes taken, There wouldn't actually be a second vote on whether to build a youth center instead of an opera house; one project or the other would appear on a single referendum." But *no* project may appear on the referendum if there occurs a stalemate among the rival factions, each one allying with a second faction to block the third faction from getting *its* proposal on a referendum.

In reality, it does not appear that any society operates entirely by majority rule. The "paradox of voting" that we have been discussing helps to explain why. If majority rule were applied comprehensively, a society might find itself *voting indefinitely*—*b* versus *c*, *a* versus *b*, *c* versus *a*, *b* versus *c* again, and so on—on many social questions. Or *never voting at all* due to jockeying for position by each faction. No wonder, then, that even the most democratic societies generally operate on the basis of some higher rule. The higher rule, or overriding factor, determines *which* either-or choice there shall be majority voting on—whether it shall be *b* versus *c,* or *a* versus *b,* or *c* versus *a.* A group that is more powerful, skillful, or dedicated than other groups may succeed in engineering the two-way choice to be voted upon in its favor. In parliamentary bodies, there are procedural rules, like Robert's Rules of Order, that facilitate regulating and limiting the votes that can be taken. A democratic society avoids chaotic fluctuations and indecisive paralysis in its legislating actions by operating on principles that override majority rule.

◆ Majority rule is not generally workable in any society. Some societies avoid the "irrational" fluctuations to which group decision making is prone by operating on a system that determines when majority voting may be used and when it may not. One way or another, the political power of existing groups or the political force of prevailing moral ideas operates to determine *which* majority (among the many different majorities) shall have its way on each public question.

SUMMARY

1. According to the logic of rational collective choice, introduced in chapter 7, each member of a coalition, or club, within a population may favor being coerced into paying a cost toward some benefit—a cost none would choose to pay if acting in isolation—because it is a "price" that each is willing to pay for coercing the rest to pay a similar cost and thus obtaining a much larger benefit that does repay one's own cost (or contribution). If by contributing I would bind the others to contribute similarly, then and only then would the benefit exceed my cost; and the same for the others in the coalition—so it pays us to act *collectively,* multilaterally, though not necessarily individually, or unilaterally. But in reality a coalition often cannot be assessed the whole cost of the collective project that it benefits from—*all* taxpayers share in the cost. Enter politics!

2. In politics-as-usual, much of the game that a pressure group plays is getting *other* groups—the government and hence society at large—to pay for one's collective benefits.

3. The Machiavellian government is glad to bestow beneficial favors on each faction, or pressure group, in return for needed political support from the faction. There would be no loss of efficiency from this reciprocal arrangement—the left hand would receive the government's "lump-sum transfer

payment" out of the government's tax revenues while the right hand was paying lump-sum assessments to pay for such transfer payments, leaving no net effect on incentives, at least on the average (only the possibility of some injustice)—were it not for some problems. The government's favors have to be hidden in the guise of a socially worthy project—such as subsidizing the leasing or construction of nationally-owned ships on the "national security" grounds that it is good to have a nationally owned merchant fleet; a government payment to a faction, being transparently a favor, might be blocked by others. Thus these pork barrel projects offered by the government to its constituents typically bring a benefit that is *less* than the production cost. The hidden favors are, in the jargon used, not "cost-effective" in this sense. So, potentially at least, *all* citizens lose from the Machiavellian government's craven antisocial campaign for political support from the constituent factions! Here, then, are apparently "collective" actions by the government that *reduce* efficiency rather than increase it. (And they use up hard-to-raise tax revenue that could otherwise have gone to pay for public projects that promote efficiency.)

4. In contemporary democracies, where people vote on issues or elect representatives to a legislature that votes on issues, a Machiavellian government seeks people's electoral support for staying in office. There results again a tendency toward pork barrel projects that are not cost-effective. However, the political process of majority voting creates some other malfunctions in collective choice making as well.

5. When there is a single issue, the middle voter on the issue has the decisive, swing vote. (So a project might fail even though benefiting the richest enormously; or might succeed despite a crushing cost to the poor. More about the cost-benefit approach to collective decisions in the next chapter.) But if there is another issue, there may be room for vote trading.

6. When there are three options to be chosen from among by an electorate or legislature by majority rule, and the voting body falls thus into three distinct interest groups (of equal size, say), then it can happen—as in the example of the Dutch opera house—that *none* of the *three proposals wins a majority* and so none is approved, even though everyone favors *any* of the three proposals to nothing at all! (But in the example of locating Brazil's capital, they circumvent the impasse by inventing a new compromise that did not originally exist, Brasilia.)

7. When there are three options it can instead happen, if people have a second and third preference besides their first preference (if they are not indifferent, in other words, to choices other than their preferred one), that *every one of the three proposals would win a majority* and so any one of them would be approved, each in its turn! This voting paradox displays the phenomenon called cycling: A can beat C, but B can beat A, but then C can beat B, but, as seen, A can beat C.

8. For these reasons many political economists conclude that political processes alone, no matter how self-denying the politicians and how informed the voters and their representatives, are not sufficient to resolve satisfactorily the issues that arise over proposals for government action. Even high-minded politics, and procedural justice, are not enough. Hence the next chapter on cost-benefit theory and ideas about fairness in a society with government and opportunities, therefore, for multilateral action.

CONCEPTS INTRODUCED

pressure groups, or factions	lump sum payments	transitivity
absolute ruler	self-selection	will of the majority
support-seeking ruler	latent function	paradox of voting
rent seeking	middle voter	procedural justice
	special interest voter	

STUDY QUESTIONS

1. "The theory of collective action, with its compelling logic, promotes the erroneous view that all government actions are driven by the logic of collection action. Consider a government in the watchmaking business. Suppose it operates the company (sets output price, designs, etc.) with the sole objective of obtaining the maximum profit possible from the business, without a care for the punctuality of the populace. Such an operation is not a "collective action" taken to stimulate or discourage (by subsidy, tax, etc.) the use of certain watches. This proves that the theory of collective action is an incomplete theory of the scope of governmental activity." Isn't every government action for the collective benefit of the group or some subgroup? Or is the statement right?

2. Write in the empty boxes the name of some real-life countries, past or present, of which you have some knowledge.

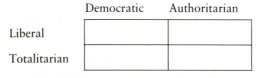

	Democratic	Authoritarian
Liberal		
Totalitarian		

3. What is the parallel between the political pork barrel and the Prisoner's Dilemma introduced in chapter 5?

4. Must a group that chooses "irrationally" be comprised of "irrational" members? Explain the fallacy there.

APPENDIX:
TRADE RESTRICTIONS AND "RENT SEEKING"
IN AN OPEN ECONOMY

The idea that, at least in a society of purely self-interested citizens, "politics" does its work imperfectly, so imperfectly that all might gain if certain ideal agreements were enforceable, has always been especially well received by observers of government legislation affecting foreign trade. Adam Smith complained that deliberations on these matters in Britain were directed by the "clamorous importunity of partial interests" rather than by "an extensive view of the general good." In the tenth of the *Federalist* papers, the one on the dangers of "faction," James Madison wrote: ". . . shall domestic manufacturers be encouraged, and in what degree, by restrictions on foreign manufacture, are questions which would be differently decided by the landed and manufacturing classes, and probably by neither with a sole regard to justice and the public good."

The history of tariffs stretches back many centuries, of course. Until the invention of better fiscal instruments, tariffs were relied upon to collect tax revenue. Perhaps they still are to a lesser degree. However, a tariff (or tariff increase) may instead have the purpose of protecting an industry from foreign competition. A tariff or tariff increase constitutes a *trade restriction* to the extent that the rate exceeds the level (perhaps zero) that would have been chosen for revenue-raising purposes alone—i.e., chosen without regard to the benefit to import-competing producers who could sell at higher prices thanks to the tariff. Likewise, quotas limiting the quantity of a good that may be imported represent a trade restriction if the purpose is not simply to obtain a lower price from foreign suppliers by purchasing less.

Even after we have thus narrowly defined the beast, there is no doubt that the beast of protectionism, in the form of restrictive tariffs and quotas, is still at large in virtually all countries.

- The recent rise of steelmaking capacity in Asia and the reentry of China into the world market has brought forth new tariff protection in Europe and North America and the introduction of "voluntary quotas" in the United States, erasing much of the trade liberalization in the 1960s and 1970s.
- Despite the elaborate treaty of the Common Market countries envisioning the elimination of protection against one another's exports, intra-European trade restrictions are now not much lighter than three decades ago, when the treaty was signed.

The age-old phenomenon of trade restrictions provides us with our most durable case study of interest-group politics.

In early thinking about interest-group legislation of trade restrictions the emphasis was at first on the influence of those groups whose wealth brought them political privilege, and later, on the effects of bloc voting. The cost to society of these trade restrictions was seen accordingly as the disincentive it placed on the consumer to buy the foreign product instead of the domestic product, which was more expensive to produce; ideally, the consumers could arrange to compensate the producers for the dismantling of the protectionist tariff and still have some gain left over—although such an arrangement would not be manageable, and thus not feasible in practice. (There is nothing wrong with this analysis, and the above chapter tends to emphasize the politician as the active player catering to various voter blocs in return for votes.)

Recent thinking about interest-group legislation, and about trade restrictions in particular, has emphasized that there is a redistribution involved: there is a transfer of rents to the factors of production engaged in the protected industry from the factors employed elsewhere (who now buy the protected product at a higher price)—not simply a loss of efficiency through disincentive effects. And the redistribution that trade restrictions create may be the germ of another kind of efficiency loss, one possibly worse than the former kind. Interest groups that see the prospect of higher rents through the imposition of a tariff will seek those rents through active promotion of the tariff while those groups who see their rents suffering as a consequence will seek to defend their rents through active opposition to the tariff. In their expenditures on lobbying and on media campaigns to sway public opinion, both sides to the conflict over the tariff absorb scarce resources, resources usable for other purposes. The value of these resources in the other uses to which they would have been put must be added when toting up the total loss of efficiency resulting from the tariff and the political process leading to it.

A simple quantitative model may serve to bring out the meaning of these ideas. Imagine that agricultural and manufacturing interests are locked in political combat over a protective tariff on imported manufactures; clearly, it would be as easy to switch to a protective quota. Americans, for example, will immediately think of the conflict between wheat farmers and auto makers; the former do not want restrictions on auto imports because it would raise the domestic price of cars and trucks to farmers and also because it would strengthen the dollar and thus lower the domestic price of wheat. (Britons will prefer to think of manufacturers' opposition to agricultural protection or the conflicting interest of the steel and coal industries over protection of the coal industry. Each country has one or more classic conflicts of this sort.) The political effort per year of the manufacturing interests, measured in units of labor, is denoted N_m; the corresponding effort of the agricultural interests is denoted N_a. The size of the prevailing tariff, given the political structure of the society, is a function of these two opposing efforts: An increase of N_m succeeds in raising the tariff, given N_a, while an increase of N_a succeeds in lowering the tariff. The other key feature of the model is the nature of the reaction of each interest group to the other: Agricultural interests increase N_a when they expect an increased N_m and thus a higher tariff; similarly, manufacturing interests intensify their N_m when they expect an increased N_a and thus a lower tariff. And each side's increased effort is some fraction of the increase expected from the other side. The problem to be solved in this model is the determination of these expenditures of resources and, if possible, the size of the resulting tariff.

The implications of the model can best be understood by reference to an illustrative scenario: Imagine that manufacturing interests catch the agricultural interests by surprise, so that N_m is at first pushed up to some positive level, N_m^o, while N_a is equal to zero; so a tariff results. But next year the agricultural interests, if they expect the level of N_m to be repeated, will react by making a positive political effort, indicated by some level of N_a greater than zero, to reduce the tariff (though they will not find it worthwhile to go to the effort to drive the tariff to zero); we may imagine that this reaction catches the manufacturers by surprise. Then, in the following year, the manufacturing interests, expecting the level of N_a to be repeated, react by stepping up their efforts (though not by so much as to restore the tariff to the first level). Where does it all end? The scenario has the two parties marching toward the *equilibrium* state—an equilibrium of correct expectations in which neither interest group is surprised by the size of the other group's opposing political effort: The agricultural interests correctly forecast N_m and the manufacturing interests correctly forecast N_a. How can we prove that the scenario converges toward this equilibrium? Since each group's expectation of the other group's N is equal to its value in the previous period, and each group reacts by increasing its own N by some fraction of the increase in the other group's N, each group's own N increases by only a fraction of the previous increase in the other group's N; so the increments in N_a and N_m become smaller and smaller, vanishing with time.

The diagrammatics of the convergence to equilibrium that is a feature of this illustrative scenario is shown in Figure 8A–1.

Of course, there are other ways in which each group might form its forecast of the other group's political effort. But even though the "players" developed different (perhaps more accurate) ways of forecasting the moves of the other side in the "game," it is quite possible that their actions would gravitate toward the aforementioned equilibrium—more quickly or slowly, as the case may be.

What can be said about the equilibrium size of the tariff in relation to what it would have been without the political efforts of the special interests? Is the equilibrium tariff larger than the lobby-free level? Clearly the lobby-

FIGURE 8A–1: The Equilibrium Levels of Lobbying over a Protective Tariff by Two Interest Groups

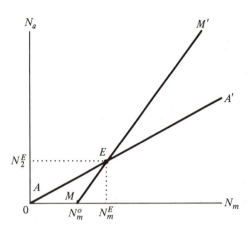

The horizontal axis measures the amount of lobbying, N_m, done by manufacturing interests for a restrictive tariff. The vertical axis measures the lobbying, N_a, against the tariff by agricultural interests.

The curve AA' describes how N_a reacts to any level of N_m that is expected. The curve MM' shows the reaction of N_m to the expected level of N_a. These curves are called reaction curves.

The equilibrium is determined by the intersection of the two reaction curves. At this intersection point, E, each side is acting exactly as anticipated by the other side in choosing its own action.

ing of the two interest groups has the net effect of *increasing* the tariff, according to the model as constructed here. When the manufacturing interests start to lobby, and increase the tariff, the agricultural interests do not counterlobby sufficiently to repeal the tariff; their defensive reaction is only enough to lessen the damage, in view of the costs of lobbying. After the manufacturing interests send lobbying reinforcements, restoring the tariff part of the way, the agricultural interests counterlobby only enough to lessen the restoration. And so on. It follows that the tariff is never set back, as the agricultural interests succeeding in reducing it on their first try, before the manufacturers renewed their attack. The equilibrium tariff is therefore *above* the no-protection level, which may be positive or zero depending on whether or not some tariff rate would be considered a good sort of tax to use (alongside other taxes) in raising the government's revenue. But note that if, contrary to the original model, the agricultural interests lobby for a tariff *cut* or a *subsidy* on manufactured imports (so $N_a > 0$ even when $N_m = 0$), it is then possible that the result is a *decreased* tariff or an outright subsidy on the importation of manufacture.

CHAPTER 9

Justifying Collective Actions:
Proposed Constitutional Principles

GILLIS:
You used to be in pictures. You used to be big.
NORMA:
I *am* big. It's the pictures that got small.

Gloria Swanson and William Holden in *Sunset Boulevard* (1950)

PROBABLY no one, on mature reflection, thinks that whatever any government does is for the best. "If the government chooses *a* over *b* it must be that *a* is socially better than *b*." A *person's* dealings with another *person* are not usually taken as being beyond criticism, after all. When two or more persons, acting collectively through the institution of a government, seem to be ganging up on a third person, making use of the coercive powers of the government to gain an advantage, the governmental action in question is no less open to scrutiny. (It is no answer to say that the business partner could go elsewhere, or the citizen could find another country. Maybe he or she does not know things are better there, or maybe things are just as bad—which does not make it more acceptable.) The collective actions undertaken by a government must be justified. Every such action ought to pass some sort of test, to adhere to certain constitutional principles; if it fails it is wrong—unjustified.

One kind of principle on which governments often act is simply procedural. Majority voting in particular, and voting methods in general, are examples of procedures by which governments often decide questions of collective action. The decisions thus reached, if every vote is fairly conducted, possess a kind of justice called procedural justice. But majority rule and other voting methods are fundamentally flawed, as the previous chapter illustrated. We have learned that to say "*a* must be socially better than *b* if *a* was chosen over *b* by *majority rule*—or it would have been had a vote been taken" is to risk a contradiction: it would in some cases imply that *b* must be socially better than *c,* and *a* socially better than *b,* so presumably *a* is also better than *c,* yet *c* socially better than *a*—an absurdity. Voting methods certainly cannot promise economic efficiency or collective rationality.

Besides, it is not a tenet of any political doctrine in the world that the will of the majority would be an altogether desirable basis for social choice anyway—assuming for the sake of argument that a rational will of the majority exists on the social question at hand. Clearly, what is good for the welfare of the majority need not be good for the welfare of everyone—or for the welfare of society, whatever our conception of social welfare or economic justice. In the succinct words of one welfare economist: "Unfortunately, . . . groups do not frequently make unanimous choices . . . [and] we are interested in the welfare of the whole group, not just the majority."*

To those whose notions of social justice place importance on individuals' rights, the inadequacy of majority will as a justification for any government action is obvious; it follows from first principles. There have been whole countries—the United States, for one—founded to establish and defend certain rights of individuals against the tyranny of sundry majorities. The classical liberalism that grew up in the eighteenth-century Enlightenment and which still survives is essentially the advocacy of certain individual liberties from governmental and quasi-governmental authority. Today, the term "liberal" in America frequently designates the advocacy of the creation of governmental and other institutions to promote human development—not a contradiction of the earlier idea of basic liberties, though an idea distinct from it. ("Of what use are the various civil liberties to a man if society does not provide education, protect health, and make other investments in human capital that would permit him to make use of his liberties?") And, everywhere, the term "libertarian" has come to designate ideas stressing the eighteenth-century notion of individual rights against the state. Whether we call it liberalism or libertarianism, the idea is the same: Might does *not* make right—nor does the sheer numerical superiority of one group of citizens over another, whether by 51 to 50 or by 100 to 1. The liberal/ libertarian challenge is not to governmental authority—there could not be

* Jan deV. Graaff, *Theoretical Welfare Economics* (London: Cambridge University Press, 1957), p. 7.

any government, or any society, without certain compulsory contributions and prohibitions—but, rather, to the scope of that authority.

The most celebrated political economists of the Enlightenment—Hume, Smith, and Ricardo—were not libertarians. They were indeed opposed to the "mercantilist" brand of governmental intervention practiced previously; they would surely have been skeptical of "central planning" by even the most benevolent planner. Their opposition to certain governmental interventions, however, was on the same grounds that they supported certain other interventions: they were against economic waste, public or private.

For the roots of what might be called libertarianism one has to turn to other Enlightenment figures, such as Immanuel Kant and Wilhelm von Humboldt. Kant advocated the principle of unanimity in collective action decisions:

... the laws ... must be absolutely incapable of doing anyone an injustice. Now if someone makes dispositions for another person, it is always possible that he may do him an injustice; but it is never possible in the case of decisions [the latter person] makes for himself, for no harm is done to a man by an act he consents to. Thus only the unanimous and combined will of everyone whereby each decides the same for all and all decide the same for each—in other words, the united will of the people—can legislate.*

Humboldt also stressed the desirability of unanimity. He thus proposed that the only collective actions that are just for the state to take are those that reduce the costs to people of what they would be doing without the aid of government. From that premise he went on to argue that the proper role of government is limited to providing the citizenry with security against foreign attack and against forcible encroachment by their fellow citizens.

A quite different view might be called borderline anarchy. In 1972 the American political philosopher Robert Nozick startled the political-philosophical world with the bold and stimulating thesis that the only just government is the "minimal state." Such a state confines itself to those collective actions without which the society would disintegrate into open strife and nomadic existence. Nozick says, "The state may not use its coercive apparatus for the purpose of getting some citizens to aid others, or in order

---

*Immanuel Kant, *The Metaphysics of Morals, Part I,* Berlin, 1797. English tr. by J. Ladd, *The Metaphysical Elements of Justice* (New York: Bobbs-Merrill, 1965), p. 78.

to prohibit activities to people for their *own* good or protection."* It is clear that Nozick's minimal state—the least government consistent with its own survival—might be minute next to Humboldt's possibly quite sizable government.

The present chapter will examine some of the principles that have been invoked—principles of justice beyond mere procedural justice—in collective-action decisions to decide collective-action questions (or, at any rate, to narrow down the range of choices left). If not majority rule, then what?

HOBBES AND COST-BENEFIT ANALYSIS

Hobbes, it was noted earlier, did not need to go beyond the easy cases: There are various collective actions that, despite their costs (of which each person may have to pay some share), not only benefit everyone but benefit each person by more than his or her share of the cost. Those easy cases were enough for Hobbes to dismiss the thought that a powerful sovereign state was unjustified and therefore a temporary aberration in the course of history.

Hobbes left unexplored the possibility that a proposal for some collective action—with a certain sprinkling, or "distribution," of benefits and costs over the members of the society—might not yield a gain for everyone, yet some feasible modification of it offering a different distribution of the costs might yield a universal gain. Table 9–1 illustrates a case in which a proposed collective action would benefit the members of three equal-sized groups unequally and, in the original proposal, burden them with equal costs. It might be Hume's project to drain that soggy meadow, or Zurich's program to build an opera house. As Table 9–1 shows, a majority of the population—the one-third belonging to group C—would actually be harmed by the collective action as proposed. Table 9–2 illustrates a proposed collective action that would be even less popular. It might be a proposal to build a youth center with the burden of paying for it spread equally among the population. As table 9–2 shows, a majority of the population—groups C and B—would be harmed by that collective action as proposed.

Neither of these illustrative cases shows a *universal* gain from the collective action as originally proposed. Yet, as the two tables show, the benefits—measured by what the beneficiaries could pay in return for the collective action without being worse off on balance—exceed in the aggregate the burdens to each person of paying for the proposed project. It is certainly

* Robert Nozick, *Anarchy, State and Utopia* (New York: Basic Books, 1974).

Table 9–1: A COLLECTIVE ACTION THAT HARMS A MINORITY

GROUP:	A	B	C	AGGREGATE
BENEFIT	80	50	20	150
BURDEN	40	40	40	120
GAIN	40	10	−20	30

The table shows the distribution of benefits and burdens of a collective action. Example: the construction and operation of an opera house and the taxation of the community to pay for it. As shown, the benefits exceed the burdens in the aggregate. But a minority, the one-third or so belonging to group C, are harmed; the burden to them, measured by what they would be willing to pay (at most) to escape the taxation, exceeds the benefit to them, measured by the most they would be willing to pay for the pleasure (when they are not being taxed for it). The excess of aggregate benefits over aggregate burden suggests, nevertheless, that a different collective action— in particular, a different distribution of the taxes or some side payment or other "pay-off" to the members of group C—might leave group C compensated, with some gain left over for the others in groups A and B.

conceivable, therefore, that the gainers from the project could *compensate* the losers and still be left with some gain. Certainly the benefits to the gainers are not so small as to rule out that compensation—the problems would be the practical ones of implementing the compensations (identifying the losers, measuring their losses, ensuring against double payments, etc.).

Table 9–2: A COLLECTIVE ACTION THAT HARMS A MAJORITY

GROUP:	A	B	C	AGGREGATE
BENEFIT	90	30	30	150
BURDEN	40	40	40	120
GAIN	50	−10	−10	30

This second table depicts the distribution of benefits and burdens of some other collective action. For example: the construction and operation of a youth center and the taxation of the community to pay for it. Here a majority, the one-third or so in group A and the one-third in group B, are harmed. Yet, as in the first table, aggregate benefit exceeds aggregate burden. So a different collective action in which the losers are compensated, and gainers still gain, is at least conceivable.

We arrive at a basic axiom of welfare economics and a rationale of cost-benefit analysis: If the aggregate benefits from a collective action would *equal* or *exceed* the aggregate burdens of paying for it, *and* if any losers from the project were actually going to be compensated by the gainers, then it would not be unjustifiable for the government (or whatever agency would administer the collective action in question) to go ahead with the project, *other things being equal.* No one would be worse off with the project than without it, and some might be better off. If the aggregate benefits exceed the aggregate burdens and the losers are compensated (without turning any gainers into losers), some persons would be better off and no one worse off. With no one worse off, where would be the harm? With some better off and none worse off, could not there be said to be a social improvement? There certainly could be, said the turn-of-the-century Italian social theorist Vilfredo Pareto. In Pareto's book *Manuel d'economie Politique* there is said to be a social improvement whenever some (meaning some or all) are better off and none worse off; in Pareto's honor, such a change has come to be called a "Pareto improvement." The axiom that Pareto improvements are a good thing has not been seriously disputed in Western political economy and moral philosophy since Pareto enunciated it. Few would condemn a society for opposing inefficiency—for seizing every opportunity for a Pareto improvement.

What if "other things" are not "equal?" What if there is a second collective project that *would pass* with flying colors the same cost-benefit and compensation tests *if* the *first* project is *rejected* and that *would not pass* those tests if the *first* project is *carried out?* Let us assume that, as a result, society will refuse to undertake both projects—if one, not the other. Hence, *either* project would be a Pareto improvement. What then?

It could be that *one* of the projects *is unjustifiable.* That is the case if for *every person* one collective action with its compensations or more-than-compensations of losers would yield a larger gain than would the other project. In this case the former collective action is a larger Pareto improvement; it is a Pareto improvement on the other Pareto improvement. This situation is a possibility, of course—and very pleasant for the politician who sees it and for the economist-advisor who brought it to his or her attention. But it will not generally be the case.

Quite to the contrary, then, it may very well be that adoption of *either* of the two projects would not be unjustifiable. That is the case if for *some persons* the first project would yield larger gains than the second project would, while for *other persons* the second would be better than the first project. In this case society has *two* justifiable courses of action. Which course it may proceed to justify will depend on the particular conception of justice that the society subscribes to (if it has any); the Rawlsian maximin principle would lead to one choice, the sum-of-utilities principle of the utilitarians would lead to another, and so on. Pareto's principle does not help to choose between alternatives both of which are efficient. Yet *the Pareto principle asserts the justice of abandoning the inefficient option: it justifies rejecting the option of saving the taxpayers the expense of either collective action.* Thus the Pareto principle serves to recommend a certain subset of the options of the government, but not (by itself) to determine a unique course of action.

Of course, in the real world, the losers from public projects are not very often compensated on the spot in the coin of the realm. Where compensation does occur it is effected through the device of log rolling, mutual back-scratching, or whatever it may be called. "You vote for our highway—or education or defense—program and we will vote for your pet project." We often see an omnibus bill that is an amalgam of special interest legislation—a Christmas tree with baubles and trinkets for everyone—and sometimes these omnibus bills are approved by a unanimous or nearly unanimous vote.

People often complain at the sight of these gaudy bills. Their hostility perhaps comes from the feeling that some legislators had to be "bribed" to add their votes to legislation—bribed with pork barrel pay-offs to their own constituents—that ought to have been supported as a matter of *principle,* out of their sense of justice (if they have any). Vote trading is not always harmless; like goods trading in some cases, it can have harmful effects. Yet vote trading may sometimes serve to convert a conflict situation into an opportunity for a social improvement—a Pareto improvement.

A UNANIMITY PRINCIPLE: THE "SCANDINAVIAN CONSENSUS"

It is natural to wonder about the other side of the coin. What if the aggregate benefits from a contemplated collective action would *not* equal or exceed the aggregate burdens involved in paying for it? Or, more generally, what if for that reason or *any other* reason the losers cannot all be compensated by the gainers? Ought it to be a constitutional principle of a society that in such cases the collective action *is* deemed unjustifiable? Such a principle, of course, would be far-reaching: It would mean that the gainers were not entitled to proceed with the collective action even if they were in the overwhelming majority and their gains were substantial; or, even if there were only a handful of them but their gains were the difference between prosperity and penury. If the sole reason the losers could not be compensated lay only in some difficulty in effecting the compensations—the losers could not be reliably identified or the gainers could not be located—the aggregate benefits might far exceed the aggregate burdens. So such a principle must seem extraordinarily stringent and demanding.

Yet a school of political economy arose around the turn of the century that advanced precisely that principle. Compensation by the gainers of those who would otherwise lose is to be a *requirement* of every collective action taken by the government. If the gains from a proposed collective action would come (in whole or in part) at the expense of outright losses to other persons, that action shall not be permitted! This was the position taken by the virtuoso Swedish economist Knut Wicksell and adopted by the Scandinavian school that he founded:

- A principle held by the Scandinavian school is that unanimity among the citizens—a consensus—is a necessary condition for undertaking any collective action, not merely (as Pareto held) a sufficient condition.
- It follows, as a corollary, that a collective action is impermissible whenever the aggregate benefit is less than the aggregate cost. For if the aggregate benefit is less than the aggregate cost, the aggregate gain of the gainers—those individuals whose own benefits exceed their own costs—must be smaller than the aggregate loss of the losers. So if one unit of benefit extracted from gainers can be converted into one unit of benefit for losers—into one unit at most—the aggregate gain must be too small to pay for compensating the losers for their losses.

In applying the principle to actual issues of the day, Wicksell was putting into practice what Kant and a few other liberal figures of the Enlightenment had preached a century earlier.

It is clear how the principle would apply to certain either-or decisions. Laws to prohibit saccharine in foods, DDT in fruit orchards, dumping of radioactive waste in unrestricted areas, carrying concealed weapons without a permit, and laws that permit newspapers publishing without a license, fluoridating the drinking water, and so forth are all collective actions of the do-or-don't variety. They are not laws that offer a carefully calibrated degree of encouragement or discouragement; they are blanket prohibitions or permissions. There are other collective actions, however, that have somehow settled the question *how much*. A decision to build a 60-inch water main is a decision not to build a 61-inch main nor a 59-inch one. A decision to staff a 60-piece marching band for the Royal Palace means not having a 61-piece band nor a 59-piece one.

The application of the Scandinavian principle of unanimous consent to this sort of collective action in which the scale of the action can be varied is at first perplexing. How in the world are the citizens of Stockholm ever to reach unanimous acceptance of the size of that band? A disciple of Wicksell provided the answer: Just as the device of compensation can (ideally, at any rate) serve to bring losers into line—if the aggregate benefits are large enough to afford that—so there must be some system of graduated compensations that can (ideally, anyway) serve to make everyone accept a band of the same size, music haters (who will be *compensated more* the larger is the band) and music lovers (who will *pay more* the larger is the band). On the Scan-

---

FIGURE 9–1: The Scandinavian Consensus over the Scale of a Collective Expenditure—the Size of the Royal Band

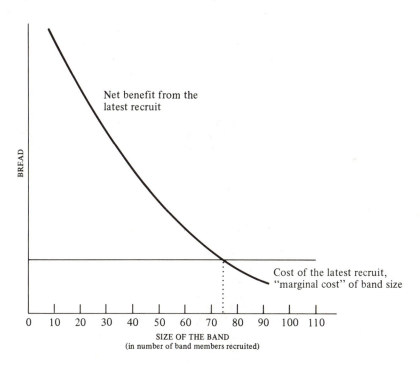

The net benefit is the sum of the amounts beneficiaries are willing to pay—*minus* the sum that victims need to be paid—for the *latest recruit* to the Royal band. The net benefit curve is downward sloping. Hence as the band is increased in size, the populace within earshot is willing to pay less and less for each *additional* recruit. As long as this *"marginal* benefit" exceeds *"marginal* cost," another member should be added—since, with compensations, no one will be harmed and some will gain.

dinavian principle, the marching band is enlarged only as far as unanimous consent can be preserved. Once the extra cost of hiring an extra bandsman exceeds the aggregate extra benefits for music lovers *net* of the aggregate extra harms (the negative benefits) suffered by the music haters, the point has been reached where compensating the losers for an extra bandsman would be impossible. Actually, such compensation might be infeasible from the start for purely administrative reasons (finding the gainers, measuring their gains, verifying the losses of those claiming to be losers, etc.). Whatever the difficulties or impediments, the principle is clear: unanimous consent is required of each additional collective action.

The Scandinavian principle—that for every person the benefit of any collective action ought to be at least as large as the cost borne—has been questioned, and we shall be getting to that. But even more basic objections are sometimes raised. Some critics object to any consideration of "benefits" in collective-action decision making. They are disturbed that collective actions should be thought about in terms of "benefit" and cost. Here are portions of the debate:

CRITICS: The crucial "benefits" that would often clinch the case for a collective action are typically not measurable. How do we measure the benefit of trial of jury, habeas corpus, our civil rights protections? How do we calculate the benefits of clean air to our grandchildren? Every judge and air inspector is invaluable.

PROPONENTS: Of course, some things are sacred—to some or all people. To obtain a collective action that would protect what they held sacred they would be willing (if required) to give everything they had (short of violating some other sacred trust). Churchill did not do a cost-benefit analysis when deciding to declare war on the Nazis, it is true; he could be sure, though, that every Briton was willing to pay more than his or her fair share of the cost (maybe to risk death) of waging the war. However we cannot be sure that every citizen, or even any citizen, would be willing to pay his or her fair share of the cost of protecting every wilderness area in the country. Merely protesting that something is sacred shouldn't make it so. The government ought to feel assured before taking a costly collective action that the benefits—for all, or at any rate for many—are commensurate with the costs. If such a liberal-humanist requirement is not met, what can justify the action?

CRITICS: But when it comes to collective actions affecting road safety or nuclear waste disposal hazards, the benefits are immeasurable, invaluable. Since human lives are priceless, how can considerations of "willingness to pay" be applicable in matters of life and death?

PROPONENTS: The fact that society has not reduced the speed limit to the point where vehicular traffic is at a perfectly safe crawl is one piece of evidence, out of thousands, that people are not willing to sacrifice much—let alone sacrifice all they have—in the interest of reducing the mortality rate. People are willing to "take a chance," which is why they risk driving, skiing, or crossing the street for inessential purposes. The benefit to a person from reduced highway mortality is simply what that person would be willing to pay for it (on the theory that the life saved may be his or her own or that of a friend or other fellow human being). Competent cost-benefit analyses of collective actions to compel the installation and wearing of seat belts in cars, for example, do make ingenious efforts to measure such benefits—by estimating, among other things, the resulting reduction in people's insurance costs.

CRITICS: In fact, though, most cost-benefit analyses are fraudulent. The *cost* of protecting a wilderness area from becoming a metropolis of oil derricks is usually clear; it is the tax revenue that must be collected to replace the oil royalties the government would forgo. But the *benefit* is underestimated if it is estimated at all, because there is no adequate means to ascertain the extent and especially the intensity of concern over the matter.

PROPONENTS: The lobbyists for the wilderness interests are no less susceptible to the temptation to defraud than other lobbyists are. A political process is needed to mediate between misestimates.

Verdict: The critics are right that cost-benefit analysis is unacceptable when it does not take into account interested citizens' values as reflected in what they would be willing to bear in higher taxes. It does not follow that cost-benefit analysis is *generally* unacceptable.

It is obvious that the Scandinavian requirement of unanimous consent could, if adopted, be applied to any proposed government expenditure of resources: to public health measures and consumer safety regulations, to investments in dams and roads. (The Scandinavian requirement is a particular *use* of cost-benefit analysis, and that analysis has long been directed to such governmental decisions.) Can the Scandinavian principle be applied to the "redistribution" of income?—to income transfers from, say, haves to have-nots? It can, and its application to such collective actions has in fact been seriously studied.

The Scandinavian principle would permit and encourage redistribution of income as far as unanimous consent obtains—and no further. Once the point is reached at which no more income can be presented to those persons dependent on state charity without someone's objecting to the cost in view of the "price—the percentage share—that he or she is being charged, and no other set of prices is possible that would obtain consensus either, state charity has reached its permissible limit, according to the principle!

What about this pretty application? Is this the solution to the heretofore unsolved dilemmas of poverty and justice? Or does it cruelly display how flawed the Scandinavian principle must be to begin with?

Most of those who object to the application of the Scandinavian principle of unanimous consent would be prepared, merely to get on with the argument, to concede that the principle is not without some appeal in *some* redistributive applications in *some* circumstances. Suppose the redistribution was pure charity in the simplest of cases—"they," the objects of charity, are too ill or handicapped, physically or mentally, to be able to participate, to contribute a thing, while "we," the productive, are (for simplicity's sake) all equal in rewards and talents. Then, *if* "we" all have the same sense of charity toward "them," it would seem morally reasonable that our charity to "them" be limited to what we consent to: the output is morally ours, since we produced it without them, so what right do they have to it? And if one (or more) of us has a *different* sense of charity toward "them," what right would they or we have to take from any such differing individual among us an amount of income from that person's original fair-and-equal share beyond what that individual consents do? The income is morally his since it is his just share of what he and the rest of us together produced. Perhaps that is a plausible position on pure charity.

But suppose the redistribution is not really pure charity. Suppose it is the result of some tinkering by the government, with the structure of rewards to the cooperative efforts of the active participants in the society: say subsidies to the employment of highly paid persons and taxes on the rewards to the low-paid persons. After all, there is no good reason why the members of society should whenever possible stick to last year's reward structure—the configuration of after-tax-and-subsidy pay rates to the various jobs and rates of return to various investments previously adopted. Society, having adopted one reward structure, *a*, may be giving consideration to substituting another reward structure, *b;* and if instead it has already adopted *b* it may be considering *a*. Then, in the former situation, with the reward structure *a* in place to begin with, it is obvious that some or all of those persons for whom a shift to reward structure *b* would be costly (would cost them income) might withhold their consent to that move—they might not want to lose the greater rewards that *a* offers them; and, in the other situation with reward structure *b*, some *other* set of persons for whom a shift to reward structure *a* would be costly might withhold *their* consent to *that* move—because they find their own rewards greater with *b*. If total output and individual effort is the same, then gainers cannot compensate losers—and have anything left of their gains. In that case, neither move would obtain unanimous consent. Application of the Scandinavian principle would compel the society to stick to whichever reward structure it happened to start with—which is absurd! In such cases the principle makes no moral sense.

The very same paradox *can* arise when the collective action being considered is the introduction (in one situation) or the removal (in the other situation) of a resource-using government program—a public expenditure rather than a redistributive tax—to raise the productivity of one group of persons at a cost to the rest of society. The government action might be a job-training program for a group of disadvantaged workers, or a mine-safety program for a group of miners, or a program to aid rural migration to urban areas.

Suppose that if the initial situation is one *without* the assistance program and with a certain prevailing structure of rewards—call it *a*—those who would benefit from introduction of the program would be unable to compensate the others. The benefits to the beneficiaries would be less than the cost of the program. The program would therefore fail the "test" that the sum of the benefits be at least as large as the costs; the gainers would be unable to "bribe" the losers into unanimous consent—the Scandinavian requirement. That is depicted by the accompanying diagram. It shows the feasibility curve relating the rent earned by each member of group 2. *Without* the assistance program, the feasibility curve is a relatively flat curve; and the corresponding reward structure chosen by society leads to the outcome indicated by point *a*. The diagram depicts a case in which introduction of the assistance program would move the feasibility curve inward *in the neighborhood of point a*. Hence, even though group 1 were to give up all its gains from the program, the losers (group 2) would not be compensated: there would be a lateral movement leftward from *a* to *a'*.

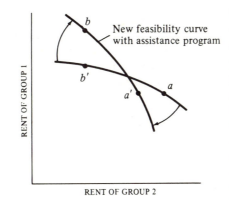

Now suppose in addition—and this is certainly a *possibility*—that if the initial situation is instead one *with* the assistance program and some accompanying structure of rewards—call it *b*—those who would benefit from the removal of the program would be unable to compensate those who would lose from removal. The way the feasibility curve *twisted* upon introduction of the assistance program depicts precisely this further possibility—it moved inward at the low end, but outward at the high end. Hence, removal of the assistance program would move the feasibility curve inward *in the neighborhood of point b*. Hence even though group 2 were to give up all its gains from the removal of the program, the losers from removal (group 1) would not be compensated: there would be a vertical movement downward from *b* to *b'*.

Thus, taking the collective action of introducing the program might not obtain unanimous consent—might not if the losers demanded to be compensated as the price for their consent. Yet, taking the collective action of removing the program *also* might not obtain unanimous consent—might not if the losers demanded compensation.

The trouble with the Scandinavian requirement is that the set of collective actions that would command unanimous consent *might depend on the collective actions taken or not taken already*—particularly, and notably, collective actions with regard to the structure of rewards in society. What a person can be bribed into consenting to may depend upon how rich that person is and how poor the people are who are asked to cough up the required bribe.

- The low-paid workers can never afford to pay more for a rise in the income tax rate (in order to raise more tax revenue with which to finance more subsidies and other aids to the working poor) than the high paid could pay out of their resulting benefits for not having that rise in the income tax rate. Yet once the increase was enacted, the low-paid beneficiaries of the tax revenue could pay more to prevent a cut of the income tax rate than the high paid could pay for obtaining that rate cut (unless the latter group can find a less inefficient way to tax).

- The low paid may be unable to afford to pay more for some productivity-enhancing program than the high paid could afford to pay (out of their share of the tax burden) to block it. Yet once that program is enacted, the low-paid beneficiaries of that program may be able to pay more to prevent its repeal than the high paid could pay for its repeal—as the previous diagram showed.

Thus, where society would end up, relying on the principle of unanimous consent, might depend (even crucially) on where it stood when it adopted that principle. In the final analysis, then, the requirement that the gainers be *able* to compensate the losers and *do it* could not deliver what it seemed to promise: It cannot serve as a method of reaching the "just economy"—the set of collective actions deemed just.

What did Wicksell and his followers say? It seems they saw the difficulty—through a glass darkly, at any rate—and felt they had the answer. "Apparently," Wicksell wrote, "justice of taxation presupposes tacitly a just distribution of income and property." Gunnar Myrdal, despite his immersion in the subject and conversations with Wicksell's disciple Erik Lindahl, could not fathom what they meant: "The decisive question is: what precisely does the assumption of a correct distribution of income and property mean? Must this condition be fulfilled *before* or *after* taxation?"*

Our analysis of the productivity-enhancing assistance program shows that "before" cannot be a correct answer. In the preceding diagram, the distribution of rents at *b*, after the program is introduced, might be the just distribution; and the distribution at *a*, before the program, might be unjust. But *a* might be the just distribution given the absence of the program; and from the initial point *a* the move to *b* cannot meet the Scandinavian requirement. So the existence of justice "before" does not make application of the Scandinavian principle acceptable.

Impatient with the question, Myrdal dismisses the possibility that "after" is a correct answer: "Clearly *not after* taxation for the theory would then be circular. Taxation would indeed be just, but only because it would be one of the causes of an *ex hypothesi* just situation. Any kind of taxation would by definition fulfill the condition of justice."†

But there is something else that Wicksell and followers ought to have said by way of explanation—and may have meant. If all the collective actions taken by society are just, so there is a just structure of rewards and a just scale to every government program, then, starting from this just state, any trial proposal to repeal or scale down a collective action or to add or scale up a collective action would injure the losers more than it would benefit the gainers (if any); so the gainers could be bribed by the losers into voting unanimously for a counterproposal to restore the original set of collective actions (at their original scale). In the just state, then, each collective action is at the scale where the "marginal aggregate benefit"—the rate at which aggregate benefit is increasing with the scale of the collective action—is

---

*Gunnar Myrdal, *The Political Element in the Development of Economic Theory*, trans. Paul Streeten (Cambridge, Mass.: Harvard University Press, 1954), p. 178.
†Ibid., p. 183.

equal to "marginal cost"—the rate at which total cost increases with the scale of the activity. Thus the condition depicted by the diagram in Figure 9–1 does correctly describe the just level of any collective action in the just state. It is not a reliable guide to collective actions, however, in actual situations, in states not known to be just already (and thus needing no action).

ECONOMIC JUSTICE AMONG THE SEVERAL

The simplest cost-benefit tests, we have seen, lead to paradoxes and conundrums. The principle of going ahead with a collective action if everyone gains would present a dilemma whenever there were two or more mutually exclusive actions both of which passed that test. The principle of going ahead with a collective action only if everyone gains might leave collective activity totally becalmed where it had navigated earlier. These conundrums would disappear, however, if everyone in society had the same sense of justice. Then there would be unanimous consent to collective actions seen as just, and unanimous dissent to collective actions seen as unjust. Those who "lost" from the collective actions that secured "justice" would have ultimately a "compensation," the satisfaction of living and working in a "just" state.

It is true that agreement on a conception of justice in the structure of rewards is not in the offing in the very near future! But people can talk about it, explore ideas. And they do, continually. And so can we.

Two topics will occupy us here:

- Why *collective* action to secure economic justice in the structure of rewards—rates of pay after tax, etc.? Why not individual action? Unilateral action. One on one.
- How, in view of evidently conflicting self-interests, can the members of society ever reach agreement on a conception of justice? Is there room, anywhere, for a sort of unanimity?

CONTRACTARIANISM: BEHIND THE "VEIL OF IGNORANCE"

Any discussion of economic justice has to come to grips with a brute fact: Nearly everyone watches out for Numero Uno. By all accounts it is normal, and healthy, to want to develop, flourish, prosper—to succeed at one's goals. Smith was apparently mistaken when he said that men have an innate "propensity to truck and barter," but it was an error over people's style, not their concerns. Most of us are always on the lookout for better terms—a more interesting or important job, greater pay or lower prices or tax savings in order to do more or have more. Not even Maoist China seems to have extinguished ambition, to have wrought a new ethos of selflessness. The image of men and women betting on themselves, struggling against rivals for scarce opportunities to achieve something distinctive, to make the most of what they have—whether rival statesmen, scientists, architects, city planners—continues to be celebrated more than scorned, in books and films. Sigmund Freud, a greater psychologist than Smith, saw risk taking and innovation as indispensable to a fully realized life.

- ◆ How, then, can people possibly detach themselves from their goals enough to support some abstract idea of justice that would subtract from their resources, from some of their rewards?
- ◆ What hope can there be for any productive discussion (much less a complete resolution) of what is just that would not inevitably be tainted by people's self-interests?

Discussions of "what is just?" still take place, all right, but some of the positions taken are thinly disguised expressions of some people's self-interests. Even those who want to think of themselves as just may have an unconscious bias toward government policies that are in their own interests. When a New York newspaper, accepting the desirability of greater tax revenue, produced a list of suggested tax increases, a reader wrote to tease them over what he saw to be (or pretended was) another example of bias:

DR. WATSON: I say, Holmes, who wrote the Nov. 15 lead editorial "Mirrors and Mr. Reagan"?

HOLMES: Elementary, my dear Watson—a person under 60 years of age, who does not smoke cigarettes, eschews alcohol, lives in the city, does not own an automobile, rents an apartment, has never worked for the Federal Government and is very much of a parochial urban mind.

WATSON: Oh, I say, Holmes—all of that?

HOLMES: Of a surety, Watson. As LaRochefoucauld says, we can all find the strength to endure the misfortunes of others.

WATSON: Oh?

HOLMES: The writer, not a cigarette smoker and at most a casual sipper of wine, has no hesitancy in asking for increases of excises on them. Being under 60, and never having been a Federal employee, the writer wishes for economies both in Social Security and in Federal pensions. Not owning a car or a home, the writer is easy with a proposed increase in gasoline taxes and with cutting the exemption for interest from income taxes.

WATSON: But, Holmes—a parochial urban mind?

HOLMES: The writer is remote from fees for harbors and airports, from irrigation and oil depletion, hence is urban. To such a mind these are areas for seeking revenue.

WATSON: Amazing, Holmes.

HOLMES: Look at it this way, Watson. If I came out for the elimination of subsidies for subways and housing, what would the writer think
of me?

WATSON: The reverse of urban—a provincial mind?

HOLMES: Excellent, Watson. Remember the Duke also said that virtues join with self-interest as the rivers join with the sea.

WATSON: You never fail to astound me, Holmes.

(A violin is heard and pipe smoke wafts in the air.)*

In fact there *are* good prima facie reasons why tax rates on the
editorial writer's pet targets ought to be comparatively high,
although possibly they are already high enough. The editorial
writer *may* have been entirely disinterested, perhaps even owns
a car and a home as positive proof. Still, the letter drives home
the possibility that the manifest intention conceals a latent self-
interest.

Fortunately, it seems to be true of most people that their sense of self-
fulfillment—those who attain it—is composed of more than a feeling of
success and competence. Their self-esteem depends also on the self-respect
that comes from feeling that their actions have been honorable, their
achievements justifiable to others. Few people, moreover, are so hermetic as
to live their lives without regard for the respect of others—just as few continue to take pride in their work without some positive reinforcement. So
most people do not want to feel they have gained by breaking the rules (or
breaking them more than the others, at any rate); nor do they want to feel
that they have by luck been the beneficiaries of unfair rules—for example,
the beneficiaries of discrimination or political advantage. On the two sides
to the fully realized life, ego and conscience, and the tension between them,
there is this epigram by one of the rabbinical sages: "If I am not for myself,
then who is for me? And if I am not for others, then who am I?"

The problem that arises, then, is *how* to "think just," not *whether* to.
What sort of "moral reasoning"—what mental experiment, which premises—will serve us in analyzing the justice or injustice of a given reward
structure, or in deciding which of two structures is less unjust? The almost
universally accepted answer is that it is necessary for each of us to put ourselves in the other's shoes. That is precisely the answer, on some readings at
least, contained in the idea of the social contract. The original philosophers
of the social contract—Locke, Rousseau, Kant—can be interpreted as advocating that each citizen ought to abide by what all citizens would have agreed
to had they been required to hammer out a binding contract in advance of

---

* William A. Huneke, Letter to the Editor, *New York Times*, November 29, 1981. Copyright ©
1981 by the New York Times Company. Reprinted by permission of the *Times* and William A.
Huneke.

knowing the luck, the breaks, that would fall on this, that, and the other citizen. "Had I known I was going to be King, I would have held out for much less extensive restrictions on my Royal Highness's powers! But I didn't know. So I really cannot complain of an injustice." Of course, the notion of some antecedent contract binding the players now is merely a figurative contract. But once people acknowledge that what they would have agreed to when they did not know in whose shoes they would be standing is just now, although they know now their actual circumstances, they have gone a long way toward reaching a consensus on the just structure of their society.

A striking application of the social-contract device to economic justice—to society's reward structure and other economic policies—is that proposed by John Rawls. Rawls carries the idea of contracting parties who do not know their positions in society to an extreme: The parties to the contract are ignorant not only of the life prospects that await them—the station in life that their natural talents, parental influences, and social contacts will offer them. The contracting parties, in Rawls's version of the social contract, are even ignorant of the proportion of people who will be unskilled workers, the proportion who will do clerical work, and so on. Hence no contracting party knows even the probabilities of landing in this or that position in society, of having one type of career or another. Why this requirement? Because Rawls thinks it unfair to make the treatment that the social contract will give to any group contingent on its relative size.

> Just as each person must decide the system of ends which it is rational for him to pursue, so a [society] of persons must decide once and for all what is to count among them as just and unjust. The choice which rational men would make in this hypothetical situation of equal liberty . . . determines the principle of justice. . . . "[J]ustice as fairness" conveys the idea that the principles of justice are agreed to in an initial situation that is fair.*

And,

> If the original position is to yield agreements that are just, the parties must be fairly situated and treated equally as moral persons. . . . Moreover . . . once knowledge of particulars [of arbitrary contingencies] is excluded, the requirement of unanimity . . . in choosing principles . . . is not out of place. . . . It enables us to say of the preferred conception of justice that it represents a genuine reconciliation of interests.†

In that hypothetical situation, what principle would persons prefer?

Rawls's "Inequality for the Benefit of Everyone"

Rawls maintains that any person who can manage to see things from the standpoint of his hypothetical contract situation would be led to adopt this striking principle: First, government programs and other social institutions that make everyone better off are perfectly just whether or not they create inequalities as a by-product. ". . . inequalities of wealth and organizational

---

* John Rawls, *A Theory of Justice* (Cambridge, Mass.: Harvard University Press, 1971), p. 12.
† Ibid., p. 141.

FIGURE 9–2: The Benefits Earned by Three Groups under Varying Strength of "Incentives"

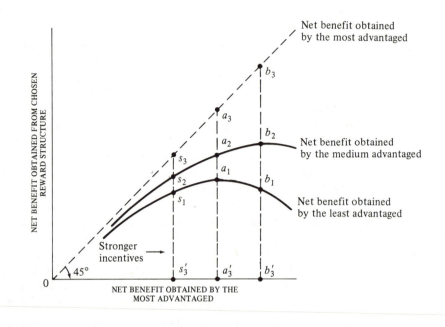

The diagram pertains to a society with three kinds of careers. The most advantaged person or group of persons has the job that offers the greatest benefit (net of any burden the job entails); the next most advantaged have the next best job; the least advantaged have the worst job. (For definiteness Rawls sometimes refers to the unskilled, the semiskilled, and the skilled. But, basically, skill is just earning power. If the greatest benefits go to performing musicians, and the next greatest benefits to those who—being unable to get musicians' jobs—do managerial work, then the musicians are the most skilled.)

Any structure of rewards adopted by the society leads to some corresponding distribution of benefits earned in each of the three sorts of jobs. For example, a certain reward structure labeled s leads to a benefit to the least advantaged indicated by point s_1; the height of the point from the horizontal axis measures the size of the benefit that would be earned by the least advan-taged under that reward structure; the same reward structure would lead to the benefit indicated by s_2 to the second most advantaged; and it would lead to the benefit for the most advantaged indicated by the height of the point s_3 on the 45° line—equivalently the distance from the origin of the point s_3' on the horizontal axis.

We can imagine, with Rawls, a reward structure that would allot the three classes of workers equal benefits and burdens (like plodding oxen in a yoke working and eating the same as one another). But the reward structure s is better for everyone, because of its incentive effects, than any such egalitarian arrangement; so that reward structure, despite the resulting inequalities, is justified. A further move from reward structure s to reward structure a is also justified, for such a move is likewise better for all. A still further move to the reward structure b, for example, would not be justified, since not everyone would gain; the least advantaged would not.

powers [that] would make everyone better off than [under any system enforcing equality] . . . accord with the general [Rawlsian] conception [of justice]."* To argue for that conclusion, Rawls suggests that the principle of equality would be the first principle to occur to anyone trying to formulate his or her notion of justice in Rawls's hypothetical contract position. That preliminary arrangement, in which everyone would have equal rights and duties and equal incomes, would provide a benchmark for judging the superiority of other arrangements:

Since it is not reasonable for [a contracting party] to expect more than an equal share in the division of social goods [i.e., income, etc.], and since it is not rational to agree to less, the sensible thing for him to do is to acknowledge as the *first* principle of justice one requiring equal distribution. . . . Thus, the [contracting] parties *start* with a principle establishing equal liberty. . . . But there is no reason why this acknowledgement should be final. If there are inequalities in the basic structure [of rewards] that work to make everyone better off in comparison with the benchmark of initial equality, why not permit them? . . . [There would be] no grounds for complaining of one another's motives [for favoring such inequalities]. A person in the [contract position] would, therefore, concede the justice of these inequalities.†

This is the "Pareto" in Rawls talking. Inequalities, or rather the collective actions that release them, are just if they make everyone better off.

And if a collective action does not make everyone better off, what then? The principle advocated by Rawls further holds that ". . . social and economic inequalities, for example inequalities of wealth and authority, are just only if they result in compensating benefits for everyone and in particular for the least advantaged members of society. [Such a principle] rule[s] out justifying institutions on the grounds that the hardships of some are offset by a greater good in the aggregate. It may be expedient but it is not just that some should have less in order that others may prosper."‡ Further,

All social values—liberty and opportunity, income and wealth, and the bases of self-respect—are to distributed equally unless an unequal distribution of any, or all, of these values is to everyone's advantage. Injustice, then, is simply inequalities that are not to the benefit of all.§

So, it seems, there is a "Wicksell" in Rawls alongside "Pareto." But Wicksell ran into trouble, it will be recalled, because he required unanimous approval of a collective action no matter what the starting situation, which made the unanimity principle unworkable as Wicksell formulated it. However, Rawls avoids any such trouble by insisting that the starting situation be the preliminary arrangement of perfect equality. It is relative to that starting point that Rawls's principle apparently requires that collective actions be a gain for all. Figure 9–2 depicts precisely that interpretation in the usual case.

* Rawls, *A Theory of Justice*, p. 62. See also p. 15.
† Ibid., pp. 150–51.
‡ Ibid., pp. 14–15.
§ Ibid., p. 62.

SUMMARY

1. In general, collective actions are apt to bring losses to some while producing gains, possibly, for others. If the political processes available cannot reliably solve these problems in a satisfactory way, what then? Political economy has long sought general principles to apply to collective actions.

2. An early principle, one going back to the liberalism / libertarianism of the Enlightenment, is unanimity. The gainers must compensate the losers, thus erasing the losses. Then the operational question becomes whether the collective action being considered is beneficial enough to permit the gainers to compensate the losers. This led to the idea of the cost-benefit test.

3. Scandinavian economists used the unanimity idea to formulate what came to be called a "Scandinavian consensus" about the scale of any public expenditures or collective action in general. If aggregate benefit of march-music lovers *net* of the aggregate negative benefit to march-music haters exceeds the cost of one bandsman, all can gain (or none lose) from a band of at least that size, and we can consider adding a second bandsman, on the same criterion, and so on. Once the extra net benefit from an extra bandsman would no longer meet or exceed the cost of hiring another, the band has reached its justifiable level.

4. But this principle of unanimity does not make sense when it comes to collective actions toward the structure of rewards to society's participants. The poor can't bribe the rich to move the country a bit to the *left* just as, generally, the rich can't bribe the poor to move the country to the *right*. Thus the principle of compensation in order to secure unanimity does not lead from *where we are now,* regardless of where we are, to a "just economy." The existing status quo, whatever one it is, is apt to have a decisive influence on whether or where any movement *away* from the status quo would be approved.

5. In contrast, Rawls uses the liberal Kantian idea of unanimity but in a novel way that skirts the above problem of initial historical conditions. In Rawls's scheme we are to imagine ourselves in a hypothetical initial condition of equality (at least approximately) and from *that* situation ask whether incentive-creating reward structures can make everyone better off, thus winning unanimous approval. Once someone raises his hand to say that a *further* move would cause him a little loss, no matter how small, "inequality" stops there.

CONCEPTS INTRODUCED

compensate	Pareto improvement	unanimity principle
cost-benefit test	Scandinavian consensus	marginal benefit

STUDY QUESTIONS

1. According to Adam Smith, the state has three functions: "[F]irst, the duty of protecting the society from violence and invasion of other independent societies; second, the duty of protecting, as far as possible, every member of society from the injustice or oppression of every other member of it; and, thirdly, the duty of erecting and maintaining certain public works and certain public institutions, which it can never be for the interest of any individual, or small number of individuals, to erect and maintain because the profit could never repay the expense to any individual or small number of individuals, though it may frequently do much more than repay it to a great society" (*The Wealth of Nations*, Book V, chap. 1, p. 681). What is the relation of this position to the idea of a cost-benefit test? Was cost-benefit the only criterion for Smith, and this test independent of the initial distribution of income and wealth; or did Smith also believe that the government had a role to play in meeting society's sense of justice?

2. What is the point of contact among Kant and Humboldt, Pareto, Wicksell and Lindahl, and Rawls?

3. Some critics of cost-benefit analysis say that a benefit to the rich should get less weight than an equal benefit to the poor. Then a project is passed if weighted benefits exceed costs. Discuss.

4. In a Rawlsian state, it is sometimes said, the benefits to the rich would get zero weight. So there would be no lectures about European painting on public TV, it is said. Discuss. Then return to question 1.

5. What does the movie quote from *Sunset Boulevard* on the opening page of the chapter have to do with many or most notions of social justice in the distribution of rewards for talent and capacity?

6. Who was Humboldt, and what was Humboldt's gift to the catalogue of libertarian thought?

Part 4

Classical Market Theory and Economic Policy

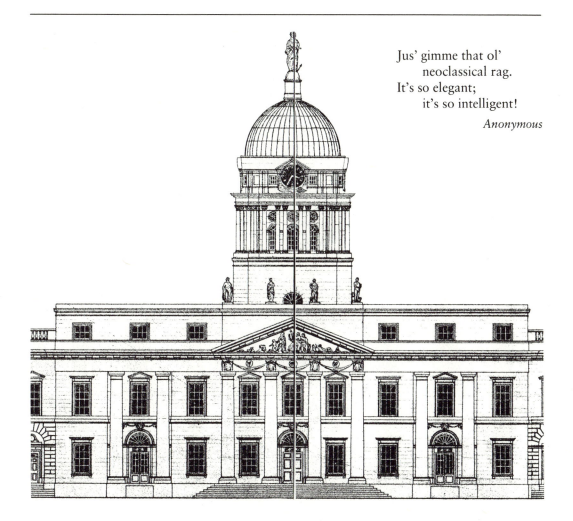

Jus' gimme that ol'
neoclassical rag.
It's so elegant;
it's so intelligent!

Anonymous

CHAPTER 10

The Classical Model of Pure Competition

DOROTHY:
Toto, this can't be Kansas anymore.

Judy Garland (to the dog) in *The Wizard of Oz* (1939)

I T is hard enough to conceive how economic *planners* might allocate the resources of a society efficiently, no matter how diligently they collected and processed information about people's resources, know how and preferences. Even if they "knew what they wanted"—whether some brand of justice, mode of social interaction, or some kind of glory—they would find themselves needing to formulate policy toward theater, track shoes, suburban living, education, retirement. In short, there would be a vast complex of questions to be resolved. To paraphrase Samuel Johnson's comment about a dog able to walk on its hind legs, the remarkable thing is not that it is done well but that it is done at all.

How much more remarkable it is if, as claimed by the classical theoreticians of the free market, from Smith to Marshall and beyond, the members of the community can allocate resources efficiently (in some uses at least) *without planning*, with only the institutions of the marketplace. This chapter will expound the main points of the classical argument. Of course, the classical theoreticians' claim is not utterly unqualified. In subsequent chapters we will take up the main qualifications that neoclassical economics makes.

HOW MARKETS WORK: THE NEOCLASSICAL THEORY

What is the classical (or neoclassical) theory of how free markets allocate resources between one industry and another, between working and not working, etc.? Noneconomists often reply, with some truth, "In classical economics, it's supply and demand, and in modern economics it isn't." There is a little more to neoclassical theory, however, than pairs of curves intersecting.

The first part of the theory derives from a basic classical maxim: Buy cheap, sell dear. In classical theory all market participants are perfectly informed. Hence each *seller,* being perfectly informed about every price quotation, would be willing to sell only to the buyer or buyers offering to pay the highest price. No supplier would find it profitable to sell for less than the highest price—up to the quantity that can be sold at that highest price, of course. Since every supplier would therefore hold out for the highest price, the terms at which the various suppliers are willing to supply will all be the same. Similarly, each *buyer,* being perfectly informed about all price data, would be willing to buy only at the lowest price—up to the limit available at that price, then at the lowest price on any further amount, and so on. Since every buyer would hold out for the best terms, the terms at which they would be willing to buy would all be identical. The reasoning leads to the first law of classical market theory:

◆ In the perfectly informed markets of classical theory, multiple prices cannot coexist in a single market—the market for any one good. If there were two or more prices for the same good, all sellers would sell at the highest price and all buyers buy at the lowest price—an impossibility! This is the *classical law of one price.*

The second proposition of the theory grows out of another classical idea: If a *seller* of a good finds he is not supplying all of the amount demanded by would-be buyers at the price he has been charging, the seller will *raise the price* charged to the point where the unmet demand—the *excess* of what is demanded over what is supplied—has been eliminated, "priced out of the market." This *rationing by price* is a more profitable way to "ration" the supply among the buyers than the other rationing methods, such as one-to-a-buyer and first come, first served. Similarly, if a *buyer* of a good finds that at the price he is paying the amount supplied to him exceeds what he is willing to buy at that price, the buyer will bargain, will "higgle and haggle," to *lower the price* until the amount offered but unbought—the amount in *excess* supply—has shrunk to zero. Why pay more? more than necessary, that is; it would be irrational. The reasoning leads to another law, what could be called the second law of classical market theory:

♦ In classical markets, where no one passes up better terms on which to buy or sell, there cannot be any buyers who desire to buy more, even paying a higher price if necessary, yet are frustrated in their attempts to do so; there is no nonprice rationing, no shortages. And there cannot be any sellers desiring to sell more, accepting a lower price if required, who are constrained from doing so; there are no surpluses, no gluts. With neither a shortage nor a surplus, the price is said to "clear the market." This is the *classical law of market clearing*.

A leading object of classical market analysis is the case of pure competition. There is said to be pure competition in a market if and only if, on the supply side, no individual seller supposes he has enough "market power" to drive up the price by restricting the amount supplied to the market—and, on the demand side, no individual buyer has enough power to drive down the price by reducing the amount bought in the market. The present chapter will focus on that case, which is, in fact, the case with which classical analysis is most closely identified. (The *other* leading case, that of a single seller with "monopoly power" or a single buyer with "monopsony power" will receive its due in chapter 12.)

Pure Competition

Under the perfect market conditions visualized by classical theory—perfect information about bids and offers, and market clearing—pure competition will result when every buyer and seller understands he is too small in relation to the size of the market to be able to exert more than a negligible effect on the market price. Every buyer knows that not buying at all, going shoeless or swearing off beer, would not make a perceptible dent in the market price, since he or she is but one buyer among millions. Similarly, every seller reckons that even withdrawing all his supply from the market would have a negligible effect on the market price because he is just one "atom" in a mass of competing sellers, sellers in "atomistic competition." Each is too small to have power.

"Atomistic competition" plus perfect market conditions is *sufficient* to make competition pure—to make each seller effectively powerless to raise the market price. But is atomistic competition *necessary*? Some present-day theorists argue that the potential existence of new competitors may have the same effect on a seller's power to drive up the price as the existence of many competitors. *If* any number of new sellers could break into the industry without incurring start-up costs—costless entry—and *if* potential entrants know that, in the event of a price war, the existing sellers can always pull their plant and equipment out to use in another industry, so new entrants need not be deterred by any threat of a fight to the death—costless exit—then the potential for new entry would also operate to deprive existing sellers of any market power. Conditions are imaginable, therefore, in which an industry is supplied by a single seller, and yet that apparent "monopolist" has no real monopoly power.

Under pure competition, then, each buyer and each seller takes the market price as a "given," as beyond his or her power to influence appreciably. Still, buyers and sellers have decisions to make. Each buyer must decide the amount to be bought—the amount demanded by him or her—at the given price. And each supplier must decide, in view of the given price, on the amount to be offered—the amount supplied. The way these buy decisions and sell decisions respond to the price—to how high or low the price is— serves to determine how high the price must be in order to clear the market. (True, a change in the amount supplied by a negligible supplier, being negligible, can make only a negligible difference in the market price; but a change in the total amount supplied by all suppliers, if it is non-negligible, makes a non-negligible difference to the market-clearing price.)

Competitive Equilibrium in a Particular Market

If a classical competitive market is in equilibrium, the expected price and the actual price are equal in that market. In equilibrium, then, decisions to plant cotton and make vacation reservations are based on expectations of prices and whatnot that will be borne out by subsequent experience.

The classical tool for determining, or explaining, the equilibrium price and the equilibrium quantity in a competitive market is supply-and-demand analysis: The *equilibrium level* of the market price is just high enough that, if suppliers expect that price to prevail, the resulting total quantity *supplied* to the market is *equal* to the total quantity that is *demanded* at that same price. A higher-than-equilibrium price, if expected by suppliers, would cause the amount supplied to exceed the amount demanded at that price—so that price could not be realized, and expectations would be disappointed. The supply-demand diagram, Figure 10–1, illustrates again how supply and demand interact to determine the level of the price that equilibrates a competitive market.

Yet there is more to the neoclassical model of competitive equilibrium than supply-and-demand curves. If buyers and sellers were often ill-informed or fickle in their decisions, their "supply" and "demand" would be useless constructs. Supply-and-demand curves have to be grounded in a *theory* of the behavior of suppliers and demanders.

FIGURE 10–1: The Determination of Equilibrium Price and Output by Supply and Demand

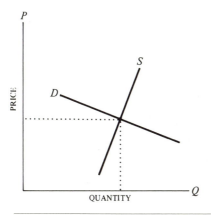

The neoclassical theory of competitive equilibrium supposes that all participants are perfectly informed as well as rational. Buyers and sellers are postulated to make *rational choices* in view of the *information* and the *expectations* they possess about all the prices, wage rates, and so on that matter to them. Further, buyers and sellers are postulated to be *completely informed* about all prices, wage rates, etc. in the present and to have correct expectations about all the prices, wage rates, and so on in the future.

> The neoclassical theory of equilibrium in a competitive market begins at the level of the behavior of the individual market participants under the ideal conditions of rationality and complete information. The total amount supplied to the market is seen as the sum of the amounts supplied by each of the individual sellers, and the total amount demanded is seen as the sum of the amounts demanded by the individual buyers. Hence, market supply is the "sum" of the individual supplies, and market demand is the "sum" of the individual demands. Figure 10–2 provides an example.

General Equilibrium, Classical Style

Barley growers are not in equilibrium if, while correctly forecasting the rewards of growing barley, they are underforecasting the price of rye to such an extent that they are going to wish they had planted less barley and more rye. The economist choosing between college teaching and business forecasting is out of equilibrium if he or she is misestimating the reward from forecasting or teaching or both. For the whole economy to be in a comprehensive equilibrium, therefore, *all* persons' expectations of *all* the prices must be correct—the prices paid for the productive services of the various kinds of labor, land, and capital (usually called wages, rents, and rentals) as well

FIGURE 10–2: Competitive Equilibrium in a Particular Market

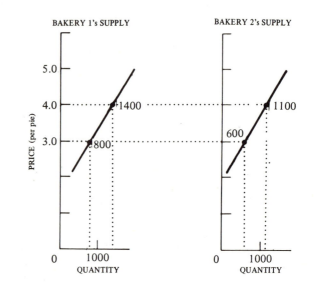

The market supply curve in Figure 10–2 shows the total amount that would be supplied to the market at any hypothetical equilibrium price. The total amount supplied at a given price is obtained by summing the amounts supplied by each of the suppliers. At the price of 3.0, for example, Bakery 1 would supply 8 hundred pizza pies and Bakery 2 would supply 6 hundred pies—for a total of 1 thousand 4 hundred (and an average of 7 hundred). Now suppose that there are 1 thousand firms. And suppose further that half the bakeries (5 hundred of them) are like Bakery 1

and half like Bakery 2. Then the average amount of pizza supplied per bakery is 7 hundred when the price is 3.0. And the *total* amount supplied by all bakeries is 7 hundred thousand as recorded in the center diagram.

The market demand curve shows the total amount that would be demanded at any hypothetical equilibrium price. The total amount demanded at a given price is calculated by summing the amounts demanded by each consumer at that price. At the price of 3.0, again, Consumer 1 would buy 3 pies and Consumer 2

as the prices of goods. This illustrates the basic concept of *general equilibrium:* everyone is right about everything—at least everything on which his or her actions depend.

- ♦ In its neoclassical version, general equilibrium means that *all* the markets, both the markets for all the goods produced and the markets for the (services of the) factors of production, are going to clear at the prices that suppliers of goods and factor services are expecting to prevail as they make their supply decisions. In the neoclassical portrait of general equilibrium, complete information as well as rationality are possessed by all.

Of course, the classical theoreticians have always realized that general equilibrium is an idealization of real life.

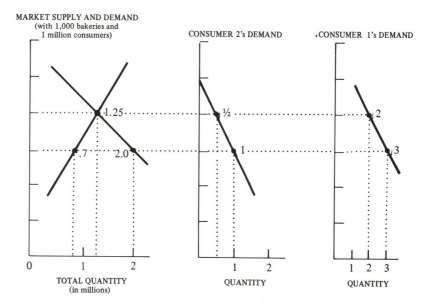

MARKET SUPPLY AND DEMAND
(with 1,000 bakeries and
1 million consumers)

CONSUMER 2's DEMAND

CONSUMER 1's DEMAND

TOTAL QUANTITY
(in millions)

QUANTITY

QUANTITY

would buy 1 pie for a total of 4 (and an average of 2). Now suppose that there are a million consumers. We illustrate the case where half of them are like the first consumer and half like the second. Hence the total amount demanded at the price of 3.0 is shown to be 2 million.

It follows that 3.0 cannot be the equilibrium price. If that were the actual and expected price, the quantity demanded would exceed the quantity supplied. So the market would not clear at that price; and we know the market always clears in classical theory! With .7 million sup-

plied, it could clear only at a price higher than 3.0—thus higher than the expected price. (A price around 5.0 would clear the market by limiting quantity demanded to .7 million.)

The equilibrium price can be seen to be *4.0*. If that is the price *expected* by sellers, 1.25 million pies will be brought to market, and the actual price necessary to clear the market will then be 4.0 also. This is the surprise-free scenario. (In equilibrium, then, half purchase half a pie, and "the other half" purchase 2 pies.)

EFFICIENCY IN PRODUCTION: THE CLASSICAL CLAIM

The most important classical claim for competitive equilibrium—for purely competitive markets operating under conditions of general equilibrium—is the claim that it achieves efficiency in production. To get some idea of what this means we ought to ask ourselves: What wouldn't be efficient? What sorts of resource allocations would be inefficient, wasteful? Two answers suggest themselves. First, there would be inefficiency *within* a particular industry if some producers (managers of the enterprises) were using too much labor, or too much capital, or too much land, while other producers were using too little; then, transferring some labor or capital or land from the former producers to the latter would result in a net increase of production in the industry. Second, there is another sort of inefficiency that could occur even if there is no inefficiency within an industry. There would be inefficiency *between* industries if one industry were using too much of one factor of production compared to another factor—say, too high a ratio of labor to land—while another industry were using too little of that factor of production compared to the other factor—too low a ratio of labor to land, in the example; then, transferring a little of that factor of production from the industry where it is used excessively to the other one, *and,* at the same time, moving some of the *other* factor of production in the reverse direction could achieve an increase in the outputs of *both* industries (or, if preferred, higher output in one and no decrease in the other). This can be proved, as will be shown below. *The theory of competitive equilibrium explains how, in that equilibrium, such inefficiencies are avoided.*

PRODUCTION EFFICIENCY WITHIN AN INDUSTRY

How does it happen that competitive equilibrium achieves production efficiency within each individual industry? Let us first sketch the argument without numerical examples and diagrams (though these will come later to make the argument more concrete). Imagine that some economic czar bent on intervening in the resource allocation occurring in some competitive industry were to reallocate a certain amount of some factor of production between one producer and another. Imagine, for example, that the czar's interference moved one unit of labor from one producer to another producer in the industry. Such a reallocation would increase total output only if the resulting *loss* of output that the *loss* of one unit of labor caused the former producer were *less* than the resulting *gain* of output capacity that the *gain* of one unit of labor permitted the latter producer. But that cannot be the result when the original resource allocation is a competitive equilibrium, as the following argument shows:

◆ First, note that the producer losing the unit of labor must have expected an extra revenue from hiring the last unit of labor *at least* as large as the wage paid to that worker—otherwise he would have lost some profit by hiring that last unit; and the producer gaining a unit of labor must have expected that the extra revenue that would have been obtained from hiring an extra unit of labor would have been *at most* as large as the wage needed to hire an extra worker—otherwise he would have profited by hiring an extra unit of labor. These points follow from the postulate that each firm achieves the maximum possible profit.

◆ Second, in a competitive equilibrium all producers face the *same* wage for the same sort of worker (and the same land rent for the identical type of land, the same rental for the same machine).

Therefore, the amount of extra revenue that the producer losing the unit of labor was expecting to obtain from hiring it must have been *at least* as large as the extra revenue that the producer gaining the unit of labor would have expected to obtain from hiring it.

◆ Third, in a competitive equilibrium all the producers face the same price for the same product being marketed and, if they must plan production ahead of time, have the same expectation of what the market price will be. Hence the price expected by each producer and used by him to figure the extra revenue that he should expect to obtain by producing more output is the same for all producers. (Call it *the* expected price.)

Therefore, the extra *output* that the producer losing the unit of labor expected to obtain from hiring it must have been *at least* as large as the extra output that the producer gaining the unit of labor would have expected to obtain from hiring it. (Why? We deduced above that the former producer expected at least as much extra revenue as the latter producer would have. And both of the producers were calculating the extra revenue to expect from producing and selling extra output with the same expectation of the price at which the industry's output will be sold. So the former producer could not have expected greater extra revenue from hiring that last worker because he expected a higher price than the other producer— which would have left open the possibility that the former producer could have expected a *lesser* extra output from hiring that last worker than would the other producer have.) Q.E.D.

An Illustration: Introducing Marginal Revenue Product

The argument may be illustrated by a numerical example. We consider two bakeries—any two of many competitive bakeries—in the bread industry. We take as given their use of land, stocks of capital equipment, etc., and focus on possible variations in a single input: the number of bakery workers.

In Table 10–1, panel A1 describes how, in Bakery 1, the output can be increased by employing more workers; panel A2 provides the analogous information about Bakery 2. These panels bring back the concept, introduced in chapter 4, of *marginal product*: the rate at which output increases with the increasing application of some input. Here the input is the number of full-time workers. So we interpret the marginal product of workers as the *increase of output resulting from the addition of the last worker*. Thus in panel A1 the marginal product associated with a total input of 71 is the

Table 10–1: VARIATION OF LABOR INPUT WITH OTHER INPUTS CONSTANT IN TWO PRODUCTION ESTABLISHMENTS: THE MARGINAL PRODUCT OF FULL-TIME WORKERS, THE EXPECTED MARGINAL REVENUE PRODUCT, AND EXPECTED MARGINAL PROFIT

| | Panel A1 | | | Panel B1 | | |
Bakery 1 Quantity of Labor	Total Product (TP)	Marginal Product (MP)	*Bakery 1* Expected Price (P^e)	Expected Marginal Revenue Product (MRP^e)	"Wage" (W)	Expected Marginal Profit ($MP \cdot P^e - W$)
67	1345	—	4	—	60	—
68	1366	21	4	84	60	—
69	1384	18	4	72	60	12
→70	1400	16	4	64	60	4 ←
71	1414	14	4	56	60	−4

| | Panel A2 | | | Panel B2 | | |
Bakery 2 Quantity of Labor	Total Product (TP)	Marginal Product (MP)	*Bakery 2* Expected Price (P^e)	Expected Marginal Revenue Product ($MP \cdot P^e$)	"Wage" (W)	Expected Marginal Profit ($MP \cdot P^e - W$)
52	1050.5	(—)	4	(—)	60	(—)
53	1068.0	17.5	4	70	60	10
54	1084.5	16.5	4	66	60	6
→55	1100.0	15.5	4	62	60	2 ←
56	1114.5	14.5	4	58	60	−2

It pays Bakery 1 to hire 70, not more; and Bakery 2 to hire 55 workers.

extra output accounted for by the addition of the 71st worker—"the marginal product of the 71st worker." (It amounts to 14 loaves, as shown.) The marginal product of the 70th worker is larger, and the marginal product of the 69th worker larger still. Evidently production is encountering *diminishing returns—decreasing marginal product of labor as successive workers are added.* Panel A2 records the sequence of marginal products of successive additions to the work force in Bakery 2. Here too the marginal product of labor is diminishing as additional workers are added.

The new concept introduced here is the *marginal revenue product:* the rate at which *revenue* received from the sale of the output increases with increasing application of some input. Having interpreted the marginal product of labor in the present example as the addition to output that resulted from adding one more full-time worker, it is natural to interpret the marginal revenue product of labor in the present example as the addition to *revenue* that resulted from adding one more worker. Further, we ought to bear in mind the distinction between the *actual* marginal revenue product— the marginal revenue product that is realized once the extra output is produced and sold on the market—and the *expected* marginal revenue product, which is just the expectation of the actual one.

- To calculate the *actual marginal revenue product* of the workers in the present example, the *marginal product* of the workers, which is the extra output sold, is *multiplied by the actual price* at which the industry output is sold. (If the additional output appreciably lowered the industry price, that complication would have to be factored into the calculation of marginal revenue product; but no such complication arises in the case of pure competition considered here.)
- To calculate the *expected marginal revenue product* of the workers in the present example, the *marginal product* of the workers is *multiplied by the "expected price"*—the price that the producer in question expects the industry output to sell at. (If the producer believed that by producing more he would lower appreciably the industry price, that complication would have to be taken into account in the calculation of marginal revenue product.)

Since each producer is out to obtain the *maximum possible expectation of profit,* according to classical theory, the number of production workers that will be hired by a producer has this obvious property: Hiring *fewer* workers would not increase the expected profit, ahd hiring *more* workers would not increase the expected profit either. It follows that the most profitable number of workers has been hired at the point where:

- the marginal revenue product expected from the *last* worker hired is enough (either more than enough or barely enough) to cover the wage rate of the workers; if it were *not* enough, there would be a reduction of expected profit from hiring the last worker, since the extra revenue expected to result from hiring him would be insufficient to pay him his wage.
- the marginal revenue product expected from hiring *one more* worker is less than enough to cover the wage that has to be paid to a worker; if it were *not* less, there would be a gain (at least no loss) in expected profit from hiring one more worker, since the extra revenue expected from hiring that worker would be sufficient to pay him his wage.

A basic competitive-equilibrium proposition of classical theory is, therefore, the following: *The point where the profit-maximizing firm stops hiring has the property that the marginal revenue product of the last worker exceeds or equals the wage, while the expected marginal revenue product of one more worker is less than the wage.*

Table 10–1 illustrates this proposition. Given a wage of 60 and the equilibrium price expectation 4.0, bakery 1 stops expanding at 70 workers and Bakery 2 at 55. Figure 10–3 depicts diagramatically the same example.

The rest of the argument is easy. If an economic czar were to move a unit of labor from Bakery 1—for a loss of output equal to 16—to Bakery 2—for a gain of output equal to 14.5, the net result would be a reduction of total

FIGURE 10–3: Expected Marginal Revenue Product and Wage Rate in
Two Bakeries

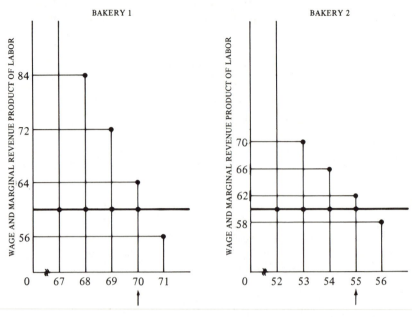

industry output obtained from the given total amount of labor working in
the industry. Furthermore, if the czar were to move a unit of labor from
Bakery 2—for a loss of output equal to 16.5—to Bakery 1—for a gain of
output equal to 14, the net result would also be a reduction of the total
output obtained from the given total input of labor to the industry.

There should be no mystery about this finding: Although some firms may
be very productive compared to others, each producer stops short of hiring
to the point where the marginal product of hiring one more worker multiplied by the expected price is less than the wage. So if a producer is "allocated" another worker by the czar while necessarily some other producer is
deprived of that worker, the result must be a reduction of the total product.
Why? Because the expected marginal revenue product *lost* by the losing
producer must be *greater* than the expected marginal revenue product *gained*
by the gaining firm—since the former must be *larger* than the wage, 60, and
the latter must be *smaller*. And since the expected price must be equal for
the two producers in competitive equilibrium, the same proposition must
hold true for the marginal products (in physical terms). So there cannot be
a gain in total industry output from any czar-conceived deviation of resource
allocation from the allocation yielded by competitive equilibrium. Q.E.D.

♦ The lesson may be summarized as follows: A pure-competition equilibrium achieves, as if by Smith's "invisible hand," an efficient allocation of all resources—land, labor, and capital—*within* any and every industry. That is, there is no way of rearranging the total amount of any factor of production that is being used by an industry—there is no reallocation of labor, land, or capital from one producer to another—that would produce a larger total output in the industry.

♦ If, contrary to the truth, there were ways of reallocating, say, labor that increased the output of the producers receiving extra labor by more than the decrease in the output of the producers having labor taken away, such a reallocation would imply that expected revenue and hence expected profit also increased more where labor was added than expected revenue and expected profit decreased where labor was taken away—since there is the same expected price and same wage everywhere. But that implies that the producers who supposedly obtained increased expected profit from getting more labor (at the going wage) could have profited earlier—before the hypothetical reallocation—by bidding some labor away from the producers who found labor less profitable, and that contradicts the premise that we started with a purely competitive equilibrium where each producer has acted to obtain the highest expected profit possible.

We are done with efficiency in production within any industry. But there is a point to make that will be useful in the next section: The contemporary economist, being impatient with clutter, asks why we should bother supposing that producers have to hire 0, 1, 2, etc., workers—as if the "amount of labor employed" had to be an integer. By the simple device of hiring part-time (and overtime) workers, a producer can vary the amount of labor input continuously, using 2.3750 workers, say, as if dialing the amount of labor the way we dial the amount of heat from a furnace or the decibels from a hi-fi rig. And even if that is not literally possible, it is close enough to being true that we might just as well pretend it is possible for the sake of the extra simplicity it brings.

In this simplification of the problem, we don't conceive of the marginal product of, say, labor as the extra product from adding one whole unit of labor—just as we don't think of the current speed of the *QE 2* as the extra distance traveled if the ship goes on sailing for one whole hour more. We conceive of the marginal productivity of labor *at a given level of the labor input* as the *rate* at which output would increase from adding labor: i.e., the extra output as a ratio to the extra (fraction of a unit of) labor when any tiny amount of labor (say, one or two man-minutes) is added—just as we think of the velocity of the *QE2 at any given moment of time* as the ratio of the extra distance traveled to the extra fraction of an hour elapsed over the next second or two.

FIGURE 10–4: Expected Marginal Revenue Product of Labor (in "Man-Hours") and the Hourly Wage Rate in 2 Bakeries

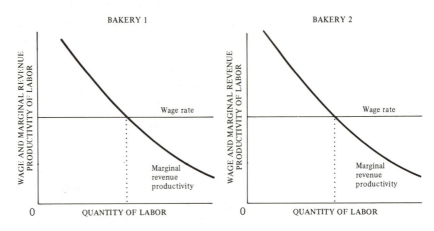

♦ As a consequence, the marginal productivity schedule may be a *continuous curve* (a continuous function), as depicted in Figure 10–4, rather than the sequence of points illustrated in Figure 10–3. Then labor is hired precisely to the point where the expected marginal revenue product just equals the wage rate—not one man-minute more, nor one less.

PRODUCTION EFFICIENCY BETWEEN ANY TWO INDUSTRIES

In a competitive equilibrium, then, each industry uses efficiently its labor, its land, and its capital. (Every grade of land and type of labor is allocated efficiently, the argument goes.) Yet an economic czar appearing on the scene might guess that the food industry is using too much of the economy's land and the cloth industry is employing too much of the economy's labor—so that by requisitioning some land from the former industry for use in the latter industry, and commandeering some labor from the latter industry for employment in the former industry, the czar could increase the output in both industries—or, at any rate, increase the output of one industry without curbing the output producible by the other one. How do we know that in competitive equilibrium the amounts of the factors of production are not allocated inefficiently *between* some pair of industries (one pair or many pairs)? What is there about classical equilibrium, with its exact profit maximization and law of one price and the rest, that would avoid inefficiency of this second (and subtler) kind? Fortunately, we now have the concepts to give a rough idea of the classical answer to that question.

To obtain the gist of the classical argument we may confine ourselves to the most convenient case—that in which each producer in both industries can dial, or fine-tune, the precise amount of each type of labor and capital and so on hired. Then, as the previous section explained, each producer will "dial" the hiring of that input precisely to the point at which the expected marginal revenue productivity of that input is exactly equal to the price per unit of that input. In our previous example, the bread industry, this means that each type of labor—for example, unskilled strong-back labor—is hired to the point where the expected marginal revenue productivity of labor is precisely equal to the corresponding wage; and each type of capital good—for example, tractors of a certain type—is hired to the point where the expected marginal revenue productivity of tractors is exactly equal to the rental on such tractors; and so on. Hence, letting P^e_{bread} stand for the expected bread price:

Wage of unskilled labor $= P^e_{bread} \times$ marginal product of unskilled labor
Rental on plain tractors $= P^e_{bread} \times$ marginal product of plain tractors
And so on.

Note, in passing, the following. When each of these equations is divided by its marginal product term, we have

$$P^e_{bread} = \frac{\text{Wage of unskilled labor}}{\text{Marginal product of labor}} = \frac{\text{Rental of plain tractors}}{\text{Marginal product of tractors}} = \text{etc.} = \text{Marginal cost}$$

Each of these ratios has a meaning. Suppose the marginal product of unskilled man-hours is 15 loaves. Then to produce one more loaf by adding just man-hours would require 1/15 more man-hours (an extra 4 minutes from someone). Suppose further the hourly money wage is 6 shekels. Then producing that extra loaf by adding only labor would cost $6 \times 1/15$ shekels. But this is exactly the ratio of the wage to the marginal product of unskilled labor. So the ratio of an input's "price" (its hire-price) to its marginal productivity is interpretable as the extra cost of producing an extra unit by adding *that* input. The equations above say that each way of adding output entails the same extra cost: *marginal cost*.

♦ Similar conditions hold, as a result of profit maximization, in every industry, of course. Take the bread and circus industries. In the circus industry, each producer will also be found hiring strong-back labor precisely to the point where the expected marginal revenue productivity of that labor (measured in gate receipts) precisely equals the wage for that sort of work; similarly, plain tractors will be found hired precisely at the point where their expected marginal revenue productivity (measured in box-office receipts) is precisely equal to the rental for those things. In the circus industry, therefore, we have the analogous conditions:

Wage of unskilled labor $= P^e_{circus} \times$ Marginal product of unskilled labor
Rental of plain tractors $= P^e_{circus} \times$ Marginal product of plain tractor
And so on.*

Here, P^e_{circus} stands for the expected price of circus admissions, of course.

The crucial observation to make now is that these two industries, like every other pair of industries, face the *same* wage for unskilled labor, the *same* rental for tractors, and so forth. Strong-back labor would all have left the farms where bread is grown to be roustabouts in the circus if the wage were higher in the latter industry than in the former. And sharp-penciled owners of tractors would not lease them at a rental below what they could get elsewhere. It follows, as night the day, that the ratio of the two marginal products in one industry is equal to the same ratio in the other industry. Both ratios are equal to the ratio of the "prices" of the two inputs.

$$\frac{\text{Marginal product of tractors in the bread industry}}{\text{Marginal product of labor in the bread industry}} = \frac{\text{Marginal product of tractors in the circus industry}}{\text{Marginal product of labor in the circus industry}} = \frac{\text{Rental (tractors) in all industries}}{\text{Wage (unskilled) in all industries}}$$

These conditions send out a clear message: Let the marginal product of tractors be 3 times (or .9 times or k times) the marginal product of labor in bread producing. Hence a czar or planner could remove one tractor from bread production and yet keep bread output constant by substituting exactly 3 workers (or .9 or k workers) in place of the tractor; and were a czar to pull out 3 workers (or .9 or k) from bread production, exactly one tractor would have to be substituted for them were it desired to keep bread output constant. Thus the ratio of the two marginal products is the rate at which the two inputs can be substituted for each other, output constant. It follows that:

- *If* that same ratio of the two marginal products in the *circus* business were *greater* than 3 (or .9 or whatever), the czar, by pulling out one *tractor* from the bread industry for use in a circus and substituting 3 workers (or .9 or whatever) pulled out of circus production, could keep *bread output constant* while making *circus output increase*—since adding one tractor to the circus industry would be more than enough to substitute for the three workers lost to the bread industry.

---

* Rearranging terms, as before, leads to the relations:

$$\frac{\text{Wage of unskilled labor}}{\text{Marginal product of labor}} = \frac{\text{Rental of plain tractors}}{\text{Marginal product of tractors}} = \cdots = P^e_{circus}$$

♦ *If* that same ratio in the circus industry were *smaller* than 3 (or whatever it is in the bread business), the czar, by pulling out 3 *workers* (or whatever) from the bread industry and substituting one tractor taken from the circus industry, could keep *bread output constant* yet make *circus output increase*—since adding three whole workers to the circus industry would be more than enough to substitute for the lost tractor.

These visions of inefficiency, these hopes for a free lunch, obviously rest on a discrepancy between the marginal product ratios in the two industries. But *in competitive equilibrium no such difference in the ratio of the marginal products occurs.* As the equations above make clear, in *all* industries the ratio of the two marginal products is equal to the *same* economy-wide ratio of the wage to the rental. Hence:

♦ In competitive equilibrium there is no inefficiency in production between industries. Production is efficient thanks to the fact that all producers face the same "factor prices" (the same cost of hiring an input) and, being profit maximizers, act to minimize their costs of producing any given amount of output by choosing between inputs (tractors, workers, etc.) with an eye to those relative factor costs.

This efficiency of production means that the production of bread and the production of circuses is at the frontier of society's production possibilities,

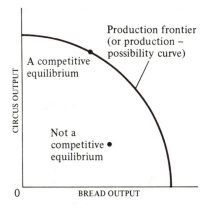

given the availability of labor and capital and land (and the rest) to that society. What has been established here is that any purely competitive equilibrium does have the virtue that it places society somewhere *on* the production-possibility curve in the accompanying diagram—not *inside* the production-possibility frontier, as would an inefficient allocation of resources.

EFFICIENCY IN CONSUMPTION: THE CLASSICAL CLAIM

Efficiency of production, it will be recalled, means that *given* amounts of the various inputs are not able, through some other allocation over the existing producers, to produce more of some good without producing less of some other. Efficiency of consumption means that *given* amounts of the outputs of the various consumer goods are not able, through some other "allocation" over the existing consumers, to produce preferred opportunities for one consumer without producing less-preferred opportunities for some other consumer or consumers.

The classical theory of competitive equilibrium makes a claim about the consumption efficiency of competitive equilibrium that is analogous to the production efficiency of that equilibrium—with some qualification. The claim is that when given totals of two or more goods are being distributed, or allocated, among the consumers, it is efficient that all the consumers face the same price for each particular good and that they be able to buy as much or as little as demanded at that price—and those are precisely the conditions that hold in pure competition: one price, which clears the market, for each good, not multiple prices and not any rationing of buyers or sellers.

Suppose, for example, that some people in a community are each deciding between a weekend trip to the oceanside resort, where it will be necessary to rent a room, and staying in town to go to the big game; there is a single price for general admission to the stadium, and all the seats are equally good. The classic case, in the classical theory of market equilibrium, is the case in which there is literally a fixed supply of both goods all of which is thrown onto the market at whatever price the market determines: So we suppose that all the identical rooms at the beachfront resort are rented, and the stadium in town is sold out. We also suppose, since we are dealing with competitive equilibrium, that prices are market-clearing and that they are known to all or correctly anticipated—so there is no one at the stadium gate with the price of admission, eager to get in, but unable to gain admittance. In this fashion, then, the classical "market" distributes the two scarce goods among the populace.

The classical argument for the efficiency of this market allocation is brilliantly clear: True, there may be some people who while having chosen the beach, would prefer, prices aside, to be at the big game instead of the beach. The Fairy Godmother could make such a person better off by transporting him or her to the game. But, then, someone else would thereby be excluded from the stadium and driven to the beach—which that latter person revealed (to us) was not his or her preference when he or she forked over the fancy price for admission to the big game! So he or she must then be made *worse* off. There can be no gain to some without a loss to some other.

Now suppose, for another example, that each person in the community can rent a number of rooms at the beach and buy a number of admissions to the stadium—over the whole season, say—instead of choosing between one room and one seat. This example is an easy extension of the previous example: The amount purchased of each good by a consumer is variable, rather than zero-or-one. Yet, as before, each consumer's purchases are limited by his or her budget and the prices of the two goods. And, as before, the total amount of rooms rented and the total number of seats "rented" in the stadium must just equal the given number available. Once again, the classical market will determine the market-clearing prices for the two goods. (*Two* goods only, provided that all weekends are alike, so a room early in the season is not a different good from a room later, etc.) Thus the "market" will distribute the two scarce goods among the consumers.

The argument showing the efficiency of this market allocation does not differ from the argument in the previous example in any essential way: Yes, there may be someone who would *prefer* at least one more game at the sacrifice of one weekend at the beach but who could not *afford* it. Yes, an economic czar could make such a person better off by awarding someone else's seat at a game to that person, and offering the vacated room to that someone else. But that latter person revealed that he or she did not prefer to give up a game for one more weekend at the beach when that person freely chose to buy as many admissions to games as he or she did! So there is no possibility—even for a czar!—of making one person better off without making some other person worse off.

To understand more deeply the claim of consumption efficiency in competitive equilibrium, consider now an example involving time and effort. Each individual in a community decides how much work to do in some activity—harvesting the corn, or picking the apple crop—in view of the rewards in compensation for the effort and inconvenience. The "work," or energy, might be measured by the number of bushels harvested. The reward structure offers a certain wage rate—really a piece rate, measured in corn (or bread or whatever) per unit of work performed. In the classic case, there is a fixed total of work demanded; the amount demanded stays constant no matter that the wage rate goes lower or higher (within some range, anyway). We may imagine, then, that the employers are going to harvest every last bushel. The reward level is then determined: It is just large enough to clear the market for work. The rate paid per unit of work performed—the piece rate per bushel—is low enough to prevent a surplus of work supplied and high enough to prevent a shortage. In this way, the classical market distributes the work to be performed (and hence efforts made, leisure lost) and the reward to be received over the population.

Could the Tooth Fairy, stepping into this scene, make anyone better off without making another worse off? The situation is not promising: Someone's work could be lightened, reward constant, but then another's work would have to be increased (since total work is given). Someone's reward could be raised, his work unchanged, but that would lower the reward left for the other workers—taking as given the produce to be left, after payment of rewards to work, as income for the employing enterprises and for the government. In desperation, the aspiring fairy might contemplate reducing someone's work, which that person evidently feels he can't afford to do himself when his work is rewarded at the market wage, *while cutting* that someone's reward by *less* than it would have cost him at the market wage rate—*enough less* to make him better off. But then another worker (or workers) would have to work more in return for an *extra reward* that is *less* than that worker would have earned had he worked that much more at the market wage rate. Since such a worker revealed his preference not to do that extra work for the extra reward obtainable at the market wage rate, compelling the worker to do it for the *lesser* extra reward would make him worse off. Therefore, no one can gain save at the expense of one or more others.

COMMENTS AND CAUTIONS

We have shown that a competitive equilibrium, as conceived in classical economics, achieves efficiency in production: Given the amounts of leisure demanded by each person, the resulting availabilities of effort are used as efficiently as possible; there is no way of causing more of one good to be produced by means of redistributing inputs among producers of that good; the only way of causing more of one good to be produced is by causing more inputs to be deployed, and that would cause less of another good to be produced. Second, it was shown that, under certain conditions at any rate, competitive equilibrium achieves efficiency in consumption: Given the bundle of outputs of the various goods that is produced, there is no way of redistributing that collection of goods in such a way as to make one person better off without making another person worse off.

However, it does *not* follow that the achievement of production efficiency plus consumption efficiency adds up to efficiency *overall*—to efficiency in the sense of Pareto. Maybe the amounts of *leisure* demanded by people are not efficient in the ideal sense at any rate—maybe everyone, to take a simple case, would benefit from working more in return for the resulting extra output. It may happen in a society that its system of taxation causes all to work less than is in their mutual interest—to work less than the ideal. Let us defer to a later chapter, chapter 13, the question of whether the best, most acceptable, kind of taxation necessarily has this distortionary effect on "incentives."

Nevertheless, it is only fair to anticipate a conclusion of that discussion of distortionary taxation: If there is in fact no ideal way of taxing—of paying for government expenditures on "goods" and paying for the "redistribution" of rewards—that should not be taken as an inescapable strike against competitive markets in favor of czarlike planners of resource allocation. The virtues of competitive equilibrium remain virtues. How impressive that, whatever the supplies of effort generated by a competitive equilibrium, given the system of taxation in place, those supplies could not produce more of one good without producing less of another. And how impressive that the resulting supplies of goods could not be redistributed to make one consumer better off without making another worse off.

SUMMARY

1. This chapter is the first to examine the properties of the resource allocation generated, under equilibrium conditions, by free markets. Our interest is in the *performance* of the market mechanism, not so much in the effects of changes in resources and tastes on the quantities and prices of the goods produced. In this chapter the focus is on the efficiency of markets when the prevailing situation is one of *pure competition* among sellers and buyers.

2. Classical market theory supposes that each participant is rational, desires the best price, and is able costlessly to be perfectly informed. From these supposed features of the marketplace the classical analysis deduces the *law of one price* and, second, the *law of market clearing*. (These laws apply to an industry under the control of a monopolist as well as to one under competition.)

3. Pure competition is associated with the situation where each seller and buyer is so "small" as to have only a negligible effect on the market price, even when he doubles or quadruples his sale or purchase. (But if a new enterprise could "enter" the industry to "contest" the market share of an existing enterprise, then even a "monopolist," although the only actual seller, might have no "monopoly power" to drive up the price by constricting output since, by doing so, the monopolist might suicidally attract new entrants.) So, under pure competition, each seller, for example, takes as given—beyond his individual control—the price he expects to receive and likewise takes as *given* the wage rate required by labor, the rent demanded by land owners, and so forth.

4. The expected *marginal revenue product* of an input is the extra *revenue* expected to be added as the result of adding an extra unit of the input. Hence it is equal, under pure competition, to the *marginal product* of the extra unit—the number of extra units of output resulting—*times* the *price*

expected to be received: Hence

$$MRP^e = MP \cdot P^e \text{ (where } ^e \text{ means "expected")}$$

If a producer chooses the number of workers and other inputs hired so as to obtain the maximum possible expected profit, as supposed, then

MRP^e of the last (or previous) worker hired $\geq W$ (W for wage) since the expected revenue benefit must exceed or cover his wage
MRP^e of an extra worker hired would be $< W$
for if such an additional worker is not hired it must be because the expected revenue benefit would *not* cover the wage cost

Similar rules describe the profit-maximizing hire of land, fuel oil, trucks, and so forth.

5. In the classical theory of the marketplace, all the sellers or suppliers take as given the *same* wage rate, the *same* land rental, and so on—since they are postulated to be perfectly informed about going wages and rents, and, by the law of one price, there *is* only *one* going wage and *one* land rent and so forth, at any particular moment. In *equilibrium* conditions, moreover, all the firms in an industry have the *same* expectation of the industry price—since, in equilibrium, everyone's expected price is *equal* to the actual price that is going to emerge; and, by the law of one price, there is going to be only *one* actual price.

6. It can then be argued that this competitive equilibrium is *efficient* in certain respects. To see that there is *efficiency in production within any particular industry* under competitive equilibrium conditions, consider this thought-experiment: A central planner with emergency powers swoops down onto the competitive-equilibrium economy to "reallocate" a worker, say, from one enterprise to another in the same industry. We now know that

the MRP^e of the worker where he is removed $\geq W$ since he was worth at least the going wage in that employment
the MRP^e of the additional worker where he is added $< W$ since one more worker was *not* hired before and hence an extra worker must not have been worth the wage cost
Hence the MRP^e from the worker's addition at one enterprise $<$ the MRP^e from the workers' removal from the other enterprise.
But since the enterprises have the *same* P^e it follows that the MP from the worker's addition in one place is $< MP$ in the other. Therefore total industry output would be *decreased* as a consequence of the reallocation by the overzealous central planner.

Hence resources are being allocated efficiently within the industry: There is no reallocation, or rearrangement, within the industry that could produce a larger quantity of the industry's product.

7. A related, more involved argument, which need not be recapitulated here, shows that there is *efficiency of production among industries:* There is no way of trading, say, labor for land or vice versa with *another* industry that could lead to an increase of either industry's capacity output without reducing the other's. Hence under *competitive equilibrium* there is *efficiency of production.*

8. There is also *efficiency in consumption,* there being no way to make one consumer better off without making any other consumer worse off.

9. There is not necessarily efficiency in the level of economic activity—total employment and so forth—because of the income tax and other "distortions." But the aforementioned efficiencies remain admirable and useful virtues.

CONCEPTS INTRODUCED

perfect information	marginal revenue product, expected and actual	efficiency in production within an industry among industries
law of one price	marginal cost	efficiency in consumption
law of market clearing	marginal productivity of a continuously variable, or perfectly divisible, input	efficiency in labor/leisure choices
pure competition, or "atomistic" competition		

STUDY QUESTIONS

1. In the classical argument explaining why competitive equilibrium yields production efficiency in an industry, what is the role played by profit maximization? By the law of one price for any one homogeneous input (such as identical land)? By correct expectations?

2. What is the role of these same features of competitive equilibrium in the classical argument why there results production efficiency *between* any two industries that are in competitive equilibrium?

3. Explain why in the neoclassical theory of competitive equilibrium marginal cost equals price.

4. Is efficiency in consumption (as this term is used here) about the mix of consumer goods produced or the allocation of given consumer goods over the consumers with purchasing power to buy them?

CHAPTER 11

Market Interferences by the Government: The Classical Objections

CHIEF (to the tribe):
The palace has outlawed our music throughout the land. But we must find a way to perform again our gypsy music!

Richard Tauber (to the chorus) in *Forbidden Music* (1936)

I N the previous chapter we considered the main part of the classical claim for free markets operating under competitive conditions. There was the argument that a competitive equilibrium yields production efficiency. There was the further argument that a competitive equilibrium yields efficiency in consumption. However, this praise of the free market would add up to little or nothing if *every* system of resource allocation, from a system of private monopolies to a system of government rationing and conscription, were *also* efficient.

The classical position is that competitive markets would yield an efficient resource allocation *and* that markets *interfered* with (by governments or private interests) do *not*. The thrust of the classical position is its forceful indictment of interferences with free markets. From Adam Smith onward to Milton Friedman and the Chicago School in this century, the classical theoreticians have damned those politicans and private individuals who act to obstruct the workings of market competition.

In this chapter we hear and weigh the classical indictment of certain governmental interferences with a competitive market—interferences such as price or wage controls, price supports, rationing, and so on. (The next chapter, on private monopoly, will consider private rather than governmental interferences with competitive markets.)

PRICE FLOORS: MINIMUM WAGES AND PRICE SUPPORTS

A government interferes with the outcome of a market when it puts a floor under the price of a good or productive service. One method of doing so is by decree. The government can establish a floor below which the price will not fall by making it illegal, and subject to penalties, for a buyer to purchase at less than that price; or for a seller to sell at less. There are a few curious examples of price floors by decree in goods markets: Municipal governments often set minimum taxi fares, provincial (or state) governments sometimes set minimum prices for milk, certain legal services. However the leading case is undoubtedly found in factor markets: It is the minimum wage.

THE MINIMUM WAGE

The standard classical analysis of the effects of a minimum wage law, and appraisal of the efficiency of such a law, supposes that markets would produce a competitive equilibrium in the absence of that law—because markets are perfectly competitive, everyone's expectations are fulfilled, and so forth. The analysis begins with the tools of supply and demand. In competitive equilibrium, the wage rate for any particular type of labor service is such that the quantity demanded is precisely matched by the quantity supplied. An effective minimum wage law—one that makes any difference—enacts a higher wage. But at that higher wage, in general, the quantity demanded is less than the quantity supplied. A surplus of that labor results.

Asked to give his views on the minimum wage law, the man-in-the-street is apt to note that those unskilled workers who retain their jobs will receive a higher wage, which is probably good—though the increased cost of hiring unskilled workers may reduce the number hired, which is certainly bad (to the extent of the reduction). In contrast, the classical economist is unable to find anything good to say about it, because he sees it as inefficient: The clearest inefficiency comes from violation of the law of one price, since only the lucky ones get the good wage. In theory, then—the *classical* theory, that is—repealing the minimum wage law would make it possible to make some better off while making none worse off, or to make everyone a little better off. How to prove it? The trick is to compensate those who would lose from repeal out of taxes levied on some who would otherwise gain:

> The classical economist can prove the point this way: Let the government abolish the minimum wage law and introduce an employment tax on hiring unskilled workers. The tax per worker is to be set at the level just high enough to make the wage cost *paid* by enterprises to hire an unskilled worker—the cost per unit of unskilled labor *including* the employment

FIGURE 11–1: A Minimum Wage Law Can Raise a Wage Rate above Its Competitive-Equilibrium Level

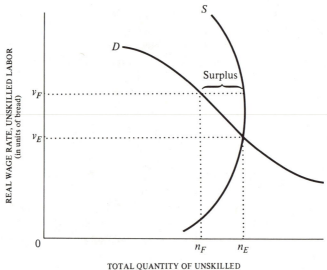

A minimum wage law, if designed to be effective, decrees that workers doing certain work must be paid not less than some "minimum wage" that exceeds the wage that would result in its absence. In the classical analysis, the latter wage rate is the competitive-equilibrium wage, labeled v_E in the diagram. The wage floor, or minimum wage, is denoted v_F. The law is "effective" in this illustration since v_F exceeds v_E.

A necessary consequence of the imposition of an above-equilibrium wage is the creation of a discrepancy between the amount of labor demanded by enterprises and the amount of labor supplied by workers. In general, the result is an excess of the quantity supplied over the quantity demanded—hence a surplus.

Since the demand curve for the productive factor is downward sloping—negatively sloped rather than vertical—the quantity of labor services hired by enterprises when faced with the minimum wage, denoted n_F, is smaller than the competitive-equilibrium level, n_E.

tax—exactly as high as it was before repeal of the minimum wage law. Since the cost of hiring unskilled labor is therefore still equal to the old wage floor, v_F in Figure 11–1, enterprises will hire the same number of unskilled workers as before—namely, n_F, the amount of unskilled labor demanded when the wage cost is v_F. So the enterprises' owners and other employees and suppliers will be unaffected by the switch. On the other hand, every unskilled worker who has been lucky enough to be employed will find that since the wage cost paid to employ him is unchanged, while the government now siphons off a portion of that payment through its employment tax, there is a fall in the wage *received*—the wage cost paid by enterprises *minus* the tax; it falls by the amount of the tax. But wait! Out of the tax revenue just collected by the employment tax, each such employee under the minimum wage law can be paid a special lump sum transfer. With this grant, he can stay employed at the old reward or retire with it, giving his job to one who wants it more.

Whenever economists think about fiats, decrees, and ukases intended to "defeat" free markets, they quickly begin to wonder about the possibilities for evasion and black markets. How do we know that the enterprises will not evade the minimum wage law by paying the floor wage "on paper," in one set of books, while actually laying out the market-clearing wage? For example, the firm could demand a "kickback" from each unskilled worker as the "price" for being hired. The situation would then look as in the first diagram on page 262. The firms all claim to be paying v_F but are actually paying v_E after netting out kickbacks and any noncash favors; and since the wage is truly v_E the enterprises actually employ the competitive-equilibrium quantity of unskilled workers, n_E.

There is a variation on this maneuver that has the advantage of being perfectly legal. While minimum wage laws aim to jack up wage rates, especially those at the low end, there is no way that the laws can hold constant the amount of strain, stress, risk, odium, tedium, and so forth that the employers will require from the employees who have gotten the legally mandated minimum wage. What is to keep the enterprises hiring unskilled workers from requiring "more" from those workers until the supply of them to the market has shrunk to the point where there is no more surplus—no more excess of amount supplied over amount demanded? Maybe nothing. In that event we have the situation in the second diagram on page 262. The market for unskilled labor

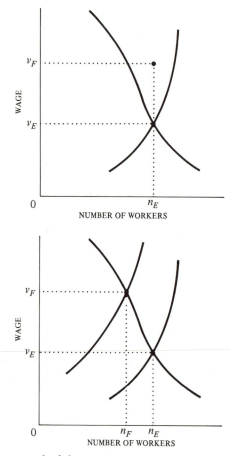

NUMBER OF WORKERS

NUMBER OF WORKERS

clears again. But the wage rates, employment levels, effort levels, and so forth are *not* those of competitive equilibrium. As seen through the lens of classical theory, employers have been presented with a nonmarket incentive to require more effort from unskilled workers. This distortion of their incentives must lead to inefficiency (though not necessarily an erasure of the gain to the unskilled workers who choose to keep their harder but better-paying jobs). From the new equilibrium *cum* distortion, with wage rate at the mandated v_F, repeal of the minimum wage law can be shown to make possible gains for all. In classical theory, competitive equilibrium without distortions yields the right level of effort. So the side effect that the minimum wage law may have on the amount of effort does not yield a redeeming side benefit that could offset its ill effects on efficiency.

PRICE SUPPORTS

Why can't there be minimum prices by decree for goods as well as factors of production—for plane trips, marriage ceremonies, cotton, bourbon, tomatoes, appendectomies . . . ? There can be, and such decrees are not uncommon. However, it is often difficult to enforce such regulations; enforcement may require expensive monitoring of licensed sellers and detection of unlicensed bootleggers. (Even in countries where the management of "capital" and normally the ownership too is largely in the hands of the state, the state-run enterprises may find themselves in competition with underground suppliers of similar goods; and the government may find it best to allow or encourage the legal enterprises to compete freely against the underground ones rather than sticking to uncompetitive prices.)

Furthermore, there is often a better or more tempting way to establish a price floor for a good. In a great many cases the government can achieve the minimum price—give or take a bit—by operating *through* the market, by *intervening* in the market rather than interfering with its operation by preventing the market from clearing. The government can raise the equilibrium market-clearing price by supplementing the demand for the good or, as we shall note later, by contracting the supply.

♦ One technique by which the government can effect a higher price for the suppliers of a good is crude but direct: It can make purchases of the good own demand to the demand of the other buyers, it can support the market price at the desired level. This is the technique of price support. See Figure 11–2.

FIGURE 11–2: Government Purchases of a Good Can Bid Up the Equilibrium Market-Clearing Price to a Support Level above Its Competitive-Equilibrium Level

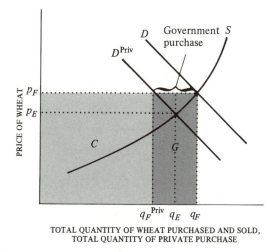

TOTAL QUANTITY OF WHEAT PURCHASED AND SOLD,
TOTAL QUANTITY OF PRIVATE PURCHASE

A government wheat purchase of the quantity indicated (in bushels, kilos, or whatever) will drive up the equilibrium market-clearing price to the desired support level, denoted by p_F. Without any government purchase, we suppose, the equilibrium market-clearing price would have been the level corresponding to competitive equilibrium, denoted p_E.

When there is no government purchase, the demand comes only from the private sector and so the private demand curve applies—the demand curve labeled D^{priv}. This demand curve measures the sum of the purchases of wheat that private individuals (nongovernmental bodies) would like to make at each possible price. At p_E this private demand curve intersects the supply curve. Hence p_E is the equilibrium market-clearing price when there is no government purchase.

At p_F there would be a surplus in the absence of any government purchase. The size of this hypothetical surplus indicates exactly the wheat quantity the government must purchase in order to make p_F (instead of p_E) the equilibrium market-clearing price. When it steps into the market to purchase that quantity, it adds precisely that amount to the overall quantity demanded by the private sector *plus* government; the overall demand curve will lie to the right of the private demand curve by just that amount, and thus intersect S at p_F.

FIGURE 11–3: Subsidization of Sales (or Purchases) of a Good Can Serve to Prop Up Suppliers' Income by Raising the Selling Price without wasting Any Output in Government Storage Bins

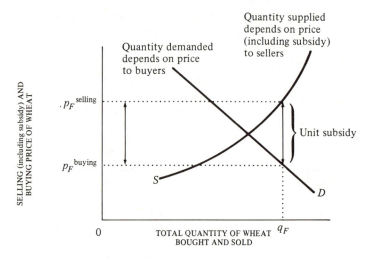

Quantity supplied depends on price (including subsidy) to sellers

Quantity demanded depends on price to buyers

SELLING (including subsidy) AND BUYING PRICE OF WHEAT

$p_F^{selling}$

p_F^{buying}

Unit subsidy

S

D

0   TOTAL QUANTITY OF WHEAT q_F
BOUGHT AND SOLD

Suppose that the aim of the government subsidy program is to bring the price received by suppliers up to the support level p_F. With a subsidy present, the price received is the sum of the unit price paid by buyers *plus* the unit subsidy paid by the government.

To calculate the required subsidy, the government must first figure that if the selling price is supported at the level p_F, the amount supplied to the market will be q_F—for, just as in Figure 11–2, q_F is the amount supplied when the price received by suppliers is p_F. But if the government is not going to make any crop purchases to support the price, and if q_F is the amount actually supplied to the market (because p_F is the level of the selling price suppliers actually receive), then q_F must also be the amount purchased by nongovernment buyers. Hence the *buying price*—the price paid on each unit by any buyer—must be just low enough to make the amount demanded by these buyers equal to q_F; otherwise, the buying price would not clear the market. The gap, or wedge, between the buying price at q_F and the selling price is exactly the size of the subsidy per unit needed to drive the selling price up to p_F.

To test understanding, consider the matter from the standpoint of buyers. The introduction of a government subsidy to suppliers of 1 shekel or 5 kopecks will reduce by exactly that amount the buying price that buyers will have to pay for any given total quantity bought: While there is no change in the selling price necessary to elicit from suppliers any given quantity supplied, a part of that selling price is now being provided by the government; hence the remaining part to be paid by the buyers of the good is reduced by exactly that much. Thus the subsidy lowers by a fixed amount the buying price that "goes with" each possible quantity supplied. This is shown

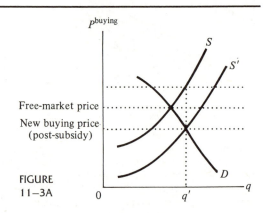

p^{buying}

S

S'

Free-market price

New buying price (post-subsidy)

D

FIGURE 11–3A

0   q'   q

Crop price-support programs were instituted in the United States on a large scale after World War II and spread later to many other countries. It did not take much experience with such price-support programs before it began to be widely sensed that such a method of boosting the prices received by producers of certain commodities—wheat, potatoes, rice, soybeans, nuts— was wasteful. The spectacle of silos full of deteriorating foodstuffs was visible evidence of some kind of inefficiency; it ought to be possible to construct another program that would be better for some or all and worse for none. In the United States two public officials, Charles Brannan and Ezra Taft Benson, earned a permanent place in American economics textbooks by advocating a plan to replace crop purchases with subsidies. Through subsidy schemes, classical analysis showed, farmers could be compensated for the fall of their prices while city folk could be made better off; or farmers made better off and urban denizens no worse; or everyone better off.

♦ The gist of the classical proof that subsidies are superior to price support is this: Let the government stop its purchases and instead offer a unit subsidy to farmers for each unit produced and sold in the market. Such a subsidy lowers the price *to the consumer* needed to elicit any given amount supplied by the farmers (since the government contributes part of the price). So if we measure the price to the consumer on the vertical axis of a diagram like Figure 11–3, the introduction of the subsidy shifts the supply curve downward. Let the government make the *subsidy just big enough to drive down the consumer price to the point where the same amount is consumed and produced as was produced before* under the support purchase program. Then *the price to the suppliers* (which includes the unit subsidy) *is the same as before;* otherwise, the farmers (canny lot) wouldn't

in Figure 11–3A by the new curve, labeled *S'*, which lies below the supply curve *(S)* by a fixed, uniform amount equal to the size of the subsidy. The new curve is a sort of supply curve as seen by buyers; it indicates the selling price *minus subsidy* at each possible quantity supplied.

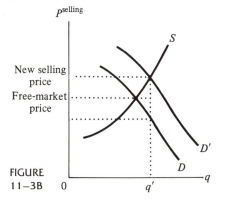

FIGURE
11–3B

Symmetrically, the subsidy may be considered from the standpoint of sellers. A government subsidy of 1 shekel will *raise* by that much the selling price that would be received by suppliers from any given total amount sold. While there is no change in the price that buyers are willing to pay for any given amount sold to them, the unit subsidy is a supplement that the government pays suppliers on each unit sold, and this fixed supplement adds exactly that much to the selling price received by suppliers. Thus the subsidy raises by a fixed amount the selling price that "goes with" each possible quantity demanded. This is shown in Figure 11–3B, by the curve *D'* that lies above the demand curve *(D)* by a fixed, uniform amount equal to the size of the subsidy. The new curve is a kind of demand curve as seen by the sellers; it shows the buying price *plus subsidy* at each possible quantity demanded.

be producing the same as before—the amount supplied would be different. So farmers are neither better nor worse off. City folks' taxes to pay for farmers' assistance, measured in city-made cloth, plus their exenditure on food is still the same rectangle it was before, bordered by $0q_F$ and $0p_F$. So it does not seem they are hurt. *And,* they are now eating more in return for this rectangle of total cloth outlay in the form of taxes plus food expenditure.

In deliberating on subsidies as substitutes for price-support purchases, politicians soon began asking whether the subsidy program would entail a greater or smaller budgetary outlay by the government. In theory, the (right) answer can go either way. As the upper diagram shows, under the subsidy program, the urban consumers lay out C_1 (in units of citymade cloth) for their wheat. The C_1 rectangle is simply the buying price of wheat (in units of cloth) *times* the amount bought. The rest of what the suppliers receive is the government outlay, G_1. The G_1 rectangle is unit subsidy *times* amount supplied.

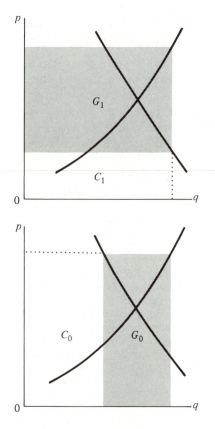

Under the crop-purchase program, the consumer outlay is C_0, which is the total quantity bought by private buyers *times* the price. And the government outlay, G_0, is the amount bought by the government times the price paid.

If the two programs are to give the same price and same revenue to the suppliers, then $C_1 + G_1 = C_0 + G_0$. It follows that the crop-purchase program would involve a lesser government outlay *($G_0 < G_1$)* if $C_0 > C_1$, and the subsidy would be "cheaper" if $C_0 < C_1$.

The question, then, boils down to whether the crop-purchase program, with its high buying price to city-folk buyers, causes them to make a larger outlay on the farm good than they would make under the low-buying-price program. Agricultural economists had the answer to that one. Yes, nearly every farm good seems to have the property that when the price goes up, the quantity demanded goes down all right, but not by so much in proportionate terms as the price goes up: The *percentage* reduction in the quantity demanded is less than the percentage increase in price, hence the outlay (price times quantity demanded) hangs higher at the higher price. If so, then the subsidy program would entail a larger budgetary outlay by the government.

For the politicians this finding was a serious drawback to the subsidy scheme. But classical economics provided a counter: While the subsidy scheme would cost city-folk some extra taxes, their savings on wheat and other farm-good purchases, thanks to the subsidized prices, would be exactly enough to pay those extra taxes. And for the same total cloth outlay, the total $C + G$ rectangle, they would get additional wheat and other farm goods—precisely the amounts that the government was buying up under the crop-purchase programs and largely wasting.

PRICE CEILINGS: MAXIMUM PRICES AND RATIONING

Society, through the long arm of the government, may also interfere with the operation of markets so as to establish a *lower* price for a good than would result if the market for that good were left free. One way by which the government can hold down the price is to establish a legal ceiling price and make it illegal (with penalties) for a seller to sell, and possibly for a buyer to buy, at a price above this maximum price. History continues to throw out fresh examples of price ceilings by decree, after classical economists had thought they were finished: War-time price controls have usually consisted largely of the enactment of such legal ceilings; in recent years many "energy" prices—natural gas and home heating oil in some countries—have been subject to ceilings despite the stiff competition in oil refining and gas extraction; and there are traditional examples as well, such as that love for sale is illegal and army draftees cannot hire others to take their place in the conscription. (Of course, the agencies that regulate certain industries also set maximum prices in some cases as well as minimum prices; but regulating the local electric company's rate structure or the telephone company's toll at coin-box pay phones is apparently, not an interference with *competitive* equilibrium, which is our subject in *this* chapter.)* Perhaps the classic cases of price ceilings, however, occur in the market for credit, where until fairly recently "usury laws" placed extensive ceilings on interest rates, and in the market for urban residential housing, where we find "rent controls" in a growing number of cities around the world.

MAXIMUM RENTALS

Let us once again suppose, proceeding in the classical vein, that the market for city apartments, because it is a perfect market, would have yielded a competitive equilibrium—in the absence of ceilings on rentals. In that would-have-been competitive equilibrium, the rental for any particular kind of apartment (2 BR, so exp. . . .) equates the quantity demanded to the total supplied. If it is effective, as we suppose, the "rent-control" program legis-lates a lower rental. At that lower rental, in general, the quantity supplied will be less than the quantity demanded. Thus there results a shortage of that kind of apartment. Figure 11–4 gives the picture. As with minimum wages, the classically-minded economist will have no difficulty demonstrat-ing, in classical terms, the inefficiency of this rent-control arrangement:

♦ Abolish the rent control, the classical argument goes, so that the rental will rise from the ceiling level, z_C in Figure 11–4, to the equilibrium level, denoted z_E. This rise of the rental presents each apartment owner with a windfall gain (or an end to windfall losses). Hence landlords can be assessed a special lump sum tax equal to $z_E - z_C$ on each such apartment owned without leaving them worse off (net of their windfall gain). The tax reve-nue thus collected can then be used to make a grant—technically called a transfer payment—in the amount $z_E - z_C$ to each family previously enjoy-ing a lease at the now-repealed rental ceiling in order to compensate each such family for the rise in the rental. Then, those families able to afford z_E but previously lacking city apartments—owing to the shortage—can swap with old tenants (who may prefer to save by moving away) or rent any new apartments (which the higher rents may stimulate) for a mutual gain!

Effective rent controls create incentives for evasion and black markets, as all interferences with the market do. For example, landlords will be tempted to demand "key money" from pro-

---

*The characteristics of a monopolistic equilibrium and the analysis of regulatory interferences with such an equilibrium by the government are the subject of the next chapter.

FIGURE 11–4: A Rent-Control Law Can Reduce an Apartment Rental below Its Competitive-Equilibrium Level

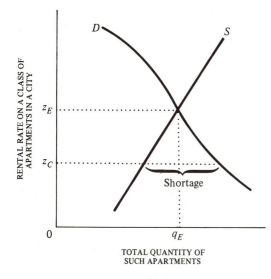

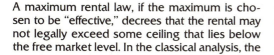

TOTAL QUANTITY OF
SUCH APARTMENTS

latter rental level is the competitive-equilibrium rental, labeled z_E in the diagram. The rental ceiling, or maximum rental, is denoted z_C. If the ceiling is effective, therefore, z_C is smaller than z_E.

The introduction of an effective ceiling necessarily creates a discrepancy between the number of apartments demanded in the city and the number supplied. The diagram shows a shortage to result from the enactment of the below-competitive-equilibrium ceiling—an excess of quantity demanded over quantity supplied.

At the lower rental, some landlords do not replace their apartment buildings with new ones as the former wear out; and some buildings may be shut down temporarily or abandoned, if their lower rental no longer covers maintenance costs. These actions account for the reduction in the amount supplied—i.e.; the "slope" possessed by the supply curve. The increase in the quantity demanded resulting from the reduction of the rental is explained by the willingness of more people from the suburbs and from other cities to move to the city and to rent an apartment there in view of the lower rental—provided such an apartment is readily available.

A maximum rental law, if the maximum is chosen to be "effective," decrees that the rental may not legally exceed some ceiling that lies below the free market level. In the classical analysis, the

spective new tenants (or induce their superintendants to demand it) as the "price" that must be paid in order to be one of the lucky ones to have an apartment at the controlled rental. Imaginably, the landlords would obtain about the same income as before the ceiling—the key money just offsetting the fall of rentals. (But that extreme case would undoubtedly not occur, since landlords would have to demand cash to prevent evidence against them in case of investigation, and some prospective tenants would be unable or, in view of the nuisance cost, unwilling to produce the whole amount necessary to give the landlord the same income as before.)

More interesting is the incentive that rent control creates for perfectly legal avoidance—as distinct from evasion. Landlords can avoid some of the cost to them of the reduction of their rentals by correspondingly reducing the quality of the existing apartments. They could always have done that, it is true. But they didn't do it before (beyond the poor level of quality they had already attained) because to do it further would have been a loss in the competitive rental that the landlord's apartment would have been able to fetch in the market. But once there is a shortage of a landlord's apartments to begin with, so that he could rent another quickly if he had one even with some reduction in its quality, then the incentive to keep up quality is eroded.

SUPPLY INTERVENTION: PUBLIC HOUSING

There are better ways than the method of decree to keep down certain prices. When the institution of a price ceiling leads to a manifest shortage, with cries of "unfair" and "do something" by the buyers left short, governments often respond by doing something: They often seek to reduce or eliminate the shortage by acting to supplement the supply. The government could dispense with decrees and rely solely on supply.

◆ A technique by which the government can establish a lower market price for the benefit of those demanding a good is simply to produce a quantity of the good itself and to sell (or lease) that quantity in order to "bid down" the market price. By thus adding its own supply to the supply of the other sellers (or lessors) it can control the market price at the level it desires.

Is such supply intervention inefficient? Is it inefficient in the same way that the demand intervention illustrated by crop purchases to support crop prices was seen to be inefficient? To discuss this question it may be well, for the sake of definiteness, to stick to our example of city housing and the government's desire to hold down apartment rentals.

It is clear that the production and leasing of additional apartments is not wasteful in the same spectacular way that purchasing wheat to let it rot is wasteful. If the government built the apartments but kept them vacant and decaying, there would be no extra supply to the *market*, and hence no resulting reduction in the market rental for such apartments. Only a complete skeptic would say that the people who took the additional apartments (when the rental on that type of apartment fell) had little use for them, which is like saying that government purchases of wheat are not appreciably wasteful because people are overeating anyway. If our skeptic is right to say that having more of the various goods is generally worthless (and having less is harmless), we can forget efficiency and political economy (to do more of something else that's worthless too!).

Yet public housing programs do contain the possibility of inefficiency. Imagine that political influence or mere bureaucratic imperfection causes some people leasing public housing to enjoy lower rentals than others are paying for the same type of apartment; it is even easier to imagine that some people will get much nicer apartments than others for the same rental because for one reason or another these apartments are all in the same official category. Then there is inefficiency, with parallels to the inefficiency resulting from minimum wages. Some people are renting their apartments only because they got a bargain, and some other people are renting their places only because they didn't get one of those bargains. The "law" of one price is not being observed here. There are two (or more) prices, or rentals; hence there are lucky and unlucky renters. The unlucky ones could "bribe" the lucky ones to vacate, if such transactions were made legally enforceable, and one or both parties would be better off and none worse off. Another mutual gain for the classical economist to celebrate!

This source of inefficiency, the establishment (intentionally or not) of two or more prices for the same good, would be avoided by a straightforward program of subsidizing the production or the leasing of rental housing. Such a subsidy would lower the rental and increase the number of apartments rented in precisely the way illustrated, in a different context, by Figure 11–3. Why, then, don't city governments use only subsidy programs rather than public housing? If cities are going to intervene in the market for housing, why not do it right? So ask classical economists. A little reflection suggests the answer: Rent control by the city government focuses its benefits on tenants who are largely residents of the city already—insiders, not outsiders. Public housing also confines its benefits to residents of the city if, as is usual, it is designed that way. But a subsidy program that assists builders or owners in order to reduce the market rental to one-and-all diffuses its benefits over outsiders as well as insiders. And, like public housing, a subsidy program costs taxpayers some money. What present residents in any city would benefit most from would be a program subsidizing the leasing of apartments by persons recorded as residents on a certain date. These original residents could be issued vouchers that are valid means of paying part of their rental, and the landlords could redeem the vouchers at the city government. But this system, while advantageous in many respects, might not be as popular as one in which the landlords received vouchers in partial payment but could not redeem them! Apropos this system, the classical economists' plea is that the original residents should be permitted to sell their vouchers to outsiders desiring to move into the city at whatever market price they bring. Then some insiders and some outsiders gain and no one loses.

RATIONS AND ALLOTMENTS

In discussing minimum prices, or parity prices, it was noted that supplementing the demand is one way to meet the problem of the surplus—or excess supply, as it is sometimes called—that must arise when suppliers expect to be able to sell at a price above the free market level. By purchasing the surplus, the government thereby eliminates it, making the market clear at the support price, though in the everyday terms of the man-in-the-street the "surplus" hasn't gone away—it is the leftover amount the government has to buy to prop up the price. It was further observed that a subsidy for the production (or consumption) of the commodity is a better solution to that problem.

There is, however, another wrong way that governments have found to meet the surplus problem. They can eliminate the surplus by contracting the amount produced and sold instead of by supplementing the amount bought. Each farmer can be issued an acreage allotment that restricts the amount of land that can be put under cultivation. Cutting back the amount of land used to grow wheat serves to raise production costs—notably, the marginal cost of growing any given quantity of wheat—and thus to shift leftward the farmer's supply curve for wheat. (Acreage restrictions are easier to enforce than direct production limitations and marketing limitations, which might tempt some farmers into smuggling extra output.) Thus the industry supply curve is moved to the left, eliminating or shrinking the surplus as desired.

What is so wrong with a system of acreage allotments? Clearly there is "something rotten" in the system when, as is ordinarily the case, the land no longer "allotted" to growing wheat (but so utilized before) is simply wasted. (True, sheer waste, of the land restricted from use in wheat growing would not occur if the land could then go into its next-best use, in growing corn or rye or whatever that might be; but if the aim of the government is to boost farmers' wheat prices, the government would be unlikely to do it at the cost of a slump in corn or rye or other grain prices brought about by an inrush of former wheat-growing land into the production of such alternative crops.) For classical economists, one of the wrongs in such an arrangement is that it causes inefficiency of production. As a consequence, everyone can be made better off by another method to prop up farmers' income:

◆ Let the government abolish acreage restrictions and impose instead a flat tax on each unit of the good—wheat, in our perennial example—produced and sold in the market. Let the size of the tax be set so that the price to the consumer is just as high—and therefore the quantity of wheat demanded by consumers just as low—as under the former acreage restriction program. Then consumers clearly are no worse off than under acreage restrictions. Apparently the farmers, however, are not getting all the revenue: Some of it is now being siphoned off by the government via the tax on wheat sales. But the government can hand back the revenue to the producers, making a transfer payment to each farmer in proportion to his production under the old system. So farmers are compensated for the switch from acreage restrictions to a tax. Indeed, farmers will now be better off. For while they may still have to get up with the chickens, they can quit work sooner, since they need not work so hard (or employ so much machinery and fertilizer) to make up for the acreage previously set aside by the restrictions. With the restrictions abolished, the given wheat output (though perhaps not "right") can now be produced efficiently—with less labor, more land. Figure 11–5 depicts aspects of the scheme.

There is another point to be made while we are on the subject of allotments, sometimes called *quotas*, sometimes *licenses*, to suppliers. Suppose that the allotments limited the amount of the crop a farmer could bring to market, the limitation varying from farmer to farmer, presumably in some rough correspondence to their respective capacities to produce. Such restrictions on production, essentially, rather than on acreage, would leave farmers with some incentive to produce efficiently. They would at least be free to use all the land they had. Nevertheless, there is no guarantee that the production limitations will be distributed across farm plots so that the marginal products of labor and capital in one farm are equal to those at another farm. Maybe some bureaucrat, no matter how able and dedicated, set the production limit too low at some farms, not realizing how wildly fertile the land was there and seeing only the size of the farms. Then land in those farms will be underutilized, owing to the production limitation; although the marginal productivities of labor and capital are still very high on that land, more hiring of labor and capital is not permitted because those farms have already run against their production ceilings. The same industry output could be produced with less total labor and total capital, therefore, by the simple device of moving some labor and capital away from the other farms, where the production ceilings do not bind and

FIGURE 11–5: Government Taxation of Sales or Purchases of a Good Can Serve to Prop Up Suppliers' Income without Mandating any Waste of Land

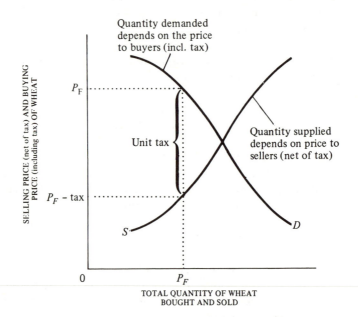

Suppose that a tax on sales of wheat is introduced, in replacement of acreage restrictions, in order to drive the buying price to the support level, p_F. In the presence of a tax, however, the selling price is equal to the buying price *minus* the unit tax. So the tax will leave the selling price received by farmers below p_F. But this is no problem, since the government can spend the tax revenue on farmers in order to return it to them.

To calculate the required tax per unit, we first note that if the buying price is going to be the support level p_F, the total quantity demanded will be the corresponding amount q_F, as shown by the demand curve. But q_F must then also be the amount supplied. Hence the *selling price*—the price received by any seller net of the tax—must be just low enough to make the amount supplied equal to q_F; otherwise, market would not clear. The gap, or wedge, between the selling price at q_F and the buying price measures exactly the tax per unit needed to make the buying price p_F.

crimp so severely, to the farms where land is being relatively underutilized.

The classical economist, ever resourceful, has a solution to this problem too (one just as good or better than a tax). Let the farmers be allowed to buy and sell to one another their "licenses," or "permits," to produce and market wheat—these permits being issued in small denominations. "Here, I don't need 20 thousand permits to sell my output, since my land is so poor, and your land's so good you could get a lot more output from just a little more labor, but you've used up your permits. So why not buy 3 thousand permits from me, and we'll both come out ahead." A perfectly competitive *market in the permits* would ensure efficient allocation of labor and capital over the various plots of land: The marginal product of labor, for example, would be equal across all farms, and ditto the marginal product of capital. (Proof: If the marginal product of labor were greater at one farm than at another, despite the law of one price (for wheat) and one wage, then a permit to produce another bushel would be worth more at the former farm than at the latter; but that cannot happen if the market for permits is in competitive equilibrium.)

RATIONING CONSUMERS

Just as there can be a "rationing" of suppliers as a device to prop up the equilibrium market price of a good, there can be rationing of consumers—or of buyers who are one or two stages away from final consumption—as a means to hold down the price. When a price ceiling is enacted to drive down the price from its free market equilibrium level and a shortage becomes manifest (recall Figure 11–4), rationing is often introduced to achieve an allocation of the short supply that is regarded as equitable (or pretended to be so regarded).

♦ In World War II, the government enacted a system of gasoline rationing that assigned each type of buyer a limit to the gasoline purchasable per week. These allotments could not be bought and sold.

♦ In early 1974, when the price of oil and hence gasoline skyrocketed, many retail gasoline stations rationed their supplies by imposing a limit of ten gallons per purchase.

Actually, once rationing is in effect, the price controls making it illegal to charge more than a certain price can be removed, since people willing to buy more of the good don't have any more of the necessary ration tickets, or coupons, legally required to effect the purchase.

Is it possible that the classical economist is opposed to consumer rationing? Is nothing sacred?? Indeed, the classical economist is vigorously opposed. But it ought to be explained that if the price of home heating oil shoots way up in late December, when the icicles are already on the windows, there may not be time for the government to institute the "better idea" of the classical economists. The classical hostility to rationing is an opposition to it as a regular and permanent practice—a sister institution intruding on the institution of the market.

There is no question that the idea of rationing has a tremendous appeal to a varied assortment of people. The classical economist feels sentenced to a life of hearing intelligent moralists demonstrate, without benefit of any economic analysis, the superiority of rationing over competitive markets.

MARIE: Everyone is entitled to equal access to the basic culture, to the opera and the circus and the rest. If you live here your Social Security number should be your ticket to a night at the opera per year. There could be some sort of user fee in order to pay the performers for showing up, but it should be far below the free market price so that everyone could afford to use his ticket. Of course, everyone will have to be rationed to one or maybe two performances, musical resources being scarce, in order to make room for all. Likewise, higher education should be tuition-free, with only modest fees, as in France.

GEOFF: I don't know about what you call culture. But I believe the basic things a man needs to go about his daily business—the bus to take him to work, coats and shoes for the kids in the winter, and his pint in the evening—those things should be free or or nearly so; and shortages should be prevented by rationing people equally, according to how much is available.

The calls for reduced prices through price controls and rationing evidently raise a challenge to the claims of classical economics on behalf of competitive markets. If the praise of competitive markets means anything, it must mean that they can do better than markets plus rationing. Obviously the classical economists have some explaining to do.

The classical reply begins by arguing that rationing, if the ration tickets (or coupons) are not legally tradable in a market, opens the door to inefficiency in consumption. Obviously it is not the best arrangement to have opera lovers always accepting their ration of a ticket each year to the ballet (as well as the opera) and ballet lovers always accepting their ration of a ticket a year to an opera, simply because it is preferable to staying home. Similarly, it is not efficient to have industrious folk quitting early at the bakery because they wouldn't have extra ration tickets to buy more admissions to the circus, even if they earned the extra dough, while normally laid-back types are working full time because with the circus at so low a subsidized price and with plenty of ration tickets in the house it is probably worth it to work full time instead of part time.

In both these illustrations of differences in taste, there is "room for a deal"—the opportunity for a mutual gain, a Pareto improvement. If the government will just permit ballet lovers to sell their opera rations in the "open market" in exchange for ballet rations (or for money with which to buy ballet rations) and opera lovers to sell their ballet rations in exchange for opera rations, both groups will be made better off. Similarly, if the government will permit the industrious people to buy some circus rations (maybe all kinds of rations!) from laid-back people, the former will work more and earn more while the latter will work less and receive more—to their mutual satisfaction. Rationing without tradability of the coupons, then, is *not* a second-best device to achieve low prices; it is a third-best scheme, at best. Tradability is better.

Now the cat is out of the bag. For if everyone can sell his ration tickets on the open market, then giving everyone a book of ration coupons is no different from giving everyone a payment of money and taxing the sale of goods so as to make them very expensive. But transfer payments to the general population—for example, Social Security in retirement—and taxes on the sale of goods, or on the earning of the money with which to buy goods (which is little different), is not rationing. It is just spending and taxing by the government. Thus the classical position is that there is nothing that rationing (without tradability) can do that ordinary government taxation and spending cannot do as well or better. In the classical system, the argument for rationing as a permanent accompaniment to the operation of markets falls to the ground.

REVIEW AND COMMENTS

We have been touring the classical economist's chamber of horrors, particularly the gallery where the most dreadful interferences with the market are exhibited. Not all the interesting sights, of course, could be inspected in such an introductory visit. For example, we neglected the custom in many countries of *giving away* a fixed number of licenses to practice medicine, typically on a first-come basis to qualified applicants, rather than auctioning the licenses and permitting an active secondhand market in them. We also omitted the important phenomenon of import quotas, which classical economists argue are inefficient next to a system of competitive bidding for licenses to import given quantities, and inefficient next to tariffs as well.

Neither have we attempted to consider the whole bill of indictment by classical economists against interferences by the government with competitive equilibrium. We focused attention on the most convincing counts in that indictment: Minimum wage laws lead to inefficiency in consumption, since some jobless workers would "buy" the jobs from the employed if only there were a mechanism by which to do it. "Parity" prices by means of government crop purchases lead to consumption inefficiency of a flagrant sort. Rent controls lead also to inefficiency in consumption, since some without rented apartments in the city would "bribe" those with apartments to relinquish them if such transactions were made legal. Acreage restrictions (and even output limitations) lead to inefficiency in production.

There is more than that to the classical indictment: There is the complaint that the minimum wage law leads to too little employment of unskilled labor, not simply to the wrong personnel in those jobs. There is the charge that farm production limitations, even if accomplished with production efficiency, lead to a deficiency of resources devoted to farming and an excess producing nonfarm goods. There is the criticism that rent controls ultimately lead to a deficiency of resources invested in city housing.

In short, there is also the classical thesis that competitive equilibrium achieves an efficient mix, or balance, of the outputs of the various goods—a mix that is not capable of any Pareto-type improvement, a change that would benefit everyone. And there is the further thesis that the sorts of quantitative interferences with the market that we have been examining are inefficient in this respect too: that they yield a mix of consumer goods that, if it were corrected by suitable measures, would permit everyone to gain as a result. This same point was hinted at in the conclusion to the previous chapter as well.

There is a third dimension to efficiency alongside efficiency in production and efficiency in consumption. We could imagine using competitive markets plus subsidies and taxes, or marketable production licenses and consumption permits, merely to determine who produces how much of the onion quota, the shoe quota, etc., and who consumes how much of this pre-fixed quota, or target. Classical economists, however, recommend relying on the "market" (provided it stays highly competitive and in equilibrium) to determine the amounts of goods produced and consumed as well. This third dimension will be taken up in the next two chapters: first, the obstacle to this third kind of efficiency raised by the power of private monopolies, second the similar obstacles raised by taxation.

SUMMARY

1. Earlier, chapter 10 presented the classical argument that a competitive equilibrium is *sufficient* to produce efficiency in production and efficiency in consumption. But it does not follow from that argument that achieving a competitive equilibrium is *necessary* to realize such efficiency in resource allocation. Maybe there are other mechanisms for allocation resources,

other than the market mechanism, that are *also* efficient in these ways. Perhaps the legislatures of the world, while constantly intervening in the marketplace in many ways, manage to preserve the efficiency of resource allocation. The *second part* of the classical argument *shows why* (according to the classical model) *certain kinds* of *interferences* with competitive markets—particularly, wage controls and price controls, price-support programs, rationing schemes, licensing requirements, and quota restrictions—*lead to inefficiency,* thus making everyone worse off than he could be. The classical claims that these interferences create inefficiency are the subject of this chapter.

2. According to classical theory, repealing the minimum wage laws, in combination with a tax on low-paid employment and use of the proceeds to pay a no-strings grant to low-paid workers lucky enough before to have one of the minimum-wage jobs, can make some or all persons better off—expanded choice!—while making no one worse off. So a consequence of the minimum wage laws, according to classical theory, is a shortfall from efficiency—a shortfall not just from the ideal efficiency that might be achievable only through ideal (but impracticable) measures but a shortfall from the practicable sort of efficiency attainable through workable (or at least approximately implementable) measures. In practice, of course, it might take a large (and therefore not costless!) bureaucracy to administer the newfangled employment taxes and grants. Nevertheless, the classical doctrine does mount a powerful case that raising the bottom wages by minimum wage decree is grotesquely inefficient compared to raising wages by the straightforward device of subsidizing the employment in the lowest-paid jobs.

3. The classical theory also demonstrates that it is inefficient in the technical economic sense of the term to prop up farmers' prices by means of a crop-purchase program, with all that rotting food. This is demonstrated by showing that a subsidy program to farmers can make some or all persons better off and none worse off. It's the idea of expanded choice again. (But there is a political catch: Government spending would be up, since the necessary subsidies would cost the government treasury more and thus require more tax revenue than would the crop-purchase program. And although the consumers could afford to pay the higher tax bill out of their savings resulting from the lower food prices to the consumer, the higher government expenditure to benefit farmers would thus become more conspicuous to the taxpayer, which would be an embarrassment to the legislators and inimical to the interests of their farmer-constituents.)

4. Rent controls can also be abolished, if accompanied by suitable companion measures, with a gain to some and a loss to none. Just offer grants to the existing beneficiaries of the rent controls, which, if they choose to

stay renting at the higher market-equilibrium rentals, will just compensate them for the rise of apartment rentals; and finance these grants out of taxes levied on the landlords that will exactly soak up the increase in their rentals. Then old tenants will realize for the first time just how scarce the space they are occupying really is. They can then decide to stay or pack up with their grants for more economical quarters and thus make available their present space to people who are willing to pay for it (and in so doing finance those grants to the old tenants).

5. Then there are the classical criticisms of consumer rationing, which has so much popular appeal. (Why should the rich get all the triple by-passes, all the taxis, and all the caviar that requires the triple by-pass?) These pesky classicists seem to be the dedicated opponents of all that we cherish! How do they argue this time? First they argue that clearly it would be better to allow anyone to trade in the secondhand market his ration coupons, or tickets, for cash or other tickets, since such voluntary exchanges between consenting adults will make everyone better off. Then he has got you, for he next points out that the government may as well give people money as give them tradable ration coupons.

CONCEPTS INTRODUCED

subsidy (on an action)
lump sum payment, or no-strings grant
tax (on an action)
lump sum tax, or assessment

interference with market outcomes
interfering with market clearing
    by legislative decree and penalties
intervening in the market through
    public purchases, subsidies, and taxes

STUDY QUESTIONS

1. "The way to run an economic system is to impose price controls on consumer goods in order to make them available to everyone. Although that step would by itself lead to "excess demand" and shortage, the way to deal with that is through rationing rather than allotting goods to those with the greatest patience in consumer queues or by the device of taxation, which the rich always get around." What are the incentive effects of such price controls and rationing on those with the peculiar talents to earn large incomes? What are the effects on efficiency in consumption? Might there be effects on efficiency in production?

2. "Why are taxis regulated through a system of licenses (called medallions)? The classical answer is that such regulation is just one more instance in which producers have in the name of 'quality service' obtained entry restrictions that brought windfall gains to the initial generation of owners. The theory of rent seeking further suggests that in the competition to acquire a valuable license the rent seekers tend to incur costs equal to the value of the licenses acquired." Explain this classical view. Can you imagine a different view?

3. In the Max Schack production *Land without Music* (released in the United States as *Forbidden Music*), public performances of gypsy music were prohibited because they were thought to reduce Ruritania's national output. In March 1985, musicians protested a New York City law prohibiting the playing of certain instruments in public restaurants the sound of which is thought to impede digestion. Evaluate the efficiency, or inefficiency, of these laws.

CHAPTER 12

Monopoly Power: The Classical Objections

JAKE GITTIS:
He used to run the Water Department?
SECRETARY:
He owned the water supply.

Jack Nicholson and Nandu Hinds in *Chinatown* (1974)

The obstacles to competitive equilibrium, classical economists acknowledge, are not all government interferences. Telephoning, burning gas on the stove, and catching an old Garbo movie on television are not goods purchased in a perfectly competitive market—and we may have to pay through the nose as a result. The newspaper business is not totally uncompetitive; but the price of the afternoon newspaper, if there is one, exceeds the "marginal cost" level, unlike competitive equilibrium prices. In several once-competitive extractive industries, competition seems to have broken down. In some labor markets, unions appear to have succeeded in obtaining better rewards for their members, whether improved conditions or higher pay, than would have resulted without their power.

The classical economist does not dispute this. From Adam Smith onward it has been recognized that businesspeople are always ready to collude at the prospect of a monopolistic gain: "People of the same trade seldom meet together, even for merriment or diversion, but the conversation ends in a conspiracy against the public or in some contrivance to raise prices."* It

* Smith, *The Wealth of Nations*, Book I, chap. 10, p. 128.

282

could be said that the classical economist views pockets of monopoly as a dentist views impacted teeth. For classical economics, the monopoly question is not whether or how much monopoly power is present but how monopoly power comes into being and, above all, what to do about it. The answers given by classical theory are the subject of this chapter.

THE NATURE OF MONOPOLY POWER

Monopoly power, a term that has come into everyday language, refers to the power of a seller to control within limits the product price or input price (wage or rental). But what precisely does that mean? A person might volunteer to take a pay cut or lower the price asked for his house, mistakenly fearing that the demand has weakened, and find the offer gleefully accepted. Or a person might demand a wage increase or raise the price asked for his house, suspecting that he had been underestimating the demand, and find that his new terms were glumly accepted. Clearly these cases are not what is meant by monopoly power. They are illustrations of a seller who is not or was not in equilibrium. They are not illustrations of a seller's power over his price under *equilibrium* conditions—when the seller has correctly estimated what the "market will bear," the best obtainable price, for the quantity he is offering.

- A seller has monopoly power if and only if he knows he can influence the equilibrium market price of the thing being offered for sale or hire—and to such an appreciable extent that the seller's behavior may very well take it into account. In contrast, the pure competitor knows that for practical purposes he may as well take the price as beyond his influence (whether because he is a drop in the bucket or because he can be replaced by an identical seller).

It is the manner in which monopoly power is commonly exercised that makes it important in political economy. The standard method by which a seller possessing monopoly power exercises influence over the price is through his control of his own supply. If the seller has monopoly power, a decrease of his own supply—a decrease of the amount he offers at each price—will cause a decrease of *industry* supply—a decrease of the total amount supplied by the industry at each price—and thus drive up the market price.

- A seller possessing some monopoly power can influence the price through the policy, or strategy, he adopts regarding his own supply: By decreasing the amount he is willing to offer at each price, he can drive up the market-clearing industry price. Evidently this power assumes that other sellers, if any, will not replace any quantity he may withdraw from the market with a counterbalancing quantity, and that the industry demand curve does not

FIGURE 12–1: Monopoly Power Is the Power of an Individual Seller, Whether or Not There Are Others, to Keep Up the Market Price Usually by Holding Back the Quantity Supplied to the Market

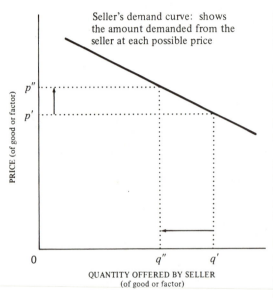

Seller's demand curve: shows the amount demanded from the seller at each possible price

PRICE (of good or factor)

QUANTITY OFFERED BY SELLER (of good or factor)

(That will only be of practical interest to a large supplier who can cut back his supply by a unit or two without disappearing!)

Either way, there is a single market price and this price must clear the market: no surplus or shortage of supply. There would never be any gain to the seller from "giving away" some or all units sold at a price below the market-clearing level (creating a shortage) or above (creating unsold supply).

The diagram views the market price from the perspective of this seller. It depicts the relationship between the price obtained by the seller, which is his view of the market price, to the *amount he supplies* to the market. This relation is aptly labeled the seller's demand curve.

The seller's demand curve is drawn so as to be downward sloping. This downward slope conveys in geometric terms the seller's *monopoly power* over price—via control of the amount the seller offers for sale. If the amount the seller supplies to the market is q', the market-clearing price must be p', since that is the price that makes the quantity demanded for the seller equal to q'. If the seller then reduces the amount he supplies from q' to q'', for example, the price must increase, from p' to p''. Reason: It takes an increase of the price to reduce the quantity demanded from the seller to q'', as the downward slope of the seller's demand curve implies.

The setting here is a classically functioning market with one variation on the classical theme: There is only a single seller, so the amount this seller supplies to the market is the total amount supplied. Or there is a seller able to contract the total amount supplied by contracting the amount he supplies, so he can influence the total supply.

have a flat stretch. Figure 12–1 summarizes in diagrammatic terms the basic idea.

There are some vivid examples of monopoly power exercised that way: Intentionally or not the pianist Vladimir Horowitz has driven up the price of Horowitz recitals by cutting back the number of recitals presented. Television showings of *The Wizard of Oz* are kept down in order to keep up the price to the stations per showing—in order not to "spoil the market." There is no real question that a seller who is the *sole* possible seller has monopoly power. The very word *monopoly* comes from the Greek for single seller. Yet we can easily conceive of a seller having monopoly power *without* being a monopolist—just as a car might have horse power without having a horse inside.

It might be mentioned for the sake of completeness that monopoly theorists distinguish an additional way, besides the method of decreasing the supply, by which the seller with monopoly power may be able to raise the price: The seller may be able to increase the demand. One technique is straightforward: "Your money or your life! It won't be healthy for you not to start paying more for our vending machines." However, that is not so much a method of exercising monopoly power as it is simple extortion disguised as monopoly power. But the other technique is not dissimilar: "If you don't pay more per unit, you will find yourself getting no units at all—from us or anyone else. Take it or leave it!" This is the exercise of monopoly power over price by threat. The seller *threatens* to decrease the supply as a means to raise the price. Those who read the indented sections will see this method of monopoly power mentioned a couple of times in this chapter, but it will not receive emphasis.

It is one thing to define the nature of the beast and quite another to explain how and where the beasts arise. Never mind Horowitz and Judy Garland and unique human talents generally. How can an enterprise, or the entrepreneur who directs it, acquire monopoly power in an industry? How can a labor union, or its organizer, obtain monopoly power in some labor market? "Could I get monopoly power over something: Be a union organizer or a robber baron?" It is an ironic point that while many classical theoreticians were demonstrating what is objectionable about monopoly power, many other classical theorists were showing how rare are the conditions under which monopoly power can arise according to classical theory.

THE CONDITIONS FOR MONOPOLY POWER

The natural starting point for analyzing the conditions under which monopoly power can arise is the case of the "constant costs" industry. With costs constant, the industry can deliver twice the output (or any other multiple or fraction) with no effect on cost per unit of output—on "unit cost." The increase of output is accomplished with a proportional increase of *all* factors of production, so the industry in its new size is simply a scaled-up replica of its former self. There might be, for example, twice as many identical plants; or all plants twice as big. It might be added that "constant costs" implies the feasibility of doubling output by doubling factor inputs, called constant returns to scale. *And* it implies that the industry is not using some specialized factor of production, like corn land or coal land of a certain richness, which *cannot* be scaled up in the same proportion because there isn't any more, or *will not* because it becomes scarcer and thus more expensive as the industry expands.

Such an industrial structure in the classical view makes monopoly power difficult or impossible to achieve. It *is* possible that the entire industry's output is supplied by a single enterprise. Yet it does not follow that such a single seller, though an apparent monopolist, has any *monopoly power*. In the constant costs industry no enterprise, even one accounting for all sales, has the power to raise the price above the competitive-equilibrium level provided there are no barriers to the entry of other enterprises into the industry. This is easily seen:

> If the single seller sets a price equal to unit cost and produces just enough to meet the amount demanded at that price, no other enterprises will be motivated to enter the industry. For if the other enterprises that might enter expect that the price is going to remain equal to unit cost, they will see no profit in entering. If the single seller decided to withdraw some of his supply so as to maintain the price above unit cost, thus earning a "pure profit," other enterprises not in the industry, noticing that the price has been high and coming to expect that it will remain so for a while, would be motivated to enter the industry by the prospect of a similar pure profit. But to maintain the price at the above-cost level in the face of the rising tide of new entrants, the original seller would have to withhold an ever-growing amount of his supply from the market—until he supplied nothing! For there is no limit to the total amount that the new entrants, none of whom is handicapped compared to the original seller, will bring to the market if the price stays high. Hence in the constant cost industry no seller has the power, *given free entry,* to keep the price above the level of unit cost—which is the competitive-equilibrium price level.

Legal Barriers to Entry: Public Sanctions and Private Threats

If a supplier or group of suppliers is to succeed in developing monopoly power, therefore, the trick is to put up barriers to entry. Banks, for example, are secure in the knowledge that new retail banks are barred. Taxicab owners can maintain a higher fare where each cab is required to have a medallion and the number of them is limited. Suppliers of professional services—

doctors and lawyers, for example—are able to restrict entry into the industry via restrictive licensing requirements. Craftsmen are often able to require lengthy apprenticeships to limit the flow of entrants. A union of skilled workers in an industry can prevent waves of nonunion labor from undercutting its above-competitive wage rate if it can somehow arrange that enterprises are permitted to hire only union labor, at the union wage scale. These time-honored methods of creating barriers to entry have traditionally involved one or another branch of the government to enforce them. The *government* certifies banks, licenses taxis, admits lawyers to the bar, enacts "union shop" legislation, and so on.

It should be added, however, that in some instances the industry "takes the law into its own hands." During the Prohibition era in America, the distillery business operated without protection of the law: New entrants were met with violence, and markets fought over gangster style. Even the history of legal industries is full of illegal restraints against entry. Hardly a year passes that farmers do not riot somewhere in the world against the arrival of trucks bearing price-busting supplies of fruit, vegetables, eggs, or poultry. It was not so many years ago that a saloon keeper could expect trouble in many cities if he made the mistake of leasing the wrong vending machines or hiring the wrong carting company. Today, when we read in the papers of complaints that there is a single seller of cement in all New York City whose price is far above those prevailing in other cities, we read between the lines the suggestion that this lone supplier is using extortionate methods to keep neighboring suppliers, whose unit costs cannot be so very much higher, from supplying cement to the New York market. Such illegal barriers to entry represent a failure by the *government,* whether through unwillingness or inability, to enforce laws against extortion. Otherwise, with constant costs, no monopoly power could survive.

This question of whether a monopoly could somehow survive the forces of competition under conditions of constant costs (or more general conditions) touches on one of the greatest contributions to economic theory, that by the classical theorist Francis Edgeworth. He introduced the idea of what is now called the *core*. An agreement, or deal, regarding trades and so forth by the members of society is "in the core" if it cannot be "blocked" in favor of some other agreement better for some and worse for none; the core is the set of all such "unblockable" agreements. Chapters 5 and 6 pictured the core of a two-person society—it is the "contract curve" of Figure 5–1 and 6–1. Edgeworth went on to show that, under certain conditions, as the number of persons in society is imagined to multiply in a certain way the core shrinks to a single agreement, a unique outcome of trades and resource allocations, etc. And that single allocation is none other than the competitive equilibrium—more precisely, the competitive equilibrium that corresponds to the settings on the government's tax and subsidy dials and to the pattern of people's initial endowments. The idea behind Edgeworth's great theorem is simple enough: that the sheer number of possible competitors causes every individual "agent" to lose his monopoly power over the price of anything he might have to sell.

Was Edgeworth mistaken in purporting to have shown that monopoly must give way to competitive equilibrium as the number of agents in the economy grows large? Certainly Edgeworth was not mistaken on his own terms, as later work has confirmed. And were Edgeworth alive to answer the question today he would undoubtedly say that monopolies assisted by *government* interference *do* disappear from the core as the number of agents grows large; for, as any classical economist can show, the government can make everyone better off by dissolving or neutralizing monopolies. Yet Edgeworth would have a harder time justifying his failure to take into account the possibility of extortionate threats against the life or property of any seller daring to compete. He could reply that he was postulating, as any classical economist would, that the government has perfect information about who is threatening what to whom; and that the government can make all better off by outlawing and effectively preventing such unproductive and counterproductive threats. In Edgeworth's view, the government could say to an enterprise that is monopolizing by extortion: "OK, you've got a pretty big stick there, so we have an idea. We'll give you this trunkful of money so you can retire in Florida and be as well off as you are today. Then people will be able to move peacefully into your market and be better off than now." Thus could Edgeworth have pointed out that monopolistic allocations obtained by extortionate threat-power are not really in the core. So Edgeworth was formally correct that monopolies do not survive, unless the government mistakenly insists on helping them, as the number of agents grows. However, Edgeworth does have to make the classical assumption that the gainers from neutralizing each monopoly are discoverable, and their gains ascertainable, so that the monopolists can actually be bought off.

In constant cost industries, then, pure competition is the rule according to classical theory. Monopoly power cannot arise without some barrier to entry. The creation of a barrier to entry by sanctions or threat requires the government's helping hand or its inability to maintain its own "monopoly of force."

Pure competition is also the rule, according to classical theory, in industries where there is increasing cost. The classical notion of a perfectly competitive equilibrium could hardly have much applicability if it were confined to an economy having only constant cost industries. Many industries engaged in mining, fishing, and livestock raising, for example, are subject to increasing cost. The increasing cost industry cannot deliver more output without incurring a higher unit cost on the additional units produced. An increase in the output of deep-water tuna, for example, is *not* accomplished by a proportional increase of *all* factors of production, because the input of fishing waters of a certain quality and proximity cannot be increased; doubling the output requires more-than-doubling the numbers of boats and men to make up for having to utilize fishing waters less rich or less close than was possible when output was smaller. As a farming community or a city expands its production, irrigation water and drinking water will eventually become difficult to come by—and thus make further expansion too costly. If the wool industry increases its output, sheep raisers must turn to grazing land inferior to the lands they previously chose. Hence the industry supply curve is upward sloping, as Figure 12–2B shows. Figure 12–2A shows the constant cost case.

An enterprise attempting to exercise monopoly power in an increasing cost industry would meet the same obstacle faced by the would-be monopolist in a constant cost industry. There can be no monopoly power without erecting some barrier to entry. The competitive price of a good in an increasing cost industry—say, fish—is equal to the unit cost in the boats catching the farthest fish—to be precise, the farthest fish caught in competitive equilibrium. An owner of a large fishing fleet, let us agree, can at least temporarily drive up the price of the sort of fish he catches above the competitive price by contracting his operations, hiring fewer men, and commissioning fewer boats as old boats and men wear out: The fewer the fish to fry, the higher their market price, given the demand. But then the market price will *exceed* the unit cost of catching fish in the farthest-going boats, since the price is up and the unit cost is down in the farthest boats because they don't have to go as far as before (industry output being down). Hence there is a "pure profit" in prospect for anyone building a boat and manning it to catch fish. And this continues to be true as long as the number of manned boats is less than the competitive level. Since the output withdrawn by the former enterprise trying to exert monopoly power can be replaced by other enter-

FIGURE 12–2: Monopoly Power Cannot Arise in Constant Cost and Increasing-Cost Industries Except by Force—Public or Private—or through Control of an Essential Resource

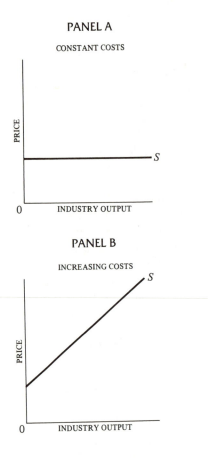

PANEL A

CONSTANT COSTS

PRICE

S

0   INDUSTRY OUTPUT

PANEL B

INCREASING COSTS

S

PRICE

0   INDUSTRY OUTPUT

FIGURE 12–2A: Constant Costs

In this case, increased or decreased levels of output can always be produced at a constant, (*i.e.*, unchanged) level of costs-per-unit-of-output—via a rise or fall in the number of firms. Hence the expected price necessary to elicit a specific industry output is a "constant," independent of the level of output. The supply curve is therefore flat.

FIGURE 12–2B: Increasing Costs

In this case, increased output requires drawing upon less productive resources for the purpose at hand—for example, more distant fishing waters. Hence the cost-per-unit of output, which an enterprise must cover to stay in business, is *increasing* with increased output. The supply curve is therefore upward sloping. An increased price is necessary to induce an increase in the amount supplied.

prises without any handicap compared to the former, it will prove impossible to keep up the price. Hence even in an increasing cost industry, no seller has the power to hold up the price above the competitive-equilibrium level, *provided there are no barriers to entry.*

ANOTHER BARRIER TO ENTRY: CORNERING A RESOURCE

The failure of the seller to wield monopoly power here lies in the seller's inability to gain control of all or most of the fish in the sea. If the seller could not only withdraw some of his own fish from the market but also keep other producers from netting more fish to replace them, he would then be able to keep up the price. *If* an entrepreneur, or organizer, can obtain substantial control of some specialized factor of production needed in an industry, that control can be used to contract the industry supply of output and thus drive up the price. It is not necessary to control all of the specialized factor in existence; to exert some monopoly power over the output price it would be enough to control the quantity of the factor used in competitive equilibrium. To have power over the price of American tobacco it would be enough to own the land in Virginia, to control the price of brandy it would be enough to own the province of Cognac. Then, when the "monopolist" pushes up the price above the competitive price level, new entrants will still enter. But if they attempt to fill in completely the output withdrawn by the "monopolist," they can do so only at a higher unit cost, since they will be driven to use inferior qualities of the specialized factor— poorer land, farther land, land shunned by the enterprises in the original competitive equilibrium. Thus handicapped by increased unit costs, they cannot drive the price back down to the competitive level. The "monopolist," in barring them from the best quality of the specialized resource, has deprived them of the means to do so.

♦ In increasing cost industries, pure competition is possible according to classical theory. It will prevail if no one can contrive any barrier to entry. But monopoly power will be found present *if* substantial control has somehow been gained over some specialized factor of production required by that industry.

The possibility of monopoly in any increasing cost industry does rest on a big "if"—namely, whether it is possible to gain the necessary control over the specialized resource. The attempt of two or more entrepreneurs to gain control over the resource may only succeed in stimulating the existing owners of the resource to hold out for prices so high as to leave little or no prospective profit for either entrepreneur attempting the consolidation. History, however, does point to some successful routes to "monopolization."

♦ Sometimes an entrepreneur has been able to act first, quietly buying a substantial share of the special resource before others do, because he was the first to see that the benefit from monopolization will more than cover the organizational costs of effecting the transactions, or he was the first to forecast those benefits and costs so optimistically. (In science being a close second with an idea is often rewarded, but not so often in business.)

♦ Sometimes a sufficiently small number of owners of the specialized factor who together have a large share of that resource have been able to cooperate in the monopolization of the industry through the operation of what is called a cartel. The participants in a cartel agree to restrict their respective outputs in step with one another and to deprive new entrants of their holdings of the specialized resource. In classical theory, such a cartel is shown to be unstable: With the price driven up, each member would want to break away to sell freely. To solve this "free rider problem," the cartel needs rules of punishment (a sort of penal code) to keep members in line for their common benefit.

The first of these routes was successfully navigated many times in the past century. (Navigation is not a bad metaphor, since the pioneer industrialists who had the vision to consolidate an industry are reminiscent of the voyager-navigators who explored and laid claim to the New World.) No one can think of Central American bananas without thinking of United Fruit, of Hawaiian pineapple without Dole, of copper mining without Anaconda, of Canadian newsprint without Lord Thompson, of Fleet Street. Frequently the entrepreneur successfully organizing the industry enjoyed the advantage of huge financial backing. Lord Thompson was said to have had a special magic with Canadian bankers. Some American enterprises attempting takeovers of American companies complain that their Canadian rivals derive an advantage from the more liberal banking regulations in Canada. It should be added that the specialized factors of production that history shows to have been successfully "monopolized" are not limited to inanimate factors such as copper ore. In the 1930s, Metro Goldwyn Meyer had under contract a substantial share of the acting talent for making motion pictures.

The second route has produced fewer successes—at least if we leave aside the "cartels of labor," which are a special case in view of the important role that government legislation plays in supporting them. The difficulty faced by a cartel is that there is a mutual benefit from a common restriction of supply; but each member of the cartel has an incentive to cheat on the agreement by producing the usual amount—or *more* if the cartel succeeds in driving up the market price—and selling underground the part not channeled or reported to the cartel. It is another instance of the "Prisoner's Dilemma," the logic of collective action, and free-rider problem. The successful cartel must be nearly cheat-proof through monitoring and harsh reprisals. Nevertheless, a few cartels have succeeded, thus far, in countries where they are not illegal. OPEC, the Organization of Petroleum Exporting Countries, is the most recent and spectacular example—although this cartel, like the former worldwide airline cartel, is peculiar in being a combine of public enterprises rather than private enterprises. No less colorful is the story of the diamond monopoly, founded a century ago by Cecil Rhodes. A man who, it is said, believed that to be born an Englishman is to win first prize in the lottery of life, Rhodes went to South Africa to expand the British Empire but left as his monument the cartel known as De Beers. The reported ruthlessness of its methods has survived down to the present. Although set up to raise the price by restricting the supply, the cartel soon saw the advantage of sharing the costs of industry advertising in order to increase the demand. The advertising campaign reached the peak of its creativity with the slogan "A Diamond Is Forever," though in fact, as a muckraking history of the industry put it, the diamond can be "shattered, chipped, discolored or incinerated to an ash."*

NATURAL MONOPOLY

According to the classical analysis we have been examining, then, free entry is the "open sesame" to pure competition in both constant cost and increasing cost industries. Contriving some barrier to entry, not excluding some government-operated barrier, is the dirty secret to monopoly power. This analysis, however, has posited constant returns to scale: An enterprise producing half that of another will need just *half* the labor and land and so on (of the same quality!) to do it—so the small or embryonic enterprise is at no disadvantage next to a large one. That guarantees that the supply withdrawn from the market by an enterprise, even a giant, will be exactly replaced by one or more other enterprises, no matter how small their scale. (The new entrants will drive the price down to the same unit cost—in the farthest boats—that the giant tried to drive the price above.)

The presence of *increasing* returns to scale opens up new fields for monopolists to conquer. Two sources of monopoly power may be mentioned:

- *Overhead cost.* A newspaper could behave like a perfect competitor, increasing its production run just to the point where marginal cost equals price. Maybe the *production* cost of the newspaper would be covered that way. (E.g., suppose that the marginal cost is a constant, so it always costs, say, three pennies extra to produce an extra copy. Then a price of three pennies will cover all production costs.) But how will the newspaper cover its overhead cost that way? It must *raise* price above the competitive level just to break even, which it can do without fear of new entrants.

- *Sunk costs.* Old Rapid Transit, before the city bought them out, used to set its price way above marginal cost and made a "pure profit" doing it

* Edward Jay Epstein, *The Rise and Fall of Diamonds* (New York: Simon & Schuster, 1982).

too. But they never had to worry, because with all that capital "sunk" in permanent tunnels they knew that no new entrant would challenge them with a competing subway line.

It is cases like these, which grew out of increasing returns to scale, that help to explain the phenomenon of *natural monopoly*. In these cases, the existing enterprise has interposed no artificial or historical barrier to the entry of any other enterprises; the existing enterprise does not have to. The cost conditions are such as to close the door to a competitive equilibrium where price equals marginal cost.

INNOVATION

No discussion of the classical theory of monopoly power is complete without considering the role of innovation. There is much truth in the popular impression that monopoly power is often traceable to technological or managerial innovation, to the discovery and application of a new product or method of production. Classical economics views the matter this way: Each day some innovation is being introduced somewhere in the economy, we may well imagine, and the innovation will enjoy a monopoly gain from the resulting opportunity to lift price above marginal cost of production. But the opportunity may well be fleeting, the gain transient. Unless the innovating enterprise has had to incur a heavy sunk cost or towering overhead cost or else contrived some barrier to entry, other enterprises, as they learn how to imitate the new product of technique, will enter or threaten to do so, and thus erode the innovator's monopoly power. Again, the government may offer to operate a barrier to entry: Patent protection may be granted to the innovator. So Polaroid has some protection against Kodak, and vice versa. By that device the monopoly gain may be prolonged. But there is no reason to extend it indefinitely. Seldom, then, are imitators kept at bay. Besides, future innovations may sweep away present ones. The gales of innovation blow both ways.

MONOPOLY POWER: THE EFFECTS AND RESULTING INEFFICIENCIES

"Where's the harm from monopoly? With each monopolistic act there are winners and losers, that's all." There is, of course, quite a lot of variety in the situations around the economy, any economy, in which monopoly power is found. Each instance of monopoly power—price fixing, wage fixing, featherbedding, tie-in sales, etc.—has its distinctive score sheet of gains and losses:

- If the local morning newspaper raises its classified advertising rates to achieve maximum possible profit, those high rates will damage consumers who use the classified pages and lessen the maximum gain that printers employed there can extract from the newspaper. (Similarly, auto makers want higher prices than auto workers (and publishers higher prices than authors).

- If the newspaper printers' union pushes up the terms to the point of maximum advantage, the newspaper's price will be driven up a little more; hence readers will lose, and the owners' maximum profit will be lessened.

- If the coal miners form a union to improve the terms of their contract, the resulting rise in the price of coal will damage users of coal; paradoxically, the price rise may benefit the mine owners more than the wage increase costs them.

Where monopoly power rears its head the issue is not invariably one of the powerful rich versus the poor, or even labor versus capital. Aware of that, the man in the street has no general view of monopoly, preferring to weigh each monopolistic situation as an individual case. He is apt to approve a monopolistic act when, as he sees it, the gainers are sufficiently deserving or their gains large enough.

A more critical view of monopoly power is often expressed, especially in the consumerism movement. "Monopolistic actions hurt the consumer. And since we are all consumers, we should unite to break up monopoly power or neutralize it wherever we find it." (True, we could imagine uniting to push up our prices and wages together—monopoly gains for all! The gains we would win as suppliers, however, would be wiped out by the consequent losses we would experience as consumers.) Certainly it is a *necessary* step in any sort of anti-monopoly argument to point out that there are losers as a result of every monopolistic action. Otherwise who could be against monopolistic behavior? It is thus important to insist that the rewards of monopoly power are not free lunches—somebody must pay. But that observation is evidently *not sufficient* to reach any anti-monopoly conclusion. So what that some consumers have to pay a little? The lettuce workers of California must feel that their disadvantaged circumstances amply justify organizing a union to force up wages and work conditions—at trivial cost to the lettuce consumer. Nurses and musicians may feel justified in demanding shorter hours if for some consumers the better performance outweighs the higher cost. (In times past, steel companies sought to justify their high prices by the good uses to which they put their profits. Hypocrisy, it has been said, is the tribute that vice pays to virtue.) In a world not perceived as very just by any known standard, every monopolist would feel irked by a crusade against *monopoly* power. "Why *us?*"

To obtain by logic the ethical conclusion that the exploitation of monopoly power is wrong requires an ethical premise. One position toward monopoly appears to be based on this moral reasoning:

1. The gain from exploitation of monopoly power is at the expense of one or more others.
2. It is not right to gain at another's expense.
∴3. The exploitation of monopoly power is not right.

Again, lettuce workers reject such a premise: Since the government neglects to arrange just rewards for their labor, through subsidies or other means, they are justified in resorting to monopolistic actions aimed at driving up their wages. Although these gains will come at the expense of lettuce consumers, the latter will still be left with some diminished gains from buying lettuce; it is not as if consumers were being forced at gunpoint to buy lettuce at punitive prices so high that they must wish they had never heard of it.

We might think, however, that the above ethical premise, premise 2, is fine *if* the reward structure was just to begin with. But recall the discussion in chapter 9 of the unanimity principle: B is working with A alone, and getting all the gains from cooperation until B's long-lost brother, B', turns up. Very possibly B' will now gain at the expense of his brother, since A is already relinquishing his share of the gains from cooperation to the lesser rewarded B. The premise isn't a workable principle in this case, because either B gains at the expense of B', by excluding him, say, or B' gains at the expense of B, by pushing himself in.

The same difficulty with the "no-gain" principle turns up when attempts are made to apply it to regulatory situations. Imagine a group of entrepreneurs embarking on a new enterprise: It could be a Broadway show, like *Evita,* or a natural gas company. The no-gain principle means that the investors shouldn't be permitted to gain from their investment beyond the *normal* return they could have obtained by investing in any of the ordinary *competitive* enterprises, like farming or book publishing; and the same goes for the royalties and salaries of the creative, managerial, or directorial talent put into a good bargaining position by the new opportunity. The application of the principle to such an enterprise has an unexpected implication: In order to make no extraordinary gain, as they would make by charging a high price, the enterprise must set a low enough price to *lose* money on the *additional* consumers brought in—to lose just enough to offset the profit (though reduced) on the original, or previous, consumers. (It is like requiring an airline to stop in Bakersfield on routes to Los Angeles in order to lose the profit.) But to do that would cause those additional consumers to gain at the expense of the producers, which is surely contrary to the principle of nonexploitation. Maybe the producers are pretty poor and would be poorer still if they had to operate in the competitive sector, where their skills would command even less money. Furthermore, it may be a waste of scarce resources to have the plane stop in Bakersfield; it would be cheaper to pay people there a compensation for having no plane service than to make the costly stop to pick them up. From the viewpoint of classical economics, the zero-gain principle constitutes very poor policy toward monopolies.

The view of monopoly power taken by classical economics is quite different. The classical position notes that every instance of monopoly power, exploited in the usual way, leads to inefficiency in the allocation of resources. The inefficiency is objectionable, since there are ways to remove the inefficiency without losses to anyone (and gains to some or all). Eliminating that monopoly power or curbing its exploitation is therefore warranted in order to correct the inefficiency.

◆ The classical position is that, if everything else is fine in the economy—the government successful at correcting previously encountered inefficiencies and avoiding ones of its own making—the exploitation of monopoly power by an enterprise or union will cause too little of the monopolized good to be demanded (and thus supplied)—and too much of one or more other goods. This distortion in the mix of goods causes an inefficiency, but also the heaven-sent opportunity to correct it: By abolishing the monopoly power, through dissolution of the monopolistic enterprise or union, or by taking countermeasures to offset the exploitation, the government can eliminate the distortion and, in the process, make all better off.*

The argument for this position begins with the meaning of monopoly power, of course. Monopoly power, it will be recalled, means the power of a seller to control the price or wage at which the good or factor service is

---

* It could be that there is another way of removing the inefficiency, a way *with losses* to some, that is preferable on the prevailing standard of justice to any way that aims to avoid losses. Then we have another way to defend the ethical premise that inefficiency is unacceptable; and we have another justified way of going about its removal.

sold. The seller with monopoly power can go on gradually raising his price, like a plane continuously gaining altitude, without arriving at a point where all the remaining buyers abruptly vanish. In contrast the seller in pure competition knows that if he dared to raise his price above the "competitive" level, the level that clears the market, those buying from him would all flock to other sellers like startled pigeons.

◆ The seller with monopoly power never has to worry that raising the price, no matter by how little, would have a catastrophic effect on the quantity bought. In the diagrammatic terms of Figure 12–1, the seller's demand curve is not flat anywhere. Hence monopoly power permits the seller to raise the price by reducing the amount offered to the market—forcing consumers to a northwestward (p, q) point up the demand curve.

The mere presence of monopoly power in some industry—an enterprise monopolizing the output, a cartel of landowners monopolizing the land, or a union monopolizing the labor supply—need not spell an allocation of resources technically different from competitive equilibrium. The monopoly power *could* be used to duplicate the technical features of competitive equilibrium: The output level would make marginal cost equal to market-clearing price, and so on. (The government could nationalize and centralize a perfectly competitive industry, turning it into a public monopoly, and choose not to alter output and inputs, price, and so forth.) But we are concerned here with private power for private gain. If the monopoly power is *exercised* to maximum *private advantage,* how does the resulting monopolistic equilibrium differ in essential features from competitive equilibrium?

THE EXERCISE OF MONOPOLY POWER OVER OUTPUT AND PRICE

The profitability of power exploited. Consider an enterprise having monopoly power over the output price in an industry and seeking the maximum profit. It will facilitate discussion to think of the monopolistic enterprise as choosing the *output* to supply, a choice also made by a perfect competitor. The amount supplied together with the demand curve then *determines* the price. We will suppose, in the classical tradition, that the enterprise knows that the quantity supplied will affect the price obtained, and how much it will affect the price; the enterprise knows its demand curve. How does knowledge of this monopoly power over the price influence the enterprise's selection of the output level? That power makes it profitable to produce *less* than the competitive-equilibrium level of industry output—less, that is, than the industry output would be if each farm or mine or factory were managed by pure competitors producing up to the point where marginal costs equals price. To see why, assume that the monpolist chose to produce the "competitive" level of industry output and produce it efficiently: At each factory the output would thus be pushed to the point where marginal cost equals price, as in competitive equilibrium. But that could *not* be the most profitable output level for the monopolistic enterprise. The monopolist could then *increase* its profit by producing a tiny bit less (and maybe a lot less). A proof:

> This proposition follows with a simple observation. Producing to make marginal cost equal to price *would be* the most profitable output *if* the monopolist had to take the price as given, as a perfect competitor does. For as long as the marginal cost is smaller than the given price, the extra total production cost from producing at a slightly higher level will be smaller than the extra revenue brought from selling the extra bit of output. (See chapter 10.) But our monopolistic enterprise *doesn't* take the price as a given. Instead it takes the downward-sloping demand curve as its given: It knows that the less it produces the higher the price will be. The monopolist knows that producing a little *less* than the level where marginal cost is equal to price at each factory will have a beneficial side effect on the price—one that the perfect competitor, viewing price as a given, does not take into account. (A very smart perfect competitor might realize that everyone's supplies must affect price at least microscopically, yet understand that his factory is just one of so many that he would receive little of the benefit from the side effect of supplying less.) So the monopolist touring his factories will decide to produce less at each factory than a perfect competitor would—less than the level where marginal cost equals price—since he will capture all the benefits of the side effect on the price. Figure 12–3 makes the point geometrically. The conclusion may be restated thus:
>
>> In deciding its output for maximum possible profit, the monopolist stops short of producing enough to drive the market-clearing price down to the marginal cost of producing. Hence less output is produced.

We consider in Figure 12–3 an enterprise that, by takeovers, has acquired substantial ownership of what was until then a perfectly competitive indus-

FIGURE 12—3: Profitability of Exploiting Monopoly Power over Industry Output and Thus Price

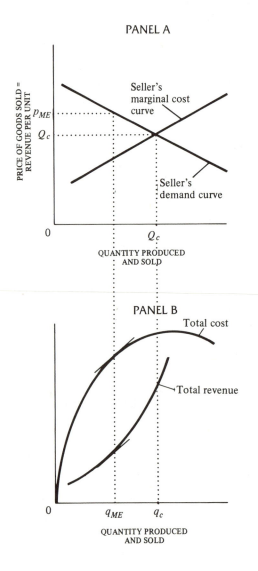

PANEL A

PRICE OF GOODS SOLD = REVENUE PER UNIT

p_{ME}

Q_c

Seller's marginal cost curve

Seller's demand curve

0   Q_c

QUANTITY PRODUCED AND SOLD

PANEL B

Total cost

Total revenue

0   q_{ME} q_c

QUANTITY PRODUCED AND SOLD

Supplying less output to the market than the competitive output level in order to put the price above the competitive price level adds to profit (or subtracts from loss)—up to a point.

try, and has found itself with some monopoly power over the total industry output and thus the industry price. Or we can consider an enterprise operating in an industry that has never heard of competition. In either case the enterprise could choose to imitate the perfect competitor: It could set its output (per week, say) to the point where it has driven down the market price to the level of its marginal cost of production. This *competitive output level,* as we may call it, is the quantity labeled q_C in Panel A of Figure 12–3. The corresponding price, labeled p_C, may be called the *competitive price level.*

However, the competitive output level cannot be the most profitable output level for the enterprise with monopoly power. Reducing output at least a little would be better for the enterprise—larger profit or a smaller loss. If the enterprise will try a reduction of its weekly output by one tiny unit, say, then the total cost of its weekly production will *decrease;* it will decrease by an amount equal to *marginal cost,* which is the extra cost incurred by producing one unit more or the extra cost saving from producing one fewer unit. But as Panel B shows, the total revenue received from its weekly sales will decrease by *less*—if it falls at all. Yes, *if* the price were not to go up as a result of the one-unit reduction in the amount supplied, *then* revenue would decrease by an amount just equal to the *price;* and such a decrease would be exactly as great as the reduction of total cost, since price is equal to marginal cost. But price *does* go up owing to the monopoly power of the supplier. And this rise in price *increases* the revenue on all the remaining units of weekly output after the experimental one-unit output reduction. Therefore, taking these *two* separate effects on revenue together, we find that revenue decreases by *less* than total cost does—and may even rise.

The main point here is a twin conclusion: that the monopolist contracts output in comparison to the competitive-equilibrium level *and* in so doing opens a wedge between price and marginal cost. By contrast, we might imagine that a monopolist is sometimes able to raise the price a certain amount without causing a reduction of the amount demanded. In that very special case, no damage could be done to the *efficiency* with which resources are allocated. Output and inputs would stay the same. The change would be purely *distributional,* against the buyers in favor of the seller.

Some economic theorists have speculated that in fact a monopolist may in some circumstances be able to raise price without causing a reduction in the amount demanded—because the monpolist may be able to forbid it! "Any buyer who does not buy as much at the new price as before will be supplied nothing at all. Take it or leave it!" By this drastic threat, the monopolist makes his "demand curve" an obsolete concept. (A curve showing maximum threat-price at each level of output replaces it.) But usually a monopolist is unable to prevent a reduction in the quantity demanded. What if the boy says he couldn't buy his year's quota of bubble gum last year because he wore braces, or he says his purchase record last year is blank because he is just starting to chew now? Furthermore, even if the monopolist could raise price some distance before causing some of the less-devoted buyers to drop out, it would *still* be profitable for the monpolist to contract output in order to get a further increase in the price obtained. So the theory that the monopolist exploits his monopoly power by contracting output in comparison to the competitive level has a lot of generality after all.

The resulting inefficiency demonstrated. What *is* the harm, though, from monopoly power exploited? If monopoly power has attacked the production of tropical fruit, the mining of precious metals, the showing of movies, then let the labor and the capital and any shiftable natural resources be deployed to make other goods—bakery goods, flowers, and so forth. What is right about the mix of goods resulting from competitive equilibrium that is not right about the mix resulting from monopolistic equilibrium?

The classical position is not, of course, that one mix of goods is morally superior to another—if people want more independent street vendors or more leisure, competitive equilibrium would have given it to them without need for monopoly to push it toward them. It is not that the exploitation of the monopoly power will bring its possessors extra profit (or perhaps the reduction of a loss), since the extra profit can readily be taxed away. Classical economics argues that inefficiency is present in any monopolistic equilibrium, no matter what people's tastes and their respective incomes are. This means not merely that Superman, with his X-ray vision into the mal-allocations, could whiz around with reallocations that would make everyone better off. It means that the government, equipped with the kind of information assumed by classical theory, could make everyone better off too. Hence the government ought to intervene against monopoly power.

What exactly is the inefficiency in monopolistic equilibrium, absent government intervention, that leaves opportunities for improving the lot of some or all and harming none? What is the waste that, with the right corrective action, makes possible such Pareto improvements?

- It is not inefficiency of production. (The monopolistic enterprise will keep to the minimum—will *minimize*—the total cost of producing any given output by using the *same* bundle of inputs that, in aggregate, would have been used to produce that output had pure competition prevailed.)
- It is not necessarily inefficiency of consumption, either. (That arises when there is not just "one price" at which all the buyers are actually buying. Although the owners of the monopolistic enterprise may be able to "get it wholesale," possibly they do not like the product.)

So what is the leak, the source of the waste? The main waste that classical economics sees in monopolistic equilibrium, without government intervention, arises from something very similar to a violation of the "law of one price": To *produce* another unit of the good the monopolistic enterprise has to pay a "price" equal to the marginal cost of production. To *buy* another unit of the good a buyer would have to pay the enterprise a *higher price*, since the price received by the monopolist exceeds marginal cost.

The disparity in "prices" seems odd. It seems to leave room for bilateral "deals" between private parties—unexploited opportunities for mutual gains. The sound of cash registers might ring in their heads as the owners of the monopolistic enterprise dream of a bargain with each buyer: "Look, we'll sell you *extra* units for less than the regular price!" However, the enterprise cannot be sure that the buyer would not simply store the extra units bought and purchase that many fewer the next time—at the regular price, or resell the extra units to a buyer who would have paid the regular price. It is even harder to attract new buyers with a lower price while preventing regular-price buyers from becoming "new" ones. Profit-seeking business management involves a constant effort to dream up new deals that will not cost more than they benefit.

The practical difficulty of extracting some gains to compensate losses. It remains for the classical economist to demonstrate that this monopolistic equilibrium is inefficient in a very practical sense—by proving that some practical government intervention (as distinct from an ideal Superman intervention) can engineer a Pareto improvement. Fortunately, seeing the nature of the waste identified makes it clear what an intervention must accomplish: The intervention by which the government can make a Pareto improvement, if any can be found, must go in the direction of stimulating *more output* from the industry where the monopoly power is—by eliminating the monopoly power or counteracting it. And the intervention must compensate (or prevent to begin with) people's losses from it so that no one is left worse off. The object of the game must be to make "deals" on behalf of the people in the market that they cannot make *by themselves* when operating one-on-one without means of enforcement.

◆ A radical intervention is to abolish the private monopoly power: either by dissolving the enterprise into smaller competitive enterprises, if that is feasible, or by nationalizing the enterprise in order to end the exploitation of the power. The owners of the monopolistic enterprise must be fully compensated if no one is to lose from the intervention. But if taxpayers are not to be hurt too, how can the government obtain the revenue to compensate the owners? Classical theory proves that the revenue can come out of the gains of the buyers who will benefit from the resulting fall of the price to the competitive level.

Proof: The lost profit suffered by the owners is *at most* the fall of price on the output in monopolistic equilibrium—*at most* $(p_{ME} - p_C) \cdot q_{ME}$ in the diagram below; for although the owners, turned into pure competitors, will produce some additional output at additional cost, the additional revenue will bring them extra profit, not loss, on that. The gain won by the buyers is *at least* that same amount; they will only gain, not lose, on the additional amounts they buy, of course. The diagram below makes the point geometrically: the gain to buyers from competition, which is C *plus* something, exceeds producers' loss, C *minus* B.

Other methods of intervening against monopoly power permit the enterprise to live but remove or counterbalance its power. An ingenious approach starts from the observation that the monopolist has contracted output below q_C in order to push p above p_C. That contraction of output would not occur, there-fore, if the government enacts a price ceiling, for-bidding the enterprise to sell at any price above p_C. Then the enterprise would have no motive to restrict output to a level below q_C. This proposition is clearly implied in Figure 12–3. However, the diagram to the left offers another per-spective on the matter. By contracting output in the first place, the monopolist

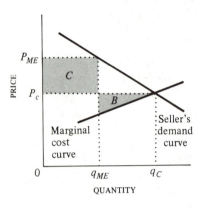

gave up an amount of profit measured by the trianglelike area labeled B in order to achieve the higher price, p_{ME}, which adds to profit the amount measured by the rectangle labeled C. If the enterprise's price is effectively frozen at the level p_C, that will cost the enterprise the area C. But then it is profitable for the enterprise to increase output from q_{ME} to q_C, thus reclaiming the profit previously sacrificed, equal to the area B. Note, however, that C must be larger than B, since the monopolist originally contracted its output in order to achieve the positive net gain C. Hence the imposition of a price ceiling on the enterprise must cause it to lose profit—to lose the "monopoly profit" resulting from the exploitation of its monopoly power. The owners of the enterprise must be compensated if no one is to lose from the intervention. In theory, however, the buyers can easily compen-sate, since they gain via a lower price at least the rectangle C.

A third method of intervention tolerates the monopoly power but operates to counterbalance its effects on output through tax-subsidy schemes that offer the enterprise an incentive to produce the competitive level of output. Under one scheme, the govern-ment in effect buys and resells to the market as much output as is necessary to drive the price back to p_C and, to make it worth-while to the monopolist, compensates the enterprise for the fall of the price suffered on output it sells directly to the market. It is clear that the amount required in compensation is again mea-sured by $C - B$. Once again, the buyers can in theory provide this compensation, and more, without losing themselves, since the gain to them from the reduction of the price to them is at least the area C. Whatever the details of any particular scheme, the enterprise is always going to have to be compensated for doing something that would be unprofitable (even loss-making) in the absence of that compensation—if no one is to lose by the intervention. So the buyers must hand over a portion of their benefits.

Every method of abolishing or neutralizing the monopoly power of an enterprise necessarily causes (other things equal) a loss of profit—the loss of the profit created by the exploitation of the monopoly power. Hence the owners of the enterprise must be compensated by the beneficiaries of the anti-monopoly action—namely, the buyers—*if* the objective is a Pareto improvement (i.e., making some or all better off without damaging any). The classical argument shows that "the numbers are there": the gains to the buyers are more than enough *in aggregate size* to compensate the losers for their losses. But how is the compensation to be extracted from the gainers? How can it be done without undoing the gain and without risking losses to some?

◆ The *ideal* solution calls for the government to assess on each individual buyer an individualized lump sum tax less than or equal to the buyer's total gain from the reduction of price plus the opportunity to take advantage of it by buying more. Each buyer's lump sum tax might be set equal to that buyer's windfall savings from paying less on the amount he would have bought at the monopolistic price. That way there is no risk of a loss, since each buyer's total gain is at least that much. But how is the government to pry loose from each buyer the needed information about how much he would have bought at the high monopolistic price?

To solve this problem the government's economists would have to solve the "free rider problem": Each buyer wants to hide his gain in the hope that will minimize his share of the payment to the owners—to be a free rider. The government's task is to create incentives for buyers to reveal the truth if they want to have a gain. In some cases there is a theoretical solution, but rarely one that is practical for the government to administer.*

---

*The best practical instrument for extracting the compensation from the gainers might seem at first to be an excise tax—a tax on each unit bought and sold. The proceeds of the tax would be handed over to the shareowners in the monopolistic enterprise. This tax too has the virtue that no one would be forced to contribute to the compensation whose gain is less than the tax as long as the price to buyers remains lower than if the government hadn't intervened against the exploitation of the monopoly power. But such a tax would be no different from a renewed exploitation of monopoly power: It drives up the price to buyers, thus contracting sales and output, with the proceeds going to the enterprise (in the case here). The effect of the excise tax would be utterly perverse.

A careful step-by-step analysis could prove that the excise tax is self-defeating. It cannot raise tax

Most classical-minded economists nevertheless suggest that opportunities to effect the desired compensation do *occasionally* arise, and should be seized:

- When a monopolistic enterprise is producing a good in common use, the owners can be compensated out of a rise in general tax rates without causing any consumer to lose on balance. After August Belmont had built the Interborough Rapid Transit, the opportunity for New York city to buy it and to use general tax revenue to lower the fare may have made everyone better off, directly or indirectly.

Most of these same economists would add that there is no persuasive reason why all anti-monopoly actions should be limited to those opportunities for a Pareto improvement:

- Classical economics does not make it a *necessary condition* for attacking a monopoly that doing so should make a Pareto improvement. There are other improvements worth having. If the members of society, on viewing the way the rewards from economic cooperation are handed out, deem some realignment of the rewards to be morally superior, economics has no brief against it. Certainly an enterprise that succeeds in cornering the supply of baby food does not have a moral entitlement to keep the profit obtainable from exploiting its monopoly power. Hence the payment of full compensation to the owners of the monopolistic enterprise, or the administrative capacity to do so, is not a general requirement.

It might seem, in view of the difficulties of compensation, that the classical doctrine toward monopoly power is in some trouble, outmoded by the complexity of economic relations in modern-day communities and countries. For the classical position is anti-monopoly and pro-competition *in general,* not merely in particular cases. "There is no such thing as a good monopoly," its creed holds. Yet neoclassical theoreticians, bringing in fresh premises and arguments as reinforcements for the battle, have sought to reestablish the hard-core classical position. One of these arguments adopts the principle of the cost-benefit test:

- It would be impractical and inappropriate for the law to distinguish a class of "good monopolies," whose exploitation of buyers is to be tolerated (because the gainers cannot be located and taxed to compensate losers), for the same reasons that the law does not distinguish a category of

---

revenue from buyers to replace the profit lost from an expansion of output (due to anti-monopoly measures). The reason is that it can make a net contribution to the owners of the industry hit by the anti-monopoly measures *only* by contracting output; it can't help simply to tax the sales and then hand the proceeds back to the industry owners unless the after-tax price paid by buyers goes up, which means contracted output. It follows that "replacing" the profit lost as a result of an expansion of output (due to the anti-monopoly measure) of one unit, thirteen, or *n* units would require a contraction of output by the same amount! Hence the price to buyers would be back to its monopolistic level as well. Back to square one.

good burglaries that the law shall do nothing to deter: impractical because it would be expensive and problematic for the courts to decide case by case whether the infeasibility of full compensation to the owners is redeemed by the moral worth of the gains; inappropriate because it is desirable to have a general rule of abolishing or neutralizing monopoly power whenever the total benefit to buyers exceeds the cost to the seller—which classical analysis claims. By making it a general rule to break up monopoly power, the law would be adding to the *sum total* of gains we obtain from exchanges with one another. Over a long life, each one of us might be made better off by application of that rule.

The other argument postulates a society where an "optimal" economic policy is designed in pursuit of some notion of justice:

♦ Where the members of a community are bent on having the "good society," or "economic justice," whatever their conception of that may be, they will not proceed to hand out licenses to private groups to monopolize particular industries the way kings awarded royal franchises in mercantilist times. Such a system would be inoptimal, unscientific! Let the government raise tax revenues and spend in accordance with its just principles and situation. Maybe the purchases of some goods will thus be taxed more heavily than others; that is a difficult question in taxation (which happens to be the subject of the next chapter). And maybe some social groups will receive larger handouts than others. *But it is obvious that it could make no sense for a particular industry to be operated by an official private monopoly licensed to obtain the greatest revenue it can, oblivious of its effects on the rest of the system. A private monopoly run for maximum profit cannot be optimal policy.*

The Exercise of Monopoly Power over Wage Rate and Employment

Consider a labor union having monopoly power over the employment and wage of a certain type of worker or workers in a certain industry—musicians, nurses, truckers, screenwriters, miners, apartment building workers. It can be seen, without delving much into the details, that the exercise of this monopoly power may be quite similar to the way that monopoly power over output and price is exercised. The union can exploit its monopoly power in the usual way: By contracting the quantity of man-hours supplied to employers hiring such labor the union can establish, or "enforce," a higher wage rate. And up to a point it will be advantageous to all or most of the workers for the union to engage in such exploitation of monopoly power. The union can enable the workers to do collectively what no single worker able to control only his own supply of labor could manage to do.

The individual worker can always act unilaterally to reduce his work week from 6 to 5 days, by moving from a 6-day to a 5-day-a-week job. And the individual worker may be aware that by causing singlehandedly that minuscule contraction in the supply of six-day-a-week labor he will cause a minuscule rise in the daily wage for 6-day-a-week work. But it does not affect him, because he won't be there to benefit from it; he will receive the daily wage for 5-day-a-week work if he moves. But if *all* workers of a certain type or in a certain industry were acting collectively to contract the length of the work week that is offered to their employers—from 6.00 days per week to 5.99, to 5.98 in successive small steps—expanded choice results.

The result is a departure from efficiency—in the ideal sense, at any rate. To "*sell*" their employers on increasing the work week by an hour, the workers would have to accept a lower hourly wage; so their reward for working an extra hour would be less than the resulting hourly wage—since the wage would be lower on all the "previous" hours worked in the week. To *hire* an additional hour of services from these workers any employer would have to pay the whole hourly wage. It is another violation of the law of "one price". Hence if the workers could be induced to work an extra hour in the week, the *benefit* to employers—while it would not be quite up to the level of the existing hourly wage, due to the diminishing returns to more man-hours—would nevertheless exceed the aforementioned "reward" that the workers would demand in compensation, which is the *cost* to the workers. In theory, then, there is room for a deal. But whether a Pareto improvement could actually be engineered is, we have seen, quite another story.

Readers of the fine print in the discussion of a monopolistic enterprise may recall a qualification there: The monopolist would like to raise the price and prevent a reduction of the amount bought by threatening to deprive consumers of a supply altogether. Labor economists often point out that the unions may likewise strive to prevent or minimize any reduction in the amount of labor hired by employers in response to the increase of the hourly wage rate. It is a question, however, whether the union by such a strategy could prevent an eventual fall of output in the industry, since capital, which is then getting less than its expected return, may go elsewhere. Besides, even if the union could raise the wage some distance before causing one or more employers to abandon the business, it might well be advantageous for the union to raise the wage farther, accepting some unavoidable fall of hours worked as a result. These two points suggest that every union will cause a departure from efficiency in the ideal sense.

SUMMARY

1. Classical economic theory, from Smith onward, does not question the presence of pockets of monopoly power in virtually every large and varied national economy. Monopoly power is said (as a matter of definition) to exist if a seller, by decreasing the quantity supplied, can drive up the equilibrium price. The big questions are how an enterprise or cartel of enterprises can gain monopoly power—which needs answering if, as is frequently the case, there are extraordinary profits to be reaped from that power that other enterprises would dearly love to capture; and, second, what to do about it, if anything?

2. A considerable amount of monopoly power around us evidently arises from government protection of the existing enterprises—banks, taxis, labor unions, and so forth—from the potential arrival of outside competition of "new entrants." The devices used here include licensing, certification, and other requirements. Violation by an entrant of these government protections is punishable by fines or imprisonment, of course. Similarly, gangster mobs can protect existing enterprises from the entry of new competitors by threats of destruction or violence. Thus an enterprise or cartel of enterprises can enjoy monopoly power through force—public or private—even in an industry that is subject to "constant costs" or "increasing costs" and thus a natural environment for the flourishing of pure competition.

3. Some monopoly power also arises through success in gaining control of some specialized resource that is an essential input for the industry. You can gain monopoly power over the price of copper ore, obviously, if you can corner the available copper-rich territory in the world.

4. Thus "barriers to entry" will generate monopoly power, and "free entry" (meaning the absence of barriers) is the open sesame to the break-up of that monopoly power.

5. The other fertile fields for monopoly power arise from the technological phenomenon of "increasing returns to scale." Because of overhead costs at each individual enterprise or production process it can happen that a single enterprise can always produce the *competitive* level of output (or any smaller level) more cheaply, at a lower aggregate cost, than if the same output were met by *two* enterprises due to the implied duplication

of overhead costs; so there is not room for two enterprises in the industry. This does not by itself imply that the single enterprise will then have monopoly power to drive up the price above the competitive level, however; but there are two important cases in which it will.

6. It may be, because of the large overhead cost of the enterprise, that an altruistic decision to behave "like a pure competitor," thus producing up to the point where "marginal cost" equals price, would leave it with not enough revenue to cover its total cost; and since its capital must be replaced from time to time, it would not be able to stay in business at such a price and output combination. So it is driven to raise its price (above marginal cost), which, although the result is a drop in output demanded by consumers, causes the loss to decrease. Though exercising monopoly power, alright, it does not earn an abnormal profit so does not have to worry about new entrants rushing in to drive the price back down.

7. In the other case, the enterprise does earn an abnormal, or excess, profit. But it does not have to worry about he entry of fresh competitors (or even polite ones) because they know that the existing enterprise has important sunk costs that it will have forever, so it will be an eternal thorn in the side of any new entrant.

8. The ill effect of monopoly power focused on by classical theory is the resulting inefficiency of resource allocation: too little output in the monopolized industry, too high a price. With ideal countermeasures at its disposal, then, a benovolent government could dissolve the monopoly power along with compensations for losses to losers out of the larger gains of gainers so as to make everyone better off (or some better and none worse).

9. As a practical matter, it is not so easy to devise a scheme that could extract the gains from the gainers, because the government lacks information about which kids would have bought the chewing gum at the monopolist's price. But breaking up a monopoly does not, in general, have to be a Pareto improvement, which all will approve of, in order to be an improvement in the sense of an act that all will feel is right and reasonable in view of society's goals.

CONCEPTS INTRODUCED

government protection	barriers to entry	overhead costs
gangster protection	free entry	sunk costs
constant cost industry	monopoly power	natural monopoly
increasing cost industry	increasing returns to scale	

STUDY QUESTIONS

1. Horticulturists and owners of plant stores have sometimes suggested that persons selling and servicing plants should be licensed by the government to ensure that this work is done by qualified people. Some economists have argued that there is no need for licensing: As long as there are reputable institutions for horticultural training, any consumer who is worried on this score will be able to find a qualified plant dealer by searching for one possessing reputable credentials (such as a training certificate on the wall).

    Why should plant dealers be keen on government licensing? Why do those economists argue against such licensing? Reach your own evaluation of the arguments pro and con. Are the arguments different in the case of veterinarians? Dentists? Obstetricians?

2. "Unfortunately, the classical doctrine toward monopoly—the harm from price being above marginal cost, and all that—is of limited usefulness. It is one thing for the government to block monopoly power wherever it threatens to arise. It is quite another thing for the government to take anti-monopoly actions, which have the effect of lowering the price, since that would cause unanticipated losses to investors—many of whom are dependent on these investments and who just paid the full market price for their shares, not dreaming that the government might force a reduction of price." Discuss.

3. Consider a monopolist described by the following data:

Labor Hired	Total Product	Marginal Product	Expected Price	Expected Revenue	Marginal Revenue Product	Wage	Marginal Profit from Labor
67	1345	—	4.060	5460.7	—	60.0	—
68	1366	21	4.050	5532.3	71.6	60.0	11.6
69	1384	18	4.025	5570.6	38.3	60.0	−21.7
70	1400	16	4.000	5600.0	29.4	60.0	−30.6

Compare this to the table for Bakery 1 in chapter 10. What change in the data gives rise to the different calculations at the right? In particular, why is the marginal-revenue-product-of-labor *smaller* (at any given level of labor input and output) in the monopolist's case than the pure competitor's? What is the consequence for the profit-maximizing level of labor input, hence output?

CHAPTER 13

Taxation and Public Expenditure: The Classical Vision

NINOTCHKA:
Why? Why should you carry other people's bags?
PORTER:
Well, that's my business, Madame.
NINOTCHKA:
That's no business. That's social injustice.
PORTER:
That depends on the tip.

Greta Garbo and George Davis in *Ninotchka* (1939)

IF the appropriate role and proper operation of the market are one leg, the Smithian leg, of classical political economy, the appropriate functions and proper policies of the government are the other leg. When David Ricardo wrote his treatise on political economy, some fifty years after Smith and Hume, his emphasis on public finance was underlined by its title.* By the latter half of the nineteenth century political economy was understood to have that Ricardian leg. The development of mathematical economics in recent decades has produced a few highly theoretical treatises on market economies without any visibly functioning government at all. But no twentieth-century treatment of political economy hops along on just the Smithian leg.

This chapter examines the neoclassical analysis of the two main questions in public finance:

---

* David Ricardo, *Principles of Political Economy and Taxation*, London, 1817. Reprinted London: J. M. Dent, Everyman Library ed., 1912.

- The question of taxation: How best to tax if tax we must? Tax land rather than labor? Wealth rather than income? Labor rather than capital? Tax consumption rather than wages or interest? Tax with progressive rates, a flat rate, or what?

- The question of public expenditure: How to decide—by which principles or criteria—the size and scope of government expenditure and subsidy? Spend on police and fire protection? Museums? Television? Subway trains? Electricity? Airline service? Against pollution? For conservation? Schools? Housing? Which? And why?

We must also consider the question of whether the "polity," be it a system of pressure groups and patronage or a pure majority-rule democracy, will "support," or sustain, the rational principles of taxation and public expenditure that the classical economist envisions being applied to the economy.

RAISING GOVERNMENT REVENUE

The government is not the sole possessor of the power to tax, as we already have noted. When an enterprise exploits its monopoly power over a good, like the local mineral water, or a factor, like copper ore, it is "taxing" the use of that good or factor. The classical economist complains that such "taxation" violates efficiency, since the users could bribe the monopolist to drop the "tax" and yet gain: The burden of the "tax" to the users must exceed the benefit to the monopolist because, besides the extra charge they pay on what they buy, there is the extra burden experienced as users choose to get along on less of the good or factor in response to the higher charge per unit—the disincentive effect of the "tax rate" as users buy less to try to "avoid the tax." The classical economist also observes that the "tax" is presumably inequitable: Even if the "tax" were perfectly efficient, like an unanticipated holdup that the victim takes no costly precautions to avoid, why should the users of the monopolist's thing be singled out to fork up the monopolist's profit as if they were to blame and the "tax" a punishment?

The "taxation" imposed by privateers, then, from yesteryear's holdups by highwaymen and the river tolls of local barons to the legal monopolies and covert collusions of the present, are no "model" of how to tax. The classical analysis, with its disapproving tone, almost suggests that no tax is a good tax.

Yet the desire of societies to tax is one of the undisputed observations in political economy. Nothing is more certain, it has been said, than death and taxes. Every society has reasons to tax, reasons that fall into these categories:

♦ To arrange the structure of rewards more nearly in line with society's prevailing notions of justice in the division of the gains from economic cooperation among society's members. Hence to tax opera divas and aerialists' earnings in order to be able to "subsidize" the ticket takers and roustabouts—through a wage subsidy to their employment or by subsidizing certain goods they consume.

♦ To contract, or shrink, the rewards that are in the form of ordinary consumer goods—bread and shoes and newspapers, as distinct from collective goods—in order to release resources that would otherwise be employed in producing those goods for use in supplying one or more collective goods: rations and ammunition for the troops to provide national security, food and medical care for the destitute and deprived to provide national self-respect, resources for scientific research or athletic achievement to provide national self-esteem, and so forth.

To these two categories a third could be added: to contract the rewards of the present generation of workers, the "active" generation, in order to make room for the just claims to rewards by the current generation of retired persons, the "inactive" generation—in the hope that the next active generation will do the same.

It is worth noting that communistic societies and equalitarian utopian communities are not exceptions in this respect. They also need to tax. A worker who receives a wage less than the marginal-product-of-his-kind-of-labor, who is therefore paid less than his "competitive-equilibrium wage," is being taxed from the standpoint of classical economic theory. Somewhat similarly, if the state has appropriated certain land or capital and not compensated the former owners with an equivalent earning asset in the form of government bonds, the government may be said to be taxing the hiring or use of that land or capital: The government pockets the marginal-product-of-land on the land it owns and uses—*minus* any interest it pays on those government bonds. Of course the proceeds of the tax will be spent on something, to subsidize the pay or hiring of unskilled workers or to subsidize "free" schools or to subsidize "free" national defense; but there is a tax there nonetheless. Hence when Poland raises the money prices of bread and coal to Polish households without also raising the wages they receive and the interest they receive on their savings deposits (both measured in terms of money), the government is raising the tax rates on labor and the land and capital—in equal proportion.

The question of taxation in such societies is thus a very direct matter of what wages to pay the workers (from the prima ballerina on down), what interest to pay savers, and what prices to charge consumers—expressed in terms of money or, what amounts to the same thing, expressed in terms of some commodity serving as a measuring rod of value, such as bread or silver. This society, in order to raise tax revenue to pay for its social objectives, must act much like a "monopolist": It must raise the price of the good or goods it is producing above the marginal cost of production. Or it must take advantage of being the sole hirer of factors and lower the pay rates received by the factors of production. Otherwise, the government will have a "zero profit" on coal, bread, and so forth with which to subsidize unskilled workers and make various expenditures.

A central problem in classical political economy, therefore, is how to tax efficiently—with ideal efficiency if that is feasible or, if not, with as little loss of efficiency as is feasible. In view of the classical economist's championing of competitive markets as supplier of most goods, the classical analysis focuses on the free market case: Individuals are free not to buy, not to work, not to save, and so on.

Taxation is a particularly sensitive issue for classical economics because of its claims in support of "the market" as an institution for allocating resources among various industries as an alternative to "central planning" of all industries by the government. The classical claims that competitive markets are efficient in production and efficient in consumption would not impress us very much if the government could do little through redistributive taxation of market incomes and expenditures to lift up the rewards from economic cooperation to the less fortunate members of society—if a society could "do justice" to disadvantaged participants only by refusing to play the market game and instead turning to the various methods of Lenin, Mao, Mussolini, or Perón.

Graduated Taxation versus the Dreaded Lump Sum

Why, the classical economist sometimes muses, should anti-market governments have all the tough, no-nonsense methods of acquiring resources? Why shouldn't societies making extensive use of free markets operate like Robin

Hood or Fidel Castro—redistributing goods by decree, drafting the number of soldiers wanted by the army, legislating production quotas to be met by farmers, conscripting people to harvest the sugar crop? Don't market-using societies handicap themselves by electing instead to obtain resources by setting tax rates on what people choose to earn or buy—since people then have an incentive to "avoid the tax" by earning or buying less of what is taxed? Maybe what free market societies need is the *lump sum* tax—a fixed levy that the taxee can do nothing to lessen, with expulsion from society the penalty for nonpayment. That would end the unfortunate incentives to earn less in order to lessen the tax due. Maybe then the system of competitive markets would be a flawless system.

The adoption of lump sum taxes, though it may be a recurrent fantasy, does not, however, reflect the real outlook of classical economics. Lump sum taxation has two serious faults, both growing out of the same problem: The size of the once-for-all tax liability that a person is saddled with has to be calculated and assessed before his career is under way; *otherwise,* the person would have an incentive to earn less or spend less before the size of the tax was determined in the hope it would lower his tax assessment, and thus the tax would fail to prevent tax-avoiding behavior. Hence, under a true lump sum tax system, the size of a person's tax liability must be decided by the government on the basis of the person's "promise" rather than any observed performance. The two resulting faults:

♦ It goes against the grain—against basic notions of justice, to be precise—to assess a tax on a person before it is known—possibly before the person knows—what the person's preferences are in the way of life styles: It is axiomatic that a person should be permitted to "opt out" of participation in society and owe the state nothing: a zero tax in recognition of the person's zero gain from zero cooperation! By the same token, a person should be permitted to opt for a small gain from economic cooperation and accordingly owe the state only a small tax. Levying a big lump sum tax on the person in the expectation that he or she will prefer to "make it big" forces the person into a cruel dilemma: to make it big in order to pay the big tax or else leave.

However, even if a "perfect" system of lump sum taxation could be devised, one where each person's talents and preferences were correctly estimated and the size of the corresponding tax set "justly," such a hypothetical system would still have another flaw:

♦ A system of lump sum taxation, even a perfect system, would take no account of the element of luck that may intervene in the final determination of people's success (or failure). What should the government do with people who are unlucky: people whose ship isn't going to come in, people who have bet on the wrong career, people too depressed to get up in the morning . . . ? Would the government insist on the taxpayer's blood, organs, and so forth—in a reenactment of *The Merchant of Venice*—if he could not come up with the bread to make payment in full? More broadly, wouldn't a tax system be objectionable that did nothing to moderate the inequalities among persons who suffer "the breaks" along the way? Economists make an interesting argument in support of such criticisms: Small-ship owners, we observe, are usually happy to buy insurance against loss at sea, although it means a lower return to their investment on the average—since the insurer would refuse the risk if he merely "broke even" on the average. Suppose accordingly that people generally dislike gambles and need to be compensated with a greater average return when accepting a greater risk. Then it would be economically inefficient for the members of society not to moderate the effects of good and bad fortune—not to *spread the risk* of bad luck by agreeing to a tax on success in order to provide insurance-type benefits for failure. As farmers willingly engage in risk sharing by chipping in when someone's barn burns down or by joining the legendary posse when a horse is stolen, so *every* member of society might prefer a tax system in which all members share in the unlucky losses of life's losers and all members share in the windfalls of life's winners *through some sort of tax on actual income or what it buys.*

No one knows exactly how important luck is in explaining inequality, but it is agreed today to be more important than was thought decades earlier. Social Darwinists such as Herbert Spencer, whose ideas were founded on those of Charles Darwin, held that inequalities in reward could be largely explained by differences in intelligence, reaction times, physical endurance, emotional drive, and other factors thought to be in part inherited. In the nature versus nurture controversy that followed, the nurturists answered the Darwinists (and other naturalists) by claiming that these inequalities could be better explained by differences in upbringing, schooling, "socializing" forces, and other factors considered a function of the social environment and therefore considered alterable. But most present-day observers contend that in a thousand success stories there is usually an element of luck together with a rational response to that luck—and similarly with society's cases of failure. When poverty began to be a subject of large-scale studies in the 1960s it became apparent that not all of society's bottom tenth were drawn from society's most disadvantaged classes, as might have been supposed. The great majority of the poor were native born, white, male—but in some sense "down on their luck." Symmetrically, studies of the great fortunes made over the past century show that in virtually all cases there was just a single stroke of "good fortune." If great wealth were a matter of talent and drive to achieve it, with little luck involved, we would expect some people to have gotten rich twice or more. Evidently the multiple innovators, such as the inventor Thomas Edison and the scientist Linus Pauling, are the exceptions. Those who latched onto one thing, such as Ivan Pavlov in psychology and Noam Chomsky in linguistics, are the rule.

These ancient injunctions against lump sum taxation have not always prevailed. In American colonial history, and long after in some sections of the country, subjects had the right to vote on certain matters at the polls but only on payment of a "poll tax." That fixed levy was the price of admission to political participation, rather than economic participation, but it was a lump sum tax nonetheless. Many countries have resorted to a lump sum tax to meet a one-time desire for revenue, or resources. Land was expropriated (generally with little or no compensation) and redistributed to peasants in the 1920s following the Mexican revolution. A huge one-time tax was levied on Norwegian corporations after they had "cleaned up" in World War II. But these applications of the lump sum tax were all exceptional, arising from singular circumstances.

Such one-time taxes have often given social reformers an idea: Why not a one-time tax on land holding, payable in land perhaps, or a one-time tax on capital, payable in capital? Then the government could live off the resulting income forever! Moreover this one-time tax would be a tax according to success rather than according to promise. It would tax workers and savers after they've made good. But in the "welfare states" of Europe and North America this radical step would solve little: There most wealth is owned by retired persons and by wage and salary earners—yes, by widows and orphans as well—who will need that wealth if they are to carry out their life plans. So the government would be obligated to offer compensation in full to most of these persons. Those not compensated in full would complain of an injustice in being taxed retroactively and without warning prior to their decisions to earn and to save. No American economist could help reflecting that such extraordinary fiscal measures have commonly been regarded as unconstitutional for many decades.

It is not evident, then, that a society "handicaps" itself when it draws back from levying the dreaded lump sum tax. Perhaps the drawbacks were apparent to the designers of the United States Constitution when they proscribed the application of the head taxes common under colonial rule. Yet it does not follow that the method of graduated taxation is ideal—the method under which the amount of tax an individual owes rises by degree with the amount earned or spent or saved or whatever constitutes the individual's tax base—or that all such methods are equal.

The "distortion" from graduated taxation. People often talk as though every sort of graduated tax, even a proportional tax rate, is a wanton act of destruction, snuffing out incentives to work and to preserve or expand the nation's wealth. It is enough to make the nonexpert suspicious: "If my tax rate goes up, why should that make me want to earn less income? I see that by choosing to make less income I would lessen my tax liability, would "avoid" some of the increase in tax liability that would otherwise result. But my objective in life is my own gain, not the government's loss." Right. Since the goal of a person is certainly not to see how small he can make his tax liability—were that his goal he would stop earning taxable income altogether—it makes no sense to claim that a person confronted by a higher tax rate will respond by earning less *in order to* avoid some of the tax. However, with regard to the graduated taxation of income or expenditure by persons, there *is* a valid argument.

The argument that financing government spending by taxation of personal income or expenditure "erodes incentives" falls into place once the proposition is stated correctly. The proposition compares the consequences of graduated taxation to those from hypothetical lump sum taxation: If some of the revenue raised by taxing the earnings or expenditure of a person were replaced by a lump sum tax of exactly the *same amount,* that person would respond by working more or at least not less. Similarly, going in the other direction: If the revenue raised from a person by the taxation of earnings or expenditure were increased but offset by a decrease of the person's lump sum tax (or increase in some lump sum payment) in the *same amount,* that person would react by earning less or at least not more. In every case the comparison is between raising revenue the graduated tax way and raising the same amount by a lump sum levy.

Then the argument for the proposition becomes clear: If I am facing a graduated tax system, I can figure, as one citizen among millions, that if I earn one more loaf of bread before tax or buy one more pint of beer the government will share in the benefit—it won't hand back to me the whole of the extra revenue collected by cutting my tax rates alone, and unfortunately the government will not share in the burden, since it won't help me to do the extra work or saving required. But if the same tax revenue were collected from me in an unalterable lump sum tax, then I could earn and

FIGURE 13–1: A Graduated Tax on Personal Income or Expenditure Drives a "Wedge" between the Marginal Product of Each Person's Labor (Allocated to Earning Taxable Income) and the Person's *After-Tax Hourly Wage Rate*. Removing the Wedge while Collecting the Same Tax Payment in a Lump Sum Would Remove the "Disincentive" to Earn and Consume More.

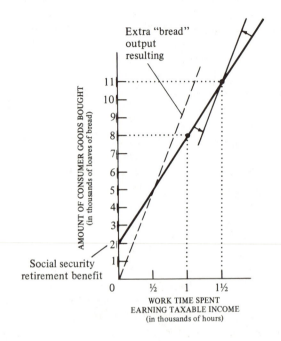

measured in terms of hours worked. A careful look shows that each additional thousand hours worked yields an additional after-tax income of 6 thousand loaves of bread. So the after-tax hourly wage rate of the person is 6.

The left-hand lighter line depicts the extra national output, also measured by its worth (market value) in units of bread, that the individual contributes. This output, like the person's after-tax income, is also a function of the individual's effort. Another careful look shows that each additional thousand hours worked by the person yields an additional national output of 10 thousand loaves. So the marginal productivity of labor of this person is 10. (Suppose this is the person's before-tax wage rate, as in competitive equilibrium. Then the tax rate is 40 percent.)

Faced with the graduated tax, the person chooses to work 1.5 thousand hours in the example and receives a retirement benefit of 2 thousand. That way he earns 15 thousand before tax and pays 6 thousand in income or expenditure taxes. Hence he receives 9 thousand after tax plus the retirement benefit. But if that tax were collected in a lump sum, the individual could "get a better deal" from working harder *than he could before,* when he had to turn over 40% of every extra penny earned to the government in income or expenditure taxes.

In the figure, the darker line depicts a person's after-tax income, measured in terms of its command over bread, as a function of the effort made,

spend as before if I like *or* I can take advantage of the improved terms at which I could buy more beer and things in return for more work—the better terms at which I could trade leisure for commodities. Rational choice dictates I earn and buy more (not less, anyway!) in response.

Sadistic teachers can tease beginning students by asking them to reconcile this neat result with what they have earlier learned about a person's supply-of-labor curve: that it can bend backward once the after-tax wage rate is very high. The sadistic question is: If the supply curve is backward bending, how do you know that the rise in the after-tax wage rate resulting from sub-

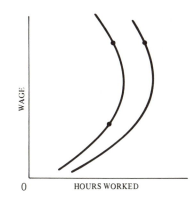

stitution of the lump sum tax in place of the graduated tax does not cause (paradoxically) a *decrease* in the amount of labor supplied—as the diagram to the left suggests is possible. But the unflappable student can reply: Since the analysis of Figure 13–1 is impeccable, the only problem is to find the mistake in the supply-curve way of looking at the matter in order to reconcile the two analyses. The mistake is that when the government raised the after-tax wage rate it also levied a lump sum tax on the person in the amount of $6,000. So for any *given* after-tax wage rate the person would actually be worse off than before and would therefore have to consume less or work more— that is, accept less leisure—or both of those things. We know that if the supply curve really is backward bending where it matters, leisure must be a good that the individual likes to take more of when he is made better off. So it must be that when he is stuck with the lump sum tax he will demand less leisure, hence supply more effort at each given after-tax wage rate. So the supply-of-effort curve *shifts rightward*. So the supply-curve analysis does *not* imply the possibility that, paraodixcally, the individual will respond by working less rather than more!

There is another pseudo-contradiction, closely related to the former one, that tends to send amateur discussions of taxation into confusion. Isn't it true, people have wisely observed, that the revenue collected by the government has to an appreciable degree been utilized for health, education, anti-poverty, and social-overhead programs that have probably *increased* the willingness and ability of many people to work and have probably added to the attractiveness of work as well? So what sense can it make, taking the larger view, to say that graduated taxation erects "disincentives" to work and save? In reply, the tax economist begins by thanking the speaker for getting that important observation off his chest and onto the table. Continuing, the tax economist notes that the proposition has been misunderstood. The propo-

sition compares the effects of the graduated tax with the consequences when, hypothetically, it is replaced by lump sum taxes
on persons raising the same amounts of revenue. If people now
work harder thanks to the government's good deeds, they would
work *harder still* if the "disincentive effect" of the graduated tax
rates were removed by substituting lump sum taxes. It *may be*
that these disincentive effects are quite serious in the sense that
there is room for large improvements in the structure of graduated taxation—even Pareto-type improvements that make everyone better off.

SUMMING UP: Classical economics must concede the unsatisfactoriness of
lump sum taxation—a head tax, a tax on "promise," and so forth. On the
other hand, graduated taxation of personal income or expenditure involves
the taxation of working or saving or both, and therefore has "disincentive
effects" on the amount of income earned. As a result, there is too little
income earned—too little work, too little savings—in the taxable commercial sector of the economy, hence too much leisure, home gardening,
and "underground" activities that escape taxation. Competitive markets
can still provide their virtuous services of ensuring that factor inputs to
the taxable sector of the economy are allocated to achieve efficiency in
production, and the goods produced are traded so as to achieve efficiency
in comsumption. (There will not be disparities in the price charged for the
same tractor or the same candy to different users.) But the supplies of
work and saving to the taxable sector are going to be less than required
for "overall" ideal efficiency.

Reactions differ to this staple theme of classical economics. One reaction
recalls the joke about a desperate situation being "hopeless but not serious."
How much *worse* is it for a person to be faced with the *flat* after-tax budget
line of Figure 13–1 than to be faced with the steeper hypothetical budget
line that "expands" the person's choice? Does it matter much to the person?
Recent evidence, psychological and econometric, suggest that in present-day
societies the "flattening" of the term of exchange has reached a degree where
it has become far from trivial.

♦ It is argued in the psychological literature that people's emotional health
  is affected by their sense of choice over their life style. Once a person feels
  it is hardly possible to alter appreciably his destiny through his own efforts
  the result is apt to be depression. This implies that a person, presented
  with an expansion of choice like that in Figure 13–1, would gain a height-
  ened feeling of autonomy from having more leverage over his income—

from being able to move up and down the steeper curve. That suggests that most persons, rather than rest content with an unchanged income (which would not be irrational), would respond vigorously to the opportunity to earn more income at improved terms. However, the sense of leverage over one's income may puff us up anyway: "Any misstep by me and I'm in the mud, so it makes a real difference how I perform."

♦ The literature of statistical economics, called econometrics, is beginning to amass evidence of the burdensomeness of government revenue collected by graduated taxation. The burden on a taxpayer can be measured in principle by the amount of income he would be willing (at most) to pay in a lump sum in order to bribe the government to rescind its tax rates. A person might, for example, be just as happy paying a lump sum tax of $7,000 as paying $6,000 in income or expenditure taxes (as in Figure 13–1). So the burden of the actual $6,000 tax payment is $7,000, the "excess burden" being $1,000. What if the tax rate goes up a little, making the burden $8,000? If the government is nearing "taxable capacity," the extra *revenue* gained might be merely $200, say. A burden of $9,000 might yield only an additional $4, say. So the burdensomeness of an extra amount (say, one unit) of tax revenue might be *five times* that amount; or *250 times* the extra amount collected; or higher! (Estimates of the number in the real world are just beginning to come in. A recent estimate of the burdensomeness of extra tax revenue in the United States is around 8 times.) A contemporary American economist, the late Arthur Okun, devised the metaphor of a leaky bucket used to carry water from the water-full to the water-less, or to a fire, to suggest the inefficiency with which the gains obtained from economic participation by one group in society can be redistributed via the tax-and-transfer system to another group. The discussion here suggests the amended metaphor of a shallow bucket that slops water over the side—the *worse the fuller the bucket.*

Another reaction to the classical theme of distortions from taxation asks why, if there is no alternative to the taxation of work and saving, do the disincentives matter? In fact, though, there are "alternatives," or choices, to select from among.

♦ A society might choose to collect and spend less tax revenue, less than the maximum obtainable, in view of the increasing burdensomeness of each extra unit collected. Perfectly true—but it is worth noting that societies are not required by rationality or logic to respond that way to the disincentives of graduated taxation. The fact that the water-bucket splashes as it is passed from hand to hand may very well fail to deter the society from filling it to the top if it is trying to put out a fire. A great many countries, particularly the "welfare states"' of northwestern Europe and some of the communist countries to the east, have seemed bent on raising as much tax revenue as they can. The conception of economic justice developed by Rawls, the so-called maximin principle, *requires* that the government collect the maximum possible tax revenue: The largest possible amount of revenue extracted from the wage income of workers and the interest income of savers is needed in order to finance the largest possible subsidy to enterprises and public agencies for the hiring, training, and so forth of the least productive workers—thus to raise the rewards of the least rewarded to the highest level. Whether a society ought, according to its moral principles, to reduce the tax bill in view of the burdensomeness of revenue raising—to scale down subsidies and expenditures for the disadvantaged or trim medical research and other public investments for future generations or cut national defense below the levels they could otherwise reach—depends upon the society's moral principles.

Here we shall concentrate on another choice to be made in regard to taxation. *Not all graduated taxes are alike.* There are "alternative" ways to raise any given total of tax revenue. The burdensomeness of the various disincentive effects have implications for the appropriate *structure* of taxation.

AVERTING INEFFICIENT TAX STRUCTURES: "TRICKLE DOWN" THEORY

Some tax structures have worse disincentive effects than other tax structures that yield the same total revenue. Some tax structures are so bad as to be inefficient in the practical sense: It is feasible—and not just with hypothetical lump sum taxes and compensations—to make everyone better off by reforming the tax structure. Classical tax analysis has discovered three sorts of pathologies in the tax structure that, if present, offer the opportunity for such an all-around gain, a so-called Pareto improvement.

Overtaxation—with a Single Proportional Tax

The idea that a society relying on graduation taxation cannot tax away all of its members' gains, which are in the nature of rents or surpluses after allowance for the effort of earning income, has already been noted above. This is the notion of maximum revenue, or *taxable capacity*. Decades ago the public gained the impression, largely from amateurs rather than professional economists, that as the rates of taxation were pushed up in such a way as to approach taxable capacity, the economy would be seized by ever more violent monetary tremors culminating in a cataclysmic hyperinflation (the nearest thing in economics to the destruction of Krypton). The public was misled, however. The tax rates might be exactly high enough to yield the maximum revenue, or *higher* than that, without people being aware of it.

If the rates of taxation prevailing in a country *exceed* the levels just large enough to bring in the maximum feasible revenue, what are the consequences?

◆ Certainly one consequence is that such taxation is pointlessly burdensome. The tax rates that have gone beyond the point of bringing in additional revenue could be reduced to lower levels sufficient to bring in the same total of tax revenue—and as a result everyone would be better off at the prospect of better after-tax wage rates and interest rates (or, equivalently, better after-tax prices at which to buy goods). Taxation at such unconstructive rates surely deserves the name *overtaxation*.

◆ Such taxation is also counterproductive, not merely unproductive, just as a monopolist suffers a *decline* of his profit from its highest possible level if he sets his price *too* high—*above* the profit-maximizing price level, so the government can expect to suffer a *decline* of the tax revenue collected from its maximum feasible level if it sets its tax rates *above* the levels sufficient to generate the maximum revenue. This point gained celebrity several years ago with the drawing of the Laffer Curve depicted in Figure 13–2. As tax rates are increased, tax revenue first rises and then falls. The reason is the same in the two situations: Once the monopolist's "mark-up" on a product or the government's tax rate on a good, say, has reached the level bringing in the maximum profit or the maximum government revenue, a further boost of the mark-up or tax rate would reduce the quantity of the good demanded by proportionately *more* than the hike in the mark-up or tax rate; so it would *decrease* the profit or tax revenue obtained.

FIGURE 13–2: The Laffer Curve

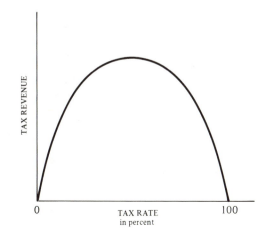

FIGURE 13–3: The Consequences of Overtaxation with a Proportional Tax Rate on Consumer Expenditure

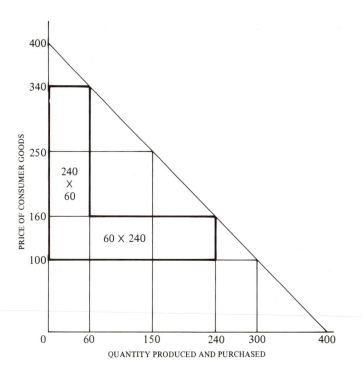

The case of "constant costs" in the consumer-good sector of the economy is depicted. Perfect competition would drive down the consumer price level to the 100 level if the taxes to pay for the government's transfer payments, subsidies, and expenditures were of the lump sum type. But the government's expenditure tax, a sort of national sales tax to consumers, drives up the post-tax competitive-equilibrium price to consumers above that level.

An expenditure tax rate is passed along entirely to consumers in the case of constant cost. So the consumer price level of 160 corresponds to a 60 percent expenditure tax rate—equivalent to a 37.5 percent tax on households' incomes, since an income of 160 would pay 60 in taxes.

This tax rate yields a tax revenue of 60 x 240, as shown. Suppose that is the revenue level desired.

The government could instead raise the same level of revenue by a much higher tax rate that drives the price level to 340. Then the tax per unit is 240 and the quantity of goods produced only 60. Here the government has *overshot* the consumer price level appropriate for raising the maximum revenue—which is 250 in the diagram, half the distance from 100 to 400.

Readers can use the analysis of chapters 11 and 12 to argue that unquestionably everyone, wage earners and interest earners, is worse off under the horrendous 340 price level than under 160.

The first point is clear enough. The second point is also familiar. A geometric depiction of these ideas is nevertheless worth having. Figure 13-3 shows the example of a proportional expenditure tax on all consumer purchases, which is similar to what the Europeans call a value-added tax.

It is possible to portray the work disincentives and burdens of the graduated taxation of wage income with the use of a supply-and-demand-for-labor diagram. For the same purpose economists often use instead another tool of analysis. In the diagram to the left, the vertical axis measures the aggregate net-of-tax-and-transfers-and-benefits income of the present young generation —the "active" population, or working generation. The horizontal axis measures their aggregate contribution of labor-time —where, to take account of differences in workers' energy or drive, we give appropriately greater weight to the man-hours of a high-marginal-product worker than to the hours of a low-marginal-product worker.

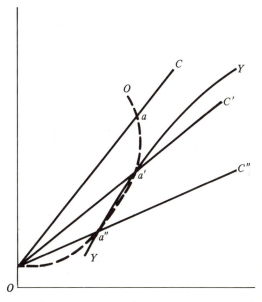

The three straight lines have a common intercept, B. The distance of B from the origin measures the total educational and medical and retirement and other "benefits" received in the aggregate by the working generation from the government. Every worker understands that his entitlement to such benefits is independent of how much he works and earns (as long as he works a little in order to qualify).

Each worker will observe his wage rate and check the papers for the proportional tax rate in order to calculate his after-tax wage rate. He will then decide accordingly how much labor-time to offer to the market, thus how much net income to earn. The aggregate amount of labor time offered will reflect the *average* after-tax wage rate of the workers. Given the average after-tax wage rate, there is a certain aggregate budget line, like *BC*, that corresponds to it. The corresponding labor-time offers decided upon by the workers *add up* to the choice of a point on *BC;* that point is labeled *a*. A higher tax rate could engineer lower after-tax wage rates, hence a lower average after-tax wage rate, and correspondingly a flatter aggregate budget line, such as *BC'*. Then the workers, in effect, would choose a point on *BC';* the point chosen is labeled *a'*. (The collection of such chosen points comprises the so-called *offer curve, BO*.)

Unfortunately the outcome at *a* cannot be an equilibrium! That follows from the fact that *a* lies *off* the curve *YY*, which measures the volume of output available to the workers: the national output *minus* the rental income on capital, which goes to the retired generation. But *a'*, with its higher tax rate, is a possible equilibrium. And so is *a"*, with its still higher tax rate. Hence there is a high-tax road and a low-tax road to the same total revenue to finance the B-level benefits. Clearly *a'* is preferred by all to *a"*. Further, an intermediate tax rate would yield a larger total revenue, being nearer the top of Laffer's Curve.

We have been discussing the proposition that tax rates generally *can* reach unconstructive, even counterproductive, levels. Is there any evidence that in actuality an across-the-board cut of tax rates might cost nothing in government revenue, even increase revenue? Or is this interesting possibility like the griffin, a species without any real-life examples? We shall certainly want to consider that question, however briefly, because it is important, and new enough that existing findings on it are not well known. It is useful to take note of the other sources of overtaxation before doing so, however.

Overtaxation of Wage Income "at the Top"

A single proportional tax system has the intriguing property that a rise in the tax rate hits everyone proportionately. In every actual country, however, it takes *many* tax rates to describe the structure of taxation rather than just one rate. Thus different incomes, different in size or source, are frequently taxed at different rates. Here we consider tax rates in relation to the *size of wage income*. The subsequent section takes up taxation of income from savings.

The disincentive effect on a person of the taxation of wage income depends in magnitude on what is called the *marginal* tax rate on the wage income the person is earning. The marginal tax rate means the rate at which the tax due increases with increasing income: the additional tax incurred from earning an additional rupee or dollar or pound of income. By contrast, the *average* tax rate of a person is simply his tax bill as a fraction of his earnings (before tax). The two rates are not generally equal, leaving aside the exceptional case of proportional taxation, and the distinction could hardly be more crucial to tax analysis:

- If the *marginal* tax rate were 100 percent on any and all additional earnings of a person, the person would clearly have no incentive whatsoever to earn any additional income *no matter how low* the person's *average* tax rate—the tax included on the income he chooses to earn expressed as a ratio to that income.

- If the *marginal* tax rate were *zero* on all income additional to what he first contemplates earning, the person would have some incentive to earn more *no matter how high* the person's *average* tax rate—no matter how heavily taxed the "first" or "previous" dollars of income.

Now, in many countries, there is what can be called *progressivity in the marginal tax rates*. When we scan the tax table we see that the marginal tax rate *rises* as our eye travels from one income bracket (with its own marginal rate) to the next higher one (with its marginal rate). It would be mathematically possible to have instead *regressivity* in the marginal tax rates—the reverse tendency of the marginal rate. (And such a society could still dedicate its tax revenue to aid the poor!) Or the marginal tax rate could arch or even undulate in attractive ways.

Classical-style tax analysis and demonstrated this startling point: It is another case of *overtaxation* to have the *marginal* tax rate *greater than zero* on additional income—extra income that could be earned but isn't being earned—of the *top* wage earners. Yes, that's right: It is wasteful of a society to penalize earners of the *biggest* wage income with a positive *marginal* rate.

- It is inefficient because the top earners are being deterred by the marginal tax rate from earning more and at no gain to the treasury. By lowering the marginal tax rate on the *first extra* dollar the government can entice the big earners to *earn* that dollar, dividing their gains between themselves and the treasury for a universal Pareto improvement. Then the government repeats, lowering the marginal rate on the *next* extra dollar, and so forth.

There is nothing faulty about the purely verbal "proof" of the proposition. If it is grasped, and it should be, it's fine. Some readers may nevertheless appreciate a more visual, geometrical presentation of the logic of the proof. Below is a diagram like that in Figure 13–1 except that the persons it refers to are solely those who earn the top income; and the relation between after-tax income received and work performed is here curvilinear—bowed out from below, to be specific—in reflection of the rising marginal tax rate as a person's wage income increases.

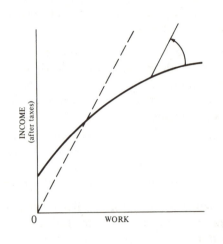

At some level of work and corresponding after-tax income an individual "has enough" in view of his wage rate and his marginal tax rate—hence the after-tax wage rate on an additional day or hour of work—and his preference for less work (at least to a point) "if the money is the same."

But why not present such a person instead with a zero marginal tax rate on the next unit of income earned?—or even on all units, for that matter. The person in question will then be better off, the jubilant beneficiary of expanded choice! If such a person does in fact work longer hours or more days as a result, he will not hurt anyone else by so doing. To argue that, we observe that the tilting of the person's after-tax budget curve, as shown, merely offers the person his marginal product on any extra work he puts in; so he will not be taking out in additional income after-tax more than he puts in. The government can ensure that other wage earners and interest receivers continue to do as well *after tax* as before. (That will require an easing of tax rates on wage income, and tightening of tax rates on interest income, if the "top dogs" are numerous enough to affect market wage rates and interest rates by their increased efforts.)

Such an argument is enough to prove that someone can be helped and no one hurt by removing the positive marginal tax rate "at the top." Of course, the rest of society will prefer, quite reasonably, to share in the top dogs' gains. So society will not want to drop the marginal tax rate abruptly to zero on the *next* dollar (and all further ones) but, rather, to reduce the marginal tax rate gradually—precisely as the text, above, suggests.

Mistakes in the Tax "Mix"

Wage income and consumer expenditure are not the only potential bases for assessing tax. Where there is labor, the chances are there is capital. Just as wage income can be taxed although it dilutes the incentive to work, so interest income can be taxed even though it blunts the incentive to save. But the two sorts of incomes are not entirely similar since, great estates aside, most savings are accumulated out of wage earnings. So the taxation of interest also dulls the incentive to work. Probably that is what people are getting at when they complain that taxing interest is "double taxation": Wages are first taxed directly, then taxed again when saved.

- It is difficult for economists to tell whether interest should be taxed or instead subsidized! Suppose all revenue came initially from wage income. The government could try a small tax on interest income and at the same time cut wage tax rates just enough to hand back to households the new revenue. But the resulting change in after-tax wage rates and after-tax interest rates may alter the households' behavior and upset the treasury's calculation. *If* households respond by offering more labor, hence paying more taxes, then it was not right to spare interest income from tax. If *less* labor is offered, drop the experimental tax and try a subsidy.

The situation we observe in all countries is that interest income is already substantially taxed, at least as heavily as wage income. Since it is at any rate possible that interest should not be taxed at all, the suspicion arises that there is overtaxation of interest in the comparative sense: A cut in interest-income tax rates and increase in wage-income tax rates calculated to give the government and households (in the aggregate) an unchanged income, provided there are no resulting incentive effects on households' behavior, might so stimulate saving and perhaps effort too that tax revenue would be greatly increased. So the increase in the wage-income tax rates could be lessened—maybe reversed.

What is the evidence? Are those American economists right who have bet that a reduction of some tax rates, perhaps even an across-the-board reduction of rates (in more-or-less equal proportion), would not cost the government some revenue?

- Recent studies of the responsiveness of saving in the United States to increases in the after-tax rate of return to saving—the net-of-tax rate of interest, in other words—estimate that reductions in the taxation of interest and profit-type income generally would stimulate an increase in the amount of saving "supplied" sufficiently to maintain or even increase the interest-tax revenue collected. However, unless the tax cuts were restricted to *new* saving, the regeneration of revenue from the increase in the tax base would take time. The effects on the amount of labor supplied have not yet been estimated with any confidence. (Although these results may not stand up, it is still possible that such interest-tax cuts when coupled with "compensating" increase in wage-tax rates would release work and saving incentives, causing a rise of revenue.)

♦ Examinations of the major tax-rate reductions in twentieth-century American history suggest that high-income taxpayers especially responded to the increased incentives to earn additional income. Particularly important, those taxpayers were induced by the rate cuts to move some of their wealth out of "tax-sheltered assets" such as mansions and farm estates into tax-yielding investments.

♦ Studies of the sharp rise after the last war in the marginal tax rates imposed on high earnings in some of the smaller countries, Great Britain and Sweden in particular, suggest that those high rates had lost as much revenue as they had gained, by prompting some of the large earners to emigrate to "tax havens" such as Monaco and the Bahamas.

Recent tax cuts in the United States and Britain have turned those economies into a living laboratory for the test of the overtaxation hypothesis. The results to date cast considerable doubt on the audacious speculation that a *general* tax rate cut would increase tax revenue. They lend some support to the theory that a cut of rates at the top would increase revenue.

THE ALLOCATIVE ROLE OF THE CLASSICAL STATE

Taxation is a means, obviously, not a purpose of the government. But to what end, or ends? It is time to sum up the place of the state in classical and neoclassical economic doctrine. At the most fundamental level, that is done in a sentence: The role of the state is to enable the members of society to enjoy the benefits of economic cooperation by enforcing their protection from one another and from threats abroad—more generally, to attack all sources of inefficiency, the removal of which can make some or all better off without harming any—and, above all, to see to it that, within the limits of the instruments available and admissible, the structure of rewards for the contributions made are deemed just according to the moral principles prevailing in the society—or at any rate, not unjust as far as these principles can be discerned

That last point has been expressed with enviable economy and forcefulness in a wide-ranging evaluation of contemporary Western economic progress: "Social justice is the sole basis for the legitimacy of the state. There is no other."* Presumably the writer did not mean that the citizen, seeing injustice, is obligated to join in an insurrection, or has a license to kill. The statement means, no doubt, that in order to obligate a person to obey all laws (pay all taxes, and so forth) and to give public support, it is not enough that the state merely supply what Rawls has tagged "procedural justice"—various legal protections, including rights against the state. The state must be seen by the person as providing substantive economic (and wider) justice. Otherwise the person has every right to oppose the state and seek its replacement by another.

When economists refer to the functions served by the classical state, or the state's classical functions, they usually mean its roles at a less fundamental level. The reference is usually to the resource-allocational roles to be performed by the government, because they are necessary or worthwhile roles that can best be performed or only performed by the government, *versus* those roles left to be performed by the market. The subject is the boundary line between the domain of the government and the domain of the market in the allocation (or influence over allocation) of resources between one use and another.

Subsidizing (and Possibly Managing) Natural Monopolies

A major category of allocative tasks of the classical state is the subsidization and possible administration of natural monopolies. By subsidizing the price of the natural monopoly with the tax money of the consumers using the good produced, whether or not the government actually takes over the monopoly, the government drives the selling price of the good produced to the level of marginal cost of production. The argument was already introduced in chapter 12, where it was shown that, failing government intervention, a natural monopoly, like any other monopoly, would tend to produce too little—at too high a price.

- ◆ Thus we find governments in the trash-hauling business, in bridge and tunnel operation, in turnpikes and railroads, and rather often in the airline business.

It might be noted that it does not matter whether the government itself performs the service (government production) or hires a private enterprise to do it (government expenditure).

However, the field of natural monopolies extends much farther. The business of protection is a natural monopoly. That is because of increasing returns to scale in that industry: If two or more protection companies were struggling over market shares, each one trying for an increasing number of clients,

---

* Fred Z. Hirsch, *The Limits to Economic Growth* (Cambridge, Mass.: Harvard University Press, 1976).

they would notice that they were duplicating resources and see the merits of merger (whether or not they could actually get together!) One security guard can guard a street the length of a whole block, and back-ups can stand ready at the central station. We could imagine a titular government, with King and a House of Rhetoric, while the real power lay with some board of crooks who operate the country's sole protection agency for their own maximum profit. In a sense, what we usually call self-rule or self-government came about when (or after) the users of protection, the paying consumers of that service, saw they could do better by "buying out" the protectors and operating the activity in the "public interest," driving the price paid in taxes and user charges down to marginal cost—usually down to zero because of the nuisance cost of collecting—rather than in the private interest of the protection enterprise. More protection results. Some of the most essential agencies of the government are from an economic standpoint natural monopolies that could be operated for a profit:

♦ Police protection and investigation are natural monopolies. So is fire protection, the sewage system, and the provision of running water.

> A distinction between these latter natural monopolies and those in the former group is that the police, fire, and other departments do not usually make a user charge for detective work, rescue work, and so forth. On the other hand, tolls and "tariffs" for bridges and tunnels, rail and air trips are the norm. Evidently there is an *insurance* element in the government's decision not to charge for rescue of a child or even a cat! So citizens become subscribers who pay a contractual fee rather like an insurance premium, instead of a user fee for use.

Providing Collective (Often Called "Public") Goods

The goods we associate with "free markets" and the "sovereign consumer" are largely *individualistic* goods, frequently called *private* goods. They have the essential property that each individual's consumption of the good subtracts from the output left over for the consumptions of the others. If the strawberries we eat this season have to add up to what is produced this season, one more strawberry for someone is one fewer strawberry for someone else.

The world also contains a variety of *collective* goods, often called *public* goods. Beliefs can be shared. Sunsets. We share safety from smallpox and polio. These are all collective goods. Like the person who didn't realize he had been speaking prose all his life, we suddenly realize that many of our enjoyments derive from collective goods: Today's television transmissions, both over-the-air (wireless) and over-the-wire (cable) TV, are collective goods—no matter whether transmitted by a private station or a public one, whether without charge or for a price—since I can turn on my set to watch without someone else having to turn his off. Knowledge is a collective good; hence scientific researchers are producers of collective goods, since you can study a medical-research paper without thereby preventing another from doing so (thanks to photo-copy machines). The good called security, or sleeping well, that comes from knowing there is a National Guard on hand to fight a dangerous forest fire or epidemic is also a collective good and the National Guard a producer of it.

If a fire starts in someone's kitchen or furnace, is the success of that person in putting it out a collective good for all of us on this side of the river? Is the decision of the fire department to put it out a collective good? No, not really. It is the presence of the fire department that is the collective good, not extinguishing someone's flaming steak (even if there is some risk of the flame's spreading). Yes, "My fire department is your fire department." But my fire is not your fire. There is, however, an external effect, or neighborhood effect, when a person starts or puts out a fire, as discussed in the next section.

Likewise, it might be thought that when a detective works on your case it is a collective good for the rest of us because "your security is our security." But suppose that I would be just as happy if the detectives sat around doing nothing until they get a call from *me,* as long as they give the appearance of catching criminals in order to deter them! In that case, their catching your thief or anyone's is not a collective good. The security from having those detectives is both *yours* and *mine.* But it would be sentimentality to say that your security is my security. There are good natural-monopoly reasons for you and I to agree to subsidize detective work in order to get the price down to marginal cost; and further insurance-type reasons for agreeing that whichever of us is robbed should pay a zero price, agreeing to pay additional taxes in place of the user charges as insurance premiums.

A characteristic of every collective good, it follows, is that there is no rationale for using a price to "ration" the use, or consumption, of the good. That is not a statement about how much production of the good would be best. (Let society produce little of it if it isn't appreciated much.) The proposition is just this: Whatever the amount produced, it is never necessary in order to avoid shortages and inefficiency of consumption that consumers be induced to consume the good in a smaller quantity or less often by means of a price charged for the quantity used. The reason: With a collective good there cannot be any problem of shortage, "excess demand," and failure of the market to clear, even at a zero price charged, since *everyone* is technologically able to consume the *whole* amount produced *simultaneously*. The classical rationale for charging consumers a price does not apply to collective goods.

If collective goods ought to come free of charge, it is quite obvious that consumers are going to have a tough time acquiring them, and in the right quantities, from the coldhearted market, where producers need to charge prices to cover their costs. If people are directed to the market to obtain a collective good, without government help, the amount supplied by the market is bound to be *less than ideal*—if any is supplied at all. *Either* producers will succeed in charging a price by managing to bar the consumer from access to the collective good—in which case some or all consumers will be driven to consume too little of the good (having to pay to watch certain sports events on television is an example), *or* producers will find they are unable to exclude any consumer from gaining access to the collective good and each consumer will refuse to pay (hoping to be a free-rider but with little expectation)—in which case producers will have no incentive to produce the collective good at all; there is no way to exclude a person from the benefits of disease prevention and clean streets, for example.

◆ Thus a great many collective goods are provided by the government, either purchased by the government for the benefit of consumers or produced by the government itself. National defense; television and radio broadcasting; protection against air pollution, water impurities, crop infestations, and epidemics; scientific research findings; museums to provide access "at cost" to art works (which are collective goods); weather and economic forecasts; and so on.

The structure of rewards in a country, no less than its climate, folklore, and language, can be viewed as a collective good, the product of legislation.

If a country carried out this classical doctrine to the letter, without exceptions, some shortcomings would become apparent. Which scientific research to commission for eventual donation to the public? Whose novels and essays to buy? Which movie script to produce?

One might guess that there is a simple solution: Let producers of scientific reports, essays, and movies take their chances by placing their new creations on the market at their own expense; then the government can offer a subsidy to users for each use that would bring the price (after subsidy) to those users down to zero—to make use free. But that will not work, for the producer knowing that he will be subsidized for the difference between the nominal charge to the user and the actual charge to the user will naturally lavish resources on production—or simply claim that his marginal cost of production is very high, so he has to get a high price.

However, if the economy had already sunk into some kind of stationary state, where all the movies to be made have been made, the government would have no problem to solve. The government could declare all patent and copyright protection henceforth unlawful. Very likely, pirated copies of high-tech designs and Professor Somebody's *Secrets of Successful Chemistry* would soon find their way onto the market in sufficient quantities to drive the price down to the cost of the ink and paper to reproduce them. If that did not happen entirely—if the owners of some Stravinski scores or Picasso oils or the prints to *The Wizard of Oz* were able to foil attempts to make copies, the government could offer a subsidy to the owners in order to bring down the price to users (theaters, opera companies, museums, and so forth) In theory, it should work. Movie houses thus would be like museums in which the cost of admission only covered the ushers and heat.

Subsidies and Taxes to Correct External ("Neighborhood") Effects

An external diseconomy occurs when the total cost of someone's action exceeds the cost of the action borne by that individual—so others have to bear some of the cost. Urban littering and overfishing were the classic examples, given in chapter 5. In those examples the members of the community or society can make themselves all better off by agreeing to tax excessive littering and fishing and spend the revenue on themselves or, better yet, use it to finance a cut in distortionary income or expenditure taxation. By now there are long handbooks on the science of such *corrective taxation.* but the idea is simple: Set the tax rate on the action at a level such that the *cost including tax* to the individual is exactly equal to the total cost of the action. In the standard terminology: Set the tax so that the private cost to the individual, including the tax, is equal to the social cost the action imposes. Of course, this scheme does require that there is enough at stake to make it worthwhile for the government to pay the costs of monitoring people in order to obtain compliance. (If people were angels there would be no need for government except to call the signals.)

◆ The great beauty of the classical answer to pollution and conservation problems is that no one in government or out need decide how much smoke is permissible or how many of a species have to be preserved. Markets can be left to determine the answers *if* all the individuals acting in the market face *corrected* after-tax costs—corrected by the addition of a tax so that they accurately reflect the social costs of the actions taken. *Then* markets will work in textbook fashion to allocate resources for efficiency in production and consumption.

There is an external economy when the total, or social, benefit of someone's action exceeds the benefit to the individual, the so-called private benefit—so others receive some of the benefit. Here the government's classical role is to subsidize the action in order to use more of it to be undertaken. Are there instances of external economies? When at age eleven Luciana Serra broke into song with the window open, the whole block burst into applause at the end! There are also beautiful people whom we like to look at. But a subsidy for open windows and state prizes for outstanding dress are not the compelling kind of example we are after. However, there are a few examples that have not already fallen into the category of collective goods.

Economists generally regard government subsidy of education as being justified on the ground that each student will produce a social benefit from his education in *excess* of his private benefit. The argument refers both to reducing illiteracy and dependency and to keeping Einsteins stimulated. Certain housing subsidies, properly directed, might serve to reduce "urban blight"; even general housing subsidies to the renting of housing would serve to drive up the price of housing and thus encourage newer units to replace decaying structures. Perhaps food-consumption subsidies, such as the food-stamp program in the United States, are justified—compared to the obvious alternative of money—on the ground that better nutrition will to some extent pay for itself in fewer hospital bills, which must be paid by the healthy population, while money won't to the same extent pay for itself. But many economists contend that these subsidies are really latent and implicit devices to redistribute income (to people whose voting behavior hinges on it), and that if the society had economic justice to begin with, "up front" by means of subsidies to the employment of ill-paid workers, then the rationale for these other subsidies would fade.

EPILOGUE TO PART 4:
THE CLASSICAL VISION OF THE "RATIONALIST" STATE

We started with a look at the Gothic economics of two-person conflict, then examined the baroque complexities of economic institutions, to behold at last the visionary market economy of classical doctrine and its neoclassical refinements. The elegance—and comparative clarity!—of the neoclassical "model" is always a relief after excursions elsewhere. We can laugh at its abstract unrealism, feel uncomfortable at its willingness to leave out so much. Still the neoclassical model is the highest intellectual achievement thus far in Western political economy. (It took 200 years to build, and they are still at work on it.)

Neoclassical political economy, as we have seen, is not so much a description of the way things are as it is a prescription for the way things ought to be (once the society has reached a consensus on principles and objectives). The neoclassical theoretician is prescribing, not assuming, the equality of marginal cost and price, and pointing to ways to a closer approximation of the two. He concedes that there are monopolistic elements at present and episodes of disequilibrium.

In particular, neoclassical doctrine is advice about the merits of markets *wisely used*, about the "use and abuse" of the profit motive—much as some uncle might advise us on the virtues of wine taken within limits. It instructs a society on the mistakes that can be made in *interfering* with markets and the mistakes that can be made in *not* interfering, in not "intervening."

- ◆ The government will have to intervene with legislation to break up any enterprises and association that, although not natural monopolies, wield "monopoly power" to raise price or wage above competitive-equilibrium level: cartels, enterprises in collusion, trusts monopolizing a resource, professional associations fixing fees, trade unions enforcing high wage rates, and so forth.

- ◆ The government will certainly have to intervene with expenditures and corrective subsidies and taxes in order to remedy the underconsumption and underproduction of goods produced by natural monopolies, the underconsumption of various collective goods, the underproduction of goods causing external economies, and the overproduction of goods causing external diseconomies that would otherwise result in competitive equilibrium.

- ◆ The government will undoubtedly have to intervene with distributional subsidies and expenditures in order to bring the structure of rewards for contributions to the economy into line—as nearly as possible in view of the disincentive effects of graduated taxation—with society's moral criteria in regard to the distribution, or "division," of the gains from economic cooperation.

That is, in capsule form, the neoclassical manual for the wise use of markets in view of their strengths, possible malfunctionings, and limitations. There is another theme in neoclassical doctrine, however.

The neoclassical theoretician further argues that a society building its economy on the neoclassical model cannot do better than that. It has to be admitted that there is a difficulty. Perfect conformity to the neoclassical principles would still not produce ideal results: If graduated taxation on incomes and expenditure is adopted, lump sum taxation being regarded as unjust, unsafe, and unsporting, the consequent disincentive effects inevitably prevent the economy from achieving ideal *overall* efficiency. Yet arguments for any sort of *nonmarket* system, or command system, must confront the "opposite" difficulty: By dictating workers' jobs and hours and retirements, and dictating their rations of bread and circus, the central planning board solves the problem of disincentives all right—but thereby risks the injustice that was one objection to lump sum taxation, land which graduated taxation has the merit of avoiding. Some workers may get no more rent, or surplus, out of that system than they would have going it alone on some mountain—no gain at all from cooperation.

> We might want to decide the issue this way: A society threatened by a disaster or attempting a recovery from one might fairly expropriate and allocate resources by decree, accepting the inevitable risks or injustice, in order to fight for its very survival. However, a society unthreatened and secure in its stability would be right to insist on eliciting the members' productive contributions to the economy by means of the incentives to work created by the market in conjunction with governmental taxation and subsidy—and resisting the lump sum tax.

Among economists, it should be added, the neoclassical doctrine appears to be winning the argument. Few economists today would dispute the desirability of using incentives to invite and welcome the contributions of people's resources to the economy rather than employing commands and public appeals. Karl Marx himself, though no friend of capitalism, came to advocate wage incentives for the *socialist state* as long as commands to work were evaded.* He should have added: Incentives are preferable to commands cruelly made to work!

This brings us to the interpretation of neoclassical doctrine. Its basic subject, we have seen, is the desirability and optimum design of *incentives*.

---

* Karl Marx, "Critique of the Gotha Program," 1891. English tr. R. C. Tucker, ed., *The Marx-Engels Reader* (New York: W. W. Norton & Co., 1972) See the passage quoted here in chapter 6, p. 143.

It is not intrinsically about market *capitalism*. The theory does assume that the owner of some trucks or factory floor space will use it or lease it for use in the way that offers the highest possible return; and the same is true of the owner of any piece of land. But the theory does *not* assume that all or indeed any of those assets used by productive enterprises are *privately owned*— owned by persons or by private pension funds owned by persons. Factory space might be held by a public trust, office space by another trust—each such trust set up by a socialist central government to administer its assets by leasing them to enterprises for the purpose of income. Likewise, the theory does not require that the producing units be private enterprises; they could be profit-maximizing public enterprises whose profit after payment of wages and rentals to the factors hired—if not "competed" away by rival public enterprises—is to be turned over to the central government treasury.

♦ The economy is on a *market system* as long as the administrators of resources and the managers of the enterprises *"play the market game,"* the enterprises looking for the lowest rentals and so forth in order to maximize profits and the "resources" looking for the highest rentals in order to maximize their returns. If the resources hired by the commercial enterprises are predominantly public owned, the system is *market socialism;* if not, it is some kind of market capitalism.

From this perspective, the neoclassical prescriptive "model" can be seen as a blueprint for the optimum design and operation of market socialism no less or more than for market capitalism. The same incentive system can be installed in either.

Night Thoughts of the Neoclassical Theoretician

Although the neoclassical model has won wide acceptance among economists, the idea of relying on competitive markets (alongside taxes and subsidies to help the poor) seems to be accepted among the public only by those with no choice. Efficiency may be approved in the abstract, by some at least, but not by anyone when it means having to accept a lower wage or move to another line of work or both. Instead of awarding the nation's highest medals to enterprises that manage to reduce their manning requirements for the same output, government officials shed tears and propose state aid, thus undermining the incentive of the workers to relocate. People appear to want to take their wage and job opportunities out of the hands of competitive markets. The real world seems seriously at variance with the neoclassical vision.

A part of the explanation, possibly, is that the neoclassical theorist has overestimated the capacity and even the willingness of people to obey the self-denying ordinances required by any notion of justice.

◆ People rationalize their associations and special legislation for higher wages on the ground that *they* are the poor if proper account of the hardship of their work is taken or on the pretext that the higher wages will enable offsetting improvements in morale and skills so there will be no harm to the rest. Enterprises justify their high prices as a spur to innovation, the "juice" of capitalism that they say neoclassical doctrine overlooks.

◆ If there is no consensus about justice, merely people voting and lobbying as they like according to their private conscience (if any), then the prevailing structure of rewards cannot be viewed as "right" and meriting our acceptance even at a cost.

The other part of the explanation, it seems clear, is that the neoclassical theory has overestimated the capacity of the market, perhaps also the willingness of people to adapt to its impersonal mechanisms. Most real-life markets are not the frictionless mechanisms portrayed in classical theory. Subsequent chapters take up the analysis of the market system from other perspectives.

SUMMARY

1. Every society has reasons to tax: First, to raise the rewards of the poorly rewarded, regrettably at the expense of the well rewarded, so that the pattern, or distribution, of rewards is in line with its notions of economic justice; second, to cut back all rewards—everyone's pay (after tax)—so as to release resources for the government's use, resources that would otherwise have been used to produce goods for individual, or private, consumption. In a capitalist economy, of course, a participant's reward is lowered by a rise in tax rates or a reduction in the subsidy; a reward is raised by the reverse. (In communist and some socialist-type economies the government operates directly on the reward of a participant or a task performed, so the tax or subsidy is only implicit.)

2. The hated lump sum tax—an inescapable and inalterable levy that must be paid no matter how badly one had done—has two drawbacks: the impossibility of gauging beforehand one's drive and ability to earn, and the inevitable influence of good or bad luck. Hence lump sum taxation would not, if it were introduced as a means to raise tax revenue, be considered a fair tax.

3. The unfortunate feature of the *graduated* tax—such as an income tax or a sales tax, where the tax due or owed increases with a decision to increase one's taxable income or one's taxable purchase and thus the tax base—is that it creates a disincentive to work; the precise idea is that it lessens incentives to work *compared* to the hypothetical lump sum tax. If the

government knew beforehand exactly how much tax revenue was going to be collected from a person through the graduated tax, and if the government then substituted a lump sum tax calculated to raise the same revenue, *then* the individual would have *expanded choice,* since he could work *more* to earn *more* bread at better terms than before, and this would no doubt cause him to work and consume more in response, so he would be better off.

4. Yes, but what significance does it have for a society that does not want, in view of the moral uncertainties, to revert to the lump sum tax? First it means that it is possible for the rate of taxation on income or expenditure or both to be so high, and thus the incentive to work so diminished, that less tax revenue is collected than would be raised by a substantially lower tax rate. There is some tax rate, if we think of a tax system with a single, or proportional, tax rate, that yields the maximum possible tax revenue; a higher tax rate than that one would be counterproductive, causing tax revenue to fall, as the tax base declines faster than the tax rate increases. The diagrammatic construction called the Laffer Curve is a convenient representation, given a paper napkin, of this two-sided relation between tax rate and tax revenue collected.

5. Another proposition emerging from the understanding of the distortiveness of graduated taxation is that there is no obvious purpose served in saddling the *highest* earners with a positive "marginal tax rate" on any *extra* income they might decide to earn. Why not hold out the carrot of a somewhat lower tax rate on the *first* extra pound or dollar earned in order to coax these highest earners to earn it? That will give them expanded choice, always welcome, and the government will get a piece of the results, in the form of extra tax revenue. Then let the government make a similar deal on the next extra dollar, and so on. Once the marginal tax rate on one more pound or dollar of earnings is zero—and even then the highest earner is unwilling to take the trouble to earn it—the government can rest secure in the knowledge that it has exhausted all opportunities for a mutual gain between the highest earner and the treasury (representing all other taxpayers).

6. Another proposition emerging from the incentive analysis of tax structures is that it could conceivably be inefficient to tax income from work and income from saving at the same rates. Choosing the "mix" of tax rates involves incentive/disincentive effects.

7. The chapter concludes with a survey of the classical conception of the role of the government. What are the connections and boundaries between the government and the "market" to be, according to classical doctrine? The main messages can fit into a telegram: The government must intervene to dissolve the power of natural monopolies, cartels, and labor unions; the government must intervene with corrective subsidies and taxes to repair

or improve the misallocations of resources caused by natural monopolies and the phenomena of external economies, external diseconomies, and collective goods; and the government must intervene with redistributional subsidies, expenditures, and the taxes to finance them in order to bring the structure of rewards for contributions made to the economy into line—as nearly as possible in view of disincentive effects of the required graduated taxation—with society's standards of economic justice; and it must provide for these without the capacities to care for themselves in line with society's prevailing standards of decency.

CONCEPTS INTRODUCED

lump sum tax	tax distortion	classical functions of the state
graduated tax	excess burden	external economy
progressive tax	Laffer Curve	external diseconomy
proportional, or flat, tax	overtaxation, or inefficient tax	political sustainability

STUDY QUESTIONS

1. "What reason is there to believe that income taxation and various expenditure taxes create a 'disincentive' to work? The rise or real wage rates over the past two centuries in industrialized countries has presumably been responsible for the marked decrease of the work week and the increase of vacation time. So, by the same token, taxes that lower real wage rates *after tax* must have the opposite effect—to increase the work week and shorten vacations and thus to increase the supply of work, or effort." Economists say, in fact, that the disincentive effects of income and expenditure taxation are comparative. Compared to what other kind of tax? Explain and discuss.

2. Distinguish between genuine tax reforms aimed at increasing the efficiency of the economy and pseudo tax reforms intended to reduce revenues. Give examples of both real and mock reforms.

3. Could the top, or maximum, of the Laffer Curve occur at an average tax rate of 90 percent? 99 percent? Where, judging by international experience, do you think it is?

4. The text discusses one conceivable justification for taxing interest. What is it? Does it apply also to a Rawlsian state desirous of obtaining the maximum possible tax revenue? Are there other justifications?

5. Carlyle caricatured classical economic policy as "anarchy plus the constable," and to this day people think of the "government as nightwatchman" when they think of the classical doctrine. Does this view correctly describe the neoclassical theory of proper economic policy presented here?

APPENDIX: THE CLASSICAL POLICY DOCTRINE ON FOREIGN TRADE AND INVESTMENT

With the discovery of comparative advantage by David Ricardo the major step was taken in understanding the gains from foreign trade. A country might be able to outproduce another country or the rest of the world in everything—Portugal, say, might have an absolute advantage in the production of wine *and* cloth, being able to produce both goods with less land and labor (per unit of output) than the other country or countries—and still have every reason to trade: to export the good or goods in which it has a comparative advantage in exchange for the good or goods in which it is at a comparative disadvantage. A country that has an absolute disadvantage in the production of every good could nevertheless improve its lot by exporting from industries where it has a comparative advantage in trade for imported goods in which it has a comparative disadvantage. But how far should foreign trade go? Granted that some trade is desirable—up to a point it is a source of potential gain for everyone in the country—what should be a country's trade policy, its so-called commercial policy? And, granted that some foreign investment is desirable, inward or outward, what should be a country's policy toward foreign capital movements?

There is no policy area in which classical economics has staked out so strong a position. On commercial policy the classical and neoclassical economists have steadily championed the policy of *free trade:* no tariffs, quotas, or other impediments (including voluntary quotas for import-supplying nations) to the free flow of goods. The basic logic of this free-trade doctrine is clear enough even in Adam Smith, well before Ricardo. Two centuries of further classical analysis, from John Stuart Mill in the nineteenth century to Paul Samuelson in the twentieth, have produced some refinements and qualifications, to be sure; but out of this constant reconsideration (as the theory becomes capable of addressing added complications) no qualifications of great practical importance have emerged.

The logic of the classical support for free trade is straightforward: If a country, say Portugal, can exchange a jug of wine for some extra cloth at certain terms, and these terms are better when Portugal cuts its wine consumption by exporting wine in trade for cloth rather than "trading with itself'' (that is, reducing wine production in order to increase its own cloth production), why shouldn't consumers be able to exchange wine for cloth—through buying less wine and more cloth—at these better terms? Why should the individual consumer be faced with a relative price for cloth—the ratio of the cloth price (in local money units) to the wine price—that is different from the terms at which the country can exchange consumption of the one good for the other? Try conscientiously as they did, the classical and neo-classical economists have found no *persuasive* reason why.

In the neoclassical analysis, the only reasons for *not* presenting the consumer with the same relative price that the country faces are reasons that arise when there would be some side effect—some effect on third parties, typically—from a decision to consume more cloth and less wine. For a fanciful example, suppose that wine drinking builds a person's resistance to some contagious disease and thereby helps to combat the spread of the disease to others. In the case of such a beneficial externality, or external economy, a tax on the consumption of cloth or a subsidy for the consumption of wine would obviously be appropriate—and a tariff on imported cloth is somewhat similar to a tax on cloth, in that it raises the price to the consumer, though it is the same as a tax only if all cloth is foreign-made.

For a less obvious example of such a side effect, suppose that less clothes buying and more wine buying would make people feel like working more, because they wouldn't need so much time away from work to shop, which would cause them to earn more taxable income and thus to produce more tax revenue (at given tax rates). In this case there is something resembling an external economy: The income tax rates must be causing people to work too little, in response to the distortion of their incentives, so a small encouragement to work a little more would have a good effect. Hence a tax on clothes consumption and/or subsidy to wine consumption would have the beneficial side effect of stimulating work and thus the supply of domestic goods—or of permitting a reduction of income tax rates. Again it should be noted, however, that a tariff is not generally the most natural way to tax a good—a tax is.

It is quite possible, however, that these essentially classical reasons for intentionally "distorting" the relative prices, or price ratios, faced by consumers do not actually apply to the country (or countries) under study. To be more realistic, it is possible there is no basis for assuming that they apply. It may be unknown whether a tariff on imports would have beneficial external effects or beneficial tax-revenue effects—or whether the truth is the other way around: that instead an import subsidy (a sort of negative tariff) would bring such a benefit. Then the classical position is that the country should follow the policy of free trade—no tariffs or other interventions in the free flow of goods in and out of the nation.

But, the reader will exclaim, may not free trade have unacceptable consequences for the distribution of income? What if, owing to the importation of cheap cloth, Portuguese workers suffer a decline in their wages when measured in wine (though their productivity in cloth making and their wage in units of cloth remain the same)? Is there not the possibility that free trade, while admirably efficient, is unjust—so that the classical presumption for free trade falls to the ground?* We must consider this question, although we have to confine ourselves to examples.

Consider this hypothetical case: In Portuguese wine making the scarce factor of production is comprised of highly skilled labor—oenologists with advanced degrees from the University of California at Davis; and in Portuguese cloth manufacture the scarce factor is unskilled labor. It would not make a difference if we had land instead of skilled labor as the scarce factor in wine growing or if we found skilled labor and land both scarce in that industry.

Now suppose that this economy has been enjoying free trade until now. And suppose that, *given* free trade, income tax rates have been set to obtain the structure of after-tax rewards that this society agrees is best. Then the thought occurs to someone that the unskilled workers, trapped in their low-wage jobs, can be better rewarded for their labor, albeit at some cost to the better-off workers in the wine industry, through the device of a tariff. Classical economics had better have an answer—and it does.

The classical reply is that the tariff is not a cost-effective way to raise the cloth workers' gains from contributing to the economy. If in fact a small tariff would bring such a benefit, the same social benefit could be achieved at a lower social cost by the more direct means of a jiggling of the tax rates on wage income: the tax rate on high incomes could be increased, thus extracting more tax revenue from the skilled labor, and the resulting budget surplus could be "spent" by a decrease in the tax rate on low incomes or an increase in the subsidy to the employment of unskilled workers. The classical analysis shows that redistributing income via the *tariff* is *doubly* burdensome: The tariff not only reduces the reward to the skilled of working harder, which has costly disincentive effects, since it reduces their after-tax wages in terms of cloth; in addition it distorts the price ratio facing skilled and unskilled workers, causing disincentives to export wine in return for cheap cloth. The classical economist would have a hard time resisting the urge to say to the advocates of the tariff: "You fellows are trying to do an end run around the wishes of society in regard to distributive justice, for if society

* Chapter 4's appendix implied only that at least *some* foreign trade would be a gain for all (compared to no trade), not that free trade would, since the home country needed to tax the imported good in order to ensure that no one lost. (It may be nevertheless that free trade would be a gain for all relative to a Rawlsian initial situation of no-trade equality.)

wanted a better deal for the unskilled it would already have petitioned its legislators to enact the implied changes in the income tax statutes. Shame on you for this deplorable lapse from our common sense of justice!"

Now consider a slightly different case. Free trade has been prevailing and society (our hypothetical Portugal) has adopted a structure of income tax rates that, *given* free trade, achieves the highest possible reward for the unskilled as measured by their after-subsidy wage rate in terms of cloth. This is a society, we suppose, aiming for Rawlsian justice. Now what if someone proposes a protective tariff on wine so as to raise the unskilled workers' rewards. On the face of it, this sounds like a proposal that can only serve to make the least-rewarded better off, and thus to be consistent with the Rawlsian principle of favoring the underdog. What says the classical economist in this case?

The classical reply is that in these circumstances the tariff would be counterproductive. If society was unable to collect more tax revenue from the skilled in aid of the unskilled, because of the acute disincentive effects of still higher tax rates on the skilled, it cannot be feasible to achieve further aid for the unskilled through a method, namely a tariff, that creates two disincentive effects instead of one. The effect of the tariff, in raising the wine price of cloth, will be to *lower* the sum of the tariff proceeds and tax revenues collected from the skilled workers. As a doubly distortionary sort of tax, the tariff cannot achieve more than what the less distortionary income tax on the skilled workers could not achieve.

If, in a classical economy, there is a reply to the classical analysis, it must differ on the assumption that society has already implemented some agreed-upon notion of justice in its income taxation (and other kinds of taxation). When there is an unresolved battle over income distribution, it is expectable that some or all groups in society will not shrink from resorting to second-best means to improve their own positions, even though all might be able to gain from a social compact to forgo these tactics.

Part 5

Romantic Rebellions

Romanticism was first born out of the sentiment of a double historical failure: the generalized spiritual bankruptcy of institutionlized religions in Europe and the blood-splashed ruin of the dream of the Enlightenment.

Michel Le Bris, Romantics and Romanticism

I call classic what is healthy, and romantic what is sick.
Goethe

CHAPTER 14

Against the Market: Critiques and Countersystems by Marx and the "New Left"

GARDENER:
I like to watch, Eve.

Peter Sellers to Shirley Maclaine in *Being There* (1980)

I F the fiction and theater of the twentieth century are any guide, working for most people is a dreary and tiresome occupation. It is a way to make a living, not to engage the imagination. If that is a fair portrait of market economies, it raises a perplexing question: How can "the market" be a pillar of the good society, as it is portrayed in the classical vision, when so many people making a living in "the market"—even many beneficiaries of its yet uncorrected injustices, some would say—appear to find so little satisfaction from it? Has some error of logic crept into the classical analysis en route to its conclusion that the market system is efficient (and just, too, if we want it to be)?

Or are inferences that the market system is inherently faulty a case of jumping to the wrong conclusion? Could it be that the tedium attributed to the market system, particularly to the market system in liberal-democratic welfare states, is due to scarcity and not to the market mechanism—not to the "mode of production," in Marx's phrase?

351

A history of political-economic thought could be built around the division among the great thinkers over which is the Right Answer—or the more nearly correct answer—to that Multiple Choice.

Here we consider some of the most fundamental critiques leveled at the classical system—the classical model of the just economy—and examine the "countermodels" that these critics have proposed instead. Although the past two centuries have produced many countermovements against the market, it will be convenient to lump the criticism of the market system into two groups—first Marx and then the New Left.

THOSE "DARK SATANIC MILLS": THE EARLY HOSTILITY TO THE INDUSTRIAL REVOLUTION

Market capitalism did not spread over Europe and North America in the sixteenth and seventeenth centuries without opposition on behalf of the older economic arrangements being challenged. To win respectability and a secure place, it was necessary for capitalism to overcome some of the economic dogma of medieval Christianity: the doctrine of the just price, the prohibition of usury, and the condemnation of luxury and sloth. The early classical tracts on behalf of free markets and the pursuit of self-interest were all consciously directed at reforming the traditional prejudice against the mores of commerce. In retrospect, the principal theme of the classical / neoclassical movement in political economy is its careful endorsement over a two-century examination of the bourgeois capitalist ethos.

The actual performance of capitalism in the first century of its untrammeled operation, however, proved nearly as threatening to its survival as the traditional opposition it had originally to overcome. Several decades after *The Wealth of Nations,* after the bright hopes of the Enlightenment, capitalism seemed to many to have brought to the working classes nothing but misery—shrinking opportunities in the countryside, punishing work and oppressive squalor in the cities. In 1848, a red-letter year in the history of political economy rivaling 1776, people took to the streets in such cities as Paris, Berlin, and Vienna to protest the economic conditions of the time; intellectuals held conferences to draw up visionary plans for reforms or radically new systems. Karl Marx wrote his epoch-making pamphlet *The Communist Manifesto* that year for a London-based secret society of German revolutionaries (causing his banishment from France and move to England, where he wrote columns on European events for the New York *Daily Tribune*). That year the political economist and philosopher John Stuart Mill published his *Principles of Political Economy,* a work that looks forward to the time when entrepreneurs have exhausted the vein of new techniques and products and a less inegalitarian "stationary state" is at hand—when, as Mill sees it, capitalism is obsolete. It was the year when the Socialist International was founded in Paris and when the composer Wagner, exiled as a dangerous socialist from Dresden, conceived the allegory of capitalism in his *Ring of the Nibelung* operas. In 1848 protests escalated to political revolutions in Italy, Germany, France, and Austria.

The backdrop of economic conditions prevailing during the Industrial Revolution has always been a subject of fluctuating opinion in economic history, particularly English conditions, where data are most easily obtained and the revolution itself occurred most dramatically. In the traditional view, the Acts of Enclosure of the eighteenth century, in which farming and grazing were "rationalized" with the introduction of property rights, fences, and commercial (mass-production) techniques, caused a redundancy of rural labor—an excess supply of labor at the former real wage of unskilled rural labor. The result was both a fall of the real wage and a push of labor into the cities to work in factories. At the same time, technological advances in the factories were driving out the domestic, or cottage, industries, in which people produced in their own homes, and creating a new, albeit lower, demand for labor in areas of urban concentration where factories might cheaply be located; so there was some pull of labor into the cities as well as push, but not necessarily enough to balance or outweight the push. In theory, then, these developments may have resulted in a drop of real wage rates for unskilled workers, despite the apparent technological progress and capital accumulation then occurring and the increased prosperity of owners of land and capital. A stalwart defender of competitive markets could have replied in defense of this Industrial Revolution: Let the government tax the owners of land and capital in order to compensate the workers for the unfortunate fall in their marginal productivity, so that all will share in the bountiful harvest of the technical progress! But no one took that position, and, in any case, the effort to redistribute incomes took a few more decades to get under way.

It is now coming to be claimed, on the basis of new statistical evidence, that workers in the cities of mid-nineteenth-century England were actually better off—in terms of real wages (wages measured by their purchasing power over the typical bundle of consumer goods bought by urban workers), life expectancy, and other quality-of-life indicators—than the rural unskilled laborers of 1780. Of course it does not follow that these measured improvements were enough to compensate the migrants to the city for the disamenities of city life—the losses in safety, quiet, clean air, sociability, and other amenities of country life. To clinch the case for a revision in our view of the effect of the Industrial Revolution on the working poor, we want evidence that rural wages (and other indicators of well-being) were also improved by the mid-nineteenth century—so rural migrants to the city were not driven out by straitened circumstances, they chose to go in order to do even better. Pending such decisive evidence we might bear in mind that the city has amenities of its own that ought to be balanced against its disamenities. After all, it wasn't rural life being extolled when Samuel Johnson proclaimed, "He that is tired of London is tired of life." Granted, Dr. Johnson said that (in the presence of Boswell) somewhat before the Industrial Revolution was at full throttle. But it has been quoted often enough ever since to suggest that the validity of its insight is little diminished to the present day.

Whatever the truth of the contentions about the worsening of the economic conditions of unskilled workers during the early decades of the Industrial Revolution, the spectacle of wide-scale poverty, on public view in the central cities, must have driven many observers of society to dream of some alternative system. More than one new system was outlined, and a few tried out. Undoubtedly, however, it was Marx's vision of communism that captured the imagination of most of those discontented with conditions under nineteenth-century capitalism.

MARX ON CAPITALISM AND COMMUNISM

Marx admired capitalism, as is often remarked, admired its dynamism next to its predecessor, feudalism. But Marx held capitalism to be morally flawed, irredeemably so by its nature. If we had been able to ask Marx whether he would not find morally acceptable a competitive-market system operated on, say, the principles of justice of John Rawls, he would evidently have replied that capitalism is incapable of so fundamentally reforming itself, because the class structure that goes with capitalism pits the capitalist class against any sort of justice for the working class—so Marx, not being fond of hypothetical questions, would not have answered the question. This notion of *economic determinism* was one of Marx's most distinctive and influential ideas. The underlying technological-psychological-geographic factors that generate the organizational institutions of a society, such as capitalism's institutions of private property and markets for labor, set up a structure of conflicting interest groups that operate to shape the way in which the benefits of that economic coordination will be distributed over the participants.

What is that moral flaw in capitalism? At a primitive level Marx's answer is that the output produced by the workers (the output in the production of which workers are engaged—not wild berries or oil but produce from farms cultivated by labor, manufactured apparel, and so forth), although wrought by their hands and energy, is not theirs to dispose of. The output belongs only to the capitalists, who own the means of production, the plant and equipment and materials (working capital) that are advantageously used in production. This fact is the root of what Marx calls "exploitation." Moreover, the production process and the design of the product are chosen by the manager for the benefit of the capitalist owners of the means of production and not that of the workers. For both these reasons the workers are "alienated" from the production process in which they are engaged.

Marx's Opposition to Return on Capital—and Its Neoclassical Defense

Going to a deeper level, Marx wants to argue further that the value of the wages paid to the workers is less than the value of the output they produce—a gap that Marx condemned as exploitation. Marx's view must have owed something to the old *labor theory of value*. According to that theory, if there were no positive rate of return earned on capital—and neglecting land—all goods would exchange at prices proportional to the labor-time embodied in them: If deep-sea fish traded for twice as much as bay fish it would be because, with all costs being ultimately wage costs and not interest or land rent, the former fish used twice as many standard man-hours to catch and bring to market—taking into account the amount of man-hours congealed, or embodied, in deep-sea and smaller boats, respectively, in the wood that serves as material, in the axes that chop that wood, and so forth. This was the case described in the labor theory of value. That theory was originated by Smith and studied (not uncritically) by Ricardo as a description of the "way things are." Marx, reasoning that labor alone is the original factor of production—not capital, since it must be produced (and no capital artifacts left by a previous civilization were found at the start), concluded that this theory was instead a prescription of the "way things ought to be": Only wages ought to be a cost, only labor ought to receive a reward, society's workers ought to receive in the aggregate all the fish and all the lumber from the boats they make and the trees they plant—with no subtraction of interest. Marx viewed the return to capital as a *surplus value* expropriated by the owners that should go to labor.

> For Marx, labor is exploited under capitalism when it is paid less than the total product, hence receives less than the total income. If the capitalist system is abandoned in favor of a totally socialist system in which all capital is owned by the state, society can end capitalist exploitation by paying the workers their total product instead of merely their "marginal product."

Marx's argument has not stood up well—whatever the right conclusions are—to more than a century of withering scrutiny. (Few arguments about the best design of society have, only a precious few.) It seems to be taken for granted by Marx that there is no "free lunch" in store for the workers unless there was an inefficiency in the allocation of resources under capitalism; this Marx does *not* assume in attacking the payment of interest. Yet Marx did conjure up the vision of a great come-and-get-it day. He left the impression that if privately owned capital is expropriated, all or a large share of the interest on that capital will then go to the workers through higher wages—in effect, a subsidy or tax cut on wage earnings.

- If that capital and the interest claim on it was largely in the hands of people in or near retirement who were counting on *spending* it to make up their loss of wage income during old-age retirement, the state would be unable to increase the consumption of the younger workers if it wished to fulfill the consumption expectations of the older people. (The government would have to provide to the elderly the interest on the expropriated capital and also pay the elderly an amount of wealth equal to the capital the old would have sold to the young during their retirement years, leaving the workers with the same consumption in their working years.)
- If instead the capital was largely in the hands of persons who were *not* going to spend their interest or the proceeds from the sale of their capital, people who were going to *save* their interest and bequeath it along with the principal to their heirs, then the state would be unable to let the workers have it if it wished to preserve saving.

The case Marx undoubtedly had in mind was one in which the capital was predominantly in the form of vast holdings belonging to a class of wealthy families who were planning to spend their interest income—the pure *rentier* who is content to live off the interest alone—and either to spend some of their capital too or, in the grand manner, to bequeath it all to the next generation in the family dynasty. Marx would surely have had no qualms about depriving such an "unproductive" class of capitalists of their income beyond a reasonable stipend from the state for those disabled or too old to work. In such a case Marx could fairly argue that a socialist expropriation of the wealth of the *rentier* class would offer each new generation of workers a come-and-get-it day in which to divide the surplus interest of the *rentiers*. But Marx's implicit assumption that a socialist *expropriation* was necessary to recover the interest siphoned off by a class of fat cats is a non sequitur.

> Society, it is now widely contended, can just as easily *tax away* the excessive interest income of a bloated *rentier* class as it can expropriate that capital for operation by the state. Neither step might take a revolution by the workers! However, if a revolution is required to expropriate private capital for use by a socialist state, that same revolution could elect to preserve capitalism while resolving to redistribute the interest to workers.

This "revisionist" contention, that taxation and public expenditure will do as well, is what distinguishes the lower-case "socialism" of the Western European socialist parties—the socialism of Richard Tawney, Beatrice and Sidney Webb, and Anthony Crossland in Britain, for example—from the upper-case "Socialism" of Marx and orthodox Marxists.

While many critics have challenged the *necessity of* abolishing capitalism in order to redistribute some or all income from *capital,* others have questioned the *desirability* of eliminating the receipt of after-tax interest income! The after-tax interest rate is seen as a useful way to govern the volume of saving.

◆ Aroused by Marx's provocative contentions, turn-of-the-century neoclassical economists in Austria and Sweden began developing a theory of capital that showed the advantageousness of rewarding savers with a rate of interest according to the rate of return on the capital investments that the saving finances—according to the marginal productivity of capital, as they termed it. They argued that the marginal productivity, or rate of return, tends to be positive, not zero. For example, if one or more persons should decide to save more, reducing by 1 ton society's consumption of fish, say, *this period,* the labor and other resources thereby released could go to work building more boats (and other fishing equipment) that might enable society *next period* to consume 1¼ tons more fish than would otherwise have been possible (given its provision for the further future); that would be a one-period rate of return of 25 percent. These theoreticians then argued that it is desirable for *efficiency of consumption* that savers be offered in reward an interest rate equal to capital's marginal productivity in order to signal savers how cheap (or expensive) future consumption is compared to present consumption—how cheap future fish are relative to fish now.

Sounding a second theme, the neoclassical theoreticians then argued that competitive market capitalism *promotes* the desired equality between the reward to saving, or after-tax rate of interest, and the rate of return to investment. According to their theory of interest, the competition of investing enterprises and of savers in the capital market, where bonds and shares are traded, causes the before-tax rate of interest prevailing in the market to equal capital's rate of return—under equilibrium, or correct-expectations, conditions at any rate. So unless the government taxes or subsidizes interest, capitalism will automatically produce the right incentive for people to save.

> Present-day neoclassical economics, though having to grapple with complications in the theory of taxation and the theory of interest, likewise opposes the Marxist abolition of all interest: Yes, the outsize holdings of wealth by big *rentiers* should be heavily taxed if they offend the prevailing morality. However, it would *not* be desirable as a general rule to tax away all the before-tax interest on all saving. (In fact, there is only an "iffy" case for *any* tax on the interest income from saving by young workers out of their wages. Introducing a tax on such interest in order to lighten taxation of wage income while keeping total tax revenue the same would create a disincentive to save without necessarily lessening the overall disincentive to work: For while the cost of present consumption measured in labor-time goes down, the cost of future consumption measured in labor-time goes up!)

What would Marx have said to that? Possibly he would have conceded the desirableness of some interest as a reward to saving (i.e., to not consuming) in some circumstances under *capitalism* but argued that in a socialist system, where most capital is under public ownership, there would be no role for interest: Central planners would determine the proper division of society's production between goods for present consumption and capital goods enabling greater future consumption. And he would no doubt have insisted that even if abolishing interest is not a valid reason for abolishing capitalism he has plenty of reasons for finding socialism superior.

But *why* would interest have no useful role to play in the socialist state? If the rate of interest can serve as an appropriate incentive device helping to motivate the right amounts of saving by persons, why not under socialism too? Marx did not bring out the point that the state could own the capital and decide in which capital goods to invest while *not* deciding each person's saving and his or her claim or entitlement to future consumption.

♦ There are *market versions* of socialism. In all versions of socialism the government does the investing in most capital goods, especially factories, shops, and offices that employ workers. In some market versions, however, each worker would be free to save, accumulating bank balances and assets in pension funds exchangeable later for future consumer goods, and the state would regulate the rate of interest offered to savers according to the rate of return on capital and taxation aspects. This way, the thrifty could save more and the others less. And possibly the reward of saving would pay for itself by encouraging a greater supply of willing labor.

Not only is the abolition of capitalism not *necessary* to stamp out interest—it is not *sufficient,* either. Socialism might benefit from paying interest.

MARX'S OPPOSITION TO COMMERCIALISM AND MARKETS

The contention that the capitalists expropriate part of the product of the working class was not the only objection to capitalism that Marx voiced. An earlier, and perhaps deeper, conviction of Marx's was that under capitalism labor is "degraded" to a commodity, something sold on the market. In the market for labor there is no room for inventiveness and imaginative problem solving, no opportunity for men or women who must work for a living to discover, exercise, and develop their talents—to achieve "self-realization." Deprived of meaningful occupations, people are led to make a "fetish" out of consumer goods, elevating them out of proportion to their worth as if to deny the greater importance of their missing satisfactions. (Here Marx seems to have anticipated Sigmund Freud.)

Marx, broadening his attack, went on to view the exchange relationship that market capitalism had introduced into social or personal interactions as spreading like a pollutant until all of people's interactions became commercial transactions for narrow personal advantage—for expanded choice, that is, rather than some transcending desire to express feelings and ideals.

Finally, there came a time when everything that men had considered as inalienable became an object of exchange, of traffic, and could be alienated. This is the time when the very things which till then had been communicated, but never exchanged; given, but never sold; acquired but never bought—virtue, love, conviction, knowledge, conscience, etc.—when everything, in short, passed into commerce. It is the time of general corruption, of universal venality.*

Champions of capitalism might want to debate with Marx the general perniciousness of commercialism today. The commercialism that is turning the economy into a university of popular art and laboratory for personal growth—that has produced Chaplin and Hitchcock, grand opera and the blues, Picasso and Warhol, Beckett and Pinter, the Beatles and Stevie Wonder, dance classes, flying lessons, and transaction therapy—can't be all bad.

* Karl Marx, *Misère de la Philosophie*, Paris, 1847. From the English translation *The Poverty of Philosophy* (London: Lawrence and Wishart, 1955). p. 29.

In some respects it may be aiding rather than hindering people's self-realization. We are not only workers, only producers, after all. We are also social actors in our roles as companion, parent, friend, and colleague, and we are political actors as well. In view of these additional roles, these additional selves, some of people's consumer spending, far from coming at the expense of their self-development, may actually promote their self-development to the extent that such spending widens their understanding of their world and themselves. For many persons whose talents have little scarcity value, the potential for self-realization will always lie primarily in the direction of their roles as marriage partner or parent.

Pressed to answer the points in Marx's indictment, defenders of capitalism seek to exonerate it from the charge of overcommercialization. The commercialism found in capitalist countries, they say, is simply a faithful reflection of the preferences of free people in our civilization. And not only in Western civilization: Industrialization in the Far East and the improved terms of trade for oil in the Middle East have occasioned the same predictable weakening of traditional social relationships and work habits, and brought about a new-found emphasis on the house, car, boat, plane, etc., which figure in "the American way of life." Capitalism, it is argued, does not force people to forgo the chance to realize their talents as artists, scientists, performers, craftspeople, in short, as *doers*, for a less meaningful life as passive consumers—mere observers who are content just with "being there." If someone wants to make shoes the old way, building the entire shoe himself from first to last, capitalism leaves him free to do so; if he chooses not to after all, despite the job satisfaction of it, the reason is the opportunity cost—by joining a shoe factory he can add more to shoe output than he can produce alone, and he will be paid as a wage that higher marginal product (minus taxes).

◆ To demonstrate that some or all people would truly prefer more satisfaction at work, despite its cost to them in reduced income with which to buy consumer goods, Marx needs to show that these people are stuck in Hume's free-rider problem: No one will do the socially desired thing by himself, left free to act or not act unilaterally, although everyone would do the right thing if he knew his actions would be matched by the others. *This Marx never did.*

The fact that Marxist regimes have arisen around the globe suggests that Marx is winning the argument and needs no help from present-day thinkers schooled in the analytical concepts of political economy (whatever his full evaluation of those regimes might be). But it could be that Marx is "winning" at the barricades for mistaken reasons. So it is only being fair to Marx to ask: Have there been subsequent defenses and extensions of

Marx's perspective that strengthen Marx's position and blunt to some degree his critics' attacks? In fact, two critiques of commercialism and profit seeking appeared only in the last decade and have attracted much attention.

In a study of what he called the "gift relationship," the late British sociologist Richard Titmuss placed the commercialization of blood giving into a disturbing perspective:

> From our study of the private market in blood in the United States, we have concluded that the commercialization of blood and donor relationships represses the expression of altruism, erodes the sense of community, lowers scientific standards, limits both personal and professional freedoms, sanctions the making of profits in hospitals, . . . places immense social costs on those least able to afford them—the poor, the sick, and the inept . . . and results in situations in which proportionately more and more blood is supplied by the poor. . . . Moreover, on four testable non-ethical criteria the commercialized blood market is bad. In terms of economic efficiency it is wasteful . . . more costly . . . [and involves more risk of contamination] . . . than voluntary systems in Britain. Freedom from disability is inseparable from altruism.*

The main point might be expressed by saying that choice is not "expanded" if the precious right to give is diminished.

In a stimulating work, the late British economist Fred Hirsch took up the challenge hurled at Marx: If anyone would be more fulfilled by putting more of his creativity into his work despite the cost in reduced money income, why doesn't he choose to do it, since competitive capitalism offers the opportunity? Hirsch's answer: The loss of relative *position* would be too painful; but if *everyone* did it there would be no such pain. Much of the quest for income is a scramble for "positional goods": "What is possible for the single individual is not possible for all individuals—and would not be even if they all possessed equal talent. . . . They do not see that opportunities open to each person separately are not open to all."†

MARX'S VISION OF COMMUNISM AND THE "NEW MAN"

However well or badly capitalism is rated on that count, measured against some ideal performance, defenders of capitalism know that the best defense is offense. How well would the system perform that Marx would put up in place of capitalism? Marx appears to have envisioned an economy coordi-

---

* Richard Titmuss, *The Gift Relationship: From Human Blood to Social Policy* (London: George Allyn and Unwin, 1971), last page.
† Fred Hirsch, *Social Limits to Growth* (Cambridge, Mass.: Harvard University Press, 1976), p. 6.

nated by some sort of central planning agency, with the objective to place under social control the production of all goods hitherto left to the market, and where the labor would be supplied by "new men"—men and women motivated not by Smithian self-interest but rather by a spirit of social cooperation. A question that has to be asked, though, is whether such a countersystem is truly feasible. To what extent was Marx reflecting the Romanticism of his time, which social thought has been compelled during the trying and disillusioning twentieth century to draw back from?

That Marx is the quintessential Romantic of economic thought seems indisputable, although he is not commonly labeled as such. Marx more than any other economist of his time powerfully expressed the growing feeling of awe and anxiety over the untamed forces of science then engulfing the industrializing countries and, at the same time, the growing hope for a visionary society of "new men" who by taming those forces would save civilization from destruction and redeem mankind's promise. Both of these themes, by the way, can be found (with some variation) in the original 1818 horror story, *Frankenstein*, by Mary Wollstonecraft Shelley (daughter of the feminist writer Mary Wollstonecraft). Inspired apparently by the excited speculations of Byron and her husband, Shelley, on how far science might venture and how it might be controlled, the story deals at one level with the disaster resulting from Dr. Frankenstein's pursuit of an uncontrolled scientific experiment, the manufacture of a human being. At another level, perhaps a subconscious one, there is an exploration of the possibility that new beings who are not made from the old mold of human being might grow up among us and flourish. But as the story unfolds, that hope meets with tragedy.

. . . the monster was not originally evil. [The new being] expressed hope "to meet with beings who, pardoning my outward form, would love me for the excellent qualities I was capable of unfolding." But the creature was shunned by everyone who came into contact with it. As a result it became a monster whose inner character was congruent with his outward appearance.*

The creature who sought friendship with the little girl by the lake is soon hunted down by a rampaging torch-wielding mob.

---

*Ellen Berscheid, "An Overview of the Psychological Effects of Physical Attractiveness," in G. W. Lucker, K. A. Ribbens, and J. A. McNamara, eds., *Psychological Aspects of Facial Form*, monograph 11, Cranio Facial Growth Series, Center for Human Growth and Development, Ann Arbor, University of Michigan, 1980, p. 23.

The Main Criticisms of the Marxist System

The critics of this Marxist countersystem question, to begin with, whether it would foster the self-realization that Marx accused capitalism of preventing. The new system, it should be noted, is not one of wantlessness or self-lessness: The citizens of the Marxist state are supposed to have a healthy interest in their own selves, and presumably they are expected to speak up and act on their own behalf within the rules of the game. So the system will have to solve the problem of how to allocate people to the various occupations and assignments with their differing promises of self-realization. A fundamental aspect of the corresponding problem in capitalism is solved very nicely by the market, according to neoclassical theory. If Abel envies Baker his post as head pie maker in the city's chief confectionary shop, and Abel appears as talented as Baker, Abel can "underbid" Baker for the job—and Baker can counterbid, and so on; ultimately, then, the pay in every job *clears the market* so that no one more able and eager than the job holder is denied that job. But under Marx's countersystem, the market is *not* to be used to allocate resources—that much is expressly clear in Marx. Hence the head pie maker does not have to bring home less bacon just because there is a surplus of workers who forecast high self-realization in that job.

- ◆ Under a centrally planned system without markets, promotion to a preferable job is likely to be either a matter of having connections in the bureaucracy, of knowing the right people, or a contest that foments personal animosities, invidious comparisons, and under-the-table trading of favors. Such a system might be quite inefficient, next to any market system, as a method of putting differing persons into their right jobs—inefficient at fostering self-realization. And so insidious a system, though allowing expression on the job, would reduce respect for work and hence people's self-respect.

This issue of bureaucracy versus the market is not confined to economywide resource allocation. It arises in the individual enterprise, including capitalist enterprises that do not face severe competition or that enjoy the cushion of a government subsidy or private support. It turns up, for example, in the private university with an endowment income to spend. The bureaucratic way to spend it is to spread it around: to raise the pay of the professorships and the professors that, through no fault of their own usually, fetch a low wage in the university labor market—up to total equality if there is enough income to go around. The lucky professors then earn a monopoly rent, one on top of the "economic rent," or "surplus," that a person might derive from just his market wage (since he would work for less); they will be envied by those who have not been successful in getting such overpaid jobs. To preserve some incentive to perform the university can "differentiate" the professorships by giving names to some of them in order to indicate their special esteem or by offering directorships and deanships having some bureaucratic power.

The market way to spend the income is to pay each professor the best estimate of his wage in the university labor market—less (more) if he especially likes (dislikes) that university. The savings can be used to hire more or better professors or to provide tuition aid and so forth. These savings, the greater incentive to perform that results, and the more suitable selection of faculty for administrative duties all point to the greater efficiency of the market way. Naturally most professors hate the market way, hate the competition. But most professors also come to feel that their respect for the importance of the enterprise in which they are participating and their own self-respect demand that their university follow the market way in spending their endowment.

Finally, the critics of the Marxist dream ask about the expense. They suggest that the Marxist method of social control over the allocation of resources—over the what and how of production, even if it did, despite doubts, promote the self-realization of the worker, might come at too high a price—so that the society could not nearly afford the abundant education, health care, housing, travel, entertainment, and so forth it could have through the ingenious institution called the market.

- Defenders of market capitalism claim that it allocates efficiently the economy's resources (over the various industries and producing sites) in the production of a given number of goods with given production techniques. That is a fair claim at least under conditions of equilibrium and other classical provisos. No such claim could fairly be made for central planning of resource allocation in an economy of appreciable complexity. (But if this "static" sort of efficiency were the market's only advantage, planned economies *might* be expected to "catch up" with endless patience and experience.)

- Advocates of market capitalism further claim that it permits and encourages outsiders and mavericks with novel or dissenting notions to introduce new products and new techniques even though if successful they will cause losses and relocations for the beneficiaries of the "status quo" situation. Writing of this receptivity to disruptive innovations, the early twentieth-century Austrian economist Joseph Schumpeter spoke of the "winds of creative destruction" to evoke this dynamic process of technical change.

Marx did not deny the achievement he himself had witnessed: "The bourgeoisie, during its role of scarce one hundred years, has created more massive and more collosal productive forces than have all preceding generations together."* He apparently foresaw the case for Marxist socialism as becoming decisive only when capitalism's creativity was largely spent, making alienation from the workplace the critical factor. But against Marx it could be argued that the end of that creativity is still not even in sight. And it could be argued too that Marx vastly underestimated the complexity of resource allocation in the industrial and post-industrial countries. None of us in this day and age makes more than the tiniest fraction of any of the goods we consume. The medieval artisans produced finished articles at least—horseshoes and wool coats, etc.—although not even they produced from scratch, building their own plant and equipment with their bare hands. Today an entire factory may be devoted to producing only a single part for later blending or assembling into a whole good or assortment of finished goods: various chemicals, machine tools, and so forth.

We who are inside the economic system are not conscious of how roundabout productive processes have become. An outside observer would be struck with the fact that almost no one in our system seems to be producing *finished* goods. Almost everyone is seen to do work of a preparatory nature, with final consumption a distant future goal. The farmer spends his time in fattening hogs, the truck driver in carrying them toward market, and the packer in advancing them further toward the last stage of consumption. A steel worker prepares pig iron, part of which will be a hammer to build a house; another bit will become part of a pig-iron furnace; which in turn will prepare pig iron to be used in making further hammers and more pig-iron furnaces; and so forth.†

It isn't really "news," therefore, when we read that some power station in the Urals has been brought to a standstill by want of a generator. That the Soviet planners are able just to keep production going most of the time boggles the mind.

Market Socialism

Engaged like everyone else in the great controversy over capitalism *versus* socialism raging at that time, and impressed by the terrible difficulty of resource allocation by central planning, some economic theorists in the 1930s came to the view that markets could be the salvation of socialism. Just as

*Karl Marx and Friedrich Engels, *Communist Manifesto,* London, 1848. Reprinted in Robert C. Tucker, ed., *The Marx-Engels Reader* (New York: W. W. Norton & Co., 1972), p. 339.

†Paul A. Samuelson, *Economics: An Introductory Analysis,* 6th ed. (New York: McGraw-Hill, 1964), p. 47.

markets have been the unsung strength of capitalism, propelling market capitalism to a far greater performance than any kind of centrally planned capitalism could manage to, so markets could be used to solve—better than central planning—the various resource-allocation questions in those areas where they also serve capitalism well. The trick is to instruct each of the state-owned productive enterprises to "play the market game": to decide output levels and input combinations in pursuit of the maximum possible profit (to be turned over, if any, to the state owner).

- ◆ Under market socialism each worker, guided by market wage rates, taxes, and the prices of things, would decide where and how long to work and choose which goods to buy with the income left for spending. And each public enterprise would respond to prevailing market wage rates and land rents and capital-good rentals in deciding the level of its production and the combination of inputs used to achieve it—with the goal of maximizing profit. If these enterprises are faced with perfect competition, or if they will dutifully act "as if" they were, the resulting equilibrium will be a *competitive equilibrium:* The wage rate of a person would measure the marginal productivity of his labor in what he is doing; the price of a product would measure the marginal cost of its production; and so forth.

It sounds simple. But how would it work? Would market socialism be implemented by employing a state-paid auctioneer in every market—for every industry and factor of production—in order to find the product price or factor price that clears the market? That certainly would be a fascinating experiment. It would be a case of "life imitating textbook"—the stylized portrait of the market mechanism found in textbooks. That kind of experiment would be taking the textbook too literally: Imagine an auctioneer for each of a million different kinds of jobs; an auctioneer for a hotel's rooms, for ice cream, and for *Pravda*. (Even in market capitalism some markets "clear" only through the speculative actions of enterprises—in absorbing inventories or accepting idle capacity.)

The way of using markets proposed by the Polish theoretician of market socialism Oskar Lange calls for the central government to set the prices, wage rates, and so forth at each stage in a trial-and-error adjustment process. Once the current list of prices, wage rates, and so forth are announced, the enterprises and households respond with their supplies and demands: Enterprises try to produce for the market the profit-maximizing amounts of their products and hire the profit-maximizing amounts of the various factors of production needed to produce these outputs. Households then decide on the amounts of the goods to buy (or to try to buy). If the market for toothpaste showed a shortage, say, the price of toothpaste would be raised—to reduce the amount demanded and increase the amount supplied; the appearance of a surplus would occasion a reduction of the price. By this process of adjustment, Lange contended, the set of prices would gravitate toward the list of prices that yields competitive equilibrium.

Elated by the thought of a whole social movement being saved from unnecessary extinction—by an unexpected application of classical economic theory—Lange suggested that socialist countries commemorate the discovery with a sculpture—not of himself but rather the Austrian anti-socialist economist who had provoked Lange by contending that socialism could not work.

Both as an expression of recognition for the great service rendered by him and as a memento of the prime importance of sound economic accounting, a statue of Professor Mises ought to occupy an honorable place in the great hall of the Ministry of Socialization or the Central Planning Board of the socialist state.*

However, Oskar Lange is now considered to have been premature in claiming to triumph over Ludwig von Mises's skepticism. Part 6 below, on the modern view of markets, accounts for some of this skepticism.

Today the theoreticians of market socialism are accused of naïveté for believing that anything like a *classical* market mechanism might really be applicable to socialist economies: It would be impractical for the central government to set a price on every good or productive service that the labor-using socialist enterprises might usefully produce—more practical to let competing enterprises set their own prices where "textbook competition" is not possible. Where the government could set prices, it would be uncertain that the government could succeed in arriving at or near the competitive-equilibrium price. (Capitalism has specialist traders who speculate on their forecasts of future prices, thus causing sharp adjustments in current prices; if the socialist government's price setters were comparatively slow-footed, a shortage might cause buyers to hoard and suppliers to hold back, thus making the shortage worse and causing the government-set price gradually to

---

* Oskar Lange, "On the Economic Theory of Socialism," in Oskar Lange and Fred M. Taylor, *On the Economic Theory of Socialism* (Minneapolis: University of Minnesota, 1938), p. 57.

overshoot the mark.) The economic theorist Friedrich Hayek might have had market socialism in mind when writing:

I am far from denying that in our system equilibrium analysis has a useful function to perform. But when it comes to the point where it misleads some of our leading thinkers into believing that the situation which it describes has direct relevance to the solution of practical problems, it is high time that we remember that it does not deal with the social process at all and that it is no more than a useful preliminary to the study of the main problem.*

Still, the methods of central planning adopted in the Soviet Union, China, and other industrially complex socialist countries in this century have functioned so poorly that pressures have continued to mount in these countries for wide experimentation with market processes of some kind or other in place of the central planners' quotas and rations.

THE NEW LEFT

Looking back at the previous discussion, one is compelled to conclude that Marx's argument against market capitalism is inadequate and his vision of a better system defective. More spectacularly, Marx's apocalyptic predictions of the immiserization and pauperization of the working class, the ever more violent cycles of boom and depression, and the disappearance of competition have come to be recognized as wrongheaded speculations not borne out by history. Nevertheless, Marx gave inspiration to diverse movements in the twentieth century that have carried on his goals. A parade of successors to Marx have sought to shore up the weaknesses of Marx's critique and to repair the defects of his alternative vision. An appraisal of the Marxian tradition in political economy could hardly stop at Marx any more than an evaluation of classical political economy could end with Smith.

Of the twentiety-century "Marxian" movements the most significant for political economy is undoubtedly the New Left. On the reorganization of society, the theme that most distinguishes the New Left from Marx is the emphasis on "industrial participation," or "economic democracy," or "workers' control." The ideal is an economy of enterprises owned and operated by the workers themselves—of producer cooperatives. It is less clear what the relationship between these enterprises might be, and their relationship to the central government.

It would not be unreasonable to suppose, in view of the antipathy toward the market system expressed by New Left theorists, that these producer cooperatives are to be brought into a system along the lines of the *syndical-*

---

* Friedrich A. Hayek, "The Use of Knowledge in Society," in *Individualism and Economic Order.* (Chicago: University of Chicago Press, 1948), p. 91.

ist, or *corporatist,* state—the sort of system pointed to, though hardly acted upon, by Mussolini in Italy and Perón in Argentina. Each industry is to be organized into a syndiate, worker-controlled or at least worker-represent-ing, and together these syndicates are to bargain over the operation of the economy—outputs, inputs, rewards. Imaginably, such syndicalism would not have to take on the worst features of twentieth-century fascism: the subordination of the individual to nationalism, intolerance of dissent, per-secution of minorities, and so forth. So many problems with this system come to mind that it is questionable whether the contraption can achieve its stated aims. If each enterprise is to be small, small enough to be on a human scale (as is often thought to be desirable), it must be asked how much auton-omy each such microcosm would be permitted—whether it would be free to produce a better plastic bag or safer tire, if such new products were more costly to produce—without having to absorb in lower wage rewards the whole increase of costs; and whether it would be free to vary the existing product at all. If, instead, each syndicate is an industry wide monopoly, it must be doubted that the individual worker would have much autonomy—to have a voice in operations, try out a new method, or just change his job.

To make possible a "decentralization" of production and work decisions, therefore, it seems necessary to imbed the producer cooperatives in some sort of market system—market socialism *without* profit-maximizing enter-prises. To a degree such a system has already left the drawing board: Leg-islation in several Western European countries has mandated labor participation in certain aspects of business management—an arrangement between capital and labor called *codetermination.* In Yugoslavia worker control is complete in some (not all) enterprises: The workers in a state-owned factory may be permitted to form a workers' council with the authority to borrow capital and to decide what to produce and sell in the market, keeping what is left over after payment of interest and land rents and mate-rial costs.

Criticis of such "alternatives" to unalloyed market capitalism ask why, if the traditional capitalist firm is inefficient in providing job satisfaction, groups of workers do not form to start worker cooperatives on their own initiative, borrowing capital from their friendly banker. The American economist Armen Alchian has described codeterminiation as "simply a proposal to transfer wealth of stockholders to employees . . . And it has no other viable eco-nomic function. That is why it does not appear voluntarily."* The oppo-nents of *mandated* codetermination (and state-sponsored worker councils *sheltered* from the competition of profit-seeking enterprises) view it as an

---

* Armen Alchian, "Private Rights to Property: The Basis of Corporate Government and Human Rights," in Karl Brunner, ed., *Economics and Social Institutions* (Boston: M. Nijhoff Pub. Co., 1979), p. 252.

attempt to achieve by management takeover a redistribution to workers that would be better achieved by increased taxation of the income from capital (leaving aside the desirability of steeper taxes on capital.)

Against this capitalist riposte, "The workers are free to form cooperatives under capitalism, and *would* if they valued them," the New Leftist could parry with, "Yes, but under capitalist injustice they can't afford to." Both ideas can be captured in the diagram to the left, in which the gain from social cooperation to the proletarian worker is measured on the vertical axis and the corresponding gain to the other class of person is on the horizontal axis. With only profit-maximizing enterprises operating, the options open to society through redistributive tax-

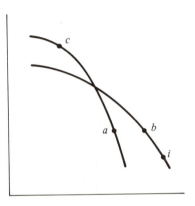

ation are described by the relatively *flat* possibility curve, or opportunity locus. With only producer cooperatives operating, the options are shown by the *steeper* opportunity locus. Critics of enforced cooperatives, codetermination, and so forth imply that the initial capitalist situation was perfectly efficient, like point *i*, and that mandated codetermination is inefficient, like point *a*. It would be better to redistribute to the proletariat via taxation, leading to a point like *b*. The defenders of cooperatives and so forth might nevertheless claim that they would become efficient, and be voluntarily chosen over profit-maximizing companies, leading to an outcome like point *c*, if society redistributed income more strongly to the proletariat.

So it is really an empirical question, a matter of judgment and guess, whether an economy of producer cooperatives might be happier for the unskilled workers than profit-seeking enterprises ever could. In a searching examination of New Left doctrine, the contemporary Swedish economist Assar Lindbeck registers doubt and skepticism:

A . . . problem for socialist market economies seems to be designing ways for individuals to take new initiatives (such as the development of new products, new firms, and new production techniques) when private ownership . . . is not permitted. . . . People who already have top posts may often be concerned mainly with the risk of losing them . . . ; the most efficient method to minimize this risk may be to avoid new adventures. It is not obvious that such problems can be avoided in a less hierarchical system of organizations *within* firms. . . . [I]t may be difficult to launch new ventures if on every occasion the majority has to be convinced that a new product is worth producing and a new method of production worth applying . . . that a plant should be moved to another region or possibly be closed down completely. We need more information about these problems, and this presumably requires practical experiments.*

Now, some such experiments are being conducted in Japan, where enterprises are consulting workers and all join in the company song.

The theoreticians of the New Left, however, are not interested in whether workers might under some circumstances opt for producer cooperatives over profit-seeking enterprises. The New Left mounts its most basic attack on capitalism precisely at this point—the irrelevance of people's preferences, the preferences they reveal in the market, as guides to their "true" wants. Certainly this has become a familiar theme in recent decades: Our preferences are "manipulated" by capitalist enterprises—we are corrupted as early as childhood by the siren song of popularity and glamour through the use of prestigious goods. (And the people who are tempted into making a living in the advertising agencies are corrupted worst of all.) Capitalism *forces* people from a life of doing to a passive existence as dull-eyed consumers driven by the incoming bills.

- The New Left has carried that theme to its ultimate extreme: Instead of an economy in which producers humbly cater to consumers' prior wants, which seems at any rate to be the classical portrait of capitalism, we find in capitalism an economy where consumers are persuaded to like what the producers choose to sell. This is the "dependence effect" and "revised sequence," in the satirical phrases of the Canadian-born critic of American-style capitalism, John Kenneth Galbraith.

- Defenders of capitalism have replied: There was no visible and pristine demand for the novels of C. P. Snow and Rubik's Cube before they were marketed; but what does that prove? Why should imaginative new products be more suspect or unwelcome than innovations in methods of production? How can the advertiser of a product survive competition from the advertiser of a better one? If we credit capitalism with finding the best available technology, why not with finding people's complex and evolving tastes?

* Assar Lindbeck, *The Political Economy of the New Left: An Outsider's View* (New York: Harper & Row, 1971), pp. 67–68.

In his assessment of the New Left claim that capitalist producers, particularly the large corporations, are sovereign over what
is bought, not consumers, Lindbeck produced some counter-
arguments and supporting evidence, which have so far not been
rebutted:

If it were true . . . that sufficient demand could be created for practically
any product that a firm decided to produce simply by advertising, it
might be difficult to explain why firms spend so much money to study
the potential markets for new products [t]he purpose of [which] is to
obtain information about consumer attitudes toward potential new
products.

Available studies also indicate that most [such] products . . . are never
launched on the market because of negative results in market research.
. . . [A]lso a very large fraction of the products that are actually launched
on markets fail . . . between one-third and one-half are withdrawn[n]
from the market within one year.

. . . [A]dvertising may have substantial effects on how consumption
of a certain type of commodity is divided among different brands. [But]
it also seems that in most countries studied the pattern of consumer
expenditure is related in very much the same way to incomes and relative prices, despite differences in the structure of domestic production
and the volume and technique of advertising . . .

Statistics on profits [of firms] do not support the idea that individual
firms can by themselves easily determine their profit levels, as often . . .
asserted by the New Left literature. It would be strange if certain firms
voluntarily had chosen zero or negative profits, while other firms obtain
profits of more than 20 percent (of the value of equity capital). . . .*

Lindbeck adds that this novel doctrine—the idea of the producer as sovereign—falls short as a theory of who gets what in
society. If there is something like free entry into the business of
shaping consumers' preferences, then how can anyone "get rich,"
or prosper more than another, in that business? How can one
enterprise enjoy disproportionate influence compared to others?
What determines which 100 or 200 enterprises will belong to
the influential oligarchy? Who gets to manipulate the manipulated?

Such is the debate between the dedicated proponents and opponents of
the New Left. Clearly, the question raised calls for thoughtful and experienced judgment? What say the disinterested judges? Most economists agree
that advertising poses economic waste and nuisance costs, not redeemed by
the cheap newspapers and free television it finances, which could be subsi-

* Lindbeck, *Political Economy of the New Left*, pp. 42–45.

dized by a tax instead of a costly industry. But few economists would agree that capitalism creates a labor force of zombies so drugged by commercialism as to have lost all instinct for seeking and finding their fulfillment. Besides, all the various countersystems—socialism, nationalism, cult communities—seem to risk making their distinctive values into obsessions. Perhaps every social system suffers the "defects of its virtues."

BEYOND THE "LEFT"

Someone once said that all of social science is a dialogue with Karl Marx. Certainly Marx had an unequaled talent at raising big questions, and deep accusations, against market capitalism. His claim that under capitalism labor is "exploited" is an example, as is his charge of the commercialization of social interchange, particularly the degradation of labor to a "commodity." However, on these themes Marx was unsatisfactory: It is not generally unjust of a society to have interest after tax, thus to reward saving. And a perfectly centralized economy—one without bargaining, without "degradation"—would be more unpleasant (as well as austere), not less.

The New Left say the ill of capitalism is its *un*freedom, the failure of people to have autonomy over their life at work. Their solution: a society built on producers' cooperatives run by the workers. The "defense" questions whether workers would "buy" it—*literally*—in view of the cost in wages, a cost they have "revealed" themselves unwilling to pay so far. The New Left replies that the workers have been brainwashed by advertising and commercialism since infancy. Not proven, say the defenders. Most economists are inclined to agree. But a view perfectly free of the cultural biases acquired in one's development is presumably unattainable. So a poll of economists would be of uncertain value.

Whatever our conclusions, it must be stressed that Marx and the "Left" represent but *one* viewpoint toward markets and capitalism. *Other* viewpoints have sprung up in the twentieth century. *Their* criticisms and proposals for reform and change are not less profound and demanding of consideration than the discussion from the "Left." The two principal *modernist* critiques of market capitalism are, in fact, the subjects of the remaining parts of this book. Thus it would seem more accurate to say that all of political economy is a debate wth Adam Smith.

SUMMARY

1. When the proponents of market capitalism had overcome the hostility to markets expressed in medieval Christianity, they had to face the disillusionment with capitalism borne of the hardships experienced during the Industrial Revolution in the early 1800s. This chapter addresses the cri-

tiques of capitalism and the outlines of countersystems put forward by Marx in the nineteenth century and by the Marxist theoreticians of the New Left in this century.

2. Marx opposes the private ownership of capital and hence the earning of interest income on such capital. But if such privately-owned capital were to be "socialized," or expropriated, it is not certain whether it would be possible as a result to increase the pay of the workers—if the government desires to replace private saving by government saving and desires to replace the consumer goods purchased by retired people with their own wealth by consumer goods offered to them by the government. If it is good to reduce the consumption of the private owners of capital, the government can always reduce the interest received by them, by taxing some or all of it away, without abolishing capitalism—that is, private ownership of capital. Second, it is nowhere demonstrated that it is a bad idea for savers to receive a reward for saving, in view of its incentive effects. In fact, even under state ownership of the actual capital goods (and private ownership of government bonds and toasters)—that is, socialism in one form or another—it is not demonstrated that it would be a bad idea to offer an interest-type reward to worker-consumers for reasons involving the resulting incentive effects.

3. Marx also opposes commercialism and markets. Defenders of the market reply that market capitalism leaves people free to devote themselves more to a life of personal development and self-expression, and less to pro-football games on TV, anytime they choose to make that trade-off.

4. Marx's own romantic vision of a communist mechanism of resource allocation is subject to some stern criticisms: the arbitrariness and insidiousness with which a centralized bureaucracy allocates people to positions, and the presumption that productivity would suffer a lot from the vain efforts of the central planning bureau to allocate resources in the entire economy. Some critics of central planning propose that market socialism would be a better mechanism for the communists to use—though there are doubts about the workability of that mechanism.

5. The New Left is probably the most significant movement for criticism and radical change of capitalism among twentieth-century thinkers who see themselves as successors in Marx's tradition hoping to improve upon him. They argue that market capitalism corrupts people's preferences, thus depriving them of real autonomy over their life as worker and consumer. They advocate a society built on producers' cooperatives run by the workers.

6. Challengers of the New Left criticism question whether workers would accept a New Left system in view of the cost in wages, a cost they have revealed themselves unwilling to pay so far. The New Left replies that the

workers have been brainwashed by advertising and commercialism since infancy. Not proven, say the challengers.

CONCEPTS INTRODUCED

economic determinism
alienation
Marxist exploitation
labor theory of value

market socialism
degradation of capitalist labor
New Man

New Left
codetermination
corruption of preferences

STUDY QUESTIONS

1. "The opposition of the Marxist to private ownership of property underestimated the importance of the potent profit-based incentive to invent and to innovate provided by market capitalism (assuming less than complete taxation of the profits!) But the critics of the Marxists have underestimated the strong incentive that managers and sientists have to succeed, to distinguish themselves, under a bureaucratic, communistic system. The advantage of a competitive market system—let's say competitive market capitalism, to be more specific—is that it operates on the basis of free entry and the 'decentralization' of investment-financing decisions: So the inventors of Walkman and *Hair!* do not require the approval of a single bureau, the Ministry of Culture, to obtain the financing to produce; nor does the introduction of computerized engine combustion and the microelectronic chip require the Minister of Production to 'sign off.' It is easier for the inventor or innovator to win a 'market test.' " Discuss these contentions.

2. "The fact that workers are free under competitive capitalism to form cooperatives in which to practice codetermination, even free to 'drop out,' but overwhelmingly choose not to do so gives the lie to the Left, old and new." What is the logic of this, and how applicable is it?

3. "The current-day advocates of so-called Industrial Policy are a throwback to yesteryear's champions of central planning, despite its obviously disqualifying defects." Discuss.

4. Does the Left, old and new, have a "monopoly" of the available criticisms of market capitalism? As an exercise, write a thirty-page essay on the views of Aristotle, Nietzsche, Acquinas, Mussolini, and others of interest.

5. For those who have seen *Being There*, or read the book by Jerzy Kosinski, in what ways does the Peter Sellers character, called Gardener but not a real gardener, embody New Left criticisms of capitalism in America and elsewhere?

Part 6

Modern Market Equilibrium Theory

. . . Painters often say that in all art the artist works essentially with colors and shapes rather than with natural objects. But the lines of a Renaissance master are complex forms which depend on already ordered shapes in nature. The painting of a cup in a still-life picture resembles an actual cup, which is itself a well ordered thing. A painting of a landscape depends on observations of elements which are complete, highly ordered shapes in themselves—like trees or mountains.

Modern painting is the first complex style in history which proceeds from elements that are not pre-ordered as closed articulated shapes. The [modernist] artist creates an order out of unordered variable elements. . . . No other art today exhibits to that degree the presence of the individual . . . and the concreteness of his procedure. This art, I believe, is deeply rooted in the self and its relation to the surrounding world.

Meyer Schapiro, "The Liberating Quality in Avant-Garde Art" (1957)

CHAPTER 15

Product Markets and the Firm: Pricing and Product Quality

HARRY LIME:

Look down there. Would you really feel any pity if one of those dots stopped moving forever? If I offered you twenty thousand pounds for every dot that stopped, would you really, old man, tell me to keep my money or would you calculate how many dots you could afford to spare?

Orson Welles (to Joseph Cotton) atop the Ferris wheel in *The Third Man* (1949)

Exasperated by the awesome claims that classical economics makes for the market mechanism—for competition—critics are often driven to sarcasm: "The magic of the market," they like to say, in parody of the classicists' bountiful praise. In fact the competent neoclassical economist acknowledges fully some limits and defects of the market: Our dependence on the government to provide collective goods, penalize external diseconomies, settle the distribution of benefits and burdens from economic cooperation, and so forth. The state plays a crucial part alongside the market. The "mystique" of the market—the supposition that the market does no wrong, that markets do not malfunction (only governments do)—is more the work of propagandists than economic scientists of *any* era.

Yet there is an element of truth in that parody. The world of neoclassical economics *is* a magical place. It is a world in which all transactions are costless:

♦ Sellers do not have to have a pricing policy and worry that their prices may be too high or low, households do not have to shop for products and shop for jobs, brokers are not needed to match buyers and sellers—the "market" does all that, free of charge. The market is able to enforce one price (the "market price") for every product and productive service specified, since *economic information,* data on prices and wages and the specifications of existing products and jobs, *is costless for sellers to transmit and costless for buyers to acquire.*

♦ There are no "producers," or entrepreneurs, making a living from scarce knowhow, no managers needed to see that workers and suppliers perform as contracted, no firms with reputations for their product and their labor relations to uphold. There is no problem of how to produce, say, textbooks or hot concrete, no problem of monitoring workers' performance or spotting a "lemon" in the used-car lot, since *economic knowledge,* knowledge about formulas and blueprints and about the performance by a worker or a product, *cannot be concealed from others.*

> In short: Build a better mousetrap and the world will instantly beat a path to your door. But if you can anyone can—without incurring any "transaction cost" for knowhow and management.

Although this neoclassical system yields hugely important insights into important questions, it seems to leave out the world of *everyday* observations! No wonder that, according to an old professional joke, a student eventually asks the professor teaching the neoclassical system: "But, sir, where are the *people* in this theory?"

In the *modern* style of market analysis, by contrast, information and knowledge hold the spotlight. In this modern view, messages are expensive to transmit, hence information is costly to find, and secrets are cheap to conceal, hence knowledge is not completely shared *in most or all markets.* The resulting focus of this modern theory is on the *roles of imperfect information and incomplete knowledge in the performance of the market economy*—on the difficulties the market players have, as consumer and as employer or employee, in acquiring information and knowledge, and the consequences of those difficulties for the functioning of markets.

♦ Each participant in the market, according to modern theory, has to rely on his *beliefs* about the desires and capacities of those he deals with (the performance of employees and product-sellers, etc.) and his *expectations* of current industry conditions (what other sellers are doing regarding price and product, etc.).

♦ Understanding that fact, each participant recognizes that the others in the market could not be completely knowledgeable about his willingness or ability as a producer or worker (no matter what he claimed) and could not be continuously informed of his every move. Each actor must deal with the others' assumptions and expectations!

With the classical magic not there—no costless "auctioneer" around to collect the amounts of the good sellers are willing to sell and buyers willing to buy at each possible price and no one, no unseen "regulator," to make sure the producer delivers the good and the worker the effort contracted for—the transactors are driven to collect their own information and make their own arrangements. The transactors have to come face to face for personal dealings. Thus some aspects of primitive exchange—the "Gothic" economics of *two-person transactions*—are typically brought back: communicating terms, perhaps bargaining, watching out for cheating and other "moral hazards," aiming for cheat-proof incentive-based agreements, and so forth.

The payoff from any new theory, of course, lies in how it expands our understanding and how it alters our attitudes and prescriptions.

♦ The modern theory of markets, largely developed just in the past two decades, has illuminated a whole universe of observations (which we will be discussing in a moment): the prevalence of the long-lived "firm," the mark-up of price above total unit cost—hence a pure profit called "good will," undue hazards in products and occupations, reputable firms and deceiving ones, "job rationing" and unemployment (even in equilibrium), discriminatory stereotyping in hiring and lending, layoff and seniority rules, and much else—a world of phenomena not understandable by neoclassical theory.

♦ It could be said, then, that by "telling it like it is" the modern theory has put its glaring light on the slimy underside of business practice. But far from all the findings are adverse. The modern theoretical developments, by contributing new insights into many business problems, have found mitigating circumstances to weigh in our evaluations of several industrial institutions—for example, the labor union, government-enforced retail price maintenance, and investment bankers.

The modern analysis of some of these phenomena will be the subject of Part 6. This analysis will be seen to modify, though not demolish, the classical analysis of markets.

The present chapter takes up the modern view of the behavior of the firm in product markets and what it implies about the equilibrium in those markets. (Then, on to the labor market, the capital market, and money.)

THE FIRM: ITS PRICING AND CUSTOMER SHARE

Why don't firms spring full-grown overnight, and disappear just as abruptly? (Why are they evergreens and perennials, not desert flowers?) Why do we find firms "Founded 1873" and even "Gegründet 1728"? (One might also wonder why they advertise their age.) In the modern view the reasons why, usually, new enterprises cannot frictionlessly slip into the ranks of established firms lie in the workings of most product markets.

One obstacle faced by a producer contemplating an attempt to break into an industry is the transaction cost of marketing the new product or distinctive service offered. The established firm can survive, possibly thrive, on its existing stock of customers, reputation, and so forth. Success breeds success, or at least survival. Word-of-mouth from the "satisfied customers" of the established firm is good enough to provide it with new, typically young customers sufficient to replace the outflow of old customers. The established firm survives because it has already paid its dues. The newcomer does not have that inherited advantage. *A new entrant bidding to enter the ranks of established firms has to start with nothing.* Hence it would have to "pay" with *below normal* prices or *above normal* service in order to get a toehold in the industry. No wonder, then, that successful new entrants into an industry are rare. And new products are often launched by established firms rather than by new ones built on the prospect of the new product only.

The *firm,* as conceived in modern theory, is typically an enterprise with an accumulated stock of *customers,* which represents some share of the market. To acquire customers or acquire more of them the firm has to make an investment—to offer temporarily a lower price or better service—in order to attract customers away from its competitors or divert incoming ones to it. The returns on such an investment—whether or not large enough to motivate the investment—come later, as with any investment, since it takes time for the "word of mouth" to spread. (Likewise it may take time for a firm to leave the business, to disinvest through high prices and poor service, since customers may need time to find a better supplier.)

In bygone times, the customer was a buyer for whom the product was made to order, or custom-built. It would have been pretentious of a street-corner newspaper vendor to speak of his customers, a delusion of grandeur. But a tailor could (and still can) refer to those to whom he sells clothes made to measure as his customers. Correspondingly, the earliest notion of a "firm" seems to have been tied to that original meaning of the word *customer.* Supplying standardized bricks or pork bellies to the market was a business for ordinary enterprises, much as classical theory depicted enterprises. In the words of an early modern thinker on the nature of the firm, the distinctive business of the firm lies in "customizing the article or service." In this view the firm is an enterprise that has acquired a clientele with whom it has entered into a kind of contract—an unwritten and unspoken "implicit" contract of a special but quite important type.

The final purchaser may want the security of a long-term contract, and owing to the difficulty of forecasting his needs he may want a general commitment that states only the limits to what the party supplying the article or service is expected to do. . . . where a simple short-term contract would be unsatisfactory, where only a long-term contract couched in terms of innumerable contingencies (not all of them imagined beforehand) would do, in such conditions we find a firm undertaking such commitments.*

Nowadays we find that notion of customer, and of the firm as "customizing" its product, a little quaint. Now my New York bank does not call me when it finds I am about to be overdrawn. Unconcerned, its computer proceeds to bounce the check. Yet the bank calls me a customer, and we do talk, exchanging information about the choices it offers and my eligibility. Both the bank and I have invested something in order to carry on this relationship. It is a customer relationship, at least in the modern sense.

Customer Markets

The term *customer market* has been used to refer to the kind of product market in which there is no auctioneer setting price to clear the market. A hallmark of customer markets is the need for price tags. There is no classical "ruling price" that imperiously coerces all the sellers to go along with it, so that it becomes superfluous to state one's own price. Competition in customer markets does not rigidly enforce a single price since the buyer and seller *do not observe* the current price set by each other seller—nor even the average of those prices. The sellers cannot each afford to trumpet repeatedly their respective prices—too few consumers would be listening or looking to repay the advertising cost. Hence no buyer has any way of canvassing the prices of all the other sellers—there are too many of them for all to be reached within the desired time. Knowing that the buyers are in the dark, the seller must speak up, setting his own price. The customer, and the comparative shopper choosing a supplier, cannot tell the price without a price tag.

A minute's thought will convince anyone that in the economy of today, at any rate the advanced economies, most of the products

* Ronald H. Coase, "The Nature of the Firm," *Economica*, November 1937, p. 393.

sold to the consumer—whether a commodity or service or mixture of both—are largely supplied on customer markets, not the auction markets of classical theory or anything like them. Some of the most vivid examples: the services of auto tow trucks, hospital emergency rooms, and funeral homes. There may not be many firms in the industry, but the unfortunate consumer cannot afford the time to shop around. Tourist hotels and roadside restaurants are similar examples, with the complication of "differentiated products"—the products are not identical. Shoe stores and supermarkets are more pedestrian examples. In Los Angeles there must a thousand such stores, each with its own assortment of items and prices. Manufacturers operate in customer markets no less than producers in the service industries, and the costs that manufacturers incur to win and keep customers is a measure of how far their markets are from the perfect market of classical theory. For example, a recent calculation showed that at the Xerox Corporation, famed for its manufactures, only one-seventh of its American work force is on the factory floor. More than half are involved in sales, customer service, and marketing. Xerox's machines could not win and retain customers if people didn't know about them (because there was no advertising or sales force) or couldn't use them (because there was no training) or couldn't maintain them (because an independent repairer would not have the same stake in their reliable performance).

The characteristic of greatest importance about true customer markets is this: *if* a supplier chose to cut its price below the "going price" in the industry, customers *elsewhere* would *not immediately know it*. If, in a local retail food market with many supermarkets and smaller stores, one of the supermarket stores were to lower some or all of its prices, and thus become the cheapest supplier (at least for consumers with certain tastes in supermarket wares), not everyone in the local market would know about it. The supermarket could hardly afford to reach all consumers with enough data to prove it was the cheapest—it could list all its own prices, if small enough type could be found, but it could not afford to list all the prices of all its competitors; it does not even know what will be the new prices of all its competitors for the week. Just as important, if the supermarket were to raise its prices, becoming more expensive than all the others, its customers would not abandon their shopping carts in the middle of the supermarket aisles and head for the nearest competitor. They would wonder whether the apparent price rise ("so far, they seem up; but maybe prices will be *down* in the next aisle") was not merely a temporary aberration, or "blip," that would be gone next week; or they would wonder whether the same price increase would not be found at the competing stores; and some might wonder whether the price rises, even if not matched by other suppliers, did not leave their supplier still cheaper than the others (by a reduced margin). They might not know where to find another convenient supplier.

◆ In customer markets, then, the response of customers to a change of prices by an individual firm, the prices of competitors remaining the same, is ordinarily going to be sluggish. It is *costly*, then, for a firm to gain customers. For an enterprise contemplating entering the industry, that is a "barrier" to entry or at least a discouraging hurdle—with consequences we now examine.

Customer-Market Equilibrium versus Classical Competitive Equilibrium

Recall the idea of equilibrium introduced in chapter 3. In an *equilibrium* the expectations of all the sellers and buyers are *realized*. In *dis*equilibrium they aren't; expectations are exceeded or disappointed.

In the auction-type markets of neoclassical theory, the expectation of a high price, or above-equilibrium price, by suppliers when they make their production decisions (how much to plant, etc.) leads to an actual price (when the crop is harvested and brought to market) that is below the expected price. Correspondingly, expectations of a low, or below-equilibrium, price by suppliers at production time leads finally to a price above the expected one. The equilibrium price is the price level which, if expected, leads to its realization—the case of the *self-fulfilling* expectation, or surprise-free outcome.*

In the customer markets of modern market theory even the expectations of the *current* average price (let alone the price of each seller no matter how small) may fail to be realizable, self-fulfillable—thus spelling disequilibrium. It is possible for a while, since price information travels slowly, that *every* firm, as it sets and resets its own price, is overestimating or underestimating the average of the prices being set simultaneously by the other firms. The expectation of a high, or above-equilibrium, average price level by the sellers when they are setting their own prices causes the actual average price—the average of the prices actually set—to fall *short* of the expected average price. Symmetrically, the expectation by the firms of a low (below-equilibrium) average price causes the actual average price—the average of the prices actually chosen by the firms—to *exceed* the expected average price. The equilibrium (average) price level is the price level that *if expected* will then be realized.†

---

* Readers who have lost all memory of this by now might wish to look again at chapter 3, pp. 69-79, esp. p. 76. It may also be recalled that the supply-demand analysis in chapter 10 dealt with the case in which the actual price equals the price expected by all the suppliers—i.e., with the equilibrium case.

† A difference of really no significance between possible disequilibrium in classical markets and possible disequilibrium in customer markets is this: In the former the current price is *observed*, so the only possibility of wrong expectations pertains to future prices. In customer markets misexpectations of current expectations can occur—hence disequilibrium from that source.

What can be said about equilibrium in customer markets, and about the equilibrium price level? We shall see that *in customer markets the equilibrium price hangs above the classical competitive-equilibrium level*, the level that would have resulted if the market had somehow been a classical instead of a modern one. That proposition leads to a corollary proposition: Since the price exceeds the unit cost of production—which includes the wage cost of labor and the interest cost (plus wear and tear) on physical capital—the owners of the customer-market firm receive a *pure profit*, which is the excess of total revenue over total labor-and-capital costs and which they keep for themselves as a kind of tax on labor and capital.

◆ Figure 15–1 depicts these two features of customer-market equilibrium, according to modern market theory, and contrasts that equilibrium to the *classical* view of what the equilibrium would be (if only the market operated classically!). The price is up, and a "pure profit" results.*

When this conclusion that the equilibrium price exceeds unit cost was reached by the fearless pioneers of modern market theory, economists brought up in classical analysis were startled and at first disbelieving. "It must be," they thought, "that the eagerness to make the maximum possible profit will motivate each firm to lower its price a little, with the plan of taking customers away from the others (and hoping later to put the price back up!), as long as the price is above costs. Thus an industry price above unit cost *could not stick*—competition will drive price down and wipe out pure profit once equilibrium is established."

That argument is valid when applied to the perfectly competitive markets of *classical* theory:

◆ In the classically competitive market the competition for customers works *frictionlessly*—cut your price a little for just a moment and new customers will instantly "beat a path to your door."

◆ In the customer markets of modern market theory, however, news of your lower price travels slowly—so a firm considering a price cut could expect the stock of customers to build up only gradually, like a slow leak of customers from the other firms. "The customers shuffle their way to the store." Hence the firm must reckon that the *pay-off* from a temporary price cut to gain market share *lies in the future*, while the *cost* of this "investing in increased customers" starts immediately. It pays to make this investment *only* if the future returns from it beat the alternative future returns that the firm could earn by keeping up the price and using the revenue saved to buy interest-paying bonds. Even if *already having* one

---

* Calling it a "pure profit" does *not* deny that a particular firm may have had to "pay"—to invest—through a cheap price for a while to capture its customers away from other firms. But firms in the aggregate do not have to make such an investment.

FIGURE 15–1: Customer-Market Equilibrium: Nonclassical Features

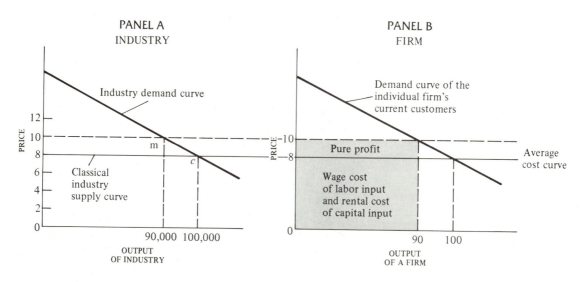

We consider an industry composed of a number of firms competing with one another in a customer market. We might think of retail haircutting in a large city; or ophthalmological checkups; or jazz clubs—to avoid the unhelpful complication of a raw material or other intermediate good. So all costs are wages or interest or space rents.

If the firms were forced to compete in the frictionless product market of classical theory, the industry would operate on its classical industry supply curve. If we suppose for simplicity that we are dealing with a constant cost industry then this supply curve would be a horizontal line. The height of this line must measure unit cost—cost per unit of output—at each and every supplier. If the market were classical, this supply curve and the industry demand curve would determine by their intersection the competitive-equilibrium price level and industry output level. This classical competitive equilibrium is depicted by the point *c* in Panel A.

But since in fact the firms do business in a customer market, their "competition" with one another, while operative to a degree, does not go so far as to drive the price all the way down to the competitive-equilibrium level. According to modern market theory the customer-market equilibrium (the real equilibrium in this customer-type market) exists at a point like *m* where price lies above, and industry output below, the classical competitive equilibrium at point *c*.

The diagram in Panel B pictures the goings-on at one firm—one of a thousand firms, all identical, each with a thousandth of the identical customers. If we suppose that the individual firm has "constant costs," to make matters very simple, the average-cost (or unit-cost) curve is also a horizontal line—with the same height as the classical industry supply curve. But this firm, like every other, sets price above its unit cost. The result is a "pure profit." It equals quantity sold *times* the "mark-up" of price over unit cost.

extra customer would be profitable, it might not be worth the investment cost to *acquire* another one. When the industry price is far above unit cost every firm calculates that "investing in more customers" *will pay*—because with the price very high the return from each extra customer is high too.

But as the price is "competed down" *toward* unit-cost level there comes a point where continued investment *no longer pays.*

♦ As for a firm deciding whether to enter the industry, it would be no easier for such a potential firm to acquire one customer than for an existing firm to acquire one more. The cost of transmitting information about its "low price" constitutes a barrier—or hurdle—to entry.

Some proofs are more convincing than others, though. When William Harvey set out to prove that human blood circulates, from the heart and back round-trip, he proved his point by

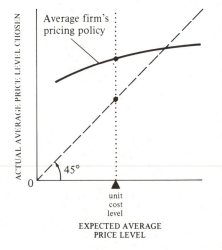

"reducing to absurdity" the previously prevailing view—the method of proof called *reductio ad absurdum.* To prove *convincingly* that the equilibrium price does lie above unit cost it is best to refute the contrary position.

So assume, contrary to the correct conclusion, that the equilibrium price *is* equal to unit cost, *despite* opportunities of firms to buy interest-paying bonds or make other investments that, like the bonds, offer an above-zero net rate of return (more cumulative returns eventually than needed to "pay back" the investment). Understand what is being assumed: If each firm expects all the others to set their price equal to the common unit cost, each firm will be content to set its own price at that level too; so *that* is the equilibrium level of the price, the self-fulfilling expectation.

But in that situation any firm could correctly figure there *would be a gain* from planning a price increase, at least a brief one, because: 1) although some customers would drift away as a result of its above-industry price, there would be no loss of profit as a consequence, since, as the firm supposes, it must ultimately lower its price back to unit cost if it is to keep any customers at all— hence, with price equal again to unit cost, there will be no real loss if the firm lost some or all of its customers; and 2) the temporary increase of revenue resulting from the temporary price hike could be used to buy some bonds yielding interest—interest forever! Hence there would be a clear gain from raising the price above the price the others are expected to set when that "expected price" is as low as unit cost. The diagram above illustrates that: When the "expected price" is equal to unit cost, the price actually set is higher than that. With all firms calculating that way, the industry price would levitate *above* the unit-cost level (even though no firm expected the others were going to be equally daring!). This finding clearly *contradicts* the original assumption, made for the sake of argument, that the equilibrium price level was *equal* to the unit cost of production. Q.E.D.*

So—*what?* How should we react on hearing that firms "mark up" their prices above unit costs and thus make a pure profit? We have already heard from neoclassical economists that firms are greedy, seeking the maximum possible profit. So we are not shocked. Should we feel offended? Maybe not, since the neoclassical Smithian theory taught us to see that greed has a place, that self-interest by buyers and sellers in the marketplace—looking for the best terms and all that—is a powerful engine for the productive employment of resources.

The harm and the medicine. The damage from the marking up of prices is like the damage from the exercise of monopoly power by a perfectly classical monopolist. By raising its price above the competitive-equilibrium level the firm is putting a tax on the consumer, who is in the end a worker and saver. We *approve* taxation by the *government*, which has no other way to raise revenue, whenever there is an overriding social purpose served by the revenue raised by the tax—a purpose that overrides or outweighs the damage from the resulting erosion of incentives to work and save. But there is no reason to approve, or excuse, taxation by private firms.

◆ If all firms raise prices, say from 8 to 10 as in Figure 15–1, that reduces the *real* wage rate—the hourly wage rate in terms of goods, or "purchasing power—from, say, $\frac{24}{8}$ to $\frac{24}{10}$. Of course the owners of these firms may be themselves workers or former workers. So the proceeds of the "tax"— the pure profit—may be received, now or later, by the wage earners themselves.

If the wage earners are themselves the sole owners of all the firms, because the workers have inherited or are going to inherit the

* A small qualification. It should be remembered that in discussing why price exceeds unit cost in customer-market equilibrium there is the crucial proviso that bonds are offering an above-zero rate of interest. *If* the rate of interest were zero in the world, which it almost never is, there *could* be a customer-market equilibrium featuring price equal to unit cost, with zero pure profit, just as in the classical theory.

ownership shares—the common stock—of their parents, there is a clear loss of efficiency resulting from the mark-up of price over cost. Perhaps the diagram to the left will convey the nature of the argument in that uncomplicated case. It is supposed, just to be very concrete, that the wage rate in terms of money is 24 (dollars, pounds, pesos, or whatever). And the neoclassical competitive price level is 8. So if there is *no* mark-up of price over cost each extra hour of work will bring 3 extra units of the good (or basket containing the representative assortment of goods). The straight line originating from the origin indicating how much *wage* income would be brought in by a family by working any number of hours will then have a slope of 3. To this wage income we have to add the family's interest income to obtain the total command over goods corresponding to any given amount of work-time earning wages. This gives the budget line *ac*. In competitive equilibrium the typical family is observed to have chosen a point like *c*.

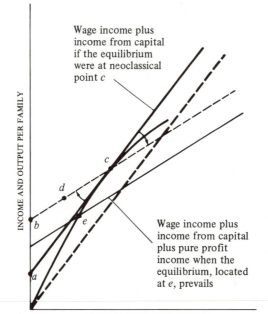

Wage income plus income from capital if the equilibrium were at neoclassical point *c*

Wage income plus income from capital plus pure profit income when the equilibrium, located at *e*, prevails

INCOME AND OUTPUT PER FAMILY

WORK-EFFORT OF THE FAMILY

But when a mark-up of price over cost arises the point *c* will not be chosen. At first the typical family will find its nonwage income bloated by the receipt of additional dividends on the ownership (or equity) shares in firms that it owns that are the result of the pure profit these firms are receiving; at the same time the family will find its wage income plus interest income reduced by an equal, offsetting amount—as long as each family keeps working and producing as much as before. Hence the curve showing the trade-off between total income and work is flattened, like the line *bc*. Though each family *could* continue working the same account as before, as under competitive equilibrium, the penalty for working less is reduced in the new situation. The new curve *bc* indicating the possible choices of the family has the slope 2.4, corresponding to the new and higher price level of 10 instead of 8. Taking account of this "expanded choice," the family is apt to choose to work *less* (and earn less accordingly), as at *d* on the line *bc*, since working less now does not entail as much sacrifice of income as it did before the mark-up. The customer-market equilibrium cannot occur at *d*, however, since in fact the marginal product of labor is still 3, not 2.4, so the economy cannot produce as much output as indicated at *d*. The true customer-market equilibrium will lie at a point like *e*—with *some* pure profit and *some* reduction of effort (compared to the neoclassical point *c*)—but not as severe as at the infeasible point *d*. Whatever the exact location of *e*, it must be worse than *c*, since *c* is best!

If on the other hand the workers inherit nothing, having to save to acquire shares, the efficiency loss is complex.

What is to be done, if anything can be? With mark-ups in customer markets "taxing" the earning of wage income and interest income too, thus penalizing effort and thrift, the government can best respond by seeking to offset the "tax" with countervailing measures designed to *spur* effort and thrift. The government might respond, for example, with the payment of a public subsidy to firms for hiring labor (and maybe capital goods as well). Such a measure could be financed by taxing away some proportion of the firms' pure profit—including the added part contributed by the employment subsidies.

♦ Hence a levy on corporations' pure profits—on corporate profits after the firms' payment of wages to labor hired, rentals to capital hired (or hired from themselves) and interest payments to lenders—when spent to subsidize employment could serve beneficially to counter the ill effects of mark-ups over cost. But it should be recorded that such a measure could only *improve* things, not cure them. (A complete cure would require the radical removal of *all* pure profit *after corporate tax*, hence a 100 percent tax on the corporate income from the employment subsidies. But that would destroy their effectiveness as inducements to firms to hire more labor!)

"UNSAFE AT ANY PRICE": THE PROBLEM
OF PRODUCT QUALITY

With the workings of customer markets on product *prices* clearly understood, it is easy to extend that theory of how customer markets work to the *quality* of the products marketed. The idea of customer markets is a tool with which to see whether and how we might be able to "make sense of"— to interpret and qualify—the present-day complaints about the unsatisfactoriness of goods sold in the market.

To complain that the goods available are simply not large enough—the chewing gum package, the ice cream scooper, a bunch of flowers all too small—is merely an indirect way of saying that the prices, the charge per unit sold, are not low enough. But frequently there is a *quality* dimension to a good that is worth distinguishing from the *quantity* dimension, or *price* dimension. When one of Woody Allen's characters grumbles about the meal she just had—"The dishes were no good and besides the portions were too small"—we may find it funny but not crazy. Maybe the meal was overpriced—priced above the marginal cost of production, thus above the competitive-equilibrium level of neoclassical theory—*and* of lesser quality than the diner would have been willing to buy (given a choice without overpricing or with equal overpricing for all qualities).

The consumer advocates of the modern day have been most emphatic about the quality of the products dished up by the market sector, much more than about the prices of products. Their most sensational complaints, undoubtedly, has been about the safety of many of the products for sale in the market. In the United States some of the "muckraking" writers of the early twentieth century wrote exposés of unsanitary conditions in the food-processing industry, no doubt hastening passage of the regulatory legislation known as the Pure Food and Drug Act. The foremost consumerist of recent years rose to fame by taking aim at the automobile industry in the classic *Unsafe at Any Speed,* the gadfly of unregulated markets, Ralph Nader.

Viewed through the lens of neoclassical theory, it should be noted, these allegations of market malfunctioning by consumerists are unsound and, if acted upon, positively harmful.

"If the consumer, in his or her wisdom, wanted a safer auto or a safer chicken (or a tastier one) in spite of the higher price producers would need to cover the cost, he or she would have leaped to buy it as soon as a producer put in on the market. Hence one or more firms, each eager to profit by getting a jump on competitors, would have rushed to the market with the safer model—if there really was a safer model that some consumers were willing to pay for. Why, then, hasn't this safer model been marketed? The realistic answer, sad though it may be to self-appointed "consumer advocates," is that the consumer does not feel able to afford the safer product, much less a perfectly safe product. And the same goes for safe occupations, safe factories, and the rest. What the consumerists are advocating, in effect, is that the consumer be taxed, via a higher price, to pay for benefits in the form of improved product safety that are not worth the costs—which is evidenced, to repeat, by the consumer's unwillingness voluntarily to buy the safer model at the higher price. The result is a loss, not a gain!—a safer car we don't have the money left to use much."*

THE CUSTOMER-MARKET VIEW

Modern market theory, by contrast, provides a ready-made model—the model of customer markets—that consumer advocates could use in reply to skeptical neoclassicists. The customer-market model suggests that the neoclassicists' rejection of the consumer movement rests on an extreme assumption of theirs, one too extreme to fit more than a few special cases. That neoclassical assumption is that anyone building a better mousetrap, a longer-life lightbulb, a less sinkable cruise ship can costlessly disseminate the knowledge of the new and better product to interested consumers. But that assumption, according to the modern theory, is not generally applicable to the contemporary economy (if any economies at all). It is simply inapplicable to customer markets:

♦ Just as the firm contemplating a reduction of its price below the average "going price" in the industry knows that it could not communicate costlessly and quickly the good news to customers at other firms—the firm would have to wait for the good news to spread by word of mouth or else pay the cost of advertising its price cut—so, likewise, the firm contemplating a *better product* could not costlessly and immediately penetrate the consciousness of the entire market with the news of the product improvement. (The firm might even have to persuade consumers that it is not lying, not hiding the knowledge that it is *not* really a better product— at least not better enough to warrant the higher price. "If I improve the product, rather than cut its price, not even my own customers would realize it.") Thus the informational frictions in customer markets impede the competitive drive toward better quality of the products as well as toward a lower price.

Of course, no consumer would have reason to worry about false advertising claims or the quality of the product if every firm were known to be perfectly honest. However, there are always a

---

* The quote is made up—fabricated—but true to the neoclassical spirit. Of course the neoclassicist does recognize the external economy generated by buying (and wearing!) seat belts—you lower everyone's insurance rate. (Recall chapter 13, pp. 337–38.) Also, the humane neoclassicist recognizes that a young mother may not know which cribs are safe and may welcome at the very least governmental instructions, warnings, gradings, and so forth!

few producers—some would say they were in a heavy majority—for whom profit outweighs the satisfaction of being honest. In one of the most recent cases, a hundred thousand Britons were "stung" by false advertising for an electronic device, called Antipic, that was claimed to make mosquitoes buzz off. The advertisements claimed that the device emitted a high-pitched hum resembling a sound they said the male mosquito makes; according to the sales pitch, there is a male hum that frightens off already mated female mosquitos— only females bite—and these females, once mated, do not want to mate again. Apparently the image of sexually harassed female mosquitoes fleeing the sound of males persuaded many thousand of Britons to part with five pounds each for the intriguing gadget. But tests by disinterested scientists showed that the scientists, stationing themselves near a mosquito-infested lily pond at Nuneham Park, near Oxford, were attacked by mosquitoes with the same frequency when the device was switched on as when it was off. The firm making Antipic replied lamely that they decided it must work in view of the testimonials of users who wrote to say that they believed it worked.

Clearly the model of customer markets does not give its endorsement to every claim of every self-styled consumer advocate. Yet the customer-market model definitely implies that customer markets stop short of offering all the product improvements that would be demanded by informed consumers despite their greater production cost—because of the *transaction cost* of informing, and in some cases convincing, interested consumers of the improvement. It implies that only the improvements that are easy to describe and demonstrate to consumers have any chance of being marketed successfully; of these, the improvements that are biggest compared to their production cost have the best chance. The model implies that improvements in automobile fuel requirements—miles per gallon—may have nearly as good a chance of reaching the consumer as a price cut; but that improvements in tire reliability or braking defect rates would not be easy to "market."

What is the medicine?

Is there anything that can be done to treat the malady of undersafe, subquality products in customer markets? Regulation is the answer, say the consumer advocates. Let the legislatures enact statutes mandating that tires meet certain government-determined specifications, that "frankfurters" must contain certain ingredients in certain proportions, and so forth. What surer way, the advocates demand to know, to get safer and better products on the market?

THE REGULATION CONTROVERSY

Critics of the regulatory movement, as it took shape in the United States during the 1960s and 1970s, have come to view it with deep skepticism. Yes, perfectly wise and selfless regulators could find plenty of helpful measures to take. But, the skeptics say, the economists' postulate of self-interest suggests that government bureaucrats who make a career out of regulating, who therefore have a vested interest in the activity of regulating, will tend naturally to overregulate: The bureaucrats will neglect to check whether their safety regulations pass the cost-benefit test or else bias the results of any cost-benefit test conducted—so the last safety gadget required on a car may produce only a negligible further improvement in safety while costing billions in higher auto manufacturing costs and car prices. And, above all, the bureaucrats, in order to build in a lifetime demand for their expertise and a need for a still larger bureau, will enmesh producing firms in a net of detailed bureaucratic rules. "Of course," as someone put it, "car brakes ought to work. But must the torsion of each screw be precisely specified?" Last, skeptics add, the power to control the product and production methods in an industry is the power to control that industry. If they can do it, the large firms in the industry will try to "capture" the regulator, to "buy" him with favors and promises of a job, in order to misuse, or pervert, the regulatory authority—to write regulations that serve primarily to keep up industry prices or keep out new products or new methods that would "spoil the market" for the existing ones.

> Every judicious economist recognizes that these are profound and important criticisms of the regulatory movement. But many, perhaps most, question whether these criticisms warrant "throwing out the baby with the bath water." Societies do not refrain from passing laws for the public safety and raising tax revenue for police departments to enforce them just because there is an ever-present danger of overzealousness by the police that would infringe upon our basic liberties and privacy if left unchecked. Likewise, societies give the go-ahead to defense departments in spite of the tendencies toward an overgrown military establishment. "The price of liberty," after all, "is eternal vigilance"; it *isn't* abstinence from all government functioning. Presumably there will always be a contest between the regulation and *de*regulation movements. The citizenry just has to hope that the better side scores points in the court of public opinion.

There are other regulatory actions the government can take, it should be added, besides requiring that products and production methods meet certain specifications. It is possible to enact and enforce laws against false and misleading advertising. In that way the government can increase the information value of advertising by firms attempting to market a safer, better, or cheaper product. It is also possible for the government to grade goods, to classify, or categorize, them. By that device the government makes it easier for a firm to advertise that it has a better product—it can advertise the government rating of its product, such as "Prime Meat" or "Grade A Maple Syrup." Here too there is the ever-present danger of abuses by the regulatory bureaus. But most economists would "think twice" before dismantling what centuries have put up.

PRICING TO SIGNAL QUALITY IN CUSTOMER MARKETS

"You can't judge a book by its cover." So goes an old adage. But if your only data on books were the covers, how else would you judge which book to buy and read? The consumer's problem of judging the quality of unknown products is another influence that may operate, alongside the information frictions discussed above, in the determination of price in customer markets—in markets where buyers cannot costlessly and instantly ascertain the prices or the product qualities (or both) of all the sellers.

When consumers are uncertain about the quality of a firm's product they will not unreasonably take the seller's price as an indication, however unreliable, of the quality. If, in the long run, the better of two rival products is generally more costly to produce, requiring a higher price in order to cover its higher cost, the consumer is quite right to make use of the price of an untried product in estimating its quality; making the best use of all available information requires the consumer to do so.

Consider, then, a typical seller that sees potential new customers constantly passing by who do not know his product; perhaps every consumer makes only a once-in-a-lifetime purchase, in which case all consumers are "new customers." The seller, aware that these uncertain consumers are going to judge the quality of his product at least partially by price, will realize that the optimum price to charge is therefore *higher* on this account. By raising his price the seller incidentally raises his demand curve, and the latter rise serves to increase the optimum price. He will raise his price as a (false) *signal* of better quality.

We have here another reason why, in markets where price or quality are not everywhere costlessly known, the price may tend to rise and to remain *above* the neoclassical perfect-competition level—where price equals marginal cost *and*, since there is no pure profit, equals unit cost as well. Even if none of the buyers returns after discovering that the seller's product is *not* of higher quality but only of higher price, there will always be new buyers for the firm to mislead by its inflated price. As the circus impresario P. T. Barnum put it, "There is a sucker born every minute." Moreover, as each firm finds that *all* the firms in the industry have pushed up their price above cost, the firm need not even plan any longer to pull back (to some degree at least) its price later, if and when the exit of old customers proves serious, since they have nowhere better to go.

> If new firms contemplate entering, attracted by the emerging pure profit, they will not necessarily be willing to undercut their established competitors, since they will have the same incentive to maintain the "inflated" price as a sign of their similar quality. If there is successful entry nevertheless, a possible effect is simply to divide the industry profit over more firms, each one using less labor and capital. (This makes sense if the whole economy is that way, all industries with a pure profit.) Or, if each firm needs a large amount of overhead capital, the industry "profit" could end up being spread over an enlarged and excessive amount of capital, all or most of it underutilized; then each firm needs its share of the profit from overpricing to help pay the interest to the bank for its capital. The restaurant industry and private hospitals are apparently examples of such overpricing and excess capacity.

Do we also have here, in the phenomenon of judging quality by price, another reason why there is too little quality in the goods offered? In one respect, yes. If a firm deciding whether to market an improved product plans to offer it at the normal price—at its "old" price, say—it will have to reckon that potential buyers will infer that a product selling for an ordinary price is an ordinary product. Hence customers who might have been inclined to try it because it is new will refuse to try it if the firm keeps the old price. However, the firm has the option to raise the price. By raising its price the firm can effectively *signal* its belief that it has a better product and that it will therefore not lose its valued customers if they try it despite its higher price. (Since the firm must have been indifferent about a small increase or decrease in the price of its unimproved product, it will presumably calculate a balance of advantage in raising the price of an improved product.) But then fewer customers can afford to try the new product.

Critics of the way customer markets behave add a further observation. When the demand curve sags in an industry, the classical response of the industry is a fall of the industry price—either because marginal cost is lower at lower output or wage rates are reduced or both; and this reduction of the price, by bolstering the quantity demanded, helps to cushion, to moderate, the decline of output. But firms in customer markets, knowing that potential new customers who happen by are unsure of the quality of their product, will figure that to reduce the price would invite these consumers to conclude that their product was cheap because inferior. This is the conundrum faced by the used-car dealer who finds he can't move his inventory at the customary price: He understands that he couldn't move it any faster at a reduced price either—because comparative shoppers, seeing a low price, would think the cars on that used-car lot were "lemons." Idle theoretical speculation, you say? Consider this true anecdote from the annals of commerce. When several years ago a well-known Broadway producer reduced the price of last-row orchestra seats to make his sell-out show affordable to students and other less well-heeled theatergoers, the princely gesture misfired: Those seats, though perfectly good, went largely unsold, as if something were wrong with them.

THE "CONTRACT" BETWEEN FIRM AND CUSTOMER*

Modern market theory contains another idea about firms in a customer market—about their policy toward price and product. The idea is that the successful firm offers its customers not just a price and product at each moment; there is a third dimension to what the firm provides. The firm makes a commitment to maintain a certain dependability in its price and reliability in its product. The loyal clientele of Famous Diner know that when the entire family, Grammy and Grandpops and the kids and all, make the trip there for Famous's Friday night complete dinner they need not fear that the management is going to jump the prices and dish up subpar meals just because there happens to be a shortage of tables, according to the management, at least. Famous Diner does not auction off its scarce tables; it resolves the problem of "excess demand" by turning away the surplus number of customers (on a first come, first served basis). Neither does Classic Cinema hike its admission if there are more people lined up for tickets than can be seated. It seems to be standard business practice of firms in customer markets never to raise price or lower quality except for "due cause," such as a recognized and presumably permanent increase in input costs.

◆ The neoclassical economics of auctioneer-type markets conditions us to believe that a seller, such as a restauranteur, *would* raise price if faced with a shortage—"to clear the market," and that doing so would be a

_____
* Optional section. This material can be skipped without loss of continuity.

good thing—"so the hungriest get the table." So it is a good question why a seller and his customers might find such business practice harmless, even beneficial.

NONVARIABLE PRICING VIEWED AS AN INSURANCE CONTRACT

There is an evident motive behind the widespread purchase of insurance. Provided the terms of the insurance are *fair,* so that the money lost *on the average* is the *same* in either case, most people prefer losing a *small* amount *for sure,* in the form of the premium payment, to the *chance* of losing a *larger* amount, in the form of expenses to replace a lost suitcase or wrecked car. For most people, the benefit from "spreading the risk" via such insurance exceeds the cost, which is zero if the premium level is fair—and even if there is *some* positive cost to cover handling and so on, there may still be a gain for some people.

This same desire to spread risks can in some cases operate to cause a firm to adopt a nonvarying-price, or single-price, policy. The insurance motive is a possible source of a mutual gain, to be divided somehow between customer and owner, from a single price.

A single price for sure instead of high prices with shortages and low prices with slack offers a gain to customers, provided the nonvarying price is set at the "fair" level (so that the price paid will be the same *on the average* under either pricing policy), that is similar to the gain offered by an insurance contract with a fair premium. Many consumers would rather pay an intermediate price for sure than face the high-price/low-price gamble. In some cases this gain is the only effect on consumers of the adoption of the fair single-price policy.

> Imagine that the patrons of Classic Cinema are all alike—same income and what not—so no one could outbid another. A patron who reaches Classic will see the movie if he or she gets a seat and head back home if not; a higher price would not create a seat and a lower price would not induce the patron to see the movie twice. So there is no attraction to the consumer in a variable-price policy. The patron might as well pay the single, intermediate price than engage in a useless gamble.

What about the owners of the firm? They also are persons. To make the argument that the adoption of a single-price policy will in some cases create the possibility of a mutual gain one wants to show that the owners of the firm will not thereby lose (or, failing that, that their losses can be offset by what the customers can afford to pay in view of their gains to compensate the owners).

Under certain conditions, the amount of profit collected on the average will not be reduced by adopting a single price that is set at the "fair" level. Since the customers are paying the same price on the average as before—the only difference being that now they pay the average each time, rather than the high-price/low-price, as we are imagining they did before—and hence still are coming to the firm to buy with the same frequency as before, the firm can afford to supply each day the same amount of meals or movie seats as it would have under the variable-price policy; then it would have the same costs as before, under the variable-price policy. It may be argued that the firm should be able to earn the same profit on the average as before.

> Since Classic Cinema's patrons are alike, except for the moments when they feel like seeing a movie, there is no patron who used to make the trip there only on the speculation of a slack night, and hence a low price, when the variable-price policy prevailed. They all paid the high price if necessary. Further, we may suppose that arriving patrons cannot easily switch to other movie theaters; that is why an excess demand, or shortage, could occur. Hence the cinema need not worry that eliminating the low price will cost it some sales.

Thus conditions may be such that both customers and owners do not lose and perhaps gain by the adoption of a single-price policy. But the argument does not apply to all conditions. (What if Famous Diner's patrons only bought a hamburger at the high price and would do the same at the single price? What if some customers are poorer? Some more mobile?) In any case, the insurance motive is not the only possible explanation of the single-price policy.

THE DISTRUST OF VARIABLE-PRICE CONTRACTS

With some imagination we can visualize Famous Diner replacing its yellowing washable price list (for dinner time, say) with an electronic board, much like the board with the current moment's price quotations at a stock exchange. Customers outside who are considering dining there would be kept posted on the latest price of the evening's special and perhaps other dishes as tables emptied causing prices to drop, and as stocks of food in the kitchen dwindled, causing prices to climb. We can imagine that Famous Diner might explain its new policy in a written statement:

"Famous Diner is proud to announce a new "contract" with its patrons. In place of our former policy of fixed prices from hour to hour and even day to day we are introducing a policy of variable prices determined according to current conditions. Although the new policy is complex in its details, made possible by an advanced computer, Famous Diner is pleased to announce that the new policy does not mean higher prices on the average for our patrons. Patrons can rest assured that anyone continuing to have the same meal as before can expect to pay the same price *on the average* as before—barring basic changes in costs and other considerations outside the control of Famous Diner. Mgmt."

Readers who recall Hume's parable of the two sheep farmers unable to monitor each other and who thus reach a workable contract will understand the look of worry that would surely cross the brows of the diner's heretofore stalwart patrons. An insightful patron would at once recognize that he had no way to observe, or monitor, the *average* price of his customary meal; he could only record the *actual* price he paid with each succeeding visit. The patron would realize that the management (or else some succeeding management) might succumb to the temptation to tinker with the "complex" pricing formula so as to allow some bargain prices to turn up occasionally but to raise considerably the average price—much as a casino would be tempted, in the absence of stiff penalities, to tinker with the "odds" in a slot machine. Then, patrons would not know whether they were being cheated or just suffering a run of bad luck. "Lately, old friend," the manager might say, "it seems that prices were higher than average whenever you were here." Thus there would never be a way for the patrons to monitor the management's fidelity to the stated contract. So they would always be vulnerable to the "moral hazard" that the management would not actually fulfill the terms of the "contract."

> The drawback of a variable-price policy for customers is the difficulty that customers would have in estimating how expensive on average the firm really is—the difficulty of verification, to borrow a term from disarmament discussion. There would be the moral hazard that firms would cheat. Strict observance by the firm of such a "contract" would not be compatible with its incentives, as contract theorists politely put it—meaning its incentive to make more profit. Hence consumers would reject it.

The difficulty of estimating, or monitoring, the average costliness has two sources: A customer would not find it costless to observe and measure the underlying conditions—such as the size of the excess demand or supply—that the firm says its price depends upon. Second, a customer, even if informed of the current situation, would not have the knowledge of what the chances, or probabilities, are of this or that condition turning up; so he would not be able to calculate the average price, the price he should expect to pay on the average. It does not help to be able to watch the dice if they are loaded and only the other player knows what the resulting odds are.

For these reasons a consumer would also be wary of buying from a firm whose policy is to vary its price with fluctuations in its costs of production. When there is an increase in the costs of producing, in average and marginal cost, the firm might calculate that its optimum price was therefore higher and so it would want (in some more perfect world at least) to pass along some or all of the increased cost of producing—even if the cost increase proves temporary, in which case it can lower its price when costs fall; clearly the firm may lose some money if it has to sell at the normal price and lose less if it can raise the price. Hence the firm would like to have an understanding with customers that entitled it to pass along such temporary cost increases whenever they occurred. But modern market theory shows why the wary consumer would balk: First, the consumer cannot observe the firm's cost and cannot ascertain that it has risen by enough to warrant the firm's price increase according to its own stated policy. Second, even if the consumer could observe each month's cost curves, he or she would not likely possess the esoteric knowledge (unless the consumer is in the same business) to be able to say what the true *average* level of cost is, hence whether this month's events warrant an above-average price. A consumer patronizing a firm on the understanding that extraordinary costs warrant extraordinary prices would realize that he was vulnerable to being cheated by the firm. The firm could constantly plead it was suffering unusual costs.

SUMMARY

1. The modern theory of market equilibrium recognizes that transaction costs, principally the costs of acquiring or transmitting information, are an important feature of real-life conditions in most markets. This recognition opens up the possibility of illuminating a great many phenomena that the classical theory, good as it is for some purposes, cannot explain. This chapter presents some portions of the modern theory of product markets.

2. The modern theory gives attention to something called the customer. The key to the customer's situation is that he or she is not costlessly informed of any change in each supplier's price. So a customer at one firm—that is, an enterprise that has customers—would not immediately know about it if another firm reduced its price, possibly making it a cheaper supplier

of the good (of which the customer is a buyer) than the firm from which he or she buys currently. Hence a firm, if it wants to increase its stock of customers—to gain a larger market share—must "invest" in a larger market share by accepting the need to set a *lower price* than the other suppliers' price (or lower than their average price) *for some time,* since it takes time for the news of the lower price to spread. Once it has the extra customers, it can put its price back up to the generally prevailing industry level.

3. So in such "customer markets" a supplier cannot simply snap its fingers to obtain more buyers; it must make a concession in its price until the desired number of additional customers have been attracted. An interesting implication is shown to follow: The "competition" of firms in such a customer market will *not* generally drive the price down to the point where revenue just covers costs of production; a positive profit remains, since the price has to cover those "investment" costs of getting customers away from other firms. This investment hurdle is a sort of barrier to entry.

4. What are the consequences of this "mark-up" of price over cost-per-unit for resource allocation? For anyone's welfare? After all, maybe everyone is an owner of shares in these firms, so everyone is a receiver of the "return" from this "customer investment" (a return frequently called "good will"). Answer: The wage rate is driven down—driven below the marginal product of labor. If you join the labor force, you will not be paid (even without regard to taxes) your marginal product—contrary to the good-old classical theory. Hence people's incentives to join the labor force, work long hours, and so forth are eroded. The situation could be corrected, though (to a degree), and in doing so people would find themselves with expanded choice; all could be made better off.

5. The same theory is next used to shed light on the determination of product quality rather than the price of the product. In the classical theory it is supposed that if you, a supplier, chose to build a better mousetrap, say, the entire population of mousetrap consumers would "beat a path to your door"—instantly, that is. The modern theory says that consumers would not immediately know your mousetrap was better, or maybe even improved! Only by the gradual spread of reports by word of mouth from satisfied users of the new trap would the information make its way through market. So if you have other lucrative investment opportunities—if you have to charge yourself an "opportunity cost" for lending to yourself funds for the better mousetrap project—you may decide to reject the mousetrap project, even though it would earn *some* positive rate of return (because consumers would pay more for the better trap as they heard about it), because it would not pay enough—that investment would be

unprofitable, uneconomical. Conclusion: although a better product would be worth it to the consumer, the transaction cost faced by suppliers in spreading the information—getting them to try it, and so forth—could deter suppliers from marketing it. There is a tendency for product quality to be too low, alongside a price that is too high.

6. The same analysis applies to product safety. Build a safer home, a better food processor, or a less flammable passenger aircraft, and who will know, in the absence of expensive marketing efforts?

7. According to the modern theory, then, product markets do not possess the perfect efficiency claimed for them by classical doctrine. So it may be possible to justify, on a case-by-case basis, certain governmental interventions in the interest of promoting efficiency. Inevitably this raises the controversy over whether regulatory agencies become the captives of the regulatees and in some instances do more harm than good.

8. Another model of how customer markets may generate an equilibrium price level that is above the competitive equilibrium level of neoclassical theory is built on "judging quality by price."

9. When consumers are not costlessly mobile, contract theory offers two reasons why a firm may choose to offer a single, or nonvarying, price to its patrons rather than having a multiple-price, or variable-price, policy in which the price is determined according to the state of the demand and other contingencies.

CONCEPTS INTRODUCED

modern versus classical view of markets	market share	implicit contract
transaction costs	customer-market equilibrium	risk spreading
customer market	pure profit	monitoring and verifying contract compliance
good will	consumerism	
	signaling by price	

STUDY QUESTIONS

1. According to neoclassical market theory, the equilibrium of a perfectly competitive industry has the property that price (actual and expected) equals marginal cost, as chapter 10 explained; and in the "long run," once capital and land have time enough to enter or leave the industry, equilibrium has the further property that price equals unit cost (cost per unit of output, or "average cost"). Hence there is no "profit" or "loss," only a normal return to capital, which is merely sufficient to pay the interest on the loan that would be needed to buy the industry's capital stock—the plant and equipment and so forth.

What is the treatment of entry in the neoclassical model that leads the model to the implication that "profit"—a return in excess of the interest on the capital stock—is eliminated?

2. According to the modern theory of some markets, the equilibrium of an industry selling in a customer market has the property that the price is above both marginal cost and unit cost. Hence the return received by a firm—the revenue from output and sales minus wages, material costs, and depreciation on capital (if it owns its capital)—exceeds the interest on a loan sufficient to buy that capital stock; so there is a "profit," or "pure profit," received by the firm.

What is the treatment of information, its transmission and acquisition, in the customer-market model that, in general, causes firms *not* to "compete" the equilibrium price down to the perfectly competitive-equilibrium level? Why is the representative firm unwilling to "invest" further via a temporary price cut (temporary if not matched by the others) to try to take customers away from the other firms? What is being supposed here about the rate of interest, or rate of return, that a firm can obtain on other investments, such as plant and equipment?

3. If each year the returns (net of capital depreciation) of firms just equal the interest on their investments in physical capital—i.e., the rentals (net of depreciation) they could obtain by renting their equipment, etc., to other producers—the zero-profit case predicted by neoclassical equilibrium theory—then the market value of these firms cannot differ from the market price, hence the replacement cost, of their capital stock: That is, the value of the equity, or common shares, must be equal to the value of the plant and equipment if there is no debt outstanding; or, in general, the value of the shares plus the debt must equal the value of the capital (since shares must equal capital minus debt). Can you see why?

Consider the tax accountant firm H & R Block, Inc., the travel agency Thomas Cook Travel, the credit-card company American Express. Are they owners of a sizable capital stock for use in their operations? How does the replacement cost of their capital stock compare to their market value—to the total value of their equity shares, or common stock, and debt? To what is the discrepancy due?

It is sometimes said that many companies are worth *less* in the capital market than the value of their capital stock figured at replacement cost. (Even the ratio of their market value to the replacement cost of the capital stock uninstalled—the equipment and factory space not yet assembled and hooked up into a turnkey, ready-to-operate plant—which is often called the "q" ratio—is estimated to be less than 1 for many firms.) Does it follow that there is something wrong with the customer-market model (unless perchance all these firms happen not to operate in customer markets, which is as bad as being "wrong")? Or are there other factors that may in some cases solve the puzzle? What if, as chapter 17 discusses, these firms are mismanaged and the shareowners cannot oust the management?

4. In the Ferris-wheel scene from *The Third Man,* quoted at the top of this chapter, Harry is venturing a justification for his dealing in dangerously impure penicillin:

a. There are no consequences from it, for if he didn't do it somebody else would.

b. Doctors and patients need not buy it. *Caveat emptor!*

c. In the capitalist ethic, one's self-interest is the sole standard.

d. There is no possibility of perfect safety; it's a matter of degree.

e. In the prevailing ethic, the small risk of death does not outweigh the vast fortune to be made.

Which one was it? How would a cost-benefit test differ? Is it possible that all persons in society would prefer a stricter safety standard than the standards favored by people as product suppliers (as employees, employers, owners) according to their sympathy for the potential victims of safety accidents?

5. It has been suggested that it is all right to permit unregulated product safety decisions by suppliers provided a consumer suffering injury can bring suit for damages. Discuss.

CHAPTER 16

Labor Markets and the Firm: "Incentive Wages" and Unemployment

DANCE-BAR MANAGER:
We hired all we need the other day.
MARIA BRAUN:
Hire me and you won't need the others.

Hannah Schygulla in *The Marriage of Maria Braun* (1980)

Marx, in a famous phrase of his, wrote of the reserve army of the unemployed. Marx had his eyes open, at least. Classical and neoclassical economists remained blind to the presence of any unemployment at all. On the other hand, Marx went nowhere with his observation. People are not continuously employed, it is true; but phone booths and ski lifts are not continuously occupied either. Does most unemployment have a different explanation? Is this special unemployment of people bad? If so, what to do about it? Unanswered questions!

♦ Marx had no explanation for the extensive unemployment he perceived as normal, or endemic, in the market system. Presumably the unfortunate conscripts into the "reserve army" are eager to be discharged from their involuntary "service" outside the factories. Why, then, are the owners of the factories so good to the workers who are fortunate enough to be working and earning a wage inside the factories? Why don't the enterprises therefore cut their wage rates?

+ Marx could offer no argument why the volume of unemployment that is normal in the market system is *too large* in some sense. Lacking a tool kit with the theoretical concepts for making such an argument, he could only take that claim for granted.

No economist would ever lose sight of the broad similarity between the markets for labor in the various lines of work and the markets for goods and factors in general: the importance of supply factors and demand factors in determining "price" and "quantity." Yet contemporary economists have come to sense that the markets for labor are, on the whole, unlike the markets for commodities and nonhuman productive factors in important respects:

+ In some markets—think of rented trucks, hotel rooms, apartments, etc.— there *are* idle resources: vacant rooms, unemployed vehicles, and so on. But we realize the problem is that the rooms and trucks cannot all pick up themselves to the places where demands strike. In contrast, the idleness of resources in the labor markets seems much larger, on the whole, than what can be explained by workers being in the wrong places. The unemployment story in most labor markets is much more than just immobility.
+ Sellers of commodities are not "rationed" in the quantities they can sell. The seller of live hogs or No. 2 fuel oil or cotton is not found carrying involuntary stocks. Every hog seller knows that, although it may be necessary to accept a small concession in the price to do it, he can move his hogs! In contrast, the supplier to most labor markets *cannot* be sure he can sell his customary services—even if he is willing to accept a wage below the going wage for the job. Sellers of labor, typically, are "rationed." Not all are hired.

If these impressions are correct—most economists have little doubt over them—it is necessary to go beyond neoclassical economics for an adequate understanding of labor markets.

The modern theory of labor-market equilibrium, built up in recent decades, offers some answers to the puzzles. It explains

+ why unemployment is normal in all or most labor markets—even under equilibrium, or surprise-free, conditions;
+ why the equilibrium volume of unemployment is larger than what could be generated by mobility costs and the accident of where demand for labor occurs;
+ why there is an element of "involuntary unemployment" in the joblessness we observe in most labor markets—an element that the suppliers of labor (workers) can do nothing to reduce;
+ why this involuntary unemployment is a bad thing—why, as a result, the equilibrium volume of unemployment is too large.

This chapter will present the gist of that modern equilibrium theory and its arguments that there is involuntary and excessive unemployment in all or most labor markets.

It will then go on to discuss two other features of labor markets illuminated by modern market theory: discrimination in hiring and the functions of labor unions. An extra, optional topic is the phenomenon of an "implicit contract," an unwritten bargain, between employer and employee about what the firm will do in the event of unanticipated disturbances—shocks to demand or to costs.

THE FIRM: ITS PERSONNEL PROBLEM AND WAGE POLICY

Modern market theory argues that there is a fundamental flaw in the neoclassical theory of how all or most labor markets work.

According to the *neoclassical* theory, the wage in every labor market *clears the market*. The wage level, in other words, is almost always at the market-clearing level. This means, among other things, that *every supplier* of labor to a labor market—everyone who is willing and able to "do the job" at the going wage—finds employment; any observed idleness must be voluntary. Hence anyone jobless at first is at no disadvantage. If, to the contrary, the number of qualified persons desiring (in view of the wage being paid) to take the job *exceeded* the number of jobs actually held, some frustrated suppliers would be unable to obtain employment in this job, and hence the market would *not* be cleared. But in such an event, neoclassical theory argues, the competition of workers for these jobs would drive down the wage until the number desiring the job just equals the number of jobs held—until, that is, the market clears.

The diagram illustrates this aspect of the neoclassical competitive process in terms of the *supply curve* for a particular labor market—labeled N^S. The wage, v, is measured along the vertical axis. The horizontal axis measures the number of persons employed, denoted N, and also the number of persons supplied, N^S.

If there were more people desiring the job than there were jobs held, the situation would be like point a, *off* and to the *left* of the supply curve. At the wage level v_1 the amount

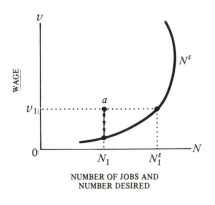

NUMBER OF JOBS AND
NUMBER DESIRED

of labor supplied, namely N_1^S, would be greater than the number of persons employed, N_1. But then the jobless would begin underbidding the job holders, the latter would match, and so on, thus driving the wage *down* in the direction of the supply curve. Market clearing implies a wage-employment outcome *on* the supply curve.*

But the proponents of modern equilibrium theory argue that labor markets cannot behave that way. They maintain that the firm simply could not operate, could not produce, if it paid each employee only the market-clearing wage for the job. Certain managerial problems that firms have dictate payment of wages to most or all employees above the market-clearing levels. The argument depends upon what modern theory sees to be the nature and problems of the firm.

What Do Firms Do? The Employee Side

The previous chapter—the first act, so to speak—introduced a principal character in the modern story of the firm—the customer. The analysis there led to an insight into what things distinguish the firm from productive enterprises in general:

◆ A firm constantly monitors and regulates its prices and products to protect or enhance its attractiveness as a supplier to its customers, so that it can go on having customers to supply in the future.

Another leading character is the employee. A great deal of the managerial functioning of the firm, in the modern view, has to do with the availability and performance of employees. The employee, like the customer, is a valuable asset of the firm and thus receives the same kid-glove treatment. Hence:

◆ A firm constantly monitors and regulates their wages and working conditions to protect its attractiveness among its employees as a desirable employer so that it can go on having employees in the future.

Besides securing the availability of employees the enterprise may have another problem to solve—that of actually getting some work out of them when they are available:

◆ A firm may have to supervise, or monitor, employees' performance in some jobs and use the "carrot and the stick"—prizes and punishments—to create an incentive for the employee to do his or her part.

---

* In very *thin* markets for labor—film directing, house painting, mountaineer-guiding, and so forth—in which the demand is intermittent, market clearing means that each supplier of the labor can improve his *chances* of a job by lowering his fee; so if he is idle at the moment it is because he is speculating that a call will come shortly. In this case, idleness may be called voluntary. In equilibrium, every supplier is able at the same wage to obtain employment with the same frequency as other identical suppliers are doing; hence newcomers are not disadvantaged.

Hence the enterprise in its modern image, called here the firm, may have as many as two personnel problems not possessed by enterprises conforming to the classical image—the task of protecting its investment in its employees and the task of obtaining a profitable performance from them. The firm's response to these nonclassical personnel problems, modern theory argues, involves adopting a nonclassical wage policy. To explore this modern argument let us first take up the second personnel problem, the problem of employees' shirking their duties at work.

The Wage As an Incentive to Deter Shirking

It is not unusual for firms to find it expensive, but not impossible, to monitor—to observe and measure—the effort of their employees in the performance of certain jobs. It would be enormously expensive to supervise every gardener or groundskeeper in a large city park or estate—and who would supervise the supervisors all the time? Police, who are especially hard to monitor, have a word for sleeping or resting while on patrol duty—they call it cooping. Even at firms in which some employees are concentrated in a small space, where any sighted person can see end to end, nonstop monitoring of employees' efforts can be quite costly.

- Is that telephone-order or telephone-complaint taker pretending to have that long transaction, or is he really talking to his girlfriend or his doctor or his stockbroker? To be sure a supervisor might have to listen in.
- Is the assembly-line worker right that he has not taken more than the permitted coffee and restroom breaks or is the spare worker who is there to fill in right that *he* is not being left with enough time for his own breaks? A referee may be needed to monitor and resolve such disputes.

Suppose now that all the firms in some industry have been following a *neoclassical wage policy* toward their employees in some or all operations. (As an example we might have in mind sales personnel in the department store industry.) Every firm, then, has been making it a practice to pay those employees only the *market-clearing wage*—a rate of pay just low enough that there is no surplus of workers (no reserve army) also desiring to have that job. (The moment some would-be salesperson appears who is willing to work for less, the industrywide wage drops until the market for sales personnel is once again cleared.) Such a wage policy would be jeopardized by the shirking problem. Yet it is imaginable it could work:

The firm would have to make it a fixed policy, known to all, to dismiss any employee the first time he or she was caught shirking a single duty. (Otherwise the firm would be filled with employees who came only to shirk until finally dismissed.) Further, the firm would have to monitor "every move" of these employees in order to detect shirking as soon as it occurred. (Otherwise an employee would start shirking and continue until first caught, then move on to another employer at the same market-clearing wage.)

Such a managerial strategy, if feasible, would be effective. It would solve the problem of shirking all right. The moment an employee shirked it would be detected, the employee would be dismissed for his misstep, and instantly the firm would bid in the perfect labor market for a new employee to replace the departed one. Hardly a second of precious employee effort would be lost in the process!

But would that managerial strategy, with its high supervision costs, be the most profitable for a firm? A wise manager would wonder whether it might not make sense to pay the firm's employees a wage *premium*, an extra wage payment beyond what the other firms (with their market-clearing wage) pay. Then, the manager would reason, the employees would be aware of the penalty they would pay if caught shirking: they would lose the premium paid by this wisely managed firm. Hence the employees would have an incentive not to be caught shirking.

♦ Then the firm could get along with intermittent (rather than continuous) monitoring—with checking employees' efforts at randomly chosen, and hence unpredictable, times—to deter shirking. The employees would sense the risk that if and when they shirk they would be caught and have to pay the penalty.

Such a managerial strategy, with a suitable increase of the pay rate and a suitable reduction in supervision costs, might *increase the firm's profit*. The saving in supervision costs resulting from the greatly reduced monitoring of the employees could outweight the increase in the firm's wage costs (plus the increase in costs to the firm resulting from any increased shirking that employees take a chance on doing). We have here an unusual application of a general principle in political economy: Rather than have a resource planner, or manager, direct every move of the resources, *it may be much more effective, less inefficient, to provide the resources with incentives to direct themselves into productive uses*.

If just one firm hit upon that more profitable management strategy there would be little more to the story. Following its decision to offer the wage premium, there would be a surplus of workers—an "excess supply"—desiring to be employees at that firm. (At the other firms there would be no shirking and a *low* wage!) But those would-be employees at the premium-paying firm, the workers who comprise the "excess supply," would not be denied employment in their preferred occupation. They certainly would not be unemployed. Most would be found employees in the other, nonpremium-paying firms. The world would neither know nor care about their yearning for what might have been, a premium-paying job.

But what are the other firms doing? If one firm would calculate a profit from paying a higher wage, why not the others? The plot thickens! For simplicity, suppose that all the firms are identical: They are in the same boat and think alike. Then, if *one* firm or more, believing the others will keep their wage at the market-clearing level, calculates a profit from raising *its* wage by 1 percent or 2 percent or whatever, *all* the firms, being like-minded and like-situated, will therefore raise their wage by the same percentage amount to the same new and higher level.

- ◆ It follows immediately that the industrywide wage will not rest at the market-clearing level at which we assumed it started. The firms, if their observations ever *did* lead them to *expect* the industry to pay that market-clearing wage, would in fact all boost their wage to a *higher level*. Hence our original position, in which the industry wage was expected to be once again the market-clearing wage level of *neoclassical* equilibrium, is *not truly an equilibrium* in our story—it is a *disequilibrium*. If firms expect one another to keep their wage at the neoclassical level, they won't actually do it. It is not a self-fulfilling expectation.

The market-clearing wage level of neoclassical equilibrium, then, is *not the equilibrium wage level* according to modern theory. Where *is* the equilibrium wage level? What is the equilibrium like? This much is immediately clear: Once all the firms have raised their wage above the market-clearing level by the same percentage amount—the same x percent, whatever x is—each firm will be disappointed: No firm will actually have obtained the wage premium, the wage differential, it expected its wage increase to achieve.

Finding that all the other firms have raised the wage to the same higher level, there are just two reactions the individual firm could have according to modern theory. The firm could raise its own wage further, thus trying again to achieve the relative advantage that it failed to obtain the first time. *Or* the firm could lower its wage a bit in view of the unexpected costliness of its strategy; but certainly the industry wage will not find its equilibrium level at the original neoclassical market-clearing level—it was *proved* to us that if firms expected that wage level industrywide they would all set a higher wage! No matter which way the firms react to their disappointment, the *equilibrium wage level will certainly be above the market-clearing wage level of neoclassical theory.* According to the modern theory we are examining, many jobs offer *incentive wages,* often called *efficiency wages,* which *exceed* the market-clearing level.

In both diagrams here, the *wage reaction curve* represents the idea that if the individual firm expects the others to set the *neoclassical* wage level, denoted v_n, the firm will set its own wage *above* that level. The *upper* diagram has the additional property that if the firm *expects* a higher wage level it will accordingly set

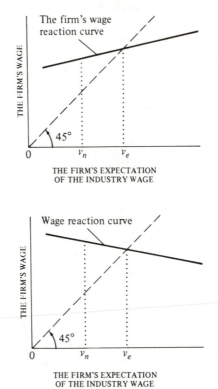

The firm's wage reaction curve

THE FIRM'S WAGE

45°

0   v_n v_e

THE FIRM'S EXPECTATION
OF THE INDUSTRY WAGE

Wage reaction curve

THE FIRM'S WAGE

45°

0   v_n v_e

THE FIRM'S EXPECTATION
OF THE INDUSTRY WAGE

its own wage still *higher than before*. (Its own wage is an increasing function of the expected industry wage.) In any case the equilibrium wage, where every identical firm's actual wage equals the expected wage, occurs at a level, v_e, above v_n.

In the lower diagram the wage reaction curve also says that if the firm expects the industrywide wage to be v_n it will set its own wage above that level. But this *lower* diagram then says that once the firm comes to *expect* a higher wage level it will set its own wage *lower* than before. Yet, clearly, this difference from the upper diagram leaves undisturbed the conclusion that the equilibrium wage level—the expectation of which induces the individual firm to choose that same wage level—occurs at some level, denoted v_e, that is nonetheless *above* v_n.

What can be said about the equilibrium besides its higher wage? What is it like? We can see right away that it is quite unlike the market-clearing position, the position that we assumed the firms began in. True, the attempts of all the firms to increase their respective relative wage are mutually defeating. (The average firm is foredoomed to pay the average wage.) Yet these frustrated attempts to offer a wage premium do have an important chain of effects. In their futile efforts to "outpay" one another the firms drive up the *normal* pay; they drive up the going wage, or competitive wage, which is the minimum a firm must pay to hire anyone. This is *before* firms decide to respond by adjusting their employee rosters. Yes, initially each firm was *happy* to pay "extra" in order to have an edge over the other firms; but now that all firms have done the same, each firm must pay more just to remain competitive with the others. This rise in the cost of hiring has, in turn, important effects:

- The rise in the cost of hiring workers will cause the firms to offer fewer jobs—there will be a *reduction in the quantity of labor demanded*. Hence less employment. Fewer jobs held.
- At the same time, this rise in the industrywide wage in the familiar case will cause an *increase in the quantity of labor supplied*—more workers seeking the job. (At the very least, there is not going to be a decrease in the quantity supplied as large as the reduction in the quantity demanded; that would mean market clearing again, this time at a higher wage, and we are taking it for granted that there is one and only one market-clearing wage level, not two.)
- Therefore, in the equilibrium, the quantity of workers supplied *exceeds* the quantity demanded. More jobs are sought than offered and held. Some people desiring such jobs cannot get one. Thus the equilibrium involves *involuntary unemployment*.

Figure 16–1 illustrates this striking feature of the labor-market equilibrium.

There is another feature to note, and a paradoxical one. Because there is some degree of unemployment in the equilibrium, firms do not have to fret that their employees will shirk all the time unless continuously monitored. The employee will be grateful that he or she is one of the lucky ones to be employed. To be discharged would mean a spell of hardship—of uncertain duration—in the reserve army of the unemployed. Hence the firm need not monitor its employees continuously. If the firm just monitors them sporadically, but frequently enough, timing its inspections in some random way, it will be able to discourage the employees from shirking and thus taking the *risk* of being caught. The equilibrium is *not* one of continuous supervision, unlike the position with which we have been imagining the firms started.

- This point helps us understand *why* the firm won't be interested in listening to unemployed workers who say, "Hire us, and we'll work for less." The firm knows that if it hired them at inferior pay they would be more interested in taking a chance on getting caught shirking than would employees (such as the ones it has) who are paid at the going wage. The firm would have to step up the frequency with which it monitors the new, and only *apparently* "cheap," employees.

This "supervision story" is *one* demonstration of a modernist theme—the tendency to involuntary joblessness in the world, even under equilibrium (correct expectations) conditions. If all labor markets are afflicted by supervision problems there will be involuntary unemployment economywide. And the applicability of the supervision story is rather general, in fact: Airlines bid up the wage paid to aircraft pilots in order to give them an incentive to

FIGURE 16–1: Equilibrium with "Incentive Wage" and Resulting "Job Rationing"

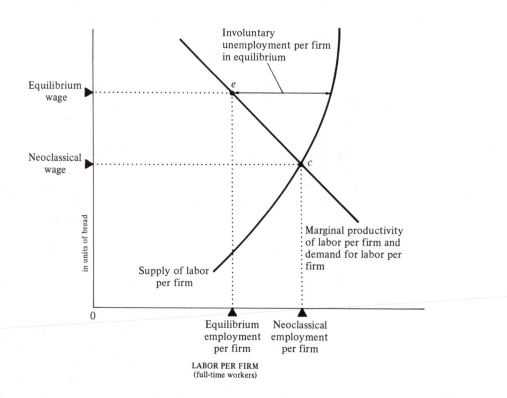

The diagram plots the supply of labor *per firm* as a function of the wage, measured in terms of a consumer good such as bread. The other curve shows how the marginal productivity of labor per firm diminishes—following the "law" of diminishing marginal productivity of labor—with increasing levels of labor per firm. The marginal productivity is likewise measured in units of the consumer good obtainable with the extra output produced.

It does not matter whether we conceive of the diagram as referring to a single industry in a multi-industry economy or as referring to the econ-omy as a whole (as if it were a one-industry economy).

According to neoclassical theory, the marginal productivity curve is the demand curve for labor under conditions of perfect competition in both the product market and the labor market. Competitive equilibrium occurs at point *c*, where the wage and the marginal productivity of labor are equal.

Modern theory, in contrast, argues that the true equilibrium is at a higher wage with lower employment as a result, such as at point *e*.

stay healthy, since it would be too expensive to give them thorough physical exams before every flight. Professional football and baseball clubs inflate the wage of their players to give them an incentive to try harder; with the evidence of the season the club can decide which players did not and sell them to another club as an object lesson. The alcoholism that has plagued production in the Soviet Union and some Western countries is also an incentive problem hinging on the costliness of monitoring the workers' behavior—in this case their behavior away from work rather than on the job. Yet *not all* the evidence of payment of "incentive wages" can be traced to the costliness of monitoring employees. Here, briefly, is another model of the "incentive wage" to demonstrate the tendency to involuntary unemployment.

THE WAGE AS AN INCENTIVE TO DETER QUITTING

A great deal of production, ever since workers left the cottage industries of preindustrial Europe involves the collaboration of highly specialized employees. Smith's legendary pin factory will be recalled. Often, however, the employees in a firm will have a certain amount of knowledge or information that is special to that firm—that is *firm-specific*. Take a firm engaged in textbook publishing. There is copy editing, art work, design, production, and so forth—all performed by specialists. But in addition these employees are walking storehouses of information about the particular projects going on at the firm, and they have some knowledge of the policies, or strategies, of the firm—*which employees elsewhere do not*.

Thus a firm in the publishing business can be said to have made an investment in its employees. The firm *uses* many kinds of capital. It makes use of photocopiers, typewriters, word processors—the stuff called physical capital. It also makes use of the human capital that is represented by the training of the artist in art school. The firm has not necessarily paid the cost of acquiring that capital, however. It did not pay for the art school, and perhaps it did not buy its photocopiers—it may have leased them. But even if it did purchase its photocopiers it does not have to worry that its photocopiers will some day walk out to join another firm: the investment is safe, at least in that respect.

♦ When the firm pays the cost, measured in time spent by managers and other employees, of "showing the ropes" to the new employee—acquainting the person with the procedures of the firm, introducing the recruit to the other employees, directing the recruit to the restroom—and pays the further cost of "familiarizing" the employee with a particular project—instructing the person about the firm's intentions regarding that project, and so on—the firm is making investments that it risks losing. The firm stands to lose such investments lock, stock, and barrel if the employee decides to quit.

Here, then, is a managerial problem, the problem of employee quitting, that is somewhat like the employee shirking problem. *If* all the firms in the publishing industry were to pay *only the market-clearing wage*, quitting would be rampant. And that would be costly for employers. The moment an employee, filled with information on the latest projects and deeply ingrained with the traditions of the old firm, decided it was time for a change of scene, the firm would have to bear the cost of breaking in a replacement. Yet as long as employers made it a practice to pay only market-clearing wages, employees would pay no penalty for moving to another firm. (The worker choosing to change firms might have to accept a lower wage at the new firm in order to unseat an existing employee—though not if, threatened with the slightest wage cut, the existing employee chose to exit, possibly, "trade places." But this cost of moving to the preferred job, if there is a cost at all, does not reflect the employer's investment and will not indemnify the employer.)

What could a firm do to meet this quitting problem? As the reader will have guessed, a smart firm would decide to pay its employees more—more than what the other firms were paying. As recipients of premium wages from their employer, these employees would have *something to lose* in the event they quit: They would lose this wage supplement, or wage bonus, that their employer—unique among the firms in the industry—was paying. That aggressive new wage policy, the firm could see, would reduce quitting.

The rest of the "quitting story" has the same plot as the shirking story. *All* the firms raise the wage in the expectation of establishing wage premium. If all the firms are identical, every firm is at each stage disappointed that the other firms have raised their wage as much. Yet after revising its expectation of the wage the others are going to be paying, no firm could afford to retreat; each firm would be impelled to try again and again to establish a wage premium as long as its quitting problem remained no less acute. (Conceivably this wage escalation could go on until the industry could not afford to hire labor.)

But this "escalation" of the industry wage *will* set in motion an equilibrating force that tends to limit the rise of the industry wage—to a level short of wiping out all jobs in the industry.

- As the industry wage is pushed up, each firm sees that the expected benefit from its own wage increase—via the reduction of turnover costs expected to result—has not materialized; only the expected cost has. Yet it can hardly afford—less than before!—to go back to the former wage even partway: It would lose its employees to its competitors as long as there is no unemployment, the labor market clearing. The cost of labor to each firm is thus pushed up. As a consequence each firm will be induced to trim its labor force, to reduce the number of jobs offered.

- The contraction in the quantity of employment offered by the industry in response to the rise in the industry wage will create unemployment in the industry—job rationing. As the industry wage climbs and industry employment shrinks, unemployment mounts. This increased unemployment lessens the firms' quitting problem—workers see there is an excess of job seekers, so they are less inclined to quit. Once the industry wage—and the unemployment!—are so high as to eliminate the firms' motive to pay a wage premium, the equilibrium wage level has been reached. *With unemployment.*

The modernist school offers two models, the shirking model and the quitting model, in support of their thesis that labor markets do not clear—that there is involuntary unemployment—even in equilibrium conditions. Do the neoclassically-minded theorists have anything to say in defense of their claim that markets, even labor markets, *do* clear? Yes. Take the quitting problem. They suggest that the very smart firm (from which the others will learn) would not attempt to solve the problem by raising its wage above the market-clearing level—that would not be very "cost-effective," since some employees would not have quit even without the elevated wage. It would be *more* profitable instead for a firm to require of each new employee a refundable deposit, to be refunded (with interest, on retirement) if the employee never quits, and to return to the employees via a wage increase the average per employee of the deposits not refunded (because some former employees have quit despite the loss of the deposit). That way, the average net remuneration per year—calculated by averaging over the quitters and stayers—would be no lower for the prospective employee contemplating joining the firm. But the firm would be exacting a stiff penalty on employees for quitting; and by setting the deposit at the right level the firm could make the employee bear the whole cost—the cost incurred by the firm in breaking in a replacement—of choosing to quit. The incentive not to quit would be stronger, and profitability accordingly greater. (Similarly, it would be more profitable instead for the firm to require an entrance fee from new employees for admission to the firm. That scheme would have the same effectiveness.) It can also be seen that profit sharing with rights fully vested—that is, retainable even if the employee quits—only *after* years of service is also a device to discourage quitting. By such diabolically ingenious devices, neoclassicists argue, every firm could deter uneconomic quitting—quits the benefit of which would have been less than the real cost—and thus achieve more profitable operation *without* having to elevate the net remuneration of its employees above the market-clearing level.

In their rebuttal the modernists make two replies (although conceding that the neoclassicists have made a useful point). The most obvious reply is that a firm relying on such a penalty—a sort of tax—to deter quitting would be suspected by naturally anxious workers of possibly operating a racket. Any worker contemplating joining the firm, and not having an insider's knowledge of its operation, would worry that he or she would be exposed to the danger—the *moral hazard*—that the firm will harass its employees until they quit, just in order to keep employees' deposits or entrance fees. Another reply is that prospective employees, to join the firm, would have to be compensated not just for the *average* loss per employee of the deposit or entrance fee; nearly every employee would also have to be compensated for the worsened variability, or speculativeness, in the pay-off: either a large pay-off, if not quitting, or a low pay-off, possibly a negative pay-off, if quitting (and thus losing the deposit). Hence workers might demand an arm and leg to take a chance on a firm adopting such anti-quitting schemes. Conclusion: We *will* see gold watches and silver trays on retirement. But we will also see net remuneration above market-clearing levels, since gold watches are not effective enough at deterring quitting.

If Involuntary Unemployment Is Bad, What Is to Be Done?

In showing the possibility of an equilibrium with involuntary unemployment, modern economic theory has taken us a long way from the neoclassical view of markets. There is no question that the Smithian image of the free market economy—everyone free to do the things that are best for himself without hurting others, so there are no unused opportunities left for mutual gains, only gains at the expense of others—has been dealt a serious blow. Recall that the young would-be worker "joining the labor force" is quite willing to strike a bargain with a firm at the mutually advantageous terms, "Hire me and I'll do it for a little less (or do it a bit better)." But the bargain cannot be struck. As the firm sees it, a person who would work for less would be *worth* that much less (if not less than that) *because the worker would have that much less "incentive" to work and the firm cannot trust the would-be employee to keep his or her end of the bargain.*

♦ This failure of labor markets to achieve certain mutually advantageous "exchanges," to which modernist theory points, is like the dilemma of mutually suspicious farmers contemplating a cooperative venture. Becoming knowledgeable about the chances that the other will "back out" and staying informed about whether the other one is "doing his agreed share" may be prohibitively expensive or impossible. Hence no deal.

There is no doubt, then, that this involuntary unemployment is bad. It is an unfortunate side effect, or third-party effect, that the employers in trying to guard against the shirking and quitting of their own employees *inflict on others*—the workers whom they would otherwise have employed in addition. The result is a failure of labor markets to achieve ideal efficiency. But what as a practical matter can be done about it? What can be done to shrink the pool of involuntarily unemployed workers—the pool that young would-be workers must swim in until fished out by an employer—without making employed workers (who may have swum in that pool) and owners of firms (who may have once been unemployed also) worse off?

There is not necessarily much or anything that could be done that would work and not harm anyone. Some things are regrettable but are not genuine *problems,* because they have no solutions! The government could campaign against shirking the way it campaigns against littering, instilling the old ethic of "An honest day's work for a day's pay." But the benefit might not repay the cost. The government might turn to cheap credit or to public works programs, useful when the economy is out of equilibrium and mired in a depression; but it would not make the equilibrium less inefficient and better for all.

- A package of governmental measures featuring a *tax on quitting* might improve everyone's "life chances," if designed just right. With quitting taxed, firms would not be driven to raise wages so high (since the benefit of a given wage hike would be smaller). The unemployment pool would shrink. All might have the prospect of a gain "on the average" over their lifetimes.

- A fiscal package containing a *tax on wages* in excess of the estimated market-clearing level might be capable of the same trick—a universal gain, or "Pareto improvement"—if the instruments are set at the right levels.

There may, then, be some unorthodox, unclassical measures the government could take to *improve* the market equilibrium, measures that work by shrinking the equilibrium pool of the involuntarily unemployed. But there do not appear to be any measures that would *perfect* the equilibrium, banishing the causes of the wasteful unemployment. The government would never have the knowledge needed to set every tax penalty and subsidy in every occupation and industry at exactly the right levels.

Socialist theoreticians suggest that socialism meets these problems. The visage of Chairman Mao, for example, conjures up a magical cooperativeness among workers. (The expression "Gung ho!" is Chinese for "Work together!") Market socialism, however, is in no better position than market capitalism to meet them. (Socialist plant managers will combat quitting, etc., with incentives.) The centrally planned socialist economies, of course, are different: They seem to be able to get young people into jobs in a hurry and keep them there. But, on the other hand, shirking and absenteeism seems to be rife in such economies. The unemployment occurs inside the production units, among the "employed." Thus socialism apparently cannot really solve the problem either.

MORE LABOR PROBLEMS

The focus by modern theory on the costly obstacles to information and knowledge contributes to the understanding of other phenomena observed in labor markets. This section will discuss a few more of the problems and puzzles in labor markets on which modern theory sheds light.

DISCRIMINATION

Discrimination covers a multitude of sins. One of the most familiar kinds of discrimination occurs when all persons in a group are "tarred with the same brush"—treated as though all are alike, without any distinctions. When the fire department sets height and weight qualifications it is discriminating: It is refusing to look at each individual applicant on his or her own merits, as if it had made a prejudgment that no one lighter or shorter could possibly be fit for the job. Why is the fire department doing it? Evidently the department is using what it *knows* or *thinks it knows* about a *group*, here the group with less-than-qualifying height and weight, in order to save costs (for the same product) or increase productivity (for the same costs), which is the same thing. By declining to consider applications of persons who do not meet the stated qualifications, which is a device called screening, the department can narrow the spending of its budget for testing applicants' capacities to potential applicants who have statistically (as a group) a better chance of passing the test—the applicants who are not so light or short; that way the department can expect to improve the yield, measured in test passers, from its testing budget. The example points to a general lesson:

♦ Some hiring discrimination by firms comes about because firms cannot costlessly inform themselves about each potential employee's capabilities. How can a firm tell? So a firm draws inferences—makes bets—about each potential employee by making use of all the information the firm does have, including information about the groups or categories to which he or she belongs and the firm's beliefs—or worse, stereotypes—about those groups. This is often called *statistical discrimination.*

Aware of this phenomenon, governments have enacted an array of fair-employment, equal-opportunity, and affirmative-action programs aimed at combating discrimination.

THE RAT RACE

In a world where workers are diverse, as just recognized, firms will naturally value all information that (in their judgment) reflects on the capabilities of a prospective employee, and, up to a point, they will pay to acquire such information—through interviewing, pre-job testing, on-the-job trials, and so forth. Aware that firms have a problem of selecting employees, centuries of young men and women trying to get ahead have hit on a strategy to get selected: Try to signal your superiority, or at least your own confidence in your superiority, by achieving something to stand out from the crowd. How to do that? Not by teen-age records for pizzas delivered or cookies sold or days atop a flag pole. Demonstrating a capacity for hard work would not be evidence to a firm that the person would be a harder-working employee than anyone else; on the contrary, the firm might worry that the person felt the world owed him or her something. However, by going on to get a college education, a master's degree, a doctorate, possibly another doctorate, the person could signal something of value to the firm: that the person probably possesses talents that make obtaining this education easier than it would be for most others (or else the person is a glutton for punishment)—and some of these talents would make the person a desirable employee. Moral:

♦ Some of the preparation done by young people for their careers is motivated not by the worth of the training acquired once employed; it is done solely to demonstrate unusual talent at acquiring certain kind of training, a talent that some firms will be looking for. As *all* would-be employees practice this strategy, the average person's signal is still average! Hence the "rat race"—a competition to "win"—may escalate to quite wasteful levels.

RECRUITING

This chapter has taken up several features of the labor market that distinguish it from product markets. Yet the themes sounded by modern theory about product markets carry over to the market for labor. (In fact, there is some analogy between one feature of the labor market already discussed, the inability of a frictionally unemployed worker to find an employer for his services at the going wage, and the inability of the modern firm to sell all the output it would like to sell at the going price.)

Recall the modernist theme that, with informational frictions present in a product market, firms competing for customers would drive down the price, all right, but *not* all the way down to the marginal cost of production: At some point the gap between price and cost is such that, as the firm sees it, to attract more customers would not repay the costly "underbidding" (for a time) that it would require. This theme can be translated to labor markets marked by similar frictions:

◆ Employers compete for employees, of course, and in the process they bid up the wage for workers' services. But modern theory recognizes that in many labor markets (not necessarily all) the firm cannot costlessly contact and communicate the desired information about the work and wages there—advertising and recruiting drives are expensive. To attract more employees from its competitors for labor it must engage in "overbidding" until the new recruits have been attracted. But since such overbidding is expensive the firms stop short of bidding the wage all the way to the neoclassical level—where the wage equals the marginal productivity of labor. Hence labor in some markets is underpaid, according to modern theory. (The firms "collect the difference" as a return to "good will"—to starting the day with a stock of contented employees already on hand!)

Job Search

It is not only workers that are diverse, heterogeneous. So are firms. Not all firms are bakeries, for example; some make ovens, some produce circuses. (Even if they merge into conglomerates, the various operating divisions may be operated somewhat independently, for reasons of "division of labor.") If nothing else they will certainly differ in their locations; not all firms can locate in the Sears building in Chicago. In such a world we will observe *frictional unemployment,* even under equilibrium conditions.

The unemployed worker may be in equilibrium: He or she may have correct expectations, not unrealistic expectations, about the going wage in his or her sort of work. It is even possible that, in the line of work, there is no job rationing—you sell your labor the way you sell fish to a grocer or restaurant. Still the worker is unemployed at the current time, because he or she has not yet found one of those employers who would be willing to offer the going wage if the worker applied and cannot afford meanwhile to take *other* work (in some less desirable job) because *finding* the desired work requires actively *looking* for it, and you cannot search for it while being actively employed in another job.

◆ Some of the unemployment found in equilibrium is frictional, as square pegs pass up less suitable positions to search for square holes, etc. This

FIGURE 16–2: Equilibrium with Costly Recruiting

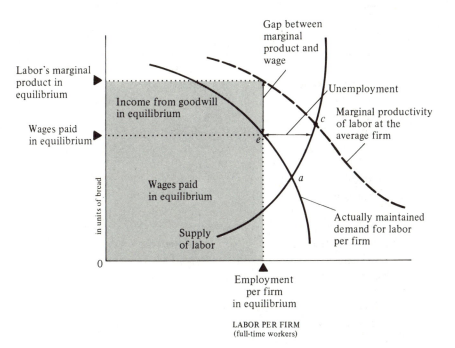

This diagram, like Figure 16–1, plots the supply of labor *per firm* and shows likewise how the marginal productivity of labor declines as the amount of employment per firm—the employment level at the "average" firm—is increased.

According to neoclassical theory the firms, if perfect competitors in both the labor market and product market, would bid up the wage and increase employment per firm to the levels indicated by point *c*. There the marginal product and wage are equal.

Modern equilibrium theory, however, argues the possibility that firms will fail to drive up the wage to the marginal product of labor because of a transactions cost—the costliness of recruiting the right sort of worker for each kind of work.

Hence, if the typical, or average, firm started at *c*, it would not replace all the employees who retire or die. There would result a surplus of workers, assuming that new suppliers of labor were arriving to keep the working-age population unchanged in size and other characteristics. These surplus workers would drive down the real wage until a new equilibrium was reached at a point like *a*. There is a consequent *gap* between the wage and the marginal product of labor.

If, however, we combine this feature of the modern equilibrium with the further feature of unemployment—either voluntary search unemployment or involuntary unemployment from job rationing or both—then the equilibrium is like point *e*. There is the gap *and* unemployment.

search activity is another manifestation of the costliness (for firms and workers) of transmitting and processing information. This is another reason, then, why *employment* is *less* than *labor supplied*.

UNSAFE MILLS

When Blake evoked those "dark Satanic mills" early in the Industrial Revolution he could not have imagined that in the not very distant future men earning their living in mines might sometimes pay an appalling death toll; that garment factories might prove fire traps for the women working in them; that someday an office building might become a towering inferno. The popular conviction today, of course, is that industrial safety was a grave problem requiring governmental legislation, and that much still remains to be done.

For the strictest neoclassical theoretician industrial safety is not a problem, not once equilibrium is attained, at any rate. Accidents do happen; similar accidents happen in the home, in children's cribs, and so forth. Each employee choosing an occupation and firm to join will balance benefits against costs, including the costs of accidents that are improbable yet terrible if they occur. Workers will be willing to pay something for extra safety at a firm by their willingness to work there for less than elsewhere. The rational firm will increase safety up to the point where still more safety would pose an extra cost exceeding what workers are willing to pay. The equilibrium outcome is efficient: more safety would be possible only at someone else's expense. Modern market theory takes a less rosy view:

◆ Modern theory, with its emphasis on the costliness of acquiring certain information, suggests that a firm offering greater safety to its employees might not be able to persuade them of the worth of what it was doing for them—and they might deny it anyway!—so the firm could not obtain an adequate reward for the extra safety.

UNIONS

Once there were unions operated by the firm, called company unions. We can see that they might perform a function. The firm genuinely wants to know about the interests—the preferences, in the more accurate lingo of the economist—of its employees. In *what form* do they want the going level of compensation? Do they prefer a bit less cash and cleaner restrooms? Do they want it in big bills or small bills? Front-loaded or in deferred compensation? Not that the owners of the firm, the stockholders, have any special concern about the employees. (Why should they care more, or even as much, about any employee than they do, or may, about malnourished children in the sub-Sahara or some friend or close relative struck by serious illness?)

The owners of the firm have an interest in knowing the most advantageous way of treating employees for a *given total expense* (and so, by the way, would any social planner who, in organizing various enterprises, valued economic efficiency).

We know, though, that these "unions" are not the real thing. In Western societies, with the traditions of individualism and independence, unions are worker-controlled, the creatures of the employees who comprise them. They express the solidarity of the employees as a group distinct and independent in its aims from the group of owners. The spread of these unions, however, has posed a problem for economic theory: How do they come into existence and survive? Certainly the early economists, Hume and Smith, Ricardo, and Marx, had no answers. They did not see any unions. The precise formulations of competitive equilibrium by the great neoclassical theorists of the twentieth century were equally unilluminating.

♦ In the neoclassical theory, there could not exist more than a handful of unions, if any. If the employees of the ABC Enterprise were to demand higher wages or anything else in their favor—cleaner restrooms, bigger pensions,—the enterprise could not afford to pay it, not one penny. If the enterprise were to pay higher compensation instantly a new competitor would spring up that would hire its labor on the equilibrium, competitive terms—and that would be able, as a result, to "undercut" the firm that was so foolish as to penalize itself with an above-competitive compensation to its employees! Knowing that, the ABC Enterprise would adamantly refuse to pay the higher wage insisted on by its recently unionized workers. And if it were so foolish *not* to refuse it would go out of business, being unable to recoup (though an above-competitive price) its above-competitive wage costs. In the neoclassical world, how can anyone get more than his marginal productivity? No one can. (The sole exception is the case of employees in a natural monopoly: By threatening strikes and other violence, *maybe* the employees can manage to obtain a share of the "pure profit"—the earnings on top of the returns to the capital invested—collected by "the gas company," "the electric company," and "the only paper in town." In these cases the workers, *if* the courts let them, *fight it out* with the owners over the distribution of the monopoly profit between owners and workers.)

In the sort of industries described by modern equilibrium theory, all that is changed. In that modernist setting there are things a union can do—functions it can perform—that will bring it into existence and permit it to survive:

♦ If the firms in an industry, and any new firms that chose to enter the industry, would find it costly to have to recruit a brand new complement of employees to replace the existing ones, the employees may possibly succeed in taking collective action to exploit the resulting opportunity: If they can threaten the firm with a large-scale withdrawal of its employees—a strike—they will have the bargaining power to wrest from the firm some of the pure profit it was earning from the "good will" of its existing employees—some of the wage savings it was enjoying by not having to pay its employees their entire marginal product.

However, to leave matters there might suggest that unions were simply clubs engaged in organized theft—the theft of the pure profit arising from the difficulty that new entrants into the industry would encounter in trying to build up a stock of employees and, for that matter, a stock of customers, a difficulty that acts as a protective wall permitting the already entrenched firms to keep their prices above cost. In one respect the situation is *better than that*. In a modernist setting there are some productive things a union can do as well:

- If some of the employees at a firm would find it costly to monitor job safety at the firm, complicated fringe benefits, the going wage at other firms and other industries, and other information the employees would like to have, these employees may be able to gain by engaging in certain collective actions: If they can form a union and manage to collect dues for it, by making dues paying a condition for continued employment, they can by this collective device perform the various and valuable "research" and "monitoring" functions that it would not pay any individual to do by himself at his own cost.

Yet in another respect the functioning of unions is worse than Robin Hood theft from owners of firms to their employees. By raising the wage that must be paid by the employer, the union tends to reduce the quantity of labor demanded, or desired, by the firm. The union may very well succeed in bargaining for an agreement that the firm will discharge no employees despite the higher wage. So the quantity of labor actually employed is not reduced at first. But the union, which is a creature of the currently existing employees, has no interest in devoting its bargaining power to protecting job opportunities for would-be new employees, who are outsiders. As the current employees, who are the insiders, die or retire, the union keeps out the outsiders in order to push up the maximum wage extractable from the firm.

- A union raises the wage that the unionized firm must pay, and eventually (if not immediately) reduces the number of jobs available. Those unlucky enough not to land one of the union jobs are left worse off than they would otherwise be unless they can form new unions at new firms.

Is this impact on nonmembers a regrettable side effect? Or, morally speaking, the main effect?

THE "CONTRACT" BETWEEN FIRM AND EMPLOYEE*

Just as a firm may be compelled to make certain commitments to a *customer* about what to do under "this or that 'contingency,' " and try to protect its reputation for keeping those commitments, so a firm may also find it necessary to enter into understandings, perhaps only "implicit," or "tacit," about how the firm will act toward the *employee* in the event of surprises, unanticipated disturbances. The inducement is similar in the two cases. The prospective customer might have to invest considerable time and expense to form the desirable business relationship with his supplier, and have to sink another investment in another supplier if the first one turns out badly; so the buyer wants *assurances* about the terms under this and that circumstance; he wants assurances that if he stands still to have his measurements taken the tailor will in reasonable time deliver a suit at the going price. Similarly, the prospective employee might have to invest in the relationship—to be interviewed, tested, indoctrinated, and to incur moving costs and to begin with the starting salary—and these investments would be lost if the employment proves to be unattractive; so the worker wants assurances about the terms of the relationship under various possible circumstances, foreseen and unforeseeable.

◆ If working in the market sector were just a matter of a specific job under specific circumstances, the terms would be specified, crisply and explicitly, in an oral or written contract (such as between me and my dentist). The relation between the firm and employee, as distinct from independent contractor, is vastly more complex, and not usually written down.

These investment-type outlays a worker must make in starting with a firm constitute some of the transaction costs of connecting workers (as well as land and capital) to productive tasks. It is the presence of such transaction costs that offers one of the major reasons why there are *firms*—why there are not just "enterprises," here today and gone when their work is done, directed by entrepreneurs who simply hire independent contractors, consultants, free lancers, people from "manpower bureaus" and never have *employees!* It would not make sense for either the worker or the enterprise to incur all those investment costs for just a single, short-lived piece of work. If we contemplate the difficulties that would be faced by an enterprise constantly going

---

* This section may be skipped without loss of continuity.

to the market to hire resources for every single task, we can see some of the other transaction costs that can be saved by operating as a firm rather than as an enterprise wedded to the market for every need: When production is organized within a firm, as noted by the British-born law-and-economics theorist Ronald Coase,

> a factor of production does not have to make a series of contracts with the factors with whom he is cooperating within the firm, as would be necessary if this cooperation were a direct result of the working of the price mechanism. . . . The contract [into which a factor enters] is one whereby the factor, for a certain remuneration (which may be fixed or fluctuating), agrees to obey the directions of an entrepreneur within certain limits.*

If we ask the economic theorist why the market mechanism is not used *at home* to decide each day who will cook dinner, who will do the dishes, and who will get to walk the dog, and if we warn the theorist that we want a deep answer, the theorist will reply, "Transaction costs." One of these transaction costs might be the pain of reopening sore points over and over again. Another is the alienation from repeated hard bargaining. Hence the implicit contract regarding division of duties in a marriage is seldom renegotiated.

What kinds of security will a worker value—be willing to pay for—in the implicit contract with an employer?

- The most obvious protection sought is the safety of not being dismissed without "due process" and "just cause," There has to be a good reason for dismissal or else the employer will have the bargaining power to demand all sorts of unenvisioned services from the employee on threat of being dismissed.

- Similarly, the worker will value protection against an arbitrary and unwarranted reduction of his wage. Unless the implicit contract provides assurance against the possibility, the worker joining the firm would be vulnerable to a wage cut on his second day—or even the first day; the firm could always manufacture some undocumented excuse that it ran into unexpected difficulties. Thus a cut in the wage, measured in terms of purchasing power over the worker's consumer goods, can be made, if at all, only for "just cause."†

---

*Ronald H. Coase, "The Nature of the Firm," *Economica*, November 1937, pp. 336–37. Bracketed words added.

†There is a recent historical footnote on this point that relates to the wages of union-organized employees. In the early 1980s, at Chrysler in the United States, Jaguar in Britain, and many other

- The worker will also want spelled out the remuneration offered, including continuation of insurance benefits, etc., in the event that the employee is "temporarily laid off." Of course, since a firm's promises of its own private unemployment insurance would not be very reliable in the event of a large or permanent misfortune, workers will naturally value—be willing to pay for—some governmental unemployment insurance as well. (Note that the worker might prefer that the income when unemployed match the income when employed, a so-called guaranteed wage, but for "incentive" reasons the firm may prefer its workers to be happier working.)

- The worker will want to have an understanding with the firm over the conditions under which he or she will be laid off (rather than someone else or no one) and, similarly, the rules for deciding promotions to more responsible, better-paying jobs.

The study of the equilibrium contract between employer and employees, called contract theory, is a new and fast-developing field of economic theory.*

SUMMARY

1. Labor markets have similarities to markets for goods and capital goods: Supply factors and demand factors have influence over "price" and "quantity" in *all* markets. Yet labor markets appear to be special: A rental truck may be idle at the current time, if it is in the wrong place at the moment. But a truck does not face a truck market that "rations" the number of jobs available for trucks: A truck owner can improve his chances of renting his truck, at the expense of another truck owner, perhaps, by indicating his willingness to accept a lower rental. In the market for capital equipment(and land), the rental is believed to reach the level that will "clear the market," leaving no idleness of trucks or only voluntary idleness (based on speculation that demand at the normal rental will reemerge in a few hours so it is best not to tie up the equipment in a lease agreement now at a bargain rate). In contrast, it appears that wage rates do not clear the labor market (at least they do not clear all the individual labor markets in the economies we commonly observe).

2. The *modern* theory of labor-market equilibrium seeks to explain the phenomenon of nonmarket-clearing in labor markets—in other words, invol-

---

firms suffering from the recession, workers saw the necessity of wage cuts to save their jobs and agreed to make large wage and work-rule concessions. (At Continental Airlines and British Coal, many did not see it that way—and many of them lost their jobs.)

*There is more on the modernist theory of employee contracts in the appendix.

untary unemployment—by pointing to personnel problems possessed by the firms that employ labor, problems not present in the *classical* theory of what enterprises do (which is not much!). One of these problems of the firm is protecting its "investment" in its employees. The other is the problem of obtaining a profitable performance from them.

3. To solve either or both of these problems the individual firm is motivated to lift the wage rate it offers above that of its competitors in the labor market—as an incentive device to deter its employees from quitting or shirking. This is the idea of the "incentive wage." As all firms resort to this stratagem, the average firm will find its higher wage is still the average one in the industry. But there is an effect: With the standard *industry wage* that each firm now *must* pay just to be "competitive" with the others *having increased,* each firm will be rationally impelled to reduce its employment roll to economize a little more on the now more expensive resource, labor. Hence employment declines, and *un*employment arises. Where do wages and employment stop? The *equilibrium* is reached once *unemployment* has risen enough that the average firm is content not to try any longer to raise its wage above the average (and indeed every firm is content to be where it is) because the volume of industry unemployment, and hence the prospective difficulty of finding a new job, *serves to deter* employees from quitting or shirking too much. (Theorists looking at labor markets from a classical perspective offer the counterargument that smart firms would find ways of deterring quitting and shirking, and conclude that "job rationing," or involuntary unemployment, may be a false impression.)

4. The inability of the unemployed labor supplier to strike a bargain with any of the firms is strongly reminiscent of the problem of Hume's two sheep raisers who are unable to bind one another to a contract. The unemployed worker can offer to work for less than the going industry wage level and swear by all he holds sacred that he will neither quit nor shirk! But the firm will not believe him; if he worked for peanuts, he would have an exceptionally strong incentive to quit at the first discovery of a job at the regular pay and to shirk, since he has less to lose if caught than an employee being paid the regular wage. The unemployed worker is a third-party victim of what is going on between employee and employee.

5. Can the the government do something about the matter to achieve a Pareto improvement (not that such an improvement is the only one worth having)? Perhaps a tax on quitting would help, with suitable use of the proceeds. Centrally planned socialist countries have apparently done well in keeping down outright joblessness, and workers are given little opportunity to quit; but at what cost in the efficiency of labor allocation and in absenteeism and shirking?

6. The chapter closes with short treatments of numerous other problems and phenomena in labor markets that modern equilibrium theory can help to illuninate: discrimination based on statistics of a group and not the person, the "rat race" to distinguish oneself, frictional unemployment and job search, frictions in recruiting specialized personnel, unsafe factories, and labor unions. (The last section, which is optional further reading, discusses the "implicit contract" between employer and employee.)

CONCEPTS INTRODUCED

job rationing

involuntary unemployment

incentive wages, or efficiency wages

equilibrium unemployment level

statistical discrimination

frictional (search) unemployment

signaling by credentials, or "rat race"

insiders and outsiders

show cause, or just cause

STUDY QUESTIONS

1. A draft of this chapter said, in discussing the supervision problem, "It would be quite expensive to set up checks to verify that the night watchman reaches every station at the appointed time" What invention (overlooked in the draft) makes it not so expensive in fact? What does that observation suggest about the generality of the need for, or gain from, "incentive wage levels?" Think of some jobs in which effort *cannot* be adequately monitored without great expense.

2. In the chapter there are diagrams showing the individual firm's wage decision as a function of its expectation of the average wage being set; the wage function is represented by a smooth curve. What if the curve slopes upward more steeply than the 45-degree line? Some economists would argue that in such a case there will be instability. Figure out their argument, making the assumption that each firm starts out expecting a wage that is *higher* than the equilibrium level, v_e. (Hint: Will this initial expectation prove to be above or below the resulting actual wage?)

3. The movie quote atop this chapter is a recognition that

   a. everything is negotiable, thus job markets clear

   b. an attitude of reserve and modesty is best in job interviews

   c. some jobs are rationed, but a snappy comeback might open some doors

   d. the mainspring driving the German "economic miracle" after the Second World War was the frighteningly high rate of unemployment prevailing there.

4. "To say that some or all labor markets do not clear is to imply that wage rates are rigid for long stretches of time, which would be stupid. Since wage settlers are not stupid, it follows that labor markets clear." Evaluate. Does the failure of wage rates to clear a labor market imply that any firm's wage rate is "sticky" in the way described? How is a firm, one that has to cope with the managerial problems of quitting and shirking, apt to adjust its wage scales when there is, say, a sharp fall in the economy's (and industry's) unemployment rate?

5. Present-day contract theory suggests that contracts *(are, are not)* apt to contain provisions for lower nominal wages (expressed in units of currency) in the event of

   a. a fall of the nominal cost of living (expressed in units of currency)

   b. a wave of employee layoffs in the industry due to a business slump

   c. a burst of gamma rays predicted by scientists to lower the productivity of labor at the firm

   d. a wave of job-seeking robots offering to do the work for less pay.

6. The optional section on the possibility of an implicit contract between firm and employee said nothing about provisions to ensure compliance of the firm with the contract—a mechanism for monitoring the firm's actions and a procedure for lodging and adjudicating complaints. Could it be that a firm would be able and willing to develop and maintain a reputation for living up to its implicit contract with its personnel, so that the contract is self-enforcing? Could it be instead that an institution like a labor union is needed to enforce the contract? In this light, try to interpret a conclusion in the recent book, *What Do Unions Do?* (New York: Basic Books, 1984) by the Harvard University labor economists Richard B. Freeman and James L. Medoff:

   > Our analysis has shown that unionism does three things to efficiency: on the monopoly side, it reduces employment in in the organized sector; on the other side, it permits labor to create, at no extra cost to management, workplace practices and compensation packages more valuable to workers, and in many settings it is associated with increased productivity.

APPENDIX: LABOR IMMOBILITY, SECTORAL UNEMPLOYMENT, AND PROTECTIONIST INDUSTRIAL POLICY

According to classical theory a market-based economy has little or no occasion for an industrial policy: Only an industry that generated external economies or monopoly power is a candidate for subsidies or, less likely, tariffs and quotas restricting foreign competition. (Chapter 13's Appendix makes a fiscal qualification.)

This classical presumption against industrial policy is no less valid when workers face serious costs of moving from one industry or firm to another, even though classical theory has always focused upon the hypothetical case of perfect mobility. Suppose the young workers joining each industry are effectively immobilized in their chosen industry for life, because of training or location costs. From the neoclassical perspective an economy of such complete immobility can best solve its resource allocation questions through the use of *local* auction-type labor markets or an equivalent sort of contract: Identical workers, all with the same *reservation wage* (the needed increase in income earned below which they would rather live on their "unemployment benefits" and home-grown tomatoes), will be employed in their industry up to the point where their marginal product (in bread) is driven down to their reservation wage (in bread); any workers left redundant will be unemployed, in a sense—laid off, and not at work, perhaps idle or tending their home gardens—but not *under*employed, since the marginal product of their labor does not warrant greater sacrifice of their leisure pursuits. The pay for laid-off and called-up workers provided by classical contracts, and the determination of who is called up, constitute another story: the laid off might be paid about as much as those called up—or *more,* if better able to spend!—and they might be chosen by drawing lots.

Modern labor-market theory, however, suggests that the resource allocation of these immobile workers is determined somewhat differently. To provide employees with certain incentives that serve efficiency the firm will want to offer higher pay to the employees it calls to work than to those laid off—higher by more than the reservation wage needed (if any) to compensate the employees for the net inconvenience, or disadvantage, of having to go to work. Such a pay differential may be needed to create an incentive for employees to keep themselves ready for work—available and in condition; and a promise of high pay to laid-off employees may lack credibility to potential recruits, since the firm might be unable to pay when business is poor and many are laid off. Further, in view of this pay differential, the firm has no incentive to call up employees to the classical point—the point where the marginal product of labor equals the employees' reservation wage. (Maybe the classical firm had an incentive to call up *too* many, but classical theory supposes that employers cannot succeed in cheating the workers of their leisure and unemployment pay—they all live in a goldfish bowl, their every move and their information costlessly observed by all.) To save on its total payroll the firm will call up a smaller number of workers, thus leaving their marginal product *above* their reservation wage. The implication is straightforward: When the firm finds it profitable to call up all the employees there is no unemployment, of course. But when there are layoffs, because "marginal productivity is weak" (in terms of bread, anyway), some or all of that unemployment constitutes *under*employment—the excess of layoffs over the classical level of layoffs. The excess unemployed would produce more if called up than their leisure is worth to them—but the firm has its reasons not to do so.

Is there anything the government can do in this hypothetical economy to reduce its inefficiency? Sometimes yes, in theory at any rate. Suppose there are two industries or sectors of industries, say, the so-called smokestack sector and the high-tech sector; and in the former there are widespread layoffs, in the latter none. In this case a small subsidy for each call-up of a laid-off worker in the smokestack sector, financed by a tax on profits in that sector, might make everyone better off—a Pareto improvement.

It is theoretically possible that a tariff or quota could be justified instead of the subsidy: Firms might find deceptive ways of obtaining the subsidies, either laying off more employees to offset the subsidized call-ups or, possibly, by fraudulent reporting. The administration of subsidies might also be costly. Hence it might be expedient simply to restrict foreign import competition in the smokestack sector, thus driving up the prices producers can get and encouraging them to increase output and employment.

The temptations to protect notwithstanding, the wiser course of action may be to refrain from tariffs and quotas on the ground that each resort to them makes it harder to resist them in inappropriate situations—the "slippery slope" consideration—and foreign governments may retaliate, so that in the end everyone (or nearly everyone) loses. The same comments apply to subsidies. Even in a modernist's kind of economy, then, there may be some practical value to adhering in some respects at least to a classical economic policy.

CHAPTER 17

Capital Markets: Finance, Banking, and Money

BIALYSTOCK:
It's so simple. We find the worst play in the world—a sure flop. I raise a million dollars. . . . We open on Broadway . . . and we close on Broadway. We take our million and fly to Rio de Janeiro.

Zero Mostel in *The Producers* (1962)

It would be no consolation for a country operating on the capitalist system to find that the competitive marketplace is wonderful at allocating *labor* among alternative uses while it makes a hash of allocating *capital*. How much of the nation's saving is being invested in pitchforks and ploughshares; how much into sinking mine shafts, oil wells; how much into apartment construction; how much into industrial research expenditures on robotics; how much into producing some new Broadway show; how much into various foreign investments, in Chinese hotel shares and Albanian airline bonds? The allocation of capital among competing productive uses is clearly of crucial importance for the success of every economic system, capitalist or other.

According to the neoclassical theoreticians who have championed the social usefulness of markets, it is one of the merits of the competitive market system that it allocates capital efficiently—less *in*efficiently, at any rate, than nonmarket systems do. Smithian "self-interest" in the markets for capital—enterprises accepting every profitable investment opportunity and wealth

437

owners eager for the highest rate of return on their savings—is seen as leading "as if by an invisible hand" to an efficient allocation of capital.

In opposition, many of the critics who dispute the social utility of markets claim that the way capitalist markets allocate capital is one of the worst defects of competitive capitalism—that the "capital markets" are the soft underbelly of capitalism. These same critics oppose the use of markets to allocate capital in socialist systems, preferring that all or most investment decisions by a nation be put under centralized governmental control.

Modern equilibrium theory finds much that is wrong with the capital markets, as with product markets and labor markets. The present chapter surveys some points made in the modernistic critique of capital markets.

The chapter concludes, in a sort of epilogue to Part 6, with reflections on the directions and limits to which a society might want to go in trying to correct or improve the defects in the market system found by the modern theory.

THE FIRM AND ITS FINANCIAL PROBLEM

In the product and labor markets of neoclassical theory, as hammered away at repeatedly in previous chapters, there are no informational frictions and no ignorance. Hence the suppliers of certain labor services and the suppliers of frozen orange juice f.o.b. N.Y. all find that their productive services and goods are perfectly liquid: The full value of any good can be instantly realized. There is no gain from casting around for a buyer, not yet discovered and not yet informed, who once found would be willing to pay more—there are no uninformed buyers, according to the theory. No one needs to be convinced that the worker can do the job, or that the orange juice is good. Perfect markets.

As seen in neoclassical theory, capital markets likewise display complete information and knowledge. An enterprise can issue new equity shares, or common stock, and find a ready market for them instantly; ownership in an enterprise is a perfectly liquid asset. And no one needs persuading about the prospects these shares have for future earnings; the prospects are known. Similarly, the enterprise has instantaneous access to credit, to loan capital, at the market rate of interest. In fact, anyone can borrow on the basis of his future income prospects (after making suitable provisions for life and other insurance)—"your word is your bond". The lenders, or creditors, somehow know that the borrower can (and will!) afford the terms. Perfect equity-capital and credit markets.

> Can the enterprise that wants to open a ski lodge where there is a large risk of rain also obtain credit? Won't potential lenders be

averse to taking such risks? Or mightn't they be willing to finance only in return for a higher rate of interest—for a premium over the risk-free rate of interest? Carrying the logic of neoclassical theory to its limits, some neo-neoclassical theorists proposed that, given enough time to develop, markets could handle perfectly the problems posed by risk: The various markets could work out *one* set of prices, wages, and interest rates that would apply under *one* outcome, or contingency—in the event it rained, for example; a *second* set of prices, etc., to apply under the second listed contingency—light and rewards to the factors of production would be contingent on the "state of the world" eventually revealed to the transactors.

In contrast, the modern theory of equilibrium in the capital markets recognizes serious imperfections in the nature of the equilibrium in those markets: Credit is not freely available at the going rate of interest, at least not usually, and new equity shares are apt not to sell for their true worth. The most important obstacles to the perfect availability of loan capital and equity capital are risks of the type called moral hazard, the workings of which will be examined below.* This type of risk can explain the financial organization of firms and the existence of financial institutions specializing in supplying loan or equity capital—banks, pension funds, and some other financial intermediaries. It can even explain the existence of money.

The Financial Hurdles of the Growing Firm

Most successful firms grow to be larger than they started; most of those that grew smaller are now no longer with us. In considering the financial problems of firms, therefore, a natural way to proceed is to study the new problems met by the firm at each stage in its financial evolution. Of course, not all firms advance from the first stage to the the last; some start at complex stages, some others never reach them.

The most primitive firm, from the financial standpoint, is the proprietorship—any single-owner (one-person or one-family) enterprise. Whatever profit or loss remains from receipts after the costs of materials and labor, and interest on any borrowings from creditors, belongs to the sole proprietor. Of course, even when the capital invested in the firm is small or nil, the proprietorship may be a vast business as measured by how much it produces—the excess of the value of its output over the value of its inputs purchased from other enterprises, which is called value added. An exhibition baseball team or a traveling modern dance troupe does not need much

---

* Moral hazard was introduced in Chapter 5, through Hume's sheep farmers and the Prisoner's Dilemma, and made subsequent appearances in Chapters 15 and 16.

capital (just gloves or leotards) but may play to millions. However, the typical firm does require some investment, at least in product development and marketing, to establish itself.

The essential feature of the proprietorship is that the amount of capital invested in the firm is limited by the proprietor's own willingness and ability to self-finance the development of the firm *and* to obtain credit. But for the proprietorship, which operates under what is called unlimited liability, there is a special drawback to borrowing: If the investment financed by the loan does not earn enough to repay the loan, both principal and interest, and if the other earnings of the firm are insufficient too, the lender could always bring suit against the proprietor in order to attach the proprietor's house, car, furniture, and so forth in repayment of the loan—should the borrower refuse to repay. In some places such a breach of contract could permit the lender to attach, or "garnishee," the defaulting borrower's future wages. In addition, in the good old days there was the penalty of debtors' prison for those with unpromising income prospects! No wonder, then, that the single proprietor is sparing in his demands for credit. To borrow a lot, under unlimited liability, is to jeopardize one's future.

To avoid landing in such jeopardy the proprietor interested in increasing the investment in the firm can turn in other directions. The proprietor may be able to find other investors who are willing to supply equity finance for the firm in exchange for part ownership, thus becoming partners. In a partnership, each investor shares the risks of the business with the other partners. The original proprietor, now a senior partner, will have to bear only *his share* of the loss from the new investment, which he did not dare to finance by borrowing. Moreover, with partners to share the risk that some investments might turn out to cause a loss for the whole company, each investor could contemplate debt financing more cheerfully than he could have as a sole proprietor. (And since there are two or more partners that a lender could sue in case of default, creditors might feel sufficiently assured to make a loan at cheaper terms than they would offer to a proprietorship. But see below.) A partnership is a form of organization most commonly found among professionals such as doctors and lawyers.

Another recourse of the firm is to incorporate in order to obtain the advantages of limited liability. Then the owner or owners of the firm are not liable to repay creditors out of their personal assets; their liability is limited to the assets of the firm, including its future earning power. Incidentally, the limited liability will protect the investors in the firm from each other: In a partnership, each partner is *liable without limit* to the full extent of his personal assets for all debts contracted by the partnership—no matter how small his ownership share.

Although protected by limited liability, the incorporated firm nevertheless must contend with obstacles and drawbacks to a new financing.

Rationing of Credit to Corporate Borrowers

Recall the theory of job rationing expounded in the previous chapter: There can be a labor-market equilibrium in which the number of workers employed is less than the amount supplied, hence involuntary unemployment. An idle worker would be prepared, given the chance, to accept a below-the-market wage in return for a job. But the flint-hearted employers refuse to lower their wages in order to avoid: 1) adverse incentive effects—workers will have less motive to perform as agreed; and 2) adverse sorting effects—the firm will find itself with a poorer selection of applicants if it offers lower wages.

There is an analogous theory of credit rationing in the loan market. The equilibrium in that market may have the feature that the maximum amount of loan capital that firms can borrow is less than the amount they would like to borrow at the market price. In fact the parallel to job rationing may be quite exact: It may be that there are some loan applicants who fail to obtain a loan at all while there are some apparently identical applicants who succeed.

Those trained in the supply-demand analysis of neoclassical theory know the right question to ask: How can it be that equilibrium in the loan market would leave some corporations willing to borrow (or to borrow more) but frustrated from doing so? Why don't the would-be borrowers "bid up" the rate of interest on loans until, finally, the only firms not borrowing are those that cannot afford the high interest cost? Why, in other words, doesn't the interest rate "clear the market?"

To understand the failure of loan markets to clear we need to grasp the position of lenders—banks, professional investors, and so forth. Lenders are confronted with a welter of investment ideas: Some geneticists have formed to market their invention of a super-pig that will lower the cost of ham. An experienced director and writer have formed a corporation to do a musical remake of *Phantom of the Opera* with Dustin Hoffman, in what would be his first singing role, playing the crazed composer. And so on.

♦ With all such investment projects the potential lender is not in a position to oversee—to monitor and evaluate at each step of the way—the management of the project. Only the managers and specialized personnel of the firm will have the knowhow and judgment, if anyone does, to steer the project to success. So they will have a free hand in deciding which chances to take and which to avoid. Any missteps on their part, not to mention bad luck, may spell a calamitous loss on the investment.

The hazard that could be faced by a lender, if lenders behaved in the manner described by neoclassical supply-demand analysis, can now be seen as follows. Suppose that there are some corporations with investment projects that are, potentially, exceptionally profitable; but these corporations cannot afford to put up any savings of their own—they have to finance entirely by borrowing. And suppose, for example, that the rate of return on these new investments would be 30 percent—provided that, as neoclassical theory assumes, managers are exercising *full care* with these investments, as if it was their own wealth at stake. According to the traditional theory, the competition of these firms for loans would (provided they are a large group) drive up the market rate of interest to the same level, to 30 percent; if the interest rate were *less,* every firm that was earning 30 percent and paying a lower rate to a lender would be the object of jealousy—other firms would rush in to spoil its good deal thus eliminating its pure profit. But consider the implications for one of these corporations that borrowed the *whole cost of the investment at these ungenerous terms:* If, by exercising full care, the firm would earn exactly the expected 30 percent return, it would all go to the lender: no profit (nothing of the return left after interest is paid) and *no loss.* If, by taking *less* than full care, the firm earns *less* than the 30 percent return, the firm still receives no profit. But again *no loss.* The manager still has his *salary,* and the employees their wages. It is the lender who has to accept less—less than the 30 percent hoped-for interest. Because of its limited liability, the entrepreneurs who own the corporation are not obligated to reach into their pockets to make up the difference between the return on the investment and the interest stipulated in the loan. Hence the borrowing firm would not have any incentive at all to take full care with its investment project. So the lender is facing the moral hazard that the borrower will not exercise due care with the borrowed capital.

Obviously a corporation whose owners can afford to finance some of the investment out of their own wealth, who can be induced by lenders to put up some "equity" in the project, *do* have some incentive to take care of the investment. But to the extent they have borrowed to finance the investment and can pay themselves a managerial salary, their incentive may be diminished—the loss to them from not taking full care may be diluted. The owners may not bear the full consequences of their own neglect.

To cope with this difficulty, creditors are willing to accept a smaller interest rate on their loans to these potentially most profitable investments in order to heighten the incentive of the borrower to take care with the investment. If a little more care serves to avoid a calamity, a serious default on the loan, the concession in the rate of interest will have proved worth it.

♦ We have therefore an answer to the question, why don't frustrated would-be borrowers outbid one another until finally the market clears? If a firm's creditor or creditors raised the interest rate to the market-clearing level, the firm would than have less incentive to make the investment "work"; and a managerial mistake or oversight might be so damaging to the return obtained on the investment as to lead to a serious default on the loan. Thus the harm or risk of harm may outweigh the good. Figure 17–1 sums up.

More could be reported about the modern theory of credit rationing. There are other adverse effects that may result if the lender should decide to push up the interest rate: The borrower (or some of the more than one borrowing firms) may be driven to "reach for a higher return," since the safest ways to conduct the business might then be insufficient to repay the loan and cover the interest. Somewhat similarly, if there are different sorts of investment projects, charging a higher interest rate may leave the lender with only a selection of the highest-risk borrowers applying for a loan—those seeking loans for low-risk investments know they would not see any profit after paying the lender's high interest. These adverse screening and adverse selection effects can be added to the adverse incentive effects discussed above—all compartments in the theory of credit rationing. However, there is not space enough here to do justice to these other (perhaps equally deserving) adverse effects.

Two objections to the modern doctrine of credit rationing should be recognized and answered. *First,* if there is an excess demand for credit, why don't lenders respond by increasing their requirements for collateral (that is, assets posted as security) from loan applicants—until the point is reached at which the excess demand for credit has vanished? Or, what is similar, why don't lenders respond by increasing the share of the investment project that borrowers finance with their own equity?

In reply it is said first of all that if the market really does eliminate the excess demand for credit through a collateral or equity requirement, that solution is not satisfactory, since some of the best investment projects may belong to borrowers who cannot meet the requirement. In any case, raising these requirements might have the effect of discouraging only the safest investments—leaving only projects with a small chance of a big return and a large chance of bankruptcy attractive to investors—so that the risks to the lender might (up to a point) actually be increased rather than lessened.

Second, instead of encouraging the borrower to practice safety by lowering the rate of interest (below the market-clearing level), why doesn't the lender reward safety by promising a bonus—a lower interest rate on future loans—in the event the borrower does not default on the present loan? This is like the gold watch as a bonus that is conditional on not quitting, on staying the course (chapter 16, p. 419). But such a bonus is not likely to solve completely the lender's hazard—just as gold watches do not. And not all demands for credit are repetitive. Some are one-shot.

FIGURE 17–1: The Modern Theory of the Equilibrium Interest Rate in the Loan Market Contrasted with the Neoclassical Supply and Demand View

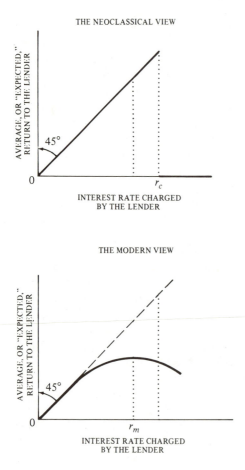

THE NEOCLASSICAL VIEW

AVERAGE, OR "EXPECTED," RETURN TO THE LENDER

45°

0

r_c

INTEREST RATE CHARGED BY THE LENDER

THE MODERN VIEW

AVERAGE, OR "EXPECTED," RETURN TO THE LENDER

45°

0

r_m

INTEREST RATE CHARGED BY THE LENDER

The upper diagram describes the situation of a lender from the neoclassical viewpoint. A lender might as well increase the interest rate charged a borrowing enterprise to the "going rate." This classical equilibrium level is denoted r_C in the diagram. (If the lender were to ask a higher interest rate the borrower would go to another lender. Hence a zero return.)

The lower diagram portrays the lender's situation from the perspective of the modern equilibrium theory. Here too there is an interest rate level that maximizes the expected return to the lender—the return that can be expected to be realized on the average. But this most profitable interest rate for the lender is reached before the borrower has lost all incentive—at r_M, less than r_C.

Where is the social harm in this credit rationing? Why should what is evidently good, or self-interested, for lenders be bad for the country? The answer is that with credit rationed instead of "auctioned off" (to the highest bidders) neoclassical style, there is no tendency for credit to go to those firms where the investment has the highest average, or expected, return. Of course, well-trained loan officers will still try to weed out crooks and whackos. But there is no presumption that the less profitable prospects will have less success in obtaining credit. In fact, lenders may give preference to loan applicants whose projects seem to be cases of "little ventured, little gained."

Penalties and Drawbacks of Equity Financing

As noted earlier, the limited liability possessed by corporations is not only a protection to the owners against creditors (a protection that will cost the owners if it subjects them to credit rationing or if they have to pay a risk premium to their creditors as a result). Limited liability also provides important protection to the owners from each other. Anyone selling off a family heirloom or a month's savings to buy equity shares in an asbestos manufacturing company can rest assured: No matter how many billions the customers or the employees may someday sue the company for, the shareowner's liability is limited to his share of the company's existing assets if it is a corporation. Having worthless shares is the worst loss possible.

♦ Hence corporate shares are a great deal safer than partnership shares. Thousands may risk a few hours' pay to buy a share or two, knowing that their loss is limited to what they are putting in.

♦ Furthermore, these corporate shares are more liquid than partnership shares would be: They can be sold to anyone—no qualifications or approvals by the other owners needed—and, if the shares are widely traded, sold in a hurry.

Thus limited liability makes it much easier to raise equity capital. But that protection is not without some costly side effects.

A difficulty faced by the corporation is that with each owner protected against a loss beyond his own possibly small share no owner has the same incentive to protect the company's investment as he would if the whole investment were his own. To a degree the partnership form solves this problem: Unprotected by limited liability, each owner is motivated to share actively in the management of the company; and each is aware that a serious mistake may jeopardize his family assets, including the family dog. But in a corporation, particularly a large "publicly held" one, who is minding the store? The owners of the corporation must employ a manager (who may be an owner or become one, of course). But that is only a start toward a solution of their problem:

The managerial problem of the corporation owners is to motivate the manager to act energetically and carefully in the interest of achieving the maximum possible return on the corporation's equity capital.

But how to achieve selfless, disinterested management of the corporation? The owners, those with an equity position in the corporation, are caught in the vise of Hume's paradox, the Prisoner's Dilemma in chapter 5.

♦ All managers have their own self-interests, which do not coincide with those of the owners. Only if the ownership could effectively "police" the manager (by penalties and rewards) could he or she be induced to serve the owners. An owner does not have the time or knowledge to study the manager's every decision-problem—not without being paid for managing. Therefore, the interests of the management and those of the ownership are divergent (aside from owner-managed firms).

The realization that the corporation results in managers having a great deal of independence from the owners goes back to the 1930s, when the Great Depression impelled critical reevaluations of prevailing economic institutions. A famous study by two American legal and business scholars argued that stockholding had grown so diversified in the typical corporation as to produce virtually a complete *separation of ownership and control*— the Berle-and-Means thesis.* They showed that nearly all of the largest corporations in the United States were publicly traded, not privately held, by the end of the 1920s; by now it is all of the largest 200. They also showed that in the typical giant corporation the entire management, all the officers and directors, owned only a minuscule fraction, some 2 or 3 percent, of the common stock outstanding.

News of a "managerial revolution" in which managers had wrested control of business from capitalists (without a shot fired) was heady stuff. But ideas of what the managers were doing with their new-found power were for the most part quite prosaic. English observers opined that the manager in making the innumerable business decisions of which the owners knew nothing would be biased in favor of "the quiet life"—for himself. To American observers of the go-go managements after the last world war that idea seemed improbable. Several Americans suggested that the managers sought the largest possible size for their companies—maximum growth. Eventually it was seen that large size might offer security (not just a power trip) to the firm and thus to the management; if profits ever got dangerously low through this strategy the management could always back-pedal by lifting prices and profit margins for a while. So the American view was not wholly at odds with the English one. The latest American thought about the self-interests of management is a doctrine propounded at Harvard Business School that holds that corporation managers are slowing the growth of productivity obtainable from corporate investment in plant and equipment by slanting these investments excessively toward short-lived projects that look for

---

* Adolph A. Berle, Jr. and Gardner C. Means, *The Modern Corporation and Private Property* (New York: Commerce Clearing House, 1932).

a quick return for the shareowners. Safety first, and the quiet life, once again.

What say the neoclassical theoreticians to all this—they who are so wedded to thinking of the enterprise as mercilessly striving for the maximum possible expected profit? Nothing, since for them owners have no problem of manager surveillance—there is no imperfect information. Even the sober modern theorist is prepared to stipulate, in the spirit of compromise, that *much* of the talk of a managerial revolution—little of it by specialists in economics, incidentally—was somewhat overblown. Owners still wield some real control. But so also does management.

This dilemma of the owners, or investors, in the corporation should not be blown out of proportion to reality. When we take our hi-fi rig for diagnosis and possible repair, we are caught in a similar dilemma. We cannot stand over the repairer to debate his analysis and challenge his proposed decisions. We lack the willingness (unless we are enthusiasts) and the ability (unless trained) to exert full control over the repairer's decisions; if we did *not* we would be repairing it ourselves. The principal in the transaction, here the hi-fi owner, does not have full control over the agent, here the repairer. But there is *some* control. The repairer can be sure we won't be contracting for his services again if the unit breaks down again in a similar-seeming way; and we can insist on certain guarantees and so forth. A corporation's owners are in a similar relationship with the corporation's management:

♦ The owners are able to take steps to obtain *some* control over the management of the corporation. Several ways have been discovered to stimulate the manager's interest in the corporation's expected, or average, profit—to reduce his incentives to play it safe, take it easy, have fun. The corporation can provide part of the manager's compensation in the form of profit sharing, deferred payments of the company's common stock, and similar schemes. The corporation can establish rules making it easy for rival managements to make takeover bids for control, which could be anticipated to lead to ouster of the existing officers.

The managerial problem of the corporation has consequences for its ability to attract equity capital. One line of argument starts from the observation that imperfect management of a corporation lowers—pretty much by definition of what we mean by imperfect—the rate of return actually obtained, and expected to be obtained in future, from its investment in bricks, mortar, good will with customers, and so forth.

♦ Imagine that imperfect management strikes a single corporation without warning. The return earned on its investment in plant, equipment, etc., is therefore reduced. Given the rate of interest wealth owners can earn by holding other companies' common stock, bonds, etc., this reduction of the corporation's return per share must spell a reduction in the market price at which shareowners in the corporation are willing to go on holding these shares.* Hence the corporation's shares will have less buying power over plant and equipment than before. (If, for example, the corporation wishes to double the number of shares outstanding, via a new issue of common stock, the newly issued shares would not fetch enough in the capital market to buy as much plant and equipment as would be needed to double the firm's productive assets.) In this way, capital markets act to deprive a badly managed corporation of new equity capital—by cutting the market valuation of any new shares.

◆ What happens when imperfect management afflicts all corporations? Do they *all* stop growing and die out? Not likely. Lower share prices inhibit capital investment by these corporations, as above. But as they *all* cut back their capital investment plans, winding up with a smaller stock of productive assets than they would otherwise have, they will find that the return per asset is increased. So share prices for the corporate sector as a whole recover to their previous level—but with less capital allocated to the corporate sector! Figure 17–2 illustrates.

There is another line of argument pointing to corporate underinvestment. The argument refers to new corporations and, equally, to new kinds of investment projects desired by already established corporations. The proposition is that capital markets *ration the supply of equity finance* for such undertakings—in addition to rationing the supply of debt finance.

◆ Consider a new corporation seeking equity capital for a new venture. The management or the investment project or both are untried. Suppose that the corporation (the entrepreneur and the management team that has researched it) believes that the new project, if undertaken, will bring a perpetual rate of return [on the investment cost incurred by the corporation] of *more* than 20 percent (per annum, say): To be definite about it, let the investment cost—the total price tag for the productive assets acquired—be, say, 100 million (pesos, pengös, pants, whatever); so the anticipated income stream would be *more* than 20 million (per annum). Suppose also that stockowners in the economy are willingly holding shares in the various corporations at share prices giving a 20 percent rate of return (per annum)—that 20 percent is the so-called cost of capital; so if the project were undertaken the corporation could anticipate that the price of the new shares issued to finance it would sell, in the aggregate, for 5

---

* To paraphrase, the price of the corporation's share will promptly drop like a stone to such a level that the *prospective rate of return to shareowners* is again equal to the *going expected rate of return* on other comparable assets.

FIGURE 17–2:   Imperfect Management in the Corporate Sector Causes Less Capital to Be Allocated There, More to Be Allocated to the Noncorporate Sector in Equilibrium

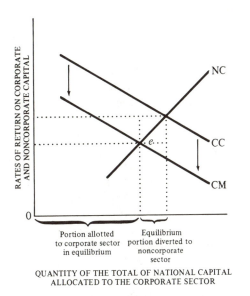

Portion allotted to corporate sector in equilibrium

Equilibrium portion diverted to noncorporate sector

QUANTITY OF THE TOTAL OF NATIONAL CAPITAL ALLOCATED TO THE CORPORATE SECTOR

The curve CC describes how the rate of return on corporate capital assets would depend upon the quantity of capital invested in the corporate sector *under neoclassical conditions*—in the absence of any managerial problem, in other words. The downward slope of this curve reflects

the now familiar principle of diminishing returns: A trillion square feet of industrial floor space in London or New York cannot earn as high a rate of return—a rental net of all expenses per cost of construction—as could a lesser stock of such industrial plant. The larger the capital stock the smaller the rate of return.

Imperfect management, as envisioned in modern theory, lowers the rate of return curve, as illustrated by the curve labelled *CM*.

If the capital saved and invested by the population is not invested in the corporate sector, where does it go? To the noncorporate sector! To houses, cars, dentists' offices, and so forth. And this sector also obeys the principle of diminishing returns: The larger the stock of capital *there* the lower is the rate of return *there*. Hence, as *less* of any given *total* quantity of capital is allocated to the *corporate* sector (and therefore more to the noncorporate sector) the *lower* is the rate of return to capital in the *noncorporate* sector. This relationship is described by the downward movement along *NC* to point e, the equilibrium.

Evidently the lower position of the modern CM curve spells less capital in the corporate sector, more capital in the noncorporate sector, and a lower (equal) rate of return in both.

times the *more* than 20 million income—once that income was generated and there for all to see; so it would be anticipated that the new stock issue would eventually sell for *more than 100 million*. Thus this project represents the technical opportunity for a gain to both parties to the deal, *since the cost of the investment project would be only 100 million while its worth would eventually be more than 100 million*. The subscribers to the new stock issue could divide the gain with the entrepreneur by paying an amount for the stock *between* the 100 million and the ultimate worth of the stock once the income is a reality.

◆ Or consider an old corporation seeking new equity capital for the same untried venture. The existing shareowners in the corporation will benefit from the project by selling the new stock for *more* than 100 million and pocketing the excess, while the new shareowners can afford to pay something more than 100 million in return for the more than 20 million annual income stream.

But Hume's enduring parable of the two or more sheep farmers wanting to cooperate (for gain, of course) but unable to effect a feasible arrangement stands as a warning. If the project were undertaken and the new issue brought to market, those invited to "subscribe" to new shares would not *know* that the project would deliver the more than 20 million of income per year. For anyone contemplating buying the new shares the prospect of that income (or anything like it) would be necessarily *uncertain*. True, that prospect *might* be genuine: Somewhere there must be some entrepreneurs and managers, with limited capital of their own, who sometimes conceive or uncover projects really offering such an attractive prospect of return. There may also be some entrepreneurs and managers, however, who are prepared to deceive the public (and deceive themselves perhaps) about the size of the prospective return on the proposed project. It should be clear that the entrepreneur and management of a new corporation always have a *motive* to deceive, since they can pocket the *excess* of what the public pays for the new issue over the cost of the investment project (100 million in the above example); in established corporations the existing shareowners may similarly gain as long as the actual return on the new project is not so much worse than the actual return on the existing assets as to offset and outweigh the gain obtained by the initial "overpayment" of the new-share purchasers.

◆ Hence the corporation, though really having found an attractive investment project, may be unable to find share purchasers venturesome enough to supply the needed finance for it—or for any scaled-down version of it.

These findings on the rationing of capital to the corporate sector, both credit rationing and equity rationing, have some notable implications for the "efficiency" with which capital markets allocate capital in a market economy:

◆ There is no tendency, as noted earlier, for capital *within* the corporate sector to go into those projects with the highest rate of return. (By contrast, in the neoclassical theory, all those projects with a rate of return greater than the cost of capital are "in"—they are actually undertaken—and all those projects with a smaller rate of return are "out," dropped.)

◆ There is no tendency for capital to migrate *between* the corporate and noncorporate sectors in search of the highest possible rate of return. The tendency, instead, is for too little capital to be allocated to the corporate sector, on the whole, and hence too much (of any *given* national total of capital) to be allocated to the noncorporate sector: to owner-occupied homes, private cars, jewelry, precious metals, various (noncorporate) foreign investments. Thus capital going to the noncorporate sector is not

FIGURE 17–3: The Consequences of Credit and Equity-Finance Rationing

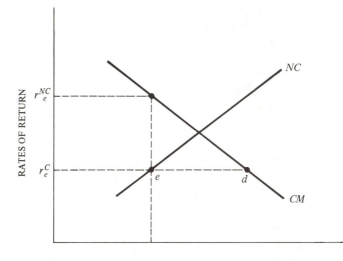

The diagram shows a discrepancy between the rate of return on corporate assets and the rate of return on other productive assets. The curves CM and NC have the same meanings as in Figure 17–2. But the equilibrium is *different* because of credit rationing and equity rationing faced by corporations. The equilibrium must be at a point, like *e* in the above figure, where there is an excess of the capital demanded by the corporate sector over the quantity supplied—an "excess demand" for capital by the corporate sector. The magnitude of this excess demand is measured by the line *ed*. (Note that the amount demanded here is the amount that the corporations could truly afford to demand—not the much larger amount that *unscrupulous* entrepreneurs would like to get their hands on.)

It follows that the equilibrium rate of return in the noncorporate sector, which is also the equilibrium level of the rate of interest, also called "the cost of capital," is less than the rate of return on productive assets invested in the corporate sector: r_e^C exceeds r_e^{NC}, as shown by the diagram. (That difference between the two rates of return does not permit an opportunity to make a gain by selling your car or dental chair for a share in ABC Corp. The shares at ABC, in the aggregate, will sell at a premium, a value in excess of the cost of the productive assets. This excess was a gain reaped by the entrepreneurs who realize the appreciation on the shares once the projects for which they managed to obtain finance paid off.)

returning the highest possible rate of return, as shown in a stylized way by Figure 17–3.

Hence, according to the modern perspective being examined here, capital markets, owing to imperfect information and resulting moral hazards, fail to possess the ideal efficiency ascribed to them by the neoclassical theory.

TAKEOVERS AND OTHER EXCITEMENTS

Existing shareowners in a corporation, as noted earlier, can try to protect themselves from management not in their interests by structuring the rules of the corporation so as to encourage a "takeover" by another corporation. If the present management is widely seen as performing poorly, one or more other corporations will then make takeover bids—tender offers for the shares of the owners. The successful bidder will remove the existing management and install a different management. Fear of such an eventuality will operate to keep the management the loyal servants of the shareowners.

♦ The vision of rival managements being able to enter into a competition for guiding each corporation has inspired the hope that such a competitive process will deprive managers everywhere of any "monopoly power" to extract income from captive shareowners—and hence lead them, as if by an invisible hand, to maximize the return on the investments entrusted them by shareowners.

This is an intriguing idea but, as viewed by the modernist theory, one with flaws and weaknesses in its argument.

A serious difficulty faced in attempted corporate takeovers arises from the fact that a corporation is a common property: The shares in the corporation are all identical; each share is worth the same as any other and is to receive equal treatment with the other shares. Yet the shares are private property, the owner of a share being free to do with it what he or she pleases. This sets the stage for a free-rider dilemma:

Suppose that, with its existing mismanagement, the corporation's shares are only worth p^{**} per share. Suppose also that the shares would be worth p^* per share if the corporate were taken over by some "raider" that could be counted on to manage it properly. It might be thought, then, that the raider can achieve success in bidding for the shares and make a profit besides by making a tender offer for the shares at any tender price that is *between* p^* and p^{**}—at any price greater than p^{**} but less than p^*. (Then the raider would have assets worth p^* for which he paid less than p^*.) But if each individual shareowner is small enough that he can refuse to tender his shares to the raider without affecting whether the raid is successful or not, it will be in each shareowner's self-interest to *hold out*—in order to be able to sell later at p^* for a *larger* gain if the raid is successful.

Since it will be in the self-interest of each individual shareowner to hold out for the entire amount that the shares would be worth under the new management, there is no profit for the raider from any attempted raid.

The difficulty facing takeover bids, then, is the free-rider problem. The same difficulty confronts the real-estate developer attempting to consolidate the properties of many owners in order to improve the existing buildings or to replace them with a better one: All could gain by cooperation, but it is in the self-interest of each property owner acting alone to hold out for the top price, leaving no gain for the would-be developer. However, there is something the shareowners can do to lessen the difficulty. They can write the charter of their corporation to provide that any shareowners who choose to hold out against a successful takeover bid will pay a penalty—they will be given less than their full share, their "pro rata" share, of the new and improved corporation. If the shares not tendered are in the minority, the takeover will go through and those who did not tender will be penalizerd with a dilution of their property rights. So no rational shareowner will hold out for the full worth of the shares. By binding themselves to suffer this penalty, through the apparently self-denying ordinance of their own corporate charter, the shareowners collectively act in their mutual interest:

◆ By penalizing shareholders holding out against a successful raid, corporate charters make the officers bear a risk if they manage badly, a larger risk the worse the management, since the worse their performance the more likely another corporation will realize it can bid successfully, and do better enough to gain.

There are limits, however, to the powers of the corporate charter to ease takeovers. One limitation arises from the transaction cost of a takeover for the raider. Just as it costs the firm something to recruit a customer or an employee, so it also costs something to conduct a raid on another corporation—clerical, legal, and other outlays. Hence, if the designers of the corporate charter have provided for only a very small penalty for dissident shareowners in the event of a takeover—which would at least have the advantage of forcing any raiders to bid close to what the corporation was judged to be worth to the raider—there may not be enough benefit in a takeover for another corporation to cover the transaction cost of a raid. Hence the most that the corporation is worth to raiders, called p^* per share above, may be notably less than the most the corporation would be worth when managed in the best interest of the shareowners.

Another limitation is governmental, and thus far poorly understood. In the public mind, perhaps understandably, takeovers are bad, not good. New managements may seize the chance to break unwritten agreements with employees or customers that are no longer (if they ever were) in the interest of the corporation's owners to keep. In any case, public legislation is often found that hampers corporate raids by prohibiting penalties for holdouts— by making dilutions of minority shareholdings more difficult. (Thus it is possible, evidently, for closed-end mutual funds to be selling at 20 percent below the value of their assets.)

As corporate managers have learned, often as early as business school, there are techniques that they can adopt in self-defense against corporate takeovers. Those having the necessary audacity or desperation have lately tried a blunt approach with some success: Finding that a corporate raider has acquired a threatening number of shares, several corporate managements have simply paid the raider a fortune—with corporate funds—*not* to make a tender offer for the corporation's shares (simply by paying the raider far more than the market price for his share holdings). Of course, the shareowners were the losers, in two ways: The corporation made a bad investment by paying an above-market price for its own stock, so the remaining shares were worth less; and the shareowners were denied the opportunity to choose a possibly superior management. It is not surprising, therefore, that in nearly all such cases the shares traded at lower, frequently much lower, prices after the management's successful manuever. (In a highly criticized case, however, that of Walt Disney Productions, the chief executive eventually resigned.)

Another technique was successfully tried by a poorly run copper company, its shares selling at a much-depressed price. The management found itself having to decide what to do with the proceeds of the sale of a subsidiary. Sensing the risk of a takeover bid, the management creatively chose to make quickly a bad investment with the proceeds so as to make the corporation a less attractive target for a corporate raid. (This provocative case was brought to the attention of students in a business school class who were asked whether, if they were directors on the board of this corporation, they would support the management's decision. To the professor's surprise all eighty students said they would do what the board did, to approve the management decision. They reasoned that the new investment in another company would probably permit them to sit on the board of that company and thus expand their business contacts.*)

In sum: Neoclassical theory recognized, of course, that the managers of enterprises wield power. In that theory, however, it is only the power to make decisions on behalf of the owners. It is hard to escape the conclusion, though, that this theory is seriously lacking. Corporate managers have the

---

*Paul Solmon and Thomas Friedman, *Life and Death on the Corporate Battlefield* (New York: Simon & Schuster, 1983).

power and the motive to run their companies for themselves—subject only to the constraints posed by the risk of takeovers, which gives them appreciable leeway.

In a few cases the power of corporate managers may be used to move imaginatively into new products and technologies. But they may use their power instead to satisfy their drive for greater empires and prestige.

THE THEORY OF MONEY

There is an asset that we have not introduced so far: money. Most of the contents of political economy can be fairly exposited and debated without any mention of money. This book has not needed so far to bring in money at all, the introductory chapter aside. The time has at last arrived, though, to speak of money—at least to offer a few prefatory remarks prior to Part 7 on monetary economics.

In actuality, of course, exchange generally involves the use of money, and has long done so, in every present-day economy. Barter deals, in which the goods ultimately wanted by the parties are traded directly for one another, are the rare exception. In commerical life, virtually every good and productive service is sold in exchange for the *same thing,* which is then used to buy goods and services in future transactions. The "money" of a society is the thing commonly used and reliably accepted as the means of payment, or "medium of exchange."

◆ Though in universal use, money differs in form from society to society, like language and cuisine. (An old *New Yorker* cartoon has an American tourist asking a vendor, "How much is it in *real* money?") In the Island of Yap a system of stone money was employed: If someone bought a good, the ownership of some of his stones was transferred to the seller—though the stones themselves might be too heavy to relocate. (In contrast, in the basement of the Federal Reserve Bank of New York they actually move gold bars from one sheikdom's pile to another's—a more primitive system.) In rural Brazil the money is largely paper currency, bank notes issued by the central bank. In the City of London and other financial centers, the money used is largely net credit balances at banking and brokerage houses—bookkeeping money "moved" from one account to another.

Those plain facts notwithstanding, there *is* no money in the world of neoclassical theory. (There is only something that serves as a unit of measure, or standard of value.) There is no particular thing, or asset, that serves as a medium of exchange.

◆ According to neoclassical theory, there is no need for a medium of exchange—for money—since, in that theory, every good is perfectly liquid: It is certain that the good can be sold immediately at the known price or sold anytime later at equally predictable terms then. No matter what good might be offered in payment to a lettuce farmer or a pianist, there will be certainty about the salability and the terms on which the good can be sold whenever some future exchange, or resale, might be desired by the payee. The supplier of lettuce will not care whether he is paid with urban land or shares in a truck fleet or warehouse receipts to platinum bars or peanuts stored somewhere, provided the payment has the agreed-upon market value. "With costs of executing transactions zero and information a free good . . . [a]ny asset is just as usable as any other for executing transactions and discharging obligations."*

♦ Carried to its logical extreme, the neoclassical view indicates no need for payments in money or goods. Anyone could elect to buy on *credit*—to buy a house or car with a personal "IOU" or have the dentist or saloon-keeper "put it on the tab." After all, in the neoclassical view contracts are completely enforceable, at negligible cost, and creditors could insure against death or accident to the debtor. (Then, too, there is or was the chivalrous code: One would not want to besmirch the family escutcheon by welching on one's debts.) Hence at the end of an honest life each person could repay his debts (with interest) with the debts of others that he had accumulated through his sales of goods and services to others. An economywide clear-inghouse could perform this service at each person's day of reckoning. Thus the neoclassical economy could be a *pure credit* economy: All are credit-worthy.

Modern market theory, in contrast, gives money an essential part to play in the market economy. The modernistic theory, with its emphasis on imperfect information, frictions, and so forth, is able to explain the widespread use of money in populous and complex economies. Imagine the moral hazard we would face daily if we accepted in payment for our services anybody's and everybody's IOUs. The seller can afford a costly credit investigation only in dealing with customers who make large or regular purchases. And no matter how encouraging the evidence, even if no evidence of past fraud or negligence turns up, there is always a chance that the customer to whom credit is extended will sometime be forced to default; moreover, the chance that a customer, if given more generous credit, would default might be impossible to estimate—and being more generous might attract a more risky selection of customers. No wonder that even relatively daring sellers ordinarily do not offer more than a week's or a month's credit—a conventional trade credit—and then only with the collateral of the goods sold, which can be repossessed.

* Karl Brunner and Allan H. Meltzer, "The Uses of Money," *American Economic Review*, December 1971, p. 804.

◆ Modernistic theory has room for the sign sometimes found posted at cash registers:

> In God we trust.
> All others pay cash.

Furthermore, modern equilibrium theory can account for the prevalence of some conventional *money* as the means of payment *rather than* whatever excess *goods* the buyer has on hand—land, shares in a truck fleet, peanuts f.o.b. N.Y. In modernistic market models, goods are *not* perfectly liquid. The pianist, dry cleaner, and stockbroker have a hard enough time, with the trying competition for customers, without accepting in payment goods they would have to devote time to finding buyers for. Hence if the seller (the pianist, etc.) wants to use the payment to purchase another good in the near future, the good received in payment might have to be dumped at a distress price to a professional broker or wholesaler who "makes a market" in the good, buying cheap and selling dear. Certainly the seller, with the awkward good received in payment, could not count on being able to find (at low cost in time and money) a buyer who was willing to sell the other good in exchange—the famous "coincidence of wants" on which barter exchange is generally based.

◆ The modernists summarize all this with a newly coined aphorism: Goods do not buy goods. Only money buys goods.

The modern understanding of the widespread use of money in every market economy leaves open the answer to the next question: What form or forms will money take? There is bound to be a political side to the answer, of course. It depends on what the government does and on what things the private sector is permitted to do. It is imaginable that the government would keep hands off: a policy of laissez faire in matters of money. What form would money taken then? And would the government keep its hands off?

◆ Left unregulated and unfettered, private enterprises would enter the business of printing their own private bank notes. Calling themselves "banks" and "investment houses," they would issue their bank notes in exchange for precious metals, jewelry, land shares, title to capital goods, and loan agreements. (There would be a technical problem at the start: It would be important to have a measuring rod, some unit of measure, in terms of which to express the prices of the various goods—so that all tinkers and all tailors would quote their prices in units of the same thing, making them easily comparable. Presumably evolving conventions could be expected to converge on some particular standard—just as every society develops one primary language.)

Few economists, if any, believe that such a laissez-faire banking system would function well. The holder of a deposit or bank notes of a bank would worry that its portfolio of assets—its loans and other holdings—would be misman-aged; visions of bankers absconding with embezzled funds to foreign havens would frighten potential depositors; the deposits at the bank might not pay the expected interest, might even earn sharply negative interest; and the bank notes might turn out to depreciate markedly in their purchasing power. Bankers could respond to these anxieties by offering guarantees of converti-bility into some particular good—warehouse certificates in some good or other (yes, gold is a possibility!). But banks can fail, so the worth of these guarantees would be little.

There is, however, another scenario. It could be that some banks would acquire enviable reputations for prudence and fidelity to their depositors. Free competition in banking, instead of drawing innumerable entrants to the business (until there was no more supernormal profit to be made there), might end up driving out all but one or a handful of banks. But this outcome too would have an unacceptable feature. No one would feel comfortable having the nation's banking concentrated in the hands of an oligarchy of one, two, or three consequently powerful firms.

◆ Laissez faire in the provision of money would fail to produce reliable money; or if perchance it did so the implications would be morally uncomfortable and, undoubtedly, politically unacceptable.

EPILOGUE TO PART 6:
THE MODERNISTS' OUTLOOK ON THE ROLE
OF THE STATE

While Part 4 offered the grand classical tour of the marketplace, its monu-ments seen at their sparkling best, Part 6 has presented a muckraking exposé of the defects of markets. We saw repeatedly the costliness of gaining infor-mation about alternative opportunities, and the exploitation of that situa-tion by profit-seeking firms. We witnessed also some of the hazards of deception or outright misrepresentation and the resulting distrust of work-ers by firms and distrust of firms by consumers, workers, and everyone else. Some of the lessons learned were:

◆ The quantity of output in the commercial sector is too small (since each firm produces too little and the costliness of finding a market—winning customers—at some point deters new firms from entering). That is, too much labor stays at home, retires early, and so forth. And the quality of that commerical output is too low as well.

◆ Too many of those who do want to work in the commercial sector find themselves involuntarily unemployed, forced to do the next best thing of keeping busy at home or looking for the occasional job vacancy (since many a firm rations its jobs to eager applicants at above-market-clearing levels instead of auctioning off positions to the lowest qualified bidders). Moreover, owing to the limited information about presumably varied job applicants, the firm is apt to resort to generalizations and stereotypes; and the job seeker is driven to invest more in credentials to distinguish himself in the rat race.

♦ Too much of the national capital avoids the nation's own commercial sector, staying home in the form of cars and owner-occupied houses and condos rather than taking shapes usable by proprietorships, partnerships, and corporations in commercial production.

Business life, in this modern view, is a reenactment (with a cast of thousands) of the malfunctions that are apt to arise in the two-person situations where neither party can perfectly observe the other's behavior—the dilemma discussed by Hume, now often called the Prisoners' Dilemma, and analyzed in chapter 5.

♦ If only the cigar customer could prove to his supplier that if an extra weekly quantity of cigars were supplied to him at a lower price he would smoke all his allotment himself and not resell any to other customers at the regular (higher) price. But it would be too costly for the cigar seller to place the smoking habits of his customers under the surveillance of television monitors. So the price stays up, and the customers' purchases stay down.

♦ If only the unemployed lathe worker could demonstrate that, if hired, he would not shirk (or not more than the existing employees, anyway), so it is worth taking him up on his offer to work for less! But even if the lathe operator could strap a TV camera to himself it would be too costly to rent one and too time-consuming to watch it continuously. (If that were *not* so, employers by implication would *not have* a shirking problem, and there would be *no* "incentive wage" above the market-clearing level to motivate hard work by the employees, and hence *no* involuntary unemployment for that reason.)

♦ If only the corporate manager could demonstrate to potential financers that the proposed investment project really is of the type that on average would yield a 3 percent return over actual cost (when the cost of capital is 2 or in any case less than 3 percent). And that the manager would exercise the fullest care to make sure that the "ship comes in." But how?

The result is that resource allocation in the market economy falls short of ideal, or full, efficiency. The self-protective behavior of the first party, springing from an awareness of the other party's selfish interests, harms the second party more than it helps the first. But the infeasibility of a self-enforcing pact, one compatible with every individual's incentives, precludes a deal for mutual gain.

There is a fallacy to beware of. It might be thought that in the *neoclassical* system, by contrast, individual actions *never* hurt others. But they can and do, according to the size of the action taken, of course. If a wine maker chooses retirement there are effects too numerous to list: The price of wine is driven up—though maybe not by a large enough amount for a statistician to detect amidst the continual fluctuations in wine prices; the wage of winery workers and the rental on vineyard land may then be driven down; and in any case resources will normally be driven out of the wine industry into other industries and thus drive down the prices of those other goods. An industrywide rush to retire by all wine makers would produce large-size effects of this sort. So there *are* losers—there is harm to someone, though maybe too small to be noticed by those harmed. In an interdependent economy with more than one factor of production and more than one good produced, it would be hard for any action of anyone not to have *some* harmful effects. But, in the neoclassical theory, unless the wine maker causes an *external* effect—an external economy or diseconomy—all the effects on others are price and wage and rental effects: No one is helped or harmed except through the changes in prices, wages, and rentals. And as a result of the totality of such changes, there are bound to be some *beneficial* effects as well, for while some people are hurt by a price change the people "on the other side of the market" are helped. Moreover, in the absence of any externalities, the gainers could compensate the losers; in that sense, the gains balance the losses. Hence the decision of the wine maker to retire does not represent any inefficiency in the workings of the market. There is, at least on efficiency grounds, no conceivable reason for the government to intervene in the wine makers' retirement decisions. (But it may be recalled that the use, indeed the necessity, of graduated taxation does pose a complication in the argument.)

What is to be done? What sort of "redesign job" can a society do to achieve some or all of those "mutual gains" that the marketplace, hobbled by informational shortcomings, has left unrealized?

It might be thought that some sort of market socialism holds the answer. But it is by no means clear that socializing the economy's enterprises holds any answer at all. If competing *socialist* enterprises, each charged to seek the highest profit income for remitting to the central government treasury, *also* operate in an environment of costly information and moral hazard, may they not behave similarly to competing *capitalist* firms—setting prices too high and quality too low, rationing jobs to motivate workers, and so forth? And may not the managers of those socialist enterprises operate in their own self-interests rather than in the interests of the state? Of course, the central government could enact codes that would constrain the operations of the socialist enterprise managers in certain ways. But so could the central government of a society intervene to regulate firms operating under market capitalism. (Since the objective here is simply to correct inefficiencies in the marketplace, the removal of which could make all citizens better off, the government would not need the prerequisite or the mandate of a revolution to proceed with the appropriate reforms.)

♦ Whether a system of market socialism could be designed more effectively than a system of market capitalism to cope with the inefficiencies arising from imperfect information, concealed knowledge, and so forth remains to be argued one way or the other. Why should the bureaucrats of socialist competing enterprises behave differently from the bureacrats managing capitalist enterprises?

Nor is the modern critique of markets sufficient, it seems, to warrant jumping from the frying pan of flawed market capitalism to the fire of *nonmarket* socialism, or communism. It used to be thought by some that society could eliminate or reduce some of the worst abuses arising from the over-zealous profit-seeking management of enterprises under capitalism by the simple means of prohibiting market competition and turning instead to centralized control: Each industry would be managed as a single enterprise, regulated in every corner, by a single public authority. The benefit, it was said, would be that the industry would not then sell rotten apples or over-charge—it would not have the motive to do so. The cost, it was conceded, would be that both the discipline imparted by competition (the spur to keep costs to a minimum) and the stimulus offered by competition (the incentive to steal a march on the competitors by innovating a new product or technique) would be lost; thus the stick and the carrot of competition would be missing, and *new* incentive problems would exist in place of the ones prevented by the prohibition of competition. However, it is now widely agreed that such an analysis is woefully naïve: We should not suppose that there is no problem of shirking under nonmarket socialism*; that there is no job rationing, particularly for the best posts; that the central authorities who allocate capital to the various enterprises can count on realistic estimates by

---

* A Soviet worker recently summed up the shirking problem this way to reporters: "They don't pay us anything, and we don't produce anything." Westerners were startled when in January 1983 the new Soviet premier, Yuri Andropov, responded to the problem by launching police sweeps of department stores and other public places in search of shirkers.

selfless industry managers of the prospective rate of return on each proposed investment project; or that an industry never lets up on quality or lets its price edge upward lest its managers feel obliged in the name of socialism to turn in their resignations and suffer lifelong dishonor.

♦ Nonmarket socialism faces some of the same problems faced by corporate market capitalism: The managers act in their own self-interest, which does not exactly coincide with the interests of the state.

It is natural, then, that a society, especially one already operating on a system of market capitalism, give first consideration to reforms of the marketplace—to governmental measures that would serve to remove or at least limit the inefficiencies, the "market failures," that costly information and concealed knowledge breed, according to modern theory. In fact, of course, attention has been given to reforms of the market, and reforms have been instituted, with a vengeance. In all of the most developed economies instituted along capitalist lines there is a vast network of regulatory agencies charged with protecting the public from the shortcomings and abuses to which the market is prone. There are agencies to protect the consumer's and worker's safety; agencies to protect the public from fraud and deceptive practices by firms in their marketing of products, employment of workers, and financing of investments; and the courts serve to protect the owners of firms against some of the more flagrant abuses suffered at the hands of their customers, employees, and managers.

The regulatory movement has now proceeded to the point where a counterreaction has set in. For some years, it is charged, there has been a bureaucratic tendency toward overregulation of markets. At the same time there are observers who contend that the economy continues to be underregulated in some quarters, whatever the possible overregulation in others. It is interesting to see, and important to recognize, that the modernist ideas of costly information and concealed information can help to explain why governmental regulation of the economy might itself be quite imperfect—why, more generally, the allocation of resources by the public sector can be expected to be rife with inefficiencies.

Information and Politics

Just as "the market" does not, generally speaking, work in the classical way and with full efficiency, for reasons of imperfect information, so the "political market"—the figurative "market" in which proposed governmental spending programs, subsidy programs, and regulatory programs compete for the public's approval in the form of "tax monies"—is also beset by imperfect information. The particular consequences of the information costs, precisely how they alter the decisions of the public sector, may be unpredictable and difficult to sort out even after the fact. Yet it is obvious that the necessity of the public sector to reach decisions under conditions of costly information will prevent its allocation of resources from being fully efficient: There would be room, if only information were costless to all and nothing concealable, for improvements that could benefit all.

In recent decades, economists have come to see that informational problems have *two* discernible patterns of effect on the public sector. On the one hand, some public programs go unfunded or underfunded because their benefits are not widely known. Hence there can be said to be a pattern of deficient government regulation and deficient government expenditure.

In the early days of discovery of the importance of information it was suggested that it was possible to say *which way* the shortage of information biased governmental decisions. During the 1950s it came to be argued by a number of political economists in the United States that the public sector was much too small: "Public squalor," in the form of littered streets and under-supplied public facilities and public amenities, "amidst private affluence" was the rallying cry. Then it was proposed that the difficulties of gathering information experienced by voters and legislators could explain *why* the public sector was too small. The American political scientist-economist Anthony Downs carefully and plausibly argued that the costs to citizens of acquiring information about the benefits to them of a proposed program and the costs to citizens of transmitting information to legislators about the benefits to them that a proposed program would bring operate to make public expenditures generally too small. The government's many capacities to do good are under-appreciated and underadvertised.*

On the other hand, many economists have come to believe that, simultaneously, informational problems have another pattern of effects on the public sector—a pattern of excessive government regulation and excessive government expenditures. In claiming that most or all government programs are excessive these critics mean that government expenditures and regulations have grown to the point of economic inefficiency: *All* could be made better off, at least in principle, by a cutback of those programs; with

---

* Anthony Downs, "Why the Government Budget Is Too Small in a Democracy," in Edmund S. Phelps, ed., *Private Wants and Public Needs*, rev. ed. (New York: W.W. Norton, 1965), pp. 76–95.

their tax savings, the gainers could *compensate* those harmed (those who got something out of those programs) and still have a net gain left—at least if the beneficiaries could be identified and the size of their benefits reliably estimated.

♦ Perhaps every other generation takes up the cry that the government has grown too big (and the odd-numbered generations claim it has gotten too small). What is new, however, is the emergence of an economic theory that predicts the inefficient giantism of established government programs.

One model of overlarge government programs turns on the idea that the public, or the voting electorate, cannot afford to acquire the information necessary to defend itself against their overgrowth. No voter acting alone has the resources to *familiarize* himself with all the existing and pending special interest legislation and to *study* the *claims* (of benefit to the general public) made on its behalf, let alone to make an independent assessment of the real benefits to himself. (And if one voter alone were to acquire the desired information what could he alone do with it?) This problem, where the benefits accrue to a tiny group while the costs are widely dispersed, was raised earlier, in chapter 8. Although the benefit, say 100 (tons of bread per year), to each small special interest group might cost the rest of the population 1,000, the costliness of acquiring information about the myriad of such special interest programs effectively nullifies the opposition to each such program. Only voter resistance to the general tax burden serves to limit the size of these programs.

To this model of bloated government spending and regulation a supporting idea could be added: If the legislators are professional politicians, with an interest in reelection, then they have an interest not only in catering to special interest groups in return for their campaign support. The legislators also have an incentive to play the demagogue: Although all the good legislation may already have been passed (for the moment, anyway), the legislator may be able to gain votes by introducing new legislation and peddling it with false claims.

♦ Just as the consumer may be duped by one or more producers into believing that certain health foods are beneficial that are not actually so, the voter may be deceived by one or more legislators into believing that certain government programs bring a net benefit that they do not actually deliver.

Another theory of over-large government programs in which information costs play an important role turns on the idea of the bureaucrats' self-interests. As with corporate managers, so with government bureaucrats: They serve themselves first and foremost, striving for power and ease, and serve the public only as a respectable means to that end—the idealistic exceptions aside. Self-interest leads the bureaucrats to become *advocates* of their agencies' programs, which they ought to be overseeing judiciously and objectively.

Markets and morality. The modern market theory has taken us a long distance from the neoclassical view of markets and the neoclassical vision of the role of the state. A whole new side of business life has been uncovered.

Smith and the other great architects of the neoclassical view understood, as deeply as anyone ever did, the moral frailty and corruptability of mankind. They took seriously the doctrine of original sin. When Smith writes that it is not to the "benevolence of the butcher" that consumers owe their daily victuals we can be sure that Smith regards it as fortunate for consumers. There would be no mercy for the consumer, Smith felt, without competition to keep producers in check. But *with* competition among sellers permitted and encouraged by the state, the individual seller of a good will have no power over the consumer, and the seller of productive services no power over the hiring enterprise. The butcher may use his friends, manipulate his family, cheat at cards and golf; but *in the butcher shop there are no moral decisions to make.* (Breach of contract aside, the most heinous offense that Smith can see is a conspiracy of sellers to try to raise the price or to get the government to do it through a tariff or minimum price law.)

The modern view of markets is quite a contrast. Knowledge—information—is power. And power corrupts. Concealed information, misleading information, misinformation, clandestine cheating, and chiseling of all sorts—these are endemic in business life. Here competition is less beneficial than Smith thought. "Do unto others before they do unto you," as they say at one business school. If your competitors are going to do it, you may have to do it to prosper, perhaps to survive. Hence it is not only large bureaucracies, with their infighting, that have a corrupting influence in economic life. So do markets, even highly competitive markets.

Society, acting through the mechanism of the government, can nevertheless do something to improve the moral climate of markets. By legislating against deceptive practices, nondisclosure, and so forth the government can make it easier for business people to resist temptations to deceive, not to disclose, and so on. By lending its moral authority in support of honesty, probity, corporate responsibility, and so forth the government can heighten the value that people place on these qualities in business dealings.

For the government to give less attention to the information problems in markets—on the grounds that the regulation costs saved would exceed the efficiency gains that would be lost—would overlook the dislike of businesspeople themselves to have to operate in an utterly vicious and sleazy moral climate where there were "no holds barred."

SUMMARY

1. One individual wants to raise capital to invest in a new football stadium, another individual wants to invest in the production of a satellite, another in the construction of a vacation resort. The markets in which it is determined which projects obtain the capital—the financing—and at what terms are generally called capital markets, or financial markets.

2. The proprietor in a proprietorship and the partners in a partnership (where we are now talking about a legal concept, not the partnership of two friendly sheep raisers, which is informal) run the risk that if an investment project earns a return that is less than the interest owed to lenders, or creditors, who helped to finance it, they are legally liable to repay the rest of the interest due out of their own pockets and their families'.

3. The corporation has only "limited liability." Its liability is limited to the assets owned by the corporation; the personal assets of the owners of the corporation are protected.

4. Two arguments are presented to the effect that the rate of interest is not necessarily driven up to equality with the prospective rate of return on the most profitable-looking investments—if the corporations with those lucrative prospects can afford to put up no capital (or negligible capital) of their own, and the owners can always collect their salaries as managers. Then creditors may find it in their interest to charge a lower rate of interest on these exceptionally promising investments to encourage the owners to take proper care to see that the project is successful. But with the rate of interest lower, and hence a larger amount of credit demanded, the lenders must "ration" out their credit—instead of "auctioning off" their credit to the highest bidder.

5. If the owners and managers are not the same people, then the limited liability of shareowners in the corporation creates another incentive problem. Since each individual shareowner's liability is limited, shareowners have little incentive to oversee the managers. With no one overseeing the managers, the efficiency and rate of return on capital of the corporation suffers. So the "capital markets" put less capital in the corporate sector, more in the noncorporate. Furthermore, distrustful share buyers may undervalue corporate shares—causing still less capital to go to the corporate sector.

6. The threat of a corporate takeover bid, with its risks to the existing management, undoubtedly helps to curb management actions that are flagrantly harmful to the shareowners. But there is a problem making the threat of takeovers unreliable. Every shareowner wants to hold out for the share price after the successful takeover—but, that way, the group

trying to take over cannot acquire enough shares. It is, once again, the problem of the "free-rider."

7. The modern theory of asset markets, with its emphasis on the problems of information and trust, leads naturally to an understanding of the role of *money* in the economy. The essential thing about money is summarized in the familiar sign: "In God we trust. All others pay cash." In short, money keeps people honest.

8. The ways in which the modern theory of markets suggests a wider role for the state, compared to the role envisioned in classical doctrine, is the subject of the preceding Epilogue to Part 6.

CONCEPTS INTRODUCED

capital, or financial, markets	credit rationing	illiquidity of a good or
equity, or equity-capital, market	rationing of equity finance	debt
	power of corporate managers	free banking
credit, or loan-capital, markets	medium of exchange versus unit of account	overregulation and under-regulation

STUDY QUESTIONS

1. Speaking recently on the issue of American banks' interest rates in the Latin American debt crisis, Robert Roosa, a prominent New York investment banker, was reported to say that "the way to preserve [a bank's] asset is sometimes to take a lower rate of [interest] so you don't lose on principal" *(International Herald Tribune,* May 16, 1984, p. 4). Are there any parallels between the incentive that a reduced interest rate may create for a foreign government borrower and the incentive created by a concession in the interest rate for a private corporate borrower? If so, should we expect credit rationing or market clearing in bank loans to overseas governments?

2. How can existing shareowners of a corporation, one about to issue a certain number of new shares or raise a certain amount of new equity finance by issuing as many new shares as needed, hope to benefit by "talking up" the prospects of the new investment that the new share issue is intended to finance? What is the effect of this hazard on a cautious public's valuation of new corporations and new corporate share offerings compared to investments in homes or in nongrowing corporations whose prospects are relatively proven?   Is there in fact a gap between the rate of return obtained typically from corporate investment in new plant and equipment, new products, and so forth and the rate of interest (after adjusting both of the aforementioned rates for the rate of inflation)?

3. "The classicists say you can't run an economy well on love, and the modernists say you can't run it well on self-interest." Is there no useful role for any self-interest? Any moral self-restraint?

4. In *Glengarry Glen Ross* by the American playwright David Mamet the plot is a contest among employees of a real-estate company. The salesman who gulls the greatest number of suckers will win a new car from the company, and the one who finishes last gets fired. Is Mr. Mamet being a classicist here or a modernist? What is the playwright apparently seeking to convey about the moral climate in real estate? Is there anything particularly hazardous about investing in real estate compared, say, to shares in a corporation?

Part 7

The Element of Disequilibrium in Modern Market Theory

In this world of rational disorder the only certainty is change.

Attributed to Jean Paul Sartre

. . . this twentieth century split . . . had a common impetus, much as a river divides into two forks. On the one hand, there were tonal composers, guided by Igor Stravinsky, who were . . . always somehow remaining within the confines of the tonal system; while on the other hand nontonal composers, led by Schoenberg, were . . . transforming the entire tonal system into a new and different poetic language.

. . . In any case, it was soon to become clear that free atonality was in itself a point of no return . . . a dead end. Where did one go from here, having abandoned all the rules?

Leonard Bernstein, The Unanswered Question (1976)

CHAPTER 18

The Classical Equilibrium Doctrine in Crisis

> RICHARD:
> I know. You know I know. I know you know I know. We know Henry
> knows, and Henry knows we know it. We're a knowledgeable family.
>
> John Castle (to Katharine Hepburn) in *The Lion in Winter* (1968)

THE monetary upheavals in Europe and then the Americas following the First World War sent tremors through classical political economy.

- Money, in the classical view, had no "real" importance in economic equilibrium. The presence of a money was important—it greased the wheels of the economic machine; but the *quantity* of money in existence, in supply, had no "real" effects: no effects on the equilibrium output of haircuts, the equilibrium employment of barbers, and the equilibrium real price of haircuts (the price in terms of bread or any other good). The quantity of money would influence powerfully the *nominal* price of haircuts, the price in terms of money—might determine whether a haircut was three francs (dollars, whatever) or thirty; but it was *neutral* toward *relative* prices— the exchange ratios at which goods could be traded for one another; a haircut would still cost, say, five loaves of bread. And it is neutral toward the volume and pattern of production; the numbers of haircuts would be the same.

471

♦ The neoclassical theory was (and is) entirely an equilibrium theory: The economic actors, workers and producers, find events conforming to their expectations. Their forecasting of prices, incomes, and so forth, on which they are basing their plans, is correctly done—it could not be better.

Money, the neoclassicists liked to say, was a "veil"—disguising reality, lending it mystery, but not truly altering the face of the economy.

In fact, people were finding their expectations shaken in one country after another as the interwar period unfolded—the turbulent period between the two world wars. Observers of that period could hardly have endorsed the classical view that they were living through an approximate equilibrium or the normal passing ups and downs of business activity.

THE CHALLENGE TO EQUILIBRIUM DOCTRINE IN THE INTERWAR PERIOD

On the Continent in the first half of the twenties, most spectacularly in Germany but also in some other countries, nominal prices and nominal wages zoomed up, and the "value of money" (what a one-mark note would buy) shriveled, faster than anyone had been able to imagine, let alone forecast. As enterprises and workers learned to forecast some inflation, then to forecast greater inflation, the rate of inflation responded by spurting that much higher—always ahead of people's forecasts!

Then, in the second half of the decade, countries began seeing falling nominal prices and a stunning slump in the level of business activity: first in Britain, eventually on the Continent, and finally (signaled by the Wall Street stock market crash of 1929) the United States and the rest. By the early 1930s the whole capitalist world was experiencing the Great Depression. Producers found themselves constantly overpredicting their competitors' nominal prices and wages; workers were continually disappointed by the paucity of vacancies and the depths to which wages kept on dropping. Few thought that prosperity was "just around the corner," but most were kept waiting longer than they anticipated.

♦ It was widely believed that, contrary to the neoclassical view, the world's economies were in a fundamental, gigantic disequilibrium; and that it was the behavior of money, particularly governmental mismanagement of money, that was responsible.

Chronologies belong to economic history, not political economy. Still, a lingering glance back at those sensational times is irresistible. The great inflations on the Continent began soon after the end of the Great War. The Treaty of Versailles that the defeated Germany signed with the Allies called for it to pay large reparations. The young economist representing Britain, John Maynard Keynes, resigned from his post to protest the terms in his tract *The Economic Consequences of the Peace*. Keynes thought that the German government would be unable to raise enough tax revenue from the taxpayer—some 25 percent of German incomes would have to be collected in taxes, he estimated—to pay the cost of buying the goods to be sent as reparations. (Now, West Germany taxes away some 50 percent of the income of its citizens, and Sweden, to cite an extreme, takes 55 percent.) In any case, the German government in those divisive years of the Weimar Republic felt itself too weak to levy higher tax rates to the degree that might have proved enough: Instead, it paid for the reparations purchases simply by printing additional quantities of paper money. As a result German prices rose, and rose further in the expectation of inflation ahead; so new money had to be printed faster; so prices rose faster. By 1922 prices were rising at the rate of 1,000 percent per year. By 1923 the rate of inflation reached one million percent. German money, held in a pocket or in a bank account, was depreciating so fast in real value, in purchasing power over goods, that it was too costly for anyone to hold for more than a few hours. Barter and foreign currencies came into use as means of payment. The German mark was being driven out of use. Finally a new currency system was instituted. The inflation was over, though employment and production did not recover to their normal levels until 1929.

In Great Britain the excitement began soon after Winston Churchill, though not fitted by training or experience to be a finance minister, took over as the Conservative government's Chancellor of the Exchequer. The British pound, often called sterling, had been "floating" in foreign currency markets, contrary to the custom of the prewar gold standard under which a country bought or sold gold in exchange for its national currency in order to stabilize the currency's value. When, during the 1923 American recession, the dollar weakened in foreign-exchange markets, the pound rose against the dollar to its old level of five dollars to the pound. Churchill then proposed a policy of fixing indefinitely the exchange rate of the pound against the dollar at this glorious old "parity" level. Keynes, alone among the economists, warned that such a high parity level for the pound would disrupt production and employment in Britain's export industries as long as their wage costs (in pounds) remained unchanged: With the pound more expensive in terms of the dollar, the overseas buyer of British coal would have to pay more dollars, or the British seller would have to receive fewer pounds; either way British coal exports would be decreased. But Churchill went ahead in 1925 with the high parity. Then the dollar strengthened in world currency markets. British coal prices (in pounds) fell sharply, so that producing up to the former level was (for the moment) not profitable. The mine owners said that to continue operations they needed a comparable fall in the coal-mining wages (in pounds). The union replied with a damaging six-month strike. Keynes reacted with a pamphlet, *The Economic Consequences of Mr. Churchill*. Unemployment moved to disturbing levels— about 10 percent—for the rest of the decade.

The climax of interwar economic history, however, was undoubtedly the Great Depression of the 1930s. The famous stock market crash on Wall Street in October 1929, still recalled as Black Friday, was the dramatic forewarning that serious disturbances for the American economy and its trading partners lay ahead. The deepest decline in production and employment occurred in the United States and Canada (among the larger countries). Output and employment declined equally sharply in Germany and somewhat less sharply in Britain. But a strong recovery started in Germany in 1933 propelled along by a series of unorthodox measures taken by Hitler's economics minister, Dr. Hjalmar Schacht. Britain soon after began to recover from its less serious slump. Meanwhile, production and employment in France grew steadily worse into the mid-thirties. American recovery only began in earnest in 1936, faltered with the recession of 1937, and resumed steadily to reach something close to prosperity in 1941, with the arrival of the Second World War.

As the Great Depression wore on it proved the most serious challenge yet to the classical case for market capitalism. Readers now might find it curious why the 1930s were especially unsettling for classical doctrine. Had not Marx and others, after all, long ago complained of the tendency of industrial capitalism to generate employment fluctuations? Of course, there were in fact fluctuations in the nineteenth century, some of them provoking much criticism. There were the "hard times" of the 1840s culminating in the crisis of 1848—the year of the *Communist Manifesto*. The very term *depression* appears to have been coined to refer to the economic slack that prevailed in the American economy over most of the 1870s. Yet these slumps pale in comparison to the Great Depression. It was by far the deepest and also the longest slump in United States history. The data on production, Chart 18–1, gives evidence of that as do the words, in letters and recollections, of the victims.

♦ The spectacle of so many out of work for so long gravely undermined faith in the value of acquisitive individualism as the Smithian pillar on which to base the economy.

SOCIAL LOSSES WHEN EMPLOYMENT FALLS SHORT OF EQUILIBRIUM

The Great Depression was a catastrophe. There was no mistaking that, then or now. As prosperity ebbed and total employment sank far beneath the equilibrium level, there was no one suggesting that the rise of unemployment was benign, that the emerging disequilibrium was as good as the equilibrium would have been. In America, there were Calvinists who thought the fortunate deserved their blessings and the unfortunate their suffering; but no one denied the suffering. If we judge the thirties by how badly off the worst-off persons were, or merely give weight in proportion to their numbers, then that decade was vastly worse than any decade before or since in this century. Awareness that the suffering was not the result of some natural disaster, of known and unavoidable cause, but rather the effect of some malfunctioning in a man-made system, and hard to diagnose, added anxiety to the pain.

A vivid record of the Great Depression has been preserved thanks to some brilliant photographers and writers who were alert to the human drama of those times. In *Down and Out in Paris and London* the British writer George Orwell explained how European derelicts in the thirties managed to survive on soup kitchens, private handouts, and the public dole. A 1938 study by the Pilgrim Trust, *Men without Work,* pointed to the emotional illness and atrophying of skills caused by prolonged joblessness. In the United States the Roosevelt administration sponsored the Federal Writers' Project to gather testimony from thousands of victims of the depression. For his 1970 book *Hard Times: An Oral History of the Great Depression in America* Studs Terkel tape-recorded the recollections of some of the survivors. Most recently a small sample of the millions of letters written to Washington by the unemployed, mostly anguished and some angry, were published in *Down & Out in the Great Depression,* edited by Robert S. McElvaine. But most striking of all are the 1930s photographs by Dorothea Lange, Carl Mydans, Berenice Abbott, and others, which capture so starkly those bleak times.

Certainly neoclassical economics views a fall of national employment below its equilibrium level as a misfortune. True, the unemployed may have more time left to spend being with the children and fixing up the house. But there will be less income with which to do those things and the other things for which income is valued. No economist has ever suggested that the benefit of the added leisure would exceed the cost in lost income, yielding a gain rather than a loss. On the contrary: Since the worker, in equilibrium, willingly *chose* to take the job, despite correct expectations of how poorly it

CHART 18–1: The National Product in the United States, Canada, United Kingdom, and Australia, 1889–1984—As Measured by Real Gross National Product (in Units of the Local Currency)

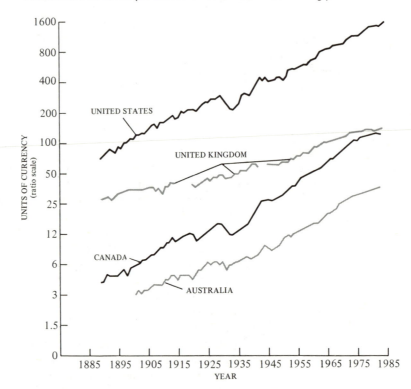

Note: The vertical axis is calibrated by the *ratio scale*. Hence equal percentage changes correspond to equal distances. The distance from 100 to 150 is the same as the distance from 400 to 600, since the ratio 150:100 is the same as the ratio 600:400.

Measuring National Product: A Brief Lesson. Economics has several ways of measuring the intensity of booms and slumps. But the most common measure gauges the level of business activity in a nation and is called the *gross national product.* It is a measure of the market value of paid and the sacrifice of leisure opportunities it entailed, the worker thus revealed his *preference* to be employed at that job instead of enjoying added leisure.

The modernist theory of market equilibrium is more emphatic. According to that theory, even the equilibrium level of employment is too small, the equilibrium unemployment level too big. That is because the phenomenon called "job rationing" causes some workers to be involuntarily employed even under equilibrium conditions—under correct expectations of wages,

the production carried out over a given time period in the commercial sector—the sector where people's labor and other productive services (whether hired by private enterprises or governmental units) are exchanged for income—not love.

In constructing a country's gross national product the government statisticians are striving to aggregate the production of apples and oranges, calculators and computers, patrolmen and detectives, the shelter of a grand mansion and the shelter of a tenement. The statisticians proceed by reasoning that if an orange sells for twice the price of an apple, then so far as consumers (who would have been willing to exchange two apples for their last orange) are concerned, the word *orange* might just as well mean double-apple, or pair-of-apples. Similarly, if the government's bill (what it spends hiring resources) for pollution control is three times its bill for pest control, the statisticians reckon that the former represents three times more "production" than the latter.

To estimate the size of a country's GNP in a particular year the statisticians can start by *adding up* the market value of the amount sold of each good—each commodity or service—by the commercial sector to households, to the government, and to exporters for sale abroad. From that total the statisticians, in order to measure total *production,* will need to subtract all sales accounted for by running down the stock of inventories on hand at year-end; and, by the same logic, they will need to add the market value of all net additions to inventories by year-end. Lastly, to include the production of capital goods, the statisticians will need to add the value of the plant and equipment sold by the domestic commercial sector to the domestic commercial enter-

prises themselves, net of any sales out of inventories of such capital goods. (It should be noted that this grand total does *not* include sales of intermediate goods by one enterprise to another, such as car radios and tires to car makers, since the sale of the whole car, with its tires and radio, has already been included. It would be double-counting to add these intermediate goods.)

In what terms are these market values to be expressed? In money terms? In terms of bread? In bygone times the statisticians contented themselves with measuring the market value of a sale by the value in money terms—by the amount of money spent if the sale was transacted with money. In effect the amount sold of each good was weighted by the money price at which it was sold (or could have been sold) during the year. When market values are expressed that way, the resulting total is the *nominal GNP,* or *money GNP;* it is often called the *GNP at current (money) prices.* But as a measure of production, or economic activity, the nominal GNP has a glaring defect: It can rise simply because of a general rise in the money prices of goods— a rise in the "price level"—despite no change whatsoever in the output of any good compared to last year.

As a consequence the statisticians have shifted to a way of expressing "market values" that avoids the misleading influence of changes in the price level. The amount sold of each good is to be weighted by the money price not in the current year but in some unchanging base year. This gives the *real GNP,* or *GNP at constant prices.* (Those interested in learning more about the measurement of national product will want to consult the appendix to this chapter.)

the frequency of job openings, and so forth. A fall of total employment below the equilibrium level only makes matters worse—by inflicting involuntary unemployment on a wider portion of the labor supply.

Times change, of course. Now there is unemployment insurance in every civilized industrial country in the world. Under such an insurance program, each worker has a portion of his wages deducted to pay the *premium* charged by the government for the workers' unemployment insurance protection. (This insurance program is always governmental, for if a private company offered unemployment insurance it would find itself besieged by insurance buyers who were already on the verge of driving their employers to discharge them.) Still, the classicist and modernist analyses remain valid:

- Unemployment insurance does not fully indemnify a person's loss of earnings if unemployment strikes. All it can do is spread in more even fashion the losses from unemployment once the catastrophe occurs—just as fire insurance can only spread the losses over the group of people who, wishing to spread their risks, have joined, perhaps compulsorily, the insurance program. The reason is that if 100 percent of income were "replaced" by the insurance plan, when unemployment strikes, we would see people "arranging" to lose their jobs—a moral hazard.
- Even 100 percent replacement of lost income could not replace the loss of self-esteem that results from losing one's job.

CLASSICAL VIEWS ON MONETARY EQUILIBRIUM

The great figures of classical economics and their early twentieth-century neoclassical successors sensed that the total employment level in any economy is sometimes knocked away from its equilibrium level by an unexpected disturbance. It was believed, however, that once the effects of the shock were fully observed the cause would be promptly diagnosed and the economy would quickly move to its new equilibrium.

- If consumers silently and unforeseeably switch from buying hats to buying jeans and running shoes, catching workers in the hat trade with their expectations too high, employment there will decrease, and decrease more than the increase of employment in jeans and shoemaking until new workers have relocated in those industries. A protracted period of disequilibrium could follow, a time of learning during which the unemployed are too slow in adjusting their off-target expectations. But it was classical doctrine that the unemployed hat workers (unless mad as a hatter) would adjust their expectations promptly, deciding either to leave for another industry or to accept a cut in their real wage—the wage measured by its command over goods, or purchasing power—in order to regain work in the hat trade.

♦ If a supply shock, or productivity shock, occurs that lowers the equilibrium level of the real wage throughout the economy, and if workers, all being caught unaware that they must accept a cut in their real wages to preserve their jobs, refuse at first to work for a lower wage in real terms—in terms of purchasing power—there will be an economywide fall of employment. This is straightforward classical economics: The insistence of workers on an above-equilibrium real wage decreases the number of workers that employers can go on hiring to some below-equilibrium level. But it was classical doctrine that workers, as soon as they perceived the new situation, would revise downward their expectations of the equilibrium level of the real wage; unemployed workers would resign themselves to having to accept a cut in their real wage, and the ensuing competition for jobs would promptly drive the real wage down—and employment up—until the new equilibrium is attained.

According to classical doctrine, then, episodes of unemployment tended to be fleeting. The market mechanism—the competition for jobs of workers and the striving of employers for the lowest possible cost—operated to bring a quick restoration of employment to its equilibrium level following any economic disturbance. Hence government intervention to promote the equilibrium level of employment was neither necessary nor useful.

THE EARLY CLASSICAL FOCUS ON EQUILIBRIUM UNDER COMMODITY MONEY

In the classical theory of the equilibration of the labor market the emphasis was always on the *real wage* demands of the workers as the key influence that limited the number of available jobs (just as the real rental demands of land owners limited the acreage rented by farmers). This must seem strange now, since in present-day economies the bulk of wage offers are quoted in units of money, not goods, and make no provision (not an explicit provision, at any rate) for adjusting the money-wage rate in proportion to the cost of living so as to preserve the real value of the terms of employment. However, the classical emphasis on the real wage demands of workers and real wage offers of employers grew naturally out of thinking in the early years of the subject about an economy in which all money is *commodity* money. The classical economists of the eighteenth century—Smith, Hume, and the rest—analyzed a world in which gold bars, gold doubloons, and the promises to pay gold of bankers and goldsmiths (so-called convertible bank notes) were the coin of the realm. The present-day system of *fiat* money, in which the government creates a paper currency not backed by gold or any other commodities (so-called inconvertible bank notes), did not become the commonly prevailing monetary system until the twentieth century.

◆ In a system of commodity money such as gold, where wages were expressed in terms of such money, a refusal of workers to accept a lower wage (in terms of the commodity money) *implied* a refusal to accept a lower real wage—provided there did not happen to be a rise in the real value of gold (i.e., an improvement in its relative price in terms of bread and other goods). In such a system, then, it would not normally be necessary to distinguish between the workers' real wage demands and their money-wage demands; they were one and the same problem, which competition would solve.

In recognition of the classical understanding of unemployment, it should be added, economists today often label as "classical unemployment" the amount of unemployment that must result *if* employers are for the most part induced to offer a wage expressed in *real* terms, and the real wage required by workers (or by firms' past contractual commitments to employees or by workers' labor unions) is *too high* to be compatible with firms' offering the equilibrium level of employment.

As the diagram below illustrates, if workers demand or firms' contractual commitments to their employees require a certain real wage, and if this required real wage is at an above-equilibrium level, employers will be driven

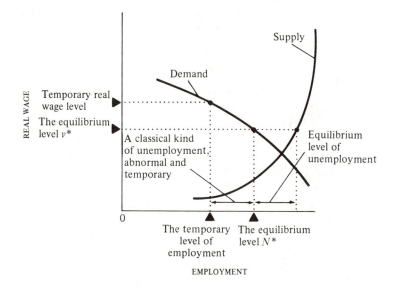

to lay off some employees or hire fewer new ones; hence employment will tend to be reduced to some below-equilibrium level, and the level of unemployment pushed above its equilibrium level. (Other simultaneous disturbances can make matters a little better or worse.) In the mid-1970s several countries on the Continent that experienced decreased employment were suspected of suffering such "classical unemployment," since *actual* real wage rates there *did not fall* after the OPEC cartel drove up the price of oil, while such a supply shock must have reduced the *equilibrium* real wage level. A truly classical economist, however, would ask proponents of this hypothesis why workers (and their unions) do not moderate their real wage demands once the observation of increased unemployment forces them to revise their expectations.

While the classical economists granted that unexpected or unperceived shocks might cause real wage rates to be fleetingly too high for employment to come up to its equilibrium level, they were firm against popular confusions on the causes of fluctuations in employment. Everyone, scholars and laymen alike, understood the sense in which the urban garment industry might be suffering from a "glut": Some error in producers' forecasts of the market-clearing price of dresses for rural womenfolk may have resulted in an oversupply, a supply for the season in excess of the equilibrium level. Next year it might be the farmers who are suffering a glut, having produced more potatoes, say, than would be demanded by cityfolk at what producers had expected the market price to be. In either case, the price will tend to fall below the expected level, as suppliers try to work off their surprisingly large unsold stocks of their product; and it is quite possible that there will be a cutback of employment—fewer dresses completed, fewer potatoes harvested and transported to the city. Unfortunately, many people slipped into the logical fallacy of believing that an economywide depression could be explained as a "general glut." The cause of such a depression was said to be general overproduction in relation to spending, or underspending in relation to production.

Readers who have come this far will probably kick themselves if they have not spotted the logical error in the idea of a "general glut": We cannot logically maintain that hard times on the farms is due to a distressingly *low farm goods prices in terms of city goods,* in terms of what farm goods will fetch in city markets, and then in the next breath say that hard times in the city are due to distressingly *low city good prices in terms of farm goods,* in terms of how much farm produce the typical city-made good can be exchanged for. The nineteenth-century French theorist Jean Baptiste Say became famous for carrying on a determined campaign against the fallacy. In what came to be known as Say's Law—what he called the *loi des débouchés*—he pointed out that the supply of goods marketed by farmers constitutes a demand for nonfarm goods, the supply of dresses represents a demand for nondresses. Say's wisdom was to see that a depression in America, say, or in the world, could not reasonably be attributed to an excessive productive capacity. On the other hand, Say's foolishness was to give the impression that, as a consequence, slumps are impossible. In place of the general-glut, or oversupply, fallacy Say invented the new fallacy that "supply creates its own demand"—as if the realization of equilibrium is somehow automatic. (As this chapter and the next show, all prices and wages in nominal, or money, terms have to undergo an adjustment, with each economic disturbance, for the equilibrium of supply and demand to be achieved. This requires the perception, cognition, and so forth of the economic actors. Equilibrium is not automatic, if it happens at all.)

Monetary Equilibrium under Fiat Money: The Neoclassical Claims

Economists with eyes fixed on the twentieth century, however, must ultimately concern themselves with the operation of market-type economies under a system of fiat money. If we inspect dollar bills, pound notes, and other specimens of paper money, we find some curious messages and strange signs.* But nowhere do they say that they are convertible into a quantity of gold or any other commodity. (The American $5 Federal Reserve Note offers to pay the bearer "five dollars," probably meaning five $1 Federal Reserve Notes.) They usually do say, "This note is legal tender for all debts, public and private." What is *not* said in this connection is just as important: The government will not enforce contracts involving payments expressed in terms of gold or other commodities or currencylike bank notes issued (to borrowers, say) by private banks. Governments like to be monopolists in the business of supplying coin and currency and to regulate the supply of (close and

---

* One of them announces "In God We Trust," which today might be interpreted as a modernist's caution that "In Secular Things (like Paper Money) You Had Better not Trust." But next to the motto is what looks like the insignia of a secret society with the caption, "A New Secular Order." So perhaps we may trust.

less close) money substitutes created by banks and other financial institutions. (A gain from doing so, called *seigniorage*, will come up in Chapter 21.) If a government did not limit its contract enforcement that way and limit the powers of private banks to compete with the government's money, there could be a "flight" out of government money into private money.

Here, in this section, we shall try to boil down matters to their simplest by supposing that all money (all things used as means of payment) is government fiat money; there are no "accounts" at private institutions called banks and investment funds that a person can write "checks" against in order to make payments—if there is a bank at all, it is a *government bank* where a person can hold a positive "credit balance" in his or her "account" if that way of holding money is preferred to holding the government's currency.*

- In this simplified world there is no difficulty at all about simply adding up the coins and currencies of the various sizes, or denominations, to form an aggregate called the "quantity of money." It makes perfect sense that a pair of five-dollar (or five-pound) notes should always be the equivalent of a ten-dollar (or ten-pound) note, since the government always manages the relative supplies of such notes in order to ensure that, in shops and markets, such notes always exchange at "par" for one another—neither ever selling at a "premium" because of a shortage of that denomination in people's holdings.

What is a "monetary equilibrium" in such a fiat money market-type economy? Evidently it means some sort of *overall general equilibrium with money*. What is the monetary condition for this equilibrium? The answer, in a nutshell, is that money must be worth in terms of the goods it will buy what people are currently expecting it will be worth when they go to exchange it for goods or other assets. In equilibrium the goods value of a unit of money (one dollar, un franc, eine Mark . . .), and hence the money value, or money price of goods, is what transactors expected.

- There is overall equilibrium in a *monetary economy* only if income earners and wealth owners, when planning how much money to hold over to the future (to next month, or week, or whatever), have *correct expectations* about the "general level" of *money prices*—the prices (in terms of money) of capital goods and land and consumer goods—currently and in the future.
- This monetary condition for overall equilibrium has to be added to the various *nonmonetary* conditions for equilibrium—in the various product markets and labor markets and asset markets—that were discussed first in chapter 3, next in the neoclassical analysis (Part 4) and then in the modernist Part 6.

*The final section of this chapter introduces private banking.

We have looked into the determination, under equilibrium conditions, of the price of fish, mousetraps, circuses, labor, and so on, in terms of bread, say. What determines how high the general level of money prices is—the *average* of the money prices of all things exchanged—under equilibrium conditions, if an equilibrium is possible? What determines, in other words, the equilibrium *money price* of bread? Two neoclassical monetary theorists of the early twentieth century, the English economist Alfred Marshall and his protégé, Alfred Pigou, both working at Cambridge, gave an answer—an answer attractive in its simplicity yet vague on details.

The neoclassicists' solution to the problem was to apply supply-and-demand analysis. The quantity of money supplied is taken to be a constant, set by the government. The quantity demanded—the amount people *plan* to hold, instead of capital assets—depends on the *value,* or purchasing power, they expect money to have. If the money price of bread is very low, then, *given* that the *relative* prices of the other goods in terms of bread are the *equilibrium* ones, the money prices of *all* goods are very low. Then the *value of money,* as the neoclassicals called it, would be very *high:* It would take a lot of bread (or any other good) to buy a unit of money—a dollar, or pound, or whatever. Thus a unit of money would buy a lot of bread or other goods. The total stock of money in circulation would have a very high purchasing power: The *real value* of the existing money supply would be very high in relation both to the existing stock of capital and other nonmoney assets and to the equilibrium level of the national product per month or per year. Imaginably, money prices could be low enough that an ordinary amount of currency in one's pocket or purse would be enough to buy the Crown Jewels or all the treasures in the National Gallery.

Such a low level of money prices, however, could not be the *equilibrium* level. Expectations of that low money price level could not be the right expectation to have. Why? If people expect to be able to buy capital assets and consumer goods at such prices, they will rush to the stock market, to real-estate offices and car lots, and to the stores with plans to exchange the excessive part of their money holdings for earning assets, consumer durables, great meals, and so forth. But the plans of everyone to reduce their money holdings cannot be fulfilled. If everyone desires (given expectations) to buy capital assets, there can be no one willing to sell. People cannot hold less money if no one is willing to hold more. (If we consider the money supply as currently *given,* held by the government at some desired level, the government will not swap bonds in return for some money; that would reduce the money supply.) The situation has the seeds of disequilibrium! The attempt of people to reduce their holdings of money can only drive prices upward and beyond the low level expected, if the actual prices were not higher already; so these expectations of the money price level would not be met.

Equilibrium can occur only if the expected money price level—hence the expected money prices of houses and bread and other things—is just high enough that money is not "burning a hole in people's pockets" and, at the same time, just low enough that people are content, in the aggregate anyway, to hold the existing stock of capital assets.

♦ If people's estimate of the level of money prices is *below* the equilibrium level, as in the case just discussed, there is an *excess supply of money,* which means an *excess demand for capital assets* (more broadly, the various assets and goods that are alternatives to money). As people try, as a result, to "get out of money into goods," they find that even if prices of capital assets were just previously at the level now expected, the excess demand for these assets implies that such prices cannot prevail. Money prices are bid up, rising above the expected level.

♦ If people's estimate of the level of money prices is *above* the equilibrium (correct expectations) level, there is an *excess demand for money,* thus an *excess supply of capital assets.* As people with nonmoney assets all try to reduce their nonmoney holdings in exchange for increased holdings of money, they drive the actual prices of houses, land, stocks, and so forth below the expected level.

> Figure 18–1, with its twin panels for money and capital, gives the supply-and-demand diagrams that neoclassical monetary theorists constructed to convey their view of how the equilibrium money-price level, and thus also the value of money, is determined.

A way of putting the monetary condition for equilibrium, then, is to say that the value of money that is expected must be just high enough that people's existing holdings of money have the expected real value—the expected purchasing power—that people want; so there is no excess demand for money, nor excess supply. Only then will the actually resulting prices be consistent with expectations. The question then arises: *How much* of their total purchasing power, their real wealth, do people want to hold in the form of money and thus how much in the alternative form of capital assets (or, more broadly, earning assets including bonds, land, and so forth)? What is the neoclassical model?

The Cambridge economists Marshall and Pigou hypothesized that the amount of purchasing power that people desire to hold in the form of money—the real value that their planned money holdings is expected to have—is proportional to their real income in terms of bread, say; the rest of their real wealth, by implication, people desire to hold in alternative forms. This is true of everyone, and the factor of proportionality is taken to be the same for all. So the expected real value of the desired quantity of money in the aggregate—the sum of the planned money holdings of all the individuals—

FIGURE 18–1: The Money-Price Level, Given the Money Supply, in Monetary Equilibrium

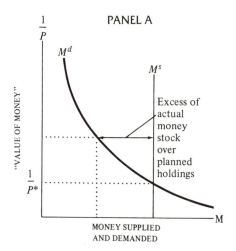
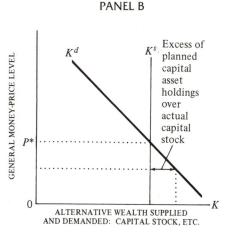

Panel A locates the equilibrium money price level at P^*. If that is the money-price level that people expect, the corresponding quantity of money that people in the aggregate will want to hold just equals the fixed amount supplied. Then the monetary condition for overall equilibrium is met.

If the money-price level is believed to be *lower,* say, hence the value of money higher, people will feel they are holding more real wealth, or purchasing power, in the form of money than they should: Capital assets, land, and so forth will be seen as bargains at such low prices. So there will be a 'decrease in the quantity of money demanded. With no change in the quantity of

money supplied, there is an excess supply of money. This excess supply is mirrored by an excess demand for alternative assets, for capital goods mostly. So actual money prices of capital assets—houses, cars, tractors, machines, etc.—could not in fact be (not for long, anyway) at the low levels expected. Actual money prices of capital assets would be bid up above the expected levels. Then producers of these capital goods would consequently bid up the money price of labor—money-wage rates. Thus the general level of money prices would be bid up. This is a disequilibrium: Expectations of money prices are disappointed and revised.

is likewise proportional to the economy's aggregate real income, which we may think of as its national product (in real terms, say, in terms of bread).

The implications of this hypothesis for the equilibrium level of the value of money, and the money price level, can be most easily traced as follows. Let P denote the general price level—the average level of money, or nominal, prices—and let P^e denote people's forecast of the price level, hence the expected level of P. Let M denote the quantity of money supplied, a given stock of currency since we are omitting bank money from the story, and let M^e denote the total of planned money holdings, hence the desired quantity of money. Finally, let Y denote the economy's aggregate real income, or national product, and let Y^e denote the total of people's expected real incomes, hence the expected level of Y. In these terms the Cambridge hypothesis says that

$$\frac{M^e}{P^e} = k\ Y \text{ or, equivalently, } M^e = k\ P^e\ Y,$$

where k, a positive constant, is the previously mentioned factor of proportionality, often dubbed the "Cambridge k"; it is desired aggregate real money holdings (on the average, from pay day to pay day) expressed as a fraction of aggregate real income (per year, say). This equation is known as the Cambridge equation of exchange.

For equilibrium, hence for $P = P^e$, the level of P^e must be such that $M^e = M$. Under equilibrium conditions, furthermore, neoclassical theory says that producers and workers will go ahead with the level of production determined by productivity and the supply and demand for labor (adding, if we like, the modern features in chapter 16). Let Y^* denote this equilibrium level of Y and Y^e. Hence this equilibrium model gives

$$M = k\ P^*\ Y^* \text{ or, equivalently, } P^* = \frac{M}{k\ Y^*}$$

for determining the equilibrium level, P^*, of the actual and expected price level, P and P^e.†

> Figure 18–2 translates to diagrammatic terms this neoclassical model of the determination of the equilibrium general price level and equilibrium aggregate output.

> For a numerical example, consider the economy of Sylvania, in which the sole commercial product is cut timber and the sole capital asset is standing timber. Suppose that Y^*, the *equilibrium* national output level, is running currently at the rate of 10 per annum (in billions of units of timber-weight, say). In the spirit of neoclassical theory we suppose that the equilibrium will be realized, perhaps after a brief interruption following any disturbance, so that the actual output level, Y, will also be equal to 10. Let the Cambridge k be 1/5. Then the desired level of *real* cash balances, M^e/P^e, which is given by kY, is equal to 2 (in billions of units of timber-weight). The desired level of *nominal* cash balances, M^e, which is determined by kYP^e, is therefore equal to $2P^e$.

† In America, it might be noted, equivalent equations were being propounded in a different guise:

$$M\ V = P\ Y \text{ and } M\ V = P^*\ Y^*,$$

where V is called the velocity (or more precisely the income-velocity) of money. Clearly, the New Haven V is the reciprocal of the Cambridge k.

FIGURE 18–2: The Neoclassical Model of Monetary Equilibrium

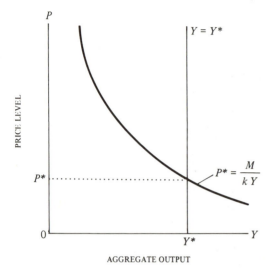

AGGREGATE OUTPUT

The height of the downward-sloping curve, representing the equation $P^* = M/kY$, measures how high the expected price level must be to induce people in the aggregate to plan to hold exactly the entire existing stock of money, no more and no less, and thus prevent an upward or downward spiraling of money prices as people vainly attempt to get into more capital assets or more money than exists.

The vertical curve, representing $Y = Y^*$, measures how large production must be if people, in their capacity as producers and suppliers of labor, etc., are not being led astray by incorrect expectations (born of disturbances), so that they produce the equilibrium output Y^*.

Neoclassical theory says that for equilibrium—for the actual price level, P, and the expected price level is to be equal—the desired level of nominal cash balance, M^e, must equal the actual level, M, hence $M = kYP^e$. In Sylvania, therefore, when M is, say, 150 (billion florins, say), then *in equilibrium* P^e equals 75 (florins per unit timber-weight). If instead P^e is less than 75, so that M^e is less than M and M/P^e is larger than 2—that is, nominal cash balances are larger than desired—cash holders will attempt to reduce their cash holdings and increase their holdings of timber. But the quantities of money and timber currently available are given. Hence the actual price of timber cannot also be 75; if it was that low at first, it would immediately be driven up by the excess supply of money, or excess demand for timber.

A composite quotation from the writings of Alfred Marshall conveys well the spirit of the theory (and the flavor of economic theorizing in those times):

In every state of society there is some fraction of their income which people find it worthwhile to keep in the form of currency; it may be a fifth, or a tenth, or a twentieth. A large command of resources in the form of currency renders their business easy and smooth, and puts them at an advantage in bargaining; but on the other hand it locks up in a barren form resources that might yield an income of gratification if invested, say, in extra furniture; or a money income, if invested in extra machinery or cattle. . . . A man fixes the appropriate fraction after balancing one against another the advantages of a further ready command and the disadvantages of putting more of his resources into a form in which they yield him no direct income or other benefit.

Let us suppose that all the inhabitants of a country, taken one with another (and including therefore all varieties of character and occupation), find it just worth their while to keep by them on the average ready purchasing power to the extent of a tenth part of their annual [real] income [plus] a fiftieth part of their property; then the aggregate [real] value of the currency of the country will tend to be equal to the sum of these amounts.*

Notice that the artful Marshall carefully allows for the possibility that the "fraction" he speaks of in the first sentence—the Cambridge k—might depend upon the "state" that the society finds itself in and thus change as the equilibrium changed. In particular, Marshall goes on to imply that how much real wealth people feel they can afford to hold in the form of currency will depend upon the *opportunity cost* of holding "barren" (noninterest-bearing) currency—as measured by the interest yield offered by alternative earning assets, such as shares in a factory or cattle ranch, or the nonpecuniary psychic yield offered by consumer durables (the Marshalls' extra furniture). Presumably a rise in the yield on such alternative assets, alternatives to holding so much wealth in the form of money, would induce people to reduce their respective individual "fractions" and thus cause a reduction in the average (mean) of these fractions—the value of the Cambridge k. Hence if the overall economic equilibrium were to change (whether or not the new equilibrium is yet realized in actuality!), and with it the expected yield on capital assets, there would be a corresponding change in the value of the Cambridge k. Years later John Maynard Keynes took the position that unpredictable shifts in the equilibrium value of k are a possible source of serious *departures* from equilibrium—of boom and slump.

THE NEUTRALITY OF MONEY IN MONETARY EQUILIBRIUM

Out of the neoclassical theory of monetary equilibrium emerges a famous theorem. It is the proposition that the quantity of money is "neutral" under equilibrium conditions: A change in the supply of money has no real effects—no effects on quantities of output produced of any good or workers hired of any type, and no effects on relative prices of produced goods and productive services. And since there is no effect on production and the real rewards to labor and capital, there is no resulting effect on the amount of real cash balances demanded by people—hence no effect on the *real value* of the money supply, in equilibrium.

---

* Quotations from Alfred Marshall, *Money, Credit and Commerce* (London: Macmillan and Co., Ltd., 1923), pp. 44–45, as compiled in John Maynard Keynes, *Treatise on Money* (London: Macmillan and Co., Ltd., 1930), p. 230. Bracketed words added.

♦ If the supply of money were twice as great as it is, that would be reflected merely by the equilibrium money price level being twice as high as a result. All money prices, money wage rates, money rentals on machines and land, etc., would be twice as high. Put concretely: If the government replaced all one-dollar bills by two-dollar bills, all five-dollar bills by ten-dollar bills, and so on, the consequence would be a doubling of the dollar prices of all goods and productive services. But no *real* effects!

This proposition has come to be known as the Quantity Theorem: Double (or halve) the quantity of money and you will exactly double (or halve) all money values.

Over the decades much ink has been spilled debating the various conditions that must be stipulated to make very sure that this "theorem" is completely right. What if there are interest-bearing government bonds outstanding? What if there are private banks? However, no one denies that the proposition contains a large grain of truth about equilibrium.

So much for the neoclassical theory of monetary equilibrium—under the simplest monetary system. It bears saying again, however, that the neoclassical economists understood more than they wrote down. They never meant to suggest that disequilibrium, even a fleeting one, is impossible—that departures from monetary equilibrium could not happen even for a moment. Suppose that somehow the supply of money fell or that the demand for purchasing power in money form—the demand for real cash balances—rose. Then the equilibrium money-price level is reduced. The new equilibrium will be reached *if and when* the level of money prices, money wages, and so forth that are expected, or believed, to be prevailing and the level actually prevailing have dropped accordingly. Unless and until that full adjustment occurs there will be disequilibrium.

One of the most thoughtful of classical economists, John Stuart Mill, suggested that in such "deflationary" situations sellers of goods (both capital assets and consumer goods), though driven sooner or later to cut their prices, do not immediately cut prices to the equilibrium level:

[At times] there is really an excess of all commodities above the money-demand [for them]; in other words, there is an under-supply of money. . . . Almost everybody is therefore a [would-be] seller and there are scarcely any buyers so that there may really be . . . what may be indiscriminately called a [general] glut of commodities or a dearth of money.*

Thus Mill, among others, recognized that money prices (and similarly money wage rates) could be too high for equilibrium. *Why* too high? Mill did not say. False hopes, a few neoclassicals suggested. Yet the neoclassicists' faith in the rapid tendency to equilibrium burned ever bright.

* John Stuart Mill, *Principles of Political Economy,* London, 1848. Reprinted London: Macmillan, 1909, Book III, chap. 14.

MONEY AND PRIVATE BANKING *

In most countries, including those with very extensive private ownership of capital, the banking system is government owned. Just in the past few years a new wave of bank nationalizations has swept over several countries: Governments moved to purchase ownership (in exchange for public debt) of banks that had been privately owned in France, Mexico, and Spain. As noted in chapter 17, the supply of money, as it is usually defined, is simply the stock of government coin and currency in the hands of the public, both households and nonbank firms, *plus* the total size of people's checking accounts at the banks—called "demand deposits" because it is understood that a deposit holder can withdraw or draw down (by writing checks) his checking-account balance "on demand," without a waiting period. In a government-owned system it is clear that the government can exercise direct and centralized control over the total supply of money: It can direct a public bank to enter one or another of the asset markets to buy a privately owned asset—bonds, corporate shares, . . . and so forth—in exchange for a deposit at the bank or for a check depositable into the seller's account at another of the public banks in the system. Voilà! The quantity of money in the economy has thus been increased. In effect the government's banking system has simply printed more bank notes, more currency, and got them into circulation by using them to purchase some assets.

◆ In economies with a government-owned and government-operated banking system there are no private banks whose actions—the purchase or sale of securities or the making or nonrenewal of loans—could have effects on the supply of money.

The other kind of banking system found in the world is composed of private banks operating under the regulation of a central bank, such as the Federal Reserve in the United States, the Bank of Canada in Canada, and the Bank of England in the United Kingdom. The central bank operates to a greater or lesser degree under government authority. The main point to be conveyed here is that in most banking systems private banks have the power to contribute to the supply of money. So does the government. Hence we may say that the quantity of money outstanding in such a system is the result of the interaction of government and private actions. Usually, in this interaction, the government has the last word. But it cannot always control the actual quantity of money in the system with precision.

The First Banks

If we looked at a dictionary we could find something about cloud banks, banks of daisies, and so forth. A bank once meant a collection, or concen-

---

* This section is not a prerequisite to understanding the subsequent chapters, though perhaps it is "required reading" for an economics education.

tration, of something; then the place where they were collected or stored—
a safe place you could "bank on." But banks stopped being mere storehouses and began to engage in the practice of banking in the economist's
sense of the term.

Economists say that the first banks were the medieval goldsmiths. As markets grew more extensive and trading far-flung, the use of money increased.
The money then was gold, which was better suited in most respects for that
role than other commodities, such as lead or deeds to distant land holdings:
It was portable, measurable, and recognizable. But it could be lost or stolen,
so it was not very safe to keep at home or in a pocket; and it would have
been a nuisance to have to go to an assay office to have your gold weighed
and checked for purity every time you wanted to spend some of it on a
consumer good or invest in a productive asset. To solve that problem people
began to deposit their gold with a goldsmith for safekeeping in exchange
for a receipt stating the quantity and quality of gold held. Even better, people then realized that to spend or invest their money they need not trek to
the goldsmith where their gold was: They could turn over some of their
goldsmith's receipts as payment to the seller, who would then make similar
use of them when making his own purchases, and so on. Thus goldsmith's
receipts came to function as paper money.

Now the *definition* of the money supply states that:

Supply of money = Gold in circulation + total value of gold receipts

But *at this stage* in our story the paper money, the gold receipts, is completely *backed* by gold held in the safes of the goldsmiths. (If somewhere a
goldsmith has absconded with his clients' deposits the corresponding gold
receipts, once the disappearance is known, will be valueless.) Hence

Gold in circulation + Value of gold receipts = Gold stock

So the supply of money is at this stage still *equal* to the total gold stock held
directly or on deposit.

True creativity occurred, however, when some observant goldsmith noticed
something: The depositors were not coming around anymore to take back
their deposits. They did not need to, because the gold receipts had become,
for most purposes, as good as gold—better, really. As long as there was
general confidence that a goldsmith held enough gold to meet any demands
for actual gold that might arise, and confidence that he in particular could
meet any depositor's demand, his depositors would continue to be willing
to hold his receipts.

♦ Of course, there were withdrawals whenever a depositor needed some
actual gold (for some special reason), yet there were also fresh flows of
gold deposited whenever a depositor received in payment some unneeded

gold. Thus there was a continual ebb and flow of the total stock of gold deposits. However, the net outflow in a week or a month was never more than a fraction, and seldom more than a small fraction, of the goldsmith's total stock of gold assets. Hence a large fraction of the goldsmith's gold stock was forever resting idle in the safe, earning no interest.

The dawning realization of all this must have set the goldsmith's mind racing: "Why not *lend* at the going rate of interest some of my gold stock, which seems at present to be greatly in excess of what is likely to be needed, and keep in reserve only as much gold as seems prudent in order to meet the occasionally heavy net outflow? As long as reserves are perceived to be ample in relation to the normal ebb and flow of deposits, what harm will there be to my depositors?" So the goldsmith made loans up to the point where his remaining reserves of gold were no longer judged excessive.

Interesting consequences followed from the goldsmith's action and those of the other goldsmiths who soon imitated. In making loans the creative goldsmith (and each imitator) *created money:* By taking gold out of idle stocks in the vaults and putting it into circulation the goldsmith adds to the stock of gold in circulation and thus to the total supply of money. (Proof: Gold in circulation, which does *not* include goldsmiths' reserves, is up, while gold receipts are not down; so the right-hand side of the previous equation, which equals the supply of money, is also up.) Nor is this proposition altered if, as might be assumed, the borrowers immediately deposit their new gold holdings, which they have just borrowed, at a goldsmith's—the goldsmith that lent them the gold or another goldsmith—in exchange for gold receipts. Then gold in circulation is not up, since the gold found its way back into the goldsmiths' vaults, but gold receipts are up, as is the supply of money. In either case the money supply goes up by the quantity of the loans made. Proof:

$$
\begin{aligned}
&\text{Gold in circulation} && + \text{Value of gold receipts} \\
={}& \text{Gold stock} - \text{Goldsmiths' reserves} && + \text{Value of gold receipts} \\
={}& \text{Gold stock} + \text{Value of gold receipts} - \text{Goldsmiths' reserves} \\
={}& \text{Gold stock} + \text{Goldsmiths' loans outstanding}
\end{aligned}
$$

Such was the alchemy of the medieval goldsmiths.

Are there any effects of the goldsmiths' loans on the economy? Or is there only make-work for government statisticians hired to keep track of the "money supply"? There is an effect and a noneffect.

♦ There are no effects of the money creation on people's real net worth—on their real wealth *net* of the real value of their liabilities. Society is certainly not richer as a result. There has been no increase of the nation's existing capital or land—not even its gold stock, which might someday find its use in people's teeth and jewelry. The increase in the goldsmiths' holdings of loan contracts, which are listed as assets, is counterbalanced by a decrease in their gold reserves, which are also assets, together with an increase in gold receipts, which are the *goldsmiths'* liabilities (since the receipt holders may demand to have them redeemed for actual gold); so there is no *net* increase in the goldsmiths' total assets *net* of their liabilities. Equally clearly, the increase in the holdings of gold and gold receipts by the nongoldsmith "public" is counterbalanced by the increase in its debts to the goldsmiths. Thus wealth in the most basic sense of the term has not been created by the creation of additional money. *But:*

♦ There *are* important effects on people's *liquidity*. These effects originate when the amazed goldsmiths find themselves with mounting stocks of depositors' gold, which are *liquid* assets—remember, gold was the money then!—that were offset only by an increase in the gold receipts they had to issue, which they found to be highly illiquid liabilities. (Hardly anyone came around to "liquidate" the liability by demanding that his receipts be redeemed for gold.) So the goldsmiths found themselves *more liquid*. When, as a result, they made some prudent loans out of their excessive reserves of liquid assets, they traded some of their new-found extra liquidity for some extra interest (interest income). Thus the nongoldsmith public became more liquid too, in exchange for payment of interest to the goldsmiths.

The impact of this increase of liquidity was the appearance of an excess demand for real assets, for land and capital equipment and so on. (In fact the goldsmiths could just as well have invested in such assets rather than lending the gold to other enterprises to make such investments.) More demand, but the same supply! The result: *An increase of the equilibrium level of money prices*—meaning prices in terms of gold. The reason: A rise of the money-price level (i.e., the general level of money prices) reduces the real value of the money supply—the money supply in terms of its purchasing power over bread and so forth. Thus a rise of the price level serves to reduce the excess supply of real cash balances and hence to reduce the excess demand for real assets. In equilibrium the price level must be just high enough that the real value of money balances is reduced to the quantity demanded.

A final point: It makes no difference to the goldsmith story if depositors instead of accepting receipts in exchange for their deposits, which they can then use as money, accept a bookkeeping entry at their favorite goldsmith's indicating their "balances," which they could then write checks against (up to the amount of the deposit balance).

Private Banking with Fiat Money

Turn now to private banking based on government-issued paper money—so-called fiat money. Once again, as in the goldsmith story, we can imagine that in the first stage *private banks* spring up that accept deposits of paper money for safekeeping. One difference, which is of some importance, is that people would not store government bank notes (currency) in return for private-bank bank notes (or bank receipts)—people would be interested in receiving bookkeeping entries of *deposit balances* in return for their surrender of government fiat money; the greater convenience for some purposes of checking-account money compared to currency-type money is another advantage that the banks can offer, besides the advantage of safety, in their campaign to attract depositors. (Remember, in the story of private banking, the government graciously leaves the banking business to private banks!) Another difference is that the private banks would not hold much of their reserves in the form of currency. The private banks would turn over most of the currency to the government in exchange for a deposit balance (a bookkeeping entry) of equal size. The government would create for this purpose an agency called the central bank—a government bank used only by the private banks. The central bank, moreover, would naturally become the government agency charged with the administration of the money supply.

In this world of fiat money and private banks, the definition of the money supply is

$$\text{Money supply} = \text{Fiat money in circulation} + \text{Demand deposit balances at private banks}$$

But note that at this stage of our story, as at the comparable stage of the goldsmith story, the banks have not done anything with their reserves of fiat money. The demand-deposit balances of people at the private banks are completely *backed* by the banks' holdings of fiat money—held either in the form of government currency or, more conveniently, in deposit balances at the central bank. Hence at this stage,

$$\text{Fiat money in circulation} + \text{Demand deposit balances} = \text{Stock of fiat money}$$

So at this stage the supply of money is still equal to the total stock of fiat money.

The parallel with the goldsmith story continues: The banks see that their reserves are excessive in relation to their ebb and flow as some deposits are drawn down (by check) and other deposits are added to (by fresh deposits of currency or of checks against deposits at other banks). So the banks will move to make loans or purchase securities with their surplus reserves. They can do that by handing over to the lender or security seller some of their holdings of currency. Or they can write "checks on themselves" and when Bank A finds its customers depositing checks on Bank B and vice versa the two banks can agree to move cash from one bank to the other only by the amount of the difference between the two totals of checks. Or, with loans, they can simply create a deposit balance for the borrowers by the stroke of a pen or an instruction to the computer. Any way they do it, the money supply is increased. It increases by exactly the amount of the loans made. Proof:

$$
\begin{aligned}
&\text{Fiat money in circulation} \quad\quad\quad\quad\quad + \text{Demand deposit balances} \\[2pt]
&= \text{Fiat money in circulation} + \underset{\text{of fiat money}}{\text{Bank reserves}} + \underset{\text{balances}}{\text{Demand deposit}} - \underset{\text{of fiat money}}{\text{Bank reserves}} \\[2pt]
&= \text{Stock of fiat money} \quad\quad\quad\quad\quad\quad + \underset{\text{and security holdings}}{\text{Bank loans outstanding}}
\end{aligned}
$$

The stock of fiat money is often called the quantity of "outside money" because this stock is determined outside the banking system—by the government, in fact; and the amount added to the supply of money by the banking system through loans and security purchases is referred to as the quantity of "inside money." The stock of fiat money has also been dubbed *high-powered money:* The term reminds us that a given level of fiat money can support a much *larger* level of the total money supply—"outside" *plus* "inside." This was just shown!

◆ Yet the above equations do not highlight a startling point: If the reserves that banks keep are only a *small fraction* of the deposit balances—that is, they lend most of what they get—and if the public holds little or no money in coin and currency—that is, the public has most of its money at the banks—then inside money may be *many times* larger than outside money. Example: Suppose the public holds nothing in fiat money (coin and currency), so the banks receive all of it. Say their reserves, then, are 100 billion—dollars, pounds, or whatever. Suppose now that the banks want (and are permitted by law) to hold reserves equal to only one-fifth of their deposit balances. When they make 80 billion of loans it winds up in the form of additional deposits of exactly 80 billion, since the borrowers want demand-deposit balances, not coin and currency. So the banks will make another 64 billion of loans—that is, four-fifths of the added 80 billion of deposits. But this 64 billion will bounce back too! The process cannot stop until finally demand-deposit balances have risen to a total of 500 billion; *then,* and only then, the banks will be content to hold in reserves the whole 100 billion—which is the fiat money the public does not want to hold. No wonder, then, that outside money is called high-powered.

Recent developments. Not many years ago it was widely understood that the central bank, if it chose, could exercise tight control over the supply of money: It could increase or decrease the supply of "outside money" and thus widen the base on which the pyramid of "inside money" is built; with less fiat money in their hands, say, the banks would have less reserves to lend. Further, the central bank could impose reserve requirements on the private banks, forcing them to hold a higher fraction of their assets in the form of fiat-money reserves; if the fractional reserve requirement was increased, say from one-fifth to one-fourth, the banks would have less in "excess reserves" from which to make loans and security purchases, so 100 billion of reserves would support a level of demand deposit balances of only 400 billion instead of 500 billion. But banks have evolved new ways of functioning:

- A bank can make loans without any reserves at first, creating deposit balances for the borrowers with "the stroke of a pen," and then borrow the fiat money needed to meet the governmental reserve requirement.
- A nonbank financial institution such as a brokerage house can, in effect, invite its customers to hold interest-bearing demand deposit balances instead of the treasury bills, commercial paper, and other short-term securities they were holding. These money market funds are not so far required to hold fiat-money reserves.
- Foreign banks, which do not have to meet our government's reserve requirement regulations, can offer to open up demand deposit balances denominated in our currency. Imaginably we might do all our banking through foreign countries "off-shore."

For these reasons banking is in a state of flux these days. What weights shall we give to the various components of the money supply? How much moneyness is there, in other words, in the deposit balances at money market funds compared to deposit balances at private banks? How about deposit balances off-shore, in distant lands? And how much liquidity is added to the economy when a brokerage house creates deposits but, for assets, purchases only highly liquid securities—which were barely less liquid than the deposits now held?

The complexity of the financial world is vastly greater than acknowledged in the Cambridge equation of exchange!

SUMMARY

1. The economic upheavals in Europe and the Western Hemisphere in the 1920s, culminating in the worldwide Great Depression, shook the faith of classical theorists in their doctrine that the economy tends rapidly to reach equilibrium in *all* markets. According to this traditional doctrine, the effect of a monetary disturbance—a shock affecting the supply of money or the willingness of people to hold money balances—vanishes quickly, like the ripples that a pebble propagates when dropped in the pond. This was the classical doctrine of monetary equilibrium. Most of this chapter is devoted to expounding what it said.

2. An economy is said to be in monetary equilibrium if—besides producers being in equilibrium by guessing the going price of their product (in terms of other products) and the going pay of their inputs, and workers being in equilibrium by guessing right about wages, etc.—people are right in their expectations about the real value, or purchasing power, of their holdings of money (i.e., the amount of real goods their holdings could be exchanged for at stores). Hence monetary equilibrium requires *correct expectations* about the *money prices* of the goods produced—or, more simply, the "value of money," measured by the purchasing power of a unit of the currency (pound note, dollar bill) in terms of "bread."

3. How is the equilibrium level of the "value of money" determined, according to the classical doctrine? What, in other words, determines the money price of bread or, more precisely, the general price level—the general (or average) level of money prices of goods? Neoclassical theory says: Each person wants to hold *on average* a level of money balances the *expected purchasing power* of which is some proportion of his *income* (per annum, say) in real terms—his pay in terms of bread, that is. The aggregate of people's real incomes is, basically, just the national output, call it Y. This leads the neoclassical theorists to say that the aggregate quantity of money desired, measured in terms of its expected purchasing power—hence the money desired expressed as a ratio to the expected price level in terms of money, (M^e/P^e)—is likewise *proportional* to national output:

$$\frac{M^e}{P^e} = k \cdot Y$$

where the coefficient, the "Cambridge k," is the factor of proportionality. We can rearrange this "Cambridge equation" to solve for what the expected price level must be in order that people plan to hold—which they have to do!—the actual supply of money, call it M_o:

$$P^e = \frac{M_o}{k \cdot Y}$$

In monetary equilibrium the actual price level equals the expected: $P = P^e$, and their common equilibrium value may be denoted P^*. Hence the above equation can be used to determine the equilibrium level of the price level:

$$P^* = \frac{M_o}{k \cdot Y^*}$$

where Y^* is the equilibrium level of national output—that is, the aggregate of the output that producers would supply in conditions of overall monetary equilibrium.

4. Next, the pièce de résistance of classical monetary doctrine, the proposition about the "neutrality of money," alias the Quantity Theorem. The

theorem: If saboteurs intending to wreak havoc on the nation's economy surreptitiously replaced every one-dollar bill with a two-dollar bill, every five-dollar bill with a ten, and similarly with bank accounts, there would be no *real* effects on the economy's equilibrium: National output would still have the same *equilibrium* value of Y^*, and the *equilibrium* price of circuses in terms of bread (the "real" price of the circus) would be the same, and so on. The only effect would be a *nominal* one: All the *money* prices would rise *in proportion* to the *money supply*—including, here, the "money price of labor," called the money-wage rate or the nominal wage. Thus the *real* value of people's money holdings in the new equilibrium would be the same as in the old. Of course, it is conceivable that the new equilibrium will not be realized—some disequilibrium may occur, at least for a while. But if the new equilibrium is reached promptly we can say, in view of the above, that the supply of money is "neutral" in the economy: It determines, given a little time for adjustment, only the money prices of things and not anything else.

5. The determination of the supply of money, from the stock of "outside money" set by the government through its central bank, via the workings of a fractional-reserve banking system, is the subject of the last section.

CONCEPTS INTRODUCED

general price level,	value of money	cost of holding money
money-price level,	Cambridge equation of exchange	real cash balances
nominal price level	money supply	outside money
monetary equilibrium	velocity of money	inside money

STUDY QUESTIONS

1. "The monetary condition for equilibrium is that the expected and actual price level provide the existing money supply with the real value, expected and actual, that people want to hold in money form rather than in earning assets." Explain. What happens to the desired real value of money holdings in the event that some or all earning assets are expected to pay a lower rate of return? What if some kinds of money begin to pay a rate of return?

2. Suppose that everyone expects a price level above the equilibrium level so that there is an excess demand for money; and everyone accordingly places sell orders with brokers and heads for vacation. If there are no stop-loss orders, how far will stock prices and so forth fall? How would expectations of the current price level be revised if brokers can locate their clients to tell the news?

3. If people desire to hold a larger amount of their real wealth in money form, the equilibrium price level is thereby reduced. Are money-wage rates, often called nominal wage rates, unchanged in the new equilibrium? Why or why not? Although everyone was willing to give up some earning assets (capital assets, etc.) to achieve the increased level of real money holdings, did people in the aggregate actually find it necessary in the end to give up earning assets? What happens to their total real wealth if the new equilibrium is reached? Would there be any difference if the government elected to "accommodate" the increased desire for real money balances by acting to increase the money supply?

APPENDIX 1: MORE ON NATIONAL INCOME AND PRODUCT

Let us take a couple of pages to be more precise about the meaning of the nominal GNP, also known as the money GNP, and its quite different twin, the real GNP.

Table 18A–1 gives a highly impressionistic accounting (with no pretense at historical accuracy except for the totals) of the national product in the United States around the time of the Great Depression. It is a mythicized America of bread and circus and tractors.

The first entry on the line labeled "Bread" indicates the money value—in billions of United States dollars—of bread produced in 1929 by American bakeries. Of course, the baking industry consumed a great deal of wheat to produce that bread. It would be double counting to add the value of *that*

Table 18A–1: REAL AND NOMINAL GNP IN MYTHIC "AMERICA" BEFORE AND DURING THE GREAT DEPRESSION

	Value of National Output at Current Prices		Average Price		Value of National Output at 1929 Prices	
	1929	1933	1929	1933	1929	1933
Circus	20	8	$ .75	$ .60	20	10
Bread	60	39	.24	.18	60	52
Wheat added to inventories	4	1	.90	.45	4	2
Tractors	12	0	900.00	800.00	12	0
	96	49*			96	64
	Nominal GNP				Real GNP	

* Individual amounts need not add to the total shown due to rounding errors.

wheat to national production, since it is already counted in the bread. But any remaining wheat production going into inventories or overseas for export must be added; that is the meaning of the 4 billion on the "Wheat" line for 1929. The money values of all the national outputs in 1929 add up to a nominal GNP of 96 billion. With the arrival of the Great Depression the nominal GNP fell by *nearly one-half*, to 49 billion, in 1933.

But *some* of the decline in the money value of the outputs of bread, wheat, and so forth was due merely to declines in *money prices*.

◆ Had the money price of circuses been *constant*, staying at 75 cents per admission, which would have been a rise of *25 percent* over the actual 60¢, the *money value* of that 1933 output would have been 25 percent higher—10 instead of 8.

When the real values of the 1933 outputs are calculated we find that the *real GNP* fell by about *one-third* from its 1929 level, not one-half.

APPENDIX 2: PRICE LEVEL AND EXCHANGE-RATE DETERMINATION IN AN OPEN ECONOMY

The coexistence of national currencies, or monies, in the world introduces a new kind of price into the picture—the rate of exchange between one money and another. In the United States and many other countries the exchange rate is defined as the amount of home currency necessary to buy a unit of the foreign currency; so a rise of the exchange rate means a depreciation of the home currency. In Britain and some other countries it is the other way around—the amount of the foreign currency needed to buy a unit of ours. Where use of the term is unavoidable (such as in equations) we use here the American definition.

The existence of foreign currencies that are bought and sold with the home currency at first poses a puzzle. To determine the money price level in our country—Portugal, for example—we have the Cambridge equation: $P^* = M/k^* \cdot Y^*$. *But now there is another relationship.* If the price of wine abroad is so many dollars and it takes so much of our currency to buy a dollar we can calculate what this wine must be selling for at home in *our* currency. If the price here were higher, foreign sellers would start selling more here, which would drive our price down; if lower, domestic sellers would start selling only abroad, which would drive our price up. Such arbitrage across markets tends to cause identical products, such as wine of the same vintage from the same bottler and vineyard, that are sold in two or more markets to sell for the equivalent price after conversion into a common money.† So, if P^f is the average price abroad, in dollars, of the goods we produce and if E is the exchange rate, or the amount of our currency needed to buy a dollar, then the average price level at home, P, is given by $P = E \cdot P^f$. So it seems at first that we have a puzzling excess of equations to determine the equilibrium price level, P^*, in our country.

Upon reflection, however, it can be seen that the *second* relationship is needed if we are to determine the *exchange rate* as well as the price level. We may think of the second relationship as determining the exchange rate, E^*, *given* the equilibrium price of our exports abroad, P^{f*}, and *given* the equilibrium price level at home, P^*. That is, $E^* = P^*/P^{f*}$. The *first* relationship determines the value of P^* for use in this E^* formula.

But what determines P^{f*}? It might be the case that our country is too small a supplier of the goods it exports to be able to affect appreciably the world price of its goods by changes (even changes that are big for us) in the amount it exports. Then P^{f*} can be taken as a constant. In this case we are done. The above equation for E^* is sufficient. We have

$$E^* = \frac{M}{k \cdot Y^*} \frac{1}{P^{f*}}, \; P^{f*} = \text{constant}.$$

Notice the implication that if M should double, E^* and P^* double also. If we think of the rest of the world as a single country with a national money supply, so that $P^{f*} = \dfrac{M^f}{k^{f*} \cdot Y^{f*}}$, then we obtain

$$E^* = \frac{M}{M^f} \frac{k^{f*} Y^{f*}}{k^* Y^*}.$$

What matters for E^* is the ratio of the two money supplies.

Another case frequently discussed is that in which the country is a sufficiently important supplier of its principal export goods in the world market that it possesses some monopoly power over the world prices of those goods. The power of Brazil over the world price of coffee, Chile over the world price of copper ore, and, to a lesser degree, Canada over the world price of wheat are good examples; Holland's power over the price of tulips, on the other hand, is a bad example, since the preponderance of Dutch exports lack this monopoly power. In this case P^{f*} is not a constant. It is lower the larger is our amount of exports; the larger the amount we sell abroad, the lower we have to go along the foreigners' demand curve for our exports. But *given* the amount of our equilibrium national output, Y^*, not purchased

---

†The law of one price, which was criticized (except as a very long-term tendency) in Part 6, especially chapter 15, is much stronger: It says that *equivalent* products, such as two wines that *taste* the same, sell for the equivalent price—i.e., the same price after exchange conversion. In contrast, the text is discussing *identical* wine that is known to be such, so information is less of a problem for buyers.

at home by residents, and thus the amount of output left for export, the corresponding P^{f*} can be calculated; we can figure out how far we are going to go down the foreigners' demand curve for our exports. So there is no difficulty. Once P^{f*} has been thus calculated, we can use the above formulae to determine E^*. The aforementioned results remain valid in this case: If our M is doubled, our E^* and our P^* both double. (Thus there is no effect on the *real* exchange rate, defined as E/P or, more accurately, as EP^f/P.) It can also be shown that if "their" M^f is doubled, P^{f*} doubles along with all other money prices abroad (including *their* exchange rate, E^f), so that E^* halves. So it is again the M ratio that matters.

To test understanding we may consider a topical example: Our government institutes increased government spending—spending that diverts labor from wine growing or expenditures to stockpile wine for future emergencies—or tax cuts that promote increased national spending on our domestic output—so that a smaller amount of our output is left for export. What are the effects on E and P^{f*} if our country has some monopoly power? The answer is a rise of P^{f*} and, if P^* is unaffected (which it will be if Y^* and k^* are unaffected), a fall of E. The latter means a strengthening of our currency in foreign-exchange markets.

CHAPTER 19

The Possibility of Monetary Disequilibrium: Keynes's General Theory of Employment*

> INSPECTOR:
> Rick, why did you come here to Casablanca?
> RICK:
> I came here for the waters.
> INSPECTOR:
> But there are no waters here in Casablanca.
> RICK:
> I was misinformed.
>
> Humphrey Bogart and Claude Rains in *Casablanca* (1942)

As the economic crisis of the interwar years persisted, teachers of economics went on explaining the neoclassical doctrine of monetary equilibrium, which was what they knew:

◆ In equilibrium, expectations are right. These expectations drive buyers and sellers to make decisions that will cause the original expectations to be fulfilled: Wages and prices will turn out as expected; fruit pickers, architects, and so on will suffer only the expected idleness "between jobs." In equilibrium, then, there is no general glut: Sellers of goods and productive services are not generally disappointed. There are no regretful feelings of having held out for too high a wage or too high a price.

---

*This chapter is made longer than the others by the inclusion of a final (optional) section, which begins on p. 527.

♦ It is possible that expectations might for a time be wrong. *If* wrong, the general level of money prices and wages might lie above the equilibrium level. At such high prices and wages there would be an "under-supply of money," as Mill called it. Then the level of production and employment could be below equilibrium. But how could such a disequilibrium occur for weeks or months at a time? Presumably, in the economy as a whole and in each individual industry, prices and wages tend to their equilibrium levels!

Thus the economists kept running up the same dead end, unable to reach a plausible explanation of the world depression around them. Finally, it seems obvious where the wrong turn was: It was in clinging to the premise that the *economy is almost always in equilibrium.*

In the early years of the Great Depression, John Maynard Keynes set out on a "long struggle of escape" from the classical doctrine of monetary equilibrium. For Keynes emancipation eventually came when he succeeded in formulating to his satisfaction "a more general theory [of a monetary economy], which includes the classical theory with which we are familiar as a special case."* Whatever the final verdict on the merits and faults of Keynes's contribution, there is no doubt that 1936, when the new theory was first published, will remain one of the landmark years in the history of economics.

This chapter will examine the two principal arguments made by Keynes in his case for a disequilibrium theory to go alongside the equilibrium theory. There is first of all his claim that money-wage rates do not tend reliably to reach their equilibrium level, and that additional unemployment—above the normal, equilibrium amount—develops as a result. Then there is his suggestion that an equilibrium may fail to exist—no equilibrium level for money wages and prices to reach—unless the government intervenes with fiscal policies to create an equilibrium.

OBSTACLES TO RAPID EQUILIBRATION: THE UNRELIABILITY OF MONEY-WAGE RATES

When a disturbance occurs in the economy, attaining the new equilibrium—if there is one and if it is attained—generally requires a new level of money prices, up or down, and a new level of money-wage rates. The Cambridge model, discussed in the previous chapter, offers a convenient way to cate-

---

* J. M. Keynes, *The General Theory of Employment, Interest and Money* (London: Macmillan and Company, 1936), p. vii.

gorize the various factors influencing the equilibrium money-price level. The Cambridge equation of exchange constitutes a formula for the height of the equilibrium money-price level, P^*:

$$P^* = \frac{M}{k^* \cdot Y^*} \tag{1}$$

The equilibrium price level is evidently compounded from three ingredients: One is the supply of money, M. The equilibrium level of the national output, Y^*, is another. The third k^*, is the equilibrium value of the Cambridge k—the value that k would have if the equilibrium is reached. The effect of the first factor was stressed in the previous chapters. The effects of the latter factors are also important:

♦ An increase in the equilibrium level of the national output—due to an increase in the supply of human or nonhuman resources—lowers the money-price level required for equilibrium.

♦ An increase in the level of real cash balances per unit of national output that people would desire to hold in equilibrium—in short, an increase in k^*, due either to a decrease in the opportunity cost of holding cash (instead of alternative assets) or an increased preference for being liquid, also lowers the equilibrium price level.

For Keynes it is an important point that k^* is *not a constant,* not a fixed coefficient, that is independent of other variables such as the rate of interest, contrary to the impression left by some of his neoclassical predecessors. In times when speculators or enterprises see prospects of a reduced rate of return from investing in new capital assets, the interest rate they are willing to pay lenders is likewise reduced; but if the interest rate is to be lower—and production, hence people's real incomes (in bread) to be the same—lenders are going to want to decrease the amount of their real wealth held in earning assets (bonds, equities, land, and so forth) and to *increase* the amount held in *real cash balances.* Hence an increase of k^* is induced by the fall in the expected rate of return on new capital. Since the k^* of the new equilibrium is thus increased, it follows that the new equilibrium will not be achieved, given M and Y^*, until the price level has sunk by enough to raise the real value of the existing stock of money to its new equilibrium level. This pet point of Keynes's begins on p. 527.

The general level of money-wage rates, of course, is a different kettle of fish. The ratio of the level of money-wage rates to the level of money prices is the wage level expressed in terms of the *product* or *products* being produced in the economy rather than in terms of *money*. It might be called the average *product wage;* it is pretty much the same thing as the average real wage, or average wage in terms of bread, say. If we denote it by the symbol *(W/P)* and denote its equilibrium level by *(W/P)**, then

$$W^* = P^* \cdot (W/P)^*$$

If we substitute for P^* here the previous formula in (1), we obtain

$$W^* = \frac{M}{k^* \, Y^*} \cdot (W/P)^* \tag{2}$$

Evidently the equilibrium money-wage level is compounded with an extra ingredient: the equilibrium level of the average product wage, *(W/P)**. Clearly:

- A decrease in the equilibrium value of the average product wage—due, say, to an oil shock (which reduces the amount of energy input that the economy's labor input has to work with) or to an influx of new workers into the labor force (which reduces the amount of capital input per worker)—lowers the money-wage level required for equilibrium.

In order to understand the difficulty about the process of equilibration that Keynes pointed to we shall focus attention, as Keynes did, on the sort of disturbance that alters the equilibrium money-wage level and the equilibrium money-price level in equal proportion—by the same percentage amount, in other words. So *(W/P)** is taken to be a constant, unaffected by the kind of disturbance we are going to study. Second, we shall focus, as Keynes did, on pure demand-side disturbances, which leave unaffected the supplies of capital and labor and energy, but not necessarily the utilization of these factors. So Y^* is also taken to be a constant. Thus we are excluding here the possibility of a supply-side disturbance affecting *(W/P)** or Y^* or both—a crop failure, an oil shock, a technological discovery, an influx of new workers or new capital, and so on.

We shall consider a pure demand-side disturbance. Such a disturbance alters the equilibrium money-wage and -price levels by disturbing k^* or M, while leaving *(W/P)** and Y^* undisturbed. But actual—as distinct from equilibrium—output and employment may be disturbed in the process of adjustment!

THE SIMPLEST MONETARY DISTURBANCES: A SPONTANEOUS INCREASE OF k

Let us consider here the simplest example of such a demand-side disturbance: An increase has just occurred in the amount of wealth that people want to hold in the form of real cash balances—under equilibrium conditions and, more broadly, under all conditions. Hence there has been an increase in k^*, the size of the Cambridge k under equilibrium conditions. It really will not matter for the rest of this introductory discussion of Keynes *why* people want to hold more real balances. However, in the interest of total clarity, let us suppose here that the increased demand for liquidity is spontaneous, exogenous: a change of tastes or a recalculation by wealth holders of what is best for them.*

- Figure 19–1 depicts an increased desire to hold real cash balances, under equilibrium conditions. It also shows the mirror image of that shift of preferences: a decreased desire to hold wealth in the form of capital goods and other nonmoney assets.

- As a result of this shift of people's preferences between money and nonmoney assets, an equilibrium is no longer possible at the *original* equilibrium money prices: If people expect that capital goods (and other alternatives to holding money) are still salable at those original prices, they will attempt to sell some of their holdings of these assets in exchange for money. But those capital goods (and other earning assets) are *there*, so they must be held! And likewise the supply of money is also taken as given at the moment. So capital cannot be swapped for money—certainly not in the aggregate. Hence there is frustration and disappointment: The old price and the old expectations are no longer consistent with equilibrium.

- But a *new* equilibrium is possible—whether or not attained! There exists a new equilibrium with a lower money price level—lower money prices of capital goods and consumer goods. If and when these prices become the ones people expect, there will be no more disappointment.

How would the developers of the neoclassical doctrine—Keynes's predecessors—have analyzed the consequences of such a disturbance in the old equilibrium? The neoclassical scenario gave quite a rosy picture:

- The flight, so to speak, from capital goods and other earning assets into money means an *excess demand* for money—and an *excess supply* of capital—figured at the original money prices of those assets. Wealth owners would like to "get out" of some of their nonmoney asset holdings and into money. But, as Mill put it, at such prices there are only sellers, no buyers.

- The immediate consequence, or "impact," of this excess supply of capital will be a slackening of new orders for newly produced capital goods; *or a*

---

* Later in this chapter, we take up an example of an *induced* increase of k^*, one induced by a fall of the interest rate firms are willing to pay.

FIGURE 19–1: The Effects on Monetary Equilibrium of an Increased Demand for Money

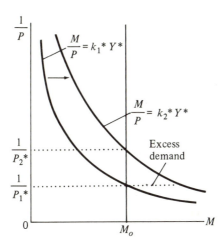

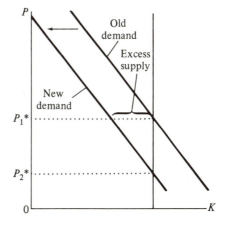

An increased demand for liquidity, hence reduced demand for illiquid assets, lowers in equal proportion the equilibrium level of all money prices and money-wage rates.

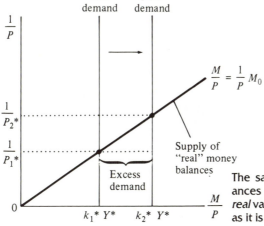

The same shift in the demand for money balances can be represented by a diagram with the *real* value of money balances (real cash balances, as it is often called) on the horizontal axis.

fall of various capital-goods prices—a fall of the stock market, property values, used capital equipment in secondhand markets; or both. But this need not result in a cutback of production and employment by capital goods-producing firms—not if those firms are quick-witted.

◆ The prospect of reduced employment demands, given the pre-existing money-wage rates, will prompt these capital-goods producers to slash their wage offers; such a firm might defend it as a "job-saving" wage cut. And the realization by the workers that wage cuts are necessary to protect their jobs will prompt them to accept those wage cuts. Lower wages will then spread to the consumer-goods industries, since firms there will be unwilling to pay above-market wages.

◆ The general fall of money-wage rates, which lowers the money costs of production, plus competition among firms, will force a reduction of consumer-good prices, besides permitting capital-goods makers to sell more cheaply. Thus there may be a stage of this adjustment process—a disequilibrium phase—in which the typical firm has underestimated the general fall of money prices; and that surprise leads it to embark on further wage cuts. However, at no point in this process are firms tempted to dismiss, or "lay off," some employees rather than simply to announce the wage cut that they assume to be sufficient to save their employees' jobs.

◆ The money-wage level and the money-price level will quickly sink by the amount necessary to restore equilibrium. In the new equilibrium, once established, the price level will be reduced by just enough, and thus the *real value of people's cash balances* will be *increased by just enough*, to *provide* exactly the *increased liquidity*—the increased real cash balances—that people suddenly desired to have. Once that new equilibrium level of money prices and money-wage rates has been reached, the "deflation" will be over:

> With people's liquidity no longer less than desired, the excess supply of capital will be gone, its cause removed. (The prices that capital-goods purchasers are willing to pay for them will no longer be depressed below the prices that capital-goods producers need to cover their costs.) Hence producers will no longer feel impelled to initiate wage cuts (beyond the previous ones).

It was *not* implied in the neoclassical analysis that a bulge of unemployment—a temporary slump of business activity—was an intrinsic, or unavoidable, feature of the equilibration process. And there was no suggestion that, if such a temporary dip in production did occur, the equilibration process would be anything but reliable and swift. This was the neoclassical line.

Keynes, drawing the opposite conclusions, found weak points in the neoclassical doctrine. In this section we take up his most general, far-reaching objections—based on his understanding of the functioning of labor markets.*

* One of Keynes's objections in this connection must be postponed. He argued that employers are not likely to calculate, when they first cut wages, that the general reduction of wages will lead to a

Keynes felt that the neoclassical scenario went haywire in its treatment of money-wage rate behavior. According to the rosy scenario, the individual worker, finding that the firm has asked its employees to accept a "job-saving" wage cut, does nothing to resist it: No one quits or even threatens to quit in an effort to repeal it. And the uncanny employer somehow knows beforehand that they wouldn't! Keynes flatly rejected this idea. "Except in a socialized community where wage policy is settled by decree," Keynes said, "there is no means of securing uniform wage reductions for every class of worker. The result can only be brought about by a series of gradual, irregular changes . . . and probably completed only after wasteful and disastrous struggles. . . ."*

Keynes's Departure from Neoclassical Analysis

Where was the error, according to Keynes, in the neoclassical analysis? Where exactly had the analysis gone wrong? Three decades after the arrival of Keynes's difficult and often cryptic book, modern-day theorists came up with an interpretation of what Keynes meant: The neoclassical scenario *assumes* that each worker, at the time he is asked to accept the job-saving wage cut, has convinced himself that the money-wage rates in *all* the jobs in the economy are about to be cut (if they haven't just been cut) in the same proportion.

> It is perfectly true that *if* the employees of a firm proposing a "job-saving" wage cut all confidently *expected* that the money-wage rates at *all* the other firms were soon going to be cut in the *same* percentage amount, the firm's cut in its money-wage rates by that amount would *not* be interpreted as a cut in its *relative* wage rates. So none of the employees would be prompted by the employer's wage cut to *quit* in order to look for a better-paying job elsewhere. Hence the firm, if it knows of and shares this expectation (that other wages are going to be cut by that amount), *could* institute this wage cut (or a smaller one) without fear of causing employees to leave.†

general reduction of prices that, since it will not have been anticipated, will require them to cut wages again, and so on, so that the process of equilibration will be drawn out. But that point does not explain why the equilibration process produces a rise of unemployment from the beginning.

* J. M. Keynes, *The General Theory of Employment, Interest and Money*, p. 267.

†There is another "if" that, for completeness, might have to be added:

> *If* the employees furthermore believed that the general reduction of money-wage rates they were expecting would soon result in a fall of consumer-good prices in the same proportion, the firm's money-wage cut of that magnitude would not be interpreted as a cut in its *real* wage rates. So none of the employees would be prompted by the employer's wage cut to resign and retire. Hence the firm, if sensing and sharing this expectation, could carry out that wage cut (or a smaller cut) without risk of driving some employees into retirement.

But on what ground did neoclassical doctrine suppose that employees have such expectations? Why should the individual employee expect a percentage cut in the money-wage rates at other firms exactly as large as the one announced by his employer? Experience teaches the contrary:

- The trouble that a firm runs into is often not entirely general: It is to some degree *specific* to the firm or to the particular industry. The firm may be experiencing a change in the demand for *its* product—its customers leaving or buying less—that *exceeds* what the other firms in the industry and what industries as a whole are experiencing. So the firm desires and plans to have *its* wages sometimes *below* (and sometimes above) the others' wages.

- Even if the latest disturbance is just a monetary shock, a pure demand-side disturbance requiring an *equal* percentage cut in all money-wage rates at *all* firms, and even if the firms have guessed that, the firms might arrive at different calculations of the general money-wage cut needed to maintain employment. So there is a chance that, by accident, a firm's calculation of the "right" wage cut *exceeds* the other firms' calculations. Such a firm, if it acts on its convictions, *would* be imposing a relative wage cut.

Every employee with any experience knows those things: that other firms are not necessarily in the same boat, and that any firm can make a mistake. An employee who thought differently about these matters would be quite strange:

SPOUSE: They cut wages at the plant?! You'll have to look for a new job!!
WORKER: Naw. I always say, if you've seen one company's wage scale you've seen them all.

Such a person would be a candidate for psychotherapy.

What is the upshot of all this? What follows from the conclusion that employees, following the demand-side disturbance, will not be prepared for the "job-saving" wage cut their employer would like to make—that they will not be expecting a general wage reduction of that size (or maybe any)? *Some jobs will not be saved.* Employment will fall—through the resulting decision by employers to lay off workers *or* by employees to quit their firm or both. Whichever way, employment cannot continue to hold up. A slump, and a costly process of adjustment, will begin.

The level of employment must decline since, with these expectations on the part of workers about the general level of money-wage rates, actual money-wage rates will not adjust to the reduced level to satisfy the employers. In other words, labor costs will not be reduced by enough to make it profitable to continue planned production and employment at the equilibrium level. If the workers are content the employers will not be. If the employers are content the workers will not be.

Modern-day economists have often found it convenient to explain the mechanism of reduced employment in supply-and-demand terms, with the labor supply curve being a *disequilibrium* supply curve—a supply curve based on false expectations!

- If the workers in the typical town or locality at first refuse a wage cut—as long as employment holds up!—the employers will be induced to lay off some workers. The ensuing decline of employment, or growth of unemployment, drives workers to make growing wage concessions. This is one path to the outcome of lower employment and lower money-wage rates.

- If the employers in the typical town at first lower their wage offers by the whole amount they judge necessary to go on hiring their employees, some employees will be induced to quit. Increasing numbers will be traveling in search of better wages ever farther from home. The ensuing rise of unemployment, or decline of employment, drives employers to improve their wage offers bit by bit until money-wage rates have "recovered" by enough that the quitting stops.

- The result, whatever the path, is the same: Employment is down, and wages decline relative to expectations.

Figure 19–2 captures the *gist* of the story. The supply curve, owing to false expectations, fails to drop as much as the demand curve.*

Keynes's break with the neoclassicists' equilibrium theory of how the labor market works—the emphasis on the imperfect mobility of labor, hence (implicitly) the costliness of transmitting and gathering information about wage rates and jobs, hence the formation of expectations based on little information—make him the first modern economist (in the sense of the term *modern* as used in this book). Yet he did not anticipate all the developments

---

* Our concern is primarily with the *present* understanding of the causes of "wage resistance" and "Keynesian unemployment," not with what Keynes thought. Nevertheless, having worked our way through a *present-day interpretation* of what Keynes meant, let us briefly compare it to what he wrote:

Whilst workers will usually resist a reduction of money wage [for the same volume of employment], it is not their practice to withdraw their labor [to retire or to search for better pay] whenever there is a rise in the price of [consumer] goods.

Since there is imperfect mobility of labor, and wages do not tend to an exact equality [within each occupation], any individual or group of individuals who consent to a reduction of money wages relatively to others will suffer a *relative* reduction in real wages, which is a sufficient justification for them to resist it.

. . . [T]he workers, though unconsciously, are instinctively more reasonable economists than the clasjical school inasmuch as they resist reductions of money wages, which are seldom or never of an all-round character . . . ; whereas they do not resist reductions of real wages [that] are associated with increases in aggregate employment and leave relative money wages unchanged unless the reduction proceeds so far . . . (J. M. Keynes, *The General Theory*, pp. 9, 14. Bracketed words added.).

FIGURE 19–2: The Money Wage and Employment in the "Average" Local Labor Market

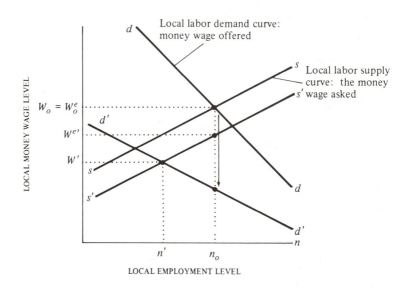

This variant of the familiar supply-and-demand diagram describes a typical *local* labor market in a hypothetical economy where there are many local markets, all somewhat remote from one another.

The demand curve shows how the wage "offered" by employers *decreases* the larger the number of workers available for employment. The demand curve slopes down for two reasons: As employment is increased at the firms, the mar-

to date in the modern economics of labor markets! Many modern theorists would say that he was not modern enough: He implies that normally every labor market *clears*—in correct-expectations equilibrium and false-expectations disequilibrium. The reason why money-wage rates do not drop as required to establish promptly the new equilibrium is that workers "resist" the wage cut necessary to prevent the slump (because they do not expect a general reduction of money-wage rates or of prices, by that amount). When the employers' labor-demand curve falls, the number of employees *working* falls because the number *resisting* increases: They are on the road, searching—or maybe picketing in protest. This is called *search unemployment*.

A more modern version of Keynes's point, that money-wage rates will not at first fall by the required amount, harks back to the theory of job rationing, introduced in chapter 16. Faced with personnel problems of quitting and shirking, this theory says, the employers respond by attempting to "outpay" one another for ginal productivity of labor is diminished. Furthermore, the larger the employment level in the typical, or average, market, and hence the greater is total economywide employment, the lower is the money price that the larger resulting volume of output can be expected to fetch in the product markets.

The local supply curve shows how the *"asked"* wage—the wage at which a given number of jobs will be accepted by workers—*increases* with the level of employment in the market. That is because, given the workers' expectations of the money-wage rates to be available in the other labor markets, an increase in the local money wage is interpreted as an increase in the wage *relative* to other markets. So fewer workers in the area go looking elsewhere for better pay.

Now suppose that there is a decline in the price at which some of the firms in the typical labor market—firms producing machinery, say—expect they can sell the output they were planning to produce. These firms notice that their customers appear to need some price concession if they are to be willing to demand the quantity that was planned.

Hence the demand curve for labor in the typical market shifts leftward and downward. At the old money wage, fewer workers would be hired. Equivalently, to employ any given number of workers the employers in the market would only be willing to offer lower money-wage rates.

But, as shown, the asking money-wage rate for any given number of jobs will be reduced by *less* than that, if at all. It is reduced only by the percentage reduction that occurs in the workers' expectation of money-wage rates in the *other* labor markets; from W_o^e to $W^{e'}$, say. They do not know that conditions are as bad generally! Hence the diagram shows a *smaller* downward shift of the *supply* curve than happens to the *demand* curve. The reason is that, as explained in the text, the workers do not revise downward their expectations of the money-wage rates they could earn in *other* local labor markets by as much as the decline in what employers can offer locally.

As a consequence, the intersection of the new demand curve with the new supply curve—based on inflated, excessive expectations of what money-wage rates are elsewhere—lies to the *left* of the old intersection. At the corresponding new level of money-wage rates, W', amount supplied equals amount of labor demanded. At the corresponding employment level, n', the asking wage and the offered wage are brought into equality. Thus in this situation the market clears.

Yet the new situation is not an equilibrium! Employment is depressed below its original, equilibrium level, n_o. Workers' expectations of wage rates elsewhere exceed the actually prevailing wage rates. Thus the workers are suffering from disequilibrium.

labor; thus they drive up the real cost of hiring labor (in bread) and, as a result, have to cut back the number of employees—until equilibrium is reached, with its corresponding pool of unemployed. According to the modernist models of labor markets, a firm never limits its labor force through a low wage—its wage rates are kept above the minimum that would be accepted; it limits its employment directly by personal decisions.

This modern theory has a quite different story to tell when an employer senses that the price buyers are willing to pay for his product has fallen, as in the case of our demand-side disturbance. This theory says that the individual firm will reduce its employment by the device of *layoffs*, temporary or permanent, of some of its employees. And if the *employer* does not expect that other employers are going to reduce *their* money-wage rates, he may very well not dare to reduce his wage rates. Why? First, he would not want to take a larger risk of losing personnel in overhead jobs who would then have to be replaced or losing ground in the battle against shirking. Second, he might not want to institute a temporary wage cut, to end when the desired number of employees had quit, because of the risk that too many employees in certain jobs would have left the firm before the "overshooting" was noticed, and the costliness of paying continuous attention to avoid that outcome. Third, the firm that cut its wage scale might lose a disproportionate share of its best employees that way. Hence the firm may very well find it preferable simply to *lay off* some of its employees—and maintain the same wage policy as before to protect against shirking and quitting.

Notice that the new situation, following the lay-offs, is not an equilibrium. The firms, not knowing that other firms were likewise affected by the slump in demand, did not expect that other firms would lay off workers too. Had they known that the unemployment level was going to shoot up, each firm might have risked a small wage cut. However, once the larger level of unemployment is noticed by firms, each will calculate that it can afford to risk paying a lower wage rate, since it knows that the higher unemployment rate and hence the greater difficulty its employees would have in finding jobs elsewhere will reduce the temptations to quit or shirk. Thus the money wage experiences its first drop, following the demand disturbance, *after* the drop of employment.*

A Simple Model of Aggregate Demand and Aggregate Supply

The previous analysis is precise about the mechanism involved in the fall of employment following the downward demand disturbance. (More precision would put some readers to sleep and make others climb the walls.) But it is not exact. It has not offered an exact formulation of the *amounts* by which employment and output, fall. It would be desirable, though, to grasp—preferably visually—the determinants (at least the main ones) of the *magnitude* of the economic decline. And it may add to our understanding of the mechanism to "work through" a simple model of employment determination that permits an exact calculation of the fall of employment resulting from the disturbance.

Our simple aggregative model contains two elements, which can be thought of as the "aggregate demand curve" and the "aggregate supply curve,"

---

*Chapter 20 discusses some added reasons for "wage stickiness" designed by the "New Keynesian" school to meet a criticism of Keynesian theory made by the "New Classical" economics.

respectively. There is no harm in thinking of the demand curve as describing the *quantity* of aggregate national output demanded at each possible money-price level; similarly, the supply curve can be interpreted as showing the quantity supplied. Equivalently, we can look at the curves from the other way:

♦ The aggregate supply curve describes the general level of money prices that producers would require to induce them to produce a certain level of output. (It describes, in other words, the money price level—averaging over the various products—they *must* expect to get in order to be willing to be ready to supply the indicated, or specified, level of output.) The curve shows how this so-called *supply price* depends upon the level of output indicated, or specified. Each such aggregate supply price schedule that could be drawn up corresponds to some given level of money-wage rates; there is a different aggregate supply curve for each different (hypothetical) level of money-wage rates.

As in Figure 19–3 below, this supply price is normally depicted as *rising* with increasing output—just as an ordinary industry supply curve is likewise upward sloping. Why? We shall suppose (along with Keynes) that the aggregate supply curve is upward sloping for the same reason that an industry supply curve is typically upward sloping: diminishing marginal productivity of labor—hence increasing marginal costs of production—as more labor is piled onto given quantities of capital and land in order

FIGURE 19–3: Aggregate Demand and Aggregate Supply

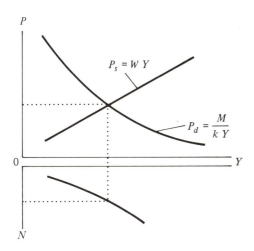

The aggregate demand curve corresponds to a given supply of money, *M,* and a particular preference for liquidity, or real money balances, as measured by *k.* An increase of *k* or a decrease of *M* shifts downward the demand curve, decreasing the demand price at each level of aggregate output (in proportion to the increase of $\frac{M}{k}$).

The aggregate supply curve corresponds to a particular level of money wage rates, *W.* An increase of *W* shifts upward the supply curve, increasing the supply price at each output level in proportion to the increase of *W.*

Note that the implied level of output, and the corresponding level of employment needed to produce it, does not necessarily equal the equilibrium levels, *Y** and *N**, of neoclassical theory!

to produce more output. So successive equal additions to the level of output require successively larger additions to the level of labor input and hence successively higher price levels to cover each successive rise in costs.

♦ The aggregate demand curve describes the level of money prices that buyers of capital goods, consumer goods, and so forth will be willing to pay when the real national income—that is, national output—is at a certain level. (It describes, then, the level of prices that producers *can* expect to get when producing at the indicated level of output.) The curve shows how this so-called *demand price* depends upon the level of output. Each such aggregate demand curve that could be drawn up corresponds to some given level of the money supply.

> As in Figure 19–3, this demand price is normally depicted as *declining* with increasing output. In this respect the curve may remind us of industry demand curves. But the reason for the downward-sloping character is rather distinctive: At greater levels of national output and therefore real income, with consequently a larger total of paychecks and divided checks being paid to households by firms, people will naturally want to hold on the average (per month or quarter-year) a larger quantity of their wealth in the form of money; but the quantity of money supplied—the money supply behind any particular demand curve—is given. When, as a result, people try vainly to get *out of goods* (capital goods) and *into money* they cause all money prices of goods to decline—until the *real* value of their average holdings of money balances has increased to the higher level desired because of their greater real income. This decline of the general level of money prices is what the downward slope of the aggregate demand schedule is describing.

In order to have an *exact* formulation of employment determination we can, as an example, take inspiration from the Cambridge equation of exchange—and go a step further. We shall suppose, in the interests of simplicity, that the Cambridge k does *not change* as the economy drifts into (and maybe eventually out of) disequilibrium. In other words, k remains *constant*—at its new value following the original disturbance.

♦ Hence our aggregate demand curve is a *Cambridge-type* relationship between the demand price, P_d, and the level of national output, Y, given M and the constant k.

$$P_d = \frac{M}{k \cdot Y}$$

This is the example of the aggregate demand curve that is shown in Figure 19–3.

Regarding the supply curve, we borrow (as Keynes did) another of the great neoclassical simplifications: We suppose that the supply price is simply the marginal cost of production. In other words, firms require only a price that just covers the extra cost of producing the last unit of output; they don't require a "mark-up" on top of that marginal cost figure. (But we could easily include such a mark-up, if a fixed one, into the present simple model.) Second, we suppose for simplicity that, with a given money-wage rate, the marginal cost level rises with the output level at a constant rate. In other words, marginal cost is proportional to the output level.*

◆ Hence our aggregate supply curve is a straight line with positive slope:

$$P_s = W \cdot Y$$

As always, the supply price is proportional to the money-wage rate the firms are paying—the cost of labor per unit. (In general we should write $b \cdot W \cdot Y$ as the formula for the supply price, where b is a positive constant; but we can make b equal 1 by the right choice of the unit—ounce, kilogram, ton,—in which to measure output.) This example of the aggregate supply curve is shown in Figure 19–3.

The system is closed (given the money-wage level) by supposing that when, at the current level of aggregate production, the demand price is less than the supply price, national output is cut back to the level at which demand price and supply price are brought into equality. And if the demand price should exceed the supply price, national output is increased to that level. Hence

$$P_d = P_s$$

Readers already understand a *part* of this. The demand price measures how low the price level would have to be, given output, to eliminate or prevent any excess demand for money—alias excess supply of capital. If the demand price should sink below the supply price, at the current level of output, the capital-goods producers (who are in the "front lines") will observe a slackening of orders for their products and/or a weakening of prices in second-hand markets for used capital goods; so they will sense the drop in what buyers of capital goods are willing to pay per unit. Realizing that the price

---

*If successive output levels 1,2,3 . . . , and hence successive increases in output 1, 1, 1 . . . need successive increases in employment 1,2,3 . . . , it follows that the needed employment rises like the square of output.

their customers are willing to pay is no longer covering their marginal costs, these producers will cut back their output. *But where does it all end?* What *limits* the decline of aggregate output? The answer: A reduction of aggregate output (accounted for by cutback of capital-goods producers) reduces people's demand for real cash balances, which is $k \cdot Y$—thus *increases* their demand for capital goods—and thus promotes a *recovery* of the *demand price*. Once the decline of aggregate output has reached the point where the demand price has recovered to a new equality with producers' supply price—the new supply price associated with the lower level of output—output declines no farther. At that point production and employment have hit bottom. (If output declined more, the demand price would rise *above* the supply price, thus inducing some or all capital-goods producers to step up their production.) At this resting point producers are no longer surprised (disappointed) by their proceeds—their sales, prices, and resulting revenues; capital-goods prices, for example, are no longer below producers' expectations, nor are customers' orders. Equilibrium has thus been restored in the *goods markets,* in particular the market for capital goods. (The disequilibrium has moved to the *labor market,* as in a game of "Button, button, who's got the button," or "Pin the tail on the donkey," or musical chairs.)

Figure 19–4 shows the *exact effects* upon output (hence employment) and the price level, at each possible level of money-wage rates, of the monetary disturbance—the increased desire to hold real cash balances, the increase of k. Before this demand shock, the economy was in equilibrium in all markets.

- Workers' expectations of the average money-wage level prevailing in the economy were correct. So the actual money-wage level, W_1, was equal to the expected money-wage level, W^e_1. The corresponding capacity level of output—the output level producible with N^* employees—is denoted Y^*.

- The money wage level, W_1, was just low enough (and just high enough) to make the *supply price* of the resulting capacity output level—the output producible with N^* employees—equal to the *demand price* at that output level. So producers of goods, producing the output level Y^*, were not finding orders or prices unexpectedly low. Thus the goods markets, or asset markets were in equilibrium too.

After the monetary disturbance, namely the increase in k, the aggregate demand curve is *lower*. Thus there is a drop in the demand price at any given level of output, such as the output level Y^*. Now it is imaginable that the money-wage level would drop immediately "in sympathy" by the same percentage amount. (It is conceivable that all workers and firms understood that the equilibrium money-wage level and money-price level had just dropped by this percentage amount *and* that they all expected wage rates generally to drop by just that amount as a result; then each firm would be motivated

FIGURE 19–4: The Demand Shock, Combined with Failure of the Money-Wage Level to Jump to Its New Equilibrium Value, Forces Output and Employment to Decline

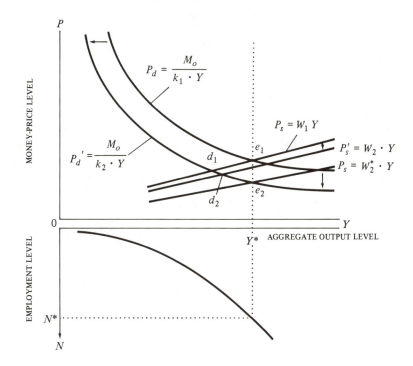

and emboldened to cut its own money-wage scales by the same percentage amount, anticipating that its employees would not "resist.") *If* money-wage rates dropped by that percentage amount, the economy would click into the new equilibrium frictionless—without a hitch. Production would continue at Y^*, employment at N^*. The resulting broken-line aggregate supply curve, which assumes that the money-wage level has magically dropped to the new equilibrium level W^*, would apply. So the supply price would fall, at any given output level such as Y^*, by the same percentage amount as the demand price fell. But this is the hypothetical possibility that Keynes rejected.

The figure deals with the case in which the money-wage rate does *not* drop by that much. It does not because workers fail at first to expect a general reduction of money-wage rates and prices by the amount of the drop (which *we* can see, but *they* can't) in the demand price. As a result, a gap opens up between the demand price and the supply price. Employment and output fall until the gap is closed.

The Persistence of the Slump—And a "Stabilizing" Monetary Policy

We have seen how, if labor markets function in the way described above, our deflationary monetary disturbance is bound to have an impact on employment—not just money-wage rates and the price level. The story is just as Keynes insisted. However, there was more to Keynes's argument. Clearly if the new theory is to explain stubborn, long-lived slumps in business activity—episodes of below-equilibrium employment stretching over a year or more—it will be necessary to explain why money-wage rates *take a long time* to fall fully to their new equilibrium level following the disturbances. Keynes was prepared for the question.

Keynes, it appears, was unwilling to rule out the possibility that the equilibration process, after the early impact on employment, might go swiftly and smoothly. But the most likely process, he felt, was a gradual one:

- The first decline of money-wage rates, if any, would be only a small fraction of the decline needed for equilibrium. Then, when a firm notices that other firms have evidently cut their wages too, it will feel it can cut its own wage rates some more without losing more employees than it is willing to lose. By this process, the firms "inch" their wage rates down, never getting very far out of line with one another.

- Each of the firms, when deciding on the size of its next wage cut, keeps on being unaware that the similar wage cutting by the other firms is going to cause prices to fall by as much. So the firms are constantly initiating wage cuts that are smaller than they would have liked if they had realized the depths to which money-wage rates and prices had to fall to "touch bottom."

Thus the recovery of employment is apt to proceed by degrees, as depicted in Figure 19–5.

Of course the same economic gods that disturbed the economy one season, sending it into a slump, could always remove the disturbance by next season. Wages would then have to turn around and head back up. But that does not seem to be the usual pattern. Many or most large disturbances do not appear, in retrospect, to have been entirely temporary: There has usually been a permanent element. Hence the recovery from a slump is often slow, as wages have some distance to go.

The finding that employment fluctuations tend to be protracted, or persistent, raises a question for government policy: If the typical recovery from a slump is painfully slow, can't a rehabilitative therapy be found to hasten the recovery? Keynes believed that there was a therapy that would normally be helpful: monetary medicine.

- When the level of money-wage rates is observed to fall the government should act to increase the supply of money—with the object of driving wage rates back to the target level.

FIGURE 19–5: The Possibility of a Painfully Slow Recovery

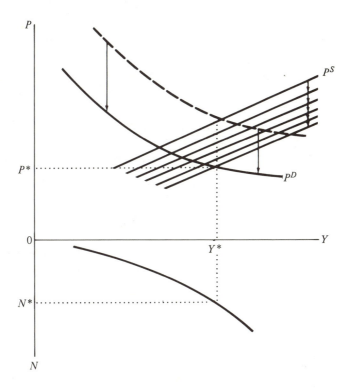

The adjustment of the average money-wage level may occur only gradually, as workers and employers need time to perceive or infer the cumulative decline of money-wage rates generally in the economy and to adjust further their own wage demands accordingly.

- ◆ When the average money wage is seen to rise above the target level the government would move to decrease the supply of money—to pull wages back down.

Thus the governmental agency that controls the size of the national money supply, namely the country's central bank, would be charged with manipulating the supply of money—raising it or lowering it in response to incoming wage statistics—in order to *stabilize* the money-wage level.

- ◆ Whenever a slump developed and so money wages tended to move below target, this monetary policy would cause the money supply to *grow*. If any small decline of wages triggered an increase of the money supply, the recovery would thereby be given a boost.

Thus the government's monetary policy of stabilizing wages could contribute to stabilizing employment. Better that than passive reliance on the slow fall of money-wage rates.

BIG SHOCKS, DEEP SLUMPS

The foregoing analysis of the effects of a monetary disturbance has delivered the single most important message Keynes wanted to convey: That money wage rates cannot be depended upon to jump from one level to another so as always to permit production and employment to continue uninterruptedly at their equilibrium levels.

The main thrust of the Keynesian analysis cannot be completed, however, without taking up an important special case.

In the previous analysis of the depth of the slump, summarized in Figure 19–4, it was *assumed* that the fall of national output and the associated recovery of the demand price would and could proceed to the point where the demand price has finally pulled up to *equality* with the supply price. But there is a possible problem: The contraction of output, it will be recalled, is *led* (we might say spearheaded) by the capital-goods producers. True, any decline of national output means a decline in some people's income—wages and so on—and consequently a decline in the demand for consumer goods; hence the consumer-goods makers may share with the capital-goods makers some of the burden of the necessary decline of total national output. Nevertheless, if there is any parallel fall of consumer-good output it could only be the *result* of the decline of national output, not the cause—the caboose, not the engine. Investment, not consumption, is the engine. With that understood the problem can be seen: What if capital-goods production falls to *zero,* and *still* there is no equality reached between the demand price and the supply price? Unquestionably that is a theoretical possibility:

- If the monetary disturbance is a sufficiently *big* shock, *all* production of capital goods may disappear—except perchance for the capital projects of nonprofit organizations, such as churches and hospitals ministering to the unemployed.

> And in fact it happened: At the bottom of the Great Depression in the hardest-hit countries, commercial firms were simply not buying new capital goods and capital-goods manufacturers were not producing any. Investment—the production of new capital goods—had vanished for all practical purposes.

What then? What determines the level of national output in this extreme case?

Keynes had a theory for that too: Although capital-goods production is nil, the GNP will not fall to zero. It will fall to the level at which consumers and the government are willing to buy the entire national output by themselves. Consumer-goods output will not fall further, once that point is reached, (as long as consumers do not reduce further their spending on consumer goods). Production of goods for the government will not fall further if the government maintains its spending.

♦ Thus Keynes saw the *spender as hero* in conditions of deep slump. More spending would generate more production. Capital-good production could not be hurt by the resulting decline of the demand price for capital goods, since this production is zero anyway! (Keynes was much criticized for overemphasizing this special case of deep slump.)

Keynes, who despised diagrams, did sketch one (with words) to summarize his model of employment determination—*given* the

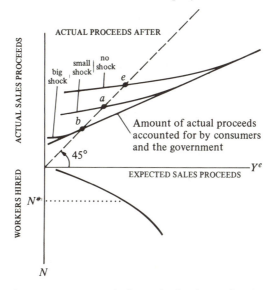

level of money-wage rates prevailing at the moment, as well as the prevailing level of the money supply. Here is a version of Keynes's diagram.

The proceeds that the firms expect to receive— the sum total of the revenue in real terms, in terms of bread, they are expecting—are measured along the horizontal axis.

The lower quadrant shows how the number of employees (the amount of labor) demanded by the firms depends on the level of expected proceeds. Equivalently, it shows the expected proceeds that the firms require to be willing to hire N workers.

The vertical axis in the upper quadrant measures the proceeds the firms actually receive or *would* receive under various conditions.

The upper quadrant shows how the size of the *actual* proceeds *depends* upon the number of workers the firms hire and pay money to, and thus upon the magnitude of the proceeds *expected* by firms.

The product market is in equilibrium if and only if *actual* and *expected* proceeds are *equal*. Then capital-goods producers are finding that the level of investment demand is up to expectations—as measured by the rate of new orders and the prices that customers are willing to pay. This equilibrium occurs where the curve depicting actual proceeds *intersects the 45-degree line*. To the *right* of that intersection actual proceeds are *below* the expected level; expectations are excessive—they must *fall* to secure equilibrium (given the position of the curve). To the *left* matters are reversed.

This chapter first discussed a *small* (or moderate) disturbance, corresponding to a small shift of the proceeds curve, which moves the economy from a position like *e* to a point like *a*. At that point there is *positive* production of capital goods—not a total collapse in that sector. But a *big* shock would drive the economy to a point like *b*. At that point only the Keynesian heroics of the consumer and the government hold up national production and employment. At point *b,* unlike *a,* more spending by consumers or the government would increase the floor level of output—the level reached in product-market equilibrium.

SUMMING UP THE SIMPLEST MODEL OF GNP AND EMPLOYMENT

We have discussed Keynes's system, his theory of employment, in the simplest possible terms. The centerpiece of this theory is the nonequilibrium behavior of money-wage rates. When the level of money wages lies above the level necessary for general, or overall, equilibrium in the economy, the level of employment will be driven below its equilibrium level as a result.

The problem is not that money-wage rates are utterly rigid—that no firm could get away with reducing its wages by a penny. That would have been a ridiculous claim in 1936, following a phenomenal slide of money-wage rates (along with employment) in the early 1930s. Money wages do decline in a slump—but mostly or entirely as a *result* of the fall of employment and the ensuing (painfully slow) process of observation and adjustment to the new situation. But there is no uncanny way by which money-wage rates can jump, following a monetary disturbance, from one equilibrium level to the new equilibrium—as if possessing the instinctual sense of a jungle cat—by just the amount necessary to prevent a slump of output and employment in the process. Nor is there, Keynes argued, a generally quick and painless route to recovery from disequilibrium once down-side, or deflationary, demand disturbances have sneaked up on the economy.

Yet the government need not stand idly by. When wage rates fall it can increase the money supply to get them back up. Keynes did not believe that such a monetary policy would prevent slumps. But he believed that it would help to combat slumps.

DISTURBANCES TO THE EXPECTED PROFITABILITY OF CAPITAL FORMATION*

The demand-side disturbance considered above was an increase in the quantity of real cash balances, M/P, that people desire to hold as a ratio to their aggregate real income, hence national output—an increase of the Cambridge k. Such a disturbance may be described this way: Wealth owners suddenly prefer to be more liquid at the *previously prevailing rate of interest* (or yields) on loans and securities. *Equivalently,* we may say that wealth owners suddenly *require a higher rate of interest* (or yield) to go on holding the existing supply of stocks and bonds and outstanding loans—as long as the previously prevailing level of liquidity, as measured by the level of real cash balances, continues to prevail.

It has been implicit that, at the time of the disturbance, there is *no* coincidental rise in anyone's expectations of the profitability of investment (in the economist's sense)—meaning investment by firms in newly produced capital goods. Hence there is no increase in the rate of interest that firms are willing to pay for loans (or that lenders find it possible and prudent to extract from borrowing firms) and no increase in expectations of firms' earnings on the investments they are about to make in new plant and equipment. We may call this concept the *expected rate of return to investment;* Keynes called it the *"marginal efficiency of capital."*

♦ Thus the disturbance causes initially a clash, or discrepancy, between the *rate of interest required* by wealth owners (as their "price" for holding illiquid assets) and the *expected rate of return to investment*—Keynes's marginal efficiency.

---

* This section can be omitted without losing the thread.

♦ This discrepancy forces a drop in stock prices, used capital-goods prices, and new orders for new capital goods. In turn, this causes output and employment to fall—since money-wage behavior isn't "smart" enough to prevent it.

Keynes worried more about a slightly different type of demand disturbance: an abrupt fall in the expected rate of return to investment. It is clear that the *actual* profitability of investment can change quite a lot from decade to decade—even when we restrict our attention to years of prosperity. However, Keynes believed that *expectations* of the profitability of investment—the opinions and hunches of speculators, entrepreneurs, and corporate managers—are subject to wide swings in a year or a month. He stressed the importance of "business confidence" and spoke of "animal spirits" to emphasize the instinctual and capricious nature of these expectations.

Suppose, then, as our second example of a demand-side disturbance, that enterprises and speculators turn gloomy, or "bearish," about the prospective returns from investment in plant and equipment; They revise downward their forecasts of the future net returns—the rentals (net of depreciation) plus any capital gains—that can be earned on existing capital and any contemplated investments in additional capital. Further, there is *no* coincidental reduction by wealth owners in the rate of interest they require—no change, in other words, in their preferences for liquidity. What are the effects of such a disturbance?

♦ This disturbance in the expected profitability of investment likewise causes a clash between the *rate of interest required by wealth owners* and the *expected rate of return to investment*—Keynes's marginal efficiency of capital.

♦ The impact is in important ways similar: Stock prices, used capital-goods prices, and orders for new capital goods decline.

♦ The near-term consequences for output and employment are also the same: a slump—which money wages fail to prevent.

This second sort of disturbance contracts employment, given people's wage expectations, just as the first disturbance studied, because it too has a deflationary effect on the price level: In both cases the new equilibrium, which is reached if and when output fully recovers from the slump, is one with a lower price level (and lower money-wage level). Hence the new equilibrium in both cases has an increased quantity of real cash balance, M_o/P^*.

♦ When the disturbance is an *increase in the preference for liquidity* and hence an increase in the required rate of interest (given the level of liquidity), the rise in the level of real cash balances achieved in the new equilibrium serves to reduce the required rate of interest back to the same level as the expected rate of return investment. *Liquidity increases* to the level sufficient to make people *once again content to hold securities and loans at the (unchanged) rate of interest that firms can pay*—namely, the expected rate of return to investment.

♦ When the disturbance is a *decrease in the expected rate of return to investment*, the rise in the level of real cash balances found in the new equilibrium serves to reduce the required rate of interest to equality with the *new* and *lower* expected rate of return to investment. Here too, *liquidity increases* to the level sufficient to make people *willing to hold the existing stock of securities and loans outstanding at the (reduced) rate of interest that firms can pay*—their expected rate of return.

The reason that the two sorts of disturbances both have a deflationary effect on the equilibrium price and wage level, and an initially contractionary effect on output and employment until wage expectations have adjusted, can be expressed in terms of the Cambridge equation of exchange. Both disturbances imply an increase in the Cambridge *k*, which means a decline of the demand-price (or aggregate demand) schedule. The first disturbance is a *spontaneous* increase in *k*: At each level of output and real income, people suddenly want to hold larger cash balances in real terms (i.e., to be more liquid) even though nothing has happened to lower the costliness of holding interestless cash rather than earning assets; if the rate of interest is not to rise above the unchanged expected rate of return to investment, and the prices of capital goods are not to sink below their production cost, which would cause output to fall, there has to be a decrease of the price level, which increases the supply of real cash balances. The second disturbance can be interpreted as an *induced* increase in *k*: At each level of output and real income there is no change in the real cash balances that people want to hold, given the rate of interest, but the expected rate of return to investment falls; if the interest rate is not to exceed the (reduced) expected rate of return to investment and the prices of capital goods not to sink below their production cost, which would cause output and real income to fall, there has to be a decrease of the price level to increase the supply of cash balances in real terms.*

---

* The point can be made with a stylized model: P_d is the price level required to bring the real value of the money supply up to the level that would be desired, kY, if the output is to be at some given level Y. The size of k is a function of the prevailing rate of interest, i, because the latter is a measure of the "opportunity cost" of holding interestless cash instead of interest-earning assets. If i falls a person can afford to hold more money, less in earning assets; k is therefore increased. Further, if firms are going to invest enough to bring output up to a given Y, the interest rate must be equal to the expected rate of return to investment, ϵ. If i exceeded ϵ, say, investment by firms would stop. That is,

$$\frac{M}{P_d} = k \cdot Y; \ k = \alpha - \beta i, \text{ where } \alpha > 0, \ \beta > 0; \ i = \epsilon$$

KEYNES'S TRUMP CARD: THE POSSIBLE NONEXISTENCE OF EQUILIBRIUM

The previous section would not perhaps have been worth the trouble if it were not for an important point raised by Keynes: It is possible for the marginal efficiency of capital to fall to *critically* low levels—so low that no equilibrium *exists:* There *is* none to be reached.

Capital investment can coexist with money because holding capital, though illiquid, promises the compensation of a substantial rate of interest or yield. But suppose the marginal efficiency of capital fell to zero or, as is conceivable, to some negative figure. In that case no one would find owning stocks and used capital goods worthwhile. Or suppose, as a less extreme case, that the marginal efficiency of capital falls to a level close enough to zero that receivers of money income—wage earners, dividend recipients, bond-coupon clippers, welfare clients, and so forth—do not find it worthwhile anymore occasionally to place a portion of their money accumulations in the stock market (and properties generally), since the transaction costs of such placements—possible brokerage fees and nuisance costs—would eat up the likely returns on such capital assets. What then?

Thus a fall of ϵ produces an *induced* increase in the value of k and decrease of P_d required for asset-market equilibrium at the given Y. Whether induced or spontaneous (as earlier), *the increase of* k *shifts down the* P_d *curve.*

The point can also be made with the accompanying diagram. The drop in the expected rate of return to investment necessitates for overall equilibrium an increase in the supply of real cash balances, hence a fall of the general price level if the nominal money supply is given, in order to restore the rate of interest to equality with the reduced expected rate of return to investment (i.e., Keynes's marginal efficiency). This fall of the price level gives the decline of the demand price—the downward shift of the aggregate demand curve. (Since we are always talking about the k *required* for *equilibrium* at a given Y, we might better call it, say, $k^*(Y)$.)

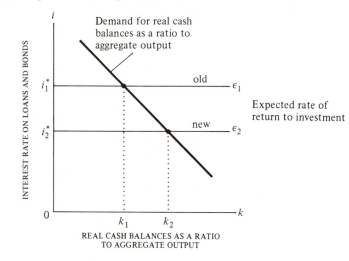

REAL CASH BALANCES AS A RATIO
TO AGGREGATE OUTPUT

Once the marginal efficiency of capital is at such a critical level the economy will sink into a deep slump; and no amount of downward adjustment by money-wage rates and downward shift of the supply-price schedule will be sufficient to bring about recovery. The reason is that the fall of the marginal efficiency of capital to a level at which no one will buy capital *no matter how large the person's real cash balances* implies that no matter how low the general price level might fall there would still be a disequilibrium in asset markets—there would still be people trying to sell capital assets (to finance retirement living, etc.) and no one willing to buy any of them, since the expected returns are not enough to cover the transactions costs. In technical terms, the demand price for output, which is the general price level needed to equilibrate the asset markets, has dropped to zero. The demand-price schedule has dropped onto the horizontal axis.

- Thus any money-wage level and corresponding supply-price schedule, no matter how low, will not be low enough to pull the general price level down to the demand price for output. There no longer exists an equilibrium at Y^* with some corresponding equilibrium wage and price level.
- As long as the marginal efficiency of capital remains critically low the economy is destined to remain mired in a deep slump: with price (equals supply price) and money-wage rates always collapsing toward zero, yet the price always above the demand price, which remains zero.

There can be no doubt that Keynes believed this theoretical possibility, a critically low marginal efficiency, to be of likely applicability to North American and European economies in the interwar years. But it does not seem that he ever gave up hope that the marginal efficiency of capital might not be in such bad shape and that, if it was, it might revive.

SUMMARY

1. This chapter is primarily devoted to the main point where Keynes and his "Keynesian" followers break with the classical doctrine of monetary equilibrium. The main point of disagreement is over the classical contention that money-wage rates and money prices tend promptly to their equilibrium levels—so that the economy does not depart from equilibrium or, if it has departed, bounces back as soon as the situation is recognized.

2. The monetary disturbance singled out for study is an increase in the demand for liquidity: There is an increase in the value of the Cambridge k (under all conditions) and hence an increase in its level under equilibrium conditions, k^*. If k^* doubles, for example, then the equilibrium levels of the money-wage rate and the money-price level, W^* and P^*, respectively, are

cut in half, given the supply of money; only by such a drop in prices can people obtain the increased amount of money balances in real terms (in terms of purchasing power over bread) that the increased k implies they want.

3. Keynes objected to the classical doctrine that actual money-wage rates and (since money cost of production is tied to wages) money prices would in fact fall promptly to their new equilibrium levels. Why? It is not in the self-interest of the individual worker to accept such a cut in his money wage, Keynes insisted, *unless* of course he believed (or could be persuaded by his employer) that the money-wage rates offered at the other firms where he might work instead were going to be cut in the same proportion. And, in general, there is no reason for him to suppose that whenever his employer speaks of a need to cut wages in order to "save jobs" the other employers are ramming through the same pay cuts. So employees will "resist" such wage cuts; and employers, knowing that, will not be willing, each one acting alone, to impose the full magnitude of the wage cut that would in fact be necessary to save all jobs. There is *some* wage cut, and some workers, hoping to recoup their old wage, quit to look elsewhere—or they all quit to join the picket line. Figure 19–2 tells the story, or one such story.

4. Suppose, following Keynes, we take the average money-wage rate currently prevailing as given. It could be "given" at the same level it was at before the monetary disturbance, before the shock to k^*; or we could take as "given" the (inadequate!) drop of the money-wage level immediately following the disturbance. If we take the money wage as given in this sense, then we can use the Cambridge equation plus a supply-side equation to determine jointly the current level of output, and the general price level.

Instead of using the Cambridge equation as a formula for the equilibrium price level, P^*, after plugging into the equation the *equilibrium* level of output, Y^*, we can read it as a demand relationship between the price level and any *arbitrary* level of output, Y:

$$P = \frac{M}{k \cdot Y}$$

We may also utilize the relationship that says how high a price producers require in order to be willing to supply a specified level of output:

$$P = W \cdot Y$$

The former relation is a sort of *aggregate demand curve* that indicates how high the level is to which people, with their holdings of the nation's money supply, would drive up the general price level: The *lower* the output level, and hence people's real incomes (in terms of bread), the less will be their need for real money balances; hence the *higher* the corresponding price level. (The same money is chasing fewer goods.) This is the *demand price* of national output. The latter relation is a sort of *aggregate supply curve* that indicates how high the level of money prices must be in order to induce producers, given the money-wage rates they are paying, to supply a specified level of national output: The *higher* the output level, and hence the higher cost-per-unit and marginal cost, the *higher* the corresponding price level. This is the *supply price* of national output. Thus the demand price decreases with output, and the supply price increases (or at least it does not decrease).

Then, to close the system, it is argued that output gravitates to the level at which the "demand price" equals the "supply price"—or, if one prefers, "aggregate output demanded" equals "aggregate output supplied." The argument: If the demand price exceeds the supply price, producers will sense that they can sell more at the same price or sell the same output at a higher price—the product market is not clearing; either way, producers will then be induced to step up output (and raise price to cover the higher costs).

5. For Keynes the principal message is that rather than count on money-wage rates to wend their way down to the new lower level that is necessary for reattaining monetary equilibrium, at the old Y^*, it would be much faster and perhaps more reliable to depend on the monetary authorities to increase the money supply—to increase M so as to offset the increase of k. How much of an increase is that? Keynes advocated that when the government sees money-wage rates beginning to slacken, presumably because of weakening conditions in the demand for labor relative to the supply, the central bank ought to begin actions that increase the money supply—in order to "stabilize" the average level of money wages in the economy. Let the central bank stabilize money-wage rates and unemployment will tend to bounce back quickly following a disturbance; don't ask the labor market, with its hopelessly uncoordinated wage setters and workers, to try to adjust the pattern of wages in order to reattain equilibrium following disturbances. Thus was born the Keynesian activism that seized governments in the 1940s around the world.

6. An interesting point is the possibility that if the aggregate demand schedule falls it may be impossible for national output to fall by enough to establish a renewed equality between demand price and supply price—because the production of capital goods cannot turn *negative*, and at some low enough level of output and real incomes (in terms of bread) consumers will insist on spending all their income—they won't reduce their spending any further. This is the case of a "deep slump," produced by a

"big shock." An interesting feature of this case is that the government could step in to replace business purchases of capital goods, which have vanished, with government purchases of goods or with tax cuts to stimulate additional consumer purchases of goods. (But in the previous case, such fiscal actions by the government might not do much good; they would crowd out production of capital goods unless they can reduce the Cambridge k—a difficult topic taken up in the appendix to this chapter.)

7. The optional Further Reading section takes up a pet point of Keynes: A downward revision of speculators' and investors' estimates of the profitability of investment—the expected rate of return *induces* an increase in k^*, which has the same effects on W^* and P^* as a spontaneous increase by borrowing the rate of interest that borrowers are willing to pay and hence lowering the equilibrium level of the interest rate. Keynes thought this speculative factor may have been the cause of the Great Depression.

CONCEPTS INTRODUCED

demand-side disturbance, or demand shock
supply-side disturbance, or supply shock
search unemployment
layoff

aggregate demand curve
aggregate supply curve
equilibrium (and disequilibrium) in the capital-goods market
expected rate of return to investment, or marginal efficiency of capital

stabilizing policy
deep slump
crowding out

STUDY QUESTIONS

1. "Keynes couldn't have known the first thing about wages if he thought that the employer cuts wages *at all*, that wages bear *any* of the impact, when aggregate demand (hence the employer's perception of his demand) falls. Keynes evidently thought wages are not cut *enough* only because a firm's workers view every wage cut with the suspicion that the firm is trying to bail itself out of a problem that is peculiar to the firm rather than economywide. In real life, employers adjust only employment, never pay or promotion. In a slump managers cut their total wage bill only by furloughing or firing employees." Discuss. If in fact wages are "perfectly sticky," bearing none of the impact of a fall of aggregate demand (and falling only when the evidence of generally higher unemployment is observed), would this "fact" invalidate Keynes's conclusion that there *is* an impact on *employment* when aggregate demand falls? Is it certain that firms do *not* "cut" wage rates indirectly by slowing down individual employees' pay raises (for seniority,

etc.) and job promotions? Is it possible that Keynes did not think that the "fact" of wage stickiness is helpful for understanding slumps without a plausible *theory*, or understanding, of such stickiness? (The next chapter ends with some New Keynesian theories of wage stickiness of a sort.)

2. The diagram below was invented by the British economist J. R. Hicks to illuminate the Keynesian mechanism by which, given nominal wage rates, a deflationary monetary shock disturbs output and interest rate away from equilibrium. Try using it to explain how the increase of k (illustrated) at first raises the interest rate—given output still at Y^* and price level at the corresponding level, $P_s(Y^*)$—as people try to dump some of their capital assets for money. Then explain why, with $i > \epsilon$ and hence $P_d < P_s$, the result is a fall of output to the point where the interest rate is again equal to ϵ, the expected rate of return.

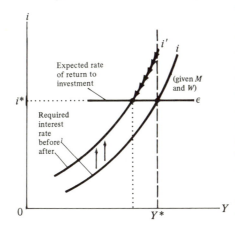

3. Here for the interested reader to study is a numerical example of the workings of the simple model of aggregate supply and demand. We focus again on a monetary shock, an increase of k. We suppose that the level of money-wage rates remained unchanged (at first) at the level W_1. Using the condition that the output level must fall to the point where the demand price and supply price are again equal we have

$$W \cdot Y = \frac{M}{k \cdot Y}$$

Borrowing from the mathematicians' tricks, we multiply both sides of the equation by Y, thus preserving the equality of left- and right-hand sides. And we divide both sides by W. Then

$$Y^2 = \frac{M}{W} \cdot \frac{1}{k}$$

So output is the square root of the money-supply-to-money-wage-level ratio divided by k. (Hence if the demand shock decreases $(1/k)$ by 19 percent, so that the square of output falls to 81 percent of its former level, as from 100 to 81, then output will fall by 10 percent, as from 10 to 9.)

The model makes it possible to calculate the decline of employment as well. If the extra employment requirement for successive equal additions to output is rising linearly, the number of workers needed for production rises with the square of output: $N = \frac{1}{2} Y^2$, say. Putting this relationship and the previous one together gives us

$$N = \frac{1}{2} \cdot \frac{M}{W} \cdot \frac{1}{k}$$

Hence in our example the employment requirement falls by 19 percent—from $\frac{1}{2}$ 100 to $\frac{1}{2}$ 81. It should be noted, however, that this calculation gives the percentage decline in the employment of so-called production workers—workers whose employment is tied to the volume of output produced. Suppose that three-quarters of the original number of employees were overhead employees instead of production workers—managers, accountants, salespersons, guards, and so on. (It can be argued that government workers belong there too.) Then total employment will fall by only *one-quarter* of 19 percent—less actually than the 10 percent fall of output.

4. "Economics never makes sense. Take the interest rate. Economists say that if the rate of return to investment expected by producers should fall, equilibrium requires a similar fall in the rate of interest, and such a fall in the equilibrium interest rate requires a lower level of wage rates at equilibrium. But if people expect lower returns, or rentals, on capital goods (plant and equipment), the *market prices* of office buildings, factory space, secondhand jet aircraft, and common stocks (which are ownership claims to capital goods) will fall in much the same proportion. They must do so to get people to go on holding these assets instead of money. So, calculated at these lower bargain prices, the expected rate of return to buying a building or a jet has not fallen at all! So how can there be a discrepancy between the expected rate of return and the rate of interest?" Discuss this hideous but very common confusion. Is the "expected rate of return to investment"—Keynes's "marginal efficiency of capital"—calculated at (possibly depressed) market prices dictated by the *demand price* or at the *supply-price* level of newly produced capital goods when their production is at the level consistent with equilibrium national output? Explain that the discrepancy between the expected rate of return (properly defined) and the interest rate corresponds to a gap between the supply price of new capital goods and the demand price.

APPENDIX: THE CROWDING-OUT CONTROVERSY IN CLOSED AND OPEN ECONOMIES

Chapter 19 has presented those themes in Keynes's great book that have proved of enduring interest to economists up to the present day. At the same time, it has shielded the reader from another of his themes, one that has been controversial for the past two or three decades and has found less and less acceptance. Keynes asserted that it is generally true, not just in deep slumps, that output and employment will rise whenever there is an increase of consumer demand—an increased "propensity" on the part of income earners to spend, a decreased "propensity" to save. The chapter conceded that consumer demand *does* have a role to play in propping up output and employment under conditions of deep slump: In such a case the consumers (and the government) are the only buyers in town, so it is not surprising that their willingness to buy more consumer goods would stimulate consumer-good production and thus total national production.

The Crowding-Out Question in a "Closed Economy"

In the standard case with which the chapter is predominantly concerned, however, it is not at all apparent that consumer demand has any influence on the level of total production and total employment. In this case total output (and thus total employment) is determined by the condition that it sinks to the level at which the demand price is equal to the supply price. So increased consumer demand can generate increased total output only by lowering the supply-price schedule or raising the demand-price schedule. But increased consumer spending will do nothing to help lower money-wage rates, so it will not lower the supply-price schedule. And it will do nothing intrinsically to increase the money supply; the government controls that, and the government could increase the stock of money with or without signs that consumers were spending more freely. So we conclude that the increased consumer demand must increase the value of k (and thus shift up the aggregate demand-price schedule) if it is to increase total production and employment. But will it? Let us hear first from the nays.

Those economists who *deny* that k will be thus increased offer a simple argument: If consumer demand increases there will indeed be a temporary rise of total output. But any rise of total production will increase the demand for money, since more wages and dividend income will then be arriving in cash pay-envelopes, electronic transfers in people's bank accounts, and checks; but the stock of money, we are supposing, is unchanged. So there is a tendency for holders of bonds and stocks and other earning assets to try to sell them (to someone!) in order to acquire larger cash balances—but no greater tendency on anyone's part to buy (far from it). So the prices of these non-money assets drop as a result.

- The fall in the price of existing office buildings, factory space, oil rigs, tankers, and so forth weakens the prices that potential buyers would be willing to pay for newly produced capital goods.
- In effect, wealth owners are now requiring a higher rate of interest—a higher yield on bonds and stocks—in order to be reconciled to holding the existing stock of earning assets despite the increased desirability of liquidity. Rates of interest on bank loans will go up similarly in sympathy. The effect of these higher rates of interest will be a slackening of the willingness of firms to issue bonds and take out loans to finance investments in new capital goods. So the demand facing capital-goods producers weakens through this channel as well.

So *capital-goods* production is *cut back*. How far is it contracted? The argument is that it is contracted until *total* national production is back to where it began: Once total production has sunk back to its initial level the rate of interest will have returned to equality with the marginal efficiency of capital since the rate of interest will then be back to its original level and the marginal efficiency will be at its initial level once total production is back at its initial level. The argument supposes that the marginal efficiency is unaltered (in particular, not pushed up) by the fact that more of the initial level of total production takes the form of consumer-goods output and less takes the form of capital-goods output. The argument also supposes (as is customary) that there is just one level of total production where the required rate of interest equals the marginal efficiency of capital. With these premises, the level of production must tend to the same level it was before the increase in consumer demand. The extra consumption spending merely *crowds out* an equal amount of investment spending.

◆ In essence the argument is that a shift in the composition of output does not alter the marginal efficiency of capital and thus the price level (and the real cash balances level) needed to bring wealth owners' required rate of interest into equality with the marginal efficiency of capital. Hence there is *no change* in the *demand price* that goes with the initial level of total output.

This was the view of the British Treasury in the 1920s.

The other view. Keynes disagreed with this Treasury view without adequately explaining the basis for his disagreement. He asserted that the marginal efficiency of capital is dependent on the *rate* of investment per year or month (or whatever): that the greater the *rate* of investment, the lower the corresponding marginal efficiency of capital. If that is in fact the case, when increased consumer-good output takes the place of some capital-goods output, the total volume of production being unchanged, the marginal efficiency will be increased. In that case there must result an increase of total production, since, without it, there would be a discrepancy between the marginal efficiency and the rate of interest.

Keynes's reasons why the marginal efficiency should depend on the *speed* with which firms are adding new plant and equipment to their capital stock are another story. It would take us beyond the introductory stage of economics to consider these reasons and present-day theories offering fresh reasons for such a dependence. They all argue that a reduction of the rate of investment, which would be implied by greater consumption-type spending if total output remains unchanged, *lowers* the *marginal cost* of producing and installing new capital, and in that way raises the *rate of return* to new investment, or marginal efficiency—which is the ratio of return to cost.

◆ The disturbance thus creates a clash between the marginal efficiency of capital and the (initially unchanged) rate of interest required by wealth owners.

- The impact is a fall in the marginal cost of supplying new capital goods while there is no change (at the initial level of national output) in the prices of common stock and used capital goods.
- As a consequence, capital goods production and national employment increase—unless and until wages rise enough to prevent that.

Expressed in terms of the Cambridge equation, k is decreased and the demand-price schedule shifts upward, reflecting the fact that the real value of cash balances must fall for the rate of interest required by wealth owners to remain equal to the higher marginal efficiency of capital; and this upward shift of the demand-price schedule, given the supply-price schedule, leads to an increase of total output and employment.

CROWDING OUT IN THE OPEN ECONOMY

Later, however, economists realized that even if there are good reasons for believing that increased consumer spending in a closed economy would stimulate increased total output—by lifting the marginal efficiency of capital and thus raising the demand price for output at each level of total production—the conclusion might not extend to an economy that is open to foreign trade and lending. Perhaps the increased consumer spending (or government spending) will simply spill over into increased imports of foreign-made goods or crowd out some exports to such an extent that total output is left unchanged. It came to be seen that this is a theoretical possibility, and perhaps not far from what actually happens. At least that is so if the country keeps the supply of money unchanged in the face of the bulge in spending rather than manipulating the money supply in order to stabilize the national currency's value against foreign currencies—to fix the exchange rate.

The argument begins with the proposition that today, with capital so mobile internationally, we will not go far wrong if we think of there being a single *world* rate of interest. The opportunity of people in "our" country to borrow or lend at this interest rate tends to prevent our rate of interest from moving up or down very much from the level of the world rate. It is further supposed that our country is not large enough to be able to influence very much the world interest rate; as an approximation, we may take the world rate as a datum, or given.

Consider again, then, the effects of an increase of consumer demand—for home goods, say, not imported goods. It follows from the above suppositions that the increased consumer spending cannot drive up the interest rate in our country and thereby induce a decrease of k, given the world interest rate; hence the increased consumer spending cannot raise the demand price (i.e., cannot shift up the demand price curve), given the money supply in our country. It is also true that the increased consumer spending can do nothing to lower the supply price of output (i.e., to shift down the supply price curve). Therefore, the increased consumer spending cannot increase total production; the level of total output is unchanged. Evidently, some export production is crowded out or some goods formerly made domestically are imported (capital goods if not consumer goods) or both. In this theory, the increased consumer spending crowds out exports net of imports—net exports, so called—rather than investment.

An interesting point to add concerns the exchange rate. When the country's policy is to hold constant the money supply, as we are supposing, it cannot hold constant its exchange rate—the cost in home currency of buying a unit of foreign currency—at the same time; the exchange rate will be freely fluctuating, its level determined by the market. There are two cases to consider:

- If our country is an important supplier of the good it exports in the world market, important enough (at least temporarily) that the amount it supplies to the world market has an effect on the world price, then the crowding out of exports pushes up the prices of these goods in terms of foreign currencies on the world market; but we are taking it for granted that the prices of domestically produced goods are unchanged in terms of the home currency. It can then be seen that the home currency must be worth more in terms of foreign currencies than before; the home currency is implied to appreciate to a higher value. If it did not appreciate, there would be a discrepancy between the price obtained for exports after conversion to the home currency at the rate of exchange between home and foreign currencies, on the one hand, and the price obtained for the same goods at home as expressed in the home currency; foreigners would rush to buy our exports at our home price instead of at the price in foreign currencies, and in so doing they would drive up the exchange value of our currency in foreign-exchange markets.

- If, as in the second case, our country is like a purely competitive firm in an industry—too small a supplier to have any significant influence on the market price—the crowding out of exports has no effect on the world price in terms of foreign currencies as well as the domestic price in terms of the home currency. It can then be seen that there is no appreciation of the home currency.

The former case may fit Canada: If consumers there go on a spending spree they may very well drive up the world price of wheat and the exchange value of the Canadian dollar. The latter case fits tiny Uruguay: Increased consumer spending there will not drive up the world wheat price nor the Uruguayan peso. In both cases, though, wheat and other exports are crowded out (to the extent that extra imports are not crowded in to meet the increased spending) by exactly enough to leave total output no higher than before the increase of consumer spending.

Why do macroeconomists consider these to be important findings, even if oversimplifications of an even more complex tangle of relationships? There is first the answer that it is surely important to understand that when "the consumer goes on strike" total output may fall by little or even not at all; the home currency will tend to depreciate, and exports will consequently increase, net of imports, so as to fill much or all of the gap left by the home consumer.

Another answer is that what applies to the spending of consumers here also applies to spending by the government (and, for that matter, investment spending by firms, which we will not pursue). Suppose there is an increase of spending on goods by the government without any increase in tax rates. We may say that the government's *fiscal deficit* is thus widened. Suppose further that, although consumers may be made uneasy by the larger public deficit, the effect is to increase the sum of spending by consumers and the government. Macroeconomists consider it important to recognize that this increased government spending may fail to boost total output, even if (as may be the case) it would have done so in a closed economy; and that the main effects may be a crowding out of exports net of imports—a widening of the so-called *trade deficit*—and an appreciation of the home currency in foreign-exchange markets.

Thus macroeconomists in seeking explanations for the striking rise of the dollar in the first half of the 1980s pointed to the marked widening of the fiscal deficit in the United States, brought by across-the-board tax cuts and enlarged military spending, and the simultaneous curbing of fiscal deficits in Europe and Japan. Yet the macroeconomist could not be sure how large a part these divergent fiscal policies play in the "strong dollar." Other factors were also at work. It is hoped that time will tell.

Temporary Fiscal Stimulus

We have been analyzing a permanent increase of domestic spending, such as an indefinite fiscal stimulus. What if the stimulus is believed to be temporary? The above analysis provides a clue.

If the current stimulus is seen to lift the foreign-exchange value of our currency, and if the stimulus is expected soon to end, speculators will be betting on a return of our currency to its normal value—thus a recovery of foreign currencies. This expectation raises the rate of interest in our country and thus decreases the value of our Cambridge k and moderates the appreciation of our currency. The result: *incomplete* crowding out of exports and thus *some* rise of national output.

CHAPTER 20

Ever since Keynes: Government Intervention vs. Reliance on "the Market"

PROFESSOR VAN HELSING:
I have devoted my life to the study of many strange things—things which perhaps mankind would be better off *not* knowing.

Edward Van Sloan in *Dracula* (1931)

KEYNES and his interpreters argued that economywide, or macroeconomic, shocks to the economy would have impacts upon aggregate production and employment—upon *quantities*, not merely nominal wages and nominal prices, as the neoclassical monetary theorists appeared to believe. Though Keynes only hinted at the basis for his position, modern-day theorists have "made sense" of Keynes's conclusions. Modern theories of how labor markets work provide reasons, *reasons involving the imperfect information that is typical in labor markets*, why disturbances, if they are unforeseen, have impacts upon output and employment. This part of "Keynesian" doctrine has stood up well to the critical scrutiny of economists. (Keynes's point that an equilibrium might not exist after the disturbance, in which case no matter how far money wages fell there could be no restoration of equilibrium, has also survived—intact but unused.)

The other theme of Keynes's is, right or wrong, of much more profound significance: He insisted that the approach to the new equilibrium, and thus the recovery of the economy from the disturbance, is apt to be terribly drawn out—in a word, retarded, or protracted. From that premise Keynes then argued that the government could improve matters by the way it exercises its control over the supply of money—by the monetary policy it adopts. While wages might be slow to fall by the amount needed (following a contractionary, or deflationary, demand shock) for reattainment of equilibrium, given the supply of money, the government could quickly increase the money supply by the amount needed for equilibrium given the level of wages. In short, if wages have to fall as a ratio to the money supply, it would be quicker to increase the denominator than to wait for the numerator to decline. Thus was born the Keynesian doctrine that an activist, or interventionist, monetary policy could serve to combat slumps.

It is worthwhile being concrete even if the details are not crucial. Keynes proposed that the money supply be managed with the objective of stabilizing the average money-wage level:

> If money-wage rates drop, the money supply ought to be boosted with the aim of bringing wages back up. If employment rises, thus creating the prospect of a fall of wages, the money supply should also be boosted to prevent a fall of wages.

Such a monetary policy would often have the side effect of shortening or preventing a slump. It would not be a magic bullet—a sure, total cure: There could be "large fluctuations in employment" nevertheless. "But the fluctuations will be less," Keynes wrote, "than with a [policy of reliance on a] flexible wage."* Succeeding "Keynesians" advocated focusing on employment instead:

> If there is a rise of unemployment above the equilibrium level or the prospect of such a rise, the government should raise the money supply to combat that rise in unemployment.

It is these latter beliefs of Keynes and his followers that have been the object of intense controversy for subsequent generations of economists—the supposition that slumps have a systematic tendency to linger, and to moderate only gradually; and the supposition that an activist policy by the government can help cure and sometimes prevent slumps. To the critics, Keynes was like a scientist who, having successfully explained that a person might feel sad after losing his dog, went on to claim that such a loss tends to produce a depression—but a depression for which the scientist has a helpful medicine. For these critics, that is medicine that society, if drawn into using it, would be better off not knowing about.

---

*Keynes, *The General Theory of Employment, Interest and Money* (London: Macmillan and Company, 1936), p. 271.

In this chapter we deal with the leading criticisms in recent decades of this part of Keynesian doctrine. These are the early monetarist attack, dating from the 1960s, and the later development of a counter-theory, which gives support to monetarism, called the New Classical macroeconomics.

THE MONETARIST COUNTER TO KEYNES

The antithesis of Keynesian activism is the doctrine called *monetarism*. The first monetarists conceded that the *best* monetary policy, if it could actually be put into practice, would contain the right dose of Keynesian activism. But, they said, in matters of monetary policy as so often in other public affairs, the best is the enemy of the good: *If the government, through the central bank it controls, is licensed to pursue an activist policy of economic stabilization, the results are apt to be worse than if the government resisted the temptation to intervene.*

In supporting this bold theme, which ran counter to the activist instinct of most economists, the monetarists first made a crude, but impressive, case of a purely empirical sort: Economic history shows that the worst episodes suffered in the past century (at least) were made worse, not better, by the managers of the money supply. The classical example is the Great Depression. In the years of the precipitous decline of wages and employment, the early 1930s, the managers of the money supply were trying, as well as they knew how, to encourage economic recovery. But their efforts were seriously misguided, disastrously so in the United States.

> With a proper understanding of the contractionary impulses that must have been at work in those years and an understanding of what steps might counteract them, the central banks around the world presumably ought to have acted to increase the supply of money—or at the very least acted to maintain the supply of money. But in fact the money supply fell sharply in the United States from 1930 to 1932. There is scattered evidence of some contraction of the money supply in other countries as well. Thus, in America at least, the management of the money supply was perverse. The United States central bank, the Federal Reserve Bank, took actions that (on the whole) *reinforced* rather than combatted the contraction being experienced in the early 1930s.

Another classic example occurred during the Vietnam War:

> Had the central bank acted promptly to decrease the money supply—or at least to hold it constant—the sharp rise in production for military purposes (procurements and personnel) in 1967 and

1968 would have increased the demand for real cash balances and put downward pressure on bond prices, stock prices, and so forth. Thus it would have soon crowded out production of new capital goods; total GNP would have subsided to normal. Instead, the Federal Reserve boosted the supply of money.

Thus a casual inspection of economic history suggested that activism in monetary policy making had compiled a dismal record.

♦ Summing up this part of their case, the monetarists concluded that reliance on activist management of the money supply had (on the whole) made the performance of the economy worse than it would have been had the government instead relied on the market process of money-wage adjustments to restore equilibrium following macroeconomic disturbances. In a slump money wages can be counted on to decline relative to the money supply; and in a boom, to rise relative to the money supply. At least money wages don't *march off in the wrong direction,* scoring a touchdown for the opposing team.

In the monetarist view, then, it is better for the government to do nothing than to pursue an activist monetary policy with the objective of stabilizing the economy. Yet the monetarists had to define what to them means to "do nothing." Does it mean that the government, through its central bank, should not print any more money—by buying bonds and other assets with newly printed currency and central-bank checks—and should not destroy money— by selling bonds or other assets in return for currency or checks cashed in for currency? (Then, if people bring more currency to the banks, the money supply will increase—through no action by the government.) Or does it mean that the government will print or destroy money as needed to stabilize the total supply of money (currency plus bank deposits)? And if so, which deposits shall be counted as part of the money supply? Or *what?*

♦ The monetarists have not been able to reach a consensus on that technical issue. Some advocate stabilizing some broad measure of the money supply—typically M2, which includes some savings deposits at banks as well as checkable (therefore moneylike) demand deposits. But there is an entire family of measures of the money supply. Some advocate stabilizing some narrow measure of the money supply—typically *M1,* which excludes savings deposits (and usually *M1B,* which includes all checkable deposits, not *M1A,* which excludes checkable deposits at nonbank institutions like mutual funds). Finally, some advocate stabilizing M0, which is only the money created by the central bank, not the money created privately when people take currency for deposit in fractional-reserve-holding private banks.

♦ There is the further technical issue of how the monetary aggregate being controlled—M2 or *M1* or M0—ought to move (if at all) *with time.* Should the path of the monetary aggregate be flat? Or should it grow at some constant percentage rate, like 3 percent or 5 percent per year? Or should the desired growth rate be adjusted from decade to decade, or epoch to epoch, as gauged appropriate for achieving the preferred rate of inflation (whichever rate that may be)? Here too the monetarists have been unable to reach a consensus.

Whatever the exact definition of "monetarist" monetary policy that is adopted, its marked contrast to activist, or interventionist, monetary policy is perfectly clear. Indeed, monetarists stress that the stability and predictability of the monetary policy rule is far more important than the particular form that the rule takes.

♦ For monetarists what is crucial for the good performance of the economy is the reliability with which the monetary authorities at the central bank follow their announced and understood rule, not the details of the rule. Money-wage rates will be set too high for achievement of the equilibrium level of employment, for example, if the participants in the labor market all expect the central bank to set the money supply at one level when in fact the bank then engineers a lower supply—thus producing a contractionary demand shock to the economy.

WHY DO THE MONETARY AUTHORITIES SO OFTEN ACT PERVERSELY? SOME EARLY MONETARIST THEORIZING

Ineptitude in the past is no guarantee, of course, of ineptitude in the future. To make a convincing case against activism in monetary policy the monetarists need to offer *reasons* why we should expect the past to repeat itself in one way or another. (The monetarists might adopt as their motto a statement by Goethe: "We learn from history that we do not learn from history.")

One reason why activist monetary policy may backfire is that it leaves the policy response up to the policy makers' judgment, which is not always predictable. So it may happen that the central bank is expected to do one thing in the interest of stability while in fact it does something different, also in the interest of stability. Then the private decision makers in the economy may be caught off base, with their wages and prices too high or too low in relation to the money supply level actually being engineered by the central bank.* In short, when the activist policy is up to the *discretion* of the central

---

* A perfect example followed the oil shock of 1974. Would the Federal Reserve decrease the money supply to stabilize prices or increase the money supply to stabilize employment? Surprisingly, they opted for the former. Later, after a major money-supply data revision, it became less clear that a significant reduction had occurred, however.

bank the result may be a *failure* of *coordination* between the bank and the private economy. Recall the pure coordination game in chapter 3: A convention, or rule, is useful.

Undoubtedly the fall of the American money supply in the early years of the Great Depression was not intended by the Federal Reserve; much of it was the accidental product of bank failures, and much of it was unmeasured and unperceived at the time. *But* the unwillingness of the Federal Reserve to try to reverse the money supply—to push it back toward its former level—was deliberate. The governors of the Federal Reserve decided against restoring the money supply, which would have revived the economy presumably, in order to prevent a rise of prices and wages to their old levels, which the governors considered "inflation." That decision in favor of "stability" of *prices* may have prolonged the depression.

In a boom the self-interest of firms and workers drives wages up; in a slump it drives them down. This mechanism tends to drive employment back to its equilibrium level. In contrast, it is not obviously in the strong self-interest of central-bank officials to decrease the money supply in booms and increase it in slumps. So it would not be a surprise if relying on the central bank to restore equilibrium might sometimes turn out badly. Yet this leads to a question: What *is* in the self-interest of the directors, or governors, of the central bank? According to a hypothesis of political economy considered in the epilogue to the modernist Part 6, every regulatory agency of the government tends to become a captive of the vested interests it is supposed to regulate. (In the pleasure-pain calculus of a regulator, friendly relations with the regulatees are more fun than adversary relations and sometimes beneficial after public office is over.) This implies that the central bank serves the *banking interests,* within the limits of its legislative mandate.

In the early months of 1932 the Federal Reserve took steps toward reversing the previous decline of the money supply. But the resulting dip of interest rates must have seemed a threat to the survival of a great many of the banks, which depend on a surplus of loan and securities interest over any payment of interest to depositors to cover their operating deficit as a supplier of consumer services. In any case, the Federal Reserve soon suspended its efforts to reverse the money supply, at or near the very bottom of the depression.

Another hazard in relying on activist monetary policy, monetarists say, is that policy makers may make their decisions on the basis of "the wrong model" of the economy—a model of how the economy works that is seriously flawed in some respect. As judged by an omniscient observer, what the central bank decides to do may often seem like pure guesswork—as if the central-bank officials were flipping a coin to reach decisions. Not possessed of perfect economic knowledge, or accurate up-to-date data, the misguided central bankers will sometimes reach the wrong decision. Of course, the private actors making decisions in the labor markets and product markets are not perfectly knowledgeable either. But, the monetarists argue, it *adds* to the fluctuations of the economy rather than diminishing those fluctuations to have the central bank intervening in the economy when, with excessive frequency, it intervenes in the wrong direction.

- A key area of ignorance is the size of the equilibrium level of unemployment. Imagine that the central-bank officials believe the equilibrium level to be, say, 4 percent of the labor force when the true equilibrium level is, say, 6 percent. If the economy happens to be moving into boom conditions, hence the unemployment rate is observed to be falling below 6 percent, the *stabilizing* policy would be to "lean against the wind": to begin *decreasing* the money supply so as to prevent the (presumably undesired) fluctuation of employment and resulting upward pressure on the trend of prices and wages. But the central bank might actually be *increasing* the money supply—it might still be combating the previous slump—if it believes that the equilibrium unemployment rate is 4 percent and it sees that the economy is not there yet. Thus the central bank might be led by its incorrect model of the economy to do the wrong thing from the viewpoint of economic stability.

An early monetarist classic that further develops the theme of mistakes in activist policy established its author, Milton Friedman, as the leading theoretician of the monetarist school. It is the first paper to analyze the capacity of activist policy to stabilize with the same conceptual tools that would be used by a biologist or engineer or operations-research analyst to study a problem of system control—the statistical concepts from probability theory. With this approach, Friedman investigates the conditions under which "countercyclical" action will succeed—in some average sense—in *reducing* instability rather than actually increasing it!

... The many proponents of full-employment policies seem to take it for granted that a full-employment policy will not be destabilizing, that this will be true regardless of the precise character of the policy, and that there is no serious problem about the magnitude of government measures to promote stability except to make them large enough. . . . [They fail] to recognize that there is a basic problem about the effectiveness of countercyclical action, that it is possible to do too much as well as too little . . .

Friedman goes on to show that there are two pitfalls in stabilization policy: the problem of inadvertently acting in the wrong direction, which we have just discussed in the paragraph above, and the problem of overdoing action that would have been the right thing if undertaken on a smaller scale. Here is Friedman's conclusion:

There is some limit to the possibilities of stabilizing the level of economic activity by policy measures intended to do so. This limit depends upon two major characteristics of the action: the extent to which the effects of the action are [in line with] the effects needed—to put it loosely, the frequency with which the effects are in the "right" direction—and the magnitude of the action taken. For any given magnitude of action the total effects of the policy may be destabilizing even if effects of the actions taken are more frequently in the "right" than in the "wrong" direction; there is some minimum frequency of "right" to "wrong" action required in order that the actions on balance [meaning on the average] be stabilizing. Similarly, for any given frequency of "right" to "wrong" actions, there is an optimum magnitude of action. More vigorous action than this, however well intended, will do more harm than good. . . . [G]ood intentions are not enough.*

Summing up this line of argument, the monetarists conclude that there are good reasons for the failures of activist monetary policy making in the past; and these same reasons should make us predict repeated failures in the future if activism should continue to be tried.

At this point in the debate between the Keynesians and the monetarists we ought to reserve judgment. For one thing, the monetarist side has recently found itself supplied with a fresh argument on its behalf offered by the New Classical school. The monetarists also make an inflation argument, which awaits the next chapter; and there is new evidence resulting from the monetarist experiments at disinflation in several countries over the past few years.

For the balance of this chapter we shall hear the novel and fundamental attack on Keynesian activism developed by proponents of the New Classical macroeconomics. (Similarities and dissimilarities to the classical, or neoclassical doctrine developed early in this century will become apparent as we proceed.)

* Milton Friedman, "The Effects of Full-Employment Policy on Economic Stability, *Essays in Positive Economics* (Chicago: University of Chicago Press, 1953), pp. 118, 131–32.

THE "NEW CLASSICAL" ATTACK ON KEYNES

The New Classical macroeconomics accepts the *first part* of Keynesian analysis: the idea that unforeseeable and thus *unanticipated* demand shocks have effects upon *quantities* as well as prices—effects' on the real GNP and employment. But it rebels against the *second part:* the Keynesian theory that recovery from a slump is characteristically drawn out, and the claim that a *regular policy* of boosting the money supply in a slump can speed it up.

New Classical macroeconomists assert that money-wage rates typically *will not* linger at excessive levels once the slump—the rise of unemployment and the first sag of wage rates and prices—is reported over radio and television and in the press. As soon as the news of the slump has been reported, money-wage rates will drop by the appropriate amount; they will drop by just the amount predicted by equilibrium theory. Then, with wages and prices having made the suitable adjustment to the disturbance, aggregate production and employment will be back on their equilibrium path! Once the news is out, the Keynesian problem—excessive money wages resulting from excessive, "inflated" wage expectations—will vanish, and so will the disequilibrium that was temporarily created by the unanticipated disturbance.

♦ Thus the New Classical macroeconomists rejected the prop—the supposition by Keynes and his modern-day interpreters that wages would adjust too slowly even after the news of the slump was out—supporting the Keynesian theory that recoveries tended to be too slow. *If* recoveries take a while, the New Classicals suggested, it is for different reasons, not for the Keynesian reason of the "wage problem."

The New Classical rejection of the Keynesian analysis of recovery led to rejection of the Keynesian policy conclusion. The case for an activist monetary policy to hasten recoveries is seriously damaged if it is not true that wages are a problem impeding recovery.

According to the New Classical argument, which we shall shortly examine, an activist monetary policy is *unnecessary*.

New Classical macroeconomists next assert that a government policy of combating slumps with an increase in the money supply would be ineffective anyway. A monetary policy of reacting to a slump by boosting the money supply seems to have common sense on its side: If a slump develops either there has been a increase in the desire for liquidity—an increase in the demand for money—or, conceivably, a decrease in the supply of money, presumably not intended by the central bank authorities whose job it is to control the money supply. In either case it seems sensible for the central bank to respond to the slump by acting to increase the supply of money; at least it seems sensible to orthodox Keynesians, who see increased money as a quick and reliable solution to the slump, and see depending on the "flexibility" of wages in the marketplace as a slow and unreliable solution. But, say the New Classicals, such a policy will not work. If the increase of the money supply is *anticipated* by the people in the market place, it will merely raise prices and money-wage rates in the same proportion; it will do nothing to stimulate an increase of production and employment.

- Thus the New Classical macroeconomists reject the Keynesian assumption that a monetary policy aimed at countering slumps, at speeding recoveries, could be effective. If the central bank announces beforehand its plan to increase the money supply or makes it a regular policy—a dependable rule—to boost the money supply in slumps, the policy action by the central bank will be anticipated in labor and product markets. And an *anticipated* increase of the money supply merely drives up wages and prices, not employment.

Thus countercyclical policy in the view of the New Classical school is *ineffective*. We turn first to this second proposition.

THE "POLICY INEFFECTIVENESS" PROPOSITION

The argument that the New Classical macroeconomists make for the ineffectiveness of "countercyclical" monetary policy is easy to grasp. They begin, in essence, by pointing to the Cambridge model of equilibrium with its equation of exchange. It implies, as will be recalled, that the equilibrium price level is proportional to the money supply; double the one and we will double the other. In the new equilibrium following an increase in the money supply, therefore, the *real* value of the money supply—the quantity of real cash balances held, M/P—will be the same as that in the previous equilibrium.

The theory says further that when we compare the two equilibriums, before and after the change of the money supply, we will find that everything real is the same: same real cash balance level, same real wealth, same supply of labor and demand for labor, and so forth; and therefore the same *real* wage rates, the same *relative* prices, and, in particular, the same equilibrium level of employment. (Hence the neoclassical proposition that money is a "veil," obscuring the face of the economy but not altering it.)

The New Classical macroeconomists next argue that this theory of the equilibrium price (and money-wage) level and equilibrium employment level *always* applies, no matter what the situation the economy has been in (or is in), provided the increase of the money supply is anticipated. They argue that the money supply increase, if anticipated by everyone, will cause everyone to *expect* a proportional increase in the general level of wage rates and prices—in the prices and wages for all the various goods and jobs. And if everyone expects the money supply, the general level of money wages, and the general level of money prices to increase by some equal percentage amount, such as 5 percent, everyone's asking wage will increase in the same proportion.

> Each worker will demand exactly that compensating increase in order to maintain the same "real" and "relative" position in a basically unchanged economic situation. "If I was about to require a money wage of X *without* this 5 percent increase of the money supply, I should *now* hold out for X + 5 percent (of X), since everyone else is going to get 5 percent more." And some workers may require the 5 percent money-wage increase in order to stay in the labor force rather than retire, since prices are expected to rise by 5 percent.

Hence to retain the same number of workers—the same quantity of labor input—as would have been hired without the increase of the money supply, firms must pay money-wage rates that are 5 percent higher than would otherwise have been necessary.

The last step in the argument: Since the workers, expecting the 5 percent increase of the money supply, must be paid 5 percent higher money wages for the same volume of employment, the firms must receive 5 percent higher prices if they are to be willing to produce the same volume of output (and thus offer the same volume of employment)—more if they are to be willing to produce more than that. As chapter 19 pointed out, the *supply price* for a given level of output is proportional to the level of money wages; so the supply price rises by 5 percent at any given level of output. But at the same time, the *demand price* is proportional to the money supply; so the demand price is also going to rise by 5 percent at any given level of output. Hence the supply price rises in the same proportion as the demand price. Thus the increase in the money supply does not succeed in raising the level of aggregate production and employment in the economy.

- The increase in money prices that people are willing to pay for goods is offset, or "neutralized," by a matching increase in the supply prices that producers require.
- The increase in money wages that firms are willing to pay workers is neutralized by a matching increase in the asking wages that workers hold out for.

Although the government's action may have been intended to stimulate employment, to promote recovery, its effect is simply to raise money wages and prices. Its power to raise employment is exactly *neutralized* by the higher wage and price requirements of workers and firms. Their *anticipation of the money supply increase* and their *correct forecast of its effects on the general wage and price levels* lead them, each one acting self-protectively, to raise their own wages and prices by just the percentage amount that neutralizes the money-supply increase—rendering it ineffective for stimulating employment. Figure 20–1 summarizes the New Classical argument.

♦ Thus do the New Classical macroeconomists argue that any countercyclical monetary policy intended (or pretended!) by the government to increase output and employment, to promote recovery and counter the slump, is *totally ineffective* as long as the public *anticipates* the government's pol-

FIGURE 20–1: The Neutrality of Monetary Policy in the New Classical Macroeconomics

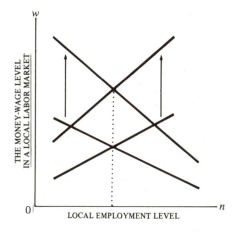

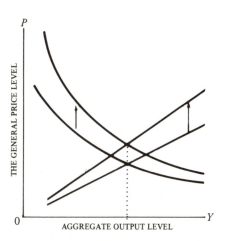

An increase of the money supply lifts demand curves, raising each demand price (at a given quantity) in proportion to the money supply. Similarly, it raises the wages offered by employers (for a given employment) in the same proportion as well. But if the money-supply change is anticipated in the marketplace, asking wages will be increased by as much, proportionately, as wages offered; hence supply prices will immediately increase in the same proportion as well. Hence the anticipated money-supply increase

does not change the level of production where demand price equals supply price. And it does not change the employment level (in the aggregate and in each geographically distinct labor market) at which wage offered equals asking wage. Hence the aggregate production and employment levels resulting will be the same levels that would have resulted without the anticipated money supply increase. A passive, do-nothing monetary policy would have the same results for output and employment.

icy. (It is true the government *can* stimulate employment by increasing the money supply by *more* than is generally anticipated in the economy, thus catching workers and firms with their expectations too low. But that is another story—for the next chapter.)

We could delve a step deeper into the chamber where the New Classical theoreticians keep the logic of their doctrine. *Why* does a money-supply increase anticipated by everyone cause *anyone*—let alone everyone—to expect a proportional increase in the general levels of wages and prices? One answer is "Because they have learned to do so, like rats subjected to repeated experiments." But this answer is not entirely satisfactory: No rat will learn to expect a proportional increase of wages and prices, upon hearing that the money supply is going to go up, unless and until the other rats learn it. If the *others* in the economy do *not* expect any resulting increase of wages, for example, then the anticipated disturbance to the money supply will *not* generate a proportional increase of wages and prices; and it *will* generate some increase of employment. *With no change in the others' expectations,* the upward shift in the curve describing the money wage offered by employers at each level of employment will simply *slide the economy rightward* (and upward) *along the curve describing the money wage asked* at each

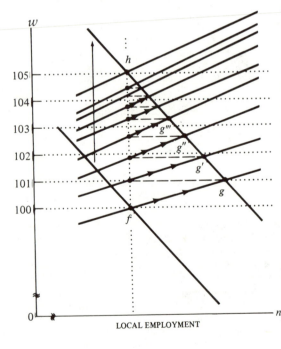

level of employment. In the diagram above, the economy would slide from *f* to a point like *g*. In the example drawn, the increase of the money supply, which we may suppose to be 5 percent, would support an increase of wages by 5 percent at the same (unchanged) level of employment—as indicated by *h* in comparison to *f*. But the outcome at *g* would leave wages only 1 percent higher.

According to the logic of New Classical theory, however, each person (worker, etc.) is led by a chain of reasoning to expect that the outcome *will* be a 5 percent general increase of wages, *not* no increase or any lesser increase—to expect the outcome at *h*. The reasoning goes this way: "If the others expect *no* increase of wages the actual wage level will rise and level off at *g*. So I must raise my asking wage in the same proportion. But *they*—all the others—know this too. So *they* will be expecting the same increase in the general level of ages as I; so they will each raise their asking wages in that proportion too. But this increase of asking wages will cause the general level of wages to increase some more—to *g′*—though not in equal proportion, of course, since the "demand curve" is not vertical. So I must raise my asking wage by that much more. But so will the others. And so on. I see that only at *h* does the process converge—with the gap between 'expected' and 'actual' vanished."

The "Policy Unnecessary" Proposition

We turn now to the first of the New Classical propositions: The "news" corrects people's expectations and thus restores equilibrium. So an activist policy is unnecessary.

We return to the scene of the previous chapter. A "deflationary" demand shock—an increase of k—has occurred. The shock did *not* have the neoclassical effect of merely causing a fall of all money-wage rates and prices in equal proportion (so as to gratify the increased thirst for real cash balances). The shock had a Keynesian impact on production and employment, particularly in the capital-goods industries. There was an impact on employment because the demand shock caught the participants in the economy unaware, *ignorant of the nature and size of the macroeconomic shock that had just gripped them*. They had no sense that the equilibrium levels of money-wage rates and money were, suddenly, sharply different from before.

> The typical worker who was employed in a particular place making a particular capital good did not know at the time the shock struck that the shock was so general—that it was occurring in all the capital-goods industries equally, that employment

and wages were going to fall more or less equally in all those industries. Workers in the consumer-goods industries may have had no suspicion at first of any disturbance at all in the economy.

Being ignorant of the shock, workers (and firms too) had no reason suddenly to expect, at the time of the shock, a sharp reduction in the general level of wage rates and prices. (And any "smart guy" who did expect it would have been wrong, since the others weren't expecting it.) Because they do not revise downward their expectations of the average money-wage level in the economy—not by enough, anyway—there is "resistance" to wage cuts; the general wage reduction needed to maintain employment doesn't take place. Figures 19–2 and 19–3 illustrated the situation.

New Classical economists concede that part of the story. *Of course* the demand shock momentarily lowers employment. The workers (and the firms too) *could not have known* at the time what was hitting them. They were caught with their expectations up instead of down and so were holding out for wages that employers could no longer pay (particularly in the capital-goods industries) for the amount of "man-hours" being used until the arrival of the demand shock. But what happens to expectations next month when radios blare out government *reports* of a *sharp rise of unemployment* last month? And a *decline of average hourly wages* last month?

♦ The New Classical macroeconomics supposes that workers and firms will inform themselves about each development in the economy once it becomes known. Then, with their knowledge of how the economy works, they will use the new information to interpret what has happened to the economy and to analyze its significance for wages, prices, unemployment, and so forth in their own industry in the future.

The New Classical macroeconomics argues that the workers, upon hearing the new reports on unemployment, wages, and so forth, and armed with their past experience in such matters, will draw the correct conclusions about what has hit them. The report on the new unemployment level, the new average wage level, and so forth will enable them to identify the kind of shock that has occurred—here, a demand shock—and to estimate the size of the shock. They will use their estimate of the scale of the shock to form new, "updated" expectations of the money-wage rates and prices that will prevail in the postshock economy.

A shock believed to be permanent. To begin with, let us suppose that the shock is believed to be "permanent." People realize that there may be future shocks, of course, but they do not expect that there is any tendency for the shock that has just occurred to reverse itself—to fade or disappear with the passage of time, or to grow. The increase in k that people estimate has occurred, on the basis of the new economic reports, is believed to be a once-

and-for-all increase, not a "blip" and not the first installment in a series of increases.

According to the New Classical macroeconomics, people will put together their information on the magnitude of the rise in unemployment together with their beliefs about the permanence of the shock in order to calculate—on the basis of the relationship observed in the past—the magnitude of the general reduction of prices and wages to expect, compared with the pre-shock levels, now that the news of the shock is out. Here is the sort of thought process involved:

"I've seen months with a 3 percent fall of employment before. In fact I've seen them all. And in those cases where the shock seems to have proved permanent, I've noticed that there is a relationship between the size of the temporary fall in employment and the size of the permanent drop in wages and prices that follows. A 3 percent fall of employment indicates something like a 5 percent drop of wages and prices."

In effect, according to the New Classical economists, the supplier of labor choosing among jobs and deciding on an acceptable wage is using the latest information on the movement of employment, the average wage, and so forth to obtain a "feel" for the magnitude of the shock, which is then used to forecast the level of wages and prices in the postshock equilibrium. They all do this. They use one macroeconomic model (such as chapter 19's model), of aggregate employment, production, wages, and prices, together with the latest information on previous employment, wages, and so forth, in order to forecast wages, prices, etc. (in the same way the economic forecaster uses the model); or, more likely, they all heed the same consensus forecast of these variables.

We have now arrived at the crux of the difference between the Keynesian theory of the retarded recovery, which could use the rehabilitative therapy of activist monetary policy, and the New Classical theory. In the Keynesian theory, the workers have to learn by experience that their expectations of wages elsewhere are "inflated," out of line with actuality. With each dose of learning, the wages that workers hold out for are cut back a bit—so the average wage falls a little, and employment recovers a little; but then another dose of learning is needed, since wages have again fallen below expectations. And so on as the new equilibrium is gradually approached.

> In the New Classical theory there is no trial-and-error process of successive approximations to the new equilibrium. Once the news of the slump is out, the new information on unemployment, wages, and so forth is used to make the *correct forecast* of the future level of the average wage. *At this point there is no tendency for people's expectations to be in error*—for wage expectations to be inflated.

It follows that the New Classical macroeconomics predicts an *immediate move to the new equilibrium* once the news is out. What was holding employment below its equilibrium level, following the shock, was the failure of some or all workers to gauge fully the extent of the decline in wage rates—particularly, at first, the decline in the capital-goods industries—and to reduce accordingly their "asking wages" by the full percentage amount required for the equilibrium level of employment. But as soon as the economic news comes out, wage expectations will cease to be inflated. No one's expectations of wages elsewhere will exceed actuality; the grass will no longer be greener elsewhere. The "resistance" to the wage cuts needed for achievement of the equilibrium employment level will be over, the recovery complete.

The New Classical macroeconomic is, at bottom, a doctrine that the economy tends to bounce back to equilibrium once the economic news, with its basic data on quantities and prices, is available for people to use in "updating" their forecasts, or expectations.

FIGURE 20–2: The *Correct* Expectation of the Average Wage Level, Following the Demand Shock, Achieves the New Postshock Equilibrium

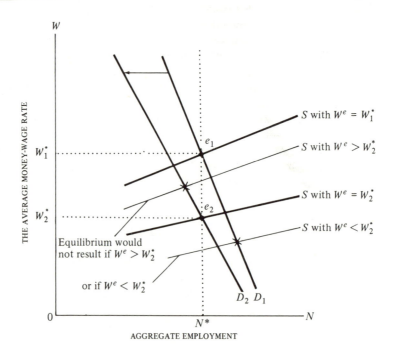

Figure 20–2 illustrates the "quantum leap" in wage expectations that the theory implies in predicting the jump back to equilibrium.

A Shock Believed to Be "Transitory"

The thoughtful reader might at this point be thinking that the New Classical macroeconomics is incredible! We all know that wages do not dart around like goldfish subjected to a disturbing rap on the bowl. There must be a little more to the doctrine that that! And there is.

The previous discussion took as an example the case of a disturbance believed to be permanent. Consider now the equally important case at the other extreme: The demand shock is believed by everybody to have been entirely temporary and already gone by the time reports of last month's unemployment and wages arrived.

In this case, according to the New Classical macroeconomics, when people hear the reports on last month's economy they will proceed to expect the same average wage level and the same prices in the economy as prevailed before the shock—since they believe that the disturbance last month was a fleeting demand shock that has no tendency to recur. In fact, some of the

---

The diagram shows how achievement of the new equilibrium, following the demand shock, depends on the workers' expectations of the average wage level prevailing elsewhere—outside the direct observation of each worker.

Each S curve indicates the average wage asked by workers at every possible employment level, N—and *given* their expectations of the average wage level, W^e. Thus the S curves are hypothetical, or conditional: Which S curve applies depends on the expected average wage level, W^e. At any particular employment level, the lower W^e, the lower the workers' asking wages. In the diagram the wage asked falls in proportion to—equally with—W^e.

The D curve shows the aggregate amount of labor demanded by firms given the average wage level, W. D_1 is the old curve, before the demand shock, and D_2 is the new curve, after the permanent shock.

A close look at the diagram reveals that if, following the downward shift of the D curve, the expected wage does not fall—or falls to a level still above W_2^*—the workers' wage expectations will prove incorrect: The actual wage, W, will be *less* than the expected wage, W^e; and, correspondingly, the employment level, N, will be below the equilibrium level, N^*.

If, instead, the expected wage falls to a level

below W_2^*, the workers' wage expectations will also prove incorrect: the actual wage will then turn out to be *more* than the expected wage. (Example: Expecting that the average wage is going to be zero won't make it so!) Correspondingly, the employment level, N, will be above the equilibrium level, N^*.

Evidently W_2^* is the correct wage expectation for the workers to have, following the demand shock. If the expected wage level, W^e, is equal to W_2^*, the actual wage level resulting will likewise turn out to be equal to W_2^*. Workers' expectation of the wage level W_2^*—and only that wage level—will prove *self-fulfilling*.

The New Classical macroeconomics supposes that the workers, on hearing reports of the initial fall of employment and of wages—and the magnitudes of these events—will be able to use this information to form the correct, self-fulfilling wage expectation. The workers will *not* go on underestimating (or underforecasting) the average wage level, and so find themselves disappointed to see that actual wages are below expectations. Neither will the workers overestimate (or overpredict) the fall of wages. They will form expectations of the average wage level W_2^*. Hence employment bounces back to the equilibrium level, N^*.

capital-goods workers who were hit by lower wages last month, when the shock struck, will sigh with relief:

"Honey, I was so durned scared it was one of those, y'know, 'structural' things, and that we was gonna have to move. But now I realize, after hearing the TV, that it is just one of those what they call monetary shocks, and 'here today, gone tomorrow.' "

What does this prove? It shows that the New Classical macroeconomics does not predict that the average money wage is volatile. When the demand shocks are believed to be *temporary*, expectations of wage levels will *not* dart from one level to another. Although wages may have weakened somewhat on impact, when the shock occurred, people will again expect the "normal" wage when the news comes out.

A Shock of Uncertain "Permanence"

We can now put the above two extreme cases together to see the implications of the New Classical macroeconomics in the realistic case: People are not sure the shock is permanent. People believe the shock could be gone by now; if not by now then perhaps next month or in another month. But they believe too that it could be permanent.

In this case, since there is thought to be a *chance* that the shock is still present, in which case k is still at its increased level, there will be *some* fall in people's expectations of the future average wage level. For example, if people are *almost* certain that the shock is still present, their expectations of the wage level after hearing the reports of increased unemployment and so forth will fall by *almost* the amount of the drop in the case where they are certain the shock is still present. But since there is also thought to be a *chance* that the shock is gone now, the expected wage level resulting after reports of last month's economy will *not* fall by the whole amount it would drop if the shock were thought certain to be permanent. For example, if people are *almost* certain the shock was temporary and gone by now, people's wage expectations will *almost* be the same as before the shock. People thus weigh the chance that the shock is continuing—say one chance in five—against the chance (four chances in five) that the shock is now over. Then, "playing the odds," they proceed to hedge against the two possibilities, continuance or noncontinuance of the shock.

But both possibilities cannot actually occur. The two events, continuation of the shock this month and noncontinuation, are mutually exclusive. Workers cannot protect themselves against both events; they can only play the odds.

We arrive then at our first conclusion about the "realistic" case: Once the news of last month's disturbance is reported, expectations of wages this month will fall *too little* to permit full recovery of employment *in the event the shock actually continues* this month (that is, k remains at its increased level). Expectations fall too little to protect against that eventuality, because people believe there is a chance the shock was temporary and gone by now. And they may be right about that, and right about the chances.

This leads to another conclusion. Suppose that in fact the shock is *permanent*. As the shock continues month after month people will presumably respond to the evidence by *revising* in their minds *the chance* that the shock is really temporary and gone by now, at last. People will *lower* their estimate of the chance that the shock is gone now and raise their estimate of the chance that the shock is continuing. Hence people's expectations of the average wage level will fall. And as a result employment will recover some more.

♦ As the chance that the shock will continue grows ever larger in people's minds, the expected level of wages sinks ever closer to the level it would reach if people were certain of continuance; and consequently the level of employment approaches ever closer to the level N^*.

Thus it may *appear* to the outside observer, and to a Keynesian economist, that there is something wrong—something pathological—about the slowness of the recovery from the shock. But the permanence of the shock was unknown, uncertain. So expectations were reasonable. Time was needed.

THE "NEW KEYNESIAN" RESPONSE TO NEW CLASSICAL MACROECONOMICS

Born the year Marx died, 1883, Keynes went to his grave with worldwide esteem, long before the development and spread of the New Classical criticisms of his theory. It has therefore been left for other economists in sympathy with the "intuition" behind Keynes's theory to *defend* or *improve on* the theory in response to the New Classical criticism.

THE STATISTICAL EVIDENCE

Readers who have delved into textbooks in other fields, in psychology and paleontology as well as some of the physical sciences, are often surprised to find that introductory texts in economics are so shorthanded in offering evidence for or against the theories being discussed. The main reason, undoubtedly, is that in a subject as complex as economics—where everything depends upon everything else (or the expectation of it, which is worse)— the interpretation of evidence is a whole field in itself, called econometrics. At best an introductory text can hope to be faithful to present findings.

For several years econometricians have been examining decades of yearly and quarterly data on output, employment, price level, and so forth in order to bring the Keynesian theory and its New Classical challenger to a *statistical test*—a sort of contest to see whether the challenger has decisively greater power to explain the data (or predict later data) than the current champion. It can be reported that, so far, the findings to date are not very favorable to the challenger.

- ◆ The econometric analyses of historical data for the United States, for example, do not support the New Classical hypothesis that countercyclical monetary policy is ineffective. In particular, statistical analysis does not refute the Keynesian tenet that even an anticipated increase of the money supply has the effect of boosting employment temporarily.

- ◆ Statistical analyses of the dynamics of employment suggest that the speed of recovery from the typical slump is not as fast as the New Classical economics predicts. (If people had gauged correctly the chances that the typical disturbance was permanent, as the New Classical economics says, they would have lowered their expectations of wages faster than they actually did; employment would have recovered faster when the disturbance was really permanent and would have overshot the mark—the N* level—when the disturbance was temporary.)

The tests of the New Classical theory have turned out better than might have been feared by the originators but *not well enough*—not yet, at any rate—to convert all or most economists to New Classical macroeconomics. *Something* is wrong, it appears likely, with the New Classical theory. Yet it is often through the rejection of a theoretically interesting model that a science progresses.

Win or lose, the salvos of ammunition hurled by the New Classical macroeconomics made an impression on the Keynesians, who see now that the wage theory of Keynes and his modern interpreters is, at best, incomplete. *Why* should Keynesians suppose that an increase of the money supply, if anticipated, will contribute to recovery from a slump, rather than just raising wages and prices? *Why* should Keynesians suppose that wage expectations respond only sluggishly to all or most slumps and to the news of them? (Keynes himself did not suppose that wages always adjust too little, only that they may do so and often will.) The Keynesians have to support their premises—or else they must shift their grounds. Hence even if dead wrong, *the New Classical macroeconomics is still important because it demands Keynesians to fortify their theoretical structure or reconstruct it.* Failure to do so may cost them some of their remaining influence.

New Keynesian Theories of Wage and Employment Decisions

The theoretical world of the New Classical macroeconomics is a highly abstract one, designed to permit rigorous (and mathematical) analysis: There, all markets open once a month—or once every "period"—after which production quietly takes place until the next month or period. In that world, then, all decisions take place periodically and simultaneously, based on new transmissions that are likewise periodic and simultaneous. For some questions that abstraction is undoubtedly helpful.

Real life is not so regular or periodic. The news usually comes out in small bits and pieces; even a *sharp* disturbance produces a slow accretion of evidence, as in plodding detective work. One day there is a curious decline in certain stock market prices, another day a sharp fall in metals prices, then some goods news followed by more bad news. By the time a production figure for the previous month is reported the experts have already predicted a decline; some decline, larger or smaller than the actual one, will already have been "discounted," as commentators say. In *this* world, it is a special day when information of significant value is received.

Information and Wage "Stickiness"

Although information is arriving continuously there are nevertheless reasons why a firm would choose to review and revise its wage scale only occasionally or perhaps periodically:

- the cost of the time spent by the manager in deciding how large a wage change to establish for each category of employee;
- the cost of transmitting the needed information about the decision, including advertising the increase or explaining the decrease; and
- the cost of overreacting or misreacting in the wrong direction compared to the smaller cost of underreaction or no reaction. (Monetarists give a similar explanation of the undesirability of "fine-tuning" of the money supply in a vain effort to achieve greater stability.) Too much wage variability by the firm may add to, not subtract from, the risks of understaffing through its effect on quitting.

The consequent possibility that money-wage rates are "sticky," "stuck" at the old equilibrium level for days and weeks following a monetary disturbance, may help to explain how a slump can develop and take time to dissolve through falling wages. As prices or sales are perceived by the firm to worsen, the firm may decide to shut the door temporarily to hiring (even replacement hiring)—expecting perhaps to reopen later—without at the same time electing now to review wages in view of the above costs of wage-scale revisions. (A decision not to incur the costs of reviewing, revising, and retransmitting the firm's wage scale this week does not imply a decision also to "hire as usual.") With wages hanging above their most profitable level (which falls with the demand shock, and falls more as other wages in the economy sag), the New Classical wage adjustment is gummed up; employment likewise fails to snap back to the neoclassical normal, or equilibrium, level, N^*. The adjustment of wages lags behind the news.

Nonsynchronous, or "Staggered," Wage Setting

The fact that firms do not review their wage rates continuously (or daily at any rate), and adjust them at the drop of a hat, could be of quite limited use to New Keynesians in their dispute with New Classical macroeconomists. *If,* as in Japan, all firms review and adjust wages simultaneously, say once a year, an important element of the New Classical model would have some validity. Wages, though unresponsive to the news all year, would take a big jump when each year is up.

New Keynesians argue that such synchronization is not the natural tendency. With only a steady trickle of news about the worsening of business, the average level of wage rates generally adjusts gradually since on any day not all firms will find it worthwhile to adjust all their wage rates; as a result, wage setting will not be synchronous. The first day's bad news, unless it is momentous, will influence the wage rates of only a small fraction of the firms: Those firms that were going to cut wage rates will cut them more and those that were going to increase wages will raise them less or not at all. The next day of bad news will likewise induce only a selective response among the firms, unless the news is of decisive importance. Eventually, if reports of unemployment and production do not improve greatly, the accumulated news (including reports of the decline in the average wage) will become sufficiently bad that the stragglers, the firms that have not so far responded, will take their turn at cutting wage rates.

This ragged, disorderly retreat of wage rates may have been the sort of process that Keynes had in mind once the economy was well into the slump. It is a far cry from the precision-drill process imagined by the New Classicals. It is crucially different in a key respect:

> On each day of this wage-cutting process, as news of the effects of some permanent demand shock continues, those firms that decide to cut their wages that day are aware that they are a minority. Contrary to the New Classical story, they do *not* suppose that their wage cuts are part of a general reduction of wage rates, all in more or less the same proportion (depending on individual circumstances), in the amount needed to restore equilibrium. If they are smart they know it will take time, and if very smart a very long time, for the general level of wages to sink to the new, lower equilibrium level that will erase the slump.

On a day that a firm decides to "unstick" and restick its wage scale, by *how much* will it choose to cut its wage rates? There is a strong possibility that the answer is—very little. Each firm may find that its best policy is to lower its wage scale *by only a fraction* of the distance between its *previous* level and what the firm estimates to be its *ultimate* equilibrium level, the level reached once all wages have fully adjusted to the lower level needed for full recovery from the aftershock slump. It is *not* generally best for the firm to "jump" its wage all the way to the ultimate equilibrium level (nor beyond for a time), because:

♦ Even if all the *other firms* did that when each decided it was the right time to cut its wages, the firm would be exposed for days and possibly weeks or months with the lowest wage around—and as a result too many of its experienced expensive-to-replace employees might quit for better-paying firms.

♦ If all the other firms are also going to cut their wages only fractionally, the firm has an even stronger reason to cut its own wages only fractionally—again, so as not to be too far "ahead" of the others.

If each firm decides to cut its wages only fractionally, by only a fraction of the amount by which the general level of wages must fall to end completely the slump of production and employment, it follows that when all firms have gotten around to cutting wages once or more (at least)—when the last firm to act has acted—the general level of wages will still have fallen by only some fraction of the amount needed for complete recovery. So the process must go on and on. When the least ripe fruit has finally dropped from its branch, all the fruit will only have dropped and attached itself to lower branches, from which it must drop again to still lower branches, and so on, never reaching—only approaching—the ground below.

♦ Even when the demand shock is permanent and believed to be permanent by everyone, the economy does *not* stage a complete recovery as soon as all firms have found it convenient to adjust their wages—in however many days it takes for the slowest to act. The recovery is drawn out, gradual. Full recovery is only approached, not reached (barring a disturbance in the reverse direction, of course!)

This description, or model, of the wage-cutting process predicts that monetary policy *can* be "effective" in combating slumps. If the government makes it a policy to boost the money supply whenever news indicating a slump is reported, that action, even if anticipated and its effects correctly expected by everyone, will be effective in shortening the slump (or, by mistake, causing a boom!). Contrary to the New Classical theory, the money-supply increase *will not* immediately drive up wages and prices in the same proportion (from the lower level to which they would have fallen at the time the money supply is increased). For in the Keynesian model, most wages would not have been cut right away without the boost to the money supply. *Those* wage rates are not going to neutralize the money-supply increase right away. As wage rates are cut successively around the economy it may be that the boost to the money supply will cause each wage cut to be smaller than it otherwise would have been. So *ultimately* the boost to the money supply will be neutralized. But this must be so, for if the economy is going to recover one way or another, the contribution that the boost of the money supply can make is *to speed the recovery, to shorten the slump*. It cannot serve as a stimulant of undiminished "effectiveness," converting depression into a permanent economic "high."

♦ Although a gradual approach to full recovery from a slump would take place without a countercyclical monetary policy, nevertheless a policy of boosting the money supply to a higher level following news of lower production in capital-goods industries and so forth will be (temporarily) effective in speeding the recovery. Provided that the money supply boost is not an overreaction to the news (either because the policy is overreactive or because the shock is largely temporary), this countercyclical policy will stabilize the economy.

This understanding of the laggard nature of the wage adjustment process and the effectiveness of countercyclical monetary policy may seem good enough. But today's economists demand an exact model of wage determination—a theoretical model, in quantitative (mathematical) terms, in which firms are trying to maximize profit and workers are choosing rationally as well. And the New Keynesian school has not so far produced such a model. The American macroeconomic theorist James Tobin suggests this failure is the cause of the unending controversy over Keynes:

... [T]he adjustment process itself has not been successfully described as optimizing [i.e., profit-maximizing and rational] behavior, [so that it] carries conviction in our profession. This failure, neither surprising nor discreditable in view of the intrinsic difficulties of the task, is the root of the chronic crisis in macroeconomics.*

But neither has the New Classical school succeeded so far in justifying certain apparently ad hoc features in their models: the unusual notion that in any interval between wage changes, a firm's employment is impervious to monetary shocks, as if the output were pre-sold; and the assumption, to which we turn next, that everyone agrees on the "right" forecasts.

The New Classicals' Premise of Correct Expectations under Fire

Theorists sympathetic to Keynes's modern outlook—the emphasis on people's limited information *and* uncertain knowledge—cannot rest their case in defense of Keynesian theory without attacking a vulnerable premise that is crucial for the New Classical argument.

The New Classical macroeconomists grant that no one's expectations are error-free. They claim, however, that although errors will be made, people

* James Tobin, *Asset Accumulation and Economic Activity* (Chicago: University of Chicago Press, 1981), pp. 36–37.

nevertheless form the *best possible forecasts* given the information they have available to them. "To err is human," but *on average* expectations are neither too high nor too low. This has come to be known as the hypothesis of *rational expectations*. But note that rational here means right—as right as possible—not merely efficient in not wasting information.

Some critics of the New Classicism have put their fingers on a problem with this premise of rational expectations. To say that people, hearing that the unemployment rate shot up 3 percentage points last month, can correctly forecast (as well as can be done with that information) the next general wage level and so forth implies that people *know* the relationship between unemployment and the next wage level when people's expectations are generally correct. But to *learn* that relationship, before their expectations are correct, they would have to study a history of unemployment and wages when expectations were *not* correct—and no one knew how the others were forming and reforming their expectations.

♦ Critics of "correct expectations" say that in a social system where all are trying simultaneously and independently to learn, these learning efforts of others may prevent each person from learning the exact truth. It is not necessarily feasible for individuals to learn the formula for the "rational forecast."

If we agree that in highly disturbed times people's expectations may be incorrect to a serious degree, we must be prepared for the possibility that a disturbance will produce a disequilibrium (i.e., disappointed expectations) on a large scale, thus a serious slump, for example. In such situations, a policy of pushing up the money supply in response to the increased unemployment will be neither unnecessary nor ineffective in promoting recovery to equilibrium.

AN "IMPLICIT" CONTRACT BARS WAGE CUTS WITHOUT "DUE CAUSE" *

Reading in these past pages on the New Classical macroeconomics the idea that employers might institute sharp cuts in money wages (sharp enough to end the slump if the shock, though permanent, is understood to be so) would make many a personnel manager smile in disbelief. It is not unusual for many of a firm's employees to have made a large investment in order to secure their positions at the firm: an arduous period, without high wages *then,* of "learning the ropes" at that firm—its plans, strategies, and methods, which are often different from those at other firms; a lengthy period of apprenticeship and testing, which a worker would not undertake without

* This section is not required for understanding the chapters that follow.

the expectation of large prizes for success; perhaps the costs of relocation, putting up with disagreeable associates; and so forth. Furthermore, once the worker has made the long journey required for a career at the firm of his or her choice, it might be too costly, maybe too late, to set out on a second one. Thus worker mobility is apt to be imperfect. Hence a worker choosing among competing employers will look for assurance in advance about the formula the firm will use in determining wages, dismissals, layoffs, and so forth.

♦ An employee, having invested in his or her position, having acquired a stake in remaining there, would be vulnerable to unscrupulous exploitation of his or her "immobility" by the firm—would be a sitting duck for "wage economies"—if there were no understandings (at least implicitly) with the firm, and if the firm did not find it important to maintain its reputation for living up to such tacit understandings.

The modern theory of the "implicit" labor contract does not say that a firm's wage rates will in no circumstances be cut. But modern economic theory emphasizes a property that an implicit contract with an employer must have in order to be useful to the employee: For employees to be able to "enforce" the contractual protections they seek or have any hope of doing so—for them to be able to "blow the whistle" on the firm when it moves to violate the personnel policy it wants to enjoy a reputation for—the conditions under which wages can be cut must be observable to the employee. The firm will have to *show cause* that, under the terms of the tacit understandings with its employees, it can proceed with a cut of money-wage rates.

♦ Firms in attempting to recruit long-term employees will have to offer contracts that promise not to cut wages except under certain verifiable conditions—and promise to raise wages when certain other conditions are observed. Workers would reject a firm whose policy was to cut wages without the agreed-upon evidence being offered in justification—if only "the firm feels that a wage cut is needed to save jobs." To cut wages a firm would have to point to evidence: a fall in the general level of prices or a rise in layoffs at the firm or, better yet since the firm cannot manipulate what the *other* firms do, a rise in layoffs at highly similar firms in the economy, or something. Tying the wage this way is called wage *indexing*.

We can now feel ourselves near to an insight. When a demand shock occurs, and capital-goods demand is hit hard—manifested by sharply lower capital-goods prices or production or both—consumer demand (for most or all consumer goods) may fall little. So prices and output in most or all consumer-good industries may fall little. Then indexed wages will fall little.

♦ If the employee contract in a firm producing *consumer* goods permits only a little reduction of money wages when the cost of living and employment in its industry fall by only a little, and if the contract protects and insulates the firm's wages from unemployment reported in capital-goods production, recovery will be sluggish. The hard times in the capital goods industries may lack much effect on wages and wage expectations elsewhere.

> Could the New Classicals escape from this new reason why money wages might adjust downward only at a sluggish pace despite ample evidence of a slump? They could argue that each firm would daringly decide to lower sharply its prices despite the little fall of its wage rates—with the understanding that if the general level of prices turned out to be sharply lower as well, as it expects, its employees must return some of their "excessive" money wages for the month. It seems doubtful, however, that workers would enjoy having money wages already received "encumbered". by contingency clauses involving evidence not available to them at the time they have to decide how much of those wages to spend. Paying employees for that privilege might cost the firm a lot—too much to be worth it.

Thus contract theory indicates how contracts will slow down the decline of the general price level needed for recovery and thus prolong the unemployment in the capital-goods sector due to the monetary shock and resulting excess demand for money. Wage indexation tends not to facilitate adjustment but rather to create inertia and momentum.

SUMMARY

1. In place of the neoclassical doctrine of monetary equilibrium Keynes substituted the doctrine that fluctuations of employment around the normal, or mean, level are inevitable, that recovery from a slump (or boom) is usually retarded, and that the central bank—by boosting the money supply in response to a dip of money-wage rates or a rise of the unemployment rate (which creates the prospect of a dip in money-wage rates)—can speed the economy's recovery from a slump. Thus Keynes and his "Keynesian" successors envisioned an "activist" central bank that would aim to stabilize the level of the average money-wage rate and in so doing dampen and shorten fluctuations of employment as well. The rise of the Keynesian insurgents in the 1940s and 1950s brought a wave of counter-insurgents, called monetarists, and, in the 1970s, a second wave, called New Classicists, who resisted the Keynesian doctrine.

2. Monetarists argue that allowing the central bank, such as America's Federal Reserve or Britain's Bank of England, discretion over the supply of money to adopt as its target—leaving it to the central bank's judgment whether the money supply should be increased or decreased in each situation—would be counterproductive, a bad idea: It would keep the private sector of the economy off balance, it would invite the central bank to placate vested interests, and it would risk the central bank's taking actions that, however well intentioned, would prove to be in the wrong direction, due to ignorance of the "numbers" or imperfect economic knowledge of how the economy works. Hence a regular policy—in short, a fixed rule—is better than year-to-year discretion on an ad hoc basis. But an aggressive rule that reached strongly to each dip of the economy could easily be worse than a passive, do-nothing rule, which the monetarists favored. The monetarist rule is that the money supply be kept on a gently rising path with a constant growth rate from year to year.

3. The New Classicals introduced a new argument against an activist monetary policy: A fixed-policy rule, they argue, would have no beneficial effect whatsoever as soon as people learned of it. If the money supply were known to be increased by a certain percentage amount whenever news of a certain sort occurred (for example, a 2 percent fall of national output), everyone would anticipate its effects: Prices and wages, both actual and expected, would all increase in the same proportion, "neutralizing" the intended effect on rational output and employment. The effort to speed the recovery of production would be thwarted by an offsetting increase of wages and prices.

4. The New Classical economics further argues that although the typical recovery is gradual, it is not retarded by some undesirable impediment standing in the way of a downward adjustment of money-wage rates and money prices to their new equilibrium levels. In the rare case where the monetary disturbance that has caused the slump (say, an increase in the Cambridge k) is known by all to be permanent, the recovery would be immediate as soon as evidence of the disturbance—news of higher unemployment, lower prices, and so forth—became available to producers and employees. The usual problem is that the disturbance is not known to be permanent; it is believed possibly to be temporary, and perhaps about to vanish. So it is in fact quite "rational" of producers and workers not to establish wages and prices that are as low as would be necessary for equilibrium if the disturbance were permanent; for if they reduced prices and wages by that much and in fact the disturbance vanished at the same time, then wages and prices would be below their equilibrium levels—there ought not to have been any reductions of wages and prices at all. To guard against the chance of that, it is rational for producers and workers to cut their wages and prices by *less* than that amount; then there is some possibility that wages and prices are too low and some possibility

that wages and prices are too high. *If,* in fact, the disturbance is a permanent one, the slump will continue. But it will gradually subside as people revise in their minds the likelihood that the disturbance is temporary—and hence accept lower and lower wages and prices.

5. It is safe to say that the statistical evidence does not give satisfactory support to the New Classical theory. It appears to make a difference, for example, whether the central bank follows a rule of steady growth of the money supply or responds with strong efforts to "stabilize" the economy (but an introductory discussion cannot go further into these econometric matters). Thus it appears that it may be possible to rescue the Keynesian doctrine of "retarded recovery" and "effective policy" against the New Classical attacks. But how?

6. The chapter continues with a discussion of the New Keynesian idea that not all wage rates and all prices are decided upon simultaneously, from day to day or quarter-year to quarter-year. It is likely that wages are adjusted nonsynchronously, in staggered fashion. If so, that will cause the recovery from a slump—even one known to be due to a permanent disturbance—to be retarded, or protracted, because each wage, when it is cut, is cut only fractionally, pending the catching-up of the other wages; it is cut only a fraction of that amount required by the new equilibrium so as not to be too far in front of the others, not all of which are going to be revised today, because some of them are already so low, and so much lower than the average, that they are not going to be cut yet.

7. Another New Keynesian reply to the New Classical theory is that the individuals in the economy, everyone on his own, cannot acquire the national expectations postulated in the theory.

CONCEPTS INTRODUCED

monetarism	policy ineffectiveness proposition	contractual indexing
activist stabilization policy		New Keynesian school
discretionary management, or policy	policy unnecessariness proposition	money-wage stickiness
New Classical school	permanent versus transitory disturbance	staggered wage setting
the "news"		rational expectations
		learning

STUDY QUESTIONS

1. Why is defining the money supply like defining Los Angeles or maybe London or Rome? (For extra credit, relate to this question the old gag, "I can spell banana but I don't know where to stop.") Why is it not entirely like that in a fairly stable environment? (What has been happening to banking regulations, overseas and offshore banking opportunities, the nonbank creation of money, and so forth?)

2. "Milton Friedman's original brand of monetarism does not claim that a philosopher-king (or philosopher-central banker) could not help to stabilize employment or wages, barring abnormally bad luck, or that Professor Friedman himself could not, only that central bankers as they are and as the pressures upon them are cannot be expected to help stabilize." Evaluate, citing the monetarist arguments. Do the fresh arguments bestowed upon monetarism by the New Classical macroeconomics fit, or reinforce, the above statement? Or do the New Classicals claim that not even Professor Friedman could stabilize through an activist monetary policy?

3. A decade after his book *The General Theory* began the "Keynesian revolution," Keynes complained about "all this modern stuff gone silly and sour" (*Economic Journal*, 1946). Whatever he may have meant then, would Keynes have been a Keynesian now? Specifically, would he have abandoned activism in monetary policy in favor of fixity (or fixed growth) of the money supply? Or would he have continued in favor of discretionary activism? Or would he have looked for something else?

4. "On page 1 of the morning papers there is a photograph of British union leader named Arthur Scargill being hauled off on charges of obstructing deliveries of Polish coal. On page 2 a paramilitary federal border patrol unit is reported to have been on training exercises that 'simulated' the forceful suppression of striking workers as a massive strike of metalworkers spreads over West Germany. So it goes. *This* is the real stuff of wages and employment—the violence and terror, force and counterforce—not your pretty models of market dynamics by thin-lipped academics." Discuss what role, if any, is played by labor unions.

5. A fringe doctrine often linked to New Classical macroeconomics asserts that whether money wages or real wages fail to drop immediately to their equilibrium level does not matter for employment: The implicit contract with employees will keep them on the job as long as doing so is not wasteful of their time—as long as their marginal product exceeds or matches their opportunity cost. There are no free lunches around, no unexploited opportunities for mutual gain. Discuss. Is the claimed willingness of the firm to overlook the high wage, and so not lay off, compatible with its incentives to reduce loss or increase profit? Do implicit contracts offer a wage to the laid-off that reduces the firm's incentive to lay off to a level that reflects the worker's benefit from leisure? If there were no layoffs, would that ensure that production would be maintained? Are prices perfectly flexible, adjusting immediately?

6. In a volume of papers that ushered in the modern theory of how monetary disturbances can have employment effects, the introduction summarizes: "The actors [in these models] have to cope ignorant of the future or even much of the present. Isolated, and apprehensive, these Pinteresque figures construct expectations of the state of the economy—over space and over time—and maximize relative to that imagined world. . . . [A] change of aggregate demand alters the relations between actual prices and expected prices. The implied alteration of expected relative prices— of expected wage rates elsewhere relative to sampled rates, of expected mean future demand prices relative to current demand prices . . . etc.—causes a change in quantity decisions, hence changes in employment" (E. S. Phelps et al., *Microeconomic Foundations of Employment and Inflation Theory* [New York: W. W. Norton, 1970], pp. 22–23). Use chapters 19 and 20 to interpret. What further development, reported here, was not then foreseen?

CHAPTER 21

Inflation: Its Causes, Effects, Reduction, and Control

TEST PILOT (to Ground Control):
I've got it. The stick must be pushed forward, not pulled back!

Michael Redgrave (to Ralph Richardson) in *Breaking the Sound Barrier* (1952)

I N macroeconomics the absorption with the worldwide slump in the thirties gave way in the decades after the Second World War to growing concern over worldwide inflation. As the crisis of the 1930s exceeded the scope of neoclassical economics in the 1930s, so the inflation of recent decades developed ahead of the capacity of economic theory to comprehend it. Inflation was eventually seen to be a phenomenon quite different from what had been believed.

INTRODUCTION TO INFLATION

Inflation, it was learned, is *not* a simple by-product of boom conditions—that is, an abnormal bulge of employment and production, which will end when the boom ends—leaving wages and prices at a higher *level* than before but not rising any more. If inflations were just signs of booms, then reducing or altogether arresting inflations by central-bank monetary action would *simply require combating booms*—either by the activist Keynesian policy of

573

contracting the money supply or by the passive monetarist method (the method of passive resistance) of refusing to "feed" booms with extra doses of money supply.

♦ The Monetarist policy is to ask the "marketplace" to find the new and higher equilibrium level of wages and prices, W^* and P^*, corresponding to whatever drop of k^* has occurred; once that new equilibrium is found, the boom will be over and wages and prices will be no longer rising.

♦ The Keynesian policy is to ask the central bank to find the new and lower money-supply level needed to *offset* the drop of k^* so that the equilibrium wage and price levels, W^* and P^*, do not increase; once it is found, output *and* price level will return to normal.

In fact, the "one-time" rise of prices and wages produced during one boom does not fall within the meaning of inflation in the economist's sense of the term. In economists' lexicon, inflation is the phenomenon of rising wages and prices despite the absence of boom conditions—despite the absence of any surprise disturbances, whether demand shocks or supply shocks. Inflation, in the economists' book, is the rise of wages and prices going on under surprise-free conditions—an equilibrium phenomenon. And the *problem* of reducing or stopping inflation is the task—maybe not feasible!—of doing that without disrupting the economy, particularly without sending it into a slump.*

♦ Rising wages and prices in equilibrium conditions signify the economy is experiencing inflation—and the same is even truer in slump conditions (since in a noninflationary economy a slump would be accompanied by a fall of wages).

♦ By contrast, an episode of rising wages and prices (during a boom) *due to an unanticipated demand shock* (say, a fall of k^*) means that they are *moving to* a higher equilibrium level—not that their equilibrium level is rising. This "jump" of the price level is a disequilibrium event. Economists are disinclined to call *any* such one-shot increase of prices by the name inflation even if it is boom-free. *Inflation* suggests an ongoing process.

In these terms, the sharp rise of prices and wages in the United States at the outbreak of the Korean War in 1951 did not indicate the presence of inflation there—not the true inflation of the economists, at any rate; it indicated the occurrence of a surprise demand shock. Plainly, the worldwide rise of general price levels that followed the Oil Shock of 1974—the tripling of oil

---

*Some economists use the specialized term *cost inflation* to designate this phenomenon; then they use "boom inflation," or "demand inflation," to designate a one-time hitch of the price level caused by an episode of boom.

prices by OPEC, the Organization of Oil Producing and Exporting Countries—did not signal the presence of inflation; just a supply shock that raised the equilibrium price level.

In the past few decades the countries of Western Europe and North America have all been experiencing inflation—a continuing rise of wages and prices as an accustomed, equilibrium phenomenon. Measured by the rate of increase of the general price level or wage level, inflation became large enough to be noticed by the latter half of the 1950s in the United States and Canada, earlier in Britain and Italy. By the end of the 1960s inflation was markedly greater everywhere (though still pretty low in West Germany) and very much on the public's mind. By the early 1980s inflation was stronger still—reaching more than 10 per cent in America and nearly 20 per cent in Britain—and uppermost in the public's list of economic problems for the government to deal with.

As doctors feel that some patients focus too much on certain complaints, so many economists have questioned whether the general public does not attach far greater importance to the inflation of recent magnitudes than it really deserves—a case of economic hypochondria. Many economists suspect the public has been deluded by an elementary theoretical error: The public thinks that if the government ended the inflation, the prices of the things they buy would stop rising all right while the prices of the things they sell—and the wages of their labor—would go on rising at the old inflationary rates! Yes, there might be a grain of truth in the conclusion; but the analysis is faulty; since one person's price paid is another's price received, a slowdown of money *prices* must slow people's aggregate money *income*.

But whether the widespread hostility toward inflation on the scale recently experienced can ultimately be justified by the best available economic theory or not is, in one respect, beside the point. If government action to rid the economy of inflation is in high demand, the political party or political leaders who can persuade the public that they have the "will and the means" to do it, more so than the others, will receive the rewards of elective office—and further rewards for their results, if any. Hence one knight after another is going to be elected to do battle with the dragon Inflation until it is slain. But since it is not known for sure how best to slay the dragon Inflation, some methods of attack will prove quite costly—and some will fail in the attempt. The method employed so far is a planned slowing down, or deceleration, of the money supply:

◆ In 1969 America's central bank head, Federal Reserve Board Chairman Arthur F. Burns, with the support of the newly elected President Richard M. Nixon formulated and instituted what they called the "Game Plan" to restore "reasonable price stability" by reducing gradually the growth of the money supply.

◆ In 1980 the Bank of England, with the encouragement of the new Conservative government led by Prime Minister Margaret Thatcher, adopted a policy, called Thatcherism, of limiting the growth of the money supply in order to choke off inflation.

◆ In 1981 Federal Reserve Board Chairman Paul M. Volcker, with the support of newly elected President Ronald Reagan, renewed its resolve to aim for lower growth-rate targets for the money supply (following an earlier try begun in 1979).

It is evident from the data in Chart 21–1 for the United States and the United Kingdom that the costs caused by these efforts, both in production lost and unemployment, have been enormous. (It is also true that the results, in inflation shed, have not been impressive to date in the United Kingdom.)

◆ The great costs incurred in the efforts to reduce inflation are reason enough for us, as citizens, to want to study the nature of inflation.

There is another interest in the study of inflation—as a case study in government failure (rather than market failure). If the public's preference is for a "flat" trend in the general price level, with money-wage rates rising or falling with the marginal productivity of labor, how did it come to happen in one country after another that inflation developed on a scale far exceeding the public's preference? Was there, as a matter of historical fact, a mistake or two along the way—misunderstanding and misestimates by

CHART 21–1: The Time-Paths of the Unemployment Rate in the United States and the United Kingdom in the Era of Inflation and Disinflation

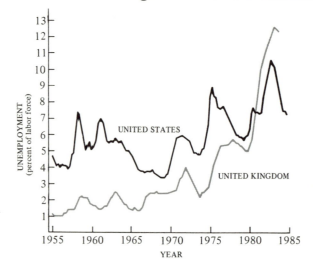

governments and their economists? Is there, in any case, a natural tendency for the government to produce faster inflation than the public prefers? If so (to either question or both), did "Keynes"—the idea of an activist monetary policy within the discretion of the central bank—enable these things to happen? If so, is there some sort of nondiscretionary system with fixed constitutionlike rules and constraints that would save us from a repetition of the recent inflation rates, assuming that governments will eventually succeed in reducing inflation to the size desired?

♦ Inflation is today being studied as a classic example, an instant classic, of government failure. Certainly it is regarded as a failure by the general public.

Here, then, is a quick survey of the inflation mechanism: its causes, effects—both benefits and costs, the methods of reducing it, and (once reduced to the desired rate) its control over the future.

CAUSES OF INFLATION

Until now we have been thinking of an economy's monetary equilibrium—the state it is in when expectations of the wage level and price level are correct—as one with no trend (up or down) in the path of the general price level, no trend in the path of the wage level, and no trend in the money supply (or aggregate output, Y, and the Cambridge k). Thus, for example, the new equilibrium wage level *tomorrow* is equal, barring another shock, to the new (postshock) equilibrium wage level today. The problem addressed by Keynes's *General Theory* was the difficulty that wages have in getting from yesterday's actual level, which we took to be equal to the old (preshock) equilibrium level, to that *new* equilibrium level. Clearly such an exposition "abstracts" from the upward trend of wages that will exist in equilibrium conditions if the productivity of labor is rising—productivity growth—or if the price level is rising—inflation.

It is not hard, however, to conceive of the monetary equilibrium of an economy experiencing inflation. It may be the *same* economy as before in every other respect. But if the economy's money supply is being pushed up fast enough relative to the growth of the economy, *its equilibrium,* whether or not attained at any time, will be one with a rising price level and rising wage level. The equilibrium price level will be rising, driven up by the growth of the money supply, along a path determined by the Cambridge equation:

$$P^* = \frac{M}{k^* \cdot Y^*}$$

This venerable equation, it will be recalled, is a formula for the *equilibrium price level* at a moment of time; it takes as *given* the equilibrium aggregate output level, Y^*. So the formula leaves open a question: whether the equilibrium aggregate output level is any different, perhaps larger, in an inflationary equilibrium than in the zero-inflation, or noninflationary, equilibrium. We know that, according to the Cambridge theory, the value of Y^* at any given moment is independent of the *level* of P^* as well as the level of M. (If *not*, the Cambridge equation would no longer imply that doubling M would double P^*—the basic Quantity Theorem from which all monetary theory starts.) But it is still possible at the same time that the value of Y^* at any moment depends on the *rate of increase* of P^* in the following sense: A faster growth of the money supply and thus a faster rise of the equilibrium price level and equilibrium wage level might possibly increase (or decrease) the current level of Y^*.

In theory, however, there is no necessary connection between the equilibrium output level and the inflation occurring in equilibrium. There are few reasons for believing that inflation or higher inflation might be accompanied by greater equilibrium production—and as many reasons to believe the truth might be the opposite. This is especially true of the equilibrium size of the unemployment rate. Later we will examine some data bearing on the matter. In any case it is safe to say the following:

♦ Nowadays nearly all economists maintain the hypothesis that the equilibrium employment level (and unemployment rate as well) is not sensitive to the presence of inflation nor to the speed of the inflation—within limits anyway. When the equilibrium unemployment rate is the same number at all different rates of inflation it is called the *natural rate of unemployment*.

At first reading it may seem as though we have just uncovered the cause of inflation—growth of the money supply in excess of the growth of aggregate output (and the growth, if any, in the Cambridge k). But such an account of the "causes" of inflation would be absurdly inadequate, and misleading too. It is superficial because we want to know the causes of the fast growth of the money supply! (And it is misleading because it may suggest that to stop inflation—without disruption—it would be enough to stop the excess growth of the money supply; more on that later.)

The Government's Temptation to Inflate

A government's decision to inflate can sometimes be seen as a mistaken calculation and sometimes as a political calculation. Both sorts of explanation are instructive. We consider first the former sort. It is not out of the question, after all, that inflation was fueled by an ill-considered and ultimately unsupportable economic model of the inflation mechanism.

A Mistaken Model of Inflation

A basic feature of Keynes's theory is that wages will be found to be falling during a slump until the cumulative fall of wages and prices is enough to remove the last traces of the slump. A picture of this evolution is presented in Figure 21–1: When unemployment is at its peak, and the recovery just starting, the decline of wages is at its greatest. As the recovery proceeds, and unemployment draws closer to its equilibrium level, the *rate* at which wages are declining is found to be less. Wages decline more slowly the lower is the level of unemployment. As the recovery approaches completion—as the unemployment rate approaches its equilibrium level—the *rate* of decrease of the wage level approaches zero.

♦ If we abstract from the possibility that the economy's equilibrium may involve inflation or productivity growth, hence a rising *equilibrium* level of money-wage rates, and more some decades than others, we see that the theory of slump and recovery *prepares us for a statistical relationship* between the *rate of change* of the *money-wage level* and the *level of the unemployment rate*. There should be a similar relationship between the rate of change of the price level and the unemployment rate.

There is no reason why such a relationship should not be traced out if the demand shock is expansionary and generates a boom. If we still confine ourselves to equilibriums without inflation and productivity growth, then, at the top of the boom, when unemployment is at its lowest, wages and the price level will be rising. The upward push of the price level acts as a self-correcting mechanism serving to produce a "recovery" from the boom: Just as *lower* asking wages, hence lower supply prices, *lift employment,* so *higher* asking wages, hence higher supply prices, *drag employment down.* As the retreat to equilibrium proceeds, and unemployment rises nearer to its equilibrium level, the *rate* at which wages and prices rise will be slower. *Wages and prices will be rising less rapidly the higher is the unemployment rate.* As the unemployment rate approaches its equilibrium level, the rate of increase of the wage level and price level approaches zero.

The idea took hold in the 1950s, after a decade of alternating booms and slumps and occasional episodes of rising prices, that the relationship between the rate of wage and price change, on the one hand, and the level of unemployment, on the other, was durable and robust. It might not be as sturdy as an oak, as accurate as a chronometer: The relationship might jiggle up and down from era to era or year to year (as extraneous influences of labor unions and structural upheavals mucked up the data). But the relationship was dependable enough, many economists came to believe, to warrant two conclusions:

♦ If a country wants to pursue a monetary policy aimed at *low* unemployment—perhaps a 3 percent unemployment rate in the United States, for example, a 2 percent rate in the United Kingdom—it must pay the piper by suffering rising prices as a consequence. The less it is willing to pay, the worse the unemployment it will get. Every country is stuck on the horns of a dilemma: It will only get the level of jobs and prosperity that it is willing to pay for with rising prices.

♦ Yet if a country is willing to pay the costs—whatever those are—of suffering a certain (more or less steady) rate of increase of the price level, the low unemployment that will buy will last forever. (In other words, the "price" of a given low unemployment rate is not an ever-worsening rate of increase of the price level.) Countries are not earthbound at some N^*; they can lift off from N^*!

This so-called trade-off between wage-and-price rise and the unemployment became known as the Phillips Curve after the Australian economist-engineer who pioneered its statistical study, W. A. Phillips.

In this downhill race to cover all the points about inflation we can hardly afford a pause to praise the great or the famous. But a word should be said about Phillips's unusual work and its extraordinary effect on economic thinking and policy making. The path-breaking event was an academic and almost amateurish-looking paper published, somewhat inauspiciously, in the little-read and rather intellectual journal of the London School of Economics.* It is the first known study of the quantitative relationship between the rate of wage or price increase, on the one hand, and the level of economic activity on the other. The ordinary well-trained econometrician would have elected to study post-World War II data in detail, using the best available econometric techniques available at the time. Phillips, however, was an electrical engineer by training, interested in economic stabilization techniques—not an econometrician. His instinct was to compile a long history of data and by constructing a diagram with points representing the data for each year to persuade readers of the existence of a trade-off relationship between the rate of wage increase and the level of the unemployment rate; and to show how little the relationship had moved around in nearly a hundred years.

That diagram struck a resonant chord in most of the economics profession around the world. In a simple drawing of a curve Phillips captured with appealing precision what many econo-

---

* W[illiam] A. Phillips, "The Relationship between the Rate of Change of Money-Wage Rates and Unemployment in the United Kingdom 1861–1957," *Economica*, November 1958.

mists were beginning to think and wanted to say. Battalions of econometricians set out to "fit" a Phillips Curve, using the most sophisticated techniques they could, to data from America, Australia, Britain, Canada—indeed, every country that had unemployment and wage or price data. Reports of finding and "estimating" the Phillips Curve appeared throughout the scholarly economic journals. (If you didn't find the curve you didn't publish.) Thus the careful quantitative studies by Phillips and his followers gave important professional support to the idea of a trade-off—to the idea that a lower level of unemployment could be "bought" at the cost of a steeper rise of wages and prices—for as long as the "buyer" might desire. (Those who didn't believe it were thought crazy, attention-seeking, or woefully biased.)

This idea that the government, through its control of the money supply, could operate the economy around a lower unemployment rate (as an average figure) if it is prepared to accept a steady upward trend of wages and prices rested on an ill-considered supposition. It may well be true that the government by engineering an unanticipated demand shock in the form of a surprise increase of the money supply could catch workers and firms with their expectations of the general wage level too low; then the result is an increase of employment and production, not merely a "classical" increase of wages and prices in proportion to the money supply. According to the modern-day expectational theories of employment disturbances:

- When a slump strikes, with actual employment N falling below N^* and the actual unemployment rate rising above u^*, unemployment is high *because workers or firms have overestimated (overpredicted) the wage level at other firms and towns—they have underestimated the general fall of wages* (hence the workers have held out for a wage higher than they generally ought to have, or the firms have kept their wage scales higher than they wish they had).

- Similarly, when a boom occurs, either by government design or accident, so that actual employment N rises above N^* and the actual unemployment rate falls below u^*, unemployment is low *because workers or firms have underestimated (underpredicted) the wage level at other firms or places—have underestimated the general rise of wages* (hence the workers did not hold out for a wage as high as they would have had they known or the firms did not raise their wage scales as high as they would have done had they known).[*]

---

[*] In the alternative model touched on in chapter 19, a slump of employment is explained by the failure of firms to expect the increased slack in the labor market (a larger "reserve army"), which would have encouraged them to cut wages in anticipation and to anticipate that the other firms will do the same, hence to cut wages even more. The reverse occurs in a boom.

So it is certainly conceivable that the government, starting from a situation of zero-inflation equilibrium, could *create a disequilibrium* by generating an unanticipated increase of the money supply.

What happens once workers and firms awaken to the fact that the general level of wages rose when no rise was expected, so that the level of wages exceeds their previous estimates? Then wages will be pushed up, and with them prices as well. The worker will want to catch up to the others, to return his relative wage to where he thought it was. This catch-up response of wages tends to cool off the boom—to *drag employment down* to its equilibrium level. A Keynesian analysis suggests that the process would take place by degrees, little by little. (If the money supply increased by 7 percent and the impact was an average wage increase of 2 percent, workers and firms, learning of that, might next aim for another 2 percent—or less if they thought the boom was receding.) A New Classical analysis suggests the process could occur in one step. (If the firms and workers believe, on hearing the news of the "7" and the "2," that the 7 percent increase of the money supply is permanent, wages would then jump up the rest of the way to equilibrium—by about 5 percent more.)

◆ Whatever the details of the reaction process following the impact of the first money-supply shock, it is clear that the money supply must be *increased again*—by 2 percent or 5 percent or whatever—in order to overcome the reaction to the first increase if the government is to *recreate the disequilibrium*—the underprediction of the general rise of wages—that is necessary to achieve the desired below-equilibrium level of the unemployment rate.

Thus a lower unemployment rate, one below the noninflation equilibrium level u^*, can be "bought" indefinitely—at the cost of a steady rise in the level of wages and prices—*if* the constant increase of wages and prices leaves the labor markets in a state of constant disequilibrium, with workers and firms constantly underestimating the rise in wages and prices. Figure 21–1 offers a pictorial summary of this step, or stage, in the argument.

But it seems unsafe and implausible to suppose that a steady upward trend of wages and prices could proceed forever with workers and firms never learning to expect the steady rate of increase that is occurring. It seems reasonable to suppose that, in fact, people would sooner or later come to *expect* the normal increase in the general level of wages and prices—*all* of it, whether it is 5 percent or a less impressive rate of increase, such as 2 percent per year. Then a worker finding a higher money wage somewhere or seeing the money wage on his current job go up, due to what is really just the normal increase (2 percent or 5 percent) in the general level of wages, *will not misinterpret it* as a fortunate improvement in his relative wage—as

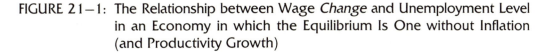

FIGURE 21−1: The Relationship between Wage *Change* and Unemployment Level in an Economy in which the Equilibrium Is One without Inflation (and Productivity Growth)

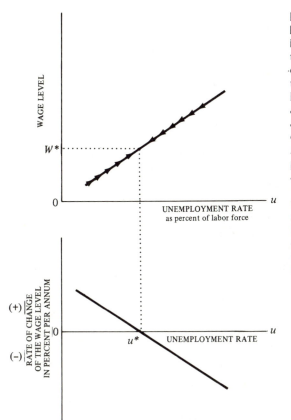

If we abstract from the possibility that the equilibrium of the economy under study is one with inflation (and perhaps productivity growth) so that the price level and wage level will be rising in equilibrium, and maybe even in the slump, the theory of employment has a simple implication: In slumps, wages and prices will be falling—if they aren't there will be no recovery. In booms, wages and prices will be rising—if not there will be no end to the boom. And, to repeat, at the *equilibrium* level of business activity, where the unemployment rate is at its equilibrium level, wages and prices will be unchanged.

These features of the process of "equilibration," of return to equilibrium, suggest that there may be a continuous, or regular, relationship between the *rate* of wage change (and price change) and the level of the unemployment rate. Of course, this relationship might not be a straight line.

better pay ("Honey, we can stop looking") or as catching up to the better pay he thought he had won earlier. Such an improvement in money pay will be (correctly) viewed as needed to avoid falling behind. Workers' asking wages will not lag behind the actual wage level. They will go up *in anticipation* that wage rates at other firms and towns will again increase at the normal rate. And firms, anticipating the same thing and counting on the normal increase of prices, will be prepared to offer these anticipatory wage increases. There will be no underestimation of the wage increase now, hence no need for "catching up" later. Thus the disequilibrium, in which the unemployment rate is low (because underestimation of the average market wage makes actual wages below-equilibrium and employment above-equilibrium), can no longer be created by a regular increase of the money supply (at the 2 or 5 percent in our examples) once people "catch on" to the normal trend of wages and prices.

♦ Once the surprise is taken out of the steady normal rise in the general wage and price level, the successive increases of the money supply generating the process will no longer have the effect of pulling employment and production up to an above-equilibrium level. The rising money supply will simply produce an *inflation equilibrium*. And on the hypothesis of a "natural rate of unemployment" in all equilibriums, the unemployment rate in that inflation equilibrium will be no better than in the *noninflation* equilibrium. Figure 21–2 summarizes.

This analysis points to one explanation of the origin of inflation in recent decades. The inflation arose by miscalculation, a result of wishful thinking. It was widely believed for more than a decade that, by steadily increasing the money supply, a government could engineer a permanent reduction in the economy's average unemployment rate, the level around which the unemployment rate would fluctuate. Several countries, including the United States and Britain, sought to take advantage of this conjectured opportunity. They chose to step up the growth rate of the money supply, at the cost of a faster rise in wages and prices, believing they would obtain reduced unemployment in return—for as long as they chose to do it.* By the early 1970s, however, it was widely conceded that this policy rested on false hopes: Wages and prices continued to rise at the faster pace that had developed by the end of the previous decade, leaving aside years of slump when wages slowed down; but the unemployment rate was back to normal—or worse.

♦ By the time government policy makers became convinced that steady inflation would do nothing to keep unemployment down once the rise of wages and prices became anticipated in labor markets it was too late: Wages and prices were continuing to rise along with the money supply, but the rising trends in wages and prices were "built in" to the expectations and routine practices of workers and firms. If the government did not offer the normal doses of increased money in keeping with the wage increases to which workers and firms were accustomed, employment would *fall below* equilibrium. For the carefree boom conditions they enjoyed in the 1960s—strawberry fields forever!—countries subsequently reaped the harvest of inflation equilibrium where rising wages and prices are the norm.

Inflation as a "Political Equilibrium"
The above explanation of how countries find themselves with inflation is certainly not the only one. And it is better as an explanation of how inflation

---

* It ought to be mentioned that some countries did not choose inflation—they "imported" it.

FIGURE 21–2: The *Anticipation* of Increased Inflation Eliminates the Boost to Employment According to the "Natural Rate" Hypothesis

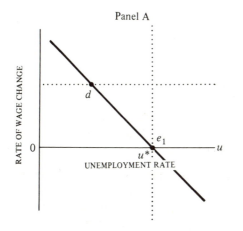

Panel A

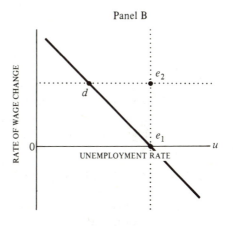

Panel B

Panel A: A permanent, steady rate of increase of wages and prices, started and fed by constant increase of the money supply, *would* achieve a permanently lower unemployment rate—lower than the noninflation equilibrium level at e_1—if people (workers and firms) *never learn to expect, or anticipate, the rising trend of wages and prices,* thus remaining in a constant state of disequilibrium, as at *d,* perpetually and forever!

Panel B: But if people sooner or later *will* learn to *expect* the steady rate of increase of the wage level and price level, the end result will be an inflation equilibrium, such as e_2. And if the unemployment rates in all these equilibriums (e_1, e_2, and others with higher inflation) are equal—all equal to the so-called natural rate of unemployment—no permanent reduction of the unemployment rate will have been achieved whatsoever!

in some countries arose than as a theory of how inflation (at some determinate rate) remains—as an explanation of lasting inflation equilibrium. There is, however, a deeper theory of inflation—a more general explanation.

Inflation may be the end result of a realistic political calculation—not necessarily a calculation merely serving the narrow self-interests of cynical politicians, though it might be that. What determines whether a country operates in an inflation equilibrium with inflation of prices at the rate of 2 percent per year or with inflation running at 10 or 20 or even 200 percent per year? What determines whethether the government would end up choosing the equilibrium e_1 or e_2 or e_3 or whichever among the various equilibriums that could result? Inevitably such questions remind the economist of others, such as: What determines whether a firm hires three employees or four? Governments and societies are more complex entities than firms, subject to inner conflicts and so forth. But as a starting point it is not so bad to answer:

Governments increase inflation until a further increase of the rate of inflation would no longer be to their net political advantage.

> If the rate of inflation in the currently prevailing inflation equilibrium is not already so high that still faster rise of wages and prices would be tempting—because of near-term or longer-term benefits—inflation will be driven higher.

A political theory of inflation, though based on that principle, cannot stand on that principle alone. To be meaningful, and eventually tested against evidence, such a theory needs to indicate the nature of the political advantages and disadvantages from more inflation (and less). In the usual theory politicians are said to make two calculations:

◆ Although the government's resort to a more rapid increase of the money supply (carried out by compliant central bankers who can always be replaced) and thus a faster rise of wages and prices would (it is agreed) bring no permanent reduction of the unemployment rate, it would, if undertaken in a surprise move to throw labor markets into disequilibrium for a while, produce a *temporary* reduction of the unemployment rate below the "natural" rate common to all equilibriums (inflationary and noninflationary). And such a reduction would please many workers who would credit such a boom with landing them in their well-paid jobs, saving them from continued looking or waiting for a good job. And it would, by temporarily increasing production and incomes, increase for a while the tax revenue of the government, thus permitting a cut of tax rates in the present or future.*

◆ However, there certainly comes a point after which higher inflation is generally regarded as *worse*, not better, all things considered. People find a steeply rising trend of wages and prices inconvenient to deal with (and a falling trend too)—the more so the steeper the trend. It sows confusion and mistakes, complicates calculations, etc. "Correcting" for inflation through various kinds of "indexation" is an imperfect remedy, creating complications and costs of its own.

From these elements, the theory goes, some determinate rate of inflation will emerge. And it will *not* be the rate of inflation that the public likes best. To see that, suppose (for illustration) that the public prefers a "flat" price

---

*Even in equilibrium conditions, faster-rising prices may serve a purpose—up to a point. With higher inflation under way, the government can and must print new money faster to keep up. And it may as well use this newly printed money each month to pay for some of its normal purchases (which it would have made anyway). Thus the government can cut taxes, obtaining more of its financing through the printing of new money all the time. (But there will come a point at which engineering still higher inflation would not help.) This subject, called the "inflation tax," is discussed more fully below.

level to any rising or falling trend. If the economy found itself *at first* in the crowd-pleasing zero-inflation equilibrium, a situation in which no one is expecting any rise of wages and prices, the economy would not remain there; for then the *advantage* to the government in power from a surprise move toward growth, or more accurately faster growth, of the money supply—the advantage being primarily or solely the temporary reduction of the unemployment rate (and the benefits from that, such as extra tax reve-nues)—would *outweigh*, so far as the politicians are concerned at least, the *disadvantage* in prospect as the resulting rise of wages and prices came to be expected (so that, barring a new move toward still faster growth of the money supply, the final result would be attainment of a new equilibrium at the natural rate of unemployment again but with a rising trend of prices and wages). Why? How is that balance of advantage argued? The argument rests on two features of the theory:

- Presumably the new equilibrium, with its upward trend of prices, is going to be permanent. (We cannot hope that politicians will choose to undo tomorrow whatever the politicians choose to do now.) And by contrast the reduction of unemployment will be only temporary. But today's poli-ticians do not care, since they are not likely to be running for office decades later. So they will "discount" *future* benefits and future costs compared to *present* ones.

- Moving from equilibrium with zero inflation to one with a little inflation is just a departure from the best equilibrium—the optimum, the top of the hill—to one not quite so good. But a temporary move of the unemploy-ment rate below its equilibrium level, no matter how small a step, would be an uphill movement, since the equilibrium level of the unemployment rate is not the optimum—the best rate is much lower—certainly in the eyes of the public (and economists too).

Hence to politicians it is definitely worth moving from zero inflation to *some* inflation (maybe not a fast rate)—at the cost of *some* move away from the top of the smooth "inflation hill"—for the sake of the move, even though only temporary, up the still steep unemployment hill. Thus politicians will accept *some* inflation—more than desired!

It is not, plainly, the easiest argument in economics to grasp! (Even a mathematical version has to go beyond elementary calculus.) But some sense of the argument is worthwhile, for it is typical of a whole class of proposi-tions about the shortsightedness of governments: They underinvest in the protection of the environment, they skimp on public education and support of scientific research, they run budgetary deficits (some of them hidden in off-budget accounts) so as to pass the burden of financing to future taxpay-ers, and they run down their international reserves and run up their foreign debts as far as suits them. The extent to which politicians (and statesmen) can do these things is a measure of their power! If they could not do these things we might have to conclude that they were servants of the "political will" of the public or useful brokers in a multilateral social bargain or legislative entrepreneurs finding new laws to gratify the public—in any case not powerful actors actively thwarting some of the diverse interests of the public for their own self-interests.

Maybe so, but how do they do it? One theory is that a government does it the same way a Machiavellian government collects and spends more taxes than everyone wants: People cannot act collectively to make such spending unconstitutional, and it is not worth it for any individual interest group to give up any benefits from the government of its own for the sake of the dent that would make in the government's profligacy. Similarly, people may see that their children are being taxed, literally or figuratively, to finance benefits for the present generation. But no person or interest group will find it worth sacrificing its own present self-interests, by throwing its support to anti-inflation dissidents, for the sake of its children—unless by doing so it would somehow bind the other groups to do likewise. (Of course, sometimes inflation goes too far!)

TRUE COSTS AND BENEFITS FROM INFLATION

We have been dealing until now with a paradox: Inflation is, like government debt, unpopular with the public. Yet governments create some of it in spite of the public. It is certainly possible, however, that the public fails to understand some of the economic aspects of inflation in arriving at its opinion. (No one would propose that the design of military weapons or appropriations for support of scientific research be decided in a general referendum to ascertain public opinion.) Thus it is possible that the *best* rate of inflation, though of course varying with circumstances, is hardly ever or never zero. Perhaps it is generally *greater* than zero.

In fact the analysis of inflation, using the best available economic theory, uncovers some benefits of inflation not suspected by the general public. The question arises; therefore, whether these underappreciated benefits might, at least in some circumstances, outweigh the true costs—leaving a gain as the net result of inflation.

The most widely conceded benefit from inflation (under equilibrium conditions), one well known to Latin Americans, has already been alluded to in the footnote on p. 586. Inflation—and, up to a point, higher inflation—increases the revenue that the government can earn through its creation of money; this revenue (like user fees) can be used to finance government spending in place of revenue obtained the old-fashioned way, by ordinary taxation.

The common sense of this "revenue from inflation" is simple enough: The higher the rate of inflation to which the economy is accustomed—the faster wages and prices are rising under equilibrium conditions—the faster must the government print money in order that the supply of money "keep up with the demand." For as prices and wages move to ever-higher levels, successively larger amounts of money balances will be required by people if they are to have the same amount of "liquidity" despite the decline in the real value of each dollar bill, pound note, or whatever. Like counterfeit notes, the newly printed money can be injected into the economy simply by using it to pay for goods—goods that might (in whole or in part) have otherwise been purchased with more conventional financing (such as earning it in the case of the counterfeiter or taxation in the case of the government.) Thus the government, by printing more money each day, can finance the same level of government expenditure with less taxation *or* it can finance a larger level of public expenditure with the same taxation (or both)—with no change in the government's real indebtedness, as measured by the real value (adjusting for inflation) of the interest-bearing public debt.

When the money injectors are deciding the dosage, however, they have to keep in mind that if inflation is created or increased a notch to a higher rate, the *expectation* of rising prices raises the prospective *nominal* return on capital goods and land—so bonds and loans must offer a comparable increase in their nominal rate of return too—but *not* necessarily the prospective nominal rate of return on *money,* and certainly not on all money. The government may elect not to pay interest on the bank-type money that some banks are required to hold—as deposit balances at the central bank in order to meet their reserve requirements. And it seems thus far to be impractical for governments to pay interest on currency (coin and bank notes), as impractical as charging a user fee for holding government currency. Thus money will be at an increased disadvantage—the opportunity cost of holding it higher. There will be a "flight" from money, therefore, into these so-called earning assets offering the prospect of the improved nominal yield. At the initial level of money wages and prices (including capital-goods prices) there will be an increased demand for capital, but no increased supply, of course—hence an excess demand; and an excess supply of money.

The *new* inflationary equilibrium path, therefore, will be one with a higher *price level*—the equilibrium price level *jumps up* to a higher starting level (from which it will rise according to the new rate of inflation)—*or else* the government must cut back the *money supply* to a reduced starting level. *Either way,* the *real* value of the money supply will be *lower* in the new equilibrium with the faster inflation. In terms of the Cambridge equation, k* *will be smaller in the faster-inflation* equilibrium. Hence each year's percentage increase in the money supply, though a large *percentage increase,* may very well represent a *smaller* amount of purchasing power—because, in real terms, it is a (higher) percentage increase from a lower base level. At some dosage, the side effect may counter the main effect.

♦ At some point, if the inflation rate is increased further, the added revenue from the still faster percentage growth of the money supply will be offset totally by the further reduction in the real value of the money supply—and its percentage increase.

So much for commonsense views. The un-common sense of the matter ties the revenue effect of higher inflation to *seigniorage.* As the creator of the economy's money supply or some part of it, the government central bank has come into ownership of earning assets—government bonds, even private bonds and land and capital in some cases. The central bank created the money supply by exchanging newly printed money for such interest-paying (or return-yielding) assets. Since these bank-owned assets generally earn interest while the bank's money generally does not, the central bank obtains a net return from these past acquisitions of earning assets. This we may call seigniorage.

If, now, the economy shifts to a new, faster-inflation equilibrium, the nominal yield on these earning assets of the central bank will be increased—exactly as explained above; while the central bank need not and perhaps cannot really pay interest (or more interest) on the money it has created. So, on this account, the *seigniorage earned by the central bank will go up*—given the price level *and* level of the money supply. But the price level must jump up or else, to prevent it, the central bank must sell off some of its earning assets in exchange for money to ensure that the money supply "jumps down" to a lower level. In the former case the *real* value of the increased seigniorage in nominal, or money, terms may therefore be decreased; in the latter case the nominal seigniorage may actually be reduced. Thus, as the inflation rate is increased to one level after another, the seigniorage may at first be increased; but as inflation becomes so high that money is driven to occupy a small place in the economy, and real cash balances become small, the seigniorage may begin to *decrease* thereafter. This un-commonsense view does not differ radically from the common-sense view.

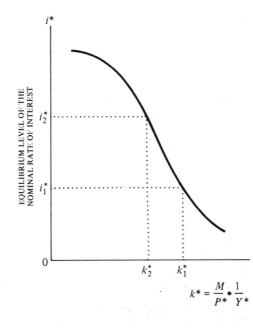

$$k^* = \frac{M}{P^*} \cdot \frac{1}{Y^*}$$

Our analysis of seigniorage is summarized in the diagram to the left. On the vertical axis is the nominal rate of return expected or promised on loans, bonds, titles to capital and land, equity shares — including any expected nominal (purely inflation-caused) capital gains. This nominal rate of interest is the "opportunity cost" of holding real wealth in interestless money balances rather than earning assets; it is the "price" of liquidity, therefore. Accordingly, the quantity of real cash balances demanded by people—their desired average holdings of money in real terms (purchasing power)—is a function of how high this "price" is. This relationship between "price" and quantity demanded is depicted by the demand curve in the diagram. Given an equilibrium with interest rate i^*, the demand curve determines the corresponding equilibrium level of real cash balances—measured on the horizontal axis and expressed as a ratio to the equilibrium level of aggregate output, Y^*. Given the level of the money supply, M, the equilibrium price level, P^*, is thus determined. The diagram shows that if, because increased inflation is now expected, the expected nominal rate of return on earning assets is increased to i_2^* from i_1^*, the equilibrium level of the *real value* of the money supply *drops* immediately to $(M/P^*)_2$ from $(M/P^*)_1$—either through a jump up of P^* or through a central-bank decision to decrease M. Therefore the government's seigniorage, which is the rectangle $i^* \cdot (M/P^*)$, may go up or down.

Even if a faster-rising trend in wages and prices does serve to increase the government's revenue—up to some point where still faster inflation would be counterproductive—this benefit is not without its cost. Although government revenue may be generated, this "inflation tax" has adverse incentive effects that are analogous to the distortionary effects of the income tax, the sales tax, and other kinds of graduated taxes. The introduction of such a tax creates an incentive for the taxpayer to reduce earnings or reduce purchases—in short, to reduce the "base" on which the tax is calculated—compared to what the taxpayer would do if the government simply seized the needed tax revenue, with no ifs or buts, in an unconditional lumpsum levy. (There may also be a reduction compared to "before," but it is the comparison to the effect of a lump sum tax that is relevant here.) An excise tax on eau de toilette, by raising the price to the consumer, induces the taxpayer to "economize" in his purchases of it—to substitute other goods in its place, almost as if he were trying spitefully to thwart the government's quest for revenue. Yet the *social cost,* in terms of leisure or other goods that are consequently foregone, of producing the quantity sold to any of these good-smelling taxpayers, has not increased; only the price has increased. So, generally speaking, the incentive to economize more on the taxed goods is inappropriate; there results a distortion, or inefficiency, in the mix of goods produced and consumed. Similarly, an increased rate of inflation, by raising the expected nominal yields on earning assets but not on money (not all money, at any rate), induces people to "economize" more in the holding of money balances—to get along on a smaller average amount of cash, in real terms, with the aim of holding more earning assets. But from society's standpoint this effort to substitute earning assets for cash is utterly wasteful and pointless.

♦ The result of the inflation-caused increase in the nominal rate of return on earning assets is a distortion of people's incentives, an inefficient allocation of resources: People are led by higher interest rates to *spend time* economizing on their money balances—running "back and forth to the bank"—and time is a precious, all-too-scarce resource. People respond that way since the nominal rate of interest is the "opportunity cost" of holding money—holding it requires giving up the interest that could have been earned by holding earning assets instead—and the "inflation tax" has increased this "price." Yet the *social cost* of providing money—in real terms or nominal terms—has not increased. So the incentive to economize more on cash balances, or liquidity, is inappropriate. (In fact, the social cost of offering people liquidity *could* in some circumstances be so close to zero that negative inflation—and thus a very *low* nominal interest rate—might be desirable on this score.) In short, high inflation prompts wasteful trips to the bank.

♦ The inducement to hold more earning assets instead of money is futile as well. Wanting to get out of some cash and into some more stocks and bonds will not, out of thin air, create a larger capital stock for society's benefit (or even create more stocks and bonds); people can only buy from each other! Only a decision of people to save more, to consume less, could do that—and then only gradually, at the cost of present enjoyments for the prospect of future ones in return. (The flight out of money into capital merely produes less money in real terms, not more capital. And consumption will not be reduced, saving increased, if the inflation tax just substitutes for other taxes, leaving revenue unchanged.)

The conclusion to be drawn, then, is that the "revenue from inflation" is not necessarily a gain, or advantage, from inflation. The cost of the inflation tax, arising from the distortion of resource allocation just pointed out, *may* very well exceed the benefit. (Even a country bent on obtaining the maximum possible tax revenue might find it best to avoid resort to the inflation tax since, by distorting resource allocations, that tax might reduce the amount of tax revenue obtainable from all the other kinds of taxes!)

> Economists testifying on the matter of inflation have to say: It is possible that the revenue benefit of more inflation—by permitting the reduction of other distorting taxes—may exceed the cost. Then a reduction of the inflation rate would be going in the wrong direction from this viewpoint. But they also have to acknowledge the possibility that the best "level" for the inflation tax rate is *zero*.

This reexamination of the merits of inflation, if any, needs one more point: It could happen, as chapter 19 pointed out, that a noninflation equilibrium—short of radical changes in taxation and subsidies—does not exist. Without inflation, the prospective nominal rate of return on capital goods is so low that, if produced and sold at their supply price, no one would want to hold them in preference to holding money! This is a problem pointed to in Keynes's *General Theory*. What to do? In such a situation, inflation has the saving virtue that it raises up the prospective nominal rate of return on capital.

> The testifying economist would have to say that total elimination of inflation in the economy might—if not now then some time—be dangerous because it might leave nominal interest rates around zero or below. The economy cannot function that way.

THE DIFFICULTY OF REDUCING INFLATION

Although we may try to understand the rise of inflation over so much of the globe in recent decades, we must be careful not to "overexplain" it to the point where governmental efforts to reduce inflation become incomprehensible! Clearly a government can go "too far" with inflation for everyone; or it can go "too far" for some substantial number of citizens. Then a new initiative may be undertaken, perhaps by a new political leadership, to reduce inflation. In the past few decades, in fact, governments in several countries have embarked on a program of intended "disinflation." The results of these experiments have been the subject of much discussion in political economy circles. A result in every case has been a distressing bulge of unemployment.

One problem of stopping (or slowing) inflation that these experiments seem to raise is the problem of persuading producers and workers to "level off" their expectations of future wages and prices in accordance with the government's intentions to "level off" the actual wages and prices (by stopping or slowing the growth of the money supply). Much of this problem, it is widely believed, can be traced to the problem of the disinflation program's "credibility." "Yesterday the government seemed willing to continue the old inflation, did it not? Then why should I revise downward my expectation of inflation this month and this year?" Then, even if the government demonstrates its resolve for a while, and inflation does come down, people may expect the government will soon reverse its field and return to the old inflation. The government is forced to persevere with its tough stance, thus permitting a slump to develop out of the clash between higher prices and no higher money supply, if it is to have any hope of vanquishing the inflation.

Some further problems add to the difficulty of gaining credibility: If people were to expect reduced inflation, business investment would suffer a fall in its expected nominal rate of return; disinflation triggers an attempted flight *from* capital back to money; so, to prevent a slump from resulting, the central bank must *increase* the money supply—which might undermine people's hopes that inflation was going to drop! Further, the money supply would have to increase in order to accommodate "catch up" increases of those wage rates that are outdated and due for an increase.

Two questions thus arise: If there is no better way than that, is the game worth the candle? And, must there not be a better way? There are some thoughts on these questions but not yet any tested answers.

EPILOGUE TO PART 7

Our examination of the political economy of business fluctuations and government stabilization in the market-based national economy is at an end.

Along the way some gains in understanding of the economics of slump and inflation must have resulted. But it was certain political questions—the big policy questions—with which we were primarily concerned: How best can the government contribute to the stability of the market-based national economy, without engaging in radical surgery to remove much of the market? And how satisfactory can we expect the resulting stability, or instability, to be? Let us collect some of the foregoing observations that are of use in trying to answer these questions.

The Achilles' heel of Keynesianism appears to be its failure to provide accountability: If the government authorities have increased the money supply, they can explain that it was necessary to prevent a slump, whatever their real motives and perceptions. If the authorities have decreased the money supply, they can reply that it was needed to prevent or stem excessive inflation. Postwar history suggests that a vague mandate to "stabilize" some unspecified mixture of things becomes a license for politicians to pursue their self-interest. Keynes himself was least open to that criticism, since he was precise, not vague, in advocating management of the money supply to stabilize the average wage level (perhaps around a trend path). But even such a well-defined objective would entail judgment, guesswork, and controversy. Frequently, as the target—be it a certain wage level, or price level, or exchange rate—becomes more and more costly to reach, it is easier to revise the target than to regain it. (But monetarism is vulnerable to the same criticism: It is often easier to adjust the target.)

Monetarism seemed at first to be the answer, as any central bank could be expected to be able to stabilize the supply of money (perhaps around a trend path). But monetarism is not very operational, since there are so many varieties of money supply, which tend to move at sharply divergent rates; and any money supply loses much of its meaning as financial institutions invent new kinds of deposits, or assets, that serve as near-money. Moreover, even if these problems were not serious, in the New Keynesian view the monetarist doctrine is overconfident about the speed with which wage rates adjust to reequilibrate the economy following a demand shock or supply shock. Much greater cushioning of the economy from such shocks would be desirable. Finally, it is a difficult and dangerous business to introduce a monetarist policy into an economy initially accustomed, or addicted, to rapid inflation—more rapid, that is, than the new monetarist goal. (But Keynesianism is subject to the same objection: Normal stabilization could not commence immediately without producing severe withdrawal pains.)

Some of those who have felt acutely dissatisfied with both monetarism and Keynesianism have expressed the hope that some third way, some better kind of monetary standard, will sometime be discovered; and some economists have proposed new kinds of monetary policy for theoretical analysis and evaluation. There have been advocates of a return to the postwar system instituted at Bretton Woods in 1946: all countries keeping fixed exchange rates with the dollar, and the dollar kept at a fixed parity with gold. But this system never operated according to design; most countries continually devalued their currency, and the United States kept losing gold reserves. Many economists are uncertain that return to the Bretton Woods system would be a step in the right direction.

Thus the prospects for stability in market-based economies is dimmer than the hopes of economists at the zenith of Keynesianism in the 1950s. Rapid inflation is still a possibility and even a serious slump must be guarded against. If the profitability of investment should decline a great deal, the rate of return to investment could decline by so much as to create the potential for a deep slump; but there is, it appears, enough economic understanding to combat it and even to prevent it. In view of how much has been learned there is in fact much cause for hope.

SUMMARY

1. What economists usually mean by inflation (or "cost inflation") is an ongoing process of rising money-wage rates and money prices despite the absence of any disequilibrating unanticipated disturbance. Of course, such a disturbance, in the form of an unanticipated increase in the money supply or an unanticipated decrease in the demand for money, does produce a one-time rise of money wages and money prices; but this is a climb of wages and price onto a higher equilibrium level, not the phenomenon of a rising equilibrium level of money wages and prices.

2. Inflation has come under intense study in recent decades not because moderate or higher inflation is immensely costly—economists are not sure that it is—but because government efforts to rid the economy of the inflation have, so far, always caused a serious slump in employment and production in the process of achieving a reduction of inflation; and because such inflation, which is now a worldwide epidemic, presents a classic case study of "government failure": If the public dislikes inflation, why do governments start it and why, once started, do they not end it before it is a very big problem?

3. One theory of the origin of inflation, particularly in the 1950s and 1960s, is that many governments at the time operated on the basis of a mistaken economic model: The model said that the central bank, through its control of the growth of the money supply, could "buy" a reduction of the unemployment rate below what we can regard as the equilibrium level, u^*, that "goes with" the level of national output, Y^*, in conditions of monetary equilibrium. Producers or workers or both can be kept off balance, in a state of disequilibrium, by the resulting growth of the money

supply. The *benefit* is that production and employment will be increased, for when the average of actual money-wage rates, W, is pulled above expectations of the average level, W^e, the result is that some unemployed workers are coaxed to stop searching or holding out for a better job (since they are led to think they have just found it). The *cost*, according to this model, is that expectations of the average wage will catch up to reality, so a new injection of money growth will be necessary, and so on; hence the "price" of engineering the lower unemployment rate is a positive rate of inflation—the higher the lower is the unemployment rate being engineered. But it was evidently a mistake to suppose that people would go on being fooled indefinitely by the government's policy of steadily increasing the money supply so as to support rising prices and wages.

4. The Natural Rate hypothesis (sometimes called the Accelerationist hypothesis) says that, to the contrary, maintaining the unemployment rate some distance *below* the equilibrium level, u^*, which the economy fluctuated around when its monetary equilibrium was one with zero inflation, would require *increasingly rapid* inflation—without any limit, reaching 1 thousand percent inflation per year and more. To express the same hypothesis another way: If the government decides to engineer a higher inflation at some constant percentage rate when until then the economy has been enjoying an equilibrium without inflation (or with a lesser inflation rate), then there will be a temporary fall of unemployment—just as described above (point 3); but as producers and workers catch on to the higher inflation, their expectation of the wage level will begin to keep pace with the actual wage level, and so each month's wage increase will no longer cause unemployment to be reduced. The economy will have the "cost" of inflation *without* the "benefit" of reduced unemployment.

5. The political theory of inflation says that a certain rate of inflation is a natural characteristic of "political equilibrium." Politicians discount severely a future benefit or cost relative to a present benefit or cost of the same size (in real terms). The costs of generating a steady inflation, starting from none, are mostly in the future, and the benefits mostly in the present—in the transition from the old equilibrium to the new. Hence politicians tend to underweigh the disadvantages of more inflation and overweigh the advantages, with the result that too much inflation is chosen. (It is not worth it for any particular interest group to give up something in order to lend support to anti-inflation dissidents if it has to act alone, because it cannot give up enough to succeed; only a multilateral pact among political factions would work, but that is hard to arrange.)

6. A cost-benefit analysis of the true costs and true benefits from inflation does not necessarily lead to the conclusion that the best rate of inflation, in equilibrium, is zero. Perhaps moderate inflation would be best if it can be counted on to stay at the best level, thus to remain moderate.

7. One problem of reducing inflation, when there is a desire by the government to do so, is people's disbelief that the government will not soon seize again the short-term advantages from returning to the old rate of inflation. The problem of falling interest rates and catch-up wage increases add to the difficult.

CONCEPTS INTRODUCED

inflation	inflation tax	political-equilibrium inflation rate
Phillips Curve	seigniorage	disinflation
natural rate of unemployment	inflation distortions	credibility
	inflation from no inflation	flight from capital

STUDY QUESTIONS

1. In the 1980s much of the inflation in European and North American economies was eliminated by the introduction of anti-inflation monetary policy. Has the political-equilibrium inflation rate fallen? Can inflation morality constrain politics? For a while? Forever?

2. It has been observed that the money supply actually speeded up in the period late 1980–late 1984, while the velocity of money—the inverse, or reciprocal, of the Cambridge *k*—moved to sharply lower level in 1981 and 1982. Does it follow from this that the Federal Reserve played no part in the reduction of inflation (and the accompanying slump) during the first half of the 1980s?

Index